Models for Writers

Short Essays for Composition

THIRTEENTH EDITION

Alfred Rosa

Paul Eschholz

University of Vermont

Boston | New York

For Bedford/St. Martin's

Vice President, Editorial, Macmillan Learning Humanities: Edwin Hill
Senior Program Director for English: Leasa Burton
Program Manager: John E. Sullivan III
High School Program Manager: Nathan Odell
Marketing Manager: Joy Fisher Williams
Director of Content Development: Jane Knetzger
Developmental Editor: Leah Rang
Assistant Editor: Stephanie Cohen
Content Project Manager: Pamela Lawson
Workflow Supervisor: Joe Ford
Production Supervisor: Robin Besofsky
Media Project Manager: Jodi Isman
Manager of Publishing Services: Andrea Cava
Project Management: Lumina Datamatics, Inc.
Composition: Lumina Datamatics, Inc.
Photo Editors: Martha Friedman/Angela Boehler
Photo Researcher: Candice Cheesman
Permissions Manager: Kalina Ingham
Text Permissions Researcher: Mark Schaefer
Senior Art Director: Anna Palchik
Text Design: Rick Korab, Korab Company Design
Cover Design: John Callahan
Cover Image: Eskemar/Getty Images
Printing and Binding: LSC Communications

Manufactured in the United States of America.

1 2 3 4 5 6   22 21 20 19 18 17

For information, write: Bedford/St. Martin's, 75 Arlington Street, Boston, MA 02116

ISBN 978-1-319-05665-0 (Student Edition)
ISBN 978-1-319-05668-1 (High School Edition)

Acknowledgments

Text acknowledgments and copyrights appear at the back of the book on pages 661–64, which constitute an extension of the copyright page. Art acknowledgments and copyrights appear on the same page as the art selections they cover.

Preface

Models for Writers, now in its thirteenth edition, continues to offer students and instructors brief, accessible, high-interest models of rhetorical elements, principles, and patterns. As important as it is for students to read while they are learning to write college-level essays, *Models for Writers* offers more than a collection of essays. Through the abundant study materials that accompany each selection, students master the writing skills they will need for all their college classes. Writing activities and assignments give students the chance to stitch together the various rhetorical elements into coherent, forceful essays of their own. This approach, which has helped several million students become better writers, remains at the heart of the book.

In this edition, we continue to emphasize the classic features of *Models for Writers* that have won praise from teachers and students alike. In addition, we have strengthened the book by introducing new selections and new perspectives, and we have emphasized the student voices that resound throughout the book. For the first time, this edition is also available with LaunchPad, which has an interactive e-book, reading quizzes, extra practice with reading and writing through LearningCurve adaptive quizzing, and more.

FAVORITE FEATURES OF *MODELS FOR WRITERS*

- **Brief, lively readings that provide outstanding models.** Most of the seventy professional selections and all seven of the sample student essays in *Models for Writers* are comparable in length (two to four pages) to the essays students will write themselves, and each clearly illustrates a basic rhetorical element, principle, or pattern. Just as important, the essays deal with subjects that we know from our own teaching experience will spark the interest of most college students. In addition, the range of voices, cultural perspectives, and styles represented in the essays will resonate with today's students. They will both enjoy and benefit from reading and writing about selections by many well-known authors, including Judith Ortiz Cofer, Stephen King, Anne Lamott, Amy Tan, Maya Angelou, David Sedaris, Langston Hughes, Bharati Mukherjee, Mary Sherry, and Martin Luther King Jr.

• **Introductory chapters on reading and writing.** Throughout the chapters in Part One, students review the writing process from fresh angles and learn how to use the essays they read to improve their own writing. Chapter 1, The Writing Process, details the steps in the writing process and illustrates them with a student essay in progress. A dedicated section on thesis statements, Develop Your Thesis, includes a clear five-step process to help students through the challenge of arriving at an effective thesis statement from a broad topic. Chapter 2, From Reading to Writing, shows students how to use the apparatus in the text, provides them with guidelines for critical reading, and demonstrates with three student essays (narrative, responsive, and argumentative) how they can generate their own writing from reading.

• **An easy-to-follow rhetorical organization.** Each of the twenty-one rhetorically based chapters in *Models for Writers* is devoted to a particular element or pattern important to college writing. Chapters 3 through 10 focus on the concepts of thesis, unity, organization, beginnings and endings, paragraphs, transitions, effective sentences, and writing with sources. Chapter 11 illustrates the importance of controlling diction and tone, and Chapter 12, the uses of figurative language. Chapters 13 through 21 explore the types of writing most often required of college students: illustration, narration, description, process analysis, definition, division and classification, comparison and contrast, cause and effect, and argument. Chapter 22, Combining Models, shows students how these writing strategies can be combined to achieve a writer's purpose.

• **Flexible arrangement.** Each chapter is self-contained so that instructors can easily follow their own teaching sequences, omitting or emphasizing certain chapters according to the needs of their students or the requirements of the course.

• **Abundant study materials.** To help students use the readings to improve their writing, every essay is accompanied by ample study materials.

Reflecting on What You Know activities precede each reading and prompt students to explore their own ideas and experiences regarding the issues presented in the reading.

Thinking Critically about This Reading questions follow each essay and encourage students to consider the writer's assumptions, make connections not readily apparent, or explore the broader implications of the selection.

Questions for Study and Discussion focus on the selection's content, the author's purpose, and the particular strategy the author used to achieve that purpose. To remind students that good writing is never one-dimensional, at least one question in each series focuses on a writing concern other than the one highlighted in the chapter.

Classroom Activities provide brief exercises that enable students to work (often in groups) on rhetorical elements, techniques, or patterns. These activities range from developing thesis statements to using strong action verbs and building argumentative evidence, and they encourage students to apply concepts modeled in the readings to their own writing. Several activities throughout the book also provide students with examples of career-related writing to demonstrate that critical reading, writing, and thinking skills are crucial beyond the college classroom. Several new activities invite students to employ different learning strategies and understand a concept through movement, visuals, or other hands-on and collaborative practice.

Suggested Writing Assignments provide at least two writing assignments for each essay, encouraging students to use the reading selection as a direct model, asking them to respond to the content of the reading, or expanding the selection topic to include their personal experience or outside research.

- **Concise and interesting chapter introductions.** Writing instructors who use *Models for Writers* continue to be generous in their praise for the brief, clear, practical, and student-friendly chapter introductions that explain the various elements and patterns. In each introduction, students will find illuminating examples—many written by students—of the feature or principle under discussion.

- **Practical instruction on working with sources.** One of the biggest challenges student writers face is incorporating supporting evidence from other writers into their essays. In Chapter 1, The Writing Process, students find clear advice on developing strong thesis statements and marshaling evidence and support. Chapter 10 models strategies for taking effective notes from sources; using signal phrases to integrate quotations, summaries, and paraphrases smoothly; synthesizing sources; and avoiding plagiarism. Further reviewing the steps and skills involved in research and synthesis, Chapter 23, A Brief Guide to Writing a Research Paper, provides one full-length MLA-style model student research paper and the cover sheet, first page, and list of references for one APA-style model student research paper (the entire paper is offered online in LaunchPad). Thus, students become more confident in joining academic conversations and in writing the kinds of essays that they will be called on to write in their college courses.

- **Targeted instruction on sentence grammar.** Chapter 24, Editing for Grammar, Punctuation, and Sentence Style, addresses editing concerns that instructors across the country have identified as the most problematic for their students, such as run-on sentences, verb tense shifts, comma splices, sentence fragments, and dangling and misplaced modifiers. Brief explanations and hand-edited examples show students how to find and correct these common errors in their own writing. Also available in this new edition are a host of online tutorials and self-paced, adaptive activities for further practice with grammatical and mechanical concepts.

- **An alternate table of contents showing thematic clusters.** The alternate table of contents (pp. xxxi–xxxvi) groups readings into twenty-four clusters, each with three to eight essays sharing a common theme. Students and instructors attracted to the theme of one essay in *Models for Writers* can consult this alternate table of contents to find other essays in the book that address the same theme.

- **Glossary of Useful Terms.** Cross-referenced in many of the questions and writing assignments throughout the book, this list of key terms defines rhetorical and literary terms that student writers need to know. Terms that are explained in the Glossary (pp. 647–60) are shown in boldface the first time they appear in a chapter.

NEW TO THE THIRTEENTH EDITION OF *MODELS FOR WRITERS*

- **Engaging, informative, and diverse new readings.** Twenty-three of the book's seventy readings are new to this edition of *Models for Writers*—ideal models by both new and established writers. We selected these essays for their brevity and clarity, for their effectiveness as models, and for their potential to develop critical thinking and writing on interesting and relevant topics. Among the new readings are Jonathan Safran Foer's "Against Meat," Chimamanda Ngozi Adichie's "We Should All Be Feminists," Jonah Berger's "The Power of Conformity," Misty Copeland's "Life in Motion," and Marie Kondo's "Designate a Place for Each Thing."

• **More attention to student writing.** A clearer design emphasizes the student writing in each chapter introduction, showing students the power of their words to serve as models for each chapter theme. A new student essay by Libby Marlowe in the Chapter 21 argument cluster on crime demonstrates how to enter a conversation and use texts from *Models for Writers* to write an effective argument.

• **Compelling new examples of argument.** A timely new argument cluster in Chapter 21, Argument, features a new group of readings on "Conflict: Using Language to Seek Resolution" by diverse voices: an expert on conflict resolution, a political journalist, and a Cincinnati police officer.

• **Updated MLA coverage.** A section in Chapter 23, A Brief Guide to Writing a Research Paper, aligns formatting and citation examples with the 2016 Modern Language Association guidelines.

• **LaunchPad for *Models for Writers*.** LaunchPad, Macmillan's customizable online course space, includes auto-scored reading comprehension quizzes and an interactive e-Book version of the text. A digital tutorial in Chapter 1 transforms the writing process into an interactive walk-through, and annotation activities in Chapter 2 allow students to practice close reading in the digital environment. The LaunchPad also offers an array of new materials, including LearningCurve adaptive quizzing, multimedia tutorials, and other resources that you can adapt, assign, and mix with your own.

ACKNOWLEDGMENTS

In response to the many thoughtful reviews from instructors who use this book, we have maintained the solid foundation of the previous edition of *Models for Writers* while adding fresh readings and writing topics to stimulate today's student writers.

We are indebted to many people for their advice as we prepared this thirteenth edition. We are especially grateful to Michael Alvarez, Southern Maine Community College; Shannon G. Blair, Central Piedmont Community College; Elizabeth Catanese, Community College of Philadelphia; Tamera Davis, Northern Oklahoma College: Stillwater; Stacey Frazier, Northern Oklahoma College; Cynthia C. Galvan, Milwaukee Area Technical College; Maria Gonzalez, Miami Dade College; Jacqueline Gray, St. Charles Community College; Nile Hartline, DMACC; Liz Mathews,

University of the Incarnate Word; Jean E. Mittelstaedt, Chemeketa Community College; Carrie Myers, Lehigh Carbon Community College; Michelle Patton, Fresno City College; Jose Reyes, El Paso Community College; Donald Stinson, Northern Oklahoma College; Stephen Turner, Milwaukee Area Technical College; Magdeleine Vandal, Carroll Community College; Robert Vettese, Southern Maine Community College; Vita Watkins, Glendale Community College; and Katherine Woodbury, Southern Maine Community College.

It has been our good fortune to have the editorial guidance and good cheer of Leah Rang, our developmental editor on this book, and Stephanie Cohen, assistant editor. We have also benefited from the great contributions to this edition by Andrew J. Hoffman, Elizabeth Catanese, and Jonathan Douglas, as well as the careful eye of Pamela Lawson, our content project manager, and the rest of the excellent team at Bedford/St. Martin's—Edwin Hill, Leasa Burton, John Sullivan, and Joy Fisher Williams—as we planned, developed, and wrote this new edition. Our special thanks go to the late Tom Broadbent—our mentor and original editor at St. Martin's Press—who helped us breathe life and soul into *Models for Writers* in its earliest editions. The lessons that he shared with us during our fifteen-year partnership have stayed with us throughout our careers.

Thanks also to Sarah Federman, who authored the new material for the *Instructor's Manual*. Our greatest debt is, as always, to our students—especially James Duffy, Trena Isley, Jake Jamieson, Zoe Ockenga, and Jeffrey Olesky, whose papers appear in this text—for all they have taught us over the years. Finally, we thank each other, partners in this writing and teaching venture for over four decades.

Alfred Rosa
Paul Eschholz

WE'RE ALL IN. AS ALWAYS.

Bedford/St. Martin's is as passionately committed to the discipline of English as ever, working hard to provide support and services that make it easier for you to teach your course your way.

Find **community support** at the Bedford/St. Martin's English Community (community.macmillan.com), where you can follow our *Bits* blog for new teaching ideas, download titles from our professional resource series, and review projects in the pipeline.

Choose **curriculum solutions** that offer flexible custom options, combining our carefully developed print and digital resources, acclaimed works from Macmillan's trade imprints, and your own course or program materials to provide the exact resources your students need.

Rely on **outstanding service** from your Bedford/St. Martin's sales representative and editorial team. Contact us or visit **macmillanlearning.com** to learn more about any of the options below.

LaunchPad for *Models for Writers:* Where Students Learn

LaunchPad provides engaging content and new ways to get the most out of your book. Get an **interactive e-Book** combined with assessment tools in a fully customizable course space; then assign and mix our resources with yours.

- A digital **tutorial** in Chapter 1 transforms the writing process into an interactive walk-through, and annotation **activities** in Chapter 2 allow students to practice close reading in the digital environment.
- **Reading comprehension quizzes** accompany every professional reading selection in this edition.
- **Diagnostics** provide opportunities to assess areas for improvement and assign additional exercises based on students' needs. Visual reports show performance by topic, class, and student as well as improvement over time.
- **Pre-built units**—including readings, videos, quizzes, and more—are easy to adapt and assign by adding your own materials and mixing them with our high-quality multimedia content and ready-made assessment options, such as **LearningCurve** adaptive quizzing and Exercise Central.
- Use LaunchPad on its own or **integrate it** with your school's learning management system so that your class is always on the same page.

LaunchPad for *Models for Writers* can be purchased on its own or packaged with the print book at a significant discount. An activation code is required. To order LaunchPad for *Models for Writers* with the print book, use ISBN 978-1-319-14476-0. For more information, go to **launchpadworks.com**

Choose from Alternative Formats of *Models for Writers*

Bedford/St. Martin's offers a range of formats. Choose what works best for you and your students:

- *Paperback* To order the paperback edition, use ISBN 978-1-319-05665-0.
- *High school* To order the hardcover high school edition, use ISBN 978-1-319-05668-1.
- *Popular e-Book formats* For details about our e-Book partners, visit **macmillanlearning.com/ebooks.**

Select Value Packages

Add value to your text by packaging one of the following resources with *Models for Writers*.

LaunchPad Solo for Readers and Writers allows students to work on what they need help with the most. At home or in class, students learn at their own pace, with instruction tailored to each student's unique needs. *LaunchPad Solo for Readers and Writers* features:

- **Pre-built units that support a learning arc.** Each easy-to-assign unit is comprised of a pre-test check, multimedia instruction and assessment, and a post-test that assesses what students have learned about critical reading, the writing process, using sources, grammar, style, and mechanics. Dedicated units also offer help for multilingual writers.
- **Diagnostics that help establish a baseline for instruction.** Assign diagnostics to identify areas of strength and for improvement and to help students plan a course of study. Use visual reports to track performance by topic, class, and student as well as improvement over time.
- **A video introduction to many topics.** Introductions offer an overview of the unit's topic, and many include a brief, accessible video to illustrate the concepts at hand.
- **Twenty-five reading selections with comprehension quizzes.** Assign a range of classic and contemporary essays each of which includes a label indicating Lexile level to help you scaffold instruction in critical reading.
- **Adaptive quizzing for targeted learning.** Most units include LearningCurve, game-like adaptive quizzing that focuses on the areas in which each student needs the most help.

• **Additional reading comprehension quizzes.** *Models for Writers* includes multiple-choice quizzes, which help you quickly gauge your students' understanding of the assigned reading. These are available in *LaunchPad Solo for Readers and Writers.*

LaunchPad Solo for Readers and Writers can be packaged with *Models for Writers* at a significant discount. For more information, contact your sales representative or visit **macmillanlearning /readwrite.**

Writer's Help 2.0 is a powerful online writing resource that helps students find answers, whether they are searching for writing advice on their own or as part of an assignment.

• **Smart search.** Built on research with more than 1,600 student writers, the smart search in Writer's Help provides reliable results even when students use novice terms, such as *flow* and *unstuck*.

• **Trusted content from our best-selling handbooks.** Choose *Writer's Help 2.0, Hacker Version*, or *Writer's Help 2.0, Lunsford Version*, and ensure that students have clear advice and examples for all of their writing questions.

• **Diagnostics that help establish a baseline for instruction.** Assign diagnostics to identify areas of strength and areas for improvement and to help students plan a course of study. Use visual reports to track performance by topic, class, and student as well as improvement over time.

• **Adaptive exercises that engage students.** Writer's Help 2.0 includes LearningCurve, game-like online quizzing that adapts to what students already know and helps them focus on what they need to learn.

• **Reading comprehension quizzes.** *Models for Writers* includes multiple-choice quizzes, which help you quickly gauge your students' understanding of the assigned reading. These are available in Writer's Help 2.0.

Writer's Help 2.0 can be packaged with *Models for Writers* at a significant discount. For more information, contact your sales representative or visit **macmillanlearning.com/writershelp2.**

Instructor Resources

You have a lot to do in your course. We want to make it easy for you to find the support you need—and to get it to you quickly.

Instructor's Manual for Models for Writers is available as a PDF that can be downloaded from **macmillanlearning.com**. Visit the instructor resources tab for *Models for Writers*. In addition to suggested answers for each selection's critical reading and study questions, the instructor's manual includes essay analysis and discussion, as well as tips to help students think critically about what they have read. Also included in the manual are two sample course plans for first-year composition courses—one fifteen weeks, one ten weeks—and a complete sample syllabus for a fifteen-week developmental English course.

COUNCIL OF WRITING PROGRAM ADMINISTRATORS (WPA) OUTCOMES STATEMENT FOR FIRST-YEAR COMPOSITION

In 2014 the Council of Writing Program Administrators updated its desired outcomes for first-year composition courses. The following chart provides detailed information on how *Models for Writers* helps students build proficiency and achieve the learning outcomes that writing programs across the country use to assess their students' work: rhetorical knowledge; critical thinking, reading, and writing; writing processes; and knowledge of conventions.

WPA Outcomes	Relevant Features of *Models for Writers*, 13e
RHETORICAL KNOWLEDGE	
Learn and use key rhetorical concepts through analyzing and composing a variety of texts	• The organization of *Models for Writers* supports students' understanding of rhetorical strategy. **Part Two** (Chs. 3–10) focuses on elements of the essay; **Part Three** (Chs. 11–12) highlights the language and style of the essay; **Part Four** (Chs. 13–22) explores the different writing strategies most often required of college students. Concise and practical **chapter introductions** explain how the elements and strategies suit authors' purposes. • **Chapter 1** shows students how to identify their **audience** (p. 20) and introduces them to **purpose** through an understanding of rhetorical methods of development (pp. 20–22). • In **Chapter 2**, students learn how to understand **context** through headnotes and how to read rhetorically and read as a writer (p. 53), analyzing and evaluating texts according to their rhetorical purpose. • Dedicated **boxes** such as Audience Questions (p. 20) and Questions to Ask Yourself as You Read (p. 45) provide additional support for analyzing and composing texts. • **Questions for Study and Discussion** following each reading focus on the author's purpose and the particular strategy used to achieve that purpose. • **Suggested Writing Assignments** following each reading prompt students to write using the rhetorical element or strategy focused on in that chapter. • A dedicated section in Chapter 21, Argument, asks students to **Consider Ethos, Logos, and Pathos** (p. 497).
Gain experience reading and composing in several genres to understand how genre conventions shape and are shaped by readers' and writers' practices and purposes	• The **seventy readings** in the book span a variety of topics, disciplines, and genres. Part Three is organized by rhetorical pattern, with three reading options per chapter to give students experience and practice. • Each reading selection features a **robust apparatus** that gives students practice analyzing and writing for a variety of purposes and in a range of styles. In addition to Questions for Study and Discussion and Suggested Writing Assignments (see above), **Classroom Activities** provide opportunities for applied learning with exercises that enable students to work (often in groups) on rhetorical elements, techniques, or patterns. Several activities connect rhetorical strategies to real-world **genres** such as application letters and memos.

WPA Outcomes	Relevant Features of *Models for Writers*, 13e *(cont.)*
Develop facility in responding to a variety of situations and contexts calling for purposeful shifts in voice, tone, level of formality, design, medium, and/or structure	• Chapter introductions explain how each rhetorical element and strategy is used to achieve an author's purpose. • **Part Two** (Chs. 3–10) emphasizes the Elements of the Essay, with dedicated chapters and model professional readings focused on organized writing: Thesis, Unity, Organization, Beginnings and Endings, Paragraphs, Transitions, Effective Sentences, and Writing with Sources. • **Part Three** (Chs. 11–12) emphasizes the Language of the Essay, with chapters dedicated to Diction/Tone and Figurative Language. • While most essays and instruction highlight the writer's chosen organization, students are introduced to the importance of structure in the section Map Your Organization in Chapter 1 (p. 23), and **Chapter 5, Organization**, focuses especially on essay structure.
Understand and use a variety of technologies to address a range of audiences	• Several of the **Classroom Activities** encourage students to engage other learning styles and use other technologies, from drawing on paper to creating storyboards. • The book's **LaunchPad** invites students to interact with the readings in a digital environment with highlighting and annotation tools. Online tutorials on important writing concepts help students learn through interaction. In addition, adaptive, game-like **LearningCurve** quizzing allows students to practice reading and writing skills.
Match the capacities of different environments (e.g., print and electronic) to varying rhetorical situations	• Research coverage in Chapter 10 and Chapter 23 gives instructions specific to research and project planning, from taking notes to finding and evaluating sources, in **both print and online spaces.** • See also the previous WPA Outcomes section, "Understand and use a variety of technologies to address a range of audiences."

CRITICAL THINKING, READING, AND COMPOSING

Use composing and reading for inquiry, learning, critical thinking, and communicating in various rhetorical contexts	• Chapter 1, The Writing Process, presents writing as **inquiry**, as a tool for **gathering ideas and exploring topics**. • Chapter 2, From Reading to Writing, gives students tools to read critically and learn to read as a writer (p. 53); students learn to understand the **rhetorical context** and the writer's choices in order to apply those tools to their own writing. • Thinking Critically about This Reading, Questions for Study and Discussion, and Suggested Writing Assignments encourage students to **write to learn** through small-stakes journal or homework writing or full essays appropriate to the rhetorical strategy of the chapter.

WPA Outcomes	Relevant Features of *Models for Writers*, 13e *(cont.)*
Read a diverse range of texts, attending especially to relationships between assertion and evidence, to patterns of organization, to the interplay between verbal and nonverbal elements, and to how these features function for different audiences and situations	• **A lively collection of seventy brief classic and contemporary essays provide outstanding models for students.** Each selection has been carefully chosen to engage students and to clearly illustrate a basic rhetorical element or pattern at work in the chapter. • **Thematic clusters** (pp. xxxi–xxxvi) offer flexibility, grouping readings by topic so students can use the selection in the book to collect and analyze information on their subject of choice. Themes include The American Dream, The Immigrant Experience, The Natural World, Social Issues and Activism, and Technology, among others. • A new **Chapter 22, Combining Models**, explains more varied organizational writing strategies, showing how to combine patterns for effective writing. • Several readings include images to encourage students to analyze the relationship between **visual and verbal elements** (see Wei-Haas, Shaughnessy, Krulwich, Morris). • **Chapter 21, Argument**, provides thorough coverage of making and **supporting claims**.
Locate and evaluate (for credibility, sufficiency, accuracy, timeliness, bias, and so on) primary and secondary research materials, including journal articles and essays, books, scholarly and professionally established and maintained databases or archives, and informal electronic networks and Internet sources	*Models for Writers* offers practical instruction on working with sources to guide students in one of their biggest writing challenges: incorporating supporting evidence from other writers into their essays. • Chapter 1, The Writing Process, offers students clear advice and steps for developing **strong thesis statements** and marshaling **evidence** and **support**. • **Chapter 10, Writing with Sources**, and **Chapter 23, A Brief Guide to Writing a Research Paper**, review the steps and skills involved in research and synthesis, with dedicated sections on Finding and Using Sources in print and online (p. 597), Evaluating Your Print and Online Sources (p. 599), and Analyzing Your Sources for Position and Bias (p. 601). The chapter includes model MLA- and APA-style research papers and models for citations. • Helpful **charts** in Chapter 23 make useful **reference tools**; see, for example, Refining Keyword Searches on the Web (p. 598) and Strategies for Evaluating Print and Online Sources (p. 599).
Use strategies—such as interpretation, synthesis, response, critique, and design/redesign—to compose texts that integrate the writer's ideas with those from appropriate sources	• The questions and prompts that accompany each reading ask students to **interpret**, **respond**, and **critique** the reading and the writer's choices, engaging in academic **conversation**. • **Chapter 10, Writing with Sources**, models strategies for taking effective notes from sources; using signal phrases to **integrate** quotations, summaries, and paraphrases smoothly; **synthesizing** sources; and avoiding plagiarism. • The Checklist for Analyzing a Writer's Position and Bias (p. 602) in Chapter 23 urges students to analyze writers' purposes and **assumptions** as they incorporate outside sources into their own writing. • A new student essay, "Shame: The Ultimate Clickbait," in the Chapter 21 argument cluster, Crime: Finding an Effective Punishment, demonstrates how to enter a conversation, **synthesize** selections from *Models for Writers*, and organize an effective written argument. • See also the previous WPA Outcomes section, "Locate and evaluate. . . ."

WPA Outcomes	Relevant Features of *Models for Writers*, 13e *(cont.)*
PROCESSES	
Develop a writing project through multiple drafts	• **Chapter 1, The Writing Process**, leads students from Prewriting through Drafting, Revising, Editing, and Proofreading to present a final draft. See, especially, Choose a Subject Area and Focus on a Topic (p. 11), Get Ideas and Collect Information (p. 12), and the step-by-step process in Develop Your Thesis (p. 14). • **Chapter 24, Editing for Grammar, Punctuation, and Sentence Style**, provides sound advice, examples, and solutions for the editing problems that trouble students most.
Develop flexible strategies for reading, drafting, reviewing, collaborating, revising, rewriting, rereading, and editing	• In Chapter 1, a sample student essay by Jeffrey Olesky (pp. 34–38) **illustrates one student's choices** during the process for each stage and is also available as an interactive tutorial activity in LaunchPad. • Most **Classroom Activities** that accompany each reading encourage students to work **collaboratively** to understand and apply rhetorical concepts and strategies in writing or other exploratory methods.
Use composing processes and tools as a means to discover and reconsider ideas	As part of the instruction on the writing process, Chapter 1 includes dedicated sections to help students **brainstorm and prewrite** with notes, clustering, and outlining: Choose a Subject Area and Focus on a Topic (p. 11) and Get Ideas and Collect Information (p. 12).
Experience the collaborative and social aspects of writing processes	• The Reflecting on What You Know and Thinking Critically about the Reading prompts that immediately precede and follow each reading selection, respectively, can be used for **group discussion and writing**. • The Classroom Activities that accompany each reading frequently ask students to **share their writing** and ideas with their classmates and discuss them, learning from each other.
Learn to give and to act on productive feedback to works in progress	Dedicated boxes in Chapter 1, such as Questions for Revising (p. 27), guide students through the writing process and assist in **peer revision** workshops.
Adapt composing processes for a variety of technologies and modalities	• The book assumes that most students compose in digital spaces, and instructions in a number of Suggested Writing Assignments and other prompts reflect and encourage this use of the digital space. • Instructions for research and collecting notes on sources in Chapter 10 and Chapter 23 assume that students are working mostly online and with technology, so the advice offers strategies for **collecting and managing data in digital formats**. • The **LaunchPad** version of *Models for Writers* offers a digital course space and an interactive e-book as well as integrated digital tutorials to teach core concepts of writing.
Reflect on the development of composing practices and how those practices influence their work	**Reflecting on What You Know** prompts before each reading ask students to discover and apply their prior knowledge to the reading selection.

WPA Outcomes | Relevant Features of *Models for Writers*, 13e *(cont.)*

KNOWLEDGE OF CONVENTIONS

Develop knowledge of linguistic structures, including grammar, punctuation, and spelling, through practice in composing and revising	• A dedicated Part Three focuses particularly on the **Language of the Essay**, drawing students' attention to the rhetorical effectiveness of diction, tone, and figurative language. • Chapters in Part Two, The Elements of the Essay, emphasize the importance of **linguistic structure** at various levels of the essay, including Transitions (Ch. 8) and Effective Sentences (Ch. 9). • **Chapter 24, Editing for Grammar, Punctuation, and Sentence Style**, covers common grammar and mechanical errors and presents clear examples of corrections to help students write with minimal errors. Coverage includes run-ons and comma splices, sentence fragments, subject-verb agreement, pronoun-antecedent agreement, verb tense shifts, misplaced and dangling modifiers, faulty parallelism, weak nouns and verbs, and academic diction and tone. • In the LaunchPad, **LearningCurve adaptive quizzing** on common grammar, mechanics, and writing topics lead students to online self-guided practice that lets them learn at their own pace.
Understand why genre conventions for structure, paragraphing, tone, and mechanics vary	• Chapter introductions for each rhetorical element in Parts Two and Three and for each rhetorical pattern in Part Four explain how each strategy serves a writer's **purpose**. • Dedicated chapters on **Paragraphs** (Ch. 7), **Tone** (Ch. 11), and **Mechanics** (Ch. 24) further emphasize rhetorical importance and variation.
Gain experience negotiating variations in genre conventions	In addition to the support in chapter introductions mentioned above, the **Classroom Activities** and **Suggested Writing Assignments** following each reading selection encourage students to apply the rhetorical strategies to real-world genres and situations and to use them in their writing.
Learn common formats and/or design features for different kinds of texts	Model student essays in the book are presented in MLA formatting. Chapter 23 features fully formatted examples of **MLA**- and **APA**-style student research papers, with annotations highlighting the **genre design conventions**.
Explore the concepts of intellectual property (such as fair use and copyright) that motivate documentation conventions	• **Chapter 10, Writing with Sources**, explains why outside sources are rhetorically useful and helps writers articulate positions in the conversation and extend their own ideas, and how doing so requires **thoughtful documentation** when **integrating** quotation, paraphrase, or summary. • A dedicated section, **Avoid Plagiarism** (p. 238), further defines and explores these concepts.
Practice applying citation conventions systematically in their own work	**Chapter 23, A Brief Guide to Writing a Research Paper**, offers detailed guidance on taking notes to avoid plagiarism as well as model citations in both **MLA and APA styles**.

Contents

Thematic Clusters

The thematic clusters that follow focus on themes that students can pursue in their own compositions. The essays themselves provide ideas and information that will stimulate their thinking as well as provide source material for their writing. The clusters—the themes and the essays associated with them—are meant to be suggestive rather than comprehensive and fairly narrow in scope rather than far-ranging. Instructors and students are, of course, not limited by our groupings and are free to develop their own thematic groupings on which to base written work.

The American Dream

Arts and Entertainment

Discoveries/Epiphanies

Education

Family and Friends

Feminism and Gender Roles

Heroes/Role Models

The Immigrant Experience

Language and Power

Medical Dilemmas

Moral Values

The Natural World

Parenting

Peer Pressure

People and Personalities

Punishment and Crime

Race in America

Sense of Place

Sense of Self

Sensual World

Social Issues and Activism

Technology

Work

Writers on Writing

Introduction for Students

Both students and teachers often agree that it is important to write well, and it is not hard to figure out why. Knowing how to write well is stressed at every rung of the educational ladder—from the early grades, through middle school, high school, and college. "You need to know how to write." This thought, often a command, has become an educational cliché, a truth so often uttered and so seemingly apparent that few people feel the need to offer any explanation for it. As the authors of *Models for Writers*, however, we feel a special obligation to offer reasons for learning to write and for doing it well. It's simple. We always learn better if we understand what and why we are learning.

No activity better develops your ability to think than writing does. Writing allows you to express what's on your mind, to examine your thoughts, and to "see" objectively what you think. When you write thoughtfully and clearly, others can better understand you. Better yet, you can know yourself better. One way of thinking about writing, then, is to see it as holding a mirror up to yourself.

Writing, unlike speaking, is usually more deliberate and allows you to examine your ideas carefully and critically by reading what you have written as you compose sentences. It's not a one-way street but an interactive process. The process of reading what you have written and then revising and refocusing what you think gives you many opportunities to improve, clarify, and best express what you want to say. At some point in the process, when you are satisfied with your thinking, you can freeze the best expression of your thoughts, for that moment at least. And that moment can be an immensely satisfying one. When you can say about what you've written, "That's exactly what I mean," you will have brought order out of chaos and certainty where none seemed possible before. No other activity can do as much for developing your critical and intellectual abilities as writing.

It should not come as a surprise, then, that employers in every field are looking for people who can read and write well, for all these reasons. Simply put, employers want to hire and retain the best minds they can to reach their business objectives, and the ability to read and write well is a clear indication of a rigorous mind. In today's workplace, there is virtually no field that doesn't require clear, accurate, and direct expression in writing, whether it be writing cover letters and résumés, internal e-mails, self-appraisals, laboratory reports, contract bids, proposals, loan or grant applications, sales reports, market analyses, journal articles, books, or any other documents. Perhaps more than anything else, your ability to organize your thoughts and present them clearly will affect your overall success not only on the job but also in life itself.

Models for Writers is designed to help you learn to write by providing you with a collection of model essays—that is, essays that are examples of good writing. Good writing is direct and purposeful and communicates its message without confusing the reader. It doesn't wander from the topic, and it answers the reader's questions. Although good writing is well developed and detailed, it also accomplishes its task with the fewest possible words and with the simplest language appropriate to the writer's topic and thesis.

We know that one of the best ways to learn to write and to improve our writing is to read. By reading, we can see how other writers have communicated their experiences, ideas, thoughts, and feelings. We can study how they have used the various elements of the essay (words, sentences, paragraphs, organizational patterns, transitions, examples, evidence, and so forth) and thus learn how we might effectively do the same. When we see how a writer like James Lincoln Collier develops his essay "Anxiety: Challenge by Another Name" (p. 85) from a strong thesis statement, for example, we can better appreciate the importance of having a clear thesis statement in our own writing. When we see the way Maya Wei-Haas uses transitions in "How Chuck Taylor Taught America How to Play Basketball" (p. 186) to link events and important ideas so that readers can recognize how the parts of her essay fit together, we have a better idea of how to write coherently.

But we do not learn only by reading. We also learn by doing—that is, by writing—and in the best of all situations, we engage in reading and writing in conjunction with each other.

Models for Writers therefore encourages you to practice what you are learning and to move from reading to writing.

- **Part One, On Reading and Writing Well** (Chapters 1–2), introduces you to the important steps of the writing process, shows you how to use apparatus that accompanies each selection in this text, provides you with guidelines for critical reading, and demonstrates with three annotated student essays how you can generate your own writing from reading. You will soon see that an effective essay has a clear purpose, often provides useful information, has an effect on the reader's thoughts and feelings, and is usually a pleasure to read. The essays that you will read in *Models for Writers* were chosen because they are effective.

All well-written essays share a number of structural and stylistic features, and these are illustrated by the various essays in *Models for Writers*. One good way to learn what these features are and how you can incorporate them into your own writing is to look at each of them in isolation. For this reason, twenty chapters of essays, each chapter with its own particular focus and emphasis, are spread over Parts Two, Three, and Four.

- **Part Two, The Elements of the Essay** (Chapters 3–10), includes eight chapters on the elements that are essential to a well-written essay. Because the concepts of thesis, unity, and organization underlie all the others, they come first in our sequence, followed closely by advice and models for strong beginnings and endings, well-developed paragraphs, clear transitions, and effective sentences. Finally, a chapter on writing with sources provides proven strategies for taking effective notes from sources; for using signal phrases to integrate quotations, summaries, and paraphrases smoothly into the text of an essay; and for avoiding plagiarism.
- **Part Three, The Language of the Essay** (Chapters 11–12), shows how writers carefully choose words to convey meaning, to create a particular tone or relationship between writer and reader, and to add richness and depth to writing through figurative language.
- **Part Four, Types of Essays** (Chapters 13–22), focuses on the types of writing that are most often required of college writing students. These types of writing are often referred to as *organizational patterns* or *rhetorical modes*.

- **Part Five, Guides to Research and Editing** (Chapters 23–24), includes a useful Chapter 23, A Brief Guide to Writing a Research Paper, with an annotated MLA-style student research paper. This chapter provides clear guidance on establishing a realistic schedule for a research project, conducting research on the Internet using directory and keyword searches, evaluating sources, analyzing sources, developing a working bibliography, taking useful notes, and using MLA and APA citation styles to document your paper. Chapter 24, Editing for Grammar, Punctuation, and Sentence Style, provides sound advice and solutions for the editing problems that trouble students most. This final section in *Models for Writers* helps you build confidence in your academic writing skills.

Studying and practicing the organizational patterns are important in any effort to broaden your writing skills. In *Models for Writers*, we look at each pattern separately because we believe that this is the simplest and most effective way to introduce them. However, it does not mean that the writer of a well-written essay necessarily chooses a single pattern and sticks to it exclusively and rigidly. Confining yourself to cause-and-effect analysis or definition throughout an entire essay, for example, might prove impractical and may yield an awkward or unnatural piece of writing. In fact, it is often best to use a single pattern to organize your essay and then to use other patterns as your material dictates. As you read the model essays in this text, you will find that a good many of them use one dominant pattern in combination with other patterns, but we have especially developed a new **Chapter 22, Combining Models**, to showcase essays that use multiple patterns.

Chapters 3 to 22 are organized in the same way. Each opens with an explanation of the element or principle under discussion. These introductions are brief, clear, and practical and usually provide one or more short examples of the feature or principle being studied, including examples from students such as yourself. Following the chapter introduction, we present three model essays (Chapter 21, with ten essays, is an exception). Each essay has a brief introduction of its own, providing information about the author and directing your attention to the way the essay demonstrates the featured technique. A Reflecting on What You Know prompt precedes each reading and invites you to explore your own ideas and experiences regarding some issue presented in the reading. Each essay is followed by four kinds of study materials—Thinking Critically about This Reading, Questions for Study and Discussion, Classroom Activity, and Suggested Writing Assignments. Read Chapter 2, From Reading to Writing, for help on improving your writing by using the materials that accompany the readings.

Models for Writers provides information, instruction, and practice in writing effective essays. By reading thoughtfully and critically and by applying the writing strategies and techniques you observe other writers using, you will learn to write more expressively and effectively.

part one

On Reading and Writing Well

You have until 01/11/19 to receive a full refund with receipt!

9781319056650 RENTAL @ 17.95	17.95
1 U MODELS FOR WRITERS	

Subtotal:	17.95
Tax:	1.08
TOTAL:	19.03
CREDIT	19.03
Change Due	0.00

151604-2-10	2019-01-08 13:44:08

KEEP YOUR RECEIPT!!!

You have until 1/11/19 to receive a full refund with receipt!

RENTAL AGREEMENT
1. I am at least 18 years of age.
2. I am entering this Textbook Rental Agreement ("Agreement") with Textbook Outlet of my own free will as of the date set out. I will return each of the textbooks rented ("Rented Materials") to Textbook Outlet where I received the

Rented Materials are part of and subject to this Agreement.

3. Failure to Return. If I fail to return each of the Rented Materials by the Due Date, or return them in an unacceptable condition (as set out below), I authorize Textbook Outlet to charge the following "Non-return Fee" to my credit card: (1) 90% of the new book price plus (2) a processing fee of 10% of new book price. Textbook Outlet is not responsible for reminding me of any Due Date. Once the Non-return Fees have been paid in respect of the Rented Materials, the Rented Materials shall belong to me.

4. Conditions upon Return. Highlighting and writing in rented textbooks is permitted and acceptable. However, Rental Materials must be returned in complete and saleable condition. Saleable condition means the spine of the book is intact, there is no water damage to the book, and all component parts of the book must be present. I am responsible for any loss or theft of the Rented Materials.

5. Cards as Security. I will not cancel or exceed the purchasing limits of the credit card above until the Rented Materials are either returned to Textbook Outlet by the Due Date in saleable condition or the Non-return Fees are paid. I will promptly notify Textbook Outlet of any changes to my personal information or my credit card information as set out above.

6. Refund. The Bookstore's standard

CHAPTER 1

The Writing Process

The essays in this book will help you understand the elements of good writing and provide ample opportunity for you to practice writing in response to the model essays. As you write your essays, pay attention to your writing process. This chapter focuses on the stages of the writing process—prewriting, writing the first draft, revising, editing, and proofreading. It concludes with a sample of one student's writing process that you can model your own writing after. The strategies suggested in this chapter for each stage of the writing process will help you overcome many of the challenges you may face while writing essays.

Writers rarely rely on inspiration alone to produce an effective piece of writing. Good writers prewrite or plan, write the first draft, revise, edit, and proofread. It is worth remembering, however, that often the process is recursive, moving back and forth among the five stages. Moreover, writing is personal; no two people go about it exactly the same way. Still, it is possible to learn the steps in the process and thereby have a reliable method for undertaking a writing task.

PREWRITING

Reading can give you ideas and information, and reading helps expand your knowledge of the organizational patterns available to you; consequently, it can help direct all your prewriting activities. During *prewriting*, you select your subject and topic, gather ideas and information, and determine the thesis and organizational pattern or patterns you will use. Once you have worked through the prewriting process, you will be ready to start on your first draft. Let's explore how this works.

Understand Your Assignment

When you first receive an assignment, read it over several times to make sure you understand what you are being asked to do. Try restating the assignment in your own words to make sure you understand it. For example, consider the following assignments:

1. Narrate an experience that taught you that every situation has at least two sides.
2. Explain what is meant by *theoretical modeling* in the social sciences.
3. Write a persuasive essay in which you support or refute the following proposition: "Violence in the media is in large part responsible for an increase in violence in American society today."

Each of these assignments asks you to write in different ways:

1. The first assignment asks you to tell the story of an event that showed you that every situation has more than one perspective. To complete the assignment, you might choose simply to narrate the event, or you might choose to analyze it in depth. In either case, you will need to explain to your reader how you came to this new understanding of multiple perspectives and why it was important to you.
2. The second assignment asks you to explain what theoretical modeling is and why it is used. To accomplish this assignment, you will first need to read about the concept to gain a thorough understanding of it, and then you'll need to define it in your own words and explain its purpose and usefulness to your readers. You will also want to demonstrate the abstract concept with concrete examples to help your readers understand it.
3. The third assignment asks you to take a position on a controversial issue for which there are many studies on both sides of the question. You will need to research the studies, consider the evidence they present, and then take a stand of your own. Your argument will necessarily have to draw on the sources and evidence you have researched, and you will need to refute the arguments and evidence presented by those experts who take an opposing position.

If, after reading the assignment several times, you are still unsure about what is being asked of you or about any additional requirements of the assignment, such as length or format, be sure to consult with your instructor.

Choose a Subject Area and Focus on a Topic

Although you will usually be given specific assignments in your writing course, you may sometimes have the freedom to write on any subject that interests you. In such a case, you may already have a specific idea in mind. For example, if you are interested in sports, you might argue against the use of performance-enhancing drugs by athletes. What happens, however, when you are free to choose your own subject and cannot think of anything to write about? If you find yourself in this situation, begin by determining a broad subject that you might enjoy writing about—a general subject such as medical ethics, amateur sports, or foreign travel. Also consider what you've recently read—essays in *Models for Writers*, for example—or your career ambitions when choosing a subject. Select several likely subjects and let your mind explore their potential for interesting topics. Your goal is to arrive at an appropriately narrowed *topic*.

A *topic* is the specific part of a subject on which a writer focuses. Subjects such as the environment, literature, and sports are too broad to be dealt with adequately in a single essay. Entire books are written about these and other subjects. Start with your broad subject and make it more specific.

Suppose, for example, you select farming and advertising as possible subject areas. The examples in the Narrowing Subjects to Topics box that follows illustrate how to narrow these broad subjects into manageable topics. Notice how each successive topic is more narrowed than the one before it. Moving from the general to the specific, the topics become appropriate for essay-length writing.

In moving from a broad subject to a particular topic, you should take into account any assigned constraints on length or format. You will also want to consider the amount of time you have to write. These practical considerations will affect the scope of your topic.

☑ For more practice, visit the LaunchPad for *Models for Writers*: LearningCurve > Main Ideas

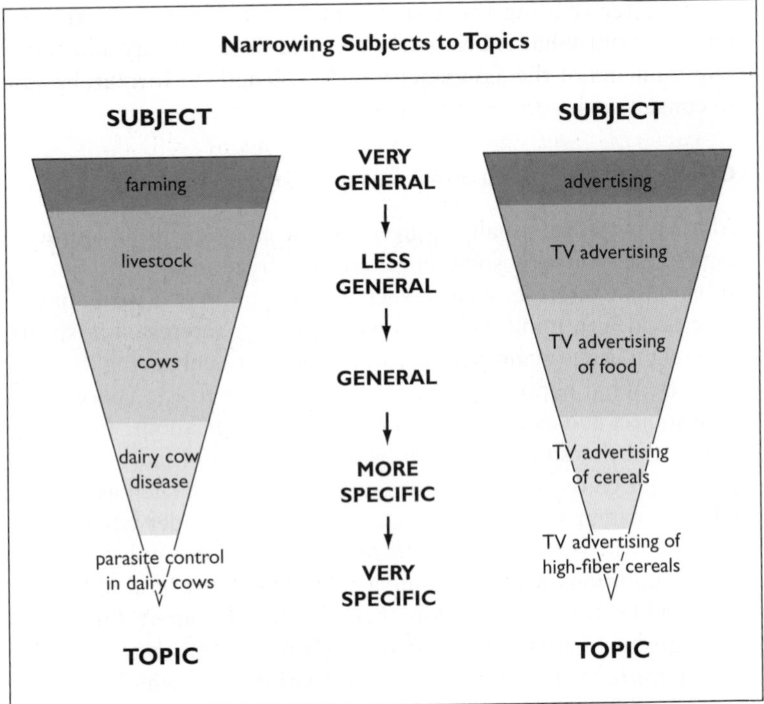

Get Ideas and Collect Information

After you have found your topic, you will need to determine what you want to say about it. The best way to do this is to gather information. Your ideas about a topic must be supported by information, such as facts and examples. The information you gather about a topic will influence your ideas about the topic and what you want to say. Here are some of the ways you can gather information:

1. *Brainstorm.* Jot down the things you know about a topic, freely associating ideas and information as a way to explore the topic and its possibilities. (See p. 30 for an example.) Try not to censor or edit your notes, and don't worry about spelling or punctuation. Don't write your notes in list form because such an organization will imply a hierarchy of ideas, which may hamper your creativity and the free flow of your thoughts. The objective of *brainstorming* is to free up your thinking before

you start to write. You may want to set aside your notes and return to them over several days. Once you generate a substantial amount of brainstormed material, you will want to study the items, attempt to see relationships among them, or sort and group the entries by using different colored highlighters.

2. *Cluster.* Another strategy for stimulating your thinking about a topic is *clustering*. Place your topic in a circle and draw lines from that circle to other circles in which you write related key words or phrases. Around each of these key words, generate more circles representing the various aspects of the key word that come to mind. (See p. 31 for an example.) The value of clustering over brainstorming is that you are generating ideas and organizing them at the same time. Both techniques work very well, but you may prefer one over the other or find that one works better with one topic than another.
3. *Research.* You may want to add to what you already know about your topic with research. Research can take many forms beyond formal research carried out in your library. For example, firsthand observations and interviews with people knowledgeable about your topic can provide up-to-date information. Whatever your form of research, take careful notes so you can accurately paraphrase an author or quote an interviewee. Chapters 10 and 23 (see pp. 225–42 and 595–605) will help with all aspects of researching a topic.

Understand What a Thesis Is

Once you have generated ideas and information about your topic, you are ready to begin the important task of establishing a controlling idea, or *thesis,* for your essay. The thesis of an essay is its main idea, the point you are trying to make. It is important because everything in your essay, all the ideas and information you have gathered, should be connected to the thesis. It is the glue that holds your writing together.

In his essay "The Ways of Meeting Oppression" (pp. 425–29), Martin Luther King Jr. offers the following thesis statement: "Oppressed people deal with their oppression in three characteristic ways." King supports his thesis by describing the three ways that oppressed people have traditionally dealt with oppression and explaining why two of those responses—acquiescing to their oppressors or violently resisting them—have not traditionally worked and are not responses he would recommend. He then works his way to the conclusion of his essay, recommending the path of nonviolent resistance as the best way to achieve social justice. His thesis statement carries with it the answer to several implied or built-in questions: What are the characteristic ways of meeting oppression, and which one is to be recommended? The structure of his essay, then, is also built into his thesis statement.

Remember that a weak thesis cannot produce a successful essay no matter how much effort you put into your writing. A strong thesis, on the other hand, will succeed, but only if it is properly supported.

Develop Your Thesis

You might think that creating a thesis requires some kind of clever thinking or special skills on your part when, in fact, it's a fairly straightforward task. Rather than staring at a blank screen or sheet of paper hoping for a thesis to magically appear, you need to look at the ideas and information you have generated about your topic and ask questions about them in order to understand the topic completely.

STEP 1: ASK QUESTIONS

Let's say that you chose or were assigned the topic of internships, the practice of employing relatively inexperienced people, often students, so that they become familiar with particular work environments and business practices. Through your reading you have learned that internships are often mutually beneficial. Interns can gain useful work-related experience, and businesses get inexpensive temporary help (which sometimes leads to permanent positions).

Now you need to more deeply inform yourself about internships by asking questions about the information and ideas you have gathered. For example,

- Why did internships develop as an educational and business practice? Where and when are they now used?
- Are there internship programs at your school? If so, what informational materials are available to you?

- Who can help you find an internship? Can you get an internship on your own?
- Do any businesses in your area offer internships?
- What are the negative aspects of an internship for both parties?
- Do you have family or friends who have employed interns? Do you have family or friends who have had internships? What information have you been able to gain from those on both sides of the relationship?
- Are interns usually paid? How are internships funded?

When the questioning starts, one question will lead to another, and the answers to these questions—often found through more reading, interviews, and discussions—will inform you about the depth and breadth of your topic. If all this is done well, you will soon begin to think like an expert on your topic.

At this point, the likelihood of developing a thesis, or a number of them, will greatly increase. It is out of the facts and ideas that you have collected and the questions you ask of that material that a thesis will come to mind.

STEP 2: LIST SEVERAL POSSIBLE THESIS STATEMENTS

After you have asked all the questions you think necessary and have supplied answers to those questions, you are ready to list possible thesis statements. Trying to develop not just one thesis but several of them can be a very helpful strategy in refining your ideas and coming up with the best possible thesis. Also, keep in mind that a thesis can be considered a *working thesis* until you are sure it conveys exactly what you want to say, or until you revise it into its final form.

Here are some theses that might be developed as a result of a deeper investigation into the topic of internships:

- All effective internship programs have five key elements.
- Research is necessary before applying to an internship program.
- Employers must have a clearly defined set of expectations for internship programs.
- Record keeping and reporting are the keys to an effective internship program.

- There are no standard practices for funding internships.
- We need a federally funded internship program.

STEP 3: CHOOSE YOUR DIRECTION

The potential theses listed in Step 2 reflect different approaches to and aspects of the topic of internships. Let's take a closer look at how each one may have been arrived at and where each might lead the writer:

- *All effective internship programs have five key elements.*

  This thesis is most likely the product of an examination of successful internship programs to learn their key elements. The supporting information might also serve to explain the establishment of an internship program or how to improve an existing one.
- *Research is necessary before applying to an internship program.*

  This thesis might be the product of learning what can go right and wrong with an internship and might even suggest what individuals need to know about a program before entering it.
- *Employers must have a clearly defined set of expectations for internship programs.*

  This thesis suggests that successful internships are the result of clear expectations for the intern and well-defined pathways for achieving success.
- *Record keeping and reporting are the keys to an effective internship program.*

  This thesis suggests that communication is important in any internship relationship. It implies that all parties should document projects, goals, and steps toward achieving those goals, as well as any or all efforts in accomplishing them.
- *There are no standard practices for funding internships.*

  This thesis suggests that the way internships are financed is not standardized and that because each internship must be arranged for individually, arrangements vary greatly.
- *We need a federally funded internship program.*

  This thesis suggests that internships are so worthwhile that they need to be made available nationally and be federally funded.

STEP 4: WRITE YOUR THESIS STATEMENT

A thesis statement should be

- the most important point you make about your topic,
- more general than the ideas and facts you use to support it, and
- focused enough to be covered in the space allotted for the essay.

A thesis statement is not a question, although it might be prompted by one or many, as we have seen with the topic of internships.

An effective method for developing a thesis statement is to begin by writing, "What I want to say is that . . ."

> What I want to say is that unless employers offer paid internships, businesses will never recruit the most qualified interns, and interns will not be able to receive the full benefits of their internships.

Later, when you delete the formulaic opening and streamline the text, you will be left with a thesis statement:

> Unless employers offer paid internships, businesses will never recruit the most qualified interns, and interns will not be able to receive the full benefits of their internships.

A good way to determine whether your thesis is too general or too specific is to consider how easy it will be to present information and examples to support it. If you stray too far in either direction, your task will become much more difficult. A thesis statement that is too general will leave you overwhelmed by the number of issues you must address. For example, the statement "Malls have ruined the fabric of American life" would lead to the question, "How?" To answer it, you would probably have to include information about traffic patterns, urban decay, environmental damage, economic studies, and so on. You would obviously have to take shortcuts, and your essay would be ineffective. On the other hand, too specific a thesis statement will leave you with too little information to present. "The Big City Mall should not have been built because it reduced retail sales at the existing Big City stores by 21.4 percent" does not leave you with many options to develop an argument.

The thesis statement is usually set forth near the beginning of the essay, although writers sometimes begin with a few sentences that establish a context for the piece. One common strategy is to position the thesis as the final sentence of the first paragraph. In the opening paragraph of an essay on the harmful effects of quick-weight-loss diets, student Marcie Turple builds a context for her thesis statement, which she presents in her last sentence:

> Americans are obsessed with thinness—even at the risk of dying. In the 1930s, people took dinitrophenol, an industrial poison, to lose weight. It boosted metabolism but caused blindness and some deaths. Since then dieters have used hormone injections, amphetamines, liquid protein diets, and, more recently, the controversial fen-phen. What most dieters need to realize is that there is no magic way to lose weight—no pill, no crash diet plan. The only way to permanent weight loss is through sensible eating and exercise. *Thesis*
>
> —Marcie Turple, student

STEP 5: REVISE YOUR THESIS STATEMENT IF NECESSARY
Remember that you are not unalterably committed to the wording of your original thesis, what writers call a *working thesis*. Just as you provide evidence to support the thesis statement, you are free to revise the statement to fit the evidence. For example, let's suppose you decide to use the following thesis statement for an essay on internships:

> We need a federally funded internship program.

You discover as you draft your essay that your evidence is largely financial. You learn that schools and businesses, especially in poorer parts of the country, refrain from establishing internships because there is little money for such efforts. You reason that if there were a federally funded program, students and businesses from any part of the country, regardless of local resources, would have an equal opportunity to participate. You then revise your working thesis to reflect this additional, more pertinent evidence:

> We need a nationwide federally funded internship program that will provide equal opportunity for all students and businesses, regardless of their regional economic differences.

Models for Writers abounds in essays with excellent thesis statements, and we often ask you to identify them. Reading essays with strong thesis statements and locating the controlling idea in each is a great way to learn how to write your own strong thesis statements. Here are some more examples of thesis statements drawn from the essays in *Models for Writers*:

James Lincoln Collier states his thesis in paragraph 20 of "Anxiety: Challenge by Another Name" (p. 85):

> The point is that the new, the different, is almost by definition scary. But each time you try something, you learn, and as the learning piles up, the world opens to you.

Collier's thesis appears near the end of his essay and consists of two sentences instead of a single statement.

Natalie Goldberg presents her thesis at the beginning of her essay in "Be Specific" (p. 330):

> Be specific. Don't say "fruit." Tell what kind of fruit—"It is a pomegranate." Give things the dignity of their names. Just as with human beings, it is rude to say, "Hey, girl, get in line." That "girl" has a name.

Notice how she offers a strong opening sentence, really a command, and then moves on to elaborate on what she means by being specific in the rest of her paragraph. It is a message she will carry through the rest of her essay as well.

Finally, in an essay about finding appropriate punishment for minor crimes, Dan M. Kahan in "Shame Is Worth a Try" (p. 557) offers the following thesis statement in paragraph 3:

> [W]hat the shame proponents seem to be getting, and the critics ignoring, is the potential of shame as an effective, cheap, and humane alternative to imprisonment.

With this thesis, Kahan expresses his argument and provides the reader with an outline of the three main points he'll expand on in his essay to support that argument.

As you read through the essays in this book, be on the lookout for thesis statements that you find especially effective: Note their placement within the essay and think about why they've caught your eye. These can serve, then, as models for you when you write your thesis statement. For more on the various ways of developing an effective thesis, see Chapter 3, Thesis (pp. 71–74).

Know Your Audience

Although it is not always possible to know who your readers are, you nevertheless need to consider your intended audience. Your attitude toward your topic, your tone, your sentence structure, and your choice of words are just some of the important considerations that rely on your awareness of audience. For a list of questions to help you determine your audience, see the box below.

Audience Questions

1. Who are my readers?
2. Is my audience specialized (for example, those in my geology lab) or more general (college students)?
3. What do I know about my audience's age, gender, education, religious affiliation, socioeconomic status, and political attitudes?
4. What do my readers need to know that I can tell them?
5. Will my audience be interested, open-minded, resistant, objective, or hostile to what I am saying?
6. Is there any specialized language that my audience must have to understand my subject or that I should avoid?
7. What do I want my audience to do as a result of reading my essay?

Determine Your Method of Development

Part Four of *Models for Writers* includes chapters on the various types of essays most often required of college students. Often these types of writing are referred to as *methods of development*, *modes*, *rhetorical patterns*, or *organizational patterns*.

Studying these organizational patterns and practicing the use of them are important in any effort to broaden your writing skills. *Models for Writers* presents each pattern separately as a way to introduce the pattern effectively and provide focus, but that does not necessarily mean that a well-written essay adheres exclusively and rigidly to a single pattern of development. Confining yourself exclusively to comparison and contrast throughout an entire essay,

☑ **For more practice, visit the LaunchPad for *Models for Writers*: LearningCurve** > Patterns of Organization for instance, might prove impractical and result in a formulaic or stilted essay. As you read the model essays in this text, you will find that many of them use a combination of patterns to support the dominant pattern, and Chapter 22 (pp. 568–71) specifically focuses on how these mixed methods of development can appear in an essay and strengthen its message. For a description of what each organizational pattern involves, see the Organizational Patterns box.

Organizational Patterns

Illustration	Using examples to illustrate a point or an idea
Narration	Telling a story or giving an account of an event
Description	Presenting a picture with words
Process Analysis	Explaining how something is done or happens
Definition	Explaining what something is
Division and Classification	Dividing a subject into its parts and placing them in appropriate categories
Comparison and Contrast	Demonstrating likenesses and differences
Cause and Effect	Explaining the causes of an event or the effects of an action
Argument	Using reason and logic to persuade someone to your way of thinking

Combining organizational patterns is probably not something you want to plan or even think about when you first tackle a writing assignment. Instead, let these patterns develop naturally as you organize, draft, and revise your materials.

If you're still undecided or concerned about combining patterns, try the following steps:

1. Summarize the point you want to make in a single phrase or sentence.
2. Restate the point as a question (in effect, the question your essay will answer).

3. Look closely at both the summary and the question for key words or concepts that suggest a particular pattern.
4. Consider other strategies that could support your primary pattern.

EXAMPLES OF COMBINED ORGANIZATIONAL PATTERNS

Summary	Question	Pattern	Supporting Patterns
Venus and Serena Williams are among the best tennis players in the history of the game.	How do Venus and Serena Williams compare with other tennis players?	*Comparison and contrast.* The writer must compare the Williams sisters with other players and provide evidence to support the claim that they are "among the best."	*Illustration* and *description.* Good evidence includes examples of the Williams sisters' superior ability and accomplishments as well as descriptions of their athletic feats.
How to build a personal website.	How do you build a personal website?	*Process analysis.* The word *how,* especially in the phrase *how to,* implies a procedure that can be explained in steps or stages.	*Description.* The writer should describe the website, especially the look and design of the site, at various points in the process.
Petroleum and natural gas prices should be federally controlled.	What should be done about petroleum and natural gas prices?	*Argument.* The word *should* signals a debatable claim and proposal, which calls for evidence and reasoning in support of the conclusion.	*Comparison and contrast* and *cause and effect.* The writer should present evidence from a comparison of federally controlled pricing with deregulated pricing, as well as from a discussion of the effects of deregulation.

Map Your Organization

After you decide what you want to write about and come up with some ideas about what you might like to say, your next task is to organize the main ideas for your essay in a way that seems both natural and logical to you. One way to map your ideas is to make an outline. In constructing this outline, if you discover that a particular organizational pattern will help you in generating ideas, you might consider using that as your overall organizing principle.

Some writers make a detailed outline and fill it out point by point, whereas others follow a general plan and let the writing take them where it will, making any necessary adjustments to the plan when they revise.

Here are some major patterns of organization you may want to use for your outline:

- Chronological (oldest to newest, or the reverse)
- Spatial (top to bottom, left to right, inside to outside, and so forth)
- Least familiar to most familiar
- Easiest to most difficult to comprehend
- Easiest to most difficult to accept
- According to similarities or differences

Notice that some of these organizational patterns correspond to the rhetorical patterns in Part Four of this book. For example, a narrative essay generally follows a chronological organization. If you are having trouble developing or mapping an effective organization, refer to the introduction and readings in Chapter 5, Organization. Once you have settled on an organizational pattern, you are ready to write a first draft.

WRITING THE FIRST DRAFT

Your goal in writing a first draft is to get your ideas down on paper. Write quickly and let the writing follow your thinking. Do not be overly concerned about spelling, word choice, or grammar because such concerns will break the flow of your ideas. After you have completed your first draft, you will go over your essay to revise and edit it.

As you write your draft, pay attention to your outline but do not be a slave to it. It is there to help you, not restrict you. Often, when writing, you discover something new about your subject; if so, follow that idea freely. Wherever you deviate from your plan, place an X in the margin, use a comment balloon, or highlight the shift to remind yourself of the change. When you revise, you can return to that part of your writing and reconsider the change you made, either developing it further or abandoning it.

It may happen that while writing your first draft, you run into a difficulty that prevents you from moving forward. Use your resources to work through the difficulty: talk about your writing with a friend or writing tutor, review your notes, or use the information in *Models for Writers*. For example, suppose you want to tell the story of something that happened to you, but you aren't certain whether you should be using the pronoun *I* so often. Turn to the essays in Chapters 11 and 14 to see how the authors use diction and tone and how other narrative essays handle this problem. You will find that the frequent use of *I* isn't necessarily a problem at all. For an account of a personal experience, it's perfectly acceptable to use *I* as often as you need to. Or suppose that after writing several pages describing someone who you think is quite a character, you find that your draft seems flat and doesn't express how lively and funny the person really is. If you read the introduction to Chapter 15, you will learn that descriptions need lots of factual, concrete detail; the selections in that chapter give further proof of this. You can use those guidelines to add details that are missing from your draft.

If you run into difficulties writing your first draft, don't be discouraged. Even experienced writers run into problems at the beginning. Just try to keep going and take the pressure off yourself. Think about your topic and consider your details and what you want to say. You may even want to go back and look over the ideas and information you've gathered.

Create a Title

What makes a good title? There are no hard-and-fast rules, but most writers would agree that an effective title hooks the reader into reading the essay, either because the title is unusual and intrigues the reader or because it asks a question and the reader is curious to know the answer. A good title announces your subject and prepares your reader for the approach you take. You can create a title while writing your first draft or after you have seen how your ideas develop. Either way, the important thing is to brainstorm for titles and not simply use the first one that comes to mind. With at least a half dozen to choose from, preferably more, you will have a much better sense of how to pick an effective title—one that does the important work of explaining your subject to the reader and that is lively and inviting. Spend several minutes reviewing the titles of the essays in *Models for Writers* in the Table of Contents, pp. xix–xxxii. You'll like some better than others, but reflecting on the effectiveness of each one will help you strengthen your own titles.

Focus on Beginnings and Endings

Beginnings and endings are important to the effectiveness of essays, but they can be difficult to write. Inexperienced writers often think that they must write their essays sequentially when, in fact, it is

Questions for Beginnings and Endings

1. Does my introduction grab the reader's attention?
2. Is my introduction confusing in any way? How well does it relate to the rest of the essay?
3. If I state my thesis in the introduction, how effectively is it presented?
4. Does my essay come to a logical conclusion, or does it just stop short?
5. How well does the conclusion relate to the rest of the essay? Am I careful not to introduce new topics or issues that I did not address in the body of the essay?
6. Does the conclusion help underscore or illuminate important aspects of the body of the essay, or is it just another version of what I wrote earlier?

better to write both the beginning and the ending after most of the rest of an essay is completed. Pay particular attention to both parts during revision.

The beginning of your essay is vitally important to its success. Indeed, if your opening doesn't attract and hold your readers' attention, readers may be less than enthusiastic about proceeding.

Your ending is almost always as important as your beginning. An effective conclusion does more than end your essay; it wraps up your thoughts and leaves readers satisfied with the presentation of your ideas and information. Your ending should be a natural outgrowth of the development of your ideas. Avoid trick endings, mechanical summaries, and cutesy comments, and never introduce new concepts or information in the ending. Just as with the writing of titles, the writing of beginnings and endings is perhaps best done by generating several alternatives and then selecting from among them. Review the Questions for Beginnings and Endings box and see Chapter 6 for more help developing your beginnings and endings.

REVISING

After you have completed a first draft, set it aside for a few hours or even until the next day. Removed from the process of drafting, you can approach the revision of your draft with a clear mind. When you revise, consider the most important elements of your draft first. You should focus on your thesis, purpose, content, organization, and paragraph structure. You will have a chance to look at grammar, punctuation, and mechanics after you revise. This way you will make sure that your essay is fundamentally solid and says what you want it to say before dealing with the task of editing.

It is helpful to have someone — a friend or a member of your writing class — listen to your essay as you read it aloud. The process of reading aloud allows you to determine if your writing sounds clear and natural. If you have to alter your voice to provide emphasis, try rephrasing the idea to make it clearer. Whether you revise your work on your own or have someone assist you, the

☑ **For more practice, visit the LaunchPad for *Models for Writers*: LearningCurve** > Supporting Details

Questions for Revising

1. Have I focused on my topic?
2. Does my thesis make a clear statement about my topic?
3. Is the organizational pattern I have used the best one, given my purpose?
4. Does the topic sentence of each paragraph relate to my thesis? Does each paragraph support its topic sentence?
5. Do I have enough supporting details, and are my examples the best ones that I can develop?
6. How effective are my beginning and my ending? Can I improve them?
7. Do I have a good title? Does it indicate what my subject is and hint at my thesis?

questions in the Questions for Revising box above will help you focus on the largest, most important elements of your essay early in the revision process.

EDITING

When you are sure you have communicated clearly what you want to say and you have done considerable work drafting and revising, you will want your work to be as accurate as possible. Editing is different from revising in that your focus is on correctness. It is also different from proofreading for careless errors in the final preparation of your essay, which we will discuss later in this chapter (pp. 28–29). During the editing stage, you check your writing for errors in grammar, punctuation, mechanics, spelling, usage, and sentence style. If your writing has editing errors, your readers may question the authority you are trying to establish as a writer—and perhaps then question your content.

You may have difficulty identifying editing errors because they are not easy to spot and take time to learn. After all, if they were easy to see, you would probably have identified and corrected them in the process of drafting and revision. For example, perhaps you forgot or were never made aware of the fact that the word *irregardless* is redundant, unacceptable usage and should be avoided. Or maybe you didn't notice that you created a nonparallel construction in one of your sentences:

INCORRECT	The scientists' typical pattern of behavior was to question, to probe, and research.
CORRECT	The scientists' typical pattern of behavior was to question, to probe, and to research.

Here the infinitive (or to + verb) verb form should be used to parallel other similar verb forms in the series.

Very often, editing errors are easier for others to see than for you to detect in your own writing, so it is a good idea to ask a classmate, roommate, or friend to edit your work in addition to the work you have done. It is not necessary to have immediate answers while editing, but it is important to raise questions and to double-check for accuracy. Chapter 24 (pp. 635–46) provides sound advice and solutions for the editing problems that trouble students most. For more guidance with these and other editing concerns, refer to a grammar handbook, make an appointment with a writing center tutor, or ask your instructor for advice.

PROOFREADING

Do not assume that because you used a spell-check or grammar-check function you've found and corrected every spelling and grammatical error. In fact, such checkers often allow incorrect or misspelled words to pass while flagging correct grammatical constructions as incorrect. Although spell-checkers and grammar-checkers are a good first line of defense against certain types of errors, there is no replacement for a human proofreader—you.

One way to proofread is to print out your essay and carefully proofread it manually. Distancing yourself from the screen and reading with a pen or pencil in hand makes it easier to avoid simply skimming the words you've written. Check to make sure you do not use *your* where you intend *you're, its* where you mean *it's,* or *to* where you want *too*. Spell-checkers often do not catch these types of errors. If you know you are prone to certain mistakes, go through your essay looking for those particular errors.

Questions for Editing and Proofreading Essays

1. Have I checked my essay for common grammatical or style errors that I am prone to make?
2. Have I corrected my editing errors with the help of my handbook?
3. Have I printed a hard copy of my essay for proofreading?
4. Have I misspelled or incorrectly typed any words? Has my spell-checker inadvertently approved commonly confused words such as *its* and *it's* or *their, there*, and *they're*?
5. Have I checked my essay for errors I make often?
6. Do all my edits and corrections appear in my hard copy?
7. Have I formatted my essay according to my instructor's directions?
8. Have I given the hard copy of my final draft a thorough review before turning it in?

Be sure to refer to the Questions for Editing and Proofreading Essays box in this section. Check to be certain you have followed your instructor's formatting guidelines. Above all, give your essay one final read-through before submitting it to your instructor.

WRITING AN EXPOSITORY ESSAY: A STUDENT ESSAY IN PROGRESS

While he was a student in a writing class at the University of Vermont, Jeffrey Olesky was asked to write an essay on any topic using a suitable method of development. After making a brief list of the subjects that interested him, he chose to write about golf. Golf had been a part of Olesky's life since he was a youngster, so he figured he would have enough material for an essay.

First, he needed to focus on a specific topic within the broad subject area of golf. Having considered a number of aspects of the game—how it's played, its rise in popularity, the controversies over the exclusion of women and minorities from private clubs—he kept coming back to how much golf meant to him. Focusing on his love of golf, he then established his tentative thesis.

Tentative Thesis

Golf has taught me a lot.

Olesky needed to develop a number of examples to support his thesis, so he brainstormed for ideas, examples, and anecdotes—anything that came to mind to help him develop his essay. These are his notes:

Brainstorming Notes

Golf is my life — I can't imagine being who I am without it.

I love to be out on the course early in the morning.

It's been embarrassing and stressful sometimes.

There's so much to know and remember about the game, even before you try to hit the ball.

The story about what my father taught me — felt badly and needed to apologize.

"You know better than that, Jeffrey."

I have pictures of me on the greens with a cut-down golf putter.

All kinds of character building goes on.

It's all about rules and playing fairly.

Wanted to be like my father.

The frustration is awesome, but you can learn to deal with it.

Golf is methodical.

I use golf to clear my head.

Golf teaches life's lessons.

Golf teaches you manners, to be respectful of others.

Golf teaches you to abide by the rules.

Golf is an internal tool.

When he thought that he had gathered enough information, he began to consider an organizational plan, a way to present his information in a logical manner. He realized that the character-building benefits of golf that he included in his brainstorming notes clustered around some key subtopics. He decided

Clustering Diagram

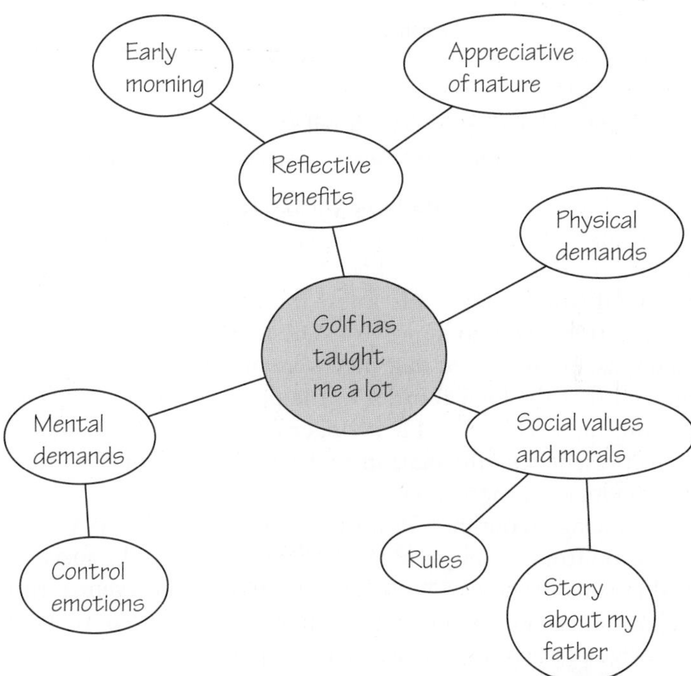

to do some clustering, drawing circles that included his ideas about golf: the physical and mental demands of the game, the social values and morals it teaches, and the reflective benefits of golf. He then sorted out his related ideas and examples and added them, mapping their relationships in this diagram.

Before beginning to write the first draft of his essay, Olesky thought it would be a good idea to list in an informal outline the major points he wanted to make. Here is his informal outline:

Informal Outline

1. Brief introductory paragraph announcing the topic
2. An expansion of the introductory paragraph and the thesis statement: Golf has taught me a lot
3. A discussion of how, above all, golf teaches one to control one's emotions

4. A discussion of how much one needs to know and remember to play golf well
5. The social values that golf teaches
6. A multiparagraph example illustrating a valuable lesson taught through golf
7. Golf provides an opportunity to reflect
8. Reflection, in turn, leads to a deeper appreciation of nature

With his outline before him, Olesky felt ready to try a rough draft of his essay. He wrote quickly, keeping his organizational plan in mind but striving to keep the writing going and get his thoughts down on paper. He knew that once he had a draft, he could determine how to improve it. Olesky wrote some fairly solid paragraphs, but he sensed that they were on different aspects of his topic and that the logical order of the points he was making was not quite right. He needed a stronger organizational plan, some way to present his information that was not random but rather showed a logical progression.

Reviewing his outline, Olesky could see that there was a natural progression from the physical lessons of the sport to the social and moral lessons to the psychological, emotional, and even spiritual benefits that one could derive. He decided therefore to move item 3 in his original organization and make it item 6 in the revision. Here is his reordered outline:

Reordered Outline

1. Brief introductory paragraph announcing the topic
2. An expansion of the introductory paragraph and the thesis statement: Golf has taught me a lot
3. A discussion of how much one needs to know and remember to play golf well
4. The social values that golf teaches
5. A multiparagraph example illustrating a valuable lesson taught through golf
6. A discussion of how, above all, golf teaches one to control one's emotions
7. Golf provides an opportunity to reflect
8. Reflection, in turn, leads to a deeper appreciation of nature

Olesky was satisfied that his essay now had a natural and logical organization: it moved from matters of lesser to greater importance to him personally. However, he now needed to revise his thesis to suit the argument he had established. He wanted his revised thesis to be focused and specific and to include the idea that the lessons and values golf has taught him could not have been learned as easily in other ways. Here is his revised thesis statement:

Revised Thesis Statement

In its simplicity, golf has taught me many lessons and values that other people have trouble learning elsewhere.

After revising the organization, he was now ready to edit his essay and to correct those smaller but equally important errors in word choice, wordiness, punctuation, and mechanics. He had put aside these errors to make sure his essay had the appropriate content. Now he needed to make sure it was grammatically correct. Here are several sample paragraphs showing the editing Olesky did on his essay:

Edited Paragraphs

Addition for clarity

Elimination of unessential information

Change of period to colon to eliminate sentence fragment and introduce appositive phrase

Correction of *it's* to *its*

Ever since I was a little boy, no older than two or three, I have had a golf club in my hand. My mother has pictures of me *as a toddler* with my father on the putting green of the local golf course. ~~that my father belonged to.~~ With a cut-down putter, the shaft ~~had been~~ reduced in length so that it would fit me, I would spend hours trying to place the small white ball into the little round hole. I'm sure at first that I took to the game to be like my father: ~~T~~to act like him, play like him, and hit the ball like him. However, it is not what I have learned about the mechanics of the golf swing or ~~all~~ *about* the facts ~~and figures~~ of the game that have caused golf to mean so much to me but rather the things golf has taught me about everyday life *in general*. In it~~'~~s simplicity, golf has taught me many lessons and values other people have trouble learning elsewhere.

Golf is a good teacher because ~~Along the same lines,~~ there are many variables and aspects to the game ~~of golf.~~ You ~~are~~ constantly hav~~ing~~e to think, analyze, and evaluate *your position and strategy.* ~~That is the difficulty of the game of golf.~~ Unlike many sports ~~once you~~ *that rely on* committ~~ed the~~*ing* action*s* to muscle memory, *golf requires* ~~there is no guarantee you will still perform well. There is~~ a phenomenal amount of information to think about and keys to remember. Legs shoulder-width apart, knees flexed, fingers interlocked, body loose . . . and you haven't even tried to hit the ball yet. But having to go about things so methodically *in golf* has enabled me to apply ~~the methods of golf~~ *the skills of patience and analysis* to many other parts of my life. I don't believe I would have nearly the same personality if golf had not played such an ~~intricate~~ *integral* role in my development.

Elimination of wordiness

Addition of specific information for clarity

Improved dicton

In addition to editing his revised paper, Olesky reexamined his title, "Character Builder." He considered a half dozen alternatives and finally settled on the use of "Golf" as a main title because it was such a key word for his topic and thesis; he used "A Character Builder" as his subtitle. He also thought about his conclusion, wondering whether it was forceful enough. After giving it considerable thought and seeking the advice of his classmates, Olesky decided to end with the low-key but meaningful final paragraphs he generated in his original draft. Here is the final version of his essay:

Final Essay

Title: suggests what the essay will be about

Jeffrey Olesky

Golf: A Character Builder

Beginning: effective opening paragraph sets the context for the essay

Golf is what I love. It is what I do, and it is who I am. In many respects, it has defined and shaped my character and personality. I couldn't possibly imagine my life without golf and what it has meant for me.

Ever since I was a little boy, no older than two or three, I have had a golf club in my hand. My mother has pictures of me as a toddler with my father on the putting green of the local golf course. With a cut-down putter, the shaft reduced in length so that it would fit me, I would spend hours trying to place the small white ball into the little round hole. I'm sure at first that I took to the game to be like my father: to act like him, play like him, and hit the ball like him. However, it is not what I have learned about the mechanics of the golf swing or about the facts of the game that have caused golf to mean so much to me but rather the things golf has taught me about everyday life in general. In its simplicity, golf has taught me many lessons and values other people have trouble learning elsewhere.

Thesis statement: sets clear expectation in the reader's mind

Transition: discussion moves to how the game influences personality

Golf is a good teacher because there are many variables and aspects to the game. You constantly have to think, analyze, and evaluate your position and strategy. Unlike many sports that rely on committing actions to muscle memory, golf requires a phenomenal amount of information to think about and keys to remember: legs shoulder-width apart, knees flexed, fingers interlocked, body loose . . . and you haven't even tried to hit the ball yet. But having to go about things so methodically in golf has enabled me to apply the skills of patience and analysis to many other parts of my life. I don't believe I would have nearly the same personality if golf had not played such an integral role in my development.

Golf requires lots of information, both physical and mental

Golf teaches life lessons

Golf has also changed and shaped my personality by repeatedly reinforcing many of the lessons of life. You know the ones I'm referring to, the rules you learn in kindergarten: treat others as you would like to be treated; respect other people and their property . . . the list goes on. Golf may not blare them out as obviously as my kindergarten teacher did, but in its own subtle, respectful tone, golf has imbued me with many of the values and morals I have today. Simply by learning the rules of such a prestigious, honest, and respected game, you gradually learn the reasoning behind them and the ways that they relate to life.

Illustration: extended example in narrative of some lessons that golf teaches

A good example of such a life lesson comes from the first time my father ever took me out on an actual golf course. I had been waiting for this day for quite some time and was so excited when he finally gave me the chance. He had gone out to play with a few of his friends early one Saturday morning in one of the larger tournaments. I was caddying for my father. Although I was too young to actually carry his bag, I would clean his golf ball, rake the bunkers for him, and do the other minor tasks that caddies do. But the fact that I was actually out "with the big boys," watching them play golf, was enough to make me happy. Besides, none of the other gentlemen my father was playing with seemed to mind that I was along for the ride.

Narrative example continues

The lesson I learned that day appears rather simple now. It came on the putting green of the second hole. My father had finished putting out, and I was holding the flagstick off to the side of the green while the other players finished. Generally, my father would come stand next to me and give me a hand, but due to circumstances we ended up on opposite sides of the green. During the next player's putt, my father lowered his eyebrows at me and nodded his head to one side a few times. Curious as to what he wanted me to do, I almost let the question slip out of my mouth. But I knew better. I had already learned the rules of not talking or moving while other golfers were hitting. I quietly stood my ground until everyone was finished and then placed the flagstick back in the hole. While walking toward the next tee box, I neared my father. Regardless of what he had wanted me to do, I thought he would commend me for not talking or moving during the ordeal.

Dialogue: shows rather than tells, and puts the reader in the scene

"You know better than that, Jeffrey," he said.

"What?" I asked curiously, disappointed that he had not praised me on a job well done.

"You never stand so that your shadow is in someone's line."

How could I be so stupid? He had reminded me a thousand times before. You never allow your shadow to fall in the line of someone's putt because it is distracting to the person putting. I rationalized to my father that maybe the man hadn't noticed or that it didn't bother him. Unfortunately, my father wasn't going to take that as an excuse. After explaining to me what I had done wrong, he suggested that I go over and apologize to the gentleman. I was still a young boy, and the figure of the older man was somewhat intimidating. This task was no easy chore because I was obviously very scared, and this is perhaps what made the lesson sink in a little deeper. I remember slowly approaching my father's friend and sheepishly looking back to my father for help. Once I realized I was on my own, I bashfully gave him my apologies and assured him that it wouldn't happen again. As you can probably guess, the repercussions were not as dramatic as I had envisioned them to be. Once my father had pointed out my mistake, I begged him to reconcile with the gentleman for me. However, in apologizing for myself, I learned a valuable lesson. Golf is important because it has taught me many social values such as this, but it can also be a personal, internal tool.

Transition: golf can also be a personal, internal tool

Golf has taught me how to deal with frustration and to control myself mentally in difficult and strenuous situations. Golf is about mastering your emotions in stressful times and prevailing with a methodical, calm mind. I have dealt with the disappointment of missing a two-foot putt on the last hole to break eighty and the embarrassment of shanking my drive off the first hole in front of dozens of people. In dealing with these circumstances and continuing with my game, I have learned how to control my emotions. Granted, golf is not the most physically strenuous sport, but it is the mental challenge of complete and utter concentration that makes it difficult. People who are not able to control their temper or to take

Organization continues to move from concrete practical concerns to those that are more abstract command of their emotions generally do not end up playing this game for very long.

Organization: Olesky moves to more philosophic influences

Golf gives me the opportunity to be reflective—time to myself when I can debate and organize the thoughts in my head. There are few places where you can find the peace and tranquility like that of a golf course in the early morning or late afternoon. When I am playing by myself, which I make an effort to do when I need to get away, I am able to reflect and work out some of the difficulties I am facing. I can think in complete quietness, but at the same time I have something to do while I am thinking. There are few places in the world offering this type of sanctuary that are easily accessible.

Organization: Olesky discusses golf's ability to bring him close to nature

It is in these morning reflections that I also gain an appreciation of my surroundings. I often like to get up early on a Saturday or Sunday and be the first one on the course. There are many things I love about the scenery of a golf course during the morning hours. I love the smell of the freshly cut grass as the groundskeepers crisscross their patterns onto the fairways and greens. I love looking back on my progress toward the tee box on the first hole to witness my solitary foot tracks in the morning dew. I love the chirp of the yellow finches as they signal the break of dawn. All these conditions help to create the feeling of contentment as I walk down the first fairway. Thinking back to those days on the putting green with my father, I realize how dear golf is to me. Golf has created my values, taught me my lessons, and been my outlet. I love the game for all these reasons.

Ending: a quiet but appropriate conclusion

CHAPTER **2**

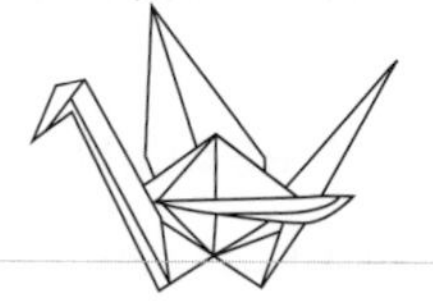

From Reading to Writing

To move from reading to writing, you need to read actively and critically, with an alert, inquiring mind. Reading critically means learning how to analyze and respond to what you read. You must be able to discover what is going on in an essay, to figure out the writer's reasons for shaping the essay in a particular way, to decide whether the result works well or poorly—and why. At first, such digging may seem odd, and for good reason. After all, we all know how to read. But do we know how to read *critically*?

Critical reading is a skill that takes time to acquire. By becoming more familiar with different types of writing, you will sharpen your critical thinking skills and learn how good writers make decisions in their writing. After reading an essay, most people feel more confident talking about the content of the piece than about the writer's style because content is more tangible. In large part, this discrepancy results from our schooling. Most of us have been taught to read for ideas. Not many of us, however, have been trained to read critically, to engage a writer and his or her writing, and to ask why we like one piece of writing and not another. Similarly, most of us do not ask ourselves why one piece of writing is more convincing than another.

When you learn to read and think critically, you begin to answer these important questions and come to appreciate the craftsmanship involved in writing. Critical reading, then, is a skill you need if you are truly to engage and understand the content of a piece of writing as well as understand the craft that shapes the writer's ideas into a presentable form. Critical reading will repay your efforts by helping you read more effectively, think more critically, and grow as a writer.

☑ **For more practice, visit the LaunchPad for *Models for Writers*: LearningCurve** > Critical Reading

READING CRITICALLY

Critical reading requires, first of all, that you commit time and effort. Second, try to take a positive interest in what you are reading, even if the subject matter is not immediately appealing. Remember that you are reading not for content alone but also to understand a writer's methods—to see firsthand the kinds of choices writers make as they write.

To get the most out of your reading, follow the five steps of the reading process:

1. Prepare yourself to read the selection.
2. Read the selection.
3. Reread the selection.
4. Annotate the text with marginal notes.
5. Analyze and evaluate the text with questions.

Step 1: Prepare Yourself to Read the Selection

Before diving into any given selection, it's helpful to get a context for the reading: What's the essay about? What do you know about the writer's background and reputation? Where was the essay first published? Who was the intended audience for the essay? How much do you already know about the subject of the reading selection?

We encourage you, therefore, to review the materials that precede each selection in this book. Each selection begins with a title, a portrait of the writer, a headnote, and a writing prompt.

- From the *title,* you often discover the writer's position on an issue or attitude toward the topic. On occasion, the title provides clues about the intended audience and the writer's purpose in writing the piece.
- The *headnote* contains three essential elements: a biographical note about the author, publication information, and rhetorical highlights of the selection. (1) The *biographical note* will tell you information on the person's life and work as well as something about his or her reputation and authority to write on the subject of the piece. (2) The *publication information* tells you when the selection was published and in what book or magazine it appeared. This information gives

you insights about the intended audience and the historical context. (3) The *rhetorical highlights* direct your attention to one or more of the model features of the selection.

- Finally, the *writing prompt*, called Reflecting on What You Know, encourages you to collect your own thoughts and opinions about the topic or related subjects before you commence reading. This prompt makes it easy for you to keep a record of your own knowledge or thinking about a topic before you see what the writer has to offer in the essay.

To demonstrate how these context-building materials can work for you, carefully review the following materials that accompany Abraham Lincoln's "The Gettysburg Address." The speech itself appears later in this chapter (p. 46).

The Gettysburg Address

Title

Abraham Lincoln

Headnote

1. Biographical note

John Parrot/Stocktrek Images/ Getty Images

Born in Hodgenville, Kentucky, in 1809, Abraham Lincoln grew up on what was our country's western frontier in Kentucky and Indiana. Largely self-educated, he went on to become a successful politician and lawyer. Lincoln served as the 16th President of the United States from March 1861 until his assassination in April 1865. Lincoln delivered his Gettysburg Address in the midst of the bitter ongoing Civil War. With the possible exception of the Declaration of Independence, no document of American history is as famous as this speech that dedicated the national cemetery at the Gettysburg battlefield on November 19, 1863. The Battle of Gettysburg was fought in the rolling countryside of southeastern Pennsylvania during the first three

2. Publication information

days of July 1863. We now know that it was the turning point of the American Civil War, leading to the emancipation of this country's slaves.

Since Lincoln delivered this speech, millions of Americans have memorized it, and countless others have quoted it or imitated its rhetoric for various purposes. As you read, look again at the familiar words with their original context in mind to see how they served Lincoln's purpose, his sense of the occasion, and his larger sense of the nation's history and destiny. Pay particular attention to the tone he uses to appeal to his audience. 3. Rhetorical highlights

Reflecting on What You Know

What have you heard or read about the Gettysburg Address? Do you think it is an important speech? Why? Do speeches, especially political speeches, ever change things? Can they affect the way people think, feel, and act? Explain. Writing prompt

From these preliminary materials, what expectations do you have for the selection? And how does this knowledge equip you to engage the selection before you read it?

- The address's title indicates the place Lincoln delivered the speech and suggests that he will have something to say about the battle at Gettysburg. Readers can assume that he will also address the larger conflict between the North and the South.
- (1) The *biographical note* reveals that Lincoln (1809–1865) lived his life between two important events in our history. He was born shortly after our country was founded and died just after the concluding battle of the conflict that threatened to tear it apart. He felt that the nation and its founding principles were in danger of failing. As the 16th President of the United States, he was well prepared and qualified to reflect on the importance of Gettysburg and the dedication of the cemetery there. (2) The *publication information* indicates that Lincoln delivered his speech on November 19, 1863, about four and a half months after the battle at Gettysburg was fought. The purpose of his speech was to dedicate the new national cemetery

at that site. (3) The *rhetorical highlights* advise you to pay particular attention to how Lincoln uses diction and tone to enhance both his purpose and sense of the occasion.

- The writing prompt asks you to reflect on what you already know about the Gettysburg Address and then consider the importance and effectiveness of speeches in general, particularly those of a political nature. After reading Lincoln's address, you can compare your initial reflections with your reactions to Lincoln's speech now.

Step 2: Read the Selection

Always read the selection at least twice, no matter how long it is. The first reading gives you a chance to get acquainted with the essay and to form your first impressions of it. With the first reading, you want to get an overall sense of what the writer is saying, keeping in mind the essay's title and the facts that you know about the writer from the essay's headnote. The essay will offer you information, ideas, and arguments—some you may have expected, some you may not have expected. As you read, you may find yourself modifying your sense of the writer's message and purpose. Does the writer reveal a bias? Any unsupported opinions? If there are any words that you do not recognize, circle them so that you can look them up later in a dictionary. Put question marks alongside any passages that are not immediately clear. You may, in fact, want to delay most of your annotating until a second reading so that your first reading can be fast and free.

Step 3: Reread the Selection

Your second reading should be quite different from the first. You will know what the essay is about, where it is going, and how it gets there. Now you can relate the parts of the essay more accurately to the whole. Use your second reading to test your first impressions against the words on the page, developing and deepening your sense of how the essay is written and how well. Because you now have a general understanding of the essay, you can pay special attention to the author's purpose and means of achieving that purpose. You can also determine whether the writer reveals a bias and whether the writer adequately supports his or her opinions. (For more information about detecting a writer's bias and determining how well the writer supports his or her opinions, see pp. 601–2.) Finally, you can look for features of organization and style that you can learn from and adapt to your own work.

Step 4: Annotate the Text with Marginal Notes

When you annotate a text, you should do more than simply underline or highlight important points to remember. It is easy to highlight so much that the efforts of your highlighting can become almost meaningless because you forget why you highlighted the passages in the first place. Instead, as you read, write down your thoughts in the margins or on a separate piece of paper. (See p. 46 for Lincoln's "Gettysburg Address" with student annotations.) Mark the selection's main point when you find it stated directly. Look for the pattern or patterns of development the author uses to explore and support that point, and jot the information down. If you disagree with a statement or conclusion, object in the margin: "No!" If you feel skeptical, indicate that response: "Why?" or "Explain." If you are impressed by an argument or turn of phrase, compliment the writer: "Good point!" Place vertical lines or stars in the margin to indicate important points.

Jot down whatever marginal notes come to mind. Most readers combine brief responses written in the margins with underlining, circling, highlighting, stars, or question marks. Refer to the What to Annotate in a Text box for some suggestions of elements you may want to mark to help you record your responses as you read.

What to Annotate in a Text

- Memorable statements of important points
- Key terms or concepts
- Central issues or themes
- Examples that support a main point
- Unfamiliar words
- Questions you have about a point or passage
- Your response to a specific point or passage

For more practice, visit the LaunchPad for *Models for Writers*: **Tutorial** > Active Reading Strategies; **LearningCurve** > Active Reading

Remember that there are no hard-and-fast rules for which elements you should annotate. Choose a method of annotation that works best for you and that will make sense when you go back to recollect your thoughts and responses to the essay. When annotating a text, don't be timid. Mark up your book as much as you like, or jot down as many responses in your notebook as you think will be helpful. Don't let annotating become burdensome. A word or phrase is usually as good as a sentence. One helpful way to focus your annotations is to ask yourself questions as you read the selection a second time.

Step 5: Analyze and Evaluate the Text with Questions

As you read the essay a second time, probe for a deeper understanding of and appreciation for what the writer has done. Focus your attention by asking yourself some basic questions about its content and form, such as those in the Questions to Ask Yourself as You Read box.

Questions to Ask Yourself as You Read

1. What does the writer want to say? What is the writer's main point or thesis?
2. Why does the writer want to make this point? What is the writer's purpose?
3. Does the writer take a position on the subject and adequately support it?
4. What pattern or patterns of development does the writer use?
5. How does the writer's pattern of development suit his or her subject and purpose?
6. What, if anything, is noteworthy about the writer's use of this pattern?
7. How effective is the essay? Does the writer make his or her points clearly?

Each essay in *Models for Writers* is followed by study questions that are similar to the ones suggested here but are specific to the essay. These questions help you analyze both the content of the

☑ For more practice, visit the LaunchPad for *Models for Writers*: LearningCurve > Interpretive Reading essay and the writer's craft. As you read the essay a second time, look for details that will support your answers to these questions, and then answer the questions as fully as you can.

An Example: Annotating Abraham Lincoln's "Gettysburg Address"

Notice how one of our students, guided by the seven preceding questions, recorded her responses to Lincoln's text with marginal notes.

Opening echoes "Declaration of Independence"

Four score and seven years ago our fathers brought forth on this continent, a new nation, conceived in Liberty, and dedicated to the proposition that all men are created equal.

Interesting repetition of "conceived" and "dedicated"

Announces purpose of solemn occasion

Now we are engaged in a great civil war, testing whether that nation, or any nation so conceived and so dedicated, can long endure. We are met on a great battle-field of that war. We have come to dedicate a portion of that field, as a final resting place for those who here gave their lives that that nation might live. It is altogether fitting and proper that we should do this.

"But" shifts focus to soldiers who fought at Gettysburg

"consecrate" feels spiritual

Ironic

Reminds "the living" of work to be done

Parallel construction emphasizes Lincoln's resolve

But, in a larger sense, we can not dedicate—we can not consecrate—we can not hallow—this ground. The brave men, living and dead, who struggled here, have consecrated it, far above our poor power to add or detract. The world will little note, nor long remember what we say here, but it can never forget what they did here. It is for us the living, rather, to be dedicated here to the unfinished work which they who fought here have thus far so nobly advanced. It is rather for us to be here dedicated to the great task remaining before us—that from these honored dead we take increased devotion to that cause for which they gave the last full measure of devotion—that we here highly resolve that these dead shall not have died in vain—that this nation, under God, shall have a new birth of freedom—and that government of the people, by the people, for the people, shall not perish from the earth.

Practice: Reading and Annotating Rachel Carson's "Fable for Tomorrow"

Before you read the following essay, think about its title; the biographical, publication, and rhetorical information in the headnote; and the writing prompt. Make some marginal notes of your expectations for the essay and write out a response to the prompt. Then, as you read the essay itself for the first time, try not to stop; take it all in as if in one breath. The second time, however, pause to annotate key points in the text, using the marginal fill-in lines provided alongside each paragraph. As you read, remember the seven basic questions mentioned earlier:

1. What does Carson want to say? What is her main point, or thesis?
2. Why does she want to make this point? What is her purpose?
3. Does Carson take a position on her subject and adequately support it?
4. What pattern or patterns of development does Carson use?
5. How does Carson's pattern of development suit her subject and purpose?
6. What, if anything, is noteworthy about Carson's use of this pattern?
7. How effective is Carson's essay? Does she make her points clearly?

Fable for Tomorrow

Title:

____

____

Rachel Carson

Headnote:

1. Biographical note:

____

____

____

____

____

Naturalist Rachel Carson (1907–1964) majored in biology at the Pennsylvania College for Women (which later became Chatham College) in the mid-1920s and earned a master's degree in marine zoology from Johns Hopkins University. Later

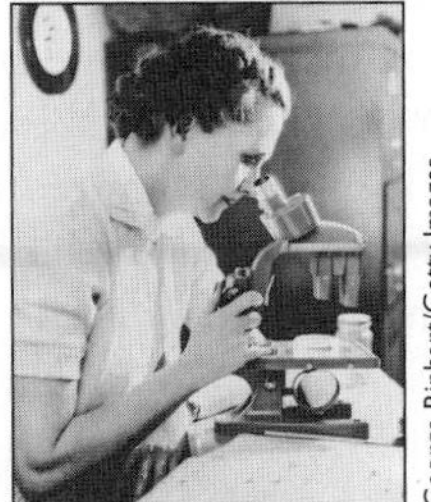
George Rinhart/Getty Images

she worked as an aquatic biologist for the U.S. Bureau of Fisheries in Washington, D.C. She wrote *Under the Sea Wind* (1941), *The Sea Around Us* (1951), and *The Edge of the Sea* (1955)—all sensitive investigations of marine life. But it was *Silent Spring* (1962), her study of herbicides and insecticides, that made Carson a controversial figure. Once denounced as an alarmist, she is now regarded as an early prophet of the ecology movement.

2. Publication information: ______

In the following fable (a short tale teaching a moral), taken from *Silent Spring*, Carson uses contrast to show her readers the devastating effects of the indiscriminate use of pesticides.

3. Rhetorical highlights: ______

Reflecting on What You Know

Hardly a week goes by that we don't hear a news story about the poisoning of the environment. Popular magazines have run cover stories about Americans' growing interest in organic foods. Where do you stand on the issue of using chemical fertilizers, herbicides, and pesticides to grow our nation's food? Do you seek out organic products when you shop? Why or why not?

Writing prompt: ______

Annotations: ______

1 There was once a town in the heart of America where all life seemed to live in harmony with its surroundings. The town lay in the midst of a checkerboard of prosperous farms, with fields of grain and hillsides of orchards where, in spring, white clouds of bloom drifted above the green fields. In autumn, oak and maple and birch set up a blaze of color that flamed and flickered across a backdrop of pines. Then foxes barked in the hills and deer silently crossed the fields, half hidden in the mists of the fall mornings.

2 Along the roads, laurels, viburnum and alder, great ferns and wildflowers delighted the traveler's eye through much of the year. Even in winter the roadsides were places of beauty, where countless

birds came to feed on the berries and on the seed heads of the dried weeds rising above the snow. The countryside was, in fact, famous for the abundance and variety of its bird life, and when the flood of migrants was pouring through in spring and fall people traveled from great distances to observe them. Others came to fish the streams, which flowed clear and cold out of the hills and contained shady pools where trout lay. So it had been from the days many years ago when the first settlers raised their houses, sank their wells, and built their barns.

3 Then a strange blight crept over the area and everything began to change. Some evil spell had settled on the community: mysterious maladies swept the flocks of chickens; the cattle and sheep sickened and died. Everywhere was a shadow of death. The farmers spoke of much illness among their families. In the town the doctors had become more and more puzzled by new kinds of sickness appearing among their patients. There had been several sudden and unexplained deaths, not only among adults but even among children, who would be stricken suddenly while at play and die within a few hours.

4 There was a strange stillness. The birds, for example — where had they gone? Many people spoke of them, puzzled and disturbed. The feeding stations in the backyards were deserted. The few birds seen anywhere were moribund; they trembled violently and could not fly. It was a spring without voices. On the mornings that had once throbbed with the dawn chorus of robins, catbirds, doves, jays, wrens, and scores of other bird voices there was now no sound; only silence lay over the fields and woods and marsh.

5 On the farms the hens brooded, but no chicks hatched. The farmers complained that they were unable to raise any pigs — the litters were small and the young survived only a few days. The apple trees were coming into bloom but no bees droned

among the blossoms, so there was no pollination and there would be no fruit.

6 The roadsides, once so attractive, were now lined with browned and withered vegetation as though swept by fire. These, too, were silent, deserted by all living things. Even the streams were now lifeless. Anglers no longer visited them, for all the fish had died.

7 In the gutters under the eaves and between the shingles of the roofs, a white granular powder still showed a few patches; some weeks before it had fallen like snow upon the roofs and the lawns, the fields and streams.

8 No witchcraft, no enemy action had silenced the rebirth of new life in this stricken world. The people had done it themselves.

9 This town does not actually exist, but it might easily have a thousand counterparts in America or elsewhere in the world. I know of no community that has experienced all the misfortunes I describe. Yet every one of these disasters has actually happened somewhere, and many real communities have already suffered a substantial number of them. A grim specter has crept upon us almost unnoticed, and this imagined tragedy may easily become a stark reality we all shall know.

Once you have read and reread Carson's essay and annotated the text, write your own answers to the seven basic questions listed on page 47. Then compare your answers with the set of answers that follows.

1. *What does Carson want to say? What is her main point, or thesis?* Carson wants to tell her readers a fable, a short narrative that makes an edifying or cautionary point. Carson draws the "moral" of her fable in the final paragraph. She believes that we have in our power the ability to upset the balance of nature, to turn what is an idyllic countryside into a wasteland. As she states in paragraph 8, "The people had done it [silenced the landscape] themselves." Human beings need to take heed and understand their role in environmental stewardship.

2. *Why does she want to make this point? What is her purpose?* Carson's purpose is to alert us to the clear danger of pesticides (the "white granular powder," paragraph 7) to the environment. Even though the composite environmental disaster she describes has not occurred yet, she feels compelled to inform her readers that each of the individual disasters has happened somewhere in a real community. Although Carson does not make specific recommendations for what each of us can do, her message is clear: to do nothing about pesticides is to invite environmental destruction.
3. *Does Carson take a position on her subject and adequately support it?* Carson takes the position that Americans should be more careful in their use of pesticides. She believes that when farmers use pesticides indiscriminately, the environment suffers unintended consequences. As her fable develops, Carson shows the widespread effects of pesticides and herbicides on the landscape. Her evidence—though controversial in 1962—adequately supports her position. Carson tells us that every one of these disasters has actually happened somewhere in America.
4. *What pattern or patterns of development does Carson use?* Carson's dominant pattern of development is comparison and contrast. In paragraphs 1 and 2, she describes the mythical town before the blight ("all life seemed to live in harmony with its surroundings"); in paragraphs 3–7, she portrays the same town after the blight ("some evil spell had settled on the community"). Carson seems less interested in making specific contrasts than in drawing a total picture of the town before and after the blight. In this way, she makes the change dramatic and powerful. Carson enhances her contrast by using vivid descriptive details that appeal to our senses to paint her pictures of the town before and after the "strange blight." The countryside before the blight is full of life; the countryside after, barren and silent.
5. *How does Carson's pattern of development suit her subject and purpose?* Carson selects comparison and contrast as her method of development because she wants to shock her readers into seeing what happens when humans use pesticides indiscriminately. By contrasting a mythical American town before the blight with the same town after the blight, Carson is able to *show* us the differences, not merely tell us about

them. The descriptive details enhance this contrast: for example, "checkerboard of prosperous farms," "white clouds of bloom," "foxes barked," "seed heads of the dried weeds," "cattle and sheep sickened," "they trembled violently," "no bees droned," and "browned and withered vegetation." Perhaps the most striking detail is the "white granular powder" that "had fallen like snow upon the roofs and the lawns, the fields and streams" (7). The powder is the residue of the pervasive use of insecticides and herbicides in farming. Carson waits to introduce the powder for dramatic impact. Readers absorb the horror of the changing scene, wonder at its cause, and then suddenly realize it is not an unseen, uncontrollable force but human beings who have caused the devastation.

6. *What, if anything, is noteworthy about Carson's use of this pattern?* In her final paragraph, Carson writes, "A grim specter has crept upon us almost unnoticed." And this is exactly what happens in her essay. By starting with a two-paragraph description of "a town in the heart of America where all life seemed to live in harmony with its surroundings," Carson lulls her readers into thinking that all is well. But then at the beginning of paragraph 3, she introduces the change: "a strange blight crept over the area." By opting to describe the preblight town in its entirety first and then contrast it with the blighted town, she makes the change more dramatic and thus enhances its impact on readers.

7. *How effective is Carson's essay? Does she make her points clearly?* Instead of writing a strident argument against the indiscriminate use of pesticides, Carson chooses to engage her readers in a fable with an educational message. In reading her story of this American town, we witness what happens when farmers blanket the landscape with pesticides. When we learn in the last paragraph that "this town does not actually exist," we are given cause for hope. Even though "every one of these disasters has actually happened somewhere," we are led to believe that there is still time to act before "this imagined tragedy" becomes "a stark reality we all shall know." When she wrote *Silent Spring* in 1962, Carson was considered an outspoken alarmist, and now almost daily we read reports of water pollution, oil spills, hazardous waste removal, toxic waste dumps, and climate change. Her warning is as appropriate today as it was when she first wrote it.

USING READING IN THE WRITING PROCESS

Reading and writing are two sides of the same coin. Many people view writing as the making of reading, but the connection does not end there. We know that one of the best ways to learn to write and to improve our writing is to read. By reading, we can begin to see how other writers have communicated their experiences, ideas, thoughts, and feelings in their writing. We can study how they have effectively used the various elements of the essay—thesis, unity, organization, beginnings and endings, paragraphs, transitions, effective sentences, diction and tone, and figurative language—to say what they wanted to say. By studying the style, technique, and rhetorical strategies of other writers, we learn how we might effectively do the same. The more we read and write, the more we begin to read as writers and, in turn, to write knowing what readers expect.

Reading as a Writer

What does it mean to read as a writer? As mentioned earlier, most of us have not been taught to read with a writer's eye, to ask why we like one piece of writing and not another. Similarly, most of us do not ask ourselves why one piece of writing is more convincing than another. When you learn to read with a writer's eye, you begin to answer these important questions. You read beyond the content to see how certain aspects of the writing itself affect you. You come to appreciate what is involved in selecting and focusing on a subject as well as the craftsmanship involved in writing: how a writer selects descriptive details, uses an unobtrusive organizational pattern, opts for fresh and lively language, chooses representative and persuasive examples, and emphasizes important points with sentence variety. You come to see writing as a series of decisions the writer makes.

On one level, reading stimulates your thinking by providing you with subjects to write about. For example, after reading Helen Keller's "The Most Important Day," you might take up your pen to write about a turning point in your life. Or by reading Carl T. Rowan's "Unforgettable Miss Bessie" and Thomas L. Friedman's "My Favorite Teacher," you might see how each of these writers creates a dominant impression of an influential person in his or her life, leading you to write about an influential person in your own life.

On a second level, reading provides you with information, ideas, and perspectives for developing your own essay. In this way, you respond to what you read, using material from what you've read in your essay. For example, after reading June Tangney's essay "Condemn the Crime, Not the Person," you might want to elaborate on what she has written and either agree with her examples or generate ones of your own. You could also qualify her argument or take issue with it. Similarly, if you want to write about the effects of new technologies and engineering on our health and well-being, you will find Julie Zhuo's "Where Anonymity Breeds Contempt" and Christina Baker Kline's "Taking My Son to College, Where Technology Has Replaced Serendipity" invaluable resources.

On a third level, critical reading can increase your awareness of how others' writing affects you, thus making you more sensitive to how your own writing will affect your readers. For example, if you have ever been impressed by an author who uses convincing evidence to support each of his or her claims, you might be more likely to back up your own claims carefully. If you have been impressed by an apt turn of phrase or absorbed by a writer's new idea, you may be less inclined to feed your readers dull, worn-out, and trite phrases.

More to the point, however, the critical reading that you are encouraged to do in *Models for Writers* will help you recognize and analyze the essential elements of the essay. When you see, for example, how a writer such as Julie Zhuo uses a strong thesis statement to control the parts of her essay calling for the elimination of anonymous comments on the Internet, you can better appreciate what a clear thesis statement is and see the importance of having one in your essay. When you see the way Maya Wei-Haas uses transitions to link key phrases and important ideas so that readers can clearly recognize how the parts of her essay are meant to flow together, you have a better idea of how to achieve such coherence in your own writing. And when you see how Martin Luther King Jr. divides the ways in which people characteristically respond to oppression into three distinct categories, you witness a powerful way in which you, too, can organize an essay using division and classification.

Another important reason, then, to master the skills of critical reading is that for everything you write, you will be your own first reader and critic. How well you are able to scrutinize your own drafts will powerfully affect how well you revise them, and revising well is crucial to writing well. So reading others' writing with a critical eye is a useful and important practice; the more you read, the more skilled you will become at seeing the rhetorical options available to you and making conscious choices in your own writing.

WRITING FROM READING: THREE SAMPLE STUDENT ESSAYS

A Narrative Essay

Reading often triggers memories of personal experiences. After reading several narratives about growing up—Maya Angelou's "Momma, the Dentist, and Me" (p. 293) and Dick Gregory's "Shame" (p. 145), in particular—and discussing with her classmates how memorable events often signal significant changes in life, student Trena Isley decided to write a narrative about such a turning point in her own life. Isley focused on the day she told her father that she no longer wished to participate in sports. Recalling that event led her to reconsider her childhood experiences of running track. Isley welcomed the opportunity to write about this difficult period in her life. As she tried to make her dilemma clear to her classmates, she found that she clarified it for herself. She came to a deeper understanding of her own fears and feelings about striking out on her own and ultimately to a better appreciation of her difficult relationship with her father. What follows is the final draft of Isley's essay.

Trena Isley

On the Sidelines

Point of view: first-person narrative

It was a Monday afternoon, and I was finally home from track practice. The coach had just told me that I had a negative attitude and should contemplate why I was on the team. My father greeted me in the living room.

"Hi, honey. How was practice?"

"Not good. Dad. Listen. I don't want to do this anymore. I hate the track team."

Opening: critical dialogue between writer and her father highlights conflict

"What do you mean *hate*?"

"This constant pressure is making me crazy."

"How so?"

"It's just not fun anymore."

"Well, I'll have to talk to Coach— "

"No! You're supposed to be my father, not my coach."

"I am your father, but I'm sure . . . "

"Just let me do what I want. You've had your turn."

He just let out a sigh and left the room. Later he told me that I was wasting my "God-given abilities." The funny part was that none of my father's anger hit me at first. All I knew was that I was free.

Flashback: writer returns to beginning of story and sets context

My troubles began the summer I was five years old. It was late June, and the sticky weather had already settled into the Champlain Valley. My father was yanking my hair into a ponytail in preparation for the first day of the summer track and field season.

As our truck pulled into the upper parking lot I could look down on the scene below. The other kids resembled ants against the massive black track, all of them parading around with no obvious purpose. I stepped out of the truck, never taking my eyes off the colony beneath me, and fell. As I stood there, both knees skinned and bleeding, the last thing I wanted to do was join the other kids. My father quickly hushed my sobs and escorted me down into the throng of children. Around the track we ran, each step stinging my knees as the tears in my eyes continued to rise. Through blurred vision I could see my father on the sidelines, holding his stopwatch in one hand and wearing a grin from ear to ear.

Echo of title

For most of my childhood I was content to let my father make me a track star. As my collection of blue ribbons grew, I was perfect in my father's eyes. By the time I was ten, college coaches were joking with me about scholarships. So I continued to run. It was fun in the beginning, and Dad always had

Organization: chronological sequence of events

nice things to say about me. I can remember him talking to my grandmother over the holidays: "Trena's got a real shot at winning the 200 meters at the state meet this year, but she's got to train hard."

Writer provides details of her track "career" and relationship with her father

I began to alter my opinion of competition as I entered my teenage years. At this point I wasn't having fun anymore. My father took me to the gym for "training" sessions four days a week before school. I knew my friends weren't getting up at 5:00 a.m., so I didn't understand why I had to. At thirteen years old all I wanted was to be considered normal. I wanted to fit in with the other kids and do regular teenage stuff.

My father didn't understand my waning interest in track. He still looked forward to my competitions and practice every morning. When my alarm would go off, I would not jump out of bed, often claiming that I didn't feel well or pretending to oversleep. When I began not winning all or even most of my races, my father pushed me to work harder. He would talk incessantly about other competitors and how often they practiced. He never stopped trying to coax me into practicing by buying me breakfast or taking me out to lunch. He tried endlessly, but I just didn't care about track. I resented him more and more with each attempt. I needed to do something that I was truly interested in. And I needed to do it alone.

Dialogue: shows the disconnect between writer and her father

"Hey, Dad, what do you think about me trying out for the school play this term? I was told I have a good shot at a part."

"I don't think you'd have time. Track practice is every day, isn't it? I've been talking with the coach, and he says the team is looking strong this year. He tells me the state meet should be tough, though. Do you need new spikes?"

"No, Dad. The ones I have are fine, but I just thought . . ."

"Great, 'cause you'll need good spikes when you run on some of those dirt tracks."

So that was that. It got so bad that my father didn't hear me unless "track" was in the sentence. I was starving for my own identity. The mold "Trena the track star" that my father had created for me was crumbling rapidly. Sadly, he wasn't noticing; however, I knew I wanted to quit the track team, but I was afraid that if I gave up sports there would be nothing left for me to be good at. The worst thing someone could be in my family was average.

Writer returns to confrontation with father in opening scene

When I finally did it — told my father the pressure was making me crazy and that I was quitting — I felt three times lighter. I came to find out, though, that this freedom did have its price. I got to sleep late, but Dad didn't ask me how my day was anymore. He didn't ask me much of anything except when I'd be home at night and with whom I was going out. He wasn't my coach anymore — he was my warden.

Every night I was grilled for details. He needed to know everyone I was with and what we were doing. When I'd tell him, he never seemed to believe me. My dreams of living on a farm and building my own house were laughed at. In the same conversation my younger sister could tell my parents that she was hoping to work for the United Nations, and she would be applauded. The shift had been made. I gained my personal and creative independence but lost a parent.

Organization: time reference "five years"

It has been five years since I retired from athletics and slipped out of my father's graces. Presently my father and I do speak, but it's all on the surface. I now realize that I didn't need the extra morning practices to be good at something. This transition was normal and healthy. It happened quickly, so quickly that I left my father holding the remains of our relationship. The problem was that neither of us bothered to reinvent one for our future as adults. It's not hard for me to understand why we still have a difficult time relating to each other. We really don't know each other very well.

Ending: writer reflects on relationship with her father

Eventually we'll be able to talk about my quitting track as just that, a small incident that marked the turn of a page in both our lives. We both have unresolved feelings that are standing in the way of our friendship. I need to stop blaming him for my blemished self-image, and he needs to realize that I can succeed without his coaching. In the end we both have to forgive each other.

A Response Essay

For an assignment following James Lincoln Collier's essay "Anxiety: Challenge by Another Name" (p. 85), Zoe Ockenga tackled the topic of anxiety. In her first draft, she explored how anxious she felt the night before her first speech in a public speaking class and how in confronting that anxiety she benefited from the course. Ockenga read her essay aloud in class, and other students had an opportunity to ask her questions and to offer constructive criticism. Several students suggested that she might want to relate her experiences to those that Collier recounts in his essay. Another asked if she could include other examples to bolster the point she wanted to make. At this point in the discussion, Ockenga recalled a phone conversation she had had with her mother regarding her mother's indecision about accepting a new job. The thought of working outside the home for the first time in more than twenty years brought out her mother's worst fears and threatened to keep her from accepting the challenge. Armed with these valuable suggestions and ideas, Ockenga began revising. In subsequent drafts, she worked on the Collier connection, actually citing his essay on several occasions, and developed the example of the anxiety surrounding her mother's decision. What follows is the final draft of her essay, which incorporates the changes she made based on the peer evaluation of her first draft.

Zoe Ockenga

Title: indicates main idea of the essay

The Excuse "Not To"

Beginning: captures readers' attention with personal experience most college students can relate to

I cannot imagine anything worse than the nervous, anxious feeling I got the night before my first speech in public speaking class last spring semester. The knots in my stomach were so fierce that I racked my brain for an excuse to give the teacher so that I would not have to go through with the dreaded assignment. Once in bed, I lay awake thinking of all the mistakes that I might make while standing alone in front of my classmates. I spent the rest of the night tossing and turning, frustrated that now, on top of my panic, I would have to give my speech with huge bags under my eyes.

Anxiety is an intense emotion that can strike at any time or place, before a simple daily activity or a life-changing decision. For some people, anxiety is only a minor interference in the process of achieving a goal. For others, it can be a force that is impossible to overcome. In these instances, anxiety can prevent the accomplishment of lifelong hopes and dreams. Avoiding the causes of stress or fear can make us feel secure and safe. Avoiding anxiety, however, may mean forfeiting a once-in-a-lifetime opportunity. Confronting anxiety can make for a richer, more fulfilling existence.

Thesis

First example: continues story introduced in opening paragraph to support thesis

The next day I trudged to class and sat on the edge of my seat until I could not stand the tension any longer. At this point, I forced myself to raise my hand to volunteer to go next simply to end my suffering. As I walked to the front of the room and assumed my position at the podium, the faces of the twenty-five classmates I had been sitting beside a minute ago suddenly seemed like fifty. I probably fumbled over a word or two as I discussed the harmful aspects of animal testing, but my mistakes were not nearly as severe as I had imagined the night before. Less than five minutes later the whole nightmare was over, and it had been much less painful than I had anticipated. As I sat down with a huge sigh of relief to listen to the next victim stumble repeatedly over how to milk dairy cows, I realized that I had not been half bad.

Although I still dreaded giving the next series of speeches, I eventually became more accustomed to speaking in front of my peers. I would still have to force myself to volunteer, secretly hoping the teacher would forget about me, but the audience that once seemed large and forbidding eventually became much more human. A speech class is something that I would never have taken if it had not been a requirement, but I can honestly say that I am better off because of it. I was forced to grapple with my anxiety and in the process became a stronger, more self-confident individual. Before this class I had been able to hide out in large lectures, never offering any comments or insights. For the first time at college I was forced to participate, and I realized that I could speak effectively in front of strangers and, more important, that I had something to say.

Second example: cites essay from Models for Writers to support thesis

The insomnia-inducing anticipation of giving a speech was a type of anxiety that I had to overcome to meet my distribution requirements for graduation. In the essay "Anxiety: Challenge by Another Name" by James Lincoln Collier, the author tells of his own struggles with anxiety. He tells of one particular event that happened between his sophomore and junior years in college when he was asked to spend a summer in Argentina with a good friend. He writes about how he felt after he made his decision not to go:

Block quote in MLA style

> I had turned down something I wanted to do because I was scared, and had ended up feeling depressed. I stayed that way for a long time. And it didn't help when I went back to college in the fall to discover that Ted and his friend had had a terrific time. (86)

The proposition of going to Argentina was an extremely difficult choice for Collier, as it meant abandoning the comfortable routine of the past and venturing completely out of his element. Although the idea of the trip was exciting, the author could not bring himself to choose the summer in Argentina because of his uncertainties.

The summer abroad that Collier denied himself in his early twenties left him with such a feeling of regret that he vowed to change his approach to life. From then on, he faced challenges that made him uncomfortable and was able to accomplish feats he would never have dreamed possible — interviewing celebrities, traveling extensively throughout Europe, parachuting, and even learning to ski at age forty. Collier emphasizes that he was able to make his life fulfilling and exciting by adhering to his belief that anxiety cannot be stifled by avoidance; it can be stifled only by confrontation (88).

Third example: introduces mother's dilemma

Anxiety prevents many individuals from accepting life's challenges and changes. My own mother is currently struggling with such a dilemma. At age fifty-three, having never had a career outside the home, my mother has been recommended to manage a new art gallery. The River Gallery, as it will be called, will be opening in our town of Ipswich, Massachusetts, this spring. An avid collector and art lover as well as a budding potter, my mother would, I believe, be exceptional at this job.

Anticipating this new opportunity and responsibility has caused my mother great anxiety. Reentering the workforce after over twenty years is as frightening for my mother as the trip to Argentina was for Collier. When I recently discussed the job prospect with my mother, she was negative and full of doubt. "There's no way I could ever handle such a responsibility," she commented. "I have no business experience. I would look like a fool if I actually tried to pull something like this off. Besides, I'm sure the artists would never take me seriously." Just as my mother focused on all the possible negative aspects of the opportunity in front of her, Collier questioned the value of his opportunity to spend a summer abroad. He describes having second thoughts about just how exciting the trip would be:

Quotation: quotes Collier to help explain mother's indecision

> I had never been very far from New England, and I had been homesick my first few weeks at college. What would it be like in a strange country? What about the language? And besides, I had promised to teach my younger brother to sail that summer. (86)

Focusing on all the possible problems accompanying a new opportunity can arouse such a sense of fear that it can overpower the ability to take a risk. Both my mother and Collier found out that dwelling on possible negative outcomes allowed them to ignore the benefits of a new experience and thus maintain their safe current situations.

Currently my mother is using anxiety as an excuse "not to" act. To confront her anxiety and take an opportunity in which there is a possibility of failure as well as success is a true risk. Regardless of the outcome, to even contemplate a new challenge has changed her life. The summer forgone by Collier roused him to never again pass up an exciting opportunity and thus to live his life to the fullest. Just the thought of taking the gallery position has prompted my mother to contemplate taking evening classes so that if she refuses the offer she may be better prepared for a similar challenge in the future. Although her decision is unresolved, her anxiety has made her realize the possibilities that may be opening for her, whether or not she chooses to take them. If in the end her answer is no, I believe that a lingering "What if?" feeling will cause her to reevaluate her expectations and goals for the future.

Conclusion: includes strong statement about anxiety that echoes optimism of thesis

Anxiety can create confidence and optimism or depression, low self-esteem, and regret. The outcome of anxiety is entirely dependent on whether the individual runs from it or embraces it. Some forms of anxiety can be conquered merely by repeating the activity that causes them, such as giving speeches in a public speaking class. Anxiety brought on by unique opportunities or life-changing decisions, such as a summer in a foreign country or a new career, must be harnessed. Opportunities forgone due to anxiety and fear could be the chances of a lifetime. Although the unpleasant feelings that may accompany anxiety may make it initially easier to do nothing, the road not taken will never be forgotten. Anxiety is essentially a blessing in disguise. It is a physical and emotional trigger that tells us when and where there is an opportunity for us to grow and become stronger human beings.

MLA-style works cited list

Works Cited

Collier, James Lincoln. "Anxiety: Challenge by Another Name." *Models for Writers,* edited by Alfred Rosa and Paul Eschholz, 13th ed., Bedford/St. Martin's, 2018, pp. 85–88.

An Argumentative Essay

James Duffy's assignment was to write a thesis-driven argument, and he was free to choose his own topic. He knew from past experience that to write a good essay, he would have to write on a topic he cared about. He also knew that he should allow himself a reasonable amount of time to find a topic and to gather his ideas. A premedical student, James found himself reading essays online and in the library that had a scientific bent. An essay in the August 8, 1983, issue of *Newsweek* entitled "A Crime of Compassion" by Barbara Huttmann caught his eye because it dealt with the issues of the right to die and pain treatment in terminally ill patients, issues that he would be confronting as a medical doctor.

James wrote this particular essay on a patient's right to choose death during the second half of the semester, after he had read a number of model arguments and had learned the importance of incorporating such elements as good paragraphing, unity, and transitions in his earlier essays. He began by brainstorming about his topic: he made lists of all the ideas, facts, issues, arguments, opposing arguments, and refutations that came to mind as a result of his own firsthand experiences with dying patients while on an internship. When he was confident that he had amassed enough information to begin writing, he made a rough outline of an organizational plan and then wrote a first draft of his essay. After conferencing with several peers as well as his instructor, James revised what he had written.

The final draft of James's essay illustrates that he had learned how the parts of a well-written essay fit together and how to make revisions that emulate some of the qualities in the model essays he had read and studied. The following is the final draft of James's essay.

James Duffy

One Dying Wish

Opening: context-setting story focuses attention on the central issue

It was an interesting summer. I spent most of my internship assisting postdoctoral students doing research in Cincinnati. One day I came across a file I will never forget. Within the thick file was the story of a fifty-something cancer patient. The man's cancer had metastasized and was now spread throughout his entire body. Over a period of two months he went under the knife seven times to repair and remove parts of his battle-weary body. He endured immeasurable pain. The final surgery on record was done in an effort to stop the pain — doctors intentionally severed the man's spinal cord.

Thesis: writer presents clear statement of position

Terminally ill patients experience intractable pain, and many lose the ability to live a life that has any real meaning to them. To force these people to stay alive when they are in pain and there is no hope for recovery is wrong. They should have the choice to let nature take its course. Forcing people to live in pain when only machines are keeping them alive is unjust.

Presentation of opposing argument: troublesome hospital policy

The hospital I was doing my internship in that summer had a policy that as long as someone was alive, they would do anything to keep him or her alive. The terminal cancer patient whose file I stumbled across fit into this category. He was on narcotics prescribed to alleviate his pain. The problem was that the doctors could not prescribe above a certain life-threatening dosage, a level far below what was necessary to manage the patient's pain. In such a situation, the doctors can't raise a dose because they risk sedating the patient to the point of heart failure.

Discussion of what writer believes is wrong with hospital policy

The hospital I was working at had fallen on hard times; the last thing they needed was to lose a large malpractice suit. If a doctor prescribes above the highest recommended dosage, his or her hospital is at risk if the patient dies. Keeping patients on life support at low dosages, however, is cruel. The doctors at many hospitals have their hands tied. They simply can't give dosages high enough to treat the pain without putting the hospital at risk, and the other option, stopping life support, is forbidden by many hospitals.

Evidence: writer uses example of his Aunt Eileen to show how patient choice and compassionate care should work

When I was fifteen, my Aunt Eileen, who was thirty-four, was diagnosed with a malignant skin cancer. The disease was caught late, and the cancer had metastasized throughout her body. At the time, Eileen had been married for eight years and had a four-year-old daughter and a six-year-old son. They were and are adorable children. When Eileen learned of the disease, she was devastated. She loved her husband and children very much and could not bear the thought of not being with them. Eileen fought the disease fiercely. She tried all the conventional treatments available. Her father and brother were both doctors, so she had access to the best possible care, but the disease did not succumb to the treatment. She tried unconventional and experimental treatments as well, but it was all for naught. The disease had an unshakable grip on her. She had wasted away to well below one hundred pounds; a tumor had grown to the size of a grapefruit on her stomach. It was the end, and everyone knew it. Luckily Eileen was able to get into a hospice center. While she was there, she was able to make peace with herself, her family, and God and die calmly without pain.

If Eileen had been forced to keep living, her pain undertreated and her body resuscitated again and again, the damage to her and her family would have been enormous. It would have been almost impossible to make peace with herself and God if she had been in pain so intense she couldn't think. The hospice personnel managed the pain and helped Eileen and her family avoid the anguish of a prolonged and painful death.

Evidence: writer introduces outside source to support his argument for patient choice

In "A Crime of Compassion," Barbara Huttmann, a registered nurse, recounts her hospital's disregard for a patient named Mac. Mac's story is one of a prolonged and painful death, without options. Mac came into the hospital with a persistent cough and walked out with a diagnosis of lung cancer. He battled the disease but lost ground fast. Over the course

Writer summarizes Huttmann's story about her patient Mac, taking care to put any directly quoted material in quotation marks followed by an in-text citation

of six months, Mac lost "his youth, . . . his hair, his bowel and bladder control, . . . and his ability to do the slightest thing for himself" (11). Mac wasted away to a mere sixty pounds. He was in constant pain, which the hospital was unable to manage. His young wife now looked "haggard" and "beaten" (11). Mac went into arrest three times some days. Every time his wife broke down into tears. The nurses ordered "code blue" every time it happened, and the hospital staff resuscitated Mac. This situation repeated itself for over a month. During one month, Mac was resuscitated fifty-two times. Mac had long ago realized the battle was over. He pleaded with his doctors and nurses to let him die. The problem was that the hospital did not issue no-code orders. A no-code order meant that if Mac went into arrest again they would let him die. Days passed as Barbara Huttmann, his nurse, pleaded for a no-code order. Each time he went into arrest his wife, Maura, took another step toward becoming psychologically crippled. As Barbara worked to resuscitate Mac, she'd look into his eyes as he pleaded for her to stop. Finally, Barbara decided enough was enough. Mac went into arrest and she did not call the code blue until she was certain he could not be resuscitated. For granting Mac his dying wish, Barbara was charged with murder.

Writer uses anti-capital punishment argument to bolster his call for more humane treatment of the terminally ill

The situation of Mac illustrates the death many people are forced to endure. These situations constitute an irony in today's society. Many complain that executions are inhumane or cruel and unusual. A principal argument of these anti–capital punishment people is that the death is not pain-free. People also think that regardless of the situation a patient should be allowed to die and should not be medicated to the point of death. Mac was forced to live on the brink of death for over a month, watching as his wife was also destroyed by his ordeal. The treatment Mac received can only be described as inhumane. To force a man to live in pain when there is no reasonable hope he will ever get better is truly cruel and unusual.

Had Mac had the option of a peaceful and pain-free death, it would have saved himself and his wife the pain of being forced to live on the edge of death for such an extended period of time. Maura must have looked into Mac's tortured eyes and wondered why he had no choices concerning his life or death. Almost any other choice would have been better than the treatment he received.

Conclusion: Writer calls for action on the rights of the terminally ill

American society needs to follow the lead of countries like the Netherlands and Belgium or a state like Oregon with its Death with Dignity Act and reevaluate the right of the terminally ill to die. Keeping people in agonizing pain for a long period is uncivilized. Everyone would agree with that. Many people do not understand, however, that prolonging the life of a terminally ill patient with unmanageable pain is the same thing. Laws need to be passed to protect doctors who accidently overmedicate a terminally ill patient in the interest of pain management. Patients also deserve the right to determine if they want to go off life support, no matter what hospital they are in. Until people demand that action be taken to resolve this issue, the terminally ill will continue to suffer.

Works Cited

Huttmann, Barbara. "A Crime of Compassion." *Newsweek*, 8 Aug. 1983, p. 11.

part two

The Elements of the Essay

CHAPTER **3**

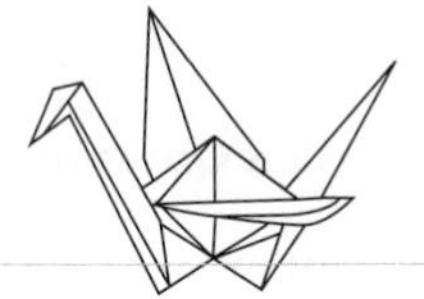

Thesis

The **thesis** of an essay is its main or controlling idea, the point the writer is trying to make. The thesis is often expressed in a one- or two-sentence statement, although sometimes it is implied or suggested rather than stated directly. The thesis statement determines the content of the essay developed in every paragraph.

Because everything you say in your composition must be logically related to your thesis, the thesis statement controls and directs the choices you make about the content of your essay. This does not mean that your thesis statement is a straitjacket. As your essay develops, you may want to modify your thesis statement to accommodate your new thinking. This urge is not only acceptable but also normal.

A thesis statement should be

- the most important point you make about your topic;
- debatable, or open to an opposing argument;
- more general than the ideas and facts used to support it; and
- appropriately focused for the length of your paper.

A thesis statement is not a question but an assertion—a claim made about a debatable issue that can be supported with evidence. The word "debatable" is important here. If your argument has no opposing argument, it is not itself an argument.

STRATEGIES FOR DEVELOPING A THESIS

Deciding on a direction for your essay and writing a thesis can be a daunting task, but below are some strategies that will help you brainstorm a working thesis. For more information on thesis statements, including steps to develop them, see Chapter 1, pages 13–19.

Ask a Question

One way to develop a working thesis is to determine what question you are trying to answer in your essay. A one- or two-sentence answer to this question often produces a tentative thesis statement. For example, a student wanted to answer a question about gendered speaking styles, and after a working answer and two drafts, she modified her thesis statement:

QUESTION:	Do men and women have different conversational speaking styles?
PRELIMINARY ANSWER:	Men and women appear to have different objectives when they converse.
MODIFIED THESIS:	Very often, conversations between men and women become situations in which the man gives a mini-lecture and the woman unwittingly turns into a captive audience.

Complete the Sentence

Another effective strategy for developing a thesis statement is to begin by writing "What I want to say is that . . ."

> What I want to say is that unless the university administration enforces a strong anti-hazing policy, the well-being of many of its student-athletes will be endangered.

Later, when you delete the formulaic opening, you will be left with a thesis statement:

> Unless the university administration enforces a strong anti-hazing policy, the well-being of many of its student-athletes will be endangered.

LOCATION OF THE THESIS

Usually the thesis is presented early in the essay, sometimes in the first sentence. Here are some examples of strong thesis statements:

> Mutual respect is the most important ingredient in a healthy marriage.

> Mark Twain's great contribution to American literature is his use of vernacular English, and this is no more pronounced than in his novel *The Adventures of Huckleberry Finn*.

> Professional sports organizations need to address the long-term effects of player concussions with rule changes and more technologically advanced equipment.
>
> Many people believe that the American legal system is flooded with frivolous lawsuits, but there is little agreement on what is meant by "frivolous."

Each of these sentences does what a good thesis statement should do: it identifies the topic and makes an assertion about it.

Often writers prepare readers for the thesis statement with one or several sentences that establish a context. Notice in the following example how the author eases the reader into his thesis about the stages of life instead of presenting it abruptly in the first sentence:

> There used to be four common life phases: childhood, adolescence, adulthood and old age. Now, there are at least six: childhood, adolescence, odyssey, adulthood, active retirement, and old age. Of the new ones, the least understood is odyssey, the decade of wandering that frequently occurs between adolescence and adulthood.
>
> —David Brooks, "The Odyssey Years"

On occasion a writer may even purposely delay the presentation of a thesis until the middle or the end of an essay. If the thesis is controversial or needs extended discussion and illustration, the writer might present it later to make it easier for the reader to understand and accept it. Appearing near or at the end of an essay, a thesis also gains prominence. For example, after an involved discussion about why various groups put pressure on school libraries to ban books, a student ended an essay with her thesis:

> The effort to censor what our children are reading can turn into a potentially explosive situation and cause misunderstanding and hurt feelings within our schools and communities. If we can gain an understanding of why people have sought to censor children's books, we will be better prepared to respond in a sensitive and reasonable manner. More importantly, we will be able to provide the best educational opportunity for our children through a sensible approach, one that neither overly restricts the range of their reading nor allows them to read all books, no matter how inappropriate. Thesis
>
> —Tara Ketch, student

Some kinds of writing do not need thesis statements. These include descriptions, narratives, and personal writing such as letters and diaries. But any essay that seeks to explain or prove a point has a thesis that is usually set forth in a formal thesis statement.

For more information on thesis statements, see Chapter 1, pages 13–19.

Lucy and Her Friends

Laura Lee

Valery Lantratov

Born in Detroit, Michigan, in 1969, Laura Lee is a producer of ballet education tours as well as a writer on diverse topics of general interest. Her publications include over a dozen nonfiction works, including *The Name's Familiar* (1999), *Bad Predictions* (2000), *The Pocket Encyclopedia of Aggravation* (2001), and *Broke Is Beautiful* (2010); a novel, *Angel* (2015); and a children's nonfiction book, *Child's Introduction to Ballet: The Stories, Music, and Magic of Classical Dance* (2007), with Meredith Hamilton. Lee's father, Albert Lee, wrote a book about weather, *Weather Wisdom* (1976), which gave her the idea for updating the book and expanding upon it. The result is *Blame It On the Rain* (2006), from which this excerpt is taken.

In this selection, Lee explores the connection between weather and one of the most famous finds in archeology: the discovery of the bones of an ancient hominid who came to be called "Lucy." As you read, pay attention to how Lee uses other examples to support her thesis that weather can be the friend of the archaeologist.

Reflecting on What You Know

Think of a time when you came upon an unexpected discovery of your own. It could be that you learned something new about a subject you thought you already understood, or maybe it was about a person in your life. What circumstances led to your discovery? How did this discovery change your understanding of that subject or person?

The entire field of archaeology[1] owes a debt to Mother Nature. The same flash floods and storms that bury and preserve bones and fossils uncover them centuries later, giving scientists and historians a new window into the past. While many archaeological discoveries are the result of painstaking research, some involve a great deal of luck—and fortunate weather. 1

Take for example Lucy. In November 1974 anthropologist Donald Johanson and his graduate student, Tom Gray, were fossil hunting in Hadar, Ethiopia. As they searched along a gully, they spotted a bone sticking out of some soil that had been eroded by a recent flash flood. The bone, hidden for millions of years in sediment and volcanic ash, was just the beginning. After three weeks of excavation, Johanson and his team found several hundred pieces of bone, all belonging to one hominid[2] female. The scientists gave her the nickname Lucy, after the Beatles song "Lucy in the Sky with Diamonds," but her official name is *Australopithecus afarensis.* 2

The Lucy skeleton was dated back about three million years, the most complete and oldest hominid skeleton to have been found at that time. Lucy was about a meter tall and walked erect, which opened new debate in the scientific community as to when and why humans started standing upright. 3

"If I had waited another few years," Johanson wrote in his book *Lucy: The Beginnings of Humankind,* "the next rains might have washed many of her bones down the gully. . . . What was utterly fantastic was that she had come to the surface so recently, probably in the last year or two. Five years earlier, she would still have been buried. Five years later, she would have been gone." 4

Violent winter storms also increased our knowledge of Native American history and culture. For years, Richard Daugherty of Washington State University had been excavating buried remains at the abandoned coastal village of Ozette. Little by little he tried to piece together the history of the Makah Indians who had once lived on the land. Their descendants told him a story of a huge mudslide that had buried the entire village. Daugherty was unable to confirm the story until 1970, when nature lent a hand. A storm sent tides raging up the beach at Ozette and washed away a bank. 5

---

[1]*archaeology:* the study of human history through fossils, artifacts, and other physical remains.

[2]*hominid:* belonging to a family of primate mammals that includes humans and their ancestors.

Under the soil was a vast deposit of artifacts dating from around 6
the time of Columbus's arrival in the New World. There were fishhooks of wood and bone, a harpoon shaft, a canoe paddle, a woven hat, and parts of inlaid boxes. The objects are now housed in a museum created by the Makah Tribal Council.

Most fortuitous[3] of all was the accidental discovery of a Stone 7
Age body by two nonscientists. German hikers Helmut and Erika Simon were walking in the mountains of the Austrian-Italian border on a particularly sunny morning in September 1991. They wandered off the trail and were startled to see a dead body in the melting ice. They assumed it was the corpse of a modern climber, and they called a rescue team. As the medics chipped him from the ice and unearthed many of his belongings, it became clear that this climber was quite a bit older than they had originally suspected.

In fact, the man's body dated from 3300 B.C. It had been pre- 8
served in ice until a fall of dust from the Sahara and an unusually warm spell melted the ice in 1991, bringing the "Ice Man" back to the surface. Since he was found in the Ötztal Alps, he was given the nickname Ötzi. What was unique about Ötzi was that he was incredibly well preserved, with his clothing and tools intact. This gave scholars a greater understanding of Ötzi's life, culture, and community.

A unique set of circumstances gave us this window into the past. 9
Soon after Ötzi died, his body had been covered with snow, which kept the predators away. Then a glacier covered him and entombed him in ice. Normally, a glacier would destroy everything in its path, but Ötzi's body was sheltered in a rock hollow.

Even more amazing was that a freak thaw unearthed him just as 10
a pair of hikers were passing. As one commentator wrote, "Over the past five thousand years the chance of finding the Ice Man existed for only six days."

Thinking Critically about This Reading

Lee argues that "archaeology owes a debt to Mother Nature" (paragraph 1). Why does Lee state this, and under what circumstances might Mother Nature be an enemy to archaeology?

[3]*fortuitous:* lucky; fortunate.

Questions for Study and Discussion

1. What is Lee's thesis? Based on her evidence, do you think her thesis has been proven? Why or why not?
2. Lee begins her excerpt with the story of Lucy, the name given to the hominid female whose bones date back three million years. Why was the discovery of Lucy so important?
3. While excavating at Ozette, Richard Daugherty heard about a village lost to a mudslide, and he was able to confirm the story when a storm unearthed artifacts from the time of Christopher Columbus. What might this suggest about memories that are passed down in an oral (as opposed to written) culture?
4. Why does Lee describe the discovery of the Ice Man in the Ötzal Alps as "the most fortuitous of all" (7)? Do you think that description is justified? Why?
5. To what extent do the discoveries Lee describes suggest that the study of archaeology itself is a product of chance? What are the larger implications of that in terms of addressing archaeology as a science?

Classroom Activity Using Thesis

A good thesis is an arguable statement that presents an answer to a question. So, sometimes the best way to construct a thesis is to start first by constructing a question. Constructing the question can lead you to an answer, or perhaps several different possible answers that you will need to consider. Which answer you choose will depend on your own opinion about the matter and what evidence you have to support your statement.

Develop a list of five questions on the subject of "censorship on the Internet." To get you started, here is one possible question: "Should anyone be able to put any information or photographs online even if it could be considered untrue or fake?"

1. ______________________________.
2. ______________________________.
3. ______________________________.
4. ______________________________.
5. ______________________________.

Now develop a preliminary thesis statement by answering one of your questions.

Suggested Writing Assignments

1. Lee points out that the objects Daugherty found are now in "a museum created by the Makah Tribal Council" (6). However, in many other circumstances, archaeologists, adventurers, and looters have taken ancient artifacts from sites and kept them for themselves or sold them to collectors or museums. Today, some countries are trying to get such objects returned, but the countries that have them claim that they have preserved the artifacts better than the original countries could and that they are available to a wider audience. Consider your own experiences of encountering objects in museums. Do you agree or disagree with the argument that artifacts should be returned to their original countries or displayed where they are most accessible to more people? Why? Write a thesis statement and main points and develop them into an outline and/or an essay.
2. Lee points out that the Ice Man was discovered not by professional archaeologists but by two hikers walking in the Alps on a sunny day. How would you react if you discovered an ancient corpse while you were out for a walk? Write an essay about what level of responsibility you would feel about reporting your discovery and how it might affect you emotionally.
3. Lee writes about three specific instances in which weather created the conditions ripe for archaeological discoveries. Research current archeological investigations. Find a particular "dig" or area where archaeological research is currently being done. Investigate the obstacles that the researchers face. Are the obstacles financial? Political? Environmental? Something else? After doing some research on the issues, construct an essay with a strong thesis statement arguing whether such research is worthwhile.

The End of Passwords

David Pogue

Stephen Lovekin/Getty Images

David Pogue, born in 1963 in Shaker Heights, Ohio, graduated from Yale with a distinction in music; he has also been awarded an honorary doctorate in music by the Shenandoah Conservatory in Virginia. He is a tech critic for Yahoo Finance, a monthly columnist for *Scientific American*, and a host for science shows on PBS's *Nova*. He has over three million books in print, on topics ranging from technology to classical music; and he is also the winner of three Emmy awards, two Webby awards, and a Loeb award for journalism. Pogue has gained a reputation as a consumer advocate for his writing in the *New York Times*, where he especially focused on technology products such as cell phones and e-readers.

In this article, which appeared in *Scientific American* in 2016, Pogue addresses an issue all users of technology— virtually all of us—face: the use of passwords. He argues that a truly effective passwords are at odds with how most people use them. As you read, pay attention to the evidence Pogue uses to support his thesis and suggest that new technology promises better, more efficient, and more dependable protection in the future.

Reflecting on What You Know

What is your approach to the use of passwords? Do you use simple, easy-to-remember passwords? Do you use multiple passwords for different websites and devices? Do you change your passwords regularly? How do you keep track of your passwords?

Our tech lives are full of pain points, but at least the world's tech geniuses seem committed to solving them. Today who complains about the things that bugged us a decade ago, such as heavy laptops, slow cellular Internet, the inability to do e-mail in planes? 1

It was only a matter of time before those geniuses started tackling one of the longest-running pain points in history: passwords. We're supposed to create a long, complex, unguessable password—capital and lowercase letters, numbers and symbols, with a few Arabic letters thrown in if possible. *For each site*. Don't reuse a password. Oh, and change them all every month. 2

Sorry, security experts. Not possible. Not for an average person, not even for you. Nobody has that kind of memory. 3

To make matters worse, passwords aren't even especially secure. See any recent headline about stolen passwords or about some company's servers being hacked. 4

It's time to kill the password. 5

Surely, in the 50 years since we started typing passwords, somebody must have invented a better security system. The answer: yes and no. Apps such as 1Password and Dashlane memorize and enter long, complicated passwords *for* you. But most of them cost money, they don't work on every Web account and the nontechie public doesn't know they exist. 6

There's also two-factor authentication, which makes you type a password *and* a code texted to your phone to log in. It's an unbelievable hassle. The masses will never go for it. 7

Finally, biometric[1] approaches can be both secure and easy because they recognize *us*, not memorized strings of text. Here there's hope. Fingerprint readers on smartphones, tablets and laptops are becoming common, cheap, convenient, and essentially impossible to hack on a large scale. So far they're primarily useful for logging us into our *machines*. Shouldn't the next step be letting us log into our Web accounts? Iris[2] scanning is another biometric technology, fast enough to work well at automated border-crossing systems and secure enough for national ID programs such as India's (it's enrolling 1.2 billion people). 8

[1]*biometric:* relating to physical or behavioral characteristics, such as voices and fingerprints, often used to identify an individual.

[2]*iris:* the colored part of the eye that also adjusts the size of the pupil (the black center).

At the moment, iris scanners are far too new and expensive to build into every phone and laptop—but almost every technology gets cheaper over time. Some scanners can be fooled by a photograph of your eye, but this problem, too, can be overcome (by tracking your pupil as you read something, for example). Bottom line: there's no insurmountable[3] problem in iris reading's future. 9

Same with voice authentication, using the unique pitch, accent and frequencies of your speaking voice as your key. It's cheap enough for wide adoption—our phones and gadgets already have microphones. Worried about bad guys faking out the system with a recording of your voice? That can't happen if the phrase you're asked to speak changes every time you log in. 10

The only roadblocks here are background noise and laryngitis.[4] And as with any biometric security solution, this approach really requires a backup system—like a password—just in case. 11

Then there's Windows Hello, a new feature of Windows 10 that lets you log in with fingerprint, iris, or facial recognition—whatever your laptop is equipped to handle. The face option is especially exciting. You just sit down at the computer, and it unlocks instantly. You can't fool it with a photograph or even a 3-D model of your head, because the Intel RealSense camera it requires includes infrared and 3-D sensors. 12

Of course, very few gadgets come with that camera preinstalled. But the RealSense concept is truly the Holy Grail:[5] secure and convenient. If the hardware ever became as ubiquitous[6] and cheap as, say, our phones' fingerprint readers, we could have a winner. 13

Clearly, the password concept is broken. Equally clearly, these new technologies can provide both the security and the convenience the world demands. Nothing's quite there yet, and we need to keep our eye on privacy concerns (who owns the databases of biometric scans, for example?). 14

But one thing is for sure: this is one pain point that's got everyone's attention. 15

---

[3]*insurmountable:* incapable of being overcome; unbeatable.

[4]*laryngitis:* inflammation of the vocal chords that causes the voice to become hoarse or raspy.

[5]*Holy Grail:* the goal of a long or difficult quest.

[6]*ubiquitous:* common; widespread.

Thinking Critically about This Reading

Pogue argues that "It's time to kill the password" (paragraph 5). Do you agree that passwords have become a problem that needs to be solved? What are the possible benefits of eliminating the need for passwords? What are the possible negative consequences of some of the alternatives that he suggests? (Glossary: **Cause and Effect**) Explain.

Questions for Study and Discussion

1. Is Pogue's thesis about a topic of importance and controversy? Why or why not? What question is Pogue trying to answer in his thesis?
2. What is the problem with passwords, as Pogue sees it? Do you share his concerns? Why or why not?
3. When Pogue presents the two-factor authentication (7), he states that the "masses will never go for it." Why is that? Do you agree?
4. What does Pogue mean by "biometric approaches" (8)? Examine each of the approaches that Pogue suggests and argue whether or not you see each one as a realistic alternative to replace passwords.
5. At the end of his essay, Pogue does raise the issue of privacy and information ownership. What are some of those concerns? How might they be resolved?

Classroom Activity Using Thesis

A strong thesis makes a claim rather than stating something obvious about the topic. One way to check whether your thesis makes a claim is to try stating its opposite as an alternative. If this new thesis seems absurd or wrong, your original thesis might benefit from greater specificity.

Imagine that you were going to write a response to Pogue's argument about passwords. Which of the following could be a thesis statement for a substantial counterargument? If you're not sure, test each one by stating its opposite. Note: Often a good thesis cannot be easily reversed because it does not frame the issues in black and white.

1. The password system for Internet security needs to be replaced immediately.
2. Costs for hardware and software that provide the most up-to-date Internet security should be subsidized by the federal government so that all Americans can afford to be secure online.
3. Hardware and software manufacturers are working hard to improve Internet security.
4. People should be smarter about creating complex passwords that cannot be guessed by Internet hackers and identity thieves.
5. Pogue is far too optimistic about the ability to lower costs for high-end computer security devices.
6. Trying to improve security is pointless because with every new advance, thieves will create new ways around them.

Now that you've eliminated some, how many potential theses are left? When writers like Pogue address complex issues, thoughtful readers can respond with an array of ideas, concerns, or questions. Look at the remaining thesis statements and discuss how each one takes a different approach to the problem.

Suggested Writing Assignments

1. Write an essay in which you respond to Pogue's concern about the use of passwords on the Internet today. Formulate a thesis sentence in which you argue whether or not his concerns are justified. Consider whether his proposed improvements are realistic. Can you envision a time when the use of passwords will disappear completely? If so, what changes would have to occur for that to become a reality? If not, why not?
2. Do you currently use biometric security? Investigate the problems associated with biometric approaches to Internet security. What are some of the potential drawbacks as well as advantages? Formulate a thesis sentence stating an argument about the future of biometric computer security and then write an essay supporting your position.

Anxiety: Challenge by Another Name

James Lincoln Collier

Photo © Miriam Berkley

James Lincoln Collier is a freelance writer with more than six hundred articles to his credit. He was born in New York in 1928 and graduated from Hamilton College in 1950. An accomplished jazz musician, Collier has often focused his nonfiction writing on American music. His best-known book is *The Making of Jazz: A Comprehensive History* (1978). With his brother Christopher, he has written a number of history books, including *A Century of Immigration: 1820–1924* (2000), *The Civil War* (2000), *The Changing Face of American Society: 1945–2000* (2001), and a series of biographies for young readers covering major figures in American history. Collier has also written a number of children's books, one of which, *My Brother Sam Is Dead* (1974), received a Newbery Honor award and was named a Notable Children's Book.

As you read the following essay, which first appeared in *Reader's Digest* in 1986, pay attention to where Collier places his thesis. Note also how his thesis statement identifies the topic (anxiety) and makes an assertion about it (that it can have a positive effect on our lives).

Reflecting on What You Know

Many people associate anxiety with stress and think of it as a negative thing. Are there good kinds of anxiety, too? Provide an example of anxiety that has been beneficial to you or to someone you know.

Between my sophomore and junior years at college, a chance came up for me to spend the summer vacation working on a ranch in Argentina. My roommate's father was in the cattle business, and he 1 wanted Ted to see something of it. Ted said he would go if he could take a friend, and he chose me.

The idea of spending two months on the fabled Argentine Pampas[1] was exciting. Then I began having second thoughts. I had never been very far from New England, and I had been homesick my first few weeks at college. What would it be like in a strange country? What about the language? And besides, I had promised to teach my younger brother to sail that summer. The more I thought about it, the more the prospect daunted[2] me. I began waking up nights in a sweat. 2

In the end I turned down the proposition. As soon as Ted asked somebody else to go, I began kicking myself. A couple of weeks later I went home to my old summer job, unpacking cartons at the local supermarket, feeling very low. I had turned down something I wanted to do because I was scared, and had ended up feeling depressed. I stayed that way for a long time. And it didn't help when I went back to college in the fall to discover that Ted and his friend had had a terrific time. 3

In the long run that unhappy summer taught me a valuable lesson out of which I developed a rule for myself: *do what makes you anxious; don't do what makes you depressed.* 4

I am not, of course, talking about severe states of anxiety or depression, which require medical attention. What I mean is that kind of anxiety we call stage fright, butterflies in the stomach, a case of nerves—the feelings we have at a job interview, when we're giving a big party, when we have to make an important presentation at the office. And the kind of depression I am referring to is that downhearted feeling of the blues, when we don't seem to be interested in anything, when we can't get going and seem to have no energy. 5

I was confronted by this sort of situation toward the end of my senior year. As graduation approached, I began to think about taking a crack at making my living as a writer. But one of my professors was urging me to apply to graduate school and aim at a teaching career. 6

I wavered. The idea of trying to live by writing was scary—a lot more scary than spending a summer on the Pampas, I thought. Back and forth I went, making my decision, unmaking it. Suddenly, I realized that every time I gave up the idea of writing, that sinking feeling went through me; it gave me the blues. 7

[1]*Pampas:* a vast plain in central Argentina.
[2]*daunted:* discouraged.

The thought of graduate school wasn't what depressed me. It was giving up on what deep in my gut I really wanted to do. Right then I learned another lesson. To avoid that kind of depression meant, inevitably, having to endure a certain amount of worry and concern. 8

The great Danish philosopher Søren Kierkegaard believed that anxiety always arises when we confront the possibility of our own development. It seems to be a rule of life that you can't advance without getting that old, familiar, jittery feeling. 9

Even as children we discover this when we try to expand ourselves by, say, learning to ride a bike or going out for the school play. Later in life we get butterflies when we think about having that first child, or uprooting the family from the old hometown to find a better opportunity halfway across the country. Any time, it seems, that we set out aggressively to get something we want, we meet up with anxiety. And it's going to be our traveling companion, at least part of the way, into any new venture. 10

When I first began writing magazine articles, I was frequently required to interview big names—people like Richard Burton,[3] Joan Rivers,[4] sex authority William Masters, baseball-great Dizzy Dean. Before each interview I would get butterflies and my hands would shake. 11

At the time, I was doing some writing about music. And one person I particularly admired was the great composer Duke Ellington. Onstage and on television, he seemed the very model of the confident, sophisticated man of the world. Then I learned that Ellington still got stage fright. If the highly honored Duke Ellington, who had appeared on the bandstand some 10,000 times over thirty years, had anxiety attacks, who was I to think I could avoid them? 12

I went on doing those frightening interviews, and one day, as I was getting onto a plane for Washington to interview columnist Joseph Alsop, I suddenly realized to my astonishment that I was looking forward to the meeting. What had happened to those butterflies? 13

Well, in truth, they were still there, but there were fewer of them. I had benefited, I discovered, from a process psychologists call "extinction." If you put an individual in an anxiety-provoking situation often enough, he will eventually learn that there isn't anything to be worried about. 14

---

[3]*Richard Burton* (1925–1984): a well-known British stage and Hollywood movie actor.
[4]*Joan Rivers* (1933–2014): a stand-up comedian and talk-show host.

Which brings us to a corollary[5] to my basic rule: *you'll never eliminate anxiety by avoiding the things that caused it.* I remember how my son Jeff was when I first began to teach him to swim at the lake cottage where we spent our summer vacations. He resisted, and when I got him into the water he sank and sputtered and wanted to quit. But I was insistent. And by summer's end he was splashing around like a puppy. He had "extinguished" his anxiety the only way he could—by confronting it. 15

The problem, of course, is that it is one thing to urge somebody else to take on those anxiety-producing challenges; it is quite another to get ourselves to do it. 16

Some years ago I was offered a writing assignment that would require three months of travel through Europe. I had been abroad a couple of times on the usual "If it's Tuesday this must be Belgium" trips, but I hardly could claim to know my way around the continent. Moreover, my knowledge of foreign languages was limited to a little college French. 17

I hesitated. How would I, unable to speak the language, totally unfamiliar with local geography or transportation systems, set up interviews and do research? It seemed impossible, and with considerable regret I sat down to write a letter begging off. Halfway through, a thought—which I subsequently made into another corollary to my basic rule—ran through my mind: *you can't learn if you don't try.* So I accepted the assignment. 18

There were some bad moments. But by the time I had finished the trip I was an experienced traveler. And ever since, I have never hesitated to head for even the most exotic of places, without guides or even advanced bookings, confident that somehow I will manage. 19

The point is that the new, the different, is almost by definition scary. But each time you try something, you learn, and as the learning piles up, the world opens to you. 20

I've made parachute jumps, learned to ski at forty, flown up the Rhine[6] in a balloon. And I know I'm going to go on doing such things. It's not because I'm braver or more daring than others. I'm not. But I don't let the butterflies stop me from doing what I want. Accept anxiety as another name for challenge and you can accomplish wonders. 21

[5]*corollary:* a proposition that follows with little or no proof required.
[6]*Rhine:* a major river and waterway of western Europe.

Thinking Critically about This Reading

Collier writes that "Kierkegaard believed that anxiety always arises when we confront the possibility of our own development" (paragraph 9). How do Collier's own experiences and growth substantiate Kierkegaard's belief in the value of anxiety?

Questions for Study and Discussion

1. What is Collier's thesis? Based on your own experiences, do you think Collier's thesis is valid? Explain.
2. What is the process known to psychologists as "extinction"?
3. What causes Collier to come up with his basic rule for himself: "Do what makes you anxious; don't do what makes you depressed" (4)? (Glossary: **Cause and Effect**) How does he develop the two corollaries to his basic rule? How do the basic rule and the two corollaries prepare you for his thesis?
4. What is Collier's purpose? (Glossary: **Purpose**)
5. What function do paragraphs 17–19 serve in Collier's essay?

Classroom Activity Using Thesis

A good thesis statement identifies the topic and makes an assertion about it. Evaluate each of the following sentences, and explain why each one either works or doesn't work as a thesis statement.

1. Americans are suffering from overwork.
2. Life is indeed precious, and I believe the death penalty helps to affirm this fact.
3. Birthday parties are loads of fun.
4. New York is a city of sounds: muted sounds and shrill sounds, shattering sounds and soothing sounds, urgent sounds and aimless sounds.
5. Everyone is talking about the level of violence in American society.

Suggested Writing Assignments

1. Building on your own experiences and the reading you have done, write an essay in which you use as your thesis either Collier's basic rule or one of his corollaries to that basic rule.
2. Write an essay using any one of the following as your thesis:

   Good manners are a thing of the past.
   We need rituals in our lives.
   To tell a joke well is an art.
   We are a drug-dependent society.
   Travel broadens one's understanding of the world.
   Stage fright is an important part of performance.
   Making decisions by "gut" feelings is irresponsible.

CHAPTER **4**

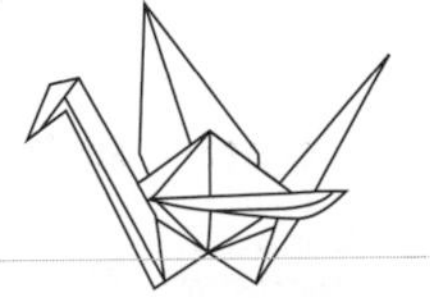

Unity

Unity is an essential quality in a well-written essay. The principle of unity requires that every element in a piece of writing—whether a paragraph or an essay—be related to the main idea. Sentences that stray from the main idea, even though they might be related to it or provide additional information, can weaken an otherwise strong piece of writing. Notice how the italicized segments in the following paragraph undermine its unity and divert our attention from its main idea:

> When I was growing up, one of the places I enjoyed most was the cherry tree in the backyard. *Behind the yard was an alley and then more houses.* Every summer when the cherries began to ripen, I used to spend hours high up in the tree, picking and eating the sweet, sun-warmed cherries. *My mother always worried about my falling out of the tree, but I never did.* But I had some competition for the cherries—flocks of birds that enjoyed them as much as I did would perch all over the tree, devouring the fruit whenever I wasn't there. I used to wonder why the grown-ups never ate any of the cherries—*my father loved all kinds of fruit*—but actually, when the birds and I had finished, there weren't many left.
>
> —Betty Burns, student

When the italicized sentences are eliminated, the paragraph is unified and reads smoothly.

Now consider another paragraph, this one from an essay about family photographs and how they allow the author to learn about her past and to stay connected with her family in the present:

First sentence gives focus and direction to the paragraph.

> Photographs have taken me to places I have never been and have shown me people alive before I was born. I can visit my grandmother's childhood home in Vienna, Austria, and walk down the high-ceilinged, iron staircase by looking through the

Subsequent sentences relate directly to the places and people mentioned in the first sentence.

small, white album my grandma treasures. I also know of the tomboy she once was, wearing lederhosen instead of the dirndls worn by her friends. And I have seen her as a beautiful young woman who traveled with the Red Cross during the war, uncertain of her future. The photograph that rests in a red leather frame on my grandma's nightstand has allowed me to meet the man she would later marry. He died before I was born. I have been told that I would have loved his calm manner, and I can see for myself his gentle smile and tranquil expression.

—Carrie White, student

A well-written essay should be unified both within and between paragraphs; that is, everything in it should be related to its **thesis**, the main idea of the essay. There are two requirements for unity:

1. The thesis itself should be clear, either through a direct statement, called the *thesis statement,* or by implication. (See Chapter 3 for more on thesis.)
2. There should be no digressions—no discussion or information that is not shown to be logically related to the thesis. A unified essay stays within the limits of its thesis.

Here, for example, is a short essay by Stuart Chase about the dangers of making generalizations. As you read, notice how carefully Chase sticks to his point.

Overgeneralizing

1 One swallow does not make a summer, nor can two or three cases often support a dependable generalization. Yet all of us, including the most polished eggheads, are constantly falling into this mental peopletrap. It is the most common, probably the most seductive, and potentially the most dangerous, of all the fallacies.

Thesis

2 You drive through a town and see a drunken man on the sidewalk. A few blocks further on you see another. You turn to your companion: "Nothing but drunks in this town!" Soon you are out in the country, bowling along at fifty. A car passes you as if you were parked. On a curve a second whizzes by. Your companion turns to you: "All the drivers in this state are crazy!" Two thumping generalizations, each

Paragraphs 2 and 3 document the thesis with examples.

built on two cases. If we stop to think, we usually recognize the exaggeration and the unfairness of such generalizations. Trouble comes when we do not stop to think—or when we build them on a prejudice.

This kind of reasoning has been around for a long time. Aristotle was aware of its dangers and called it "reasoning by example," meaning too few examples. What it boils down to is failing to count your swallows before announcing that summer is here. Driving from my home to New Haven the other day, a distance of about forty miles, I caught myself saying: "Every time I look around I see a new ranch-type house going up." So on the return trip I counted them; there were exactly five under construction. And how many times had I "looked around"? I suppose I had glanced to right and left—as one must at side roads and so forth in driving—several hundred times. 3

4 In this fallacy, we do not make the error of neglecting facts altogether and rushing immediately to the level of opinion. We start at the fact level properly enough, but *we do not stay there*. A case or two and up we go to a rousing oversimplification about drunks, speeders, ranch-style houses—or, more seriously, about foreigners, African Americans, labor leaders, teenagers.

Paragraph 4 explains how overgeneralizing occurs.

5 Why do we overgeneralize so often and sometimes so disastrously? One reason is that the human mind is a generalizing machine. We would not be people without this power. The old academic crack: "All generalizations are false, including this one," is only a play on words. We *must* generalize to communicate and to live. But we should beware of beating the gun; of not waiting until enough facts are in to say something useful. Meanwhile it is a plain waste of time to listen to arguments based on a few hand-picked examples.

Paragraph 5 analyzes why people overgeneralize. For a conclusion, Chase restates his thesis in different words.

–Stuart Chase, *Guides to Straight Thinking*

An essay may be longer, more complex, and more wide-ranging than this one, but to be effective, it must also avoid digressions and remain close to the author's main idea.

A good way to check that your essay is indeed unified is to underline or highlight your thesis and then explain to yourself how each paragraph in your essay is related to the thesis. If you find a paragraph that does not appear to be logically connected, you can revise it so that the relationship is clear. Similarly, it is useful to make sure that each sentence in a paragraph is related to the topic sentence. (See pp. 162–64 for a discussion of topic sentences.)

My Favorite Teacher

Thomas L. Friedman

Thomas L. Friedman, foreign affairs columnist for the *New York Times,* was born in Minneapolis, Minnesota, in 1953. He graduated from Brandeis University in 1975 and received a Marshall Scholarship to study modern Middle East studies at St. Antony's College, Oxford University, where he earned a master's degree. He has worked for the *New York Times* since 1981, first in Lebanon, then in Israel, and since 1989 in Washington, D.C. He has won three Pulitzer Prizes. His 1989 best seller, *From Beirut to Jerusalem,* received the National Book Award for nonfiction. Friedman's most recent books include *The World Is Flat: A Brief History of the Twenty-First Century* (2005); *Hot, Flat, and Crowded: Why We Need a Green Revolution—and How It Can Renew America* (2008); *That Used to Be Us: How America Fell Behind in the World It Invented and How We Can Come Back* (2011), co-written with Michael Mandelbaum; and *Thank You for Being Late* (2016).

In the following essay, which first appeared in the *New York Times* in 2001, Friedman pays tribute to his tenth-grade journalism teacher. As you read Friedman's profile of Hattie M. Steinberg, note the descriptive detail he selects to create a unified, dominant impression of "a woman of clarity in an age of uncertainty."

Reflecting on What You Know

If you had to name your three favorite teachers to date, who would be on your list? Why do you consider each of the teachers a favorite? Which one, if any, are you likely to remember twenty-five years from now? Why?

Last Sunday's *New York Times Magazine* published its annual review of people who died last year who left a particular mark on the world. I am sure all readers have their own such list. I certainly do. Indeed, someone who made the most important difference 1 in my life died last year—my high school journalism teacher, Hattie M. Steinberg.

I grew up in a small suburb of Minneapolis, and Hattie was the legendary journalism teacher at St. Louis Park High School, Room 313. I took her intro to journalism course in 10th grade, back in 1969, and have never needed, or taken, another course in journalism since. She was that good. 2

Hattie was a woman who believed that the secret for success in life was getting the fundamentals right. And boy, she pounded the fundamentals of journalism into her students—not simply how to write a lead or accurately transcribe a quote, but, more important, how to comport yourself in a professional way and to always do quality work. To this day, when I forget to wear a tie on assignment, I think of Hattie scolding me. I once interviewed an ad exec for our high school paper who used a four-letter word. We debated whether to run it. Hattie ruled yes. That ad man almost lost his job when it appeared. She wanted to teach us about consequences. 3

Hattie was the toughest teacher I ever had. After you took her journalism course in 10th grade, you tried out for the paper, *The Echo*, which she supervised. Competition was fierce. In 11th grade, I didn't quite come up to her writing standards, so she made me business manager, selling ads to the local pizza parlors. That year, though, she let me write one story. It was about an Israeli general who had been a hero in the Six-Day War,[1] who was giving a lecture at the University of Minnesota. I covered his lecture and interviewed him briefly. His name was Ariel Sharon.[2] First story I ever got published. 4

Those of us on the paper, and the yearbook that she also supervised, lived in Hattie's classroom. We hung out there before and after school. Now, you have to understand, Hattie was a single woman, nearing 60 at the time, and this was the 1960s. She was the polar opposite of "cool," but we hung around her classroom like it was a malt shop and she was Wolfman Jack.[3] None of us could have articulated it then, but it was because we enjoyed being harangued[4] by her, disciplined by her, and taught by her. She was a woman of clarity in an age of uncertainty. 5

[1]*Six-Day War:* the short but pivotal war in June 1967 between Israel and the allied countries of Egypt, Syria, and Jordan.

[2]*Ariel Sharon* (1928–2014): Israeli general and politician, elected prime minister of Israel in 2001.

[3]*Wolfman Jack:* pseudonym of Robert Weston Smith (1938–1995), a famous American rock-and-roll radio disc jockey.

[4]*harangued:* given a long, scolding lecture.

We remained friends for 30 years, and she followed, bragged about, and critiqued every twist in my career. After she died, her friends sent me a pile of my stories that she had saved over the years. Indeed, her students were her family—only closer. Judy Harrington, one of Hattie's former students, remarked about other friends who were on Hattie's newspapers and yearbooks: "We all graduated 41 years ago; and yet nearly each day in our lives something comes up—some mental image, some admonition[5] that makes us think of Hattie." 6

Judy also told the story of one of Hattie's last birthday parties, when one man said he had to leave early to take his daughter somewhere. "Sit down," said Hattie. "You're not leaving yet. She can just be a little late." 7

That was my teacher! I sit up straight just thinkin' about her. 8

Among the fundamentals Hattie introduced me to was the *New York Times*. Every morning it was delivered to Room 313. I had never seen it before then. Real journalists, she taught us, start their day by reading the *Times* and columnists like Anthony Lewis and James Reston. 9

I have been thinking about Hattie a lot this year, not just because she died on July 31, but because the lessons she imparted seem so relevant now. We've just gone through this huge dot-com-Internet-globalization bubble—during which a lot of smart people got carried away and forgot the fundamentals of how you build a profitable company, a lasting portfolio, a nation state, or a thriving student. It turns out that the real secret of success in the information age is what it always was: fundamentals—reading, writing, and arithmetic; church, synagogue, and mosque; the rule of law; and good governance. 10

The Internet can make you smarter, but it can't make you smart. It can extend your reach, but it will never tell you what to say at a P.T.A. meeting. These fundamentals cannot be downloaded. You can only upload them, the old-fashioned way, one by one, in places like Room 313 at St. Louis Park High. I only regret that I didn't write this column when the woman who taught me all that was still alive. 11

Thinking Critically about This Reading

What do you think Friedman means when he states, "The Internet can make you smarter, but it can't make you smart" (paragraph 11)?

[5]*admonition:* a cautionary advice or warning.

Questions for Study and Discussion

1. Friedman claims that his high school journalism teacher, Hattie M. Steinberg, was "someone who made the most important difference in my life" (1). What descriptive details does Friedman use to support this thesis? (Glossary: **Thesis**)
2. Hattie M. Steinberg taught her students the fundamentals of journalism—"not simply how to write a lead or accurately transcribe a quote, but, more important, how to comport yourself in a professional way and to always do quality work" (3). According to Friedman, what other fundamentals did she introduce to her students? Why do you think he values these fundamentals so much?
3. Friedman punctuates his description of Steinberg's teaching with short, pithy sentences. For example, he ends paragraph 2 with the sentence "She was that good" and paragraph 3 with "She wanted to teach us about consequences." Identify several other short sentences Friedman uses. What do these sentences have in common? How do short sentences like these affect you as a reader? Explain.
4. Why do you think Friedman tells us three times that Steinberg's classroom was number 313 at St. Louis Park High School?
5. What details in Friedman's portrait of his teacher stand out for you? Why do you suppose Friedman chose the details that he did? What dominant impression of Hattie M. Steinberg do they collectively create? (Glossary: **Dominant Impression**)
6. According to Friedman, what went wrong when the "huge dot-com-Internet-globalization bubble" (10) of the late 1990s burst? Do you agree?

Classroom Activity Using Unity

Mark Wanner, a student, wrote the following essay using this thesis statement:

> In order to provide a good learning environment in school, the teachers and administrators need to be strong leaders.

Unfortunately, some of the sentences disrupt the unity of the essay. Find these sentences, eliminate them, and reread the essay.

Strong School Leaders

School administrators and teachers must do more than simply supply students with information and a school building. They must also provide students with an atmosphere that allows them to focus on learning within the walls of the school. Whether the walls are brick, steel, or cement, they are only walls, and they do not help to create an appropriate atmosphere. Strong leadership both inside and outside the classroom yields a school in which students are able to excel in their studies because they know how to conduct themselves in their relationships with their teachers and fellow students. 1

A recent change in the administration of Eastside High School demonstrated how important strong leadership is to learning. Under the previous administration, parents and students complained that not enough emphasis was placed on studies. Most of the students lived in an impoverished neighborhood that had only one park for several thousand residents. Students were allowed to leave school at any time of the day, and little was done to curb the growing substance abuse problem. "What's the point of trying to teach algebra to students who are just going to get jobs as part-time sales clerks, anyway?" Vice Principal Iggy Norant said when questioned about his school's poor academic standards. Mr. Norant was known to students as Twiggy Iggy because of his tall, thin frame. Standardized test scores at the school lagged well behind the state average, and only 16 percent of the graduates attended college within two years. 2

Five years ago, the school board hired Mary Peña, former chair of the state educational standards committee, as principal. A cheerleader in college, Ms. Peña got her BA in recreation science before getting her master's in education. She immediately emphasized the importance of learning, replacing any faculty members who did not share her high expectations of the students. Among those she fired was Mr. Norant; she also replaced two social studies teachers, one math teacher, four English teachers, and a lab instructor who let students play Gameboy in lab. She also established a code of conduct, which clearly stated the rules all students had to follow. Students were allowed second chances, but those who continued to conduct themselves in a way that interfered with the other students' ability to learn were dealt with quickly and severely. "The attitude at Eastside has changed so much since Mary Peña arrived," said math teacher Jeremy Rifkin after Peña's second year. "Students come to class much more relaxed and ready to learn. I feel like I can teach again." Test scores at Eastside are now well above state averages, and 68% of the most recent graduating class went straight to college. 3

—Mark Wanner, student

Suggested Writing Assignments

1. Friedman believes that "the real secret of success in the information age is what it always was: fundamentals—reading, writing, and arithmetic; church, synagogue, and mosque; the rule of law; and good governance" (10). Do you agree? What are the fundamentals that you value most? Write a unified essay in which you discuss what you believe to be the secret of success today.
2. Who are your favorite teachers? What important differences did these people make in your life? What characteristics do these teachers share with Hattie M. Steinberg in this essay, Miss Bessie in Carl T. Rowan's "Unforgettable Miss Bessie" (p. 369), or Anne Mansfield Sullivan in Helen Keller's "The Most Important Day" (p. 101)? Using examples from your own school experience as well as from one or more of the essays noted above, write an essay in which you explore what makes a great teacher. Be sure to choose examples that clearly illustrate each of your points.

The Most Important Day

Helen Keller

Helen Keller (1880–1968) was born in Tuscumbia, Alabama. At the age of eighteen months, she was afflicted by a disease that left her blind and deaf. With the aid of her teacher, Anne Mansfield Sullivan, she was able to overcome her severe handicaps, to graduate from Radcliffe College, and to lead a productive and challenging adult life. In the following selection from her autobiography, *The Story of My Life* (1902), Keller tells of the day she first met Anne Sullivan, a day she regarded as the most important in her life.

Mara Vivat/Getty Images

As you read, note that Keller maintains unity within her narrative by emphasizing the importance of the day her teacher arrived, even though her story deals with the days and weeks following.

Reflecting on What You Know

Reflect on the events of what you consider "the most important day" of your life. Briefly describe what happened. Why was that particular day so significant?

The most important day I remember in all my life is the one on which my teacher, Anne Mansfield Sullivan, came to me. I am filled with wonder when I consider the immeasurable contrast between the two lives which it connects. It was the third of March, 1887, three months before I was seven years old. 1

On the afternoon of that eventful day, I stood on the porch, dumb,[1] expectant. I guessed vaguely from my mother's signs and from the hurrying to and fro in the house that something unusual was about to happen, so I went to the door and waited on the steps. The afternoon sun penetrated the mass of honeysuckle that covered the porch and fell on my upturned face. My fingers lingered almost unconsciously on the familiar leaves and blossoms which had just come forth to greet the sweet southern spring. I did not know what the future held of marvel or 2

[1]*dumb:* unable to speak; mute.

surprise for me. Anger and bitterness had preyed upon me continually for weeks and a deep languor[2] had succeeded this passionate struggle.

Have you ever been at sea in a dense fog, when it seemed as if a tangible white darkness shut you in, and the great ship, tense and anxious, groped her way toward the shore with plummet and sounding-line,[3] and you waited with beating heart for something to happen? I was like that ship before my education began, only I was without compass or sounding-line, and had no way of knowing how near the harbor was. "Light! Give me light!" was the wordless cry of my soul, and the light of love shone on me in that very hour. 3

I felt approaching footsteps. I stretched out my hand as I supposed to my mother. Someone took it, and I was caught up and held close in the arms of her who had come to reveal all things to me, and, more than all things else, to love me. 4

The morning after my teacher came she led me into her room and gave me a doll. The little blind children at the Perkins Institution[4] had sent it and Laura Bridgman[5] had dressed it; but I did not know this until afterward. When I had played with it a little while, Miss Sullivan slowly spelled into my hand the word "d-o-l-l." I was at once interested in this finger play and tried to imitate it. When I finally succeeded in making the letters correctly I was flushed with childish pleasure and pride. Running downstairs to my mother I held up my hand and made the letters for doll. I did not know that I was spelling a word or even that words existed; I was simply making my fingers go in monkeylike imitation. In the days that followed I learned to spell in this uncomprehending way a great many words, among them *pin, hat, cup* and a few verbs like *sit, stand,* and *walk*. But my teacher had been with me several weeks before I understood that everything has a name. 5

One day, while I was playing with my new doll, Miss Sullivan put my big rag doll into my lap also, spelled "d-o-l-l" and tried to make me understand that "d-o-l-l" applied to both. Earlier in the day we had had a tussle over the words "m-u-g" and "w-a-t-e-r." Miss Sullivan had 6

[2]*languor:* sluggishness.
[3]*plummet . . . line:* a weight tied to a line that is used to measure ocean depth.
[4]*Perkins Institution:* the first school for blind children in the United States, opened in 1832 and located in South Boston during her time there. The school moved to Watertown, Massachusetts, in 1912.
[5]*Laura Bridgman* (1829–1889): a deaf-blind girl who was educated at the Perkins Institution in the 1840s.

tried to impress it upon me that "m-u-g" is *mug* and that "w-a-t-e-r" is *water,* but I persisted in confounding the two. In despair she had dropped the subject for the time, only to renew it at the first opportunity. I became impatient at her repeated attempts and, seizing the new doll, I dashed it upon the floor. I was keenly delighted when I felt the fragments of the broken doll at my feet. Neither sorrow nor regret followed my passionate outburst. I had not loved the doll. In the still, dark world in which I lived there was no strong sentiment or tenderness. I felt my teacher sweep the fragments to one side of the hearth, and I had a sense of satisfaction that the cause of my discomfort was removed. She brought me my hat, and I knew I was going out into the warm sunshine. This thought, if a wordless sensation may be called a thought, made me hop and skip with pleasure.

We walked down the path to the well-house, attracted by the fra- 7
grance of the honeysuckle with which it was covered. Someone was drawing water and my teacher placed my hand under the spout. As the cool stream gushed over one hand she spelled into the other the word *water,* first slowly, then rapidly. I stood still, my whole attention fixed upon the motions of her fingers. Suddenly I felt a misty consciousness as of something forgotten—a thrill of returning thought; and somehow the mystery of language was revealed to me. I knew then that "w-a-t-e-r" meant the wonderful cool something that was flowing over my hand. The living word awakened my soul, gave it light, hope, joy, set it free! There were barriers still, it is true, but barriers that could in time be swept away.

I left the well-house eager to learn. Everything had a name, and 8
each name gave birth to a new thought. As we returned to the house every object which I touched seemed to quiver with life. That was because I saw everything with the strange, new sight that had come to me. On entering the door I remembered the doll I had broken. I felt my way to the hearth and picked up the pieces. I tried vainly to put them together. Then my eyes filled with tears; for I realized what I had done, and for the first time I felt repentance and sorrow.

I learned a great many new words that day. I do not remember 9
what they all were; but I do know that *mother, father, sister, teacher* were among them—words that were to make the world blossom for me, "like Aaron's rod,[6] with flowers." It would have been difficult to

[6]*Aaron's rod:* in Jewish and Christian traditions, a rod similar to Moses's staff that, in the high priest Aaron's hands, had miraculous power.

find a happier child than I was as I lay in my crib at the close of that eventful day and lived over the joys it had brought me, and for the first time longed for a new day to come.

Thinking Critically about This Reading

Keller writes that "'Light! Give me light!' was the wordless cry of [her] soul" (paragraph 3). What was the "light" Keller longed for, and how did receiving it change her life?

Questions for Study and Discussion

1. What is Keller's thesis? (Glossary: **Thesis**) What question do you think Keller is trying to answer? Does her thesis answer her question?
2. Do Keller's paragraphs support her thesis, or is there any part of this passage that breaks the unity of Keller's work?
3. What was Keller's state of mind before Anne Sullivan arrived to help her? To what does she compare herself? (Glossary: **Analogy**) How effective is this comparison? Explain.
4. Why was the realization that everything has a name important to Keller?
5. How was the "mystery of language" (7) revealed to Keller? What were the consequences for her of this new understanding of the nature of language?
6. Keller narrates the events of the day Sullivan arrived (2–4), the morning after she arrived (5), and one day several weeks after her arrival (6–9). (Glossary: **Narration**) Describe what happens on each day, and explain how these separate incidents support Keller's thesis.

Classroom Activity Using Unity

Write a unified paragraph that makes a clear statement about the following list of items. Then compare your paragraph with another student's work. How did each of you establish relationships among the items on the list? How does your writing help your reader make these connections?

A coffee maker
A toaster oven
A stove
A cookbook
A frying pan

Suggested Writing Assignments

1. Think about an important day in your own life. Using the thesis statement "The most important day of my life was __________," write an essay in which you show the significance of that day by recounting and explaining the events that took place, as Keller does in her essay. Before you write, you might find it helpful to reflect on your response to the Reflecting on What You Know prompt for this reading. Review your list to be sure that there are no items that break the unity. In other words, are there any events that you have listed that do not belong because they are not part of that same day or fail to shed light on the events of that day?
2. For many people around the world, the life of Helen Keller symbolizes what a person can achieve despite seemingly insurmountable obstacles. Her achievements have inspired people with and without disabilities, leading them to believe they can accomplish more than they ever thought possible. Consider the role of people with disabilities in our society, develop an appropriate thesis, and write an essay on the topic. Be sure that the specific details that you incorporate in the essay are unified; that is, details should relate directly to the thesis and topics that support the thesis.
3. Keller was visually and hearing impaired from the age of eighteen months, which meant she could neither read nor hear people speak. She was eventually able to read and write using braille, a system of "touchable symbols" invented by Louis Braille. Write an essay in which you put forth the thesis that the invention of braille has liberated countless numbers of people who have shared Keller's visual impairment. Use examples that relate directly to your thesis about braille.

Against Meat

Jonathan Safran Foer

Emily Berl/Getty Images

Jonathan Safran Foer was born in 1977 in Washington, D.C., and educated at Princeton University, where he took an introductory writing course from Joyce Carol Oates. He is the author of the award-winning and best-selling novels *Everything Is Illuminated* (2002) and *Extremely Loud and Incredibly Close* (2005), both of which have been made into motion pictures, as well as the book art piece *Tree of Codes* (2012). His most recent novel is *Here I Am* (2016). He is currently a writer-in-residence at New York University. This selection is adapted from his third book, the nonfiction *Eating Animals* (2010), in which becoming a new father urges him to confront the cultural importance and ethics of our eating habits.

As you read, pay attention to Foer's sympathetic portrayal of food as a center of family life, despite his vegetarian convictions. Note how each of his arguments against eating meat is unified by his desire to lead what he sees as a moral life.

Reflecting on What You Know

Reflect on the meals that are part of your family history and tradition. What sorts of food were served, and who cooked it? What impact has food had on your experience of family?

Seconds after being born, my son was breast-feeding. I watched him with an awe that had no precedent[1] in my life. Without explanation or experience, he knew what to do. Millions of years of evolution had wound the knowledge into him, as it had encoded beating into his tiny heart and expansion and contraction into his newly dry lungs. 1

Almost four years later, he is a big brother and a remarkably sophisticated little conversationalist. Increasingly the food he eats is 2

[1]*precedent:* an example or model, usually set by an earlier occurrence or long practice.

digested together with stories we tell. Feeding my children is not like feeding myself: it matters more. It matters because food matters (their physical health matters, the pleasure they take in eating matters), and because the stories that are served with food matter.

Some of my happiest childhood memories are of sushi "lunch 3
dates" with my mom, and eating my dad's turkey burgers with mustard and grilled onions at backyard celebrations, and of course my grandmother's chicken with carrots. Those occasions simply wouldn't have been the same without those foods—and that is important. To give up the taste of sushi, turkey or chicken is a loss that extends beyond giving up a pleasurable eating experience. Changing what we eat and letting tastes fade from memory create a kind of cultural loss, a forgetting. But perhaps this kind of forgetfulness is worth accepting—even worth cultivating (forgetting, too, can be cultivated). To remember my values, I need to lose certain tastes and find other handles for the memories that they once helped me carry.

My wife and I have chosen to bring up our children as vegetari- 4
ans. In another time or place, we might have made a different decision. But the realities of our present moment compelled us to make that choice. According to an analysis of U.S.D.A.[2] data by the advocacy group Farm Forward, factory farms now produce more than 99 percent of the animals eaten in this country. And despite labels that suggest otherwise, genuine alternatives—which do exist, and make many of the ethical questions about meat moot—are very difficult for even an educated eater to find. I don't have the ability to do so with regularity and confidence. ("Free range," "cage free," "natural" and "organic" are nearly meaningless when it comes to animal welfare.)

According to reports by the Food and Agriculture Organization of 5
the U.N.[3] and others, factory farming has made animal agriculture the No. 1 contributor to global warming (it is significantly more destructive than transportation alone), and one of the Top 2 or 3 causes of all of the most serious environmental problems, both global and local: air and water pollution, deforestation, loss of biodiversity. . . . Eating factory-farmed animals—which is to say virtually every piece of meat

[2]*U.S.D.A.:* United States Department of Agriculture; government branch overseeing food, farming, nutrition, and related public policies.

[3]*U.N.:* the United Nations, an international organization founded after World War II to confront global issues affecting humanity, such as human rights and climate change.

sold in supermarkets and prepared in restaurants—is almost certainly the single worst thing that humans do to the environment.

Every factory-farmed animal is, as a practice, treated in ways that would be illegal if it were a dog or a cat. Turkeys have been so genetically modified[4] they are incapable of natural reproduction. To acknowledge that these things matter is not sentimental. It is a confrontation with the facts about animals and ourselves. We know these things matter. 6

Meat and seafood are in no way necessary for my family—unlike some in the world, we have easy access to a wide variety of other foods. And we are healthier without it. So our choices aren't constrained. 7

While the cultural uses of meat can be replaced—my mother and I now eat Italian, my father grills veggie burgers, my grandmother invented her own "vegetarian chopped liver"—there is still the question of pleasure. A vegetarian diet can be rich and fully enjoyable, but I couldn't honestly argue, as many vegetarians try to, that it is as rich as a diet that includes meat. (Those who eat chimpanzee look at the Western diet as sadly deficient of a great pleasure.) I love calamari, I love roasted chicken, I love a good steak. But I don't love them without limit. 8

This isn't animal experimentation, where you can imagine some proportionate good at the other end of the suffering. This is what we feel like eating. Yet taste, the crudest of our senses, has been exempted from the ethical rules that govern our other senses. Why? Why doesn't a horny person have as strong a claim to raping an animal as a hungry one does to confining, killing and eating it? It's easy to dismiss that question but hard to respond to it. Try to imagine any end other than taste for which it would be justifiable to do what we do to farmed animals. 9

Children confront us with our paradoxes[5] and dishonesty, and we are exposed. You need to find an answer for every why—Why do we do this? Why don't we do that?—and often there isn't a good one. So you say, simply, because. Or you tell a story that you know isn't true. And whether or not your face reddens, you blush. The shame of parenthood—which is a good shame—is that we want our children to be more whole than we are, to have satisfactory answers. My children not 10

---

[4]*genetically modified:* containing a genetic structure that has been altered to produce desired results.

[5]*paradoxes:* contradictions.

only inspired me to reconsider what kind of eating animal I would be, but also shamed me into reconsideration.

And then, one day, they will choose for themselves. I don't know what my reaction will be if they decide to eat meat. (I don't know what my reaction will be if they decide to renounce their Judaism, root for the Red Sox or register Republican.) I'm not as worried about what they will choose as much as my ability to make them conscious of the choices before them. I won't measure my success as a parent by whether my children share my values, but by whether they act according to their own. 11

In the meantime, my choice on their behalf means they will never eat their great-grandmother's singular dish. They will never receive that unique and most direct expression of her love, will perhaps never think of her as the greatest chef who ever lived. Her primal story, our family's primal story, will have to change. 12

Or will it? It wasn't until I became a parent that I understood my grandmother's cooking. The greatest chef who ever lived wasn't preparing food, but humans. I'm thinking of those Saturday afternoons at her kitchen table, just the two of us—black bread in the glowing toaster, a humming refrigerator that couldn't be seen through its veil of family photographs. Over pumpernickel ends and Coke, she would tell me about her escape from Europe, the foods she had to eat and those she wouldn't. It was the story of her life—"Listen to me," she would plead—and I knew a vital lesson was being transmitted, even if I didn't know, as a child, what that lesson was. 13

Thinking Critically about This Reading

Foer states that "taste, the crudest of our senses, has been exempted from the ethical rules that govern our other senses" (paragraph 9). What does he mean? Do you agree? Explain and support your opinion with examples.

Questions for Study and Discussion

1. Foer states that millions of years of evolution are behind his infant son's instinct to breastfeed (paragraph 1). How does this relate to his later argument about his decision to become a vegetarian? (Glossary: **Argumentation**)
2. Foer argues that changing what people eat can create a "cultural forgetting" (3). What does he mean by this? How then

can he justify becoming a vegetarian, which means no longer eating the foods he used to eat?

3. Foer names animal agriculture—and, specifically, factory farming—as the biggest contributor to global warming and the cause of other environmental problems (5). Why does this matter so much to him? Does he think the actions that he and his family are taking will have any effect on these global problems? Explain.
4. Foer admits that a vegetarian diet is not as "rich" as a diet that includes meat (8). Does this admission weaken his overall argument, or does it make his decision to become a vegetarian more sympathetic and realistic? Why?
5. Why does Foer state that his grandmother's "primal story, our family's primal story, will have to change" (12)? Is such a thing possible?
6. In his conclusion, Foer brings together the idea of food and family by reflecting on his own childhood memories with his grandmother (13). How does the ending unify Foer's essay? (Glossary: **Beginnings and Endings**)

Classroom Activity Using Unity

Write a list of foods that have had special relevance to you, whether because of the person who cooked the food, the occasion or place where it was eaten, the cultural or personal history behind the food, or any other significant reason. In a group, compare your lists of foods with your classmates' lists. Make a "map" of the foods, drawing connections between them based on why they're important. What does this say about your group's "society"? Does it reveal anything important about your shared values and ethics or your cultural practices? More broadly, how does food connect us?

Suggested Writing Assignments

1. Foer makes a moral argument for vegetarianism based on the environmental harm done by factory farms and the suffering of the animals in those farms. Do you agree that his reasons are important, whether or not you're a vegetarian? Write a unified essay in which you argue whether you found his reasoning convincing (or convicting). Be sure to include reasons

to support your thesis; you may want to do some library or Internet research for more points for or against vegetarianism.

2. Explore the listings of restaurants in your area. Consider what types of food seem most popular, who attends which restaurants, and occasions for eating out. Write a unified essay in which you argue why certain types of food are more popular in your community than others. Be specific.
3. Write a unified essay about your own experiences with food and family. Include important details about the types of food associated with special family members and occasions and the emotional relevance and importance of the food to you. Be sure all of your paragraphs and examples support the thesis of your essay.

CHAPTER 5

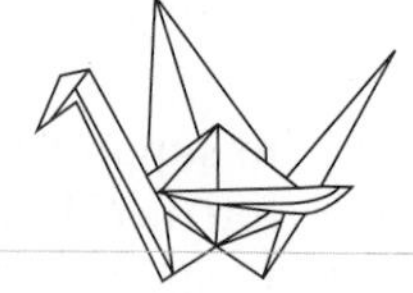

Organization

In an essay, ideas and information cannot be presented all at once; they have to be arranged in some order. That order is the essay's **organization.**

The pattern of organization in an essay should be suited to the writer's subject and **purpose.** For example, if you are writing about your experience working in a fast-food restaurant and your purpose is to tell about the activities of a typical day, you might present those activities in chronological order. If, on the other hand, you wish to argue that working in a bank is an ideal summer job, you might proceed from the least rewarding to the most rewarding aspect of this job; this is called *climactic order.*

Some common patterns of organization are chronological order, space order, and logical order.

CHRONOLOGICAL ORDER

Chronological order, or time order, is used to present a sequence of events as they occurred. A personal narrative, a report of a campus incident, or an account of a historical event can be most naturally and easily related in chronological order. In the following paragraphs, student writer Jeffrey Olesky uses chronological order to recount an important lesson he learned. You can read Olesky's entire essay on pages 34–38 of this book.

> The lesson I learned that day appears rather simple now. It came on the putting green of the second hole. My father had finished putting out, and I was holding the flagstick off to the side of the green while the other players finished. Generally, my father would come stand next to me and give me a hand, but due to circumstances we ended up on opposite sides of the green. During

> the next player's putt, my father lowered his eyebrows at me and nodded his head to one side a few times. Curious as to what he wanted me to do, I almost let the question slip out of my mouth. But I knew better. I had already learned the rules of not talking or moving while other golfers were hitting. I quietly stood my ground until everyone was finished and then placed the flagstick back in the hole. While walking toward the next tee box, I neared my father. Regardless of what he had wanted me to do, I thought he would commend me for not talking or moving during the ordeal.
>
> "You know better than that, Jeffrey," he said.
>
> "What?" I asked curiously, disappointed that he had not praised me on a job well done.
>
> "You never stand so that your shadow is in someone's line."
>
> How could I be so stupid? He had reminded me a thousand times before. You never allow your shadow to fall in the line of someone's putt because it is distracting to the person putting. I rationalized to my father that maybe the man hadn't noticed or that it didn't bother him. Unfortunately, my father wasn't going to take that as an excuse. After explaining to me what I had done wrong, he suggested that I go over and apologize to the gentleman. I was still a young boy, and the figure of the older man was somewhat intimidating. This task was no easy chore because I was obviously very scared, and this is perhaps what made the lesson sink in a little deeper. I remember slowly approaching my father's friend and sheepishly looking back to my father for help. Once I realized I was on my own, I bashfully gave him my apologies and assured him that it wouldn't happen again. As you can probably guess, the repercussions were not as dramatic as I had envisioned them to be. Once my father had pointed out my mistake, I begged him to reconcile with the gentleman for me. However, in apologizing for myself, I learned a valuable lesson. Golf is important because it has taught me many social values such as this, but it can also be a personal, internal tool.

Of course, the order of events can sometimes be rearranged for special effect. For example, an account of an auto accident may begin with the collision itself and then flash back in time to the events leading up to it. The description of a process—such as framing a poster or serving a tennis ball—almost always calls for a chronological organization.

When analyzing a causally related series of events, writers often use a chronological organization to clarify for readers the exact sequence of events. In the following example, the writer examines sequentially the series of malfunctions that led to the near disaster at the Three Mile Island nuclear facility in Harrisburg, Pennsylvania, showing clearly how each one led to the next:

> On March 28, 1979, at 3:53 A.M., a pump at the Harrisburg plant failed. Because the pump failed, the reactor's heat was not drawn off in the heat exchanger and the very hot water in the primary loop overheated. The pressure in the loop increased, opening a release valve that was supposed to counteract such an event. But the valve stuck open and the primary loop system lost so much water (which ended up as a highly radioactive pool, six feet deep, on the floor of the reactor building) that it was unable to carry off all the heat generated within the reactor core. Under these circumstances, the intense heat held within the reactor could, in theory, melt its fuel rods, and the resulting "meltdown" could then carry a hugely radioactive mass through the floor of the reactor. The reactor's emergency cooling system, which is designed to prevent this disaster, was then automatically activated, but when it was, apparently, turned off too soon, some of the fuel rods overheated.
>
> –Barry Commoner, *The Politics of Energy*

SPACE ORDER

Space order is used when describing a person, place, or thing. This organizational pattern begins at a particular point and moves in some direction, such as left to right, top to bottom, east to west, outside to inside, front to back, near to far, around, or over. In describing a house, for example, a writer could move from top to bottom, from outside to inside, or in a circle around the outside.

In the following paragraph, the subject is a baseball, and the writer describes it from the inside out, moving from its "composition-cork nucleus" to the print on its stitched cowhide cover:

> It weighs just over five ounces and measures between 2.86 and 2.94 inches in diameter. It is made of a composition-cork nucleus encased in two thin layers of rubber, one black and one red, surrounded by 121 yards of tightly wrapped blue-gray wool yarn, 45 yards of white wool yarn, 54 more yards of blue-gray wool yarn, 150 yards of fine cotton yarn, a coat of rubber cement, and a cowhide (formerly horsehide) exterior, which is held together with 216 slightly raised red cotton stitches. Printed

certifications, endorsements, and outdoor advertising spherically attest to its authenticity.

–Roger Angell, *Five Seasons: A Baseball Companion*

LOGICAL ORDER

Logical order can take many forms, depending on the writer's purpose. Often-used patterns include general to specific, most familiar to least familiar, and smallest to biggest. Perhaps the most common type of logical order is order of importance. Notice how the writer uses this order in the following paragraph:

> The Egyptians have taught us many things. They were excellent farmers. They knew all about irrigation. They built temples which were afterwards copied by the Greeks and which served as the earliest models for the churches in which we worship nowadays. They invented a calendar which proved such a useful instrument for the purpose of measuring time that it has survived with few changes until today. But most important of all, the Egyptians learned how to preserve speech for the benefit of future generations. They invented the art of writing.
>
> –Hendrick Willem Van Loon, *The Story of Mankind*

By organizing the material according to the order of increasing importance, the writer places special emphasis on the final sentence.

A student essay on outdoor education provides another example of logical order. In the paragraph that follows, the writer describes some of the special problems students have during the traditionally difficult high school years. She then explains the benefits of involving such students in an outdoor education curriculum as a possible remedy, offers a quotation from a noteworthy text on outdoor education to support her views, and presents her thesis statement at the end of the paragraph—all logical steps in her writing.

Statement of the problem

> For many students, the normally difficult time of high school is especially troublesome. These students may have learning disabilities, emotional-behavioral disorders, or low self-esteem, or they may be labeled "at-risk" because of socioeconomic background, delinquency, or drug and alcohol abuse. Any combination of these factors contributes negatively to students' success in school. Often the traditional public or private

high school may not be the ideal environment in which these students can thrive and live up to their highest potential. Outdoor education can benefit these high schoolers and provide them with the means necessary to overcome their personal issues and develop skills, knowledge, and self-esteem that will enable them to become successful, self-aware, emotionally stable, and functional adults. In their book *Outdoor Education*, authors Smith, Carlson, Donaldson, and Masters state poignantly that outdoor education "can be one of the most effective forces in the community to prevent human erosion as well as land erosion; it can be one of the means of saving youngsters from the education scrap heap" (49). Outdoor education builds a relationship between students and the natural environment that might not be formed otherwise and gives students a respect for the world in which they live. Aspects of outdoor education should be implemented in the curriculums of high schools in order to achieve these results in all students.

A possible remedy is offered and explained

Authorities are quoted to support the suggested solution

The thesis is given after a preliminary discussion to increase its acceptability

—Jinsie Ward, student

Although logical order can take many forms, the exact rationale always depends on the topic of the writing. For example, in writing a descriptive essay about a place you visited, you can move from the least striking to the most striking detail to keep your readers interested and involved in the description. In an essay explaining how to pick individual stocks for investment, you can start with the point that readers will find the least difficult to understand and move on to the most difficult point. (That's how many teachers organize their courses.) Or in writing an essay arguing for more internships and service learning courses, you can move from your least controversial to your most controversial point, preparing your reader gradually to accept your argument.

A simple way to check the organization of an essay is to outline it once you have a draft. Does the outline represent the organizational pattern—chronological, spatial, or logical—that you set out to use? Problems in outlining will naturally indicate sections that you need to revise.

A View from the Bridge

Cherokee Paul McDonald

Courtesy of Cherokee Paul McDonald

A fiction writer, memoirist, and journalist, Cherokee Paul McDonald was raised and schooled in Fort Lauderdale, Florida. In 1970, he returned home from a tour of duty in Vietnam and joined the Fort Lauderdale Police Department, where he rose to the rank of sergeant. In 1980, after receiving a degree in criminal science from Broward Community College, McDonald left the police department to become a writer. He worked a number of odd jobs before publishing his first book, *The Patch,* in 1986. In 1991, he published *Blue Truth,* a memoir. His novel *Summer's Reason* was released in 1994, and his memoir of the Vietnam War titled *Into the Green: A Reconnaissance by Fire,* was published in 2001.

"A View from the Bridge" was originally published in *Sunshine* magazine in 1990. As you read, notice how McDonald organizes his narrative. He tells us what the narrator and the boy are doing, but he also relies heavily on their dialogue to structure his story, which unfolds as the two talk. McDonald makes the story come alive by showing us, rather than by simply telling us, what happens.

Reflecting on What You Know

Make a list of your interests, focusing on those to which you devote a significant amount of time. Do you share any of these interests with people you know? What does a shared interest do for a relationship between two people?

I was coming up on the little bridge in the Rio Vista neighborhood of Fort Lauderdale, deepening my stride and my breathing to negotiate the slight incline without altering my pace. And then, as I neared the crest, I saw the kid. 1

He was a lumpy little guy with baggy shorts, a faded T-shirt and heavy sweat socks falling down over old sneakers. 2

Partially covering his shaggy blond hair was one of those blue 3
baseball caps with gold braid on the bill and a sailfish patch sewn onto
the peak. Covering his eyes and part of his face was a pair of those
stupid-looking '50s-style wrap-around sunglasses.

He was fumbling with a beat-up rod and reel, and he had a little 4
bait bucket by his feet. I puffed on by, glancing down into the empty
bucket as I passed.

"Hey, mister! Would you help me, please?" 5

The shrill voice penetrated my jogger's concentration, and I was 6
determined to ignore it. But for some reason, I stopped.

With my hands on my hips and the sweat dripping from my nose I 7
asked, "What do you want, kid?"

"Would you please help me find my shrimp? It's my last one and 8
I've been getting bites and I know I can catch a fish if I can just find
that shrimp. He jumped outta my hand as I was getting him from the
bucket."

Exasperated, I walked slowly back to the kid, and pointed. 9

"There's the damn shrimp by your left foot. You stopped me for *that*?" 10

As I said it, the kid reached down and trapped the shrimp. 11

"Thanks a lot, mister," he said. 12

I watched as the kid dropped the baited hook down into the canal. 13
Then I turned to start back down the bridge.

That's when the kid let out a "Hey! Hey!" and the prettiest tar- 14
pon[1] I'd ever seen came almost six feet out of the water, twisting and
turning as he fell through the air.

"I got one!" the kid yelled as the fish hit the water with a loud 15
splash and took off down the canal.

I watched the line being burned off the reel at an alarming rate. 16
The kid's left hand held the crank while the extended fingers felt for
the drag setting.

"No, kid!" I shouted. "Leave the drag alone . . . just keep that 17
damn rod tip up!"

Then I glanced at the reel and saw there were just a few loops of 18
line left on the spool.

"Why don't you get yourself some decent equipment?" I said, but 19
before the kid could answer I saw the line go slack.

"Ohhh, I lost him," the kid said. I saw the flash of silver as the fish 20
turned.

---

[1]*tarpon:* a large, silvery fish.

"Crank, kid, crank! You didn't lose him. He's coming back toward you. Bring in the slack!" 21

The kid cranked like mad, and a beautiful grin spread across his face. 22

"He's heading in for the pilings,"[2] I said. "Keep him out of those pilings!" 23

The kid played it perfectly. When the fish made its play for the pilings, he kept just enough pressure on to force the fish out. When the water exploded and the silver missile hurled into the air, the kid kept the rod tip up and the line tight. 24

As the fish came to the surface and began a slow circle in the middle of the canal, I said, "Whooee, is that a nice fish or what?" 25

The kid didn't say anything, so I said, "Okay, move to the edge of the bridge and I'll climb down to the seawall and pull him out." 26

When I reached the seawall I pulled in the leader, leaving the fish lying on its side in the water. 27

"How's that?" I said. 28

"Hey, mister, tell me what it looks like." 29

"Look down here and check him out," I said. "He's beautiful." 30

But then I looked up into those stupid-looking sunglasses and it hit me. The kid was blind. 31

"Could you tell me what he looks like, mister?" he said again. 32

"Well, he's just under three, uh, he's about as long as one of your arms," I said. "I'd guess he goes about 15, 20 pounds. He's mostly silver, but the silver is somehow made up of *all* the colors, if you know what I mean." I stopped. "Do you know what I mean by colors?" 33

The kid nodded. 34

"Okay. He has all these big scales, like armor all over his body. They're silver too, and when he moves they sparkle. He has a strong body and a large powerful tail. He has big round eyes, bigger than a quarter, and a lower jaw that sticks out past the upper one and is very tough. His belly is almost white and his back is a gunmetal gray. When he jumped he came out of the water about six feet, and his scales caught the sun and flashed it all over the place." 35

By now the fish had righted itself, and I could see the bright-red gills as the gill plates opened and closed. I explained this to the kid, and then said, more to myself, "He's a beauty." 36

---

[2]*pilings:* support columns driven vertically into the ground or ocean floor.

"Can you get him off the hook?" the kid asked. "I don't want to 37
kill him."

I watched as the tarpon began to slowly swim away, tired but still 38
alive.

By the time I got back up to the top of the bridge the kid had his 39
line secured and his bait bucket in one hand.

He grinned and said, "Just in time. My mom drops me off here, 40
and she'll be back to pick me up any minute."

He used the back of one hand to wipe his nose. 41

"Thanks for helping me catch that tarpon," he said, "and for help- 42
ing me to see it."

I looked at him, shook my head, and said, "No, my friend, thank 43
you for letting *me* see that fish."

I took off, but before I got far the kid yelled again. 44

"Hey, mister!" 45

I stopped. 46

"Someday I'm gonna catch a sailfish and a blue marlin and a giant 47
tuna and *all* those big sportfish!"

As I looked into those sunglasses I knew he probably would. I 48
wished I could be there when it happened.

Thinking Critically about This Reading

Near the end of the story, why does the narrator say to the boy, "No, my friend, thank you for letting *me* see that fish" (paragraph 43)? What happens to the narrator's attitude as a result of his encounter with the boy? What lesson do you think the narrator learns?

Questions for Study and Discussion

1. How does McDonald organize his essay? What period of time would you estimate is covered in this essay?
2. What clues lead up to the revelation that the boy is blind? Why does it take McDonald so long to realize it?
3. Notice the way McDonald chooses and adjusts some of the words he uses to describe the fish to the boy in paragraphs 33–36. Why does he do this? How does he organize his description of the fish so that the boy can visualize it better?
4. By the end of the essay, we know much more about the boy beyond that he is blind, but after the initial description,

McDonald characterizes him only indirectly. As the essay unfolds, what do we learn about the boy, and how does the author convey this knowledge?

5. McDonald tells much of his experience through dialogue. (Glossary: **Dialogue**) What does this dialogue add to the narration? (Glossary: **Narration**) What would have been lost had McDonald not used dialogue?
6. What is the connotation of the word *view* in the title? (Glossary: **Connotation/Denotation**) Of the word *bridge*?

Classroom Activity Using Organization

In groups of two or three, take turns describing a specific beautiful or remarkable thing to the others as if they were blind. You may want to bring in an actual object to observe while your classmates cover their eyes. Help each other find the best words to create a vivid verbal picture. Using paragraphs 33–36 of McDonald's story as a model, write a brief description of your object, retaining the informal style of your speaking voice.

Suggested Writing Assignments

1. Recall a time when you and one other person held a conversation that helped you see something more clearly—visually, in terms of understanding, or both. Using McDonald's narrative as an organizational model, tell the story of that moment, re-creating the dialogue exactly as you remember it.
2. McDonald's "A View from the Bridge" is just one "fish story" in the long and rich tradition of that genre. In its own way, the story plays on the ironic notion that fishing is a quiet sport but one in which participants come to expect the unexpected. (Glossary: **Irony**) For the narrator in the story, there is a lesson in not merely looking but truly seeing, in describing the fish so that the blind boy can "see" it. It is interesting that a sport in which "nothing happens" can be the source of so much storytelling. Write an essay in which you tell a "fish story" of your own, one that reveals a larger, significant truth or life lesson. Pay particular attention to the pattern of organization you choose, and be sure to revise your essay to tighten up your use of that pattern. If possible, incorporate some elements of surprise as well.

Grant and Lee: A Study in Contrasts

Bruce Catton

Library of Congress, Prints & Photographs Division, Courtesy Katherine Young [LC-USZ62-132904].

Bruce Catton (1897–1978) grew up in Petoskey, Michigan. As a young man, he left his studies at Oberlin College to serve in World War I and never returned to complete his degree. He became a journalist and a historian, publishing several books of popular history on the Civil War, including the Pulitzer Prize–winning *A Stillness at Appomattox* (1953) and *Two Roads to Sumter* (1963).

In this essay, Catton compares the two generals who met to negotiate the terms for the surrender of the Confederate Army. As you read, notice how Catton uses a logical organization to show the "complete contrast" between Ulysses S. Grant and Robert E. Lee as well as the fact that "these two great soldiers had much in common."

Reflecting on What You Know

What do you know about the causes of the Civil War? How would you explain the contrast between the North and the South? Do you see these contrasts still at work today?

When Ulysses S. Grant and Robert E. Lee met in the parlor of a 1
modest house at Appomattox Court House, Virginia, on April 9, 1865, to work out the terms for the surrender of Lee's Army of Northern Virginia, a great chapter in American life came to a close, and a great new chapter began.

These men were bringing the Civil War to its virtual finish. To be 2
sure, other armies had yet to surrender, and for a few days the fugitive Confederate government would struggle desperately and vainly, trying to find some way to go on living now that its chief support was gone. But in effect it was all over when Grant and Lee signed the papers. And the little room where they wrote out the terms was the scene of one of the poignant, dramatic contrasts in American history.

They were two strong men, these oddly different generals, and 3
they represented the strengths of two conflicting currents that, through them, had come into final collision.

Back of Robert E. Lee was the notion that the old aristocratic con- 4
cept might somehow survive and be dominant in American life.

Lee was tidewater Virginia, and in his background were family, 5
culture, and tradition . . . the age of chivalry transplanted to a New World which was making its own legends and its own myths. He embodied a way of life that had come down through the age of knighthood and the English country squire. America was a land that was beginning all over again, dedicated to nothing much more complicated than the rather hazy belief that all men had equal rights and should have an equal chance in the world. In such a land Lee stood for the feeling that it was somehow of advantage to human society to have a pronounced inequality in the social structure. There should be a leisure class, backed by ownership of land; in turn, society itself should be keyed to the land as the chief source of wealth and influence. It would bring forth (according to this ideal) a class of men with a strong sense of obligation to the community; men who lived not to gain advantage for themselves, but to meet the solemn obligations which had been laid on them by the very fact that they were privileged. From them the country would get its leadership; to them it could look for the higher values—of thought, of conduct, of personal deportment—to give it strength and virtue.

Lee embodied the noblest elements of this aristocratic ideal. 6
Through him, the landed nobility justified itself. For four years, the Southern states had fought a desperate war to uphold the ideals for which Lee stood. In the end, it almost seemed as if the Confederacy fought for Lee; as if he himself was the Confederacy . . . the best thing that the way of life for which the Confederacy stood could ever have to offer. He had passed into legend before Appomattox. Thousands of tired, underfed, poorly clothed Confederate soldiers, long since past the simple enthusiasm of the early days of the struggle, somehow considered Lee the symbol of everything for which they had been willing to die. But they could not quite put this feeling into words. If the Lost Cause, sanctified by so much heroism and so many deaths, had a living justification, its justification was General Lee.

Grant, the son of a tanner on the Western frontier, was everything 7
Lee was not. He had come up the hard way and embodied nothing in particular except the eternal toughness and sinewy fiber of the men

who grew up beyond the mountains. He was one of a body of men who owed reverence and obeisance to no one, who were self-reliant to a fault, who cared hardly anything for the past but who had a sharp eye for the future.

These frontier men were the precise opposites of the tidewater aristocrats. Back of them, in the great surge that had taken people over the Alleghenies and into the opening Western country, there was a deep, implicit dissatisfaction with a past that had settled into grooves. They stood for democracy, not from any reasoned conclusion about the proper ordering of human society, but simply because they had grown up in the middle of democracy and knew how it worked. Their society might have privileges, but they would be privileges each man had won for himself. Forms and patterns meant nothing. No man was born to anything, except perhaps to a chance to show how far he could rise. Life was competition. 8

Yet along with this feeling had come a deep sense of belonging to a national community. The Westerner who developed a farm, opened a shop, or set up in business as a trader, could hope to prosper only as his own community prospered—and his community ran from the Atlantic to the Pacific and from Canada down to Mexico. If the land was settled, with towns and highways and accessible markets, he could better himself. He saw his fate in terms of the nation's own destiny. As its horizons expanded, so did his. He had, in other words, an acute dollars-and-cents stake in the continued growth and development of his country. 9

And that, perhaps, is where the contrast between Grant and Lee becomes most striking. The Virginia aristocrat, inevitably, saw himself in relation to his own region. He lived in a static society which could endure almost anything except change. Instinctively, his first loyalty would go to the locality in which that society existed. He would fight to the limit of endurance to defend it, because in defending it he was defending everything that gave his own life its deepest meaning. 10

The Westerner, on the other hand, would fight with an equal tenacity for the broader concept of society. He fought so because everything he lived by was tied to growth, expansion, and a constantly widening horizon. What he lived by would survive or fall with the nation itself. He could not possibly stand by unmoved in the face of an attempt to destroy the Union. He would combat it with everything he had, because he could only see it as an effort to cut the ground out from under his feet. 11

So Grant and Lee were in complete contrast, representing two diametrically opposed elements in American life. Grant was the modern man emerging; beyond him, ready to come on the stage, was the great age of steel and machinery, of crowded cities and a restless burgeoning vitality. Lee might have ridden down from the old age of chivalry, lance in hand, silken banner fluttering over his head. Each man was the perfect champion of his cause, drawing both his strengths and his weaknesses from the people he led. 12

Yet it was not all contrast, after all. Different as they were—in background, in personality, in underlying aspiration—these two great soldiers had much in common. Under everything else, they were marvelous fighters. Furthermore, their fighting qualities were really very much alike. 13

Each man had, to begin with, the great virtue of utter tenacity and fidelity. Grant fought his way down the Mississippi Valley in spite of acute personal discouragement and profound military handicaps. Lee hung on in the trenches at Petersburg after hope itself had died. In each man there was an indomitable quality . . . the born fighter's refusal to give up as long as he can still remain on his feet and lift his two fists. 14

Daring and resourcefulness they had, too; the ability to think faster and move faster than the enemy. These were the qualities which gave Lee the dazzling campaigns of Second Manassas and Chancellorsville and won Vicksburg for Grant. 15

Lastly, and perhaps greatest of all, there was the ability, at the end, to turn quickly from war to peace once the fighting was over. Out of the way these two men behaved at Appomattox came the possibility of a peace of reconciliation. It was a possibility not wholly realized, in the years to come, but which did, in the end, help the two sections to become one nation again . . . after a war whose bitterness might have seemed to make such a reunion wholly impossible. No part of either man's life became him more than the part he played in their brief meeting in the McLean house at Appomattox. Their behavior there put all succeeding generations of Americans in their debt. Two great Americans, Grant and Lee—very different, yet under everything very much alike. Their encounter at Appomattox was one of the great moments of American history. 16

Thinking Critically about This Reading

Catton says that although there were a few days in which the Confederates continued to struggle against the Union forces, the war was effectually "all over when Grant and Lee signed the papers" (paragraph 2). Is this true not only for the military action but also for the cultural conflict, which Catton describes in his essay? Why or why not?

Questions for Study and Discussion

1. Catton organizes his essay logically to compare and contrast the two important historical figures of Grant and Lee. Are there any other types of organization at work in this essay—chronological, spatial, or logical? Where?
2. In paragraphs 5 and 6, Catton discusses Robert E. Lee at length. Which of Lee's characteristics does he emphasize? The following paragraphs, 7–9, focus on Ulysses S. Grant. Which of Grant's characteristics does he emphasize? How are the two men's values in opposition to each other?
3. After making broad comparisons of these two men, Catton focuses in on the point at which he thinks "the contrast between Grant and Lee becomes most striking" (10). Explain how the two generals understand the society to which each belongs. How do they believe they are responsible to this society?
4. Discuss the imagery Catton uses in paragraph 12 to suggest that Lee is a representative of the past whereas Grant looks forward to the future. How does he help readers picture this contrast?
5. Although the two men are fundamentally different, toward the end of the essay, Catton turns to consider what they have in common. What qualities of "marvelous fighters" (13) do Grant and Lee share?

Classroom Activity Using Organization

The following passage is taken from the late Stephen E. Ambrose's book *Crazy Horse and Custer: The Parallel Lives of Two American Warriors* (1975). Carefully read and analyze the passage, in which Ambrose compares and contrasts Chief Crazy Horse and General George Armstrong Custer. Then answer the questions that follow.

> It was bravery, above and beyond all other qualities, that Custer and Crazy Horse had in common. Each man was an

> outstanding warrior in war-mad societies. Thousands upon thousands of Custer's fellow whites had as much opportunity as he did to demonstrate their courage, just as all of Crazy Horse's associates had countless opportunities to show that they equaled him in bravery. But no white warrior, save his younger brother, Tom, could outdo Custer, just as no Indian warrior, save his younger brother, Little Hawk, could outdo Crazy Horse. And for both white and red societies, no masculine virtue was more admired than bravery. To survive, both societies felt they had to have men willing to put their lives on the line. For men who were willing to do so, no reward was too great, even though there were vast differences in the way each society honored its heroes.
>
> Beyond their bravery, Custer and Crazy Horse were individualists, each standing out from the crowd in his separate way. Custer wore outlandish uniforms, let his hair fall in long, flowing golden locks across his shoulders, surrounded himself with pet animals and admirers, and in general did all he could to draw attention to himself. Crazy Horse's individualism pushed him in the opposite direction—he wore a single feather in his hair when going into battle, rather than a war bonnet. Custer's vast energy set him apart from most of his fellows; the Sioux distinguished Crazy Horse from other warriors because of Crazy Horse's quietness and introspection. Both men lived in societies in which drugs, especially alcohol, were widely used, but neither Custer nor Crazy Horse drank. Most of all, of course, each man stood out in battle as a great risk taker.

What is Ambrose's point in these two paragraphs? How does he use comparison and contrast to make this point? How has he organized his paragraphs? How else might he have organized them? Explain.

Suggested Writing Assignments

1. Think of two historical figures who have a connection through events, beliefs, or impact. Write three different paragraphs or short essays using different types of organization: chronological, spatial, and logical. You will likely have to use different information about these figures in each version (for example, a spatial organization of Catton's Grant and Lee essay might have discussed the geography of the war or of Appomattox). Then reflect on which type of organization worked best and why.

2. Catton convinces readers that the contrast between these two men is not only stark but also "poignant" because each man represents a larger trend in American society. Choose someone who you think represents an important current trend in public life, and write an essay analyzing what he or she stands for. Like Catton, you can use both strict facts (Lee is from tidewater Virginia) and more figurative characterizations (Lee is like a knight out of the age of chivalry) to capture the person's essence.

Where Anonymity Breeds Contempt

Julie Zhuo

AP Photo/Jeff Chiu

Julie Zhuo was born in Shanghai, China, but her family moved to Texas when she was five. She attended Stanford University, where she completed both a bachelor's and a master's degree in computer science. Zhuo began working at Facebook in 2006 and is currently a vice president of product design. She also writes a weekly online series called "The Year of the Looking Glass" on Medium, featuring her thoughts on creative pursuits, management problems, and the business of social media.

In the following essay, which appeared in the Opinion Pages of the *New York Times* in November 2010, Zhuo gives readers a definition of the term *trolling* and offers examples to show why it is problematic. As you read, pay attention to how Zhuo organizes her essay around logical ideas and evidence to support her thesis, which answers a question that arises from this discussion of trolling: what can we do to combat the problem?

Reflecting on What You Know

Do you think people interact differently online than they do face to face? Why or why not? Think of an example that supports your answer.

There you are, peacefully reading an article or watching a video on the Internet. You finish, find it thought-provoking, and scroll down to the comments section to see what other people thought. And there, lurking among dozens of well-intentioned opinions, is a troll. 1

"How much longer is the media going to milk this beyond tired story?" "These guys are frauds." "Your idiocy is disturbing." "We're just trying to make the world a better place one brainwashed, ignorant idiot at a time." These are the trollish comments, all from anonymous 2 sources, that you could have found after reading a CNN article on the rescue of the Chilean miners.

Trolling, defined as the act of posting inflammatory, derogatory or provocative messages in public forums, is a problem as old as the Internet itself, although its roots go much farther back. Even in the fourth century B.C., Plato touched upon the subject of anonymity and morality in his parable of the ring of Gyges. 3

That mythical ring gave its owner the power of invisibility, and Plato observed that even a habitually just man who possessed such a ring would become a thief, knowing that he couldn't be caught. Morality, Plato argues, comes from full disclosure; without accountability for our actions we would all behave unjustly. 4

This certainly seems to be true for the anonymous trolls today. After Alexis Pilkington, a 17-year-old Long Island girl, committed suicide earlier this year, trolls descended on her online tribute page to post pictures of nooses, references to hangings and other hateful comments. A better-known example involves Nicole Catsouras, an 18-year-old who died in a car crash in California in 2006. Photographs of her badly disfigured body were posted on the Internet, where anonymous trolls set up fake tribute pages and in some cases e-mailed the photos to her parents with subject lines like "Hey, Daddy, I'm still alive." 5

Psychological research has proven again and again that anonymity increases unethical behavior. Road rage bubbles up in the relative anonymity of one's car. And in the online world, which can offer total anonymity, the effect is even more pronounced. People—even ordinary, good people—often change their behavior in radical ways. There's even a term for it: the online disinhibition effect. 6

Many forums and online communities are looking for ways to strike back. Back in February, Engadget, a popular technology review blog, shut down its commenting system for a few days after it received a barrage of trollish comments on its iPad coverage. 7

Many victims are turning to legislation. All 50 states now have stalking, bullying or harassment laws that explicitly include electronic forms of communication. Last year, Liskula Cohen, a former model, persuaded a New York judge to require Google to reveal the identity of an anonymous blogger who she felt had defamed her, and she has now filed a suit against the blogger. Last month, another former model, Carla Franklin, persuaded a judge to force YouTube to reveal the identity of a troll who made a disparaging comment about her on the video-sharing site. 8

But the law by itself cannot do enough to disarm the Internet's trolls. Content providers, social networking platforms and community sites must also do their part by rethinking the systems they have in place for user commentary so as to discourage—or disallow—anonymity. Reuters, for example, announced that it would start to block anonymous comments and require users to register with their names and e-mail addresses in an effort to curb "uncivil behavior." 9

Some may argue that denying Internet users the ability to post anonymously is a breach of their privacy and freedom of expression. But until the age of the Internet, anonymity was a rare thing. When someone spoke in public, his audience would naturally be able to see who was talking. 10

Others point out that there's no way to truly rid the Internet of anonymity. After all, names and e-mail addresses can be faked. And in any case many commenters write things that are rude or inflammatory under their real names. 11

But raising barriers to posting bad comments is still a smart first step. Well-designed commenting systems should also aim to highlight thoughtful and valuable opinions while letting trollish ones sink into oblivion. 12

The technology blog Gizmodo is trying an audition system for new commenters, under which their first few comments would be approved by a moderator or a trusted commenter to ensure quality before anybody else could see them. After a successful audition, commenters can freely post. If over time they impress other trusted commenters with their contributions, they'd be promoted to trusted commenters, too, and their comments would henceforth be featured. 13

Disqus, a comments platform for bloggers, has experimented with allowing users to rate one another's comments and feed those ratings into a global reputation system called Clout. Moderators can use a commenter's Clout score to "help separate top commenters from trolls." 14

At Facebook, where I've worked on the design of the public commenting widget, the approach is to try to replicate real-world social norms by emphasizing the human qualities of conversation. People's faces, real names and brief biographies ("John Doe from Lexington") are placed next to their public comments, to establish a baseline of responsibility. 15

Facebook also encourages you to share your comments with your friends. Though you're free to opt out, the knowledge that what you 16 say may be seen by the people you know is a big deterrent to trollish behavior.

This kind of social pressure works because, at the end of the day, most trolls wouldn't have the gall to say to another person's face half the things they anonymously post on the Internet. 17

Instead of waiting around for human nature to change, let's start to rein in bad behavior by promoting accountability. Content providers, stop allowing anonymous comments. Moderate your comments and forums. Look into using comment services to improve the quality of engagement on your site. Ask your users to report trolls and call them out for polluting the conversation. 18

In slowly lifting the veil of anonymity, perhaps we can see the troll not as the frightening monster of lore, but as what we all really are: human. 19

Thinking Critically about This Reading

Zhuo points out several legal efforts to curb "trolling" but argues that "the law by itself cannot do enough" to stop abusive comments (paragraph 9). Where does she think the responsibility lies? Do you agree? Why or why not?

Questions for Study and Discussion

1. What is Zhuo's thesis, and where does she state it?
2. What problem does Zhuo address in this essay? How does her thesis offer an approach to this problem?
3. Why does Zhuo think Plato's story about the ring of Gyges (4) is relevant to Internet users?
4. How does Zhuo define the "online disinhibition effect" (6)? Which of Zhuo's examples of this effect do you find most powerful? (Glossary: **Definition**)
5. Zhuo identifies anonymity as a source of the problem. How does she think Internet culture allows, or even encourages, users to remain anonymous?
6. At the beginning of her essay, Zhuo says a troll can lurk "among dozens of well-intentioned opinions" (1). What does this say about the balance of thoughtful responses and inflammatory comments online? How much of the latter do you think it takes to derail a discussion?

Classroom Activity Using Organization

Consider the ways in which you might organize a discussion of the seven famous films listed below. For each film, we have provided some basic information: the date it was released to theaters, stars of the film, the total income in the United States, and Oscars won. You may choose to add in your own current film choice as a point of comparison or add another category of information for comparison, such as genre or runtime.

Film	Release Date	Featured Actors	Gross Income (USA)	Academy Awards
Gone with the Wind	January 17, 1940	Clark Gable, Vivien Leigh	$198,655,278	Best Picture; Best Actress in a Leading Role; Best Actress in a Supporting Role; Best Director; Best Writing, Screenplay; Best Cinematography, Color; Best Art Direction; Best Film Editing
The Godfather	March 24, 1972	Marlon Brando, Al Pacino, James Caan	$134,821,952	Best Picture; Best Actor in a Leading Role; Best Writing, Screenplay Based on Material from Another Medium
Singin' in the Rain	April 11, 1952	Gene Kelly, Donald O'Connor, Debbie Reynolds	$1,729,345	None

Titanic	December 19, 1997	Leonardo DiCaprio, Kate Winslet	$658,672,302	Best Picture; Best Director; Best Cinematography; Best Art Direction-Set Direction; Best Costume Design; Best Sound; Best Film Editing; Best Effects, Sound Effects Editing; Best Effects, Visual Effects; Best Music, Original Song; Best Music, Original Dramatic Score
Toy Story	November 22, 1995	Tom Hanks, Tim Allen	$191,796,233	None
Pulp Fiction	October 14, 1994	John Travolta, Uma Thurman, Samuel L. Jackson	$107,930,000	Best Writing, Screenplay Written Directly for the Screen
Lord of the Rings: The Fellowship of the Ring	December 19, 2001	Elijah Wood, Ian McKellen, Orlando Bloom	$313,837,577	Best Cinematography; Best Makeup; Best Music, Original Score; Best Effects, Visual Effects

Source: *Internet Movie Database*, 2 Dec. 2016, *imdb.com.*

Suggested Writing Assignments

1. Find a newspaper article posted in the past weeks and survey the comments section. Do your findings support Zhuo's assertions about trolling? Write an essay that summarizes what you observe. Think carefully about how you want to organize your essay: in chronological order? by types of responses? by profiles of commentors? by frequency of comments on a point? Be sure to support your thesis about online commenting behavior.

2. Though Zhuo is optimistic in offering her solution to the problem, her thesis about how to curb trolling depends on a skeptical view about when humans behave morally. Do you agree with her that we are far more likely to be moral when we're being watched? Is there a better way to assure moral behavior? Write an essay supporting Zhuo's call for "full disclosure" or arguing for an alternative way to encourage more responsible interactions. Be sure to organize your supporting details in a way that most effectively defends your thesis.

CHAPTER **6**

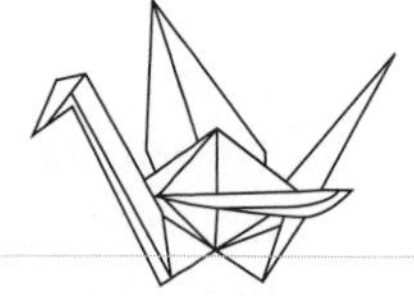

Beginnings and Endings

"Begin at the beginning and go on till you come to the end: then stop," advised the King of Hearts in *Alice in Wonderland*. "Good advice, but more easily said than done," you might be tempted to reply. Certainly, no part of writing essays can be more daunting than coming up with effective **beginnings and endings**. In fact, many writers believe that beginnings and endings are the most important parts of any piece of writing, regardless of its length. Even before coming to your introduction, your readers will usually know something about your intentions from your title. Titles such as "The Case against Medical Marijuana," "Laptop or Tablet: Which Should You Buy?," and "What Is a Migraine Headache?" indicate both your subject and your approach and prepare your readers for what follows.

BEGINNINGS

What makes for an effective beginning? Not unlike a personal greeting, a good beginning should catch a reader's interest and then hold it. The experienced writer realizes that many readers would rather do almost anything than make a commitment to read, so the opening—or *lede*, as journalists refer to it—requires a lot of thought and much revising to make it right and to keep the reader's attention from straying. The inexperienced writer, on the other hand, knows that the beginning is important but tries to write it first and to perfect it before moving on to the rest of the essay. Although there are no "rules" for writing introductions, we can offer one bit of general advice: wait until the writing process is well under way or almost completed before focusing on your opening. Following this advice will keep you from spending too much time on an introduction that you will undoubtedly revise.

More important, once you actually see how your essay develops, you will know better how to introduce it to your reader.

In addition to capturing your reader's attention, a good beginning usually introduces your thesis and either suggests or actually reveals the structure of the composition. Keep in mind that the best beginning is not necessarily the most catchy or the most shocking but the one most appropriate for the job you are trying to do.

There are many effective ways of beginning an essay. Following are a few of the most popular strategies.

Anecdote

Introducing your essay with an **anecdote**—a brief narrative drawn from current news events, history, or your personal experience—can be an effective way to capture your reader's interest. In the following example, the writer introduces an essay on choosing her career path by recounting the moment she first encountered her most inspiring teacher.

> Picture this: it is my first day of AP European History, sophomore year of high school. I sit slumped over in my desk, listening to my teacher babbling on about some revolution or uprising somewhere in the world. I struggle to stay awake, wondering how I am ever going to get through this class today, let alone this year. All of a sudden a man enters our classroom, walks right up to my history teacher (who is sitting at a desk in the front of the classroom lecturing), whips out a hankie and a rubber band, and creates something like a keffiyeh (a traditional Middle Eastern head covering) on the head of my bald history teacher. My classmates and I wait in anxious anticipation for the outburst of angry words that are sure to follow. To our surprise and delight, Mr. C (our history teacher) cracks a smile, and we all burst into laughter. He introduces this strange man as our English teacher, Mr. R. This mysterious Mr. R then proceeds to walk to the far end of the classroom, hoist himself up onto a desk, and walk across each student's desk to the other side of the room. This accomplished, he waves a final farewell and exits the classroom. This would be the English teacher I would never forget. He would be the one to inspire me to pursue a career in education.
>
> —Karen Vaccaro, student

Analogy and Comparison

An **analogy**, or comparison, can be useful in getting readers to think about a topic they might otherwise reject as uninteresting or unfamiliar. In the following multiparagraph example, William Zinsser introduces a subject few would consider engrossing—bloated, sloppy writing—with a comparison to disease. By pairing these two seemingly unrelated concepts, he both introduces and illustrates the idea he will develop in his essay: writing is a demanding craft, and to keep one's writing disease-free, one must edit with a watchful eye.

> Clutter is the disease of American writing. We are a society strangling in unnecessary words, circular constructions, pompous frills, and meaningless jargon.
>
> Who can understand the clotted language of everyday American commerce: the memo, the corporation report, the business letter, the notice from the bank explaining its latest "simplified" statement? What member of an insurance or medical plan can decipher the brochure explaining his costs and benefits? What father or mother can put together a child's toy from the instructions on the box? Our national tendency is to inflate and thereby sound important. The airline pilot who announces that he is presently anticipating experiencing considerable precipitation wouldn't think of saying it may rain. The sentence is too simple—there must be something wrong with it.
>
> But the secret of good writing is to strip every sentence to its cleanest components. Every word that serves no function, every long word that could be a short word, every adverb that carries the same meaning that's already in the verb, every passive construction that leaves the reader unsure of who is doing what—these are the thousand and one adulterants that weaken the strength of a sentence. And they usually occur in proportion to education and rank.
>
> –William Zinsser, "Simplicity," *On Writing Well*

Dialogue/Quotation

Although relying heavily on the ideas of others can weaken an effective introduction, opening your essay with a quotation or a brief **dialogue** can attract a reader's attention and succinctly illustrate a particular attitude or point you want to discuss. In the following example, the writer introduces an essay about the three main types of stress in our lives by recounting a brief dialogue with one of her roommates.

> My roommate, Megan, pushes open the front door, throws her keys on the counter, and flops down on the couch.
>
> "Hey, Megan, how are you?" I yell from the kitchen.
>
> "I don't know what's wrong with me. I sleep all the time, but I'm still tired. No matter what I do, I just don't feel well."
>
> "What did the doctor say?"
>
> "She said it sounds like chronic fatigue syndrome."
>
> "Do you think it might be caused by stress?" I ask.
>
> "Nah, stress doesn't affect me very much. I like keeping busy and running around. This must be something else."
>
> Like most Americans, Megan doesn't recognize the numerous factors in her life that cause her stress.
>
> —Sarah Federman, student

Facts and Statistics

For the most part, you should use **facts** and statistics to support your argument rather than let them speak for you, but presenting brief and startling facts or statistics can be an effective way to engage readers in your essay.

> One out of every five new recruits in the United States military is female.
>
> The Marines gave the Combat Action Ribbon for service in the Persian Gulf to twenty-three women.
>
> Two female soldiers were killed in the bombing of the USS *Cole*.
>
> The Selective Service registers for the draft all male citizens between the ages of eighteen and twenty-five.
>
> What's wrong with this picture?
>
> –Anna Quindlen, "Uncle Sam and Aunt Samantha"

Irony or Humor

It is often effective to introduce an essay with irony or humor. Humor signals to the reader that your essay will be entertaining to read, and **irony** can indicate an unexpected approach to a topic. Paul W. Merrill begins his ironic instructional essay on how to write poorly by establishing a wry tone, even poking fun at himself, stating that "the author . . . can write poorly without half trying."

> Books and articles on good writing are numerous, but where can you find sound, practical advice on how to write poorly? Poor writing is so common that every educated person ought to know something about it. Many scientists actually do write poorly, but they probably perform by ear without perceiving clearly how their results are achieved. An article on the principles of poor writing might help. The author considers himself well qualified to prepare such an article; he can write poorly without half trying.
>
> The average student finds it surprisingly easy to acquire the usual tricks of poor writing. To do a consistently poor job, however, one must grasp a few essential principles:
>
> 1. Ignore the reader.
> 2. Be verbose, vague, and pompous.
> 3. Do not revise.
>
> –Paul W. Merrill, "The Principles of Poor Writing," p. 384

There are several other good ways to begin an essay; the following opening paragraphs illustrate each approach.

Short Generalization

> Washington is a wonderful city. The scale seems right, more humane than other places. I like all the white marble and green trees, the ideals celebrated by the great monuments and memorials. I like the climate, the slow shift of the seasons here. Spring, so southern in feeling, comes early, and the long, sweet autumns can last into December. Summers are murder, equatorial—no question; the compensation is that Congress adjourns, the city empties out, eases off. Winter evenings in Georgetown with the snow falling and the lights just coming on are as beautiful as any I've known.
>
> –David McCullough, *Brave Companions: Portraits in History*

Startling Claim

> I've finally figured out the difference between neat and sloppy people. The distinction is, as always, moral. Neat people are lazier and meaner than sloppy people.
>
> –Suzanne Britt, "Neat People vs. Sloppy People"

Strong Proposition

For the ambulatory individual, access for the mobility-impaired on the University of Texas at Austin (UT) campus is easy to overlook. Automatic door entrances and bathrooms with the universal handicapped symbol make the campus seem sufficiently accessible. But for many students and faculty at UT, including me, maneuvering the UT campus in a wheelchair is a daily experience of stress and frustration. Although the university has made a concerted and continuing effort to improve access, students and faculty with physical disabilities still suffer from discriminatory hardship, unequal opportunity to succeed, and lack of independence.

The university must make campus accessibility a higher priority and take more seriously the hardship that the campus at present imposes on people with mobility impairments. Better accessibility would also benefit the numerous students and faculty with temporary disabilities and help the university recruit a more diverse body of students and faculty.

—Manasi Deshpande, student

Rhetorical Questions

Where does the universe begin? Where does it end? The universe is so immense that it is difficult to wrap our minds around the sheer magnitude of it. Yet, despite the immensity of our universe, there is only one known planet that can support life as we know it. That planet, of course, is Earth — a unique and precious sphere teeming with life, beauty, mysteries, and wonder. Unfortunately, we tend to take our valuable home for granted, for it is easy to forget just how much our actions impact the environment. Why do we ignore those who point out the negative effects of our behaviors and ask us to change our ways, especially when it comes to the issue of global warming? Evidence shows that humans are largely responsible for causing this phenomenon, yet we continue to engage in old habits that only make it worse. Global warming is a serious issue affecting everyone, and so it is up to all of us to be more aware of our actions and change our harmful behaviors in order to protect our one and only home — and us.

—Kristen Sadowski, student

The Beginnings to Avoid box lists some examples of how *not* to begin an essay. You should always *avoid* using beginnings such as these in your writing.

Beginnings to Avoid

Apology
I am a college student and do not consider myself an expert on intellectual property, but I think file sharing and movie downloads should be legal.

Complaint
I'd rather write about a topic of my own choice than the one that is assigned, but here goes.

Dictionary
Webster's New Collegiate Dictionary defines the verb *to snore* as follows: "to breathe during sleep with a rough hoarse noise due to vibration of the soft palate."

Platitude/Cliché
America is the land of opportunity, and no one knows that better than Martha Stewart.

Reference to Title
As you can see from my title, this essay is about why we should continue to experiment with embryonic stem cells.

ENDINGS

An effective ending does more than simply indicate where the writer stopped writing. A strong conclusion may do the following:

- summarize
- inspire the reader to further thought or action
- return to the beginning by repeating key words, phrases, or ideas
- restate the thesis
- predict an outcome
- recommend a course of action or way of thinking
- surprise the reader by providing a particularly convincing example to support a thesis

Indeed, there are many ways to write a conclusion, but the effectiveness of any choice must be measured by how appropriately it fits what comes before it.

The following selections illustrate some approaches to conclusions:

Restatement of the Thesis

In an essay contrasting the traditional Hispanic understanding of the word *macho* with the meaning it has developed in mainstream American culture, Rose Del Castillo Guilbault begins her essay with a succinct, two-sentence paragraph offering her thesis:

> What is *macho*? That depends which side of the border you come from.

She concludes her essay by restating her thesis, but in a manner that reflects the detailed examination she has given the concept of macho in her essay:

> The impact of language in our society is undeniable. And the misuse of *macho* hints at a deeper cultural misunderstanding that extends beyond mere word definitions.
>
> –Rose Del Castillo Guilbault, "Americanization Is Tough on 'Macho'"

Figurative Language

In the following conclusion to her essay on global warming (you can read her introduction on p. 141), Kristen Sadowski summarizes the points she has made in her essay, ending with a clever use of figurative language to drive home her point. (See the introduction to Chapter 12, pp. 303–4, for a detailed discussion of figurative language.)

> Clearly, there are numerous ways for us to reduce our greenhouse gas emissions and prevent global warming from worsening. In fact, there are so many ways that it can be overwhelming. But we do not have to change our lifestyles entirely or implement every single solution. Instead, we can be more aware of our actions and make small changes here and there until we are comfortable with our newly formed habits. Often, changing our behaviors can be the hardest thing for us to do, especially if we are content with our current way of life. By making conscious efforts to become more environmentally responsible, however, we can all be successful in our attempts to make the world a better place. One person acting alone cannot impact global warming, but individuals acting together can make a huge difference. The Earth has a fever, and we have the medicine of our actions to keep that fever at bay.
>
> —Kristen Sadowski, student

Overview of Argument

In the following conclusion to her essay "Title IX Just Makes Sense," Jen Jarjosa offers an overview of her argument and concludes by predicting the outcome of the solution she advocates:

> There have undeniably been major improvements in the treatment of female college athletes since the enactment of Title IX. But most colleges and universities still don't measure up to the actual regulation standards, and many have quite a ways to go. The Title IX fight for equality is not a radical feminist movement, nor is it intended to take away the privileges of male athletes. It is, rather, a demand for fairness, for women to receive the same opportunities that men have always had. When colleges and universities stop viewing Title IX budget requirements as an inconvenience and start complying with the spirit and not merely the letter of the law, collegiate female athletes will finally reach the parity they deserve.
>
> —Jen Jarjosa, student

If you are having trouble with your conclusion—which is not an uncommon occurrence—it may be because of problems with your essay itself. Frequently, writers do not know when to end because they are not sure about their overall purpose. For example, if you are taking a trip and your purpose is to go to Chicago, you will know when you get there and will stop. But if you don't really know where you are going, it's very difficult to know when to stop.

It's usually a good idea in your conclusion to avoid such overworked expressions as "In conclusion," "In summary," "I hope I have shown," or "Finally." Your conclusion should also do more than simply repeat what you've said in your opening paragraph. The most satisfying essays are those in which the conclusion provides an interesting way of wrapping up ideas introduced in the beginning and developed throughout, so that your reader has the feeling of coming full circle.

You might find it revealing as your course progresses to read with special attention the beginnings and endings of the essays throughout *Models for Writers*. Take special note of the varieties of beginnings and endings, the possible relationship between a beginning and an ending, and the general appropriateness of these elements to the writer's subject and purpose.

Shame

Dick Gregory

Ethan Miller/Getty Images

Dick Gregory—activist, comedian, and nutrition expert—was born in St. Louis, Missouri, in 1932. While attending Southern Illinois University on an athletic scholarship, Gregory excelled in track, winning the university's Outstanding Athlete Award in 1953. In 1954, he was drafted into the army. After his discharge, he immediately became active in the civil rights movement led by Martin Luther King Jr. In the 1960s, Gregory was an outspoken critic of U.S. involvement in Vietnam, which in turn led to his run for the presidency in 1968 as a write-in candidate for the Freedom and Peace Party. Two of his books from this era are *No More Lies: The Myth and Reality of American History* (1971) and *Dick Gregory's Political Primer* (1972). Throughout his life he has crusaded for economic reforms and minority rights and spoken out on antidrug issues. In 2000, he published *Callus on My Soul,* the second volume of his autobiography. In 2015, Gregory received a star on Hollywood's Walk of Fame, over fifty years after he first broke into the public spotlight as a stand-up comedian.

In the following episode from *Nigger* (1964), the first volume of his autobiography, Gregory narrates the story of a childhood experience that taught him the meaning of shame. Through his use of dialogue, he dramatically re-creates the experience for readers. Notice how he begins this essay in the shelter of home and ends with the feeling that his lesson in shame exposes him to the eyes of "the whole world."

Reflecting on What You Know

We all learn many things in school beyond the lessons we study formally. Some of the extracurricular truths we learn stay with us for the rest of our lives. Write about something you learned in school—something that has made life easier or more understandable for you—that you still find useful.

I never learned hate at home, or shame. I had to go to school for that. 1
I was about seven years old when I got my first big lesson. I was in love with a little girl named Helene Tucker, a light-complexioned little girl with pigtails and nice manners. She was always clean and she was smart in school. I think I went to school then mostly to look at her. I brushed my hair and even got me a little old handkerchief. It was a lady's handkerchief, but I didn't want Helene to see me wipe my nose on my hand. The pipes were frozen again, there was no water in the house, but I washed my socks and shirt every night. I'd get a pot, and go over to Mister Ben's grocery store, and stick my pot down into his soda machine. Scoop out some chopped ice. By evening the ice melted to water for washing. I got sick a lot that winter because the fire would go out at night before the clothes were dry. In the morning I'd put them on, wet or dry, because they were the only clothes I had.

Everybody's got a Helene Tucker, a symbol of everything you 2
want. I loved her for her goodness, her cleanness, her popularity. She'd walk down my street and my brothers and sisters would yell, "Here comes Helene," and I'd rub my tennis sneakers on the back of my pants and wish my hair wasn't so nappy[1] and the white folks' shirt fit me better. I'd run out on the street. If I knew my place and didn't come too close, she'd wink at me and say hello. That was a good feeling. Sometimes I'd follow her all the way home, and shovel the snow off her walk and try to make friends with her Momma and her aunts. I'd drop money on her stoop late at night on my way back from shining shoes in the taverns. And she had a Daddy, and he had a good job. He was a paper hanger.

I guess I would have gotten over Helene by summertime, but some- 3
thing happened in that classroom that made her face hang in front of me for the next twenty-two years. When I played the drums in high school it was for Helene and when I broke track records in college it was for Helene and when I started standing behind microphones and heard applause I wished Helene could hear it, too. It wasn't until I was twenty-nine years old and married and making money that I finally got her out of my system. Helene was sitting in that classroom when I learned to be ashamed of myself.

It was on a Thursday. I was sitting in the back of the room, in a 4
seat with a chalk circle drawn around it. The idiot's seat, the trouble-maker's seat.

---

[1]*nappy:* shaggy or fuzzy.

The teacher thought I was stupid. Couldn't spell, couldn't read, 5
couldn't do arithmetic. Just stupid. Teachers were never interested in finding out that you couldn't concentrate because you were so hungry, because you hadn't had any breakfast. All you could think about was noontime, would it ever come? Maybe you could sneak into the cloakroom and steal a bite of some kid's lunch out of a coat pocket. A bite of something. Paste. You can't really make a meal of paste, or put it on bread for a sandwich, but sometimes I'd scoop a few spoonfuls out of the paste jar in the back of the room. Pregnant people get strange tastes. I was pregnant with poverty. Pregnant with dirt and pregnant with smells that made people turn away, pregnant with cold and pregnant with shoes that were never bought for me, pregnant with five other people in my bed and no Daddy in the next room, and pregnant with hunger. Paste doesn't taste too bad when you're hungry.

The teacher thought I was a troublemaker. All she saw from the 6
front of the room was a little black boy who squirmed in his idiot's seat and made noises and poked the kids around him. I guess she couldn't see a kid who made noises because he wanted someone to know he was there.

It was on a Thursday, the day before the Negro payday. The eagle 7
always flew on Friday. The teacher was asking each student how much his father would give to the Community Chest. On Friday night, each kid would get the money from his father, and on Monday he would bring it to the school. I decided I was going to buy me a Daddy right then. I had money in my pocket from shining shoes and selling papers, and whatever Helene Tucker pledged for her Daddy I was going to top it. And I'd hand the money right in. I wasn't going to wait until Monday to buy me a Daddy.

I was shaking, scared to death. The teacher opened her book and 8
started calling out names alphabetically.

"Helene Tucker?" 9

"My daddy said he'd give two dollars and fifty cents." 10

"That's very nice, Helene. Very, very nice indeed." 11

That made me feel pretty good. It wouldn't take too much to top 12
that. I had almost three dollars in dimes and quarters in my pocket. I stuck my hand in my pocket and held onto the money, waiting for her to call my name. But the teacher closed her book after she called everybody else in the class.

I stood up and raised my hand. 13

"What is it now?" 14

"You forgot me." 15

She turned toward the blackboard. "I don't have time to be play- 16
ing with you, Richard."

"My Daddy said he'd . . ." 17

"Sit down, Richard, you're disturbing the class." 18

"My Daddy said he'd give . . . fifteen dollars." 19

She turned around and looked mad. "We are collecting this money 20
for you and your kind, Richard Gregory. If your Daddy can give fifteen dollars you have no business being on relief."

"I got it right now, I got it right now, my Daddy gave it to me to 21
turn in today, my Daddy said . . ."

"And furthermore," she said, looking right at me, her nostrils get- 22
ting big and her lips getting thin and her eyes opening wide, "we know you don't have a Daddy."

Helene Tucker turned around, her eyes full of tears. She felt sorry 23
for me. Then I couldn't see her too well because I was crying, too.

"Sit down, Richard." 24

And I always thought the teacher kind of liked me. She always 25
picked me to wash the blackboard on Friday, after school. That was a big thrill, it made me feel important. If I didn't wash it, come Monday the school might not function right.

"Where are you going, Richard?" 26

I walked out of school that day, and for a long time I didn't go 27
back very often. There was shame there.

Now there was shame everywhere. It seemed like the whole world 28
had been inside that classroom, everyone had heard what the teacher had said, everyone had turned around and felt sorry for me. There was shame in going to the Worthy Boys Annual Christmas Dinner for you and your kind, because everybody knew what a worthy boy was. Why couldn't they just call it the Boys Annual Dinner; why'd they have to give it a name? There was shame in wearing the brown and orange and white plaid mackinaw[2] the welfare gave to three thousand boys. Why'd it have to be the same for everybody so when you walked down the street the people could see you were on relief? It was a nice warm mackinaw and it had a hood, and my Momma beat me and called me a little rat when she found out I stuffed it in the bottom of a pail full of garbage way over on Cottage Street. There was shame in running over to Mister Ben's at the end of the day and asking for his rotten peaches,

[2]*mackinaw:* a short, double-breasted wool coat.

there was shame in asking Mrs. Simmons for a spoonful of sugar, there was shame in running out to meet the relief truck. I hated that truck, full of food for you and your kind. I ran into the house and hid when it came. And then I started to sneak through alleys, to take the long way home so the people going into White's Eat Shop wouldn't see me. Yeah, the whole world heard the teacher that day, we all know you don't have a Daddy.

Thinking Critically about This Reading

In paragraph 28, Gregory states, "Now there was shame everywhere. It seemed like the whole world had been inside that classroom, everyone had heard what the teacher had said, everyone had turned around and felt sorry for me." What did Gregory's teacher say, and why did it hurt him so greatly?

Questions for Study and Discussion

1. How do the first three paragraphs of the essay help establish a context for the narrative that follows? (Glossary: **Narration**)
2. What does Gregory mean by "shame"? What precisely was he ashamed of, and what in particular did he learn from the incident?
3. In a word or phrase, how would you describe Gregory's tone? (Glossary: **Tone**) What specific words or phrases in his essay lead you to this conclusion?
4. What is the teacher's attitude toward Gregory? In arriving at your answer, consider her own words and actions as well as Gregory's opinion.
5. What role does money play in Gregory's experience? How does money relate to his sense of shame?
6. Specific details can enhance the reader's understanding and appreciation of a subject. (Glossary: **Details**). Gregory's description of Helene Tucker's manners or the plaid of his mackinaw, for example, makes his account vivid and interesting. Cite several other specific details he gives, and consider how the essay would be different without them.
7. Reread this essay's first and last paragraphs and compare how much each one emphasizes shame. (Glossary: **Beginnings and**

Endings). Which emotion other than shame does Gregory reveal in the first paragraph, and does it play a role in the last one? Is the last paragraph an effective ending? Explain.

Classroom Activity Using Beginnings and Endings

Gregory begins his essay with a startling claim: that at school he learned about shame. Pick two from among the eight other methods for beginning essays discussed in the introduction to this chapter and use them to write alternative openings for Gregory's essay. Share your beginnings with others in the class and discuss their effectiveness.

Suggested Writing Assignments

1. Using Gregory's essay as a model, write an essay narrating an experience that made you feel especially afraid, angry, surprised, embarrassed, or proud. Include details that allow your readers to know exactly what happened. Pay attention to how you use your first and last paragraphs to present the emotion your essay focuses on.
2. Most of us grow up with some sense of the socioeconomic class that our family belongs to, and often we are aware of how we are, or believe we are, different from people of other classes. Write an essay in which you describe a possession or an activity that you thought revealed your socioeconomic standing and made you self-conscious about how you were different from others. Using Gregory's essay as a model, let your first and last paragraphs dramatize this realization by showing how your self-consciousness changed as you understood how others viewed you.

The Case for Censoring Hate Speech

Sean McElwee

Courtesy Sean McElwee

Sean McElwee grew up in Connecticut and graduated from King's College. He writes about current events and economics for publications including the *Atlantic*, the *New Republic*, *Rolling Stone*, *Alternet*, *Salon*, and *Reason*. McElwee is currently a writer based in New York City and an analyst for Demos, a public policy organization.

In "The Case for Censoring Hate Speech," McElwee answers the objections of free-speech advocates. According to McElwee, the idea for this essay came from "reading about the experiences of women, minorities and LGBT youth who had been harassed on websites like Twitter and Reddit." His goal was to "show that by allowing racism, homophobia and misogyny, these websites don't make speech more free, but rather, more constrained." McElwee did a lot of research in preparation for writing this essay, reading articles, conducting interviews, and gathering information on worldwide hate-speech laws. As you read, pay attention to how McElwee begins by setting the context for his argument and leading to a strong claim.

Reflecting on What You Know

The First Amendment to the Constitution states that "Congress shall make no law . . . abridging the freedom of speech." When or how do you think we should, for the public good, place restrictions on this right?

For the past few years speech has moved online, leading to fierce debates about its regulation. Most recently, feminists have led the charge to purge Facebook of misogyny that clearly violates its hate speech code. Facebook took a small step two weeks ago, creating a feature that will remove ads from pages deemed "controversial." But 1 such a move is half-hearted; Facebook and other social networking websites should not tolerate hate speech and, in the absence of a government mandate, adopt a European model of expunging offensive material.

Stricter regulation of Internet speech will not be popular with the libertarian-minded citizens of the United States, but it's necessary. A typical view of the case for expunging hate speech comes from Jeffrey Rosen, who argues in *The New Republic* that, 2

> given their tremendous size and importance as platforms for free speech, companies like Facebook, Google, Yahoo, and Twitter shouldn't try to be guardians of what Waldron calls a "well-ordered society"; instead, they should consider themselves the modern version of Oliver Wendell Holmes's fractious marketplace of ideas—democratic spaces where all values, including civility norms, are always open for debate.

This image is romantic and lovely but it's worth asking what this actually looks like. Rosen forwards one example: 3

> Last year, after the French government objected to the hash tag "#unbonjuif"—intended to inspire hateful riffs on the theme "a good Jew . . ."—Twitter blocked a handful of the resulting tweets in France, but only because they violated French law. Within days, the bulk of the tweets carrying the hash tag had turned from anti-Semitic to denunciations of anti-Semitism, confirming that the Twittersphere is perfectly capable of dealing with hate speech on its own, without heavy-handed intervention.

It's interesting to note how closely this idea resembles free market fundamentalism: simply get rid of any coercive rules and the "marketplace of ideas" will naturally produce the best result. Humboldt State University compiled a visual map that charts 150,000 hateful insults aggregated over the course of 11 months in the U.S. by pairing Google's Maps API with a series of the most homophobic, racist and otherwise prejudiced tweets. The map's existence draws into question the notion that the "Twittersphere" can organically combat hate speech; hate speech is not going to disappear from Twitter on its own. 4

The negative impacts of hate speech cannot be mitigated by the responses of third-party observers, as hate speech aims at two goals. First, it is an attempt to tell bigots that they are not alone. Frank Collins—the neo-Nazi prosecuted in *National Socialist Party of* 5

America v. Skokie (1977)—said, "We want to reach the good people, get the fierce anti-Semites who have to live among the Jews to come out of the woodwork and stand up for themselves."

The second purpose of hate speech is to intimidate the targeted minority, leading them to question whether their dignity and social status is secure. In many cases, such intimidation is successful. Consider the number of rapes that go unreported. Could this trend possibly be impacted by Reddit threads like /r/rapingwomen or /r/mensrights? Could it be due to the harassment women face when they even suggest the possibility they were raped? The rape culture that permeates Facebook, Twitter and the public dialogue must be held at least partially responsible for our larger rape culture. 6

Reddit, for instance, has become a veritable potpourri of hate speech; consider Reddit threads like /r/nazi, /r/killawoman, /r/misogny, /r/killingwomen. My argument is not that these should be taken down because they are offensive, but rather because they amount to the degradation of a class that has been historically oppressed. Imagine a Reddit thread for /r/lynchingblacks or /r/assassinatingthepresident. We would not argue that we should sit back and wait for this kind of speech to be "outspoken" by positive speech, but that it should be entirely banned. 7

American free speech jurisprudence relies upon the assumption that speech is merely the extension of a thought, and not an action. If we consider it an action, then saying that we should combat hate speech with more positive speech is an absurd proposition; the speech has already done the harm, and no amount of support will defray the victim's impression that they are not truly secure in this society. We don't simply tell the victim of a robbery, "Hey, it's okay, there are lots of other people who aren't going to rob you." Similarly, it isn't incredibly useful to tell someone who has just had their race/gender/sexuality defamed, "There are a lot of other nice people out there." 8

Those who claim to "defend free speech" when they defend the right to post hate speech online are in truth backwards. Free speech isn't an absolute right; no right is weighed in a vacuum. The court has imposed numerous restrictions on speech. Fighting words, libel and child pornography are all banned. Other countries merely go one step further by banning speech intended to intimidate vulnerable groups. The truth is that such speech does not democratize speech, it monopolizes speech. Women, LGBTQ individuals and racial or religious minorities feel intimidated and are left out of the public sphere. On Reddit, 9 for example, women have left or changed their usernames to be more male-sounding lest they face harassment and intimidation for speaking on Reddit about even the most gender-neutral topics. Even outside of the intentionally offensive sub-reddits (i.e., /r/imgoingtohellforthis) misogyny is pervasive. I encountered this when browsing /r/funny.

Those who try to remove this hate speech have been criticized 10
from left and right. At *Slate*, Jillian York writes, "While the campaigners on this issue are to be commended for raising awareness of such awful speech on Facebook's platform, their proposed solution is ultimately futile and sets a dangerous precedent for special interest groups looking to bring their pet issue to the attention of Facebook's censors."

It hardly seems right to qualify a group fighting hate speech as an 11
"interest group" trying to bring their "pet issue" to the attention of Facebook censors. The "special interest" groups she fears might apply for protection must meet Facebook's strict community standards, which state:

> While we encourage you to challenge ideas, institutions, events, and practices, we do not permit individuals or groups to attack others based on their race, ethnicity, national origin, religion, sex, gender, sexual orientation, disability or medical condition.

If anything, the groups to which York refers are nudging Facebook towards actually enforcing its own rules.

People who argue against such rules generally portray their oppo- 12
nents as standing on a slippery precipice, tugging at the question "what next?" We can answer that question: Canada, England, France, Germany, The Netherlands, South Africa, Australia and India all ban hate speech. Yet, none of these countries have slipped into totalitarianism. In many ways, such countries are more free when you weigh the negative liberty to express harmful thoughts against the positive liberty that is suppressed when you allow for the intimidation of minorities.

As Arthur Schopenhauer said, "the freedom of the press should 13
be governed by a very strict prohibition of all and every anonymity." However, with the Internet the public dialogue has moved online, where hate speech is easy and anonymous.

Jeffrey Rosen argues that norms of civility should be open to dis- 14
cussion, but, in today's reality, this issue has already been decided; impugning someone because of their race, gender or orientation is not acceptable in a civil society. Banning hate speech is not a mechanism to further this debate because the debate is over.

As Jeremy Waldron argues, hate speech laws prevent bigots from "trying to create the impression that the equal position of members of vulnerable minorities in a rights-respecting society is less secure than implied by the society's actual foundational commitments." 15

Some people argue that the purpose of laws that ban hate speech is merely to avoid offending prudes. No country, however, has mandated that anything be excised from the public square merely because it provokes offense, but rather because it attacks the dignity of a group—a practice the U.S. Supreme Court called in *Beauharnais v. Illinois* (1952) "group libel." Such a standard could easily be applied to Twitter, Reddit and other social media websites. While Facebook's policy as written should be a model, its enforcement has been shoddy. Again, this isn't an argument for government intervention. The goal is for companies to adopt a European-model hate speech policy, one not aimed at expunging offense, but rather hate. Such a system would be subject to outside scrutiny by users. If this is the standard, the Internet will surely remain controversial, but it can also be free of hate and allow everyone to participate. A true marketplace of ideas must co-exist with a multi-racial society open to people of all genders, orientations and religions, and it can. 16

Thinking Critically about This Reading

What does McElwee mean by calling Americans "libertarian-minded" (paragraph 2)? Compare that attitude with what he tells us about countries like Canada, England, and France.

Questions for Study and Discussion

1. What is the example that McElwee uses to begin his essay? What is effective about this example? Are there weaknesses to this approach?
2. Near the beginning of the essay, McElwee uses direct quotations from Rosen. Later, he summarizes Rosen's argument, using his own language. How do these different uses of the source serve different purposes?
3. Which websites does McElwee think have the worst problems with hate speech, and why? What does he suggest websites could do to improve the situation?

4. In this essay, McElwee responds to an argument by Jeffrey Rosen. Why does he object to Rosen's position on free speech? What, for example, does he think is wrong with the evidence Rosen cites about how Twitter reacted to the hashtag #unbonjuif?
5. What does McElwee believe are the two goals of hate speech? Do you agree or disagree, and why?
6. How does he answer the concern that limiting hate speech is like "standing on a slippery precipice"(12)? What does he say to the charge that restricting hate speech is just about avoiding giving offense to people who are overly sensitive?
7. McElwee closes his article by responding to the objection that banning hate speech is just a way to "avoid offending prudes." What is the advantage to ending his essay on this note? What are some drawbacks? How else might he have ended the same article more effectively?

Classroom Activity Using Beginnings and Endings

Carefully read the following three possible beginnings for an essay on the famous practical joker, Hugh Troy. What are the advantages and disadvantages of each? Which one would you select as an opening paragraph? Why?

> Whether questioning the values of American society or simply relieving the monotony of daily life, Hugh Troy always managed to put a little of himself into each of his stunts. One day he attached a plaster hand to his shirt sleeve and took a trip through the Holland Tunnel. As he approached the tollbooth with his toll ticket between the fingers of the artificial hand, Troy left both ticket and hand in the grasp of the stunned tollbooth attendant and sped away.

> Nothing seemed unusual. In fact, it was a rather common occurrence in New York City. Five men dressed in overalls roped off a section of busy Fifth Avenue in front of the old Rockefeller residence, hung out MEN WORKING signs, and began ripping up the pavement. By the time they stopped for lunch, they had dug quite a hole in the street. This crew was different, however, from all the others that had descended upon the streets of the city. It was led by Hugh Troy—the world's greatest practical joker.

Hugh Troy was born in Ithaca, New York, where his father was a professor at Cornell University. After graduating from Cornell, Troy left for New York City, where he became a successful illustrator of children's books. When World War II broke out, he went into the army and eventually became a captain in the 21st Bomber Command, 20th Air Force, under General Curtis LeMay. After the war he made his home in Garrison, New York, for a short while before finally settling in Washington, D.C., where he lived until his death.

Suggested Writing Assignments

1. Although McElwee works with many sources, the disagreement between Jeffrey Rosen and Jeremy Waldron seems to be the catalyst of this essay. Choose a subject you would like to write about and find articles stating two opposing views. Write an essay summarizing the points these two authors make. Focus on creating a good, attention-getting beginning to your essay.
2. Look up the law banning hate speech in one of the countries McElwee mentions in paragraph 12. Write an essay analyzing the language of the law. How does it compare with our own First Amendment? (Glossary: **Comparison and Contrast**) Be sure to end your essay with an effective conclusion. You may wish to inspire the reader to combat hate speech, speculate about the long-term effects of hate speech, or propose another solution, among other options.

Can Music Bridge Cultures and Promote Peace?

Omar Akram

Tibrina Hobson/Getty Images

Omar Akram is a world-famous pianist, composer, recording artist, and cultural ambassador who has had a major influence in shaping New Age and World Music. Born in 1964 in New York City, he is the son of a United Nations diplomat and grew up in various places around the world, absorbing a variety of cultures and their musical traditions. Since he was a very active child, his parents gave him piano lessons, which both quieted him and allowed for social engagement as he grew. Akram's albums include *Opal Fire* (2002), *Free as a Bird* (2004), *Secret Journey* (2007), and *Daytime Dreamer* (2013). His *Echoes of Love* won a Grammy for Best New Age Album in 2013, the first Grammy awarded to someone of Afghan descent, and it catapulted him to international fame. His followers find peace and solace in the quietude of his melodies, rhythms, and harmonies, characteristics that he attributes to his multicultural exposure.

In the following essay, published in the *Huffington Post* on August 12, 2013, Akram explores the idea that music has the power not only to entertain but also to embrace and transcend cultures, to move across borders, and to open hearts. As you read, notice how Akram begins his essay with a brief personal narrative that both engages his readers and introduces his topic of music, culture, and world peace.

Reflecting on What You Know

Some of us are interested in only one or a limited number of musical styles and genres, such as blues or jazz. Others are more eclectic and wide-ranging in their tastes and will listen to almost any music. We may never know exactly what shaped our musical tastes, but where and when we grew up, our gender, age, personality, and moods are worth contemplating. What kind of music do you like, and why do you find it so satisfying? Where do you think your musical preferences originated? Have your musical tastes changed? Why?

I met Fidel Castro[1] when I was 14 years old. I was at one of my father's diplomatic functions, and I had the opportunity to strike up a conversation with Castro about music. He knew I played the piano and asked me if I'd been to any of the local African jazz clubs. I was too young to enter the clubs at the time, but to my surprise the dictator wielded his power to get me in. I entered some of Cuba's best jazz clubs by simply using his name, and no one questioned it. I would go on stage and play the piano between sets, and the musicians would improvise with me and encourage me to play. This is one of the most powerful ways I was able to absorb the culture, and bring it with me in my own art. 1

After I was thrust into the international spotlight as the first Afghan American to win a Grammy award this year, I learned some important lessons about the power of music. I was born in New York as the son of a UN diplomat. I've lived all around the world, from the U.S. to the Czech Republic, Cuba, Switzerland and Afghanistan. Although my parents are from Afghanistan, I've never felt confined by the borders of just one culture, and I've learned to weave these many cultures into my compositions. One reason why I think my music in particular has been able to easily flow between international borders is because there is no singing or language. I receive letters from amazing fans all around the world who are able to create their own images and impressions about what my music means because they are not being directed by words or a certain language. It is the reason I started playing instrumental music. 2

The Grammy win brought me a lot of attention, both from the Afghan media and the people of Afghanistan. Afghanistan is a very divided country that is made up of many different ethnicities and social groups. After being on the radio and television I heard from everyone. The people there can hardly ever unite behind anything, and after I won the Grammy award there was a shared sense of accomplishment. It was a kind of unity I've never seen that I was very happy to be a part of. 3

I've received very touching letters and e-mails from people all around the world. I once received a letter from a man in Iraq who had just lost his family and his job. He was on the brink of committing suicide and someone gave him my CD. He told me that the music gave him the hope to move on. A woman in Australia wrote to me about her 4

[1]*Fidel Castro* (1926–2016): Cuban revolutionary leader who served as president of Cuba from 1976 to 2008.

father who had terminal cancer. She said that after playing my music for him his whole demeanor changed, and now he leaves it playing in the background 24/7. I've received letters ranging from an overworked father in the U.S. who is soothed by my music during his grueling commute to work, to an electricity-deprived family in Afghanistan who were mystified after hearing music unlike anything they are used to through the radio. I guess you could say music at its best could provide a sort of positive culture shock.

5 Music can positively affect people on many different levels. It can be a tool to communicate culture and a remedy for suffering just as much as it is a form of entertainment. I've learned to meld cultures and bring in instruments from around the world without hesitation. Embrace the culture you are from. It's who you are and it is a part of what makes you unique. In some ways, you can promote diplomacy through music, but it's important to understand that diplomacy does not always have to be political. Don't be afraid of who you are and where you are from. When you keep an open mind and an open heart to the many cultures of the world, you can turn your musical instrument into an instrument of peace.

Thinking Critically about This Reading

What do you think Akram's purpose is in this essay? Is he arguing a point, sharing a personal experience, or making an observation about music? What insight, if any, does his title give you into his purpose? Explain.

Questions for Study and Discussion

1. How did you respond to Akram's opening sentence? How does his opening paragraph as a whole introduce the subject of his essay?
2. Why does Akram believe that his music has been able to cross international borders and bridge cultures?
3. Akram claims to have learned "some important lessons about the power of music" (paragraph 2) after winning a Grammy award. What exactly do you think he learned? Explain.
4. In paragraph 4, Akram describes some of the letters and e-mails he has received from total strangers. What impact did

these little stories have on you? What do they add to his essay as a whole? (Glossary: **Example**)

5. Do you think the final paragraph closes Akram's essay effectively? How is this ending related to his opening paragraph?

Classroom Activity Using Beginnings and Endings

Read six to eight opening paragraphs for essays not in Chapter 6, and try to choose selections you have not yet read. Which openings make you want to read the whole essay? What was it about these beginnings that "hooked" you? Share the paragraphs you chose and your observations about them with your classmates or a small group. What generalizations can you draw about successful beginnings?

Suggested Writing Assignments

1. Akram believes that "music can positively affect people on many different levels. It can be a tool to communicate culture and a remedy for suffering just as much as it is a form of entertainment" (5). In what ways has music been a part of your life? What impact does music have on you? Using Akram's essay as a model, write an essay in which you explore the role that music plays in your life. Before beginning to write, you may find it helpful to review what you wrote in response to the Reflecting on What You Know prompt for this essay.
2. Write an essay in which you answer the question Akram asks in his title. Akram answers the question for himself by reflecting on his international experiences with music. Have you ever attended a concert (classical, jazz, rock, etc.) given by a group from another culture or country? What did you learn about the culture? Have you participated in or witnessed a community- or school-sponsored cultural exchange program that focused on music? How did the program affect the participants and the audiences?

CHAPTER **7**

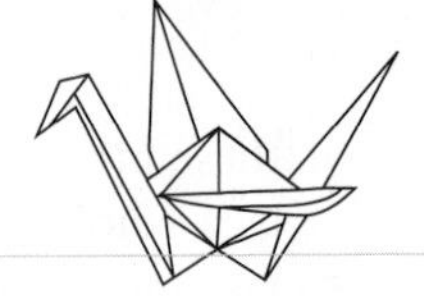

Paragraphs

Within an essay, the **paragraph** is the most important unit of thought. Like the essay, it has its own main idea, often stated directly in a topic sentence. Like a good essay, a good paragraph is unified: it avoids digressions and develops its main idea. Paragraphs use many of the rhetorical strategies that essays use—strategies like classification, comparison and contrast, and cause and effect. As you read the following three paragraphs, notice how each writer develops his or her topic sentence with explanations, concrete details and statistics, or vivid examples. The topic sentence in each paragraph is italicized.

> *Happiness is a slippery concept, a bundle of meanings with no precise, stable definition.* Lots of thinkers have taken a shot at it. "Happiness is when what you think, what you say, and what you do are in harmony," proposed Gandhi. Abraham Lincoln argued "most people are about as happy as they make up their minds to be." Snoopy, the beagle-philosopher in *Peanuts*, took what was to my mind the most precise stab at the underlying epistemological problem. "My life has no purpose, no direction, no aim, no meaning, and yet I'm happy. I can't figure it out. What am I doing right?"
>
> –Eduardo Porter, "What Happiness Is," p. 416

> The problem of substance abuse is far more complex and far more pervasive than any of us really knows or is willing to admit. *Most stories of illegal drugs overshadow Americans' struggles with alcohol, tobacco, food, and nonprescription drugs—our so-called legal addictions.* In 2000, for example, 17,000 deaths were attributed to cocaine and heroin. In that same year, 435,000 deaths were attributed to tobacco and 85,000 to alcohol. With the exception of a marked increase in heroin- and opioid-related deaths to about 47,000, in more recent years these figures have

remained in about the same proportion. It's not surprising, then, that many sociologists believe we are a nation of substance abusers—drinkers, smokers, overeaters, and pill poppers. Although the statistics are alarming, they do not begin to suggest the heavy toll of substance abuse on Americans and their families. Loved ones die, relationships are fractured, children are abandoned, job productivity falters, and the dreams of young people are extinguished.

–Alfred Rosa and Paul Eschholz

Photographs have let me know my parents before I was born, as the carefree college students they were, in love and awaiting the rest of their lives. I have seen the light blue Volkswagen van my dad used to take surfing down the coast of California and the silver dress my mom wore to her senior prom. Through pictures I was able to witness their wedding, which showed me that there is much in their relationship that goes beyond their children. I saw the look in their eyes as they held their first, newborn daughter, as well as the jealous expressions of my sister when I was born a few years later. There is something almost magical about viewing images of yourself and your family that you were too young to remember.

–Carrie White, student

Many writers find it helpful to think of the paragraph as a very small, compact essay. Here is a paragraph from Martin Luther King Jr.'s essay "The Ways of Meeting Oppression" (p. 425).

Violence as a way of achieving racial justice is both impractical and immoral. It is impractical because it is a descending spiral ending in destruction for all. The old law of an eye for an eye leaves everybody blind. It is immoral because it seeks to humiliate the opponent rather than win his understanding; it seeks to annihilate rather than to convert. Violence is immoral because it thrives on hatred rather than love. It destroys community and makes brotherhood impossible. It leaves society in monologue rather than dialogue. Violence ends by defeating itself. It creates bitterness in the survivors and brutality in the destroyers. A voice echoes through time saying to every potential Peter, "Put up your sword." History is cluttered with the wreckage of nations that failed to follow this command.

This paragraph, like all well-written paragraphs, has several distinguishing characteristics:

- It is *unified* in that every sentence and every idea relates to the main idea, stated in the italicized topic sentence.
- It is *coherent* in that the sentences and ideas are arranged logically, and the relationships among them are made clear by the use of effective transitions.
- Finally, it is *adequately developed* in that it presents a short but persuasive argument supporting its main idea.

How much development is "adequate" development? The answer depends on many things—how complicated or controversial the main idea is, what readers already know and believe, how much space the writer is permitted. Nearly everyone agrees that the Earth circles around the sun; a single sentence would be enough to make that point. A writer arguing that affirmative action has outlived its usefulness, however, would need many sentences—indeed, many paragraphs—to develop that idea convincingly.

PARAGRAPH LENGTH

How long should a paragraph be? In modern essays, most paragraphs range from 50 to 250 words, but some run a full printed page or more, and others may be only a few words long. The best answer is that a paragraph should be long enough to develop its main idea adequately. When some writers find a paragraph running very long, they break it into two or more paragraphs so that readers can pause and catch their breath. Other writers forge ahead, relying on the unity and coherence of their paragraph to keep their readers from getting lost.

Articles and essays that appear in magazines and newspapers (especially online versions) often have relatively short paragraphs, some of only one or two sentences. Short paragraphs are a convention in journalism because of the narrow columns, which make paragraphs of average length appear very long. But often you will find that these journalistic paragraphs could be joined together into a few longer paragraphs. Longer, adequately developed paragraphs are the kind you should use in all but journalistic writing.

The Art of Communal Bathing

Jamie Mackay

Courtesy Jamie Mackay

Jamie Mackay is a writer and translator. As an academic researcher, he wrote about European society on topics such as Italy's Five Star Movement and the emergence of new social classes. In 2014, he left his research position to become an investigative journalist. His many articles have appeared in *New Statesman*, *Italy Magazine*, *Il Manifesto*, and *Aeon*. Mackay is a cofounder of the Precarious Europe project, a media platform dedicated to documenting the experiences and perspectives of Europe's young people. He is also an editor at *openDemocracy*, an independent global media platform. With Niki Seth-Smith and Dan Hind, Mackay edited *Rethinking the BBC: Public Media in the 21st Century* (2016). Mackay currently lives in Florence, Italy, and is at work on a book titled *When Thinking Is the Screaming of the Soul.*

In the following essay, which first appeared on February 7, 2017, in *Aeon*, a digital magazine of ideas and culture, Mackay puts forth some provocative reasons for why we should reinvent and reinstate the practice of communal bathing. As you read, notice how he has crafted his paragraphs with strong topic sentences and created unity with the supporting sentences.

Reflecting on What You Know

Do you have any experience with communal bathing, such as showering with other team members after a game or workout? Does communal showering serve purposes other than getting a group of people clean in an efficient way? Would you prefer to shower or bathe alone or communally? Why?

For most of the history of our species, in most parts of the world, bathing has been a collective act. In ancient Asia, the practice was a religious ritual believed to have medical benefits related to the 1 purification of the soul and body. For the Greeks, the baths were associated with self-expression, song, dance, and sport, while in Rome they served as community centers, places to eat, exercise, read, and debate politics.

But communal bathing is rare in the modern world. While there are places where it remains an important part of social life—in Japan, Sweden, and Turkey, for example—for those living in major cities, particularly in the Anglosphere, the practice is virtually extinct. The vast majority of people in London, New York, and Sydney have become used to washing alone, at home, in plexi-glass containers—showering as a functional action, to clean one's own private body in the fastest and most efficient way possible. 2

The eclipse of communal bathing is one symptom of a wider global transformation, away from small ritualistic societies to vast urban metropolises populated by loose networks of private individuals. This movement has been accompanied by extraordinary benefits, such as the mass availability and movement of services and commodities, but it has also contributed to rampant loneliness, apathy and the emergence of new psychological phenomena, from depression to panic and social anxiety disorders. "Urban alienation," a term much-used by sociologists at the start of the 20th century, has become a cliché for describing today's world. 3

It is difficult to imagine a more powerful counter-image to the dominant picture of modernity than the archetypal bathhouse. Of course, these spaces vary greatly. The Japanese *sento*, with its strict rules and fastidious emphasis on hygiene, could hardly be more different from the infamously squalid wash houses of Victorian Britain. Hungary's vast *fürdo*, some of which spread over several floors, provide a different emotional experience to the intensity of the *lakȟóta* sweat-lodge of Native America. What links all these examples, however, is the role such spaces have in bringing together people who might otherwise remain separate, and placing them in a situation of direct physical contact. It is this aspect of proximity that remains significant today. 4

Reintroducing bathhouses with such a principle in mind could be a means of tackling the loneliness of living in contemporary megacities. These would not be the luxury spas and beauty salons that promise eternal youth for those who can afford them, nor the gay bathhouses of the world's metropolises, but real public spaces: cheap, multi-purpose and accessible to all. 5

Today, many people are turning to yoga, mindfulness, and other mind-body practices as a private means of resolving the sense of "disembodiment" that can arise from a cramped life spent in metro carriages and hunched over computer screens. The bathhouse could provide a similar space to focus on the body but, crucially, it would do so at the collective level, bringing corporeality[1] and touch back into the sphere of social interaction. The Japanese call this *hadaka no tsukiai* ("naked association") or, in the words of a new generation, "skinship." 6

This is a simple principle: that being physically present with one another makes us more aware of ourselves, and those around us, as biological—not purely linguistic and intellectual—organisms. The ghostly figures that slide past on trains and buses can, in such a space, cease to appear as abstract ideas or numbers and become human once again. 7

It is often forgotten that the Roman baths were a space where people of different social classes would wash side by side. Throughout the Empire, the bathhouse played a democratizing role in which different races and ages were brought into contact. According to the historian Mary Beard, even the emperor, admittedly protected by bodyguards and a team of slaves, would frequently bathe with the people. This naked cosmopolitanism was an important reference point for citizens and, as many histories attest, a key part of Rome's appeal. Directly experiencing other real bodies, touching and smelling them, is also an important way of understanding our own bodies which otherwise must be interpreted through the often distorted, sanitized and Photoshopped mirrors of advertising, film, and other media. 8

Living in a society where actual nudity has been eclipsed by idealized or pornographic images of it, many of us are, independently of our will, disgusted by hairy backs, flabby bellies, and "strange-looking" nipples. The relatively liberal attitude towards such issues in countries such as Denmark, where nudity in the bathhouse is the norm, and in some cases mandatory, exemplifies how the practice might help renormalize a basic sense of diversity and break through the rigid laws that regulate the so-called "normal body." 9

The bathhouses of the future, by reinventing the historical social functions of their ancient originals and combining their most attractive aspects to build a new model, would compensate for the erosion of public spaces elsewhere. They could serve as libraries or performance spaces, or host philosophical debates or chess championships: they might, like the 10

[1]*corporeality*: the existence or state of having a body.

Moroccan *hammam*[2], have gardens, allotments[3] or other green spaces, to bring urban dwellers in touch with plants, flowers, and animals.

Politically, too, they could be part of a wider effort to construct sustainable economic models. Last year at the UN climate change conference in Paris, countries agreed to phase out gas boilers and replace them with carbon-friendly alternatives. Although boilers do not pollute to the same degree as cars, airplanes, or cattle farms, our individual commitments to private washing is part of an unsustainable burden on the planet. Solar-powered public baths could lighten the load. 11

It's churlish[4] to simply disregard the public bath as an object of classical nostalgia. Communal bathing is a near-universal trait among our species and has a meaning that extends far beyond personal hygiene. There are pragmatic reasons to re-invent the practice, to be sure, but its anthropological diversity suggests that there might be a more fundamental need for this ancient and deeply human art. 12

Thinking Critically about This Reading

What do you think Mackay means when he says that communal bathing's "anthropological diversity suggests that there might be a more fundamental need for this ancient and deeply human art" (paragraph 12)? According to Mackay, what have people lost by not having public bathhouses available to them? Do you agree with him? Why or why not?

Questions for Study and Discussion

1. What is Mackay's purpose in this essay? (Glossary: **Purpose**)
2. How does Mackay explain the relative absence of communal bathing in the modern world?
3. Evaluate paragraphs 3, 4, and 8 for paragraph integrity by asking the following questions:
   - Does the paragraph have a clear topic sentence?
   - Does the author develop the paragraph clearly and effectively?

[2]*hammam*: a Turkish bath; a series of steam rooms.
[3]*allotments*: something assigned or shared in a particular amount, like space.
[4]*churlish*: rude or sullen.

- Is the paragraph unified?
- Is the paragraph coherent?

4. How does paragraph 7—a short, two-sentence paragraph—function in the context of this essay? In what ways does it conclude the first six paragraphs and introduce the final five?
5. Analyze the transitions between paragraphs 1 and 2, paragraphs 4 and 5, and paragraphs 10 and 11. (Glossary: **Transitions**) What techniques does Mackay use to smoothly move his readers from one aspect of his subject to the next?
6. Mackay paraphrases historian Mary Beard as part of his discussion of the Roman baths (8). What does this appeal to authority add to this paragraph and to the essay as a whole? (Glossary: **Evidence; Ethos**)
7. What is Mackay's vision for bathhouses in the future? How easy would it be to actually build such a model? Explain.

Classroom Activity Using Paragraphs

Carefully read the following set of related sentences and select one to use as a topic sentence. Then rearrange the other sentences to create an effective paragraph. Be ready to explain why you chose the order that you did.

1. PGA golfer Fred Divot learned the hard way what overtraining could do.
2. Divot's case is typical, and most researchers believe that too much repetition makes it difficult for the athlete to reduce left-hemisphere brain activity.
3. Athletes who overtrain find it very difficult to get in the flow.
4. "Two weeks later, all I could think about was mechanics, and I couldn't hit a fairway to save my life!"
5. Athletes think about mechanics (left hemisphere) rather than feel (right hemisphere), and they lose the ability to achieve peak performance.
6. "I was playing well, so I thought with a little more practice, I could start winning on tour," Divot recalled.

Suggested Writing Assignments

1. After reading Mackay's essay, consider what you think about the issue. What parts of his argument do you agree or disagree with? Write an essay in which you argue for or against the establishment of a communal bathhouse in your community. Make sure that each paragraph accomplishes a specific purpose and supports your thesis.
2. Mackay says that "living in a society where actual nudity has been eclipsed by idealized or pornographic images of it, many of us are, independently of our will, disgusted by hairy backs, flabby bellies and 'strange looking' nipples" (9). What is your current attitude about nudity? Has your attitude always been the same, or has it evolved as you've grown older? Perhaps your attitude is affected—for better or worse—by childhood memories of communal bathing, perhaps with siblings, or at a summer or sports camp. Do you remember a time when you became uncomfortable about the prospect of being naked with others? What happened? Write an essay in which you explore your feelings about nudity. Check that you have used transitions within each paragraph and between paragraphs to enhance the flow of ideas throughout your essay.

My Rosetta

Judith Ortiz Cofer

Miriam Berkley

Judith Ortiz Cofer (1952–2016) was born in Hormigueros, Puerto Rico. As a young girl, she moved with her family to Paterson, New Jersey, and when she was fifteen, the family settled in Augusta, Georgia. Cofer earned a BA in English from Augusta College and an MA from Florida Atlantic University. She is the author of numerous books, including *The Cruel Country* (2015), a memoir; *If I Could Fly* (2011), a novel; *A Love Story Beginning in Spanish* (2005), a collection of poems; *The Meaning of Consuelo* (2003), a novel; *The Latin Deli: Prose and Poetry* (1993); and *Silent Dancing* (1990), a collection of poetry and essays. Cofer wrote in several genres and for audiences of varied ages, but her writing is unified by the influence of oral storytelling, commentary on how immigrants negotiate dual identities, and concern with gender issues and the empowerment of women. Cofer was honored for her writing with grants and awards from the National Endowment for the Arts, the Georgia Council for the Arts, and the Witter Bynner Foundation. She was awarded an honorary doctorate in Humane Letters from Lehman College in New York in 2007. She taught at the University of Georgia for twenty-six years before her retirement in 2013.

In this essay from her book *Woman in Front of the Sun: On Becoming a Writer* (2000), Cofer remembers a woman who played a small but significant role in her life. As you read, pay attention to how her paragraphs have a strong topic sentence that describes Sister Rosetta, with specific details and humorous comparisons to support her description.

Reflecting on What You Know

What adults outside of your family have most influenced your life? What do you think made them so important you? How did they help you grow?

Sister Rosetta came into my life in 1966, at exactly the right moment. I was fourteen, beginning to stretch my bones after the long sleep of childhood, and the whole nation seemed to be waking up along with me. Each day the transistor radio I took everywhere informed me that the streets were alive with rebellion. Rock and roll filled the airwaves with throbbing sounds like those the heart makes when you are young and still listening to it—sounds that made me want to dance, yell, break out of my parents' cocoon of an apartment, sprout wings, and fly away from my predictable life and (what I feared most) a predictable future as a good Catholic barrio woman. Instead I was signed up for classes leading to my confirmation in the Catholic Church, spiritual preparation for the bishop's symbolic slap in the face: turn the other cheek, girl, you are now one of us humble followers of Christ. But my teacher in the ways of Christian humility, Sister Rosetta, was anything but the docile bride of Jesus I had expected. 1

She was not an attractive woman. Her face, although bright with wit, belonged on an Irish guy with a tough job, perhaps a construction foreman or a cop. If a nun's coif had not framed those features—the slightly bulbous nose, plump red-veined cheeks, and close-set eyes—this could have been the face of a heavy drinker or a laborer. She walked without grace but with a self-assured step we could hear approaching on the hardwood floors of the church basement where our lessons were held after school on cold winter afternoons in Paterson, New Jersey. Her rosary swinging from side to side on her habit's skirts, she strode in and slammed on the desktop whatever she was carrying that day. Then she'd lift herself onto the desk and face us, hands on hips as if to say, *What a shit job this is.* 2

And it was. Common knowledge had it that Sister Rosetta was assigned all the routine work of the convent by the Mother Superior to keep her busy and out of trouble. There was a rumor among us public school kids that Sister Rosetta had been arrested for taking part in a civil rights demonstration. And that she had been sent to our mainly Puerto Rican parish so that Father Jones, our saintly missionary pastor, could keep her under his wing. We found it funny to think of the shy, skinny man standing up to Sister Rosetta. 3

"OK, my little dumplings," Sister Rosetta would greet us, squinting like a coach about to motivate her team. "Today we are going to get in touch with our souls through music. Now listen carefully. You've never heard anything like this." Out of curiosity at first, then in near 4 rapture, that day I listened to the exotic music of Ravi Shankar emerge from the old turntable Sister Rosetta had dragged in. The celestial notes of his sitar enveloped me in a gauzy veil of sound, stirring me in a new way. Sister had tacked the album cover on the corkboard, and as I looked deeply into Shankar's onyx eyes he seemed to look back: in his gaze there were answers to questions I was almost ready to ask.

5 She must have noticed my enchantment, because Sister Rosetta handed me that record album as I was walking out of her overheated classroom. All she said was, "Bring it back without a scratch." Much to my mother's annoyance, I played Shankar's music every day after school in my room while I did my homework. She called it *los gatos peleando*, the cat-fight album; but to me the high, lingering notes were an alarm clock bringing me out of myself, out of ignorance and into the realm of the senses. For my thirteenth birthday I had received my own turntable and a Felipe Rodriguez album of Puerto Rican *boleros*, the romantic ballads my parents danced to at parties. I played the record occasionally for their sake, but Rodriguez's deep-throated laments about lost loves and weak women in tears did not appeal much to me. I liked the leaping, acrobatic images that Shankar's music induced, replacing my childhood dreams of flight.

Thinking Critically about This Reading

At the beginning of "My Rosetta," Cofer claims that Sister Rosetta appeared in her life "at exactly the right moment." What was special about this time in her life? Find passages from the essay that show how Cofer was feeling at this moment in time.

Questions for Study and Discussion

1. How are the topic sentences and the structure of the first two paragraphs similar? Why do you think Cofer organized the opening this way?
2. Why does Cofer fear being a "good Catholic barrio woman" (paragraph 1)? Explain this vision of her future and why she rejects it.
3. In paragraphs 4 and 5, Cofer's style of paragraphs changes. What rhetorical strategy does she use in these paragraphs? Is it effective? Why or why not? (Glossary: **Rhetorical Modes**)

4. Cofer sets up the first appearance of Sister Rosetta by telling us she is "anything but the docile bride of Jesus" (1). How does the description of her in paragraph 2 contradict that stereotypical picture of a nun?
5. What is Sister Rosetta's reputation among the public school students? Do you see any connections between her situation and Cofer's?
6. Explain the difference of opinion between Cofer and her mother over the Ravi Shankar album. How does the music Cofer's parents prefer compare to it?

Classroom Activity Using Paragraphs

Cofer uses only five paragraphs to paint the picture of Sister Rosetta and the effect she had on the young Cofer. Examine each of the paragraphs and determine what the topic sentence is for each, whether stated explicitly or implied. Highlight or underline it, and circle or make a list of the supporting details in each paragraph. Based on these descriptive paragraphs, draw a picture of what you think Sister Rosetta looks like. Don't worry if you're not the best artist. If you're working in a group, you can choose one artist and give feedback and direction or create a brief comic that depicts the actions Sister Rosetta might take based on your impression of her.

Suggested Writing Assignments

1. Choose someone close to you and write an essay describing him or her to a stranger. Using "My Rosetta" as a model, describe both physical appearance and characteristic gestures as a way to communicate personality. Focus on creating strong topic sentences to state the main idea of each paragraph and use only details that support that idea.
2. Write a personal essay about a time in your life when your view of the world was changing. First, create an outline of your essay. Organize your story into different stages, each of which will be developed into a paragraph. Write a topic sentence for each paragraph and then list what details you would include to support that topic sentence. When your outline is complete, write the essay using transitional words and phrases to give the paragraphs unity and coherence.

The Home Place

Jimmy Carter

AP Photo/Richard Drew

James Earl Carter Jr. was the thirty-ninth president of the United States. Born in the small town of Plains, Georgia, in 1924, he earned a BS from the U.S. Naval Academy and served for seven years as a naval officer. He completed two terms as a Georgia state senator and served as its governor before running for the presidency in 1976. During his term as president, he worked to combat energy shortages at home through conservation and other measures. He advocated for human rights abroad, helping to negotiate the Panama Canal Treaty and a peace agreement between Egypt and Israel. However, he faced continued economic problems at home and was defeated in his second run for the White House. After his presidency, Carter continued his service to the country, taking an active part in peace negotiations; in 2002, he was awarded the Nobel Peace Prize for his efforts at promoting peaceful conflict resolution around the world.

In this excerpt from his memoir, *An Hour before Daylight* (2001), Carter describes the workings of his father's peanut farm. Each paragraph focuses on a different part of the farm, describing in loving detail the carpentry shop, the barn, and the unreliable water pump. In Carter's mind, these physical features of the farm, plus the men who work there, form "a fascinating system, like a huge clock."

Reflecting on What You Know

What are your most vivid memories from childhood? What details do you recall when you think about your childhood home?

I still have vivid memories of the home place where I spent my boyhood. There was a dirt tennis court next to our house, unknown on any other farm in our area, which Daddy laid out as soon as we moved there and kept clean and relatively smooth with a piece of angle iron nailed to a pine log that a mule could drag over it every 1 week or so. Next was my father's commissary store, with the windmill in back, and then a large fenced-in garden. A two-rut wagon road ran from our back yard to the barn, which would become the center of my life as I matured and eagerly assumed increasing responsibilities for the work of a man.

Beyond the garden and alongside this small road was a combination blacksmith and carpenter shop surrounded by piles of all kinds of scrap metal, where everyone on the farm knew that rattlesnakes loved to breed. This is where we shod mules and horses, sharpened plow points, repaired machinery, made simple iron implements, and did woodwork, with Daddy providing the overall supervision. He was skilled with the forge and anvil, and did fairly advanced blacksmith work. This is one of the first places I was able to work alongside him. I could turn the hand crank on the forge blower fast enough to keep the charcoal fire ablaze, and to hold some of the red-hot pieces on the anvil with tongs while Daddy shaped them with a hammer and then plunged them, hissing, into water or oil for tempering. It required some skill to keep a plow point completely flat on the steel surface; otherwise a hammer blow would bring a violent and painful twisting, with the tongs and red-hot metal sometimes flying out of my hands. There was almost always something broken around the farm, and only rarely would anything be taken to town for welding. I learned a lot from Daddy, and also from Jack Clark, a middle-aged black man who was something of a supervisor on our farm and did most of the mule- and horse-shoeing. 2

In front of the shop was a large Sears, Roebuck grinding stone, and we would sit on a wooden seat and pedal to keep the thick disc spinning, with the bottom of the stone running in half an automobile tire filled with water. This was a busy place where we sharpened hoes, axes, scythes, knives, and scissors. Daddy didn't believe in paying for something we could do ourselves, so he also had an iron shoemaker's last in the shop that he used for replacing worn-out heels and soles for the family's shoes. As I got older, I helped with all the jobs in the shop, but was always most interested in working with wood, especially in shaping pieces with froe, plane, drawknife, and spokeshave. 3

The centerpiece of our farm life, and a place of constant exploration for me, was our large, perfectly symmetrical barn. It had been built by an itinerant Scottish carpenter named Mr. Valentine, whose basic design was well known in our farming region. Daddy was very proud of its appearance and its practical arrangement, which minimized labor in handling the large quantities of feed needed for our 4 livestock. There were special cribs, bins, and tanks for storing oats, ear corn, velvet beans, hay, fodder, and store-bought supplements, including molasses, a bran called "shorts," and cottonseed meal. The sheep, goats, and cattle were usually kept in stalls separate from each other and from the mules and horses, and animals requiring veterinary care could also be isolated while being treated. Hogs had their own pens, and were not permitted inside the barn.

Before I was big enough for real fieldwork, Daddy encouraged me 5
to spend time with Jack Clark, knowing that it was the best way for me to be educated about farm life, as Jack kept up a constant stream of comments about the world as he knew or envisioned it.

Jack was very black, of medium height, and strongly built. He had 6
surprisingly long arms, and invariably wore clean overalls, knee-high rubber boots, and a straw hat. Knowing (or at least claiming) that he spoke for my father, he issued orders or directions to the other hands in a somewhat gruff voice, always acting as the final arbiter over which field each hand would plow and which mule he would harness. He ignored the grumbled complaints. When all the other workers were off to their assigned duties, Jack was the sole occupant of the barn and the adjacent lots—except when I was following behind him like a puppy dog and bombarding him with questions. We became close friends, but there was always some restraint as to intimacy between us. For instance, although my daddy would pick me up on occasion to give me a hug or let me ride on his shoulders, this would have been inconceivable with Jack, except when he might lift me over a barbed-wire fence or onto the back of a mule or horse.

Radiating from the barn was a maze of fences and gates that let 7
us move livestock from one place to another with minimal risk of their escape. This was one of my earliest tasks, requiring only a modicum of skill and the ability to open and close the swinging gates. Within the first array of enclosures was a milking shed that would hold four cows at a time, adequate to accommodate our usual herd of eight to a dozen Jerseys and Guernseys that we milked in two shifts, twice a day. Later, we had a dozen A-frame hog-farrowing structures, which I helped my daddy build after bringing the innovative design home from my Future Farmer class in school. One shelter was assigned to each sow when birthing time approached, and the design kept the animals dry, provided a convenient place for feed and water, and minimized the inadvertent crushing of the baby pigs by their heavy mamas. Except during extended dry seasons, the constantly used lots for hogs and milk cows were always ankle deep in mud and manure, which made bare feet much superior to brogans.

8 A little open shed near the barn enclosed a pump that lifted about two cups of water from our shallow well with each stroke. It was driven by a small two-cycle gasoline engine that we cranked up and let run once or twice a day, just long enough to fill several watering troughs around the barn and sheds. This was the only motor-driven device on the farm, and was always viewed with a mixture of suspicion and trepidation. We were justifiably doubtful that it would crank when we needed it most, dreading the hour or two of hand pumping as the only alternative source of water for all the animals. Between the pump house and barn was a harness shed, an open-ended building where we stored a buggy, two wagons, and all the saddles, bridles, and other harness needed for an operating farm. Also near the barn was a concrete dipping-vat about four feet deep, filled with a pungent mixture containing creosote, through which we would drive our cattle, goats, and newly sheared sheep to protect them, at least temporarily, from flies and screwworms.

9 The farm operation always seemed to me a fascinating system, like a huge clock, with each of its many parts depending on all the rest. Daddy was the one who designed, owned, and operated the complicated mechanism, and Jack Clark wound it daily and kept it on time. I had dreams that one day I would be master of this machine, with its wonderful intricacies.

10 The workers on our place, all black, lived in five small clapboard houses, three right on the highway, one set farther back from the road, and another across the railroad tracks directly in front of our house. This was the community in which I grew up, all within a stone's throw of the barn.

Thinking Critically about This Reading

How does Carter show his role on the farm changing over time? As he describes the place, which features remind him of the times he took on more—and more difficult—work?

Questions for Study and Discussion

1. Carter uses the paragraphs of this essay to lead readers on a tour of the farm. Where does he start and end? Where does he stop along the way? How do his paragraphs help to focus our attention on different locations around the farm?
2. In this excerpt, Carter characterizes his father indirectly, not by telling us who he was but by showing us his habits and tendencies. Which details do you think tell readers the most about him?

3. Jack Clark is important to the running of the farm. Carter introduces him in paragraph 2, and then offers a fuller portrait of him in paragraph 6. How does he develop this paragraph on Jack Clark's character? What information does he think is important for readers to know about him?
4. Carter discusses his increasing mastery of farm tasks and his role in the way the farm was run. What does he learn about the farm from his father? From Jack Clark? What does he contribute from his class at school?
5. The water pump, the only motorized device on the farm, was "viewed with a mixture of suspicion and trepidation" (paragraph 8). Using this quotation as a starting point, discuss the attitude of the family toward change and innovation.
6. Carter begins paragraph 9 with the metaphor of the farm as a well-kept machine. Why is this an apt way of thinking about it? How does the paragraph extend this metaphor? (Glossary: **Figure of Speech**)
7. The farm is the site of Carter's family business, but he also calls it a community. In what ways is this true?

Classroom Activity Using Paragraphs

In a business setting, writing usually has clear tasks to accomplish. The following paragraphs are from the opening of a proposal by a research consultant firm. Read the paragraphs, and then write a brief description of each paragraph's purpose. What information does each paragraph provide for the clients? In a group, compare notes and discuss how the writers develop each paragraph to achieve its purpose. Does the proposal style of writing differ from the kind of essays you write for class? How?

PROPOSAL TO PROVIDE MENTAL HEALTH CARE AND TREATMENT FOR THE VETERAN HOMELESS SUFFERING FROM POST-TRAUMATIC STRESS DISORDER (PTSD) IN GILBERT COUNTY

DAS Veterans Outreach presents a proposal to the Gilbert County Board of Supervisors to partner with Royal Consulting, LLC, to provide care to veterans who are homeless or otherwise indigent and suffering from the effects of post-traumatic stress disorder (PTSD) under the auspices of the recent United States

Veterans Administration mental health care block grant, otherwise referred to as the Coker Grant. DAS Veterans Outreach has experience across the state in locating, identifying, and assisting this special portion of the homeless population in receiving treatment and counseling. Royal Consulting's background in finance and operations of non-profit programs throughout Colorado offers an ideal complement to DAS Veterans Outreach's experience in the field. Though awareness of PTSD in the military has grown, it remains stigmatized, and when left untreated, can lead to self-destructive behavior and conditions like homelessness. The veteran homeless often need treatment and care that is far beyond their means and usually receive no help until the situation is exacerbated to the point where they end up in an emergency room, jail, or morgue. We are confident and excited about the possibility of extending mental health services to the veteran homeless suffering from PTSD in Gilbert County.

DAS Veterans Outreach is a non-profit organization working towards the goal of staffs necessary to complete all of the components of the proposed program: to locate and identify potential veteran homeless; provide initial diagnoses and treatment plans; and follow up with patients and their counselors. The comprehensive approach offers the ability to control both costs and quality of service. Because of DAS Veterans Outreach prior experience with Gilbert County Mental Health Services and with the Veterans Affairs Hospital located in Shaw, Colorado, we feel ideally suited to bring these services to those homeless suffering from PTSD. Royal Consulting's extensive experience with accounting for medium-scale government-funded projects such as this means that public funds will be tracked and accounted for using the most accurate and up-to-date methods. Taxpayers will be able to see and understand exactly how their money is being spent.

Our proposal follows the following organization: In Section 1, we discuss the approach, consider challenges we may face in dealing with the veteran homeless and their resistance to outside help, and offer strategies to reduce and counter these challenges. Section 2 details the work plan, including issues of staffing, and the overall project time line. We also address where services will be located to best reach the homeless. Section 3 describes the management plan and organizational and staff qualifications at both DAS Veterans Outreach and Royal Consulting, as well as résumés for staff, including the mental health personnel who will be contracted for this work. Section 4 presents our detailed budget and budget narrative. Finally, the Appendix contains our references.

Suggested Writing Assignments

1. Write a description of your campus or school. Following Carter's lead, make your virtual tour vivid for readers by focusing each of your paragraphs on one important feature of the place.
2. In the process of describing the "home place," Carter gives readers a clear picture of his father, though he does so indirectly. For example, rather than telling us his father was frugal and self-sufficient, he writes, "Daddy didn't believe in paying for something we could do ourselves," and describes how he repaired the family's shoes (3). Write an essay that paints a picture of a parent or another family member using that person's characteristic ways of speaking or acting to convey his or her personality. (Glossary: **Illustration**)

CHAPTER 8

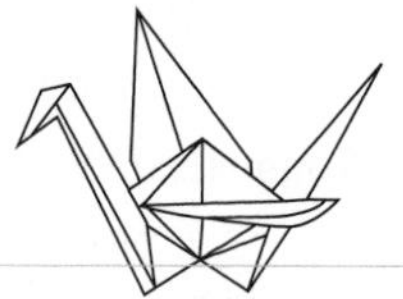

Transitions

A **transition** is a word or phrase used to signal the relationships among ideas in an essay and to join the various parts of an essay together. Writers use transitions to relate ideas within sentences, between sentences, and between paragraphs. The three major transitional strategies are

- transitional expressions
- repetition
- pronoun references

Perhaps the most common type of transition is the transitional expression. Following is a list of transitional expressions categorized according to their functions.

Transitional Expressions

Addition
and, again, too, also, in addition, further, furthermore, moreover, besides

Cause and Effect
therefore, consequently, thus, accordingly, as a result, hence, then, so

Comparison
similarly, likewise, by comparison

Concession
to be sure, granted, of course, it is true, to tell the truth, certainly, with the exception of, although this may be true, even though, naturally

Contrast
but, however, in contrast, on the contrary, on the other hand, yet, nevertheless, after all, in spite of

Example
for example, for instance

Place
elsewhere, here, above, below, farther on, there, beyond, nearby, opposite to, around

Restatement
that is, as I have said, in other words, in simpler terms, to put it differently, simply stated

Sequence
first, second, third, next, finally

Summary
in conclusion, to conclude, to summarize, in brief, in short

Time
afterward, later, earlier, subsequently, at the same time, simultaneously, immediately, this time, until now, before, meanwhile, shortly, soon, currently, when, lately, in the meantime, formerly

Besides transitional expressions, there are two other important ways to make transitions: by repeating key words and ideas and by using pronoun references. This paragraph begins with the phrase "Besides transitional expressions," which contains the transitional word *besides* and also repeats wording from the last sentence of the previous paragraph. Thus, the reader knows that this discussion is moving toward a new but related idea. Repetition can also give a word or an idea emphasis: "Foreigners look to America as a land of freedom. Freedom, however, is not something all Americans enjoy."

Pronoun references avoid monotonous repetition of nouns and phrases. Without pronouns, these two sentences are wordy and tiring to read: "Jim went to the concert, where he heard Beethoven's Ninth Symphony. Afterward, Jim bought a recording of the Ninth Symphony." A more graceful and readable passage results if two pronouns are substituted in the second sentence: "Afterward, he bought a recording of it." The second version has another advantage in that it is now more tightly related to the first sentence. The transition between the two sentences is smoother.

In the following example, notice how Rachel Carson uses transitional expressions, repetition of words and ideas, and pronoun references:

> Under primitive agricultural conditions the farmer had few insect problems. *These* arose with the intensification of agriculture—the devotion of immense acreages to a single crop. *Such a system* set the stage for explosive increases in specific insect populations. Single-crop farming does not take advantage of the principles by which nature works; *it* is agriculture as an engineer might conceive it to be. Nature has introduced great variety into the landscape, but man has displayed a passion for simplifying *it*. *Thus he* undoes the built-in checks and balances by which nature holds the species within bounds. One important natural *check* is a limit on the amount of suitable habitat for each species. *Obviously then,* an insect that lives on wheat can build up its population to much higher levels on a farm devoted to wheat than on one in which wheat is intermingled with other crops to which the insect is not adapted.
>
> *The same thing* happens in other situations. A generation or more ago, the towns of large areas of the United States lined their streets with the noble elm tree. *Now* the beauty *they* hopefully created is threatened with complete destruction as disease sweeps through the elms, carried by a beetle that would have only limited chance to build up large populations and to spread from tree to tree if the elms were only occasional trees in a richly diversified planting.
>
> –Rachel Carson, *Silent Spring*

Pronoun reference

Repeated key idea

Pronoun reference

Transitional expression; pronoun reference

Pronoun reference

Repeated key word

Transitional expression

Repeated key idea

Transitional expression; pronoun reference

Carson's transitions in this passage enhance its **coherence**—that quality of good writing that results when all sentences and paragraphs of an essay are effectively and naturally connected.

In the following four-paragraph sequence about a vegetarian's ordeal with her family at Thanksgiving each year, the writer uses transitions effectively to link one paragraph to another.

The holiday that I dread the most is fast approaching. The relatives will gather to gossip and bicker, the house will be filled with the smells of turkey, onions, giblets, and allspice, and I will be pursuing trivial conversations in the hope of avoiding any commentaries upon the state of my plate.

Reference to key idea in previous paragraph

Do not misunderstand me: I am not a scrooge. I enjoy the idea of Thanksgiving — the giving of thanks for blessings received in the past year and the opportunity to share an unhurried day with family and friends. The problem for me is that I am one of those freaky, misunderstood people who — as my family jokingly reminds me — eats "rabbit food." Because all traditional Western holidays revolve around food and more specifically around ham, turkey, lamb, or roast beef and their respective starchy accompaniments, it is no picnic for us vegetarians.

Repeated key word

The mention of the word *vegetarian* has, at various family get-togethers, caused my Great-Aunt Bertha to rant and rave for what seems like hours about those "liberal conspirators." Other relations cough or groan or simply stare, change the subject or reminisce about somebody they used to know who was "into that," and some proceed either to demand that I defend my position or try to talk me out of it. That is why I try to avoid the subject, but especially during the holidays.

Transitional time reference

Repeated key idea

In years past I have had about as many *successes as failures in steering comments about my food toward other topics.* Politics and religion are the easiest outs, guaranteed to immerse the family in a heated debate lasting until the loudest shouter has been abandoned amidst empty pie plates, wine corks, and rumpled linen napkins. I prefer, however, to use this tactic as a last resort. Holidays are supposed to be for relaxing.

–Mundy Wilson-Libby, student

How Chuck Taylor Taught America How to Play Basketball

Maya Wei-Haas

Valerie Grant

Maya Wei-Haas was born in Ann Arbor, Michigan, in 1986. She graduated from Smith College, summa cum laude, with a BS in geology and earned her doctorate in environmental chemistry from the Ohio State University in 2015. She has earned numerous awards and accolades, including the American Chemical Society (ACS) Ellen C. Gonter Graduate Student Paper Award in 2015. She worked in San Pedro, Belize, as a coral reef educator and in Alaska as a nutrient research assistant at the Toolik Field Station. Wei-Haas was an American Geophysical Union (AGU) 2015 AAAS Mass Media Fellow for *National Geographic,* where she published frequently in the "Weird and Wild" column. She has also written for AGU's *Eos* and *The Plainspoken Scientist*. She maintains her own website at mayaweihaas.com, where she posts stories and photographs from her many journeys across the world, particularly in the Arctic and Antarctica.

In this article, initially published on Smithsonian.com, where she was an assistant editor for science and innovation, Wei-Haas tells the history of the white Converse Chuck Taylor All-Star shoe, one of the most popular sneakers in the history of sports shoes. As you read, notice how Wei-Haas uses transitions of time and repetition as she traces the history of the shoe from the beginnings of basketball itself, telling the story of the shoe through decades of change in sports, the economy, and footwear.

Reflecting on What You Know

Think about items that you own, such as shoes, clothing, phones, or other commercial products. How many of them are attached to the name of a famous athlete or entertainer, such as Michael Jordan, LeBron

James, or Katy Perry? What role does the fame of such a person play in your interest in purchasing the product?

It was 1936, and the U.S. men's basketball team stepped onto the rain-soaked outdoor courts sporting bright white Converse shoes—patriotic blue and red pinstripes wrapping around each sole. The Americans were taking on the Canadians in the Olympic finals, and the conditions were miserable. As it poured, water inundated[1] the courts, turning them into a "sea of mud," according to the *New York Times*. But, in a painfully low-scoring game, the U.S. ultimately won 19-8. 1

This was basketball's inaugural year in the games and the first of seven consecutive Olympic gold medals for the U.S. men's team. But it also marked the first appearance of the iconic "Olympic white" Chuck Taylor shoes—a design still around to this day. 2

The history of the shoe is nearly as old as the game of basketball itself, and in a way both matured together. In 1891, YMCA physical educator James Naismith invented the indoor game, played with a soccer ball and two peach baskets, to keep his students fit during the frigid Massachusetts winters. Seventeen years later, Marquis Converse founded his Converse Rubber Shoe Company, also in Massachusetts, to produce rubber galoshes[2], a far cry from the canvas kicks the company is known for today. 3

The company churned out these protective boots for the wet spring, winter and fall, but sales inevitably dropped during the dry summer months. After two years of Converse firing his employees at the beginning of the slump and rehiring when the rains returned in autumn, the entrepreneur made a bid to keep his most skilled workers year-round. He started making a non-skid, canvas-topped shoe. 4

The first version was a low-top oxford kind of shoe, says Sam Smallidge, the head archivist at Converse. But these dressy sneaks quickly became associated with sports, specifically the rapidly spreading basketball craze. In 1922, the Converse Rubber Company hired a charismatic athlete named Charles "Chuck" Taylor as part salesman, part player-coach for the shoe's club team, the Converse All Stars. "It was all about promotion," says Abraham Aamidor, author of the book *Chuck Taylor, All Star*. "The team 5

[1]*inundated*: flooded; overwhelmed.
[2]*galoshes*: rain boots.

was not in a league, but would travel through small Midwestern towns and challenge the local hot shots to a game."

By Aamidor's count, the All Stars played about 30 games a year. In addition to these games, Taylor hosted clinics to teach people the relatively new sport. Sporting goods stores sent representatives to the clinics to sell Converse All Star shoes to the captive audience—touting[3] the kicks as the best basketball shoes around. "What Converse was doing was teaching America to play basketball," says Smallidge. But in addition to this, these clinics "allowed Converse to cement this relationship with basketball itself as being the premiere basketball shoe." 6

The clinics would often include a basketball game and a sideshow featuring Chuck and free-throw fiend Harold "Bunny" Levitt, according to Aamidor. "Chuck did his trick shots and Bunny Levitt never missed a free throw," he says. The duo would then pass out pocket-sized instruction books on how to play the game. Taylor traveled all over the country hosting clinics and promoting the shoes. Shoe sales were booming, but all was not well with the company. In the mid-1910s, competing rubber companies ventured into the production of rubber galoshes, which were still a Converse classic. So Marquis Converse tried to edge in on the competition's money-maker: rubber tires. 7

At the time, tires were a rapidly changing technology, and Converse couldn't keep pace. The Great Depression only added to the company's troubles, says Smallidge. "He sunk so much of his money into this tire business, so when the tire business collapsed, it kind of dragged the rest of the company down with it," he says. In 1929 Marquis Converse lost the company. The business changed hands several times. Hodgman Company had a brief stint, but its president died in a freak hunting accident soon after the merger, says Smallidge. Businessmen Joseph, Harry and Dewey Stone bought the floundering company in 1932. "The Converse name had lost its glitter," says Aamidor. "The company was in trouble." 8

Taylor, then the company's sales manager, decided to market himself as a great basketball player and add his name to the shoe, Aamidor explains. "He neither was a great player, nor did he play on some of the great teams that he said he played on," says 9

[3]*touting*: promoting; talking up.

Aamidor. But he did have moderate abilities with basketball and the connections in the field to make an impact. Though many—if not all—basketball coaches knew "it was a bunch of hooey," he says, they accepted the act and moved on. Taylor signed a contract with Converse to add his name in 1933, and the change went into effect the following year, says Smallidge. The All Star became the Chuck Taylor All Star.

As Taylor's popularity and infamy as a big-shot basketball player 10
grew, he continued to work the road selling shoes. It was his personal touches as a salesman that made all the difference, says Aamidor. For big college tournaments, Taylor often attended himself to support the teams and care for the shoes. If there were problems with stitching, fit or damages, Taylor was on hand to make the repair. "This would be like buying a basketball that has a Lebron James signature on it," says Aamidor, "and when you want to get it inflated to the right pressure, there's Lebron James doing it for you."

Similar to today, what people wore in large part came down to 11
marketing. "Chucks weren't the only canvas shoes with rubber bottoms," says Aamidor. Other shoe manufacturers at the time, such as Spalding and BF Goodrich, had similar options. "But they [Chucks] were the most expensive ones and the most elite ones," he adds.

Courtesy of United States Olympic Committee

The U.S. men's basketball team took the gold medal at the 1936 Olympics while sporting their Olympic white Chuck Taylor All Stars.

Converse's ultimate goal was to make shoes with the grippiest soles around. The tread pattern became fixed in the mid-1930s, and the patented design is still used in today's Chucks.

When the first Olympic team formed in 1936, and needed team sneaks, the company was a *shoe*-in. Converse debuted the "Olympic White All Stars" that year—a departure from the traditional black high tops. The shoe remained the Olympic shoe of choice for decades, but its popularity in sports began to peter out in the 1970s when players started expecting lucrative endorsement contracts. Converse didn't pay athletes to wear their products until 1975, when they gave Julius "Dr. J" Erving an endorsement deal. But even then, the company just couldn't keep pace with the massive deals and clothing lines that other companies began offering their players. The 1984 games was Converse's Olympic swan song. The company was the official footwear sponsor of the games, and the U.S. men's basketball team won gold sporting Converse's latest leather sneaks. 12

Even so, paralleling the company's popularity decline in the professional sports world was a growing following in rock culture. The introduction of seven colors of the shoe in 1971 bolstered this movement, and shoe sales pivoted from the courts to the streets. "Really it's the only clothing that you'll ever see old men, young girls, hipsters in New York, [all wearing]," says Aamidor, of Converse's now broad appeal. "Anybody is likely to be wearing those shoes." 13

These days, Chuck Taylor—the man—has been lost somewhere in history. He was inducted into the Basketball Hall of Fame in 1969, and died later that year. He is no longer remembered in his invented persona of a basketball star or as a spectacular salesman. Many people even assume the name is like Betty Crocker, says Aamidor—a brand name only. 14

But Taylor was indeed flesh and blood. His love of basketball and Converse shoes helped build the sport into a classic American game. 15

Thinking Critically about This Reading

In paragraph 9, Abraham Aamidor states that Chuck Taylor was not a "great player, nor did he play on some of the great teams that he said he played on." How did Chuck Taylor build his fame in order to sell shoes? What other athletes or aspects of sports can you name whose deeds are more mythical than real?

Questions for Study and Discussion

1. How does Wei-Haas use the Chuck Taylor All Star shoe to transition from her story of the United States–Canada gold medal game in 1936 to the origins of basketball in 1891?
2. How did basketball achieve popularity in its early days? What contributed to its success?
3. Wei-Haas points out that the Converse company almost went out of business by trying to compete in the tire-making industry. What were some of the problems that Converse faced?
4. Why is the story of Chuck Taylor himself crucial to understanding the appeal of the Chuck Taylor All-Star shoe?
5. What time transitions does Wei-Haas use to move the story of the shoe through the decades?
6. To what does the author attribute the continued popularity of the Chuck Taylor All-Star shoe? Did you find the evolution in the consumer of the shoe surprising? Why or why not?

Classroom Activity Using Transitions

Instructions for constructing and hanging a tire swing appear here in scrambled order. First, read all nine sentences carefully. Next, arrange the sentences in what seems to you to be a logical sequence. Finally, identify places where transitional expressions, repetition of words and ideas, and pronoun references give coherence to the instructions.

1. Attach your tire to the rope with another tight square knot. (Make sure your tire is hanging with the holes on the bottom.)
2. After it's clean, drill a few holes, evenly spaced, along the bottom half of the tire to act as a drain for rainwater.
3. Then, using a ladder, loop your protected rope over the branch, and secure the rope to the branch with a tight square knot.
4. First, pick a sturdy branch that is high enough to accommodate the length of your rope and strong enough to support your weight.
5. After it's secured, spread some mulch around the base of your tire swing to absorb any falls.

6. Then find a tire that is large enough to comfortably fit one person.
7. Now test your swing and have some fun!
8. Next, clean the tire thoroughly before getting to work.
9. When your tire is ready to be hung, get your rope and place rubber tubing over the section that will rest over the branch. (The tubing will help protect your rope from fraying.)

Suggested Writing Assignments

1. Write about your own experience of learning how to play a sport or perform another activity, such as playing a musical instrument or learning how to cook. How did you start to learn? What challenges or problems did you face, and how did you overcome them? When did you realize that you had succeeded? Make deliberate use of transitions to help your reader follow the timeline and identify the key points in your development.
2. Wei-Haas is writing about how two things developed at the same time, one helping the other: the canvas-topped sneaker and the game of basketball. Think about other situations when two different products had an impact on each other in terms of growth of popularity, design, or development. Write an essay tracing the development of the two, making effective use of transitional words and phrases, particularly expressions for cause and effect, comparison, contrast, and example.

The Phantom Toll Collector

Roland Merullo

Roland Merullo is an American novelist, nonfiction writer, and memoirist who was born in Boston in 1953 and raised in Revere, Massachusetts. He earned his BA and MA in Russian Language and Literature at Brown University and has traveled extensively in Micronesia, Russia, and Italy. His many books, some of which have been translated into Croatian, Chinese, Korean, German, Portuguese, and Spanish, include the following: *Leaving Losapa* (1991), *Revere Beach Boulevard* (1993), *In Revere, In Those Days* (2002), *Breakfast with Buddha* (2007), *Fidel's Last Days* (2008), *Lunch with Buddha* (2012), *Vatican Waltz* (2013), *Dinner with Buddha* (2015), and *The Delight of Being Ordinary* (2017). Critics of his work have noted his thoughtfulness and grace in dealing with the emotional lives of his characters.

In "The Phantom Toll Collector," first published as an opinion essay in the *Boston Globe* on July 27, 2016, Merullo reminisces about the time he was a highway toll collector for a summer. As you read, notice how effectively Merullo uses repetition of key words and ideas as well as transitional words and phrases to signal the relationships among the ideas in his essay and to emphasize his emotional responses to the events he recollects.

Reflecting on What You Know

As we grow older there is a tendency to look back on our lives with both regret and delight that we no longer are as we once were. As you reflect back on years gone by, what conclusions can you draw about your personal life experiences? Are you wistful about your younger days? Are you happy to be free of them? Was life better back then, or worse, and for what specific reasons? Have your memories reshaped your experiences?

The Massachusetts Turnpike Authority announced recently that its tollbooths would be replaced by electronic license plate readers. 1

EZPass holders won't notice much of a difference—a bit less disruption to the trip—but those motorists accustomed to actually handing money to a human being will have their plates scanned by high-speed overhead cameras and receive a bill in the mail.

The news bothered me, not because I stop to pay cash at Allston or Springfield, but because I used to be one of those guys standing in the little booth. Between my junior and senior years in college, my father got me a job collecting tolls at the Sumner and Callahan tunnels. If I remember right, the pay was $4.80 an hour, triple the minimum wage in those days. But even for someone who'd built swimming pools and scraped slop off food trays, the work wasn't easy. 2

Anyone who deals with the public knows there's a particular weight to engaging humanity in all its various manifestations. Workers for the Registry of Motor Vehicles are often maligned for being cranky, but try dealing, day after day, with some of the personalities that fan across the human spectrum, and see what happens to your sunny nature. 3

One of the difficult aspects of the job was the way it twisted ordinary interaction. For most drivers, you might as well have been a machine: in goes the dollar, out comes the 75 cents change. Multiplied by 10,000 in a given month, this perversion of human encounter could wear on you. These were pre-GPS days, though, and every so often someone would ask directions to Logan, Revere Beach, or Mass. General, and you'd enjoy a few seconds of conversation. 4

On a regular alternating basis, collectors took a shift "inside." You'd go along the catwalk, sucking carbon monoxide, and take refuge in the glass booth, mid-tunnel. There you'd sit for a stultifying hour, ready to report an accident or emergency. 5

Other breaks in the monotony were created by the . . . what's the nice word? . . . eccentrics. One sweaty afternoon, a cabbie paid, then hooked a thumb over his shoulder. "Look at the crazies I get, will ya," he said, and in the back seat was a couple, clad as they were at birth, involved in the act that sometimes leads to birth. Another time, a dark sedan pulled up to my booth, two hard-looking characters in front. The driver turned to his passenger and pointed to me, "This the guy?" he asked. The passenger leaned forward, eyed me for a few seconds, shook his head and off they went. 6

For the most part, though, the days were a blur of greasy bills and slippery quarters, a parade of expressionless faces. 7

That summer the collectors organized a softball team. We played half a dozen games, one of them against inmates on a field near the Deer Island jail. These were quiet guys, well behaved, doing time for 8 marijuana possession or child support arrears, and, for them, the game broke up a different kind of monotony.

One of my softball teammates fixed me up with his beautiful East Boston cousin, and then, as September approached, offered another kind of favor. “Ro,” he said, “why don’t you try to get on fulltime when you’re done with college? I could put in a word for you.” 9

He was offering me what mattered so much to him: the guarantee of a job. For life, if he didn’t screw up too badly. Now, though, like so many other guarantees of that sort, this one has disappeared. Cameras instead of humans. Automated phone machines instead of live operators. Intelligent gas pumps instead of attendants. Self-checkout at the supermarket. 10

And so the gleaming vehicle of progress speeds on, faster and faster, no time to stop for a chat, or even to ask directions. 11

Thinking Critically about This Reading

Increasingly we are shifting from activities that involve interactions with others to interactions with machines. For example, we now pump our own gas, we pay a robotic machine to wash our cars, and we use high-tech monitors to tell us what’s wrong with our cars. What are the pros and cons of such a change? What are we gaining and what are we losing? Are you more accepting of mechanization in some situations and not others?

Questions for Study and Discussion

1. What transitional expressions has Merullo used in paragraphs 1–3 to indicate contrast? (Glossary: **Comparison and Contrast**) Explain how each works.
2. Merullo uses transitional expressions that indicate concession or acceptance. Identify several of these transitions and explain how they work.
3. In paragraph 6, Merullo gives two examples from his time as a toll collector that broke the monotony. What is the purpose of each of these anecdotes? (Glossary: **Anecdote**)
4. What does Merullo mean when he writes in paragraph 4, “One of the difficult aspects of the job was the way it twisted ordinary interaction”?
5. Is Merullo for or against the elimination of toll collectors on highways? What evidence can you provide for your answer? (Glossary: **Evidence**).

Classroom Activity Using Transitions

Read the following three paragraphs from a student's narrative essay. Provide transitions between sentences and paragraphs so that the narrative flows smoothly.

> Last year, I got lost on a hike during an extended camping trip in Oregon. I lost the path where a storm had washed it out and could not find my way back. I walked in the rain all day, desperate to find a road that would lead me to some sign of humanity. I tried not to panic, but I was cold and exhausted, and I had no extra clothes or any gear with me to make camp for the night.
>
> I picked a direction and hoped it would lead me before long to a gas station or a restaurant—anyplace where I could get something hot to drink. After about twenty minutes I came to a little diner, but I could tell from first sight that it was closed. The sign wasn't lit, and it looked like the lights were off inside, too.
>
> One of the workers let me in through the kitchen and gave me the last of a pot of coffee, which wasn't that hot anymore, but I was not feeling picky by that point. I had not had cell phone reception since the morning, but she let me use the diner's phone to call my friends. She had to lock up and leave before they arrived, but she sent me out to wait under the front awning with a piece of pie in a napkin and a wool scarf that she said had been sitting in the lost-and-found box for months.

Suggested Writing Assignments

1. Using Merullo's essay as an model, reflect on a summer job you had that has changed in recent years. For example, is babysitting the same job it used to be? What is different now about the responsibilities, pay, and training? Be sure to pay particular attention to your use of transitions. You may want to revise your essay after reviewing the chart of Transitional Expressions on pages 182–83.
2. Write an essay in which you describe how your perception of someone or some event important in your life changed. How did you feel about the person or event at first? How do you feel now? What brought about the change? What effect did the transition have on you? Make sure that your essay is coherent and flows well: use transitional expressions to help the reader follow the story of *your* transition.

Teammates Forever Have a Special Connection

Dan Shaughnessy

Boston Globe/Getty Images

Born in 1953, Dan Shaughnessy is a native of Groton, Massachusetts. After graduating from the College of the Holy Cross in Worcester, Massachusetts, he began his career in 1977 as a sports writer covering the Baltimore Orioles for the *Baltimore Evening Sun*. He moved to the *Boston Globe* in 1981 and has been covering the Boston Red Sox in baseball and the Boston Celtics in basketball ever since. Shaughnessy has published books on sports, too, including *The Curse of the Bambino* (2004), which covered the heated Yankees–Red Sox rivalry, followed by *Reversing the Curse* (2006) after the Red Sox finally won the World Series in 2004. He was named the recipient of the 2016 J. G. Taylor Spink Award "for meritorious contributions to baseball writing" by the Baseball Writers' Association of America, the same group that votes on the induction of baseball players into the Hall of Fame.

In this article, originally published in the *Boston Globe* on June 24, 2016, Shaughnessy remembers his old baseball teammate, Stanley J. Kopec Jr. As you read, pay attention to how Shaughnessy moves from remembering the past to discussing the present, from team sports to individual sports, from teams to families, and back to his old teammate.

Reflecting on What You Know

With whom do you have special connections? It could be teammates, but it could also be other people that you have worked with on a common goal: fellow cast members in a play, people in a band, members of a club, employees at a job, or any other similar situation. What do these people mean to you now? What might they mean to you in the future?

Stanley J. Kopec Jr. died of brain cancer at his home in Pepperell at the age of 63 last week. He taught math, worked in high tech for three decades, and loved to play golf. By all accounts, he lived a quiet and happy life in Central Massachusetts. He leaves his wife, his sister, and extended family members. His obituary read, "As genuine as they come, there was not a bone of pretense in his body." 1

I know that's true. Fifty years ago, Stan was my baseball teammate. We always called him "Woody." 2

I lost touch with Woody a long time ago. We connected a few times at reunions and funerals — and occasionally he'd send me an e-mail about something in the world of sports — but life and choices simply sent us in different directions. 3

When a friend sent me a text notifying me of Woody's passing, I got to thinking about the bonds we form as teammates. 4

Woody played third base for the Groton Little League Braves in the mid-1960s. A chunky 10-year-old, he batted right, threw right, wore dark-rimmed glasses, and could really hit. I think he led the league in homers in his final year of Little League. We remained teammates through Babe Ruth summers and a couple of high school seasons. As a teenager, he was quiet, steady, and really good with the glove. We all knew he was better at math than the rest of us, but he wasn't one to brag about anything. He didn't slam his helmet when he struck out. He didn't call attention to himself. Just like the obit said, "there was not a bone of pretense." 5

If you play team sports, you have dozens, maybe hundreds of folks like this in your life. Through the random elements of geography, age, and skill level, you are thrown together with people who share the same goals as yourself. They become your daily sports family. Just like with real family, you don't get to choose who they are. And just like with real family, they can make you feel great, or they can make you miserable. 6

Boxers, golfers, gymnasts, skaters, and tennis players don't have the same experience. They're out there by themselves. They alone control their success or failure. There is nobody with whom to share glory. Likewise, there is no one to blame. It's all on you. We all know some team players who would have been better off in individual sports. 7

If you play team sports, you spend more time with your teammates than just about anyone else. You share things with them that no one else knows. You have your own language. You have inside jokes. A word to a teammate triggers a memory and a laugh. And only you and your teammates know what you are laughing about. 8

Courtesy of Dan Shaughnessy

Stanley J. Kopec Jr. (bottom row, second from the left) and Dan Shaughnessy (top row, second from the last on the right).

These bonds are forged through the sheer volume of time you spend with one another and the ways you learn to cope. A shortstop and second baseman develop their own signal system to tell one another who's covering second on the next pitch. Two guys who never get to play bond on the bench, sitting side by side, telling jokes and no doubt agreeing that they are getting screwed over by the coach. They are teammates. 9

Some teammates don't like each other. It's inevitable. Teammates do not ask to be put together, but the success of the team usually requires that they learn to live and work with one another. It's a life lesson. You learn that you don't have to like the other guy, but you're going to have to figure out how to work with him. Go back and listen to Denzel Washington's speech in *Remember the Titans*, when coach Herman Boone has his team visit the Gettysburg battleground and tells them, "I don't care if you like each other or not, but you will respect each other." 10

This dynamic never changes, not even at the highest levels of professional team sports. Pedro Martinez and Curt Schilling didn't particularly like one another, but for one season they put their personal stuff on the shelf and worked together to deliver a World Series championship to Boston. 11

When Larry Bird told us that Dennis Johnson was the best teammate he ever played with, Larry was not pretending that DJ was a better player or in any way a better guy than Kevin McHale. He was simply paying DJ the highest compliment he could deliver. Larry was telling us that DJ would do anything it took to win. DJ did not need to feed his ego. He did not need "touches." He would take the charge. He would wear himself out *guarding* Magic Johnson. And when Larry stole the ball on the inbounds pass against the Pistons, DJ would know that his job was to immediately cut to the basket. 12

The top of Mickey Mantle's plaque in Yankee Stadium's Monument Park says nothing about Mantle's seven championship rings, three MVP awards, or 536 homers. It reads: 13

Mickey Mantle

"A Great Teammate"

A teammate is someone with whom you shared . . . hits, runs, errors, and maybe coffee frappes after the games. Wins and losses. You had a common goal. You went through changes together. You grew up and probably grew apart. But wherever you go and whatever you do, your former teammates are part of your history. There was a time when the thing you were doing together felt like the thing that mattered most. 14

RIP, Stanley Kopec. 15

Thinking Critically about This Reading

In paragraph 6, in speaking of teammates, Shaughnessy states, "And just like real family, they can make you feel great, or they can make you miserable." What does this suggest about the similarities of both families and teams? Is a "family" the best metaphor to use, or is there a more appropriate comparison? (Glossary: **Metaphor**)

Questions for Study and Discussion

1. In paragraph 1, Shaughnessy cites a line from Kopec's obituary: "As genuine as they come, there was not a bone of pretense in his body." What does that mean? Why is that a desirable quality in a person?
2. Why do you suppose Shaughnessy makes the comment that Kopec did not slam his helmet when he struck out (paragraph 5)?

What does this comment suggest compared with the behavior of many of today's major leaguers?

3. Which paragraphs use pronouns to transition from one paragraph to the next? Is this the most effective transitional device in each case, or should Shaughnessy have used another means to make the transition?
4. Shaughnessy makes comparisons between team sports and individual sports, saying some teammates would have been better suited to individual sports (7). What qualities would make one not suited for team sports?
5. Shaughnessy points out that sometimes teammates do not particularly like each other but must learn to get along for the common good. Why does he bring up this potentially negative aspect of team sports?
6. How does the word "teammate" work as a transitional device to connect paragraphs 13 and 14? (Glossary: **Transition**)

Classroom Activity Using Transitions

The following sentences and clauses from the beginning of Lewis Carroll's *Alice's Adventures in Wonderland* have been rearranged. Place the sentences in what seems to you to be a coherent sequence by relying on language signals such as transitions, repeated words, pronouns, and temporal references. Be prepared to explain your reasons for the placement of each sentence.

1. but when the Rabbit actually took a watch out of its waistcoat-pocket, and looked at it, and then hurried on, Alice started to her feet,
2. In another moment down went Alice after it, never once considering how in the world she was to get out again.
3. Alice was beginning to get very tired of sitting by her sister on the bank, and of having nothing to do:
4. There was nothing so very remarkable in that; nor did Alice think it so very much out of the way to hear the Rabbit say to itself, "Oh dear! Oh dear! I shall be late!" (when she thought it over afterwards, it occurred to her that she ought to have wondered at this, but at the time it all seemed quite natural);

5. So she was considering in her own mind (as well as she could, for the hot day made her feel very sleepy and stupid), whether the pleasure of making a daisy-chain would be worth the trouble of getting up and picking the daisies, when suddenly a White Rabbit with pink eyes ran close by her.
6. once or twice she had peeped into the book her sister was reading, but it had no pictures or conversations in it, "and what is the use of a book," thought Alice "without pictures or conversations?"
7. and burning with curiosity, she ran across the field after it, and fortunately was just in time to see it pop down a large rabbit-hole under the hedge.
8. for it flashed across her mind that she had never before seen a rabbit with either a waistcoat-pocket, or a watch to take out of it,

Suggested Writing Assignments

1. Shaughnessy's article is a remembrance of a childhood friend. Write an essay describing a good friend of yours, how you met, what you do together, and how you envision life as friends in the future. Make sure that you use effective transitions to help your readers follow the timeline of your relationships and the shifts in your discussion between your description, your past, your present, and your future as friends.
2. Write about the role of sports in the lives of young people today. Are sports still a positive influence, as Shaughnessy's article claims, or have sports today become a problem, with the promise of money and fame creating an allure that only a few can ever achieve? Consider also the influence of performance-enhancing drugs, the push toward professionalism at amateur levels, and the emphasis on winning rather than simply competing. Be sure to use effective transitional expressions and devices in your writing to help your readers follow your argument.

CHAPTER **9**

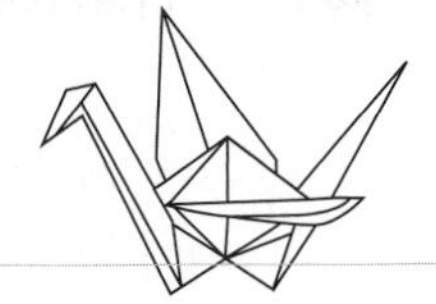

Effective Sentences

Although it often takes an entire essay or book to convey an idea, it is important to pay attention to each individual sentence, too. The way in which ideas are crafted into sentences and the variety of the types of sentences that we use can have a huge impact on readers' understanding and enjoyment of a text. Using different sentence patterns will not only keep readers interested in a text but can also make the ideas we are conveying more powerful.

Each of the following paragraphs describes the Canadian city of Vancouver, British Columbia. Although the content of both paragraphs is essentially the same, the first paragraph is written in sentences of nearly the same length and pattern, whereas the second paragraph uses sentences of varying length and pattern.

Unvaried Sentences

> Water surrounds Vancouver on three sides. The snow-crowned Coast Mountains ring the city on the northeast. Vancouver has a floating quality of natural loveliness. There is a curved beach at English Bay. This beach is in the shape of a half moon. Residential high-rises stand behind the beach. They are in pale tones of beige, blue, and ice-cream pink. Turn-of-the-century houses of painted wood frown upward at the glitter of office towers. Any urban glare is softened by folds of green lawns, flowers, fountains, and trees. Such landscaping appears to be unplanned. It links Vancouver to her ultimate treasure of greenness. That treasure is thousand-acre Stanley Park. Surrounding stretches of water dominate. They have image-evoking names like False Creek and Lost Lagoon. Sailboats and pleasure craft skim blithely across Burrard Inlet. Foreign freighters are out in English Bay. They await their turn to take on cargoes of grain.

Varied Sentences

Surrounded by water on three sides and ringed to the northeast by the snow-crowned Coast Mountains, Vancouver has a floating quality of natural loveliness. At English Bay, the half-moon curve of beach is backed by high-rises in pale tones of beige, blue, and ice-cream pink. Turn-of-the-century houses of painted wood frown upward at the glitter of office towers. Yet any urban glare is quickly softened by folds of green lawns, flowers, fountains, and trees that in a seemingly unplanned fashion link Vancouver to her ultimate treasure of greenness—thousand-acre Stanley Park. And always it is the surrounding stretches of water that dominate, with their image-evoking names like False Creek and Lost Lagoon. Sailboats and pleasure craft skim blithely across Burrard Inlet, while out in English Bay foreign freighters await their turn to take on cargoes of grain.

The difference between these two paragraphs is dramatic. The first is monotonous because of the sameness of the sentence structure and because the ideas are not related to one another in a meaningful way. The second paragraph is much more interesting and readable; its sentences vary in length and are structured to clarify the relationships among the ideas. Sentence variety, an important aspect of all good writing, should be used to express ideas precisely and to emphasize the most important ideas within each sentence. Sentence variety includes the use of *subordination, periodic and loose sentences, dramatically short sentences, active and passive voice, coordination,* and *parallelism.*

Subordination

Subordination, the process of giving one idea less emphasis than another in a sentence, is one of the most important characteristics of an effective sentence and a mature prose style. Writers subordinate ideas by introducing them either with subordinating conjunctions (*because, if, as though, while, when, after*) or with relative pronouns (*that, which, who, whomever, what*). Subordination not only deemphasizes some ideas but also highlights others that the writer believes are more important.

☑ **For more practice, visit the LaunchPad for *Models for Writers*: LearningCurve** > Coordination and Subordination

There is nothing about an idea—*any* idea—that automatically makes it primary or secondary in importance. The writer decides what to emphasize, and he or she may choose to emphasize the less profound or noteworthy of two ideas. Consider, for example, the following sentence: "Melissa was reading a detective story while the national election results were being televised." Everyone, including the author of the sentence, knows that the national election is a more noteworthy event than that Melissa was reading a detective story. But the sentence concerns Melissa, not the election, and so her reading is stated in the main clause, while the election news is subordinated in a dependent clause.

Generally, writers place the ideas they consider important in main clauses, and other ideas go into dependent clauses. Consider the following examples:

> When she was thirty years old, she made her first solo flight across the Atlantic.
>
> When she made her first solo flight across the Atlantic, she was thirty years old.

The first sentence emphasizes the solo flight; in the second sentence, the emphasis is on the pilot's age.

Periodic and Loose Sentences

Another way to achieve emphasis is to place the most important words, phrases, and clauses at the beginning or end of a sentence. The ending is the most emphatic part of the sentence, the beginning is less emphatic, and the middle is the least emphatic of all. The two preceding sentences about the thirty-year-old pilot put the main clause at the end, achieving special emphasis. The same thing occurs in a much longer kind of sentence, called a *periodic sentence,* in which the main idea is placed at the end, closest to the period. Here is an example from the *New Yorker's* Talk of the Town feature:

> On the afternoon of the first day of spring, when the gutters were still heaped high with Monday's snow but the sky itself had been swept clean, we put on our galoshes and walked up the sunny side of Fifth Avenue to Central Park.
>
> –John Updike

By holding the main clause back, Updike keeps his readers in suspense and so puts the most emphasis possible on his main idea.

A *loose sentence,* on the other hand, states its main idea at the beginning and then adds details in subsequent phrases and clauses. Rewritten as a loose sentence, Updike's sentence might read like this:

> We put on our galoshes and walked up the sunny side of Fifth Avenue to Central Park on the afternoon of the first day of spring, when the gutters were still heaped high with Monday's snow but the sky itself had been swept clean.

The main idea still gets plenty of emphasis, since it is contained in a main clause at the beginning of the sentence. A loose sentence resembles the way people talk: it flows naturally and is easy to understand.

Dramatically Short Sentences

Another way to create emphasis is to use a *dramatically short sentence.* Especially when following a long and involved sentence, a short declarative sentence helps drive a point home. Here are two examples:

> The qualities that Barbie promotes (slimness, youth, and beauty) allow no tolerance of gray hair, wrinkles, sloping posture, or failing eyesight and hearing. Barbie's perfect body is eternal.
>
> –Danielle Kuykendall, student

> Be specific. Don't say "fruit." Tell what kind of fruit—"It is a pomegranate." Give things the dignity of their names. Just as with human beings, it is rude to say, "Hey, girl, get in line." That "girl" has a name. (As a matter of fact, if she's at least twenty years old, she's a woman, not a "girl" at all.) Things, too, have names. It is much better to say "the geranium in the window" than "the flower in the window." "Geranium"—that one word gives us a much more specific picture. It penetrates more deeply into the beingness of that flower. It immediately gives us the scene by the window—red petals, green circular leaves, all straining toward sunlight.
>
> –Natalie Goldberg, "Be Specific," pp. 330–31

Active and Passive Voice

Since the subject of a sentence is automatically emphasized, writers may choose to use the *active voice* when they want to emphasize the doer of an action and the *passive voice* when they want to downplay or omit the doer completely. Here are two examples:

> High winds pushed our sailboat onto the rocks, where the force of the waves tore it to pieces.
>
> Our sailboat was pushed by high winds onto the rocks, where it was torn to pieces by the force of the waves.
>
> –Liz Coughlan, student

The first sentence emphasizes the natural forces that destroyed the boat, whereas the second sentence focuses attention on the boat itself. The passive voice may be useful in placing emphasis, but it has important disadvantages. As the examples show, and as the terms suggest, active-voice verbs are more vigorous and vivid than the same verbs in the passive voice. Then, too, some writers use the passive voice to hide or evade responsibility. "It has been decided" conceals who did the deciding, whereas "I have decided" makes it all clear. So the passive voice should be used only when necessary, as it is in this sentence.

Coordination

Often a writer wants to place equal emphasis on several facts or ideas. One way to do so is to give each its own sentence. For example, consider these three sentences about golfer Michelle Wie.

> Michelle Wie selected her club. She lined up her shot. She chipped the ball to within a foot of the pin.

But a long series of short, simple sentences quickly becomes tedious. Many writers would combine these three sentences by using **coordination**. The coordinating conjunctions *and, but, or,*

☑ **For more practice, visit the LaunchPad for *Models for Writers*: LearningCurve** > Active and Passive Voice *nor*, *for*, *so*, and *yet* connect words, phrases, and clauses of equal importance:

> Michelle Wie selected her club, lined up her shot, and chipped the ball to within a foot of the pin.
>
> –Will Briggs, student

By coordinating three sentences into one, the writer makes the same words easier to read and also shows that Wie's three actions are equally important parts of a single process.

Parallelism

When parts of a sentence are not only coordinated but also grammatically the same, they are parallel. **Parallelism** in a sentence is created by balancing a word with a word, a phrase with a phrase, or a clause with a clause. Here is a humorous example from the beginning of Mark Twain's *Adventures of Huckleberry Finn:*

> Persons attempting to find a motive in this narrative will be prosecuted; persons attempting to find a moral in it will be banished; persons attempting to find a plot in it will be shot.
>
> –Mark Twain

Parallelism is often found in speeches. For example, in the last sentence of the Gettysburg Address, Lincoln proclaims his hope that "government of the people, by the people, for the people, shall not perish from the earth." (See Chapter 2, p. 46, for the complete text of Lincoln's Gettysburg Address.)

☑ For more practice, visit the LaunchPad for *Models for Writers*: LearningCurve > Parallelism

White Lies

Erin Murphy

Erin Murphy was born in New Britain, Connecticut, in 1968 and grew up in Richmond, Virginia. She earned a BA in English from Washington College in 1990 and an MFA in English and poetry from the University of Massachusetts in 1993. Murphy is author of six collections of poetry, including *Too Much of This World* (2008), winner of the Anthony Piccione Poetry Prize, and *Word Problems* (2011), winner of the Paterson Prize for Literary Excellence. She is also coeditor of a poetry anthology, *Making Poems: Forty Poems with Commentary by the Poets* (2010) and *Creating Nonfiction: Twenty Essays and Interviews with Writers* (2016). Other awards include a National Writers' Union Poetry Award; a Dorothy Sargent Rosenberg Poetry Prize; a Foley Poetry Award; and fellowships from the Pennsylvania Council on the Arts, the Maryland State Arts Council, and the Virginia Center for the Creative Arts. Her poems have appeared in dozens of journals and several anthologies, including *180 More: Extraordinary Poems for Every Day,* edited by Billy Collins. She is on the faculty at Pennsylvania State University's Altoona College, where she teaches English and creative writing; she has received several teaching awards, including the university-wide Alumni Award for Excellence in Teaching.

First published in 2010 in *Brevity*, the following essay has been nominated for a Pushcart Prize. Murphy comments on her writing of the narrative and how she feels about it now: "This is a story that I carried with me for thirty years before I wrote about it. Now that I am a mother, I have a heightened awareness of the kind of bullying that is all too common in schools. When my own children came home with stories about classmates being ostracized, I thought of Connie and her candy. For decades, I've felt sympathy for Connie; from my current perspective, I also feel tremendous sympathy for her mother." As you read, notice how Murphy captures the reader's attention by crafting effective sentences.

Reflecting on What You Know

At what point do repeated mocking comments directed at our classmates and school friends cross the line into bullying? Have you engaged in such mocking comments? Have you been bullied? Have you come to anyone's rescue who was being bullied? Explain.

Arpi, a Lebanese girl who pronounced *ask* as *ax* no matter how many times the teacher corrected her, must have been delighted by the arrival of Connie, the new girl in our fifth grade class. Connie was albino, exceptionally white even by the ultra-Caucasian standards of our southern suburb. Only her eyelids had color: mouse-nose pink, framed by moth-white lashes and brows. 1

We had been taught that there was no comparative or superlative for *different*. Things were either different or the same, the teacher said. Likewise for *perfect*—something was either perfect or not. But surely Arpi thought of Connie as *more different* than herself. Arpi may have had a name that sounded all too close to Alpo, a brand of dog food, but at least she had a family whose skin and hair and eyes looked like hers. Connie, by comparison, was alone in her difference. She was, perhaps, *most different. Differentest.* 2

This was confirmed by the ridicule, which was immediate and unrelenting: *Casper, Chalk Face, Q-Tip.* Connie, whose shoulders hunched in a permanent parenthesis, pretended not to hear the names or the taunting questions: *What'd ya do, take a bath in bleach? Who's your boyfriend—Frosty the Snowman?* She sat in the front of the classroom, and if she felt the boys plucking white hairs from her scalp, she didn't react. The teacher, who was serving the last nine months of a thirty-year sentence in the public school system, spent the bulk of each day perusing magazines and L.L. Bean catalogs in the back of the room. As far as I know, she never intervened. 3

All of this changed in mid-October when Connie's father got a job at a candy factory, news Connie announced tentatively one rainy day during indoor recess. 4

Can he get us candy? 5

Yes. 6

Any kind? As much as we want? For free? 7

Yes, yes, yes. 8

And so the daily ritual began. Kids placed orders for Reese's Cups, Baby Ruth bars, Hubba-Bubba bubble gum. Connie kept a log of the requests in a pocket-sized notebook. The next day, she would tote 9 a box full of candy into the classroom and distribute the promised sweets to eager hands. Overnight, Connie became the center of attention. Girls—even Marcia Miller, the first in our class to wear mascara—would beg to sit by Connie at lunch so they could update their orders.

And what about me? What was my role? Did I request my 10
favorites—Three Musketeers and coconut-centered Mounds bars? Or did I, as I have told myself and others in the years since, refuse to contribute to such cruelty? Or, in a more likely scenario, did I dump out my loot triumphantly at home one afternoon, only to be scolded by my mother? I don't remember, my memory obscured, I'm sure, by the wishful image of myself as a precocious champion of social justice. And I don't remember if I actually witnessed—or just imagined—Connie and her mother at the 7-Eleven one day after school. They were in the candy aisle. Her mother was filling a cardboard box. And Connie, bathed in unflinching fluorescence, was curved over her notebook making small, careful check marks.

Thinking Critically about This Reading

In her essay, Murphy introduces an interesting technique for an essay writer. Murphy explains:

> This essay hinges on the use of what the writer Lisa Knopp calls "perhapsing." Sometimes when we're writing, we can't recall the exact details of our experiences. In this case, we can "perhaps" or speculate about what actually happened. In the final paragraph of "White Lies," I speculate about whether I saw or dreamt about Connie and her mother in the convenience store. The result of this rhetorical strategy is two-fold: it establishes me as a reliable narrator and allows me to question my own motives in "re-membering" (as in the opposite of "dismembering") the past.

How well does this strategy work for Murphy in her final paragraph? Explain.

Questions for Study and Discussion

1. Murphy's first sentence contains a lot of detail and uses parallelism to introduce Arpi and Connie. What is the effect of this beginning? (Glossary: **Beginnings and Endings**)

2. Murphy's story is brief, but how well does she satisfy the five essential features of good narration—a clear context; well-chosen details; a logical, often chronological organization; an appropriate and consistent point of view; and a meaningful point or purpose? Explain.
3. What point does Murphy make about the lack of comparative and superlative forms for some adjectives? Does reality support the grammatical rule? Explain.
4. Paragraph 4 is a single long sentence, followed by a series of very brief paragraphs consisting of short sentences. What is the effect of this? Examine other parts of Murphy's story. How does she vary her sentences and to what effect? (Glossary: **Sentence**)
5. What is Murphy's attitude toward Connie's classroom teacher? Why does she include information about her? (Glossary: **Attitude**)
6. What is the point of Murphy's story?
7. In the story, is Connie's mother a hero, or is she someone whose actions are ethically questionable, even wrong? Explain.
8. Assuming that the events in the convenience store actually took place, what motivates Connie's mother's actions? If you had been Connie's mother, what would you have done in her situation?

Classroom Activity Using Effective Sentences

Repetition can be an effective writing device to emphasize important points and to enhance coherence. Unless it is handled correctly, however, it can often result in a tedious piece of writing. Rewrite the following paragraph, either eliminating repetition or reworking the repetitions to improve coherence and to emphasize important information.

> Daycare centers should be available to all women who work and have no one to care for their children. Daycare centers should not be available only to women who are raising their children alone or to families whose income is below the poverty line. All women who work should have available to them care for their children that is reliable, responsible, convenient, and does not cost an exorbitant amount. Women who work need and must demand more daycare centers. No woman should be prevented from working because of the lack of convenient and reliable mother's child care.

Suggested Writing Assignments

1. Retell the story of "White Lies" from either Connie's or her mother's point of view or tell of a similar situation drawn from your own experiences as a schoolchild. Where does your story begin? What information do you need to tell it? What information might you have to supply by using the "perhapsing" strategy Murphy employs at the end of her essay? Murphy's theme is one of prejudice and marginalization, so if you are telling a story from your childhood you might want to base your narrative on a similar situation when you felt isolated and powerless or perhaps one in which you witnessed or were responsible for someone else feeling like an outsider.
2. Write a brief essay in which you tell of a time one or both of your parents came to your rescue when you thought yourself to be in a tight spot. Did they intervene in answer to your request for help, or did they simply see that you were in need? Were you thankful for your parents' help, or did their involvement make the situation worse? How did the "rescue" work out? Make sure to vary your sentences, using short and long sentences; periodic and loose sentences; and where appropriate, subordination, coordination, and parallelism.

Salvation

Langston Hughes

Historical/Getty Images

Born in Joplin, Missouri, Langston Hughes (1902–1967) became an important figure in the African American cultural movement of the 1920s known as the Harlem Renaissance. He wrote poetry, fiction, and plays, and he contributed columns to the *New York Post* and an African American weekly, the *Chicago Defender.* He is best known for *The Weary Blues* (1926) and other books of poetry that express his racial pride, his familiarity with African American traditions, and his understanding of blues and jazz rhythms. In his memory, New York City designated his residence at 20 East 127th Street in Harlem as a landmark, and his street was renamed Langston Hughes Place.

In the following selection from his autobiography, *The Big Sea* (1940), notice how, for the sake of emphasis, Hughes varies the length and types of sentences he uses. The effect of the dramatically short sentence in paragraph 12, for instance, derives from the variety of sentences preceding it.

Reflecting on What You Know

What role does religion play in your family? Do you consider yourself a religious person? Have you ever felt pressure from others to participate in religious activities? How did that make you feel?

I was saved from sin when I was going on thirteen. But not really saved. It happened like this. There was a big revival at my Auntie Reed's church. Every night for weeks there had been much preaching, singing, praying, and shouting, and some very hardened sinners had been brought to Christ, and the membership of the church had grown by leaps and bounds. Then just before the revival ended, they held a special meeting for children, "to bring the young lambs to the fold." My aunt spoke of it for days ahead. That night I was escorted to the 1 front row and placed on the mourners' bench with all the other young sinners, who had not yet been brought to Jesus.

My aunt told me that when you were saved you saw a light, and something happened to you inside! And Jesus came into your life! And God was with you from then on! She said you could see and hear and feel Jesus in your soul. I believed her. I had heard a great many old people say the same thing and it seemed to me they ought to know. So I sat there calmly in the hot, crowded church, waiting for Jesus to come to me. 2

The preacher preached a wonderful rhythmical sermon, all moans and shouts and lonely cries and dire pictures of hell, and then he sang a song about the ninety and nine safe in the fold, but one little lamb was left out in the cold. Then he said: "Won't you come? Won't you come to Jesus? Young lambs, won't you come?" And he held out his arms to all us young sinners there on the mourners' bench. And the little girls cried. And some of them jumped up and went to Jesus right away. But most of us just sat there. 3

A great many old people came and knelt around us and prayed, old women with jet-black faces and braided hair, old men with work-gnarled hands. And the church sang a song about the lower lights are burning, some poor sinners to be saved. And the whole building rocked with prayer and song. 4

Still I kept waiting to *see* Jesus. 5

Finally all the young people had gone to the altar and were saved, but one boy and me. He was a rounder's son named Westley. Westley and I were surrounded by sisters and deacons praying. It was very hot in the church, and getting late now. Finally Westley said to me in a whisper: "God damn! I'm tired o' sitting here. Let's get up and be saved." So he got up and was saved. 6

Then I was left all alone on the mourners' bench. My aunt came and knelt at my knees and cried, while prayers and songs swirled all around me in the little church. The whole congregation prayed for me alone, in a mighty wail of moans and voices. And I kept waiting serenely for Jesus, waiting, waiting—but he didn't come. I wanted to see him, but nothing happened to me. Nothing! I wanted something to happen to me, but nothing happened. 7

I heard the songs and the minister saying: "Why don't you come? My dear child, why don't you come to Jesus? Jesus is waiting for you. He wants you. Why don't you come? Sister Reed, what is this child's name?" 8

"Langston," my aunt sobbed. 9

"Langston, why don't you come? Why don't you come and be saved? Oh, Lamb of God! Why don't you come?" 10

Now it was really getting late. I began to be ashamed of myself, holding everything up so long. I began to wonder what God thought about Westley, who certainly hadn't seen Jesus either, but who was now sitting proudly on the platform, swinging his knickerbockered legs and grinning down at me, surrounded by deacons and old women on their knees praying. God had not struck Westley dead for taking his name in vain or for lying in the temple. So I decided that maybe to save further trouble, I'd better lie, too, and say that Jesus had come, and get up and be saved. 11

So I got up. 12

Suddenly the whole room broke into a sea of shouting, as they saw me rise. Waves of rejoicing swept the place. Women leaped in the air. My aunt threw her arms around me. The minister took me by the hand and led me to the platform. 13

When things quieted down, in a hushed silence, punctuated by a few ecstatic "Amens," all the new young lambs were blessed in the name of God. Then joyous singing filled the room. 14

That night, for the last time in my life but one—for I was a big boy twelve years old—I cried. I cried, in bed alone, and couldn't stop. I buried my head under the quilts, but my aunt heard me. She woke up and told my uncle I was crying because the Holy Ghost had come into my life, and because I had seen Jesus. But I was really crying because I couldn't bear to tell her that I had lied, that I had deceived everybody in the church, that I hadn't seen Jesus, and that now I didn't believe there was a Jesus any more, since he didn't come to help me. 15

Thinking Critically about This Reading

Why does Hughes cry on the night of his being "saved"? What makes the story of his being saved so ironic? (Glossary: **Irony**)

Questions for Study and Discussion

1. What is salvation? Is it important to young Hughes that he be saved? Why does he expect to be saved at the revival meeting?
2. Hughes varies the length and structure of his sentences throughout the essay. How does this variety capture and

reinforce the rhythms and drama of the evening's events? Explain.

3. What would be gained or lost if the essay began with the first two sentences combined as follows: "I was saved from sin when I was going on thirteen, but I was not really saved"?
4. Identify the coordinating conjunctions in paragraph 3. (Glossary: **Coordination**) Rewrite the paragraph without them. Compare your paragraph with the original, and explain what Hughes gains by using coordinating conjunctions.
5. Identify the subordinating conjunctions in paragraph 15. (Glossary: **Subordination**) What is it about the ideas in this last paragraph that makes it necessary for Hughes to use subordinating conjunctions?
6. How does Hughes's choice of words, or diction, help establish a realistic atmosphere for a religious revival meeting? (Glossary: **Diction**)

Classroom Activity Using Effective Sentences

Using coordination or subordination, rewrite each set of short sentences as a single sentence. Here is an example:

ORIGINAL: This snow is good for Colorado's economy. Tourists are now flocking to ski resorts.

REVISED: This snow is good for Colorado's economy because tourists are now flocking to ski resorts.

1. I can take the 6:30 express train. I can catch the 7:00 bus.
2. Miriam worked on her research paper. She interviewed five people for the paper. She worked all weekend. She was tired.
3. Juan's new job kept him busy every day. He did not have time to work out at the gym for over a month.
4. The Statue of Liberty welcomes newcomers to the United States. It was a gift of the French government. It was completely restored for the nation's two hundredth birthday. It is more than 120 years old.
5. Carla is tall. She is strong. She is a team player. She is the starting center on the basketball team.
6. Betsy loves Bach's music. She also likes Scott Joplin.

Suggested Writing Assignments

1. Like the young Hughes, we sometimes find ourselves in situations in which, for the sake of conformity, we do things we do not believe in. Consider one such experience you have had, and write an essay about it. What in human nature makes us occasionally act in ways that contradict our inner feelings? As you write, pay attention to your sentence variety.
2. At the end of his essay, Langston Hughes suffers alone. He cannot bring himself to talk about his dilemma with his aunt or uncle or other people in the church. Have you ever found yourself in a predicament with no one to turn to for advice or help? Why can it be so difficult for us to seek the help of others? Write an essay in which you explore answers to this question. Consider examples from your own experience and what you have seen and read about other people. Look for opportunities where your sentence variety can enhance the interest and drama of your essay.

We Should All Be Feminists

Chimamanda Ngozi Adichie

rune hellestad/Getty Images

Chimamanda Ngozi Adichie was born in 1977 in Nigeria, where she was raised in the house that had formerly been occupied by famous Nigerian writer Chinua Achebe. Her father, the country's first professor of statistics, taught at the University of Nigeria, and her mother was the first female registrar at the university. Adichie excelled in her studies of medicine and pharmacy while also editing the campus medical student magazine, *The Compass*. Eventually, she left Nigeria for the United States to study at Drexel University in Philadelphia, transferring later to Eastern Connecticut University and eventually receiving a master's degree in creative writing from Johns Hopkins University. While Adichie was still an undergraduate, she began working on her first novel, *Purple Hibiscus*, which was released late in 2003 and earned her the Commonwealth Writer's Prize: Best First Book. Her other books include *Half of a Yellow Sun* (2006), *The Thing Around Your Neck* (2009), and *Americanah* (2013). She has received numerous awards and recognitions, including a MacArthur Foundation "Genius Grant" in 2008.

In this excerpt, adapted from her acclaimed TED Talk titled "We Should All Be Feminists," Adichie speaks about the negative connotations she has confronted surrounding the word "feminist." She confronts in plain terms and everyday examples the oppression of women and the role that gender plays in society. As you read, notice how Adichie varies her sentence structure to achieve dramatic effect for her serious ideas while still using a conversational tone.

Reflecting on What You Know

What does the word "feminism" mean to you? Do you consider yourself a feminist? Why or why not?

We do a great disservice to boys in how we raise them. We stifle the humanity of boys. We define masculinity in a *very* narrow way. Masculinity is a hard, small cage, and we put boys inside this cage. We teach boys to be afraid of fear, of weakness, of vulnerability. We teach them to mask their true selves, because they have to be, in Nigerian-speak, a *hard man*. In secondary school, a boy and a girl go out, both of them teenagers with meager pocket money. Yet the boy is expected to pay the bills, always, to prove his masculinity. (And we wonder why boys are more likely to steal money from their parents.) 1

What if both boys and girls were raised *not* to link masculinity and money? What if their attitude was not "the boy has to pay," but rather, "whoever has more should pay"? Of course, because of their historical advantage, it is mostly men who *will* have more today. But if we start raising children differently, then in fifty years, in a hundred years, boys will no longer have the pressure of proving their masculinity by material means. 2

But by far the worst thing we do to males—by making them feel they have to be hard—is that we leave them with *very* fragile egos. The *harder* a man feels compelled to be, the weaker his ego is. And then we do a much greater disservice to girls, because we raise them to cater to the fragile egos[1] of males. We teach girls to shrink themselves, to make themselves smaller. We say to girls, "You can have ambition, but not too much. You should aim to be successful but not too successful, otherwise you will threaten the man. If you are the breadwinner in your relationship with a man, pretend that you are not, especially in public, otherwise you will emasculate him." 3

But what if we question the premise[2] itself? Why should a woman's success be a threat to a man? What if we decide to simply dispose of that word—and I don't know if there is an English word I dislike more than this—*emasculation*. 4

A Nigerian acquaintance once asked me if I was worried that men would be intimidated by me. I was not worried at all—it had not even occurred to me to be worried, because a man who would be intimidated by me is exactly the kind of man I would have no interest in. 5

Still, I was struck by this. Because I am female, I'm expected to aspire to marriage. I am expected to make my life choices always keeping in mind that marriage is the most important. Marriage can 6

---

[1]*ego*: a person's opinion of himself or herself.

[2]*premise*: an unstated argument or assumed position.

be a good thing, a source of joy, love and mutual support. But why do we teach girls to aspire to marriage, yet we don't teach boys to do the same? I know a Nigerian woman who decided to sell her house because she didn't want to intimidate a man who might want to marry her. I know an unmarried woman in Nigeria who, when she goes to conferences, wears a wedding ring because she wants her colleagues to—according to her—"give her respect." The sadness in this is that a wedding ring will indeed automatically make her seem worthy of respect, while not wearing a wedding ring would make her easily dismissible—and this is in a modern workplace. I know young women who are under so much pressure—from family, from friends, even from work—to get married that they are pushed to make terrible choices. Our society teaches a woman at a certain age who is unmarried to see it as a deep personal failure. While a man at a certain age who is unmarried has not quite come around to making his pick.

It is easy to say, "But women can just say no to all this." But the 7 reality is more difficult, more complex. We are all social beings. We internalize ideas from our socialization. Even the language we use illustrates this. The language of marriage is often a language of ownership, not a language of partnership. We use the word *respect* for something a woman shows a man, but not often for something a man shows a woman. Both men and women will say, "I did it for peace in my marriage." When men say it, it is usually about something they should not be doing anyway. Something they say to their friends in a fondly exasperated way, something that ultimately proves to them their masculinity—"Oh, my wife said I can't go to clubs every night, so now, for peace in my marriage, I go only on weekends." When women say "I did it for peace in my marriage," it is usually because they have given up a job, a career goal, a dream.

We teach females that in relationships, compromise is what 8 a woman is more likely to do. We raise girls to see each other as competitors—not for jobs or accomplishments, which in my opinion can be a good thing, but for the attention of men. We teach girls that they cannot be sexual beings in the way boys are. If we have sons, we don't mind knowing about their girlfriends. But our daughters' boyfriends? God forbid. (But we of course expect them to bring home the perfect man for marriage when the time is right.)

We police girls. We praise girls for virginity but we don't praise 9 boys for virginity (and it makes me wonder how exactly this is supposed to work out, since the loss of virginity is a process that usually involves two people of opposite genders). Recently a young woman was gang-raped in a university in Nigeria, and the response of many young Nigerians, both male and female, was something like this: "Yes, rape is wrong, but what is a girl doing in a room with four boys?"

Let us, if we can, forget the horrible inhumanity of that response. 10
These Nigerians have been raised to think of women as inherently guilty. And they have been raised to expect so little of men that the idea of men as savage beings with no self-control is somehow acceptable.

We teach girls shame. *Close your legs. Cover yourself.* We make 11
them feel as though by being born female, they are already guilty of something. And so girls grow up to be women who cannot say they have desire. Who silence themselves. Who cannot say what they truly think. Who have turned pretence into an art form. I know a woman who hates domestic work, but she pretends that she likes it, because she has been taught that to be "good wife material," she has to be—to use that Nigerian word—*homely*. And then she got married. And her husband's family began to complain that she had changed. Actually, she had not changed. She just got tired of pretending to be what she was not.

The problem with gender is that it prescribes how we *should* be 12
rather than recognizing how we are. Imagine how much happier we would be, how much freer to be our true individual selves, if we didn't have the weight of gender expectations.

Thinking Critically about This Reading

Adichie concludes, "Imagine how much happier we would be, how much freer to be our true individual selves, if we didn't have the weight of gender expectations." What does she mean by this? Do the examples she uses effectively convey the "weight" of gender expectations? Explain.

Questions for Study and Discussion

1. Adichie argues that the current definition of masculinity is a "hard, small cage" (paragraph 1). How does she support this statement?
2. Adichie says that men are required to be "hard," yet doing so weakens their ego. How does this happen? What examples does she use to support her statement?

3. Analyze Adichie's sentences in paragraph 3. How does she use sentence structure to heighten a sense of contrast between our treatment of genders?
4. Why does Adichie dislike the word "emasculation" (5) so much?
5. In paragraph 6, Adichie repeats the phrase "I know . . . ." How does repetition of this phrase help her make her point? What other examples of repetition can you find in her writing? (Glossary: **Repetition; Parallelism**)
6. Adichie says that the language of marriage is a "language of ownership, not a language of partnership" (7). What examples does she give to support this? Can you think of other examples that she does not use?
7. This essay was originally adapted from a speech. What aspects of her sentence structure seem more reflective of oral communication than written? Provide specific examples.

Classroom Activity Using Effective Sentences

Mark the sentences in Adichie's article according to what different types and devices she uses: long or short sentences, periodic or loose sentences, subordination, coordination, and parallelism. Make the markup visual to illuminate patterns or tendencies in her writing. Try highlighting in different colors or using a mixture of solid underlining or dashes. How often does Adichie use active voice, and when does she use the passive voice? When you are finished, what can you say about Adichie's writing style based on her sentences? Is there a trend? Discuss your results with others in your class. Talk about how you can use similar techniques in your own essays.

Suggested Writing Assignments

1. Adichie is concerned with how men and women are affected by gender stereotypes. In what ways have you been affected by cultural expectations of the roles men and women should play? Write an essay in which you examine how you may have incorporated those gender roles into your own life and how you may have rejected or resisted those cultural expectations. Supply specific details to support your thesis. (Glossary: **Thesis**) Use clear, effective, and varied sentence structures in your essay to make your writing more interesting and expressive.

2. One of Adichie's controlling ideas is that not only will women benefit from feminism, but men will, too. Consider the points she makes about gender roles that men are forced to conform to and how her examples support the argument that feminism will free men as well as women from stereotypical expectations. Write an essay showing how men will or will not benefit from feminism. You may wish to watch Adichie's TED Talks speech online, called "We Should All Be Feminists," to get a fuller understanding of her argument. As you write, be sure to use a variety of sentence structures — active and passive, subordinated and coordinated, loose and periodic — as well as sentences demonstrating parallelism to create an essay with a lively and varied style.

CHAPTER 10

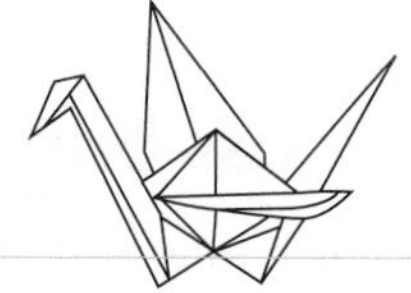

Writing with Sources

Some of the writing you do in college will be based on your personal experiences, but many of your college assignments will ask you to do some research—to write with sources. Although most of us can do basic research—locate and evaluate print and online sources, take notes from those sources, and document those sources—we have not necessarily learned how to integrate these sources effectively and purposefully into our essays. (For more information on basic research and documentation practices, see Chapter 23.) Your purpose in writing with sources is not to present quotations that report what others have said about your topic. Your goal is to take ownership of your topic by analyzing, evaluating, and synthesizing the materials you have researched. By learning how to view the results of research from your own perspective, you can arrive at an informed opinion of your topic. In short, you become a participant in a conversation with your sources about your topic.

To help you on your way, this chapter provides advice on the following:

1. Using outside sources in your writing (p. 226)
2. Summarizing, paraphrasing, and quoting sources (p. 228)
3. Integrating summaries, paraphrases, and direct quotations into the text of your essay using signal phrases (p. 233)
4. Synthesizing sources (p. 235)
5. Avoiding plagiarism when writing with sources (p. 238)

In addition, one student essay and two professional essays model different ways of engaging meaningfully with outside sources and of reflecting that engagement in writing.

USE OUTSIDE SOURCES IN YOUR WRITING

Each time you introduce an outside source into your essay, be sure that you are using that source in a purposeful way. Outside sources can be used to

- support your thesis,
- support your points with statements from noted authorities,
- offer memorable wording of key terms or ideas,
- extend your ideas by introducing new information, and
- articulate opposing positions for you to argue against.

Consider Don Peck's use of an outside source in the following passage from his essay "They're Watching You at Work," published in the December 2013 issue of the *Atlantic*.

> Ever since we've had companies, we've had managers trying to figure out which people are best suited to working for them. The techniques have varied considerably. Near the turn of the 20th century, one manufacturer in Philadelphia made hiring decisions by having its foremen stand in front of the factory and toss apples into the surrounding scrum of jobseekers. Those quick enough to catch the apples and strong enough to keep them were put to work.
>
> In those same times, a different (and less bloody) Darwinian process governed the selection of executives. Whole industries were being consolidated by rising giants like U.S. Steel, DuPont, and GM. Weak competitors were simply steamrolled, but the stronger ones were bought up, and their founders typically were offered high-level jobs within the behemoth. The approach worked pretty well. As Peter Cappelli, a professor at the Wharton School, has written, "Nothing in the science of predictions and selection beats observing actual performance in an equivalent role."

Here Peck quotes Peter Cappelli, a business school professor, to support his point that observations of workers in action have often been used to make hiring decisions.

The following passage comes from "Nature in the Suburbs," an essay that first appeared in *A Guide to Smart Growth: Shattering Myths, Providing Solutions*. The essay was adapted and published separately by the Heritage Foundation in 2004. Here environmentalist Jane S. Shaw uses several sources to substantiate her belief that "there is no reason to be pessimistic about the ability of wildlife to survive and thrive in the suburbs."

> This new ecology is different, but it is often friendly to animals, especially those that University of Florida biologist Larry Harris calls "meso-mammals," or mammals of medium size. They do not need broad territory for roaming to find food, as moose and grizzly bears do. They can find places in the suburbs to feed, nest, and thrive, especially where gardens flourish.
>
> One example of the positive impact of growth is the rebound of the endangered Key deer, a small white-tailed deer found only in Florida and named for the Florida Keys. According to *Audubon* magazine, the Key deer is experiencing a "remarkable recovery." The news report continues: "Paradoxically, part of the reason for the deer's comeback may lie in the increasing development of the area." Paraphrasing the remarks of a university researcher, the reporter says that human development "tends to open up overgrown forested areas and provide vegetation at deer level—the same factors fueling deer population booms in suburbs all over the country."

Note that in the last sentence of the second paragraph, Shaw is careful to say that she is quoting the *Audubon* reporter's paraphrase of a university researcher's thoughts and not the reporter's.

Sometimes source material is too long and detailed to be quoted directly in its entirety. In such cases, a writer will choose to summarize or paraphrase the material in his or her own words before introducing it in an essay. For example, notice how Scott Barry Kaufman, PhD, summarizes a lengthy creative-achievement study for use in his essay "Dreams of Glory," which appeared in the March 2014 issue of *Psychology Today*.

> Imagining future selves pays dividends long after school ends. In one of the longest and most comprehensive studies of creative achievement ever conducted, psychologist E. Paul Torrance followed a group of elementary school children for more than 30 years. He collected a wide variety of indicators of creative and scholastic promise. Strikingly, he found that the best predictor of lifelong personal and publicly recognized creative achievement—even better than academic indicators such as school grades and IQ scores—was the extent to which children had a clear future-focused image of themselves.

Here Kaufman introduces his summary by citing Torrance's name and giving his professional credentials (research psychologist). After briefly identifying the subjects and the length of the study as well as the data collected, Kaufman concludes with a pointed statement of Torrance's conclusion.

Finally, in the following passage from *The Way We Really Are: Coming to Terms with America's Changing Families* (1998), Stephanie Coontz uses outside sources to present the position that she will argue against.

> The fallback position for those in denial about the socioeconomic transformation we are experiencing is to admit that many families are in economic stress but to blame their plight on divorce and unwed motherhood. Lawrence Mead of New York University argues that economic inequalities stemming from differences in wages and employment patterns "are now trivial in comparison to those stemming from family structure." David Blankenhorn claims that the "primary fault line" dividing privileged and nonprivileged Americans is no longer "race, religion, class, education, or gender" but family structure. Every major newspaper in the country has published editorials and opinion pieces along these lines. This "new consensus" produces a delightfully simple, inexpensive solution to the economic ills of America's families. From Republican Dan Quayle to the Democratic Party's Progressive Policy Institute, we hear the same words: "Marriage is the best anti-poverty program for children."
>
> Now I am as horrified as anyone by irresponsible parents who yield to the temptations of our winner-take-all society and abandon their family obligations. But we are kidding ourselves if we think the solution to the economic difficulties of America's children lies in getting their parents back together. Single-parent families, it is true, are five to six times more likely to be poor than two-parent ones. But correlations are not the same as causes. The association between poverty and single parenthood has several different sources, suggesting that the battle to end child poverty needs to be fought on a number of different fronts.

By letting the opposition articulate its own position, Coontz reduces the possibility of being criticized for misrepresenting her opponents while setting herself up to give strong voice to her thesis.

LEARN TO SUMMARIZE, PARAPHRASE, AND QUOTE FROM YOUR SOURCES

When taking notes from your print and online sources, you must decide whether to summarize, paraphrase, or quote directly. The approach you take is largely determined by the content of the source passage and the way that you envision using it in your essay. Each technique—summarizing, paraphrasing, and quoting—will help you incorporate source material into your essays. Making use of all three of these techniques rather than relying on only one or two will keep your text varied and interesting.

Summary

When you **summarize** material from one of your sources, you capture in condensed form the essential idea of a passage, an article, or an entire chapter. Summaries are particularly useful when you are working with lengthy, detailed arguments or long passages of narrative or descriptive background information in which the details are not germane to the overall thrust of your essay. You simply want to capture the essence of the passage because you are confident that your readers will readily understand the point being made or do not need to be convinced of its validity. Because you are distilling information, a summary is always shorter than the original; often a chapter or more can be reduced to a paragraph, or several paragraphs to a sentence or two. Remember, in writing a summary you should use your own words.

Consider the following paragraphs, in which Richard Lederer compares big words with small words in some detail:

> When you speak and write, there is no law that says you have to use big words. Short words are as good as long ones, and short, old words—like *sun* and *grass* and *home*—are best of all. A lot of small words, more than you might think, can meet your needs with a strength, grace, and charm that large words do not have.
>
> Big words can make the way dark for those who read what you write and hear what you say. Small words cast their clear light on big things—night and day, love and hate, war and peace, and life and death. Big words at times seem strange to the eye and the ear and the mind and the heart. Small words are the ones we seem to have known from the time we were born, like the hearth fire that warms the home.
>
> –Richard Lederer, "The Case for Short Words," pp. 526–27

☑ **For more practice, visit the LaunchPad for *Models for Writers*: LearningCurve >** Summarizing

A student wishing to capture the gist of Lederer's point without repeating his detailed contrast created the accompanying summary note.

Summary Note

> Short Words
>
> Lederer favors short words for their clarity, familiarity, durability, and overall usefulness.
>
> Richard Lederer, "The Case for Short Words," 526–27

Paraphrase

When you **paraphrase** material from a source, you restate the information in your own words instead of quoting directly. Unlike a summary, which gives a brief overview of the essential information in the original, a paraphrase seeks to maintain the same level of detail as the original, to aid readers in understanding or believing the information presented. Your paraphrase should closely parallel the presentation of ideas in the original, but it should not use the same words or sentence structure as the original. Even though you are using your own words in a paraphrase, it's important to remember that you are borrowing ideas and therefore must acknowledge the source of these ideas with a citation.

How would you paraphrase the following passage from "The Ways of Meeting Oppression" by Martin Luther King Jr.?

> If the American Negro and other victims of oppression succumb to the temptation of using violence in the struggle for freedom, future generations will be the recipients of a desolate night of bitterness, and our chief legacy to them will be an endless reign of meaningless chaos. Violence is not the way.
>
> –Martin Luther King Jr., "The Ways of Meeting Oppression," p. 427

Paraphrase Note

> Nonviolence
>
> African Americans and other oppressed peoples must not resort to taking up arms against their oppressors because to do so would lead the country into an era of turmoil and confusion. Confrontation will not yield the desired results.
>
> Martin Luther King Jr., "The Ways of Meeting Oppression," 427

In most cases, it is best to summarize or paraphrase material—which by definition means using your own words—instead of quoting verbatim (word for word). Capturing an idea in your own words demonstrates that you have thought about and understood what your source is saying.

Direct Quotation

With a **direct quotation**, you copy the words of your source exactly, putting all quoted material in quotation marks. When you make a direct quotation note, check the passage carefully for accuracy, including punctuation and capitalization. Be selective about what you choose to quote. Reserve direct quotation for important ideas stated memorably, for especially clear explanations by authorities, and for arguments by proponents of a particular position in their own words.

Consider the accompanying direct quotation note. It quotes a sentence from Julie Zhuo's "Where Anonymity Breeds Contempt" (p. 129), arguing that anonymity encourages uncivil, trollish comments.

Direct Quotation Note

> Effects of Anonymous Comments
>
> "Psychological research has proven again and again that anonymity increases unethical behavior. Road rage bubbles up in the relative anonymity of one's car. And in the online world, which can offer total anonymity, the effect is even more pronounced. . . . There's even a term for it: the online disinhibition effect."
>
> Julie Zhou, "Where Anonymity Breeds Contempt," 130

On occasion you'll find a long, useful passage with some memorable wording in it. Avoid the temptation to quote the whole passage; instead, try combining summary or paraphrase with direct quotation. Consider the following paragraph from Mary Sherry's "In Praise of the F Word":

> Passing students who have not mastered the work cheats them and their employers who expect graduates to have basic skills. We excuse this dishonest behavior by saying kids can't

> learn if they come from terrible environments. No one seems to stop to think that—no matter what environments they come from—most kids don't put school first on their list unless they perceive something is at stake. They'd rather be sailing.
>
> –Mary Sherry, "In Praise of the F Word," p. 517

In the accompanying quotation and paraphrase note, notice how the student is careful to put quotation marks around all words borrowed directly.

Quotation and Paraphrase Note

Passing Not the Answer

Students and prospective employers are often deceived when students are passed through the school system, even if their work doesn't merit passing. The public "excuse[s] this dishonest behavior by saying kids can't learn if they come from terrible environments." But has anyone ever questioned the fact that "most kids," in spite of environment, "don't put school first on their list unless they perceive something is at stake"? Without an incentive, students will choose most anything over school.

Mary Sherry, "In Praise of the F Word," 517

If you are taking notes on the computer instead of by hand, you must be especially careful. You will need to avoid the temptation to simply copy and paste in an unorganized fashion from online sources, a practice that will likely lead to unintentional plagiarism (see pp. 238–42). Make sure you identify all summaries, paraphrases, and direct quotations appropriately and carefully distinguish them from your own ideas as you take notes and annotate sources. Keep track of the sources you are working with for each of your notes. It is important to stay organized and be methodical when it comes to note taking.

INTEGRATE BORROWED MATERIAL INTO YOUR TEXT

Whenever you want to use borrowed material (such as a summary, a paraphrase, or a direct quotation), your goal is to integrate these sources smoothly and logically and not disrupt the flow of your essay or confuse your readers. It is best to introduce borrowed material with a **signal phrase**, which alerts readers that borrowed information is about to be presented.

A signal phrase consists of at least the author's name and a verb (such as "Stephen King contends"). Signal phrases help readers follow your train of thought. When you integrate a summary, paraphrase, or quotation into your essay, vary your signal phrases and choose verbs for the signal phrases that accurately convey the tone and intent of the writer you are citing. A signal phrase also offers an opportunity to introduce the writer's bias, perspective, or expertise on the issue. (See pp. 601–2 for more on bias.) If a writer is arguing, use the verb *argues* (or *asserts, claims,* or *contends*); if a writer is contesting a particular position or fact, use the verb *contests* (or *denies, disputes, refutes,* or *rejects*). Verbs that are specific to the situation in your essay will bring your readers into the intellectual debate (and avoid the monotony of all-purpose verbs like *says* or *writes*). The following examples show how you can vary signal phrases to add precision to your essay:

> To summarize Amy Tan's observations about the English language, . . .
>
> Social activist and nutrition guru Dick Gregory demonstrates that . . .
>
> Mary Sherry, a literacy teacher and educational writer, advocates . . .
>
> June Tagney rejects the belief that "shame" . . .
>
> Bharati Mukherjee, an immigrant who chose to embrace United States citizenship, exposes . . .

Additional Signal Phrase Verbs

acknowledges	compares	grants	reasons
adds	confirms	implies	reports
admits	declares	insists	responds
believes	endorses	points out	suggests

Well-chosen signal phrases help you integrate summaries, paraphrases, and quotations into the flow of your essay. Besides, signal phrases let your reader know who is speaking and, in the case of summaries and paraphrases, exactly where your ideas end and someone else's begin. Never confuse your reader with a quotation that appears suddenly, with no introduction. Unannounced quotations leave your reader wondering how the quoted material relates to the point you are trying to make. Look at the following student example. The quotation is from Nancy Gibbs's "The Magic of the Family Meal," an essay that appeared in *Time* magazine on June 4, 2006.

Unannounced Quotation

> Older Americans love to reminisce about the value of family dinners that they enjoyed during their childhoods, the ones that Norman Rockwell immortalized in his cover illustrations for the *Saturday Evening Post*. These dinners were times when family members caught up with one another, exchanged ideas, got to know each other. It was there at the dining table that children learned their family's values, history, and culture. But family dinners gradually became less frequent as parents got caught up in careers and children became involved in more and more activities. As more people caught meals on the run, some began to realize that something was now missing. Not surprisingly, family dinners are now back in the news. "[T]he more often families eat together, the less likely kids are to smoke, drink, do drugs, get depressed, develop eating disorders, and consider suicide, and the more likely they are to do well in school, delay having sex, eat their vegetables, learn big words, and know which fork to use" (Gibbs). When was the last time you ate dinner with your family?

In the following revision, the student integrates the quotation into the text by means of a signal phrase, in which she gives the writer's name and position, as well as a brief description of the article in which the quotation appeared. The student provides this context so that the reader can better understand how the quotation fits into the discussion.

Announced Quotation

> Older Americans love to reminisce about the value of family dinners that they enjoyed during their childhoods, the ones that Norman Rockwell immortalized in his cover illustrations for the

> *Saturday Evening Post*. These dinners were times when family members caught up with one another, exchanged ideas, got to know each other. It was there at the dining table that children learned their family's values, history, and culture. But family dinners gradually became less frequent as parents got caught up in careers and children became involved in more and more activities. As more people caught meals on the run, some began to realize that something was now missing. Not surprisingly, family dinners are now back in the news. *Time* magazine editor Nancy Gibbs, in her report on the resurgence in family dining, emphasizes that "the more often families eat together, the less likely kids are to smoke, drink, do drugs, get depressed, develop eating disorders, and consider suicide, and the more likely they are to do well in school, delay having sex, eat their vegetables, learn big words, and know which fork to use." When was the last time you ate dinner with your family?

SYNTHESIZE SEVERAL SOURCES TO DEEPEN YOUR DISCUSSION

Synthesis enables you to weave together your own ideas with the ideas of others—the sources you have researched for your essay—in the same paragraph, so as to deepen your discussion or to arrive at a new interpretation or conclusion. By learning how to synthesize the results of your research from your own perspective, you can arrive at an informed opinion of your topic.

When you synthesize several sources in your writing, you create a conversation among your sources in which you take an active role. Sometimes you will find yourself discussing two or three sources together to show a range of views regarding a particular topic or issue—this is called *informational* or *explanatory synthesis*. At other times you will have opportunities to play your sources against one another so as to delineate the opposing positions—this is called *persuasive* or *argument synthesis*.

In the following example from her essay "The Qualities of Good Teachers," student Marah Britto uses informational synthesis to combine her own thoughts about good teachers with the thoughts of three other writers whose essays appear in *Models for Writers* (parenthetical citations refer to pages in this text). In doing so, she explains the range of attributes that distinguish good teachers from their peers.

> We have all experienced a teacher who in some way stands out from all the others we have had, a teacher who has made an important difference in each of our lives. While most of us can agree on some of the character traits—dedication, love for students, patience, passion for his/her subject—that such teachers have in common, we cannot agree on that special something that sets them apart, that distinguishes them from the crowd. For me, it was my sixth-grade teacher Mrs. Engstrom, a teacher who motivated with her example. She never asked me to do anything that she was not willing to do herself. How many teachers show their love of ornithology by taking a student out for a bird walk at 5:30 in the morning, on a school day no less? For Thomas L. Friedman, it was his high school journalism teacher, Hattie M. Steinberg. In "My Favorite Teacher," he relates how her insistence upon the importance of "fundamentals" (96) made a lifelong impression on him, so much so that he never had to take another journalism course. For Carl T. Rowan, it was his high school English, history, and civics teacher, Miss Bessie Taylor Gwynn, whose influence he captures in "Unforgettable Miss Bessie." Miss Bessie taught Rowan to hold himself to high standards, to refuse "to lower [his] standards to those of the crowd" (370). And for Russell Baker, it was Mr. Fleagle, his high school English teacher. He recalls how prim and proper and predictable Mr. Fleagle was in the classroom. But that all changed after Mr. Fleagle read one of Baker's essays aloud. In doing that, his teacher had opened Baker's eyes to "a calling" and had given him "the happiest moment of [his] entire school career" (328). Interestingly, isn't it mutual respect and appreciation that is at the heart of any memorable student-teacher bond?

This second example is taken from student Bonnie Sherman's essay "Should Shame Be Used as Punishment?" Here she uses argument synthesis deftly to combine Hawthorne's use of shame in *The Scarlet Letter* with two opposing essays about shame as punishment, both of which appear in this text. Notice how Sherman uses her own reading of *The Scarlet Letter* as evidence to side ultimately with Professor Kahan's position.

> Shame has long been used as an alternative punishment to more traditional sentences of corporeal punishment, jail time, or community service. American colonists used the stocks to publicly humiliate citizens for their transgressions. In *The Scarlet Letter*, for example, Nathaniel Hawthorne recounts the story of how the

> community of Boston punished Hester Prynne for her adulterous affair by having her wear a scarlet letter "A" on her breast as a badge of shame. Such punishments were controversial then and continue to spark heated debate in the world of criminal justice today. Like June Tangney, psychology professor at George Mason University, many believe that shaming punishments — designed to humiliate offenders — are unusually cruel and should be abandoned. In her article "Condemn the Crime, Not the Person," she argues that "shame serves to escalate the very destructive patterns of behavior we aim to curb" (553). Interestingly, Hester Prynne's post-punishment life of community service and charitable work does not seem to bear out Tangney's claim. In contrast, Yale Law School professor Dan M. Kahan believes that Tangney's "anxieties about shame . . . seem overstated," and he persuasively supports this position in his essay "Shame Is Worth a Try" by citing a study showing that the threat of public humiliation generates more compliance than does the threat of jail time (558).

Instead of simply presenting your sources in a quotation here and a summary there in your essay, look for opportunities to use synthesis — to go beyond an individual source by relating several of your sources to one another and to your own thesis. Use the following checklist to help you with synthesis in your writing.

Checklist for Writing a Synthesis

1. Start by writing a brief summary of each source that you will be referring to in your synthesis.
2. Explain in your own words how your sources are related to one another and to your own ideas. For example, what assumptions do your sources share? Do your sources present opposing views? Do your sources illustrate a range or diversity of opinions? Do your sources support or challenge your ideas?
3. Have a clear idea or topic sentence for each paragraph before starting to write.
4. Combine information from two or more sources with your own ideas to support or illustrate your main idea.
5. Use signal phrases and parenthetical citations to show your readers the source of your borrowed materials.
6. Have fresh interpretations or conclusions as a goal each time you synthesize sources.

AVOID PLAGIARISM

Honesty and accuracy with sources are essential. Any material that you have borrowed word for word must be placed within quotation marks and be properly cited. Any idea, explanation, or argument that you have paraphrased or summarized must be documented, and you must show clearly where the paraphrased or summarized material begins and ends. In short, to use someone else's idea—whether in its original form or in an altered form—without proper acknowledgment is to be guilty of **plagiarism**.

You must acknowledge and document the source of your information whenever you do any of the following:

- Quote a source word for word
- Refer to information and ideas from another source that you present in your own words as either a paraphrase or a summary
- Cite statistics, tables, charts, graphs, or other visuals

You do not need to document the following types of information:

- Your own observations, experiences, ideas, and opinions
- Factual information available in many sources (information known as *common knowledge*)
- Proverbs, sayings, or familiar quotations

For a discussion of MLA style for in-text documentation practices, see pages 606–8 of Chapter 23. For a discussion of APA style, see pages 623–25 of Chapter 23.

The Council of Writing Program Administrators offers the following helpful definition of *plagiarism* in academic settings for administrators, faculty, and students: "In an instructional setting, plagiarism occurs when a writer deliberately uses someone else's language, ideas, or other (not common knowledge) material without acknowledging its source." Accusations of plagiarism can be substantiated even if plagiarism is accidental. A little attention and effort during the note-taking stage can go a long way toward eliminating inadvertent plagiarism. Check all direct quotations against the wording of the original, and double-check your paraphrases to be sure that you have not used the writer's wording or sentence structure.

It is easy to forget to put quotation marks around material taken verbatim or to use the same sentence structure and most of the same words—substituting a synonym here and there—and treat it as a paraphrase. In working closely with the ideas and words of others, intellectual honesty demands that we distinguish between what we borrow—acknowledging it in a citation—and what is our own.

While writing, be careful whenever you incorporate one of your notes into your paper. Make sure that you put quotation marks around material taken verbatim, and double-check your text against your notes—or, better yet, against the original if you have it on hand—to make sure that your quotation is accurate. When paraphrasing or summarizing, make sure you do not inadvertently borrow key words or sentence structures from the original.

Using Quotation Marks for Language Borrowed Directly

When you use another person's exact words or sentences, you must enclose the borrowed language in quotation marks. Without quotation marks, you give your reader the impression that the wording is your own. Even if you cite the source, you are guilty of plagiarism if you fail to use quotation marks. The following examples demonstrate both plagiarism and a correct citation for a direct quotation.

Original Source

> So Grant and Lee were in complete contrast, representing two diametrically opposed elements in American life. Grant was the modern man emerging; beyond him, ready to come on the stage, was the great age of steel and machinery, of crowded cities and a restless burgeoning vitality.
>
> –Bruce Catton, "Grant and Lee: A Study in Contrasts," p. 125

Plagiarism

> So Grant and Lee were in complete contrast, according to Civil War historian Bruce Catton, representing two diametrically opposed elements in American life. Grant was the modern man emerging; beyond him, ready to come on the stage, was the great age of steel and machinery, of crowded cities and a restless burgeoning vitality (125).

Correct Citation of Borrowed Words in Quotation Marks

"Grant and Lee were in complete contrast," according to Civil War historian Bruce Catton, "representing two diametrically opposed elements in American life. Grant was the modern man emerging; beyond him, ready to come on the stage, was the great age of steel and machinery, of crowded cities and a restless burgeoning vitality" (125).

Using Your Own Words and Word Order When Summarizing and Paraphrasing

When summarizing or paraphrasing a source, you must use your own language. Pay attention to word choice and word order, especially if you are paraphrasing. Remember that it is not enough simply to use a synonym here or there and think that you have paraphrased the source; you *must* restate the original idea in your own words, using your own style and sentence structure. In the following examples, notice how plagiarism can occur when care is not taken in the wording or sentence structure of a paraphrase. Notice that in the acceptable paraphrase, the student writer uses her own language and sentence structure.

Original Source

Stereotypes are a kind of gossip about the world, a gossip that makes us prejudge people before we ever lay eyes upon them. Hence it is not surprising that stereotypes have something to do with the dark world of prejudice. Explore most prejudices (note that the word means prejudgment) and you will find a cruel stereotype at the core of each one.

–Robert L. Heilbroner, "Don't Let Stereotypes Warp Your Judgments," *Think* magazine, June 1961, p. 43

Unacceptably Close Wording

According to Heilbroner, we prejudge other people even before we have seen them when we think in stereotypes. That stereotypes are related to the ugly world of prejudice should not surprise anyone. If you explore the heart of most prejudices, beliefs that literally prejudge, you will discover a mean stereotype lurking (43).

Unacceptably Close Sentence Structure

Heilbroner believes that stereotypes are images of people, images that enable people to prejudge other people before they have seen them. Therefore, no one should find it surprising that stereotypes are somehow related to the ugly world of prejudice. Examine most prejudices (the word literally means prejudgment) and you will uncover a vicious stereotype at the center of each (43).

Acceptable Paraphrase

Heilbroner believes that there is a link between stereotypes and the hurtful practice of prejudice. Stereotypes make for easy conversation, a kind of shorthand that enables us to find fault with people before ever meeting them. If you were to dissect most human prejudices, you would likely discover an ugly stereotype lurking somewhere inside them (43).

Review the following Avoiding Plagiarism box as you proofread your final draft and check your citations one last time. If at any time while you are taking notes or writing your essay you have a question about plagiarism, consult your instructor for clarification and guidance before proceeding.

Avoiding Plagiarism

Questions to Ask about Direct Quotations

- Do quotation marks clearly indicate the language that I borrowed verbatim?
- Is the language of the quotation accurate, with no missing or misquoted words or phrases?
- Do the brackets or ellipsis marks clearly indicate any changes or omissions I have introduced?
- Does a signal phrase naming the author introduce each quotation?
- Does the verb in the signal phrase help establish a context for each quotation?
- Does a parenthetical page citation follow each quotation?

Questions to Ask about Summaries and Paraphrases

- Is each summary or paraphrase written in my own words and style?
- Does each summary or paraphrase accurately represent the opinion, position, or reasoning of the original writer?
- Does each summary or paraphrase start with a signal phrase so that readers know where my borrowed material begins?
- Does each summary or paraphrase conclude with a parenthetical page citation?

Questions to Ask about Facts and Statistics

- Do I use a signal phrase or some other marker to introduce each fact or statistic that is not common knowledge so that readers know where the borrowed material begins?
- Is each fact or statistic that is not common knowledge clearly documented with a parenthetical page citation?

How to Teach Children That Failure Is the Secret to Success

Tara Haelle

Tara Haelle was born in Alameda County, California, in 1978. She has both a bachelor's and a master's degree from the University of Texas at Austin, the latter in photojournalism. She specializes in writing about health and science and has numerous publication credits, having published in *Scientific American, Slate, Forbes,* and *Politico,* among many others. Haelle has taken on the anti-vaccine movement and delivered a TEDx talk in Oslo, Norway, "Why Parents Fear Vaccines." Her first book, co-authored with Emily Willingham, is *The Informed Parent: A Science-Based Resource for Your Child's First Four Years* (2106). She has also published nonfiction children's books: *Seasons, Tides, and Lunar Phases* (2016); *Edible Sunlight* (2016); *Insects as Predators* (2016); and *Insects as Parasites* (2016).

In this article, which was initially published in the National Public Radio Web site column Health News on May 6, 2016, Haelle writes about how parents can have a good or bad influence on how children respond to their own failures. As you read, pay attention to how Haelle integrates quotations from experts and published studies to support the thesis rather than just rely on her own personal experiences. (Note that Haelle's article was published online, with a journalistic style that does not necessarily require the same more formal or complete citations that you will need to use in academic writing. For more on citation style, see Chapter 23.)

Reflecting on What You Know

How were you raised to think about failure? Were you punished for failure, or did you learn to accept failure as a part of the learning process? Were failures in some areas of your life accepted while others were not? Consider the impact these issues have on your attitude toward failure today, especially as it applies to your education.

Is failure a positive opportunity to learn and grow, or is it a negative experience that hinders success? How parents answer that question has a big influence on how much children think they can improve their intelligence through hard work, a study says. "Parents are a really critical force in child development when you think about how motivation and mindsets develop," says Kyla Haimovitz, a professor of psychology at Stanford University. She coauthored the study, published in *Psychological Science* with colleague Carol Dweck, who pioneered research on mindsets. "Parents have this powerful effect really early on and throughout childhood to send messages about what is failure, how to respond to it." 1

Although there's been a lot of research on how these forces play out, relatively little looks at what parents can do to motivate their kids in school, Haimovitz says. This study begins filling that gap. "There is a fair amount of evidence showing that when children view their abilities as more malleable and something they can change over time, then they deal with obstacles in a more constructive way," says Gail Heyman, a professor of psychology at the University of California at San Diego who was not involved in this study. 2

But communicating that message to children is not simple. "Parents need to represent this to their kids in the ways they react about their kids' failures and setbacks," Haimovitz says. "We need to really think about what's visible to the other person, what message I'm sending in terms of my words and my deeds." In other words, if a child comes home with a D on a math test, how a parent responds will influence how the child perceives their own ability to learn math. Even a well-intentioned, comforting response of "It's OK, you're still a great writer" may send the message that it's time to give up on math rather than learn from the problems they got wrong, Haimovitz explains. 3

She and Dweck conducted a series of smaller studies to explore how the interactions between parents' failure and intelligence mindsets affected their children's beliefs about intelligence. First they interviewed 73 parents and their fourth- and fifth-grade children about their beliefs on failure and intelligence. The parents were mostly mothers with at least a college degree; they lived in the San Francisco Bay Area. The questions focused on whether they viewed intelligence as something that could change and whether they saw failure as positive, facilitating growth and enhancing productivity or as negative, debilitating and inhibiting learning. 4

The way children perceived "being smart" was not related to how their parents perceived intelligence, but it was related to how their parents reacted toward failure. "Parents who had more of a failure-is-debilitating mindset had children who were significantly more likely to believe that intelligence is fixed," they found, even after accounting for how parents perceived their children's academic success. "The more parents believed that failure is debilitating, the more likely their children were to see them as concerned with their performance outcomes and grades rather than their learning and improvement," the study found. 5

Then the researchers surveyed 160 different parents online to find out how they would respond to their child coming home with a failing quiz grade. Those who saw failure as negative were more likely to worry about their child's abilities in that subject or to comfort their child about not being talented in all subjects. But parents who saw failure as an opportunity were more likely to ask their child what they learned from the quiz, what they still can learn and whether asking the teacher for help would be useful. 6

Through two more surveys of 102 Bay Area parents and their children and 100 fourth and fifth-grade students, the researchers found that children could correctly identify their parents' beliefs about failure but not necessarily about intelligence—and it was the former that matched up with the children's own beliefs about intelligence. Finally, the researchers conducted a randomized experiment with 132 parents to discover whether parents' failure beliefs directly cause their children's beliefs through parents' reactions to failure: they did. "The takeaway is that when your child is struggling on something or has setbacks, don't focus on their abilities, focus on what they can learn from it," Haimovitz says. One way, she says, is to ask a child: "How can you use this as a jumping-off point?" 7

But it's unclear how much the study's findings relate to children of various ethnic, racial and socioeconomic backgrounds. Related research Heyman has done in China revealed a mixed bag in terms of results. "Cultures have very different beliefs about effort and ability, and asking subtly different questions you can get different answers," Heyman says. 8

Whereas academic success often correlates with athletic or social success among white students, the same is not necessarily true among black or Latino students, according to Cleopatra Abdou, an assistant professor of psychology at the University of Southern California. What 9 is consistent across cultures, however, is the powerful influence that beliefs people internalize as children follow them through life. "The messages we get from our parents, whether explicitly or symbolically or subconsciously, stay with us and are very hard to unlearn and to overcome" if they're not helpful, she says. "Sometimes we have internalized faulty beliefs or beliefs that don't serve us."

Further, taking the learn-from-failure message too far might backfire eventually. "If you're being told this message you can learn anything and you've done everything you can and you're not getting anywhere, then maybe at a certain point you're going to say I just don't believe this," she adds. Further, children's mindsets can also be influenced by their temperament, such as their tolerance for frustration, Heyman says. "One thing we do know in recent years, there's too much blaming of parents," Heyman says. "Temperament is extremely important and it's biologically based, and to deny that causes all kinds of problems." 10

The challenge for parents is to support children without setting them up for failure. "There's this very difficult fine line between parents and teachers helping children enough so that they can do things on their own that they couldn't do otherwise but not to help them so much that they expect other people to do it for them and don't get pulled up to a higher level," Heyman says. "You slowly pull back as the kids get better on their own, but not let them flail around so much that they get frustrated and give up." 11

Thinking Critically about This Reading

Much of the argument in Haelle's article rests on how parents view failure, but underpinning that is the question of the nature of intelligence and the learning process: is intelligence a fixed quality, or is it something that can change? What do you think about intelligence? What effect does the question of intelligence have on the ability of children to learn in school?

Questions for Study and Discussion

1. Haelle states that parents have a "big influence on how much children think they can improve their intelligence through hard work" (paragraph 1). Did this statement surprise you? Why or why not?

2. In paragraph 2, Haelle quotes a psychologist, Gail Heyman, who was not involved in the study conducted by Kyla Haimovitz and Carol Dweck. What is the advantage of consulting a third party for comment on the issues that the study is based on?
3. You're probably familiar with the old saying, "Do as I say, not as I do." How does this relate to Haimovitz's statement, "We need to really think about what's visible to the other person, what message I'm sending in terms of my words and my deeds" (3)? Why are words given equal importance here?
4. In paragraph 4, Haelle begins a more detailed discussion of the study conducted by Haimovitz and Dweck. What did you learn from the methods they used to conduct the study? What effect(s) do you think their methodology may have had on their results?
5. Haimovitz states, "One way [to deal with failure] is to ask a child, 'How can you use this as a jumping-off point?' " (7). What does she mean by this? In your own experience with failure, how helpful would this advice be to you?
6. Haelle concedes that other experts point out there may be cultural limits to the study's findings (8–9). What is the importance of those limits on learning?
7. Haelle quotes Heyman: "There's too much blaming of parents" (10). Do you agree? If this is true, what does that say about the study done by Haimovitz and Dweck?

Classroom Activity Using Writing with Sources

When you write from sources, your sources need to have credibility and authority within the subject area of your writing, and you need to cite those authorities accurately. For example, in paragraph 2, Haelle states that Kyla Haimovitz is a professor of psychology at Stanford University, but Haimovitz's Web site shows that she was a doctoral candidate at Stanford, not a professor. Errors like this can affect a reader's trust in an author's work. In most situations, without further information, you will not know who the experts are and how to separate quality information from uninformed or overly biased statements. Therefore, use research from credible, reliable, and current sources and present that material accurately and responsibly. (For more on evaluating sources, see Chapter 23, pp. 599–601.)

Below is a list of subject areas. Working with a group, pick one and answer the following questions: What types of sources would you use to support an argument in that subject area? Who would be the subject matter experts (by personal name, occupation, position, or experience)? What sorts of textual information would you need to support arguments in these areas? How current must the material be in the subject area to still be relevant? If you have access to library sources or the Internet, find specific examples of books, periodicals, databases, and/or websites that could be used to support your arguments. Share your findings with the class.

Subject Areas

The incarceration of minors	Homelessness
Charter schools	Divorce in America
Cyberterrorism	Eating disorders
Working in the circus	Global music trends
Childhood friendships	Fitness culture

Suggested Writing Assignments

1. Haelle's article addresses the idea that intelligence can be improved through hard work, which is revealed through students' performance in school. Research the relationship between intelligence and educational achievement. Write an essay, using sources, in which you argue whether the two are the same or if it's a mistake to judge intelligence by performance in an educational setting.
2. Haelle quotes Gail Heyman in paragraph 10: "Temperament is extremely important, and it's biologically based." Research how much biology determines personality versus environmental factors. Write an essay, using sources, in which you argue whether nature (biology) or nurture (environment) is the primary determinant of a child's personality.

The English-Only Movement: Can America Proscribe Language with a Clear Conscience?

Jake Jamieson

Courtesy of Jake Jamieson

An eighth-generation Vermonter, Jake Jamieson was born in Berlin, Vermont, and grew up in nearby Waterbury. He graduated from the University of Vermont in 1996 with a degree in elementary education and a focus in English. After graduation, he "bounced around" California and Colorado before landing in the Boston area, where he directed the product innovation and training department at iProspect, a search-engine marketing company. Jamieson then moved back to Montpelier, Vermont, where he started his own Web design company.

Jamieson wrote the following essay while he was a student at the University of Vermont and has updated it for inclusion in this book. As a believer in the old axiom "If it isn't broken, don't fix it," Jamieson thinks that the official-English crowd wants to fix a system that seems to be working just fine. In this essay, he tackles the issue of legislating English as the official language of the United States. As you read, notice how he uses outside sources to present various pieces of the English-only position. He then tries to undercut that position by using his own thinking and examples as well as the opinions of experts who support him. Throughout his essay, Jamieson uses MLA style for his in-text citations and his list of works cited.

Reflecting on What You Know

It is now possible to visit many countries and be understood in English, regardless of other languages that are spoken in the host country. If you were to emigrate, how hard would you work to learn the predominant language of your chosen country? What advantages would you gain by learning that language, even if you could get by in English? How would you feel if the country had a law that required you to use its language in its schools and businesses? Write down your thoughts about these questions.

Many people think of the United States as a giant cultural "melting pot" where people from other countries come together and bathe in the warm waters of assimilation. In this scenario, the newly arrived immigrants readily adopt American cultural ways and learn to speak English. For others, however, this serene picture of the melting pot analogy does not ring true. These people see the melting pot as a giant cauldron into which immigrants are tossed; here their cultures, values, and backgrounds are boiled away in the scalding waters of discrimination. At the center of the discussion about immigrants and assimilation is language: should immigrants be required to learn English, or should accommodations be made so they can continue to use their native languages? 1

Those who argue that the melting pot analogy is valid believe that immigrants who come to America do so willingly and should be expected to become a part of its culture instead of hanging on to their past. For them, the expectation that immigrants will celebrate this country's holidays, dress as Americans dress, embrace American values, and most importantly speak English is not unreasonable. They believe that assimilation offers the only way for everyone in this country to live together in harmony and the only way to dissipate the tensions that inevitably arise when cultures clash. A major problem with this argument, however, is that there is no agreement on what exactly constitutes the "American way" of doing things. 2

Not everyone in America is of the same religious persuasion or has the same set of values, and different people affect vastly different styles of dress. There are so many sets of variables that it would be hard to defend the argument that there is only one culture in the United States. Currently, the one common denominator in America is that the majority of us speak English, and because of this a major movement is being staged in favor of making English the country's "official" language while it is still the country's national and common language. Making English America's "official" language would change the ground rules and expectations surrounding immigrant assimilation. According to the columnist and social commentator Charles Krauthammer, making English the "official" language has important implications: 3

> "Official" means the language of the government and its institutions. "Official" makes clear our expectations of acculturation. "Official" means that every citizen, upon entering America's most sacred political space, the voting booth, should minimally be able to identify the words *president* and *vice president* and *county commissioner* and *judge*. The immigrant, of course, has the right to speak whatever he wants. But he must understand that when he comes to the United States, swears allegiance, and accepts its bounty, he undertakes to join its civic culture. In English. (112)

Many reasons are given to support the notion that making English the official language of the land is a good idea and that it is exactly what this country needs, especially in the face of the growing diversity of languages in metropolitan areas. Indeed, in a recent survey one Los Angeles school reported sixty different languages spoken in the homes of its students (Natl. Education Assn., par. 4).

Supporters of English-only contend that all government communication must be in English. Because communication is absolutely necessary for democracy to survive, they believe that the only way to ensure the existence of our nation is to make sure a common language exists. Making English official would ensure that all government business, from ballots to official forms to judicial hearings, would have to be conducted in English. According to former senator and presidential candidate Bob Dole, "Promoting English as our national language is not an act of hostility but a welcoming act of inclusion." He goes on to state that while immigrants are encouraged to continue speaking their native languages, "thousands of children [are] failing to learn the language, English, that is the ticket to the 'American Dream'" (qtd. in Donegan 51). Political and cultural commentator Greg Lewis echoes Dole's sentiments when he boldly states, "To succeed in America . . . it's important to speak, read, and understand English as most Americans speak it. There's nothing cruel or unfair in that; it's just the way it is" (par. 5). 4

For those who do not subscribe to this way of thinking, however, this type of legislation is anything but the "welcoming act of inclusion" that it is described to be. Many of them, like Myriam Marquez, readily acknowledge the importance of English but fear that "talking in Spanish—or any other language, for that matter—is some sort of litmus test used to gauge American patriotism" ("Why and When" 528). Others suggest that anyone attempting to regulate language is 5 treading dangerously close to the First Amendment and must have a hidden agenda of some type. Why, it is asked, make a language official when it is already firmly entrenched and widely used in this country without legislation to mandate it? According to language diversity advocate James Crawford, the answer is plain and simple: "discrimination." He states that "it is certainly more respectable to discriminate by language than by race" or ethnicity. He points out that "most people are not sensitive to language discrimination in this nation, so it is easy to argue that you're doing someone a favor by making them speak English" (qtd. in Donegan 51). English-only legislation has been criticized as bigoted, anti-immigrant, mean-spirited, and steeped in nativism by those who oppose it, and some go so far as to say that this type of legislation will not foster better communication, as is the claim, but will instead encourage a "fear of being subsumed by a growing 'foreignness' in our midst" (Underwood 65).

For example, when a judge in Texas ruled that a mother was abusing her five-year-old girl by speaking to her only in Spanish, an uproar ensued. This ruling was accompanied by the statement that by talking to her daughter in a language other than English, the mother was "abusing that child and . . . relegating her to the position of house maid." The National Association for Bilingual Education (NABE) condemned this statement for "labeling the Spanish language as abuse." The judge, Samuel C. Kiser, subsequently apologized to the housekeepers of the country, adding that he held them "in the highest esteem," but stood firm on his ruling (qtd. in Donegan 51). One might notice that he went out of his way to apologize to the housekeepers he might have offended but saw no need to apologize to the millions of Spanish speakers whose language had just been belittled in a nationally publicized case. 6

This tendency of official-English proponents to put down other languages is one that shows up again and again, even though they maintain that they have nothing against other languages or the people who speak them. If there is no malice intended toward other languages, why is the use of any language other than English tantamount to lunacy according to an almost constant barrage of literature and editorial opinion? In a recent listing of the "New Year's Resolutions" of various conservative organizations, a group called U.S. English, Inc., stated that the U.S. government was not doing its job of convincing immigrants that they "must learn English to succeed in this country." Instead, according to Stephen Moore and his associates, "in 7 a bewildering display of irrationality, the U.S. government makes it possible to vote, file a tax return, get married, obtain a driver's license, and become a U.S. citizen in many languages" (46).

Now, according to this mindset, not only is speaking any language other than English abusive, but it is also irrational and bewildering. What is this world coming to when people want to speak and make transactions in their native language? Why do they refuse to change and become more like us? Why can't immigrants see that speaking English is quite simply the right way to go? These and many other questions like them are implied by official-English proponents when they discuss the issue. 8

Conservative attorney David Price argues that official-English legislation is a good idea because most English-speaking Americans prefer "out of pride and convenience to speak their native language on the job" (A13). This statement implies not only that the pride and convenience of non-English-speaking Americans is unimportant but that their native tongues are not as important as English. The scariest prospect of all is that this opinion is quickly gaining popularity all around the country. It appears to be most prevalent in areas with high concentrations of Spanish-speaking residents. 9

To date, a number of official-English bills and one amendment to the Constitution have been proposed in the House and Senate. There are more than twenty-seven states—including Missouri, North Dakota, Florida, Massachusetts, California, Virginia, and New Hampshire—that have made English their official language, and more are debating the issue every day. An especially disturbing fact about this debate—and it was front and center in 2007 during the discussions and protests about what to do with America's 12.5 million illegal immigrants—is that official-English laws always seem to be linked to anti-immigration legislation, such as proposals to limit immigration or to restrict government benefits to immigrants. 10

Although official-English proponents maintain that their bid for language legislation is in the best interest of immigrants, the facts tend to show otherwise. University of Texas Professor Robert D. King strongly believes that "language does not threaten American unity." He recommends that "we relax and luxuriate in our linguistic richness and our traditional tolerance of language differences" (64). A decision has to be made in this country about what kind of message we will send to the rest of the world. Do we plan to allow everyone in this country the freedom of speech that we profess to cherish, or will we decide to reserve it only for those who speak English? Will we hold firm to our belief that 11 everyone is deserving of life, liberty, and the pursuit of happiness in this country? Or will we show the world that we believe in these things only when they pertain to ourselves and people like us? "The irony," as Hispanic columnist Myriam Marquez observes, "is that English-only laws directed at government have done little to change the inevitable multicultural flavor of America" ("English-Only Laws" A10).

Works Cited

Donegan, Craig. "Debate over Bilingualism: Should English Be the Nation's Official Language?" *CQ Researcher,* 19 Jan. 1996, pp. 51–71.

King, Robert D. "Should English Be the Law?" *The Atlantic Monthly,* Apr. 1997, pp. 55–64.

Krauthammer, Charles. "In Plain English: Let's Make It Official." *Time,* 12 June 2006, p. 112.

Lewis, Greg. "An Open Letter to Diversity's Victims." *GregLewis.org,* 12 Aug. 2003, www.greglewis.org/CulturalCommentary/081203.htm.

Marquez, Myriam. "English-Only Laws Serve to Appease Those Who Fear the Inevitable." *Orlando Sentinel,* 10 July 2000, p. A10.

---. "Why and When We Speak Spanish in Public." *Models for Writers,* edited by Alfred Rosa and Paul Eschholz, 12th ed., Bedford/St. Martin's, 2015, pp. 527–29.

Moore, Stephen, et al. "New Year's Resolutions." *National Review,* 29 Jan. 1996, pp. 46–48.

National Education Association. "NEA Statement on the Debate over English Only." Teacher's College, U of Nebraska, Lincoln, 27 Sept. 1999. Address.

Price, David. "English-Only Rules: EEOC Has Gone Too Far." *USA Today,* 28 Mar. 1996, final ed., p. A13.

Underwood, Robert L. "At Issue: Should English Be the Official Language of the United States?" *CQ Researcher*, 19 Jan. 1996, p. 65.

Thinking Critically about This Reading

Jamieson claims that "there are so many sets of variables that it would be hard to defend the argument that there is only one culture in the United States" (paragraph 3). Do you agree with him, or do you see a dominant American culture with many regional variations? Explain.

Questions for Study and Discussion

1. What question does Jamieson seek to answer in his essay? How does he answer this question?
2. How does Jamieson respond to the people who argue that the melting pot analogy is valid? Do you agree with his counterargument?
3. Former senator Bob Dole believes that English "is the ticket to the 'American Dream'" (4). In what ways can it be considered the ticket?
4. For what purpose does Jamieson quote Greg Lewis in paragraph 4? What would have been lost had he dropped the Lewis quotation? Explain.
5. James Crawford believes that official-English legislation is motivated by "discrimination" (5). What do you think he means? Do you think that Crawford would consider Bob Dole's remarks in paragraph 4 discriminatory? Explain.
6. In paragraph 6, Jamieson presents the example of the Texas judge who ruled that speaking to a child only in Spanish constituted abuse. What point does this example help Jamieson make?
7. Jamieson is careful to use signal phrases to introduce each of his quotations and paraphrases. How do these signal phrases help readers follow the flow of the argument in his essay?
8. In his concluding paragraph, Jamieson leaves his readers with three important questions. How do you think he would answer each one? How would you answer them?

Classroom Activity Using Writing with Sources

Using the examples on page 230 as a model, write a paraphrase for each of the following paragraphs—that is, restate the original ideas in your own words, using your own style and sentence structure.

> The great offense of the cell phone in public is not the intrusion of its ring, although that can be infuriating when it interrupts a tranquil moment. It is the fact that even when the phone does not ring at all, and is being used quietly and discreetly, it renders a public place less public. It turns the boulevardier into a sequestered

individual, the flaneur into a figure of privacy. And suddenly the meaning of the street as a public place has been hugely diminished.

–Paul Goldberger, "Disconnected Urbanism"

The history of a nation is more often the result of the unexpected than of the planned. In many cases it turns on momentous events. In 1968, American history was determined by a garbage men's strike. As Martin Luther King Jr. and the members of the SCLC commenced planning the Poor Peoples' March on Washington, the garbage men of Memphis, Tennessee, were embroiled in a wage dispute with Mayor Henry Loeb. On February 12th, the garbage men, most of whom were black, went on strike. What began as a simple dispute over wages soon developed into a full-fledged racial battle between the predominantly black union, local 1733, and the white power structure of the City of Memphis.

–Robert L. Walsh and Leon F. Burrell, *The Other America*

Compare your paraphrases with those of your classmates.

Suggested Writing Assignments

1. It's no secret that English is the common language of the United States, but few of us know that the country has been cautious about promoting a government-mandated official language. Why do you suppose the federal government has chosen to take a hands-off position on the language issue? If it has not been necessary to mandate English in the past, why do you think people now feel a need to declare English the "official language" of the United States? Do you think this need is real? Write an essay in which you articulate your position on the English-only issue. Support your position with your own experiences and observations as well as with several outside sources.
2. Is the English-only debate a political issue, a social issue, an economic issue, or some combination of the three? In this context, what do you see as the relationship between language and power? Write an essay in which you explore the relationship between language and power as it pertains to non-English-speaking immigrants living and functioning within an English-speaking culture.

The Clan of One-Breasted Women

Terry Tempest Williams

American author, naturalist, conservationist, and activist Terry Tempest Williams was born in Corona, California, in 1955 and grew up in Utah, where she is descended from six generations of Mormon pioneers. Williams received a degree in English and biology in 1978 and an MS in environmental education in 1984 from the University of Utah. After graduation, she taught on a Navajo reservation in Montezuma Creek, Utah; she has also been naturalist-in-residence at the Utah Museum of Natural History. A prolific writer, her essays have appeared in the *New Yorker,* the *Nation, Orion,* the *New York Times,* and *The Best American Essays* (2000). Williams is best known for her award-winning *Refuge: An Unnatural History of Family and Place* (1991), a book that interweaves memoir with a chronicle of the flooding of the Bear River Migratory Bird Refuge in 1983. Williams's other books include *Pieces of White Shell: A Journey to Navajoland* (1984), *An Unspoken Hunger* (1994), *Desert Quartet: An Erotic Landscape* (1995), *Red: Patience and Passion in the Desert* (2001), *The Open Space of Democracy* (2004), *Finding Beauty in a Broken World* (2008), and *When Women Were Birds* (2012). She has also written two books for children, *The Secret Language of Snow* (1984) and *Cattails* (1985). In 2009, Williams was featured in Ken Burns's PBS series *The National Parks: America's Best Idea.* In 2014, on the 50th Anniversary of the Wilderness Act, Williams was awarded the Sierra Club's John Muir Award, an honor granted for leadership in the American conservation movement. Currently, Williams is the Provostial scholar at Dartmouth College.

"The Clan of One-Breasted Women" first appeared as the epilogue to her acclaimed *Refuge.* This essay has since been published worldwide. In it, Williams explores the connection between radioactive fallout from aboveground nuclear testing on the Nevada desert during the 1950s and early 1960s and the high incidence of cancer occurring not only in her own family but in other Utah families as well. As you read, pay attention to how Williams weaves personal narrative together with researched evidence to make her writing more powerful.

Reflecting on What You Know

Today people are much more aware of the health risks caused by radiation and chemicals lurking in our environment than they were, say, fifty or sixty years ago. What do you know about the potential dangers of nuclear energy facilities, chemical fertilizers and pesticides, exhaust from the cars we drive, and preservatives and other additives in the foods we eat? Are you aware of any environmental contamination issues in the area where you grew up? Explain.

I belong to a Clan of One-Breasted Women. My mother, my grandmothers, and six aunts have all had mastectomies. Seven are dead. The two who survive have just completed rounds of chemotherapy and radiation. 1

I've had my own problems: two biopsies for breast cancer and a small tumor between my ribs diagnosed as "a border-line malignancy." 2

This is my family history. 3

Most statistics tell us breast cancer is genetic, hereditary, with rising percentages attached to fatty diets, childlessness, or becoming pregnant after thirty. What they don't say is living in Utah may be the greatest hazard of all. 4

We are a Mormon family with roots in Utah since 1847. The word-of-wisdom, a religious doctrine of health, kept the women in my family aligned with good foods: no coffee, no tea, tobacco, or alcohol. For the most part, these women were finished having their babies by the time they were thirty. And only one faced breast cancer prior to 1960. Traditionally, as a group of people, Mormons have a low rate of cancer. 5

Is our family a cultural anomaly? The truth is we didn't think about it. Those who did, usually the men, simply said, "bad genes." The women's attitude was stoic. Cancer was part of life. On February 16, 1971, the eve before my mother's surgery, I accidently picked up the telephone and overheard her ask my grandmother what she could expect. 6

"Diane, it is one of the most spiritual experiences you will ever encounter." 7

I quietly put down the receiver. 8

Two days later, my father took my three brothers and me to the hospital to visit her. She met us in the lobby in a wheelchair. No bandages were visible. I'll never forget her radiance, the way she held herself in a purple velour robe and how she gathered us around her. 9

"Children, I am fine. I want you to know I felt the arms of God around me." 10

We believed her. My father cried. Our mother, his wife, was thirty-eight years old. 11

Two years ago, after my mother's death from cancer, my father and I were having dinner together. He had just returned from St. George where his construction company was putting in natural gas lines for towns in southern Utah. He spoke of his love for the country: the sandstoned landscape, bare-boned and beautiful. He had just finished hiking the Kolob trail in Zion National Park. We got caught up in reminiscing, recalling with fondness our walk up Angel's Landing on his fiftieth birthday and the years our family had vacationed there. This was a remembered landscape where we had been raised. 12

Over dessert, I shared a recurring dream of mine. I told my father that for years, as long as I could remember, I saw this flash of light in the night in the desert. That this image had so permeated my being, I could not venture south without seeing it again, on the horizon, illuminating buttes and mesas. 13

"You did see it," he said. 14

"Saw what?" I asked, a bit tentative. 15

"The bomb. The cloud. We were driving home from Riverside, California. You were sitting on your mother's lap. She was pregnant. In fact, I remember the date, September 7, 1957. We had just gotten out of the Service. We were driving north, past Las Vegas. It was an hour or so before dawn, when this explosion went off. We not only heard it, but felt it. I thought the oil tanker in front of us had blown up. We pulled over and suddenly, rising from the desert floor, we saw it, clearly, this golden-stemmed cloud, the mushroom. The sky seemed to vibrate with an eerie pink glow. Within a few minutes, a light ash was raining on the car." 16

I stared at my father. This was new information to me. 17

"I thought you knew that," my father said. "It was a common occurrence in the fifties." 18

It was at this moment I realized the deceit I had been living under. Children growing up in the American Southwest, drinking contaminated milk from contaminated cows, even from the contaminated breasts of their mother, my mother—members, years later, of the Clan of One-Breasted Women. 19

It is a well-known story in the Desert West, "The Day We Bombed Utah," or perhaps, "The Years We Bombed Utah."[1] Above ground atomic testing in Nevada took place from January 27, 1951, through July 11, 1962. Not only were the winds blowing north, covering "low use segments of the population" with fallout and leaving sheep dead in their tracks, but the climate was right. The United States of the 1950s was red, white, and blue. The Korean War was raging. McCarthyism was rampant. Ike was it and the Cold War was hot. If you were against nuclear testing, you were for a Communist regime. 20

Much has been written about this "American nuclear tragedy." Public health was secondary to national security. The Atomic Energy Commissioner, Thomas Murray, said, "Gentlemen, we must not let anything interfere with this series of tests, nothing."[2] 21

Again and again, the American public was told by its government, in spite of burns, blisters, and nausea, "It has been found that the tests may be conducted with adequate assurance of safety under conditions prevailing at the bombing reservations."[3] Assuaging public fears was simply a matter of public relations. "Your best action," an Atomic Energy Commission booklet read, "is not to be worried about fallout." A news release typical of the times stated, "We find no basis for concluding that harm to any individual has resulted from radioactive fallout."[4] 22

On August 30, 1979, during Jimmy Carter's presidency, a suit was filed entitled "Irene Allen vs. the United States of America." Mrs. Allen was the first to be alphabetically listed with twenty-four test cases, representative of nearly 1200 plaintiffs seeking compensation from the United States government for cancers caused from nuclear testing in Nevada. 23

---

[1]John G. Fuller, *The Day We Bombed Utah* (New York: New American Library, 1984). [All notes are Williams's.]

[2]Ferenc M. Szasz, "Downwind from the Bomb," *Nevada Historical Society Quarterly*, Fall 1987 Vol. XXX, No. 3, p. 185.

[3]Philip L. Fradkin, *Fallout* (Tucson: University of Arizona Press, 1989), 98.

[4]Ibid., 109.

Irene Allen lived in Hurricane, Utah. She was the mother of five children and had been widowed twice. Her first husband with their two oldest boys had watched the tests from the roof of the local high school. He died of leukemia in 1956. Her second husband died of pancreatic cancer in 1978. 24

In a town meeting conducted by Utah Senator Orrin Hatch, shortly before the suit was filed, Mrs. Allen said, "I am not blaming the government, I want you to know that, Senator Hatch. But I thought if my testimony could help in any way so this wouldn't happen again to any of the generations coming up after us . . . I am really happy to be here this day to bear testimony of this."[5] 25

God-fearing people. This is just one story in an anthology of thousands. 26

On May 10, 1984, Judge Bruce S. Jenkins handed down his opinion. Ten of the plaintiffs were awarded damages. It was the first time a federal court had determined that nuclear tests had been the cause of cancers. For the remaining fourteen test cases, the proof of causation was not sufficient. In spite of the split decision, it was considered a landmark ruling.[6] It was not to remain so for long. 27

In April 1987, the 10th Circuit Court of Appeals overturned Judge Jenkins' ruling on the basis that the United States was protected from suit by the legal doctrine of sovereign immunity, the centuries-old idea from England in the days of absolute monarchs.[7] 28

In January 1988, the Supreme Court refused to review the Appeals Court decision. To our court system, it does not matter whether the United States government was irresponsible, whether it lied to its citizens or even that citizens died from the fallout of nuclear testing. What matters is that our government is immune. "The King can do no wrong." 29

In Mormon culture, authority is respected, obedience is revered, and independent thinking is not. I was taught as a young girl not to "make waves" or "rock the boat." 30

"Just let it go— " my mother would say. "You know how you feel, that's what counts." 31

---

[5]Town meeting held by Senator Orrin Hatch in St. George, Utah, April 17, 1979, transcript, 26–28.

[6]Fradkin, op. cit., 228.

[7]*U.S. v. Allen*, 816 Federal Reporter, 2d/1417 (10th Circuit Court 1987), cert. denied, 108 S. Ct. 694 (1988).

For many years, I did just that—listened, observed, and quietly formed my own opinions within a culture that rarely asked questions because they had all the answers. But one by one, I watched the women in my family die common, heroic deaths. We sat in waiting rooms hoping for good news, always receiving the bad. I cared for them, bathed their scarred bodies and kept their secrets. I watched beautiful women become bald as cytoxan, cisplatin, and adriamycin were injected into their veins. I held their foreheads as they vomited green-black bile and I shot them with morphine when the pain became inhuman. In the end, I witnessed their last peaceful breaths, becoming a midwife to the rebirth of their souls. But the price of obedience became too high. 32

The fear and inability to question authority that ultimately killed rural communities in Utah during atmospheric testing of atomic weapons was the same fear I saw being held in my mother's body. Sheep. Dead sheep. The evidence is buried. 33

I cannot prove that my mother, Diane Dixon Tempest, or my grandmothers, Lettie Romney Dixon and Kathryn Blackett Tempest, along with my aunts contracted cancer from nuclear fallout in Utah. But I can't prove they didn't. 34

My father's memory was correct, the September blast we drove through in 1957 was part of Operation Plumbbob, one of the most intensive series of bomb tests to be initiated. The flash of light in the night in the desert I had always thought was a dream developed into a family nightmare. It took fourteen years, from 1957 to 1971, for cancer to show up in my mother—the same time Howard L. Andrews, an authority on radioactive fallout at the National Institutes of Health, says radiation cancer requires to become evident.[8] The more I learn about what it means to be a "downwinder," the more questions I drown in. 35

What I do know, however, is that as a Mormon woman of the fifth generation of "Latter-Day-Saints," I must question everything, even if it means losing my faith, even if it means becoming a member of a border tribe among my own people. Tolerating blind obedience in the name of patriotism or religion ultimately takes our lives. 36

When the Atomic Energy Commission described the country north of the Nevada Test Site as "virtually uninhabited desert terrain," my family members were some of the "virtual uninhabitants." 37

[8]*Fradkin*, op. cit., 116.

One night, I dreamed women from all over the world circled a blazing fire in the desert. They spoke of change, of how they hold the moon in their bellies and wax and wane with its phases. They mocked at the presumption of even-tempered beings and made promises that they would never fear the witch inside themselves. The women danced wildly as sparks broke away from the flames and entered the night sky as stars. 38

And they sang a song given to them by Shoshone grandmothers: 39

Ah ne nah, nah
nin nah nah—
Ah ne nah, nah
nin nah nah—
Nyaga mutzi
oh ne nay—
Nyaga mutzi
oh ne nay—[9]

The women danced and drummed and sang for weeks, preparing themselves for what was to come. They would reclaim the desert for the sake of their children, for the sake of the land. 40

A few miles downwind from the fire circle, bombs were being tested. Rabbits felt the tremors. Their soft leather pads on paws and feet recognized the shaking sands while the roots of mesquite and sage were smoldering. Rocks were hot from the inside out and dust devils hummed unnaturally. And each time there was another nuclear test, ravens watched the desert heave. Stretch marks appeared. The land was losing its muscle. 41

The women couldn't bear it any longer. They were mothers. They had suffered labor pains but always under the promise of birth. The red hot pains beneath the desert promised death only as each bomb became a stillborn. A contract had been broken between human beings and the land. A new contract was being drawn by the women who understood the fate of the earth as their own. 42

Under the cover of darkness, ten women slipped under the barbed wire fence and entered the contaminated country. They were trespassing. They walked toward the town of Mercury in moonlight, taking 43

---

[9]This song was sung by the Western Shoshone women as they crossed the line at the Nevada Test Site on March 18, 1988, as part of their "Reclaim the Land" action. The translation they gave was: "Consider the rabbits how gently they walk on the earth. Consider the rabbits how gently they walk on the earth. We remember them. We can walk gently also. We remember them. We can walk gently also."

their cues from coyote, kit fox, antelope squirrel, and quail. They moved quietly and deliberately through the maze of Joshua trees. When a hint of daylight appeared they rested, drinking tea and sharing their rations of food. The women closed their eyes. The time had come to protest with the heart, that to deny one's genealogy with the earth was to commit treason against one's soul.

At dawn, the women draped themselves in mylar, wrapping long streamers of silver plastic around their arms to blow in the breeze. They wore clear masks that became the faces of humanity. And when they arrived on the edge of Mercury, they carried all the butterflies of a summer day in their wombs. They paused to allow their courage to settle. 44

The town which forbids pregnant women and children to enter because of radiation risks to their health was asleep. The women moved through the streets as winged messengers, twirling around each other in slow motion, peeking inside homes and watching the easy sleep of men and women. They were astonished by such stillness and periodically would utter a shrill note or low cry just to verify life. 45

The residents finally awoke to what appeared as strange apparitions. Some simply stared. Others called authorities, and in time, the women were apprehended by wary soldiers dressed in desert fatigues. They were taken to a white, square building on the other edge of Mercury. When asked who they were and why they were there, the women replied, "We are mothers and we have come to reclaim the desert for our children." 46

The soldiers arrested them. As the ten women were blindfolded and handcuffed, they began singing: 47

You can't forbid us everything
You can't forbid us to think—
You can't forbid our tears to flow
And you can't stop the songs that we sing.

The women continued to sing louder and louder, until they heard the voices of their sisters moving across the mesa. 48

Ah ne nah, nah
nin nah nah—
Ah ne nah, nah
nin nah nah—
Nyaga mutzi
oh ne nay—
Nyaga mutzi
oh ne nay—

"Call for re-enforcement," one soldier said. 49

"We have," interrupted one woman. "We have—and you have no 50 idea of our numbers."

On March 18, 1988, I crossed the line at the Nevada Test Site and 51 was arrested with nine other Utahns for trespassing on military lands. They are still conducting nuclear tests in the desert. Ours was an act of civil disobedience. But as I walked toward the town of Mercury, it was more than a gesture of peace. It was a gesture on behalf of the Clan of One-Breasted Women.

As one officer cinched the handcuffs around my wrists, another 52 frisked my body. She found a pen and a pad of paper tucked inside my left boot.

"And these?" she asked sternly. 53

"Weapons," I replied. 54

Our eyes met. I smiled. She pulled the leg of my trousers back over 55 my boot.

"Step forward, please," she said as she took my arm. 56

We were booked under an afternoon sun and bussed to Tonapah, 57 Nevada. It was a two-hour ride. This was familiar country to me. The Joshua trees standing their ground had been named by my ancestors who believed they looked like prophets pointing west to the promised land. These were the same trees that bloomed each spring, flowers appearing like white flames in the Mojave. And I recalled a full moon in May when my mother and I had walked among them, flushing out mourning doves and owls.

The bus stopped short of town. We were released. The officials 58 thought it was a cruel joke to leave us stranded in the desert with no way to get home. What they didn't realize is that we were home, soul-centered and strong, women who recognized the sweet smell of sage as fuel for our spirits.

Thinking Critically about This Reading

In paragraph 20, Williams tells us that "the United States of the 1950s was red, white, and blue. The Korean War was raging. McCarthyism was rampant. Ike was it and the Cold War was hot. If you were against nuclear testing, you were for a Communist regime." Why do you think that Williams thought it was important for readers to know what the United States was like during these years? Explain.

Questions for Study and Discussion

1. How did you respond to Williams's opening three paragraphs? Together, did they work well as a beginning for you? Explain why or why not.
2. What "new information" (paragraph 17) does Williams learn while talking with her father over dinner shortly after her mother had died from cancer? Of what importance is this new information?
3. How does Williams use outside sources to support the idea that "public health was secondary to national security" (21)?
4. In paragraph 35, Williams paraphrases Howard L. Andrews. How does Williams signal where the paraphrase begins and ends? For what purpose does Williams bring Andrews into the discussion at this point?
5. Why did Williams remain silent about her suspicions about the nuclear testing for so long? What ultimately convinced her that she should speak out?
6. Williams has organized her essay into three sections—paragraphs 1–19, 20–29, and 30–58. How are the three sections related? Why do you think Williams ordered her essay in this way? (Glossary: **Organization**)
7. Why did the Shoshone women cross the line at the Nevada Test Site and enter the "contaminated country"? Why did Williams join them? What did Williams mean when she told the soldier frisking her that her pen and pad of paper were "weapons" (54)?

Classroom Activity Using Writing with Sources

For each of the following quotations, write an acceptable paraphrase and then a paraphrase with a partial quotation that avoids plagiarism (see pp. 230–32 and 240–42). Pay careful attention to the word choice and sentence structure of the original.

> The sperm whale is the largest of the toothed whales. Moby Dick was a sperm whale. Generally, male toothed whales are larger than the females. Female sperm whales may grow thirty-five to forty feet in length, while the males may reach sixty feet.
>
> –Richard Hendrick, *The Voyage of the Mimi*

Astronauts from over twenty nations have gone into space, and they all come back, amazingly enough, saying the very same thing: the earth is a small, blue place of profound beauty that we must take care of. For each, the journey into space, whatever its original intents and purposes, became above all a spiritual one.

–Al Reinhert, *For All Mankind*

One of the usual things about education in mathematics in the United States is its relatively impoverished vocabulary. Whereas the student completing elementary school will already have a vocabulary for most disciplines of many hundreds, even thousands of words, the typical student will have a mathematics vocabulary of only a couple of dozen words.

–Marvin Minsky, *The Society of Mind*

Suggested Writing Assignments

1. In paragraph 36, Williams emphatically states, "Tolerating blind obedience in the name of patriotism or religion ultimately takes our lives." Using examples from your own experience, observation, and reading, write an essay in which you agree or disagree with Williams's position.
2. Poet and environmentalist Wendell Berry has said that "it is impossible to care more or differently for each other than we care for the land." What do you think he means? Like the Western Shoshone women who crossed the government line at the Nevada Test Site as part of their "Reclaim the Land" action, we are all stewards of the earth. What responsibilities do you think we have toward the land? Toward one another? How can humans work in partnership with the land? Using your own experiences as well as research in the library and on the Internet, write an argumentative essay that answers these questions.

part three

The Language of the Essay

CHAPTER 11

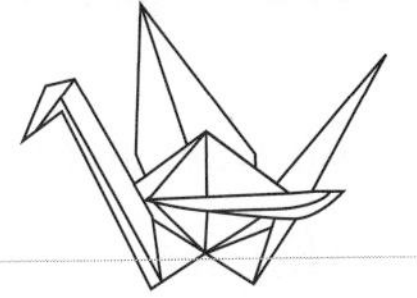

Diction and Tone

DICTION

Diction refers to a writer's choice and use of words. Good diction is precise and appropriate: the words mean exactly what the writer intends, and the words are well suited to the writer's subject, purpose, and intended audience.

Careful writers do not merely come close to saying what they want to say; rather, they select words that convey their exact meaning. Perhaps Mark Twain put this idea best when he said, "The difference between the right word and the almost right word is the difference between lightning and the lightning bug." Inaccurate, imprecise, or inappropriate diction fails to convey the writer's intended meaning and may cause confusion and misunderstanding for the reader.

Connotation and Denotation

Both **connotation** and **denotation** refer to the meanings of words. Denotation is the dictionary meaning of a word—its literal meaning. Connotative meanings are the associations or emotional overtones that words have acquired. For example, the word *home* denotes a place where someone lives, but it connotes warmth, security, family, comfort, affection, and other more private thoughts and images. The word *residence* also denotes a place where someone lives, but its connotations are legal, colder, and more formal.

Many words in English have synonyms, or words with very similar denotations—for example, *mob, crowd, multitude,* and *bunch*. Deciding which to use depends largely on the connotations of each synonym and the context in which the word is to be used. For example, you might say, "There was a crowd at the lecture," but not "There was a mob at the lecture." Good writers are sensitive to both the denotations and the connotations of words.

Abstract and Concrete Words

Abstract words name ideas, conditions, and emotions—things nobody can touch, see, or hear. Some abstract words are *love, wisdom, cowardice, beauty, fear,* and *liberty.* People often disagree about abstract things. You might find a forest beautiful, whereas someone else might find it frightening—and neither of you would be wrong. Beauty and fear are ideas; they exist in your mind. **Concrete** words refer to things we can touch, see, hear, smell, and taste, such as *sandpaper, soda, birch tree, smog, cow, sailboat, rocking chair,* and *pancake.* If you disagree with someone on a concrete issue—for example, you claim that the forest is mostly birch trees, whereas the other person says it is mostly pine—only one of you can be right, and both of you can be wrong; the kinds of trees that grow in the forest is a concrete fact, not an abstract idea.

Good writing balances ideas and facts, and it also balances abstract and concrete diction. If the writing is too abstract and has too few concrete facts and details, it will be unconvincing and tiresome. If the writing is too concrete and devoid of abstract ideas and emotions, it will seem mundane and dry.

General and Specific Words

General and **specific** do not necessarily refer to opposites. The same word can often be either general or specific, depending on the context: *Dessert* is more specific than *food* but more general than *chocolate cream pie.* Being specific is like being concrete: chocolate cream pie is something you can see and taste. Being general, on the other hand, is like being abstract. Food, dessert, and even pie are large classes of things that bring to mind only general tastes or images.

Good writing moves back and forth from the general to the specific. Without specific words, generalities can be unconvincing and even confusing: the writer's idea of "good food" may be very different from the reader's. But writing that does not connect its specific details to each other through generalization often lacks focus and direction.

Clichés

A word, phrase, or expression that has become trite through overuse is called a **cliché.** Let's assume your roommate has just returned from an evening out. You ask her, "How was the concert?" She responds, "The concert was okay, but they had us *packed in there like sardines*. How was your evening?" And you reply, "Well, I finished my term paper, but the noise here is enough to *drive me crazy*. The dorm is a real *zoo*." The italicized expressions were once vivid and colorful, but through constant use they have grown stale and ineffective. Experienced writers always try to avoid such clichés as *believe it or not, at the end of the day, the bottom line is, last but not least, hits the spot, let's face it, sneaking suspicion, step in the right direction*, and *went to great lengths*. They strive to use fresh language.

Jargon

Jargon, or technical language, is the special vocabulary of a trade or profession. Writers use jargon with an awareness of their audience. If their audience is a group of co-workers or professionals, jargon may be used freely. If the audience is general, jargon should be used sparingly and carefully so that readers can understand it. Jargon becomes inappropriate when it is overused, used out of context, or used pretentiously. For example, computer terms like *input, output,* and *feedback* are sometimes used in place of *contribution, result,* and *response* in other fields, especially in business. Using computer jargon outside of talking about computers may be excluding or dehumanizing. For example, if a manager asks her direct report what his "output" has been for the past year, she may be implying that he is only a machine that receives and processes information according to a program, not an individual contributing to the company.

Formal and Informal Diction

Diction is appropriate when it suits the occasion for which it is intended. If the situation is informal—a friendly e-mail, for example—the writing may be colloquial; that is, its words may be chosen to suggest the way people talk with one another. If, on the other hand, the situation is formal—an academic paper or a research report, for example—the words should reflect this formality. Informal writing tends to be characterized by slang, contractions, references to the reader, and concrete nouns. Formal writing tends to be impersonal, abstract, and free of contractions and references to the reader. Formal writing and informal writing are the extremes. Most writing falls between these two extremes and is a blend of the formal and informal elements that best fit the context.

TONE

Tone is the attitude a writer takes toward the subject and the audience. Tone is conveyed by the voice we use to express ourselves in our writing. The tone may be friendly, hostile, bitter, sarcastic, angry, serious, mocking, whimsical, humorous, enthusiastic, skeptical, indifferent, facetious, sad, and so on.

As you read the following paragraphs, notice how each writer creates a different tone and how that tone is supported by the diction—the writer's particular choice and use of words.

Nostalgic

> When I was six years old, I thought I knew a lot. How to jump rope, how to skip a rock across a pond, and how to color and stay between the lines—these were all things I took great pride in. Nothing was difficult, and my days were carefree. That is, until the summer when everything became complicated and I suddenly realized I didn't know that much.
>
> –Heather C. Blue, student

Angry

> That man over there says that women need to be helped into carriages, and lifted over ditches, and to have the best place everywhere. Nobody ever helps me into carriages, or over mud-puddles, or gives me any best place! And ain't I a woman? Look at me! Look at my arm! I have ploughed and planted, and gathered into barns, and no man could head me! And ain't I a woman? I could work as much and eat as much as a man—when I could get it—and bear the lash as well! And ain't I a woman? I have borne thirteen children, and seen them most all sold off to slavery, and when I cried out with my mother's grief, none but Jesus heard me! And ain't I a woman?
>
> –Sojourner Truth, "Ain't I a Woman?"

Sarcastic

Ultimately, the plutocratic takeover of rural America has a downside for the wealthy too. The more expensive a resort town gets, the farther its workers have to commute to keep it functioning. And if your heart doesn't bleed for the dishwasher or landscaper who commutes two to four hours a day, at least shed a tear for the wealthy vacationer who gets stuck in the ensuing traffic. It's bumper to bumper westbound out of Telluride, Colorado, every day at 5, or eastbound on Route 1 out of Key West, for the Lexuses as well as the beat-up old pickup trucks.

–Barbara Ehrenreich, "This Land Is Their Land"

Objective or Academic

In 2006 an American big-game hunter from Idaho shot and killed the first documented wild polar-grizzly bear hybrid, a mostly white male covered in patches of brown fur with long grizzly-like claws, a humped back, and eyes ringed by black skin. Four years later a second-generation "pizzly" or "grolar" was shot. After hearing reports of the bears, Brendan Kelly, then an Alaska-based biologist with the National Oceanic and Atmospheric Administration, started to wonder which other species might be interbreeding as a result of a changing Arctic landscape.

–Katherine Bagley, "Climate Change Is Causing Some Mixed-Up Wildlife"

Business or Professional

The renovation of the County Courthouse is progressing on schedule and within budget. Although the cost of certain materials is higher than our original bid indicated, we expect to complete the project without exceeding the estimated costs because the speed with which the project is being completed will reduce overall labor expenses.

–Tran Nuguélen, project engineer

Dramatic

Every day you walk on it, your baby crawls across it, and your dog rolls around on it. Your child may accidentally drop a piece of candy on it and eat the candy anyway. All the while you are unaware that your floor is made with a toxic chemical that has proven to cause various types of cancer and other serious health risks. Vinyl flooring — one of today's most affordable, durable, and easily installed flooring options — is manufactured using vinyl chloride.

–Mina Raine, student

Ironic

Once upon a time there was a small, beautiful, green and graceful country called Vietnam. It needed to be saved. (In later years no one could remember exactly what it needed to be saved from, but that is another story.) For many years Vietnam was in the process of being saved by France, but the French eventually tired of their labors and left. Then America took on the job. America was well equipped for country saving. It was the richest and most powerful nation on earth. It had, for example, nuclear explosives on hand and ready to use equal to six tons of TNT for every man, woman, and child in the world. It had huge and very efficient factories, brilliant and dedicated scientists, and most (but not everybody) would agree, it had good intentions. Sadly, America had one fatal flaw — its inhabitants were in love with technology and thought it could do no wrong. A visitor to America during the time of this story would probably have guessed its outcome after seeing how its inhabitants were treating their own country. The air was mostly foul, the water putrid, and most of the land was either covered with concrete or garbage. But Americans were never much on introspection, and they didn't foresee the result of their loving embrace on the small country. They set out to save Vietnam with the same enthusiasm and determination their forefathers had displayed in conquering the frontier.

–The Sierra Club, "Vietnam Defoliation: A Fable for Our Times"

The diction and tone of an essay are subtle forces, but they exert a tremendous influence on readers. They are instrumental in determining how we will feel while reading an essay and what attitude we will have toward its argument or the points it makes. Readers react in a variety of ways. An essay written informally but with a largely angry tone may make one reader defensive and unsympathetic; another may believe that the author is being unusually honest and courageous and may admire these qualities and feel moved by them. Either way, the diction and tone of the piece have made a strong emotional impression. As you read the essays in this chapter and throughout this book, see if you can analyze how the diction and tone shape your reactions.

How Do Plants Know Which Way Is Up and Which Way Is Down?

Robert Krulwich

Born in 1947, Robert Krulwich earned a BA in history from Oberlin College and a JD from Columbia Law School, but he left the path toward a law career to cover the Watergate hearings for Pacifica Radio. He went on to work as a journalist for a number of publications and news programs, including *Rolling Stone, 48 Hours, Nightline,* and *NOVA.* Krulwich has won Emmy Awards for his reports on computers and privacy, savings and loan bailouts, and the history of Barbie dolls. He was also awarded the 2010 Essay Prize from the Iowa Writers' Workshop. *TV Guide* called him "the most inventive network reporter in television." He is currently a correspondent for National Public Radio and cohost of the Peabody Award–winning show *Radiolab.*

In this essay for NPR, Krulwich uses writing and illustrations to answer a simple question, leading to a rather complex series of scientific hypotheses. As you read, pay attention to how he avoids jargon, translating the scientists' research findings into language easy for general readers to understand.

Reflecting on What You Know

What do you know about the scientific method, which researchers employ to answer their questions about the world? What would you hypothesize about how plants grow right side up?

Think of a seed buried in a pot. Like this one: 1

It's dark down there in the potting soil. There's no light, no sunshine. So how does it know which way is up and which way is down? It *does know.* Seeds routinely send shoots up toward the sky, and roots the other way. Darkness doesn't confuse them. Somehow, they get it right . . . 2

More intriguing, if you turn a seedling (or a whole bunch of seedlings) upside down, as Thomas Andrew Knight of the British Royal Society did around 200 years ago, the tips and roots of the plant will sense, "Hey, I'm upside down," and will wiggle their way to the right direction, doing a double U-turn, like this: 3

How do they know? According to botanist Daniel Chamovitz, Thomas Knight 200 years ago assumed that plants must sense gravity. They feel the pull of the Earth. Knight proved it with a crazy experiment involving a spinning plate. 4

He attached a bunch of plant seedlings onto a disc (think of a 78 rpm record made of wood). The plate was then turned by a water wheel powered by a local stream, "at a nauseating speed of 150 revolutions per minute for several days." 5

If you've ever been at an amusement park in a spinning tea cup, you know that because of centrifugal force you get pushed *away from* the center of the spinning object toward the outside. 6

Knight wondered, would the plants respond to the centrifugal pull of gravity and point their roots to the outside of the spinning plate? When he looked . . . 7

. . . that's what they'd done. Every plant on the disc had responded to the pull of gravity, and pointed its roots to the outside. The roots pointed out, the shoots pointed in. So Thomas Knight proved that plants can and do sense gravitational pull.

But he couldn't explain how. 8

We humans have teeny crystalline stones floating in our ear cavities that literally sink in response to gravity, telling us what's up and what's down. What do plants have? 9

Strangely, this is a real puzzle. We still don't know for sure how plants do it. There is a team of botanists, John Kiss and his colleagues at Miami University in Ohio, who have a promising idea, but at the moment it's just a very educated guess. 10

Plants have special cells right down at the tip — the very bottom — of their roots. And if you look closely, inside these cells there are dense, little ball like structures called "statoliths" — which comes from the Greek, meaning "stationary stone." You can see them here. 11

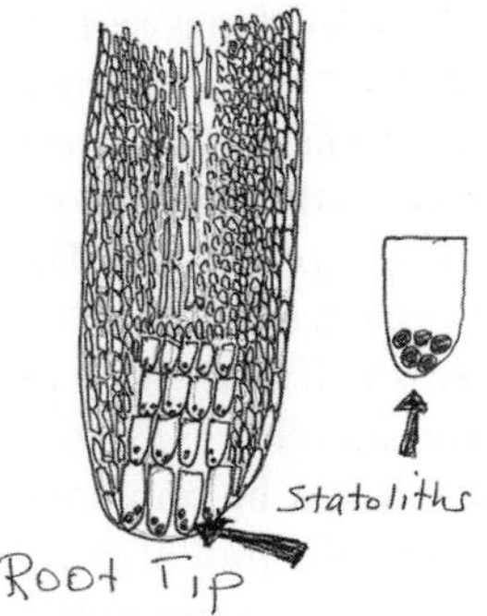

I think of them as pebbles inside a jar. If the jar is upright, the pebbles, naturally, fall to the bottom. 12

If I put the jar on its side, the pebbles will roll to the side of the jar, the new bottom, and lie there. 13

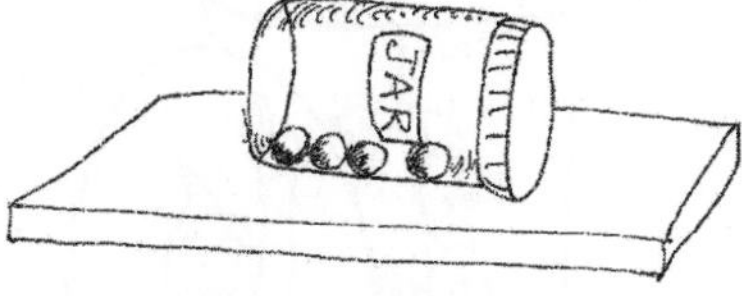

If I turn the jar upside down, the pebbles will drop into the cap, which used to be the top but is now the bottom. 14

Basically these little pebbly things *respond to gravity.* In a plant 15
cell, gravity pulls them to the "bottom," and once they find a resting place, they can send signals to neighboring cells in the plant essentially saying, "OK guys! We now know where Down is. Those of you that need to go down (root cells), go this way! Those of you who need to go up (the shoot on top), go the other way!"

This, suggests Professor Kiss, is how plants figure out where 16
"down" is. They use little statolith balls as gravity receptors.

His idea got a boost when he sent some seedlings into space 17
(to the space station) where the pull of gravity is close to zero, figuring if the statoliths just float randomly and don't drop to the bottom of their cells, the plants won't know which way is down. And sure enough, he reported that plants growing in space did not send their roots in any specific direction. The roots just went every which way.

So the next time you pass a tree, a flower, a grapevine, grasses, 18
bushes, vegetables, any plant that seems to be reaching for the sky, that plant may be going up not just because it wants to be kissed by the sun, but also because down at its bottom, in cells rooted in the Earth, it's got itty bitty rocks telling it, "go thattaway!"

Thinking Critically about This Reading

What role do the illustrations play in Krulwich's explanation? What do they add to his writing? Which do you find most effective?

Questions for Study and Discussion

1. How would you describe the tone of this essay? What is Krulwich's attitude toward the question he poses?
2. The first researcher Krulwich mentions is Thomas Andrew Knight, who performed his experiments on plants around two hundred years ago. What have scientists been able to determine about how plants grow since then? What do they still not know for sure?
3. How does Krulwich use analogies to illustrate the scientists' findings? (Glossary: **Analogy**) For example, see the analogy of the record in paragraph 5. Can you find other places where he helps readers visualize his subject?
4. Krulwich uses active verbs to convey the lively, even dramatic process of experimentation. The researchers he writes about *wonder*, *assume*, and *prove*. Identify other strong verb choices throughout the essay. What do they contribute to Krulwich's explanation of the science?
5. One of the few scientific terms Krulwich uses in his essay is "statolith." How would you define this word? What information does Krulwich offer to help you form this definition?
6. How does the behavior of plants in the space station support the current understanding of how these statoliths work?

Classroom Activity Using Diction and Tone

Writers create and control tone in their writing in part through the words they choose. For example, the words *laugh, cheery, dance,* and *melody* help create a tone of celebration. Make a list of the words that come to mind when considering each of the following tones:

humorous	authoritative	tentative
angry	triumphant	repentant

Compare your lists of words with those of others in the class. What generalizations can you make about the connotations associated with each of these tones?

Suggested Writing Assignments

1. Choose a subject on which you have some expertise—an adventurous favorite food, a cult comic series, or an uncommon job experience, for example. Write an introduction to your subject for a general audience, "translating" any specialized terminology for the reader. Consider including images, as Krulwich did, to help your reader understand the subject (but be sure to correctly cite the images; see Chapter 23).
2. Write an exploratory essay on a question you feel is unsolved, something that is, as Krulwich writes of the gravitational sense of plants, "a real puzzle." Using Krulwich's essay as a model, allow your essay to follow your mental process as you think about this question. What information can you gather, and from what sources? In what areas do you feel you have adequate knowledge, and where does that knowledge end? What leaves you wondering?

Me Talk Pretty One Day

David Sedaris

Ralph Orlowski/Getty Images

David Sedaris was born in 1956 in Binghamton, New York, and grew up in Raleigh, North Carolina. He briefly attended Western Carolina University and Kent State University but ultimately graduated from the Art Institute of Chicago in 1987. Before becoming a writer, Sedaris worked as a mover, an office temp, a housekeeper, and an elf in a department store Christmas display — an experience he wrote about in his celebrated essay "Santaland Diaries." He has contributed to National Public Radio, *Harper's, Details*, the *New Yorker*, and *Esquire* and has won several awards, including the James Thurber Prize for American Humor. Sedaris often writes about his quirky Greek family and his travels with his partner, Hugh Hamrick, with whom he currently lives in London. His essays and stories have been collected in several best-selling books, including *Barrel Fever* (1994), *Holidays on Ice* (1997), *Naked* (1997), *Dress Your Family in Corduroy and Denim* (2004), *When You Are Engulfed in Flames* (2008), *Squirrel Seeks Chipmunk: A Modest Bestiary* (2010), and *Let's Explore Diabetes with Owls* (2013), whose audio version was nominated for a Grammy Award for Best Spoken Word Album.

The following essay about taking French lessons in Paris first appeared in *Esquire* in March 1999 and later became the title piece for Sedaris's fourth book, *Me Talk Pretty One Day* (2000). As you read, pay attention to how he uses his words to play with the ideas of language, understanding, and belonging.

Reflecting on What You Know

Have you ever been in a situation in which you did not speak the prevalent language — for example, in a foreign country, in a language class, or among a group of people who spoke a language other than yours? How did you feel about not being able to communicate? How, if at all, did you get your thoughts across to others?

At the age of forty-one, I am returning to school and having to think of myself as what my French textbook calls "a true debutant." After paying my tuition, I was issued a student ID, which allows me a discounted entry fee at movie theaters, puppet shows, and Festyland, a far-flung amusement park that advertises with billboards picturing a cartoon stegosaurus sitting in a canoe and eating what appears to be a ham sandwich. 1

I've moved to Paris in order to learn the language. My school is the Alliance Française, and on the first day of class, I arrived early, watching as the returning students greeted one another in the school lobby. Vacations were recounted, and questions were raised concerning mutual friends with names like Kang and Vlatnya. Regardless of their nationalities, everyone spoke what sounded to me like excellent French. Some accents were better than others, but the students exhibited an ease and confidence I found intimidating. As an added discomfort, they were all young, attractive, and well dressed, causing me to feel not unlike Pa Kettle[1] trapped backstage after a fashion show. 2

I remind myself that I am now a full-grown man. No one will ever again card me for a drink or demand that I weave a floor mat out of newspapers. At my age, a reasonable person should have completed his sentence in the prison of the nervous and the insecure—isn't that the great promise of adulthood? I can't help but think that, somewhere along the way, I made a wrong turn. My fears have not vanished. Rather, they have seasoned and multiplied with age. I am now twice as frightened as I was when, at the age of twenty, I allowed a failed nursing student to inject me with a horse tranquilizer, and eight times more anxious than I was the day my kindergarten teacher pried my fingers off my mother's ankle and led me screaming toward my desk. "You'll get used to it," the woman had said. 3

I'm still waiting. 4

The first day of class was nerve-racking because I knew I'd be expected to perform. That's the way they do it here—everyone into the language pool, sink or swim. The teacher marched in, deeply tanned from a recent vacation, and rattled off a series of administrative announcements. I've spent some time in Normandy,[2] and I took a 5

[1]*Pa Kettle:* someone who is simple or unsophisticated; the name of a character in a series of comic movies popular in the 1950s.
[2]*Normandy:* a province in northwestern France.

monthlong French class last summer in New York. I'm not completely in the dark, yet I understood only half of what this teacher was saying.

"If you have not *meismslsxp* by this time, you should not be in this room. Has everybody *apzkiubjxow*? Everyone? Good, we shall proceed." She spread out her lesson plan and sighed, saying, "All right, then, who knows the alphabet?" 6

It was startling because a) I hadn't been asked that question in a while, and b) I realized, while laughing, that I myself did not know the alphabet. They're the same letters, but they're pronounced differently. 7

"Ahh." The teacher went to the board and sketched the letter *A*. "Do we have anyone in the room whose first name commences with an ahh?" 8

Two Polish Annas raised their hands, and the teacher instructed them to present themselves, giving their names, nationalities, occupations, and a list of things they liked and disliked in this world. The first Anna hailed from an industrial town outside of Warsaw and had front teeth the size of tombstones. She worked as a seamstress, enjoyed quiet times with friends, and hated the mosquito. 9

"Oh, really," the teacher said. "How very interesting. I thought that everyone loved the mosquito, but here, in front of all the world, you claim to detest him. How is it that we've been blessed with someone as unique and original as you? Tell us, please." 10

The seamstress did not understand what was being said, but she knew that this was an occasion for shame. Her rabbity mouth huffed for breath, and she stared down at her lap as though the appropriate comeback were stitched somewhere alongside the zipper of her slacks. 11

The second Anna learned from the first and claimed to love sunshine and detest lies. It sounded like a translation of one of those Playmate of the Month data sheets, the answers always written in the same loopy handwriting: "Turn-ons: Mom's famous five-alarm chili! Turn-offs: Insincerity and guys who come on too strong!!!" 12

The two Polish women surely had clear notions of what they liked and disliked, but, like the rest of us, they were limited in terms of vocabulary, and this made them appear less than sophisticated. The teacher forged on, and we learned that Carlos, the Argentine bandoneon[3] player, loved wine, music, and, in his words, "Making sex with the women of the world." Next came a beautiful young Yugoslavian who identified herself as an optimist, saying that she loved everything life had to offer. 13

[3]*bandoneon:* a small accordion popular in South America.

The teacher licked her lips, revealing a hint of the sadist[4] we would later come to know. She crouched low for her attack, placed her hands on the young woman's desk, and said, "Oh, yeah? And do you love your little war?"[5] 14

While the optimist struggled to defend herself, I scrambled to think of an answer to what had obviously become a trick question. How often are you asked what you love in this world? More important, how often are you asked and then publicly ridiculed for your answer? I recalled my mother, flushed with wine, pounding the table late one night, saying, "Love? I love a good steak cooked rare. I love my cat, and I love . . ." My sisters and I leaned forward, waiting to hear our names. "Tums," our mother said. "I love Tums." The teacher killed some time accusing the Yugoslavian girl of masterminding a program of genocide, and I jotted frantic notes in the margins of my pad. While I can honestly say that I love leafing through medical textbooks devoted to severe dermatological conditions, it is beyond the reach of my French vocabulary, and acting it out would only have invited unwanted attention. 15

When called upon, I delivered an effortless list of things I detest: blood sausage, intestinal paté, brain pudding. I'd learned these words the hard way. Having given it some thought, I then declared my love for IBM typewriters, the French word for "bruise," and my electric floor waxer. It was a short list, but still I managed to mispronounce IBM and afford the wrong gender to both the floor waxer and the typewriter. Her reaction led me to believe that these mistakes were capital crimes in the country of France. 16

"Were you always this *palicmkrexjs*?" she asked. "Even a *fiuscrzsws tociwegixp* knows that a typewriter is feminine." 17

I absorbed as much of her abuse as I could understand, thinking, but not saying, that I find it ridiculous to assign a gender to an inanimate object incapable of disrobing and making an occasional fool of itself. Why refer to Lady Flesh Wound or Good Sir Dishrag when these things could never deliver in the sack? 18

The teacher proceeded to belittle everyone from German Eva, who hated laziness, to Japanese Yukari, who loved paintbrushes and soap. Italian, Thai, Dutch, Korean, Chinese—we all left class foolishly 19

[4]*sadist:* one who finds pleasure in being cruel to others.

[5]*". . . your little war":* the Balkan War (1991–2001), which consisted of armed conflict and genocide in the territory of the former Yugoslavia.

believing that the worst was over. We didn't know it then, but the coming months would teach us what it is like to spend time in the presence of a wild animal. We soon learned to dodge chalk and to cover our heads and stomachs whenever she approached us with a question. She hadn't yet punched anyone, but it seemed wise to prepare ourselves against the inevitable.

Though we were forbidden to speak anything but French, the teacher would occasionally use us to practice any of her five fluent languages. 20

"I hate you," she said to me one afternoon. Her English was flawless. "I really, really hate you." Call me sensitive, but I couldn't help taking it personally. 21

Learning French is a lot like joining a gang in that it involves a long and intensive period of hazing. And it wasn't just my teacher; the entire population seemed to be in on it. Following brutal encounters with my local butcher and the concierge[6] of my building, I'd head off to class, where the teacher would hold my corrected paperwork high above her head, shouting, "Here's proof that *David* is an ignorant and uninspired *ensigiejsokhjx*." 22

Refusing to stand convicted on the teacher's charges of laziness, I'd spend four hours a night on my homework, working even longer whenever we were assigned an essay. I suppose I could have gotten by with less, but I was determined to create some sort of an identity for myself. We'd have one of those "complete the sentence" exercises, and I'd fool with the thing for hours, invariably settling on something like, "A quick run around the lake? I'd love to. Just give me a minute to strap on my wooden leg." The teacher, through word and action, conveyed the message that, if this was my idea of an identity, she wanted nothing to do with it. 23

My fear and discomfort crept beyond the borders of my classroom and accompanied me out onto the wide boulevards, where, no matter how hard I tried, there was no escaping the feeling of terror I felt whenever anyone asked me a question. I was safe in any kind of a store, as, at least in my neighborhood, one can stand beside the cash register for hours on end without being asked something so trivial as, "May I help you?" or "How would you like to pay for that?" 24

My only comfort was the knowledge that I was not alone. Huddled in the smoky hallways and making the most of our pathetic 25

[6]*concierge:* a doorman in a French apartment building.

French, my fellow students and I engaged in the sort of conversation commonly overheard in refugee camps.

"Sometimes me cry alone at night." 26

"That is common for me also, but be more strong, you. Much 27 work, and someday you talk pretty. People stop hate you soon. Maybe tomorrow, okay?"

Unlike other classes I have taken, here there was no sense of 28 competition. When the teacher poked a shy Korean woman in the eyelid with a freshly sharpened pencil, we took no comfort in the fact that, unlike Hyeyoon Cho, we all knew the irregular past tense of the verb "to defeat." In all fairness, the teacher hadn't meant to hurt the woman, but neither did she spend much time apologizing, saying only, "Well, you should have been paying more attention."

Over time, it became impossible to believe that any of us would 29 ever improve. Fall arrived, and it rained every day. It was mid-October when the teacher singled me out, saying, "Every day spent with you is like having a cesarean section." And it struck me that, for the first time since arriving in France, I could understand every word that someone was saying.

Understanding doesn't mean that you can suddenly speak the lan- 30 guage. Far from it. It's a small step, nothing more, yet its rewards are intoxicating and deceptive. The teacher continued her diatribe, and I settled back, bathing in the subtle beauty of each new curse and insult.

"You exhaust me with your foolishness and reward my efforts 31 with nothing but pain, do you understand me?"

The world opened up, and it was with great joy that I responded, 32 "I know the thing what you speak exact now. Talk me more, plus, please, plus."

Thinking Critically about This Reading

Sedaris's French teacher tells him that "every day spent with you is like having a cesarean section" (paragraph 29). Why is Sedaris's ability to recount this insult significant? What does the teacher's "cesarean section" metaphor mean?

Questions for Study and Discussion

1. Sedaris's tone is humorous. What words in particular help him create this tone? Did you find yourself smiling or laughing

out loud as you read his essay? If so, what specific passages affected you this way?

2. What is your impression of Sedaris and his classmates? What words and phrases does he use to describe himself and them?
3. Why do you think Sedaris uses nonsense jumbles of letters—*meismslsxp* and *palicmkrexjs,* for example—in several places? How would his essay be different had he used the real words instead?
4. What does Sedaris realize in the final four paragraphs? What evidence does he provide of this realization?

Classroom Activity Using Diction and Tone

Good writers rely on strong verbs—verbs that contribute significantly to what is being said. Sportswriters, for example, are acutely aware of the need for strong action verbs because they must repeatedly describe similar situations. It is not enough for them to say that a team wins or loses; they must describe the type of win or loss more precisely. As a result, verbs such as *beat*, *bury*, *edge*, *shock*, and *trounce* are common in sports headlines. In addition to describing the act of winning, each of these verbs makes a statement about the quality of the victory. Like sportswriters, we all write about actions that are performed daily. If we were restricted to using only the verbs *eat*, *drink*, *sleep*, and *work* for each of these activities, our writing would be repetitious, monotonous, and most likely wordy.

Together with a small group of classmates, list as many verbs as you can that could be used in place of these four. What connotative differences do you find in your lists of alternatives? What is the importance of these connotative differences for you as writers? In which writing situations would you use certain words but not others?

Suggested Writing Assignments

1. Write a narrative essay recounting a humorous incident in your life. (Glossary: **Narration**) Use the following questions to start thinking about the incident: Where were you? What happened? Who witnessed the incident? Did you think it was humorous at the time? Do you view it differently now? Why or why not? Choose words and phrases for your narrative that convey a humorous tone.

2. "Refusing to stand convicted on the teacher's charges of laziness," Sedaris explains, "I'd spend four hours a night on my homework, working even longer whenever we were assigned an essay" (23). Write an essay in which you evaluate Sedaris's teacher. Given that she inspired Sedaris to apply himself to his work, do you think she was an effective teacher? Would her methods have the same effect on you? Why or why not? (Glossary: **Cause and Effect**)
3. As Sedaris's essay illustrates, fitting in often depends on our ability to communicate with authenticity—using the appropriate pronunciation, terminology, or slang—to a particular audience. (Glossary: **Audience; Jargon; Slang**) Have you ever felt alienated by a group because you didn't use its lingo appropriately, or have you ever alienated someone else for the same reason? Write a narrative essay in which you recount one such event. (Glossary: **Narration**) Be sure to use diction and tone creatively to convey your meaning. Before you begin, you might find it helpful to refer to your response to the Reflecting on What You Know prompt for this selection.

*Momma, the Dentist, and Me**

Maya Angelou

Syracuse Newspapers/Frank Ordonez/ The Image Works

Best-selling author and poet Maya Angelou (1928–2014) was an educator, historian, actress, playwright, civil rights activist, producer, and director. She is best known as the author of *I Know Why the Caged Bird Sings* (1970), the first book in a series that constitutes her complete autobiography, and for poems such as "Still I Rise" and "On the Pulse of the Morning," a characteristically optimistic poem on the need for personal and national renewal that she read at President Bill Clinton's inauguration in 1993. Starting with her beginnings in St. Louis in 1928, Angelou's autobiography presents a life of joyful triumph over hardships that tested her courage and threatened her spirit. It includes the titles *All God's Children Need Traveling Shoes* (1986), *The Heart of a Woman* (1997), and *A Song Flung Up to Heaven* (2002). Her final book was *Mom & Me & Mom* (2013), a memoir of her relationship with her mother. At the time of her death, Angelou was the Reynolds Professor of American Studies at Wake Forest University and had received more than fifty honorary degrees.

In the following excerpt from *I Know Why the Caged Bird Sings,* Angelou narrates what happened, and what might have happened, when her grandmother, the "Momma" of the story, took her to a local white dentist. As you read, consider Angelou's word choices and how they contribute to the story's success, particularly as you gauge the effect of the italicized paragraphs.

Reflecting on What You Know

When you were growing up, were you ever present when one or both of your parents were arguing with another adult about a matter concerning you? What were the circumstances? Narrate the events that brought about the controversy and show how it was

*This title is original to *Models for Writers*, Thirteenth Edition, and does not appear in the Maya Angelou work.

resolved. Were you embarrassed by your parents' actions, or were you happy that they stood up for you?

The angel of the candy counter had found me out at last, and was 1
exacting excruciating penance for all the stolen Milky Ways, Mounds, Mr. Goodbars, and Hersheys with Almonds. I had two cavities that were rotten to the gums. The pain was beyond the bailiwick[1] of crushed aspirins or oil of cloves. Only one thing could help me, so I prayed earnestly that I'd be allowed to sit under the house and have the building collapse on my left jaw. Since there was no Negro dentist in Stamps, nor doctor either, for that matter, Momma had dealt with previous toothaches by pulling them out (a string tied to the tooth with the other end looped over her fist), pain killers, and prayer. In this particular instance the medicine had proved ineffective; there wasn't enough enamel left to hook a string on, and the prayers were being ignored because the Balancing Angel was blocking their passage.

I lived a few days and nights in blinding pain, not so much toy-
ing with as seriously considering the idea of jumping in the well, and 2
Momma decided I had to be taken to a dentist. The nearest Negro dentist was in Texarkana, twenty-five miles away, and I was certain that I'd be dead long before we reached half the distance. Momma said we'd go to Dr. Lincoln, right in Stamps, and he'd take care of me. She said he owed her a favor.

I knew there were a number of whitefolks in town that owed her
favors. Bailey and I had seen the books which showed how she had lent 3
money to Blacks and whites alike during the Depression, and most still owed her. But I couldn't aptly remember seeing Dr. Lincoln's name, nor had I ever heard of a Negro's going to him as a patient. However, Momma said we were going, and put water on the stove for our baths. I had never been to a doctor, so she told me that after the bath (which would make my mouth feel better) I had to put on freshly starched and ironed underclothes from inside out. The ache failed to respond to the bath, and I knew then that the pain was more serious than that which anyone had ever suffered.

Before we left the Store, she ordered me to brush my teeth and then 4
wash my mouth with Listerine. The idea of even opening my clamped jaws increased the pain, but upon her explanation that when you go to a doctor you have to clean yourself all over, but most especially the part that's to be examined, I screwed up my courage and unlocked my teeth.

[1]*bailiwick:* a specific area of interest, skill, or authority.

The cool air in my mouth and the jarring of my molars dislodged what little remained of my reason. I had frozen to the pain, my family nearly had to tie me down to take the toothbrush away. It was no small effort to get me started on the road to the dentist. Momma spoke to all the passers-by, but didn't stop to chat. She explained over her shoulder that we were going to the doctor and she'd "pass the time of day" on our way home.

Until we reached the pond the pain was my world, an aura that haloed me for three feet around. Crossing the bridge into whitefolks' country, pieces of sanity pushed themselves forward. I had to stop moaning and start walking straight. The white towel, which was drawn under my chin and tied over my head, had to be arranged. If one was dying, it had to be done in style if the dying took place in whitefolks' part of town. 5

On the other side of the bridge the ache seemed to lessen as if a whitebreeze blew off the whitefolks and cushioned everything in their neighborhood—including my jaw. The gravel road was smoother, the stones smaller, and the tree branches hung down around the path and nearly covered us. If the pain didn't diminish then, the familiar yet strange sights hypnotized me into believing that it had. 6

But my head continued to throb with the measured insistence of a bass drum, and how could a toothache pass the calaboose,[2] hear the songs of the prisoners, their blues and laughter, and not be changed? How could one or two or even a mouthful of angry tooth roots meet a wagonload of powhitetrash children, endure their idiotic snobbery, and not feel less important? 7

Behind the building which housed the dentist's office ran a small path used by servants and those tradespeople who catered to the butcher and Stamps's one restaurant. Momma and I followed that lane to the backstairs of Dentist Lincoln's office. The sun was bright and gave the day a hard reality as we climbed up the steps to the second floor. 8

Momma knocked on the back door and a young white girl opened it to show surprise at seeing us there. Momma said she wanted to see Dentist Lincoln and to tell him Annie was there. The girl closed the door firmly. Now the humiliation of hearing Momma describe herself as if she had no last name to the young white girl was equal to the physical pain. It seemed terribly unfair to have a toothache and a headache and have to bear at the same time the heavy burden of Blackness. 9

[2]*calaboose:* a jail.

10 It was always possible that the teeth would quiet down and maybe drop out of their own accord. Momma said we would wait. We leaned in the harsh sunlight on the shaky railings of the dentist's back porch for over an hour.

11 He opened the door and looked at Momma. "Well, Annie, what can I do for you?"

12 He didn't see the towel around my jaw or notice my swollen face.

13 Momma said, "Dentist Lincoln. It's my grandbaby here. She got two rotten teeth that's giving her a fit."

14 She waited for him to acknowledge the truth of her statement. He made no comment, orally or facially.

15 "She had this toothache purt' near four days now, and today I said, 'Young lady, you going to the Dentist.'"

16 "Annie?"

17 "Yes, sir, Dentist Lincoln."

18 He was choosing words the way people hunt for shells. "Annie, you know I don't treat nigra, colored people."

19 "I know, Dentist Lincoln. But this here is just my little grandbaby, and she ain't gone be no trouble to you . . ."

20 "Annie, everybody has a policy. In this world you have to have a policy. Now, my policy is I don't treat colored people."

21 The sun had baked the oil out of Momma's skin and melted the Vaseline in her hair. She shone greasily as she leaned out of the dentist's shadow.

22 "Seem like to me, Dentist Lincoln, you might look after her, she ain't nothing but a little mite.[3] And seems like maybe you owe me a favor or two."

23 He reddened slightly. "Favor or no favor. The money has all been repaid to you and that's the end of it. Sorry, Annie." He had his hand on the doorknob. "Sorry." His voice was a bit kinder on the second "Sorry," as if he really was.

24 Momma said, "I wouldn't press on you like this for myself but I can't take No. Not for my grandbaby. When you come to borrow my money you didn't have to beg. You asked me, and I lent it. Now, it wasn't my policy. I ain't no moneylender, but you stood to lose this building and I tried to help you out."

25 "It's been paid, and raising your voice won't make me change my mind. My policy . . ." He let go of the door and stepped nearer Momma.

---

[3]*mite:* a very small creature.

The three of us were crowded on the small landing. "Annie, my policy is I'd rather stick my hand in a dog's mouth than in a nigger's."

He had never once looked at me. He turned his back and went through the door into the cool beyond. Momma backed up inside herself for a few minutes. I forgot everything except her face which was almost a new one to me. She leaned over and took the doorknob, and in her everyday soft voice she said, "Sister, go on downstairs. Wait for me. I'll be there directly." 26

Under the most common of circumstances I knew it did no good to argue with Momma. So I walked down the steep stairs, afraid to look back and afraid not to do so. I turned as the door slammed, and she was gone. 27

Momma walked in that room as if she owned it. She shoved that silly nurse aside with one hand and strode into the dentist's office. He was sitting in his chair, sharpening his mean instruments and putting extra sting into his medicines. Her eyes were blazing like live coals and her arms had doubled themselves in length. He looked up at her just before she caught him by the collar of his white jacket. 28

"Stand up when you see a lady, you contemptuous scoundrel." Her tongue had thinned and the words rolled off well enunciated. Enunciated and sharp like little claps of thunder. 29

The dentist had no choice but to stand at R.O.T.C.[4] *attention. His head dropped after a minute and his voice was humble. "Yes, ma'am, Mrs. Henderson."* 30

"You knave, do you think you acted like a gentleman, speaking to me like that in front of my granddaughter?" She didn't shake him, although she had the power. She simply held him upright. 31

"No, ma'am, Mrs. Henderson." 32

"No, ma'am, Mrs. Henderson, what?" Then she did give him the tiniest of shakes, but because of her strength the action set his head and arms to shaking loose on the ends of his body. He stuttered much worse than Uncle Willie. "No, ma'am, Mrs. Henderson, I'm sorry." 33

With just an edge of her disgust showing, Momma slung him back in his dentist's chair. "Sorry is as sorry does, and you're about the sorriest dentist I ever laid my eyes on." (She could afford to slip into the vernacular[5] *because she had such eloquent command of English.)* 34

---

[4]*R.O.T.C.:* Reserve Officers Training Corps of the U.S. military.

[5]*vernacular:* the everyday language spoken by people of a particular country or region.

"I didn't ask you to apologize in front of Marguerite, because I 35
don't want her to know my power, but I order you, now and herewith. Leave Stamps by sundown."

"Mrs. Henderson, I can't get my equipment . . ." He was shaking 36
terribly now.

"Now, that brings me to my second order. You will never again 37
practice dentistry. Never! When you get settled in your next place, you will be a veterinarian caring for dogs with the mange, cats with the cholera, and cows with the epizootic. Is that clear?"

The saliva ran down his chin and his eyes filled with tears. "Yes, 38
ma'am. Thank you for not killing me. Thank you, Mrs. Henderson."

Momma pulled herself back from being ten feet tall with eightfoot 39
arms and said, "You're welcome for nothing, you varlet,[6] *I wouldn't waste a killing on the likes of you."*

On her way out she waved her handkerchief at the nurse and 40
turned her into a crocus sack of chicken feed.

Momma looked tired when she came down the stairs, but who 41
wouldn't be tired if they had gone through what she had. She came close to me and adjusted the towel under my jaw (I had forgotten the toothache; I only knew that she made her hands gentle in order not to awaken the pain). She took my hand. Her voice never changed. "Come on, Sister."

I reckoned we were going home where she would concoct a brew 42
to eliminate the pain and maybe give me new teeth too. New teeth that would grow overnight out of my gums. She led me toward the drugstore, which was in the opposite direction from the Store. "I'm taking you to Dentist Baker in Texarkana."

I was glad after all that I had bathed and put on Mum[7] and Cashmere 43
Bouquet talcum powder. It was a wonderful surprise. My toothache had quieted to solemn pain, Momma had obliterated the evil white man, and we were going on a trip to Texarkana, just the two of us.

On the Greyhound she took an inside seat in the back, and I sat 44
beside her. I was so proud of being her granddaughter and sure that some of her magic must have come down to me. She asked if I was scared. I only shook my head and leaned over on her cool brown upper arm. There was no chance that a dentist, especially a Negro dentist, would dare hurt me then. Not with Momma there. The trip was

---

[6]*varlet:* a rascal; lowlife.
[7]*Mum:* a brand of deodorant.

uneventful, except that she put her arm around me, which was very unusual for Momma to do.

The dentist showed me the medicine and the needle before he deadened my gums, but if he hadn't I wouldn't have worried. Momma stood right behind him. Her arms were folded and she checked on everything he did. The teeth were extracted and she bought me an ice cream cone from the side window of a drug counter. The trip back to Stamps was quiet, except that I had to spit into a very small empty snuff can which she had gotten for me and it was difficult with the bus humping and jerking on our country roads. 45

At home, I was given a warm salt solution, and when I washed out my mouth I showed Bailey the empty holes, where the clotted blood sat like filling in a pie crust. He said I was quite brave, and that was my cue to reveal our confrontation with the peckerwood dentist and Momma's incredible powers. 46

I had to admit that I didn't hear the conversation, but what else could she have said than what I said she said? What else done? He agreed with my analysis in a lukewarm way, and I happily (after all, I'd been sick) flounced into the Store. Momma was preparing our evening meal and Uncle Willie leaned on the door sill. She gave her version. 47

"Dentist Lincoln got right uppity. Said he'd rather put his hand in a dog's mouth. And when I reminded him of the favor, he brushed it off like a piece of lint. Well, I sent Sister downstairs and went inside. I hadn't never been in his office before, but I found the door to where he takes out teeth, and him and the nurse was in there thick as thieves. I just stood there till he caught sight of me." Crash bang the pots on the stove. "He jumped just like he was sitting on a pin. He said, 'Annie, I done tole you, I ain't gonna mess around in no niggah's mouth.' I said, 'Somebody's got to do it then,' and he said, 'Take her to Texarkana to the colored dentist' and that's when I said, 'If you paid me my money I could afford to take her.' He said, 'It's all been paid.' I tole him everything but the interest been paid. He said, ''Twasn't no interest.' I said, ''Tis now. I'll take ten dollars as payment in full.' You know, Willie, it wasn't no right thing to do, 'cause I lent that money without thinking about it. 48

"He tole that little snippety nurse of his'n to give me ten dollars and make me sign a 'paid in full' receipt. She gave it to me and I signed the papers. Even though by rights he was paid up before, I figger, he gonna be that kind of nasty, he gonna have to pay for it." 49

Momma and her son laughed and laughed over the white man's evilness and her retributive[8] sin. 50

I preferred, much preferred, my version. 51

Thinking Critically about This Reading

What does Angelou mean when she states, "On the other side of the bridge the ache seemed to lessen as if a whitebreeze blew off the whitefolks and cushioned everything in their neighborhood—including my jaw" (paragraph 6)? How long did Angelou's pain relief last? Why?

Questions for Study and Discussion

1. What is Angelou's purpose in relating this story? (Glossary: **Purpose**)
2. Compare and contrast the content and style of the interaction between Momma and the dentist that is given in italics with the one given at the end of the narrative. (Glossary: **Comparison and Contrast**)
3. How does the diction in the quotations differ from the diction Angelou uses in her narration as she tells the story? What effect does this difference have on your experience as a reader?
4. Angelou tells her story chronologically and in the first person. (Glossary: **Point of View**) What are the advantages of first-person narration? How does this point of view choice affect her diction and tone?
5. Identify three similes Angelou uses in her narrative. (Glossary: **Figure of Speech**) Explain how each simile serves her purpose. (Glossary: **Purpose**)
6. Why do you suppose Angelou says she prefers her own version of the episode to that of her grandmother?
7. This is a story of pain—and not just the pain of a toothache. What words does Angelou use to describe the pain of the toothache, and how does that enhance the impression of her pain? What other pain does she tell of in this autobiographical piece, and what word does she use to describe it?

---

[8]*retributive:* demanding something in repayment, especially punishment.

Classroom Activity Using Diction and Tone

Writers of all sorts have to match their language to the occasion for writing. In the Gettysburg Address, the text of which follows, President Abraham Lincoln was presented with the grave and monumental occasion of commemorating lives lost in war. He declares it "fitting and proper" that the nation designate part of the battlefield as a memorial. Read the speech and then discuss how Lincoln finds a similarly "fitting and proper" diction for his speech. Which words or phrases best reflect the seriousness of the occasion?

> Four score and seven years ago our fathers brought forth on this continent, a new nation, conceived in Liberty, and dedicated to the proposition that all men are created equal.
>
> Now we are engaged in a great civil war, testing whether that nation, or any nation so conceived and so dedicated, can long endure. We are met on a great battle-field of that war. We have come to dedicate a portion of that field, as a final resting place for those who here gave their lives that that nation might live. It is altogether fitting and proper that we should do this.
>
> But, in a larger sense, we can not dedicate—we can not consecrate—we can not hallow—this ground. The brave men, living and dead, who struggled here, have consecrated it, far above our poor power to add or detract. The world will little note, nor long remember what we say here, but it can never forget what they did here. It is for us the living, rather, to be dedicated here to the unfinished work, which they who fought here have thus far so nobly advanced. It is rather for us to be here dedicated to the great task remaining before us—that from these honored dead we take increased devotion to that cause for which they gave the last full measure of devotion—that we here highly resolve that these dead shall not have died in vain—that this nation, under God, shall have a new birth of freedom—and that government of the people, by the people, for the people, shall not perish from the earth.

Suggested Writing Assignments

1. Write a few paragraphs about an actual event—either a personal event or a historic event—adopting one of the particular tones listed on pages 274–76. Then write about the same event using two different tones so that you have three versions of the

same event. How did you create the different tones? Does one tone work better for recounting the event than another? Why?

2. Every person who tells a story puts his or her signature on it in some way—by the sequencing of events, the amount and type of details used, and the tone the teller employs. Consider a time when you and a relative or friend experienced the same interesting sequence of events differently, then tell the story of those events from your unique perspective. (Glossary: **Point of View**) Once you have done so, try telling the story from what you imagine the other person's perspective to be. Perhaps you even heard the other person actually tell the story, using word choice to inject his or her personality. What is the same in both versions? How do the renditions differ?

CHAPTER **12**

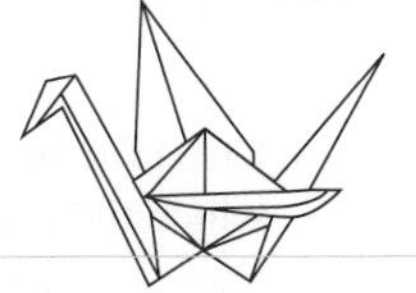

Figurative Language

Figurative language is language used in an imaginative rather than a literal sense. Although it is most often associated with poetry, figurative language is used widely in our daily speech and in our writing. Prose writers have long known that figurative language brings freshness and color to writing and also helps clarify ideas. For example, when asked by his teacher to explain the concept of brainstorming, one student replied, "Well, brainstorming is like having a tornado in your head." This figurative language helps others imagine the whirl of ideas in this young writer's head as he brainstorms a topic for writing.

The two most common **figures of speech** are the simile and the metaphor. A **simile** compares two essentially different ideas or things and uses *like* or *as* to link them.

> I was taught that candles are like house cats—domesticated versions of something wild and dangerous.
>
> –Sloane Crosley, *I Was Told There'd Be Cake*

> I walked toward her and hailed her as a visitor to the moon might salute a survivor of a previous expedition.
>
> –John Updike, *Assorted Prose*

A **metaphor** compares dissimilar ideas or things without using *like* or *as*.

> She was very old and small and she walked slowly in the dark pine shadows, moving a little from side to side in her steps, with the balanced heaviness and lightness of a pendulum in a grandfather clock.
>
> –Eudora Welty, *A Worn Path*

> Charm is the ultimate weapon, the supreme seduction, against which there are few defenses.
>
> –Laurie Lee, *I Can't Stay Long*

To expand the richness of a particular comparison, writers sometimes use several sentences or even a whole paragraph to develop a metaphor. Such a comparison is called an *extended metaphor*.

> The point is that you have to strip down your writing before you can build it back up. You must know what the essential tools are and what job they were designed to do. If I may belabor the metaphor on carpentry, it is first necessary to be able to saw wood neatly and to drive nails. Later you can bevel the edges or add elegant finials, if that is your taste. But you can never forget that you are practicing a craft that is based on certain principles. If the nails are weak, your house will collapse. If your verbs are weak and your syntax is rickety, your sentences will fall apart.
>
> –William Zinsser, *On Writing Well*

Another frequently used figure of speech is personification. In personification, the writer attributes human qualities to ideas or objects.

> The moon bathed the valley in a soft, golden light.
>
> –Corey Davis, student

> Blond October comes striding over the hills wearing a crimson shirt and faded green trousers.
>
> –Hal Borland, *Borland Country*

> Procrastination is the thief of time. Collar him.
>
> –Charles Dickens, *David Copperfield*

In all the preceding examples, notice how the writers' use of figurative language enlivens their prose and emphasizes their ideas. Each vividly communicates an idea or the essence of an object by comparing it to something concrete and familiar. In each case, too, the figurative language grows out of the writer's thinking, reflecting the way he or she sees the material. Be similarly honest in your use of figurative language, keeping in mind that figures of speech should never be used merely to dress up your writing. Above all, use them to develop your ideas and clarify your meaning for the reader.

The Flight of the Eagles

N. Scott Momaday

Ulf Andersen/Getty Images

N. Scott Momaday was born in Lawton, Oklahoma, in 1934 and lived on the Kiowa reservation with his parents and grandparents. After a year, his family moved to Arizona, where he lived most of his life. Both of his parents worked as teachers on Indian reservations, which exposed Momaday to the cultures and languages of the tribes of the Southwest United States, particularly the Navajo, Apache, and Pueblo. Momaday eventually taught on a Pueblo reservation himself before moving to California to complete MA and PhD degrees at Stanford University. In 1969, his novel *House Made of Dawn* won a Pulitzer Prize and initiated what critic Kenneth Lincoln called a Native American renaissance in literature. Since that time, Momaday has published numerous books, including *The Way to Rainy Mountain* (1969), *The Ancient Child* (1989), *The Man Made of Words: Essays, Stories, Passages* (1997), and *Again the Far Morning: New and Selected Poems* (2011).

In this excerpt from *House Made of Dawn*, Momaday uses dense, inventive language—including figures of speech—to paint a precise picture of two birds in flight. As you read, notice how Momaday's similes help you visualize the scene.

Reflecting on What You Know

Seeing birds in flight is a relatively common experience, so we might take it for granted. Close your eyes and visualize a bird flying. How would you describe the way it moves through the air?

They were golden eagles, a male and a female, in their mating flight. They were cavorting, spinning and spiraling on the cold, clear columns of air, and they were beautiful. They swooped and hovered, leaning on the air, and swung close together, feinting and screaming with delight. The female was full-grown, and the span of her broad wings was greater than any man's height. There was a fine flourish to her motion; she was deceptively, incredibly fast, and her pivots and wheels were wide and full-blown. But her great weight was streamlined and perfectly controlled. She carried a rattlesnake; it hung shining from her feet, limp and curving out in the trail of her flight. Suddenly her wings and tail fanned, catching full on the wind, and for an instant she was still, widespread and spectral in the blue, while her mate flared past and away, turning around in the distance to look for her. Then she began to beat upward at an angle from the rim until she was small in the sky, and she let go of the snake. It fell slowly, writhing and rolling, floating out like a bit of silver thread against the wide backdrop of the land. She held still above, buoyed up on the cold current, her crop and hackles gleaming like copper in the sun. The male swerved and sailed. He was younger than she and a little more than half as large. He was quicker, tighter in his moves. He let the carrion drift by; then suddenly he gathered himself and swooped, sliding down in a blur of motion to the strike. He hit the snake in the head, with not the slightest deflection of his course or speed, cracking its long body like a whip. Then he rolled and swung upward in a great pendulum arc, riding out his momentum. At the top of his glide he let go of the snake in turn, but the female did not go for it. Instead she soared out over the plain, nearly out of sight, like a mote receding into the haze of the far mountain. The male followed.

Thinking Critically about This Reading

Why does Momaday pay such careful attention to what others might ignore—the intricate movements of two birds? What meaning does he find in their paired flight?

Questions for Study and Discussion

1. Near the beginning of the passage, Momaday personifies the birds as "screaming with delight." What does this seemingly human emotion add to the scene he depicts? Do you notice any other instances of personification?
2. Circle all of the active verbs in the first three sentences of the paragraph. Why does Momaday choose these words? What picture do they paint in your mind?

3. How would you describe Momaday's tone in this passage? What words or phrases do you think best convey his attitude toward the eagles? (Glossary: **Tone**)
4. Discuss how the two birds contrast with each other. How does Momaday describe the differences in their appearance?
5. The interaction that Momaday witnesses between the birds centers on the rattlesnake. How does he use similes to help readers picture their movements?
6. How does Momaday begin the paragraph? How does he end it? How do these sentences shape the very short story he tells about the eagles?

Classroom Activity Using Figurative Language

What is the most unusual event you have witnessed? Using the figures of speech you have learned (simile, metaphor, and personification), write six sentences that describe the event so that your readers can appreciate it. First state what the event was, then present your sentences in either a connected paragraph or a series of separate sentences. Share your description with your classmates to determine how effectively you have conveyed the dominant impression you wished to create.

Suggested Writing Assignments

1. Write a single carefully crafted paragraph in which you describe in detail your close observations of some small event in nature—the movement of trees in the wind, a bee buzzing around a flower, or a person feeding pigeons in a park. Use similes, metaphors, or personification to communicate what you observed to a reader.
2. Momaday pays careful attention in this passage to the way the birds move. For example, he uses the metaphor of a pendulum to convey the shape of the bird's flight. Write a personal essay about something that requires movement—for example, walking or cycling to school, cooking dinner, or playing a sport. Think about how those movements feel to you as you perform them and how they might look to an outside observer. As you compose your essay, focus on metaphors or other figures of speech that add a sense of motion.

The Barrio

Robert Ramirez

Courtesy of Robert Ramirez

Robert Ramirez was born in Edinburg, Texas, in 1949. After graduating from the University of Texas–Pan American, he taught writing and held the positions of cameraman, reporter, anchor, and producer for the local news on KGBT-TV, the CBS affiliate in Harlingen, Texas. He is retired from working as an alumni fundraiser for the University of Texas–Pan American, now known as University of Texas Rio Grande Valley.

The following essay first appeared in *Pain and Promise: The Chicano Today* (1972), edited by Edward R. Simmen. Notice how Ramirez uses figurative language, particularly metaphors, to awaken the reader's senses to the sights, sounds, and smells that are the essence of the barrio.

Reflecting on What You Know

Where did you grow up? What do you remember most about your childhood neighborhood? How did it feel as a young person to live in this world? Do you still call this neighborhood "home"? Explain.

1 The train, its metal wheels squealing as they spin along the silvery tracks, rolls slower now. Through the gaps between the cars blinks a streetlamp, and this pulsing light on a barrio streetcorner beats slower, like a weary heartbeat, until the train shudders to a halt, the light goes out, and the barrio is deep asleep.

2 Throughout Aztlán[1] (the Nahuatl term meaning "land to the north"), trains grumble along the edges of a sleeping people. From Lower California, through the blistering Southwest, down the Rio Grande[2] to the muddy Gulf, the darkness and mystery of dreams engulf communities fenced off by railroads, canals, and expressways.

[1]*Aztlán:* the mythical place of origin of the Aztec peoples.
[2]*Rio Grande:* a river flowing from southwest Colorado to Texas and Mexico and into the Gulf of Mexico.

Paradoxical[3] communities, isolated from the rest of the town by concrete columned monuments of progress, and yet stranded in the past. They are surrounded by change. It eludes their reach, in their own backyards, and the people, unable and unwilling to see the future, or even touch the present, perpetuate the past.

Leaning from the expressway or jolting across the tracks, one enters a different physical world permeated by a different attitude. The physical dimensions are impressive. It is a large section of town which extends for fifteen blocks north and south along the tracks, and then advances eastward, thinning into nothingness beyond the city limits. Within the invisible (yet sensible) walls of the barrio are many, many people living in too few houses. The homes, however, are much more numerous than on the outside. 3

Members of the barrio describe the entire area as their home. It is a home, but it is more than this. The barrio is a refuge from the harshness and the coldness of the Anglo world. It is a forced refuge. The leprous people are isolated from the rest of the community and contained in their section of town. The stoical pariahs of the barrio accept their fate, and from the angry seeds of rejection grow the flowers of closeness between outcasts, not the thorns of bitterness and the mad desire to flee. There is no want to escape, for the feeling of the barrio is known only to its inhabitants, and the material needs of life can also be found here. 4

The *tortillería* [tortilla factory] fires up its machinery three times a day, producing steaming, round, flat slices of barrio bread. In the winter, the warmth of the tortilla factory is a wool *sarape* [blanket] in the chilly morning hours, but in the summer, it unbearably toasts every noontime customer. 5

The *panadería* [bakery] sends its sweet messenger aroma down the dimly lit street, announcing the arrival of fresh, hot sugary *pan dulce* [sweet rolls]. 6

The small corner grocery serves the meal-to-meal needs of customers, and the owner, a part of the neighborhood, willingly gives credit to people unable to pay cash for foodstuffs. 7

The barbershop is a living room with hydraulic chairs, radio, and television, where old friends meet and speak of life as their salted hair falls aimlessly about them. 8

The pool hall is a junior level country club where *'chucos* [young men], strangers in their own land, get together to shoot pool and 9

[3]*paradoxical:* seemingly contradictory.

rap, while veterans, unaware of the cracking, popping balls on the green felt, complacently play dominoes beneath rudely hung *Playboy* foldouts.

The *cantina* [canteen or snackbar] is the night spot of the barrio. It is the country club and the den where the rites of puberty are enacted. Here the young become men. It is in the taverns that a young dude shows his *machismo* through the quantity of beer he can hold, the stories of *rucas* [women] he has had, and his willingness and ability to defend his image against hardened and scarred old lions. 10

No, there is no frantic wish to flee. It would be absurd to leave the familiar and nervously step into the strange and cold Anglo community when the needs of the Chicano[4] can be met in the barrio. 11

The barrio is closeness. From the family living unit, familial relationships stretch out to immediate neighbors, down the block, around the corner, and to all parts of the barrio. The feeling of family, a rare and treasurable sentiment, pervades and accounts for the inability of the people to leave. The barrio is this attitude manifested on the countenances[5] of the people, on the faces of their homes, and in the gaiety of their gardens. 12

The color-splashed homes arrest your eyes, arouse your curiosity, and make you wonder what life scenes are being played out in them. The flimsy, brightly colored, wood-frame houses ignore no neon-brilliant color. Houses trimmed in orange, chartreuse, lime-green, yellow, and mixtures of these and other hues beckon the beholder to reflect on the peculiarity of each home. Passing through this land is refreshing like Brubeck,[6] not narcoticizing like revolting rows of similar houses, which neither offend nor please. 13

In the evenings, the porches and front yards are occupied with men calmly talking over the noise of children playing baseball in the unpaved extension of the living room, while the women cook supper or gossip with female neighbors as they water the *jardines* [gardens]. The gardens mutely echo the expressive verses of the colorful houses. The denseness of multicolored plants and trees gives the house the appearance of an oasis or a tropical island hideaway, sheltered from the rest of the world. 14

---

[4]*Chicano:* an American of Mexican descent.

[5]*countenances:* facial expressions that indicate mood or character.

[6]*Dave Brubeck* (1920–2012): pianist, composer, and conductor of "cool" modern jazz.

Fences are common in the barrio, but they are fences and not the walls of the Anglo community. On the western side of town, the high wooden fences between houses are thick, impenetrable walls, built to keep the neighbors at bay. In the barrio, the fences may be rusty, wire contraptions or thick green shrubs. In either case you can see through them and feel no sense of intrusion when you cross them. 15

Many lower-income families of the barrio manage to maintain a comfortable standard of living through the communal action of family members who contribute their wages to the head of the family. Economic need creates interdependence and closeness. Small bare-footed boys sell papers on cool, dark Sunday mornings, deny themselves pleasantries, and give their earnings to *mamá*. The older the child, the greater the responsibility to help the head of the household provide for the rest of the family. 16

There are those, too, who for a number of reasons have not achieved a relative sense of financial security. Perhaps it results from too many children too soon, but it is the homes of these people and their situation that numbs rather than charms. Their houses, aged and bent, oozing children, are fissures[7] in the horn of plenty. Their wooden homes may have brick-pattern asbestos tile on the outer walls, but the tile is not convincing. 17

Unable to pay city taxes or incapable of influencing the city to live up to its duty to serve all the citizens, the poorer barrio families remain trapped in the nineteenth century and survive as best they can. The backyards have well-worn paths to the outhouses, which sit near the alley. Running water is considered a luxury in some parts of the barrio. Decent drainage is usually unknown, and when it rains, the water stands for days, an incubator of health hazards and an avoidable nuisance. Streets, costly to pave, remain rough, rocky trails. Tires do not last long, and the constant rattling and shaking grind away a car's life and spread dust through screen windows. 18

The houses and their *jardines*, the jollity of the people in an adverse world, the brightly feathered alarm clock pecking away at supper and cautiously eyeing the children playing nearby, produce a mystifying sensation at finding the noble savage[8] alive in the twentieth century. It is easy to look at the positive qualities of life in the barrio, and look at them with a distantly envious feeling. One wishes 19

---

[7]*fissures:* narrow openings or cracks.

[8]*noble savage:* in literature, an idealized concept of uncivilized human.

to experience the feelings of the barrio and not the hardships. Remembering the illness, the hunger, the feeling of time running out on you, the walls, both real and imagined, reflecting on living in the past, one finds his envy becoming more elusive, until it has vanished altogether.

Back now beyond the tracks, the train creaks and groans, the cars 20
jostle each other down the track, and as the light begins its pulsing, the barrio, with all its meanings, greets a new dawn with yawns and restless stretchings.

Thinking Critically about This Reading

What evidence does Ramirez give to support the following claim: "Members of the barrio describe the entire area as their home. It is a home, but it is more than this" (paragraph 4)?

Questions for Study and Discussion

1. What is the barrio? Where is it? What does Ramirez mean when he states, "There is no want to escape, for the feeling of the barrio is known only to its inhabitants, and the material needs of life can also be found here" (4)?
2. Ramirez uses Spanish phrases throughout his essay. Why do you suppose he uses them? What is their effect on the reader? He also uses the words *home, refuge, closeness*, and *family*. What do they connote in the context of this essay? (Glossary: **Connotation/Denotation**) In what ways, if any, are they essential to the writer's purpose? (Glossary: **Purpose**)
3. Identify several metaphors and similes that Ramirez uses in his essay, and explain why they are particularly appropriate.
4. In paragraph 6, Ramirez uses personification when he refers to the aroma of freshly baked sweet rolls as a "messenger." Cite other words or phrases that Ramirez uses to give human characteristics to the barrio.
5. Explain Ramirez's use of the imagery of walls and fences to describe a sense of cultural isolation. What might this imagery symbolize? (Glossary: **Symbol**)
6. Ramirez begins with a relatively positive picture of the barrio but ends on a more disheartening note. (Glossary: **Beginnings and Endings**) Why does he organize his essay in this way? What might the effect have been had he reversed these images?

Classroom Activity Using Figurative Language

Create a metaphor or simile that would be helpful in describing each item in the following list. To illustrate the process, the first one has been completed for you.

1. Skyscraper: The skyscraper sparkled like a huge glass needle.
2. Sound of an explosion
3. Intelligent student
4. Crowded bus
5. Slow-moving car
6. Pillow
7. Narrow alley
8. Greasy french fries
9. Hot sun
10. Dull knife

Compare your metaphors and similes with those written by other members of your class. Which metaphors and similes seem to work best for each item on the list? Why? Do any seem tired or clichéd?

Suggested Writing Assignments

1. In paragraph 19, Ramirez states, "One wishes to experience the feelings of the barrio and not the hardships." Explore his meaning in light of what you have just read and any experience or knowledge you may have of "ghetto" living. In what way can it be said that the hardships of such living are a necessary part of its "feelings"? How might barrio life change, for better or for worse, if the city were to "live up to its duty to serve all the citizens" (18)?
2. Write a brief essay in which you describe your own neighborhood. (Glossary: **Description**) You may find it helpful to review what you wrote in response to the Reflecting on What You Know prompt for this selection.

Polaroids

Anne Lamott

Araya Diaz/Getty Images

Born in San Francisco in 1954, Anne Lamott is a graduate of Goucher College in Baltimore and the author of seven novels; *Imperfect Birds* (2010) is the most recent of them. She has also written a food-review column for *California* magazine and a book-review column for *Mademoiselle*. In 1993, she published *Operating Instructions: A Journal of My Son's First Year,* in which she describes her own adventures as a single parent. Lamott has also written five books about her thoughts on faith: *Traveling Mercies: Some Thoughts on Faith* (1999), *Plan B: Further Thoughts on Faith* (2005), *Help, Thanks, Wow: The Three Essential Prayers* (2012), *Stitches: A Handbook on Meaning, Hope and Repair* (2013), and *Small Victories: Spotting Improbable Moments of Grace* (2014).

The following selection is a chapter from Lamott's popular book about writing, *Bird by Bird* (1994). The entire essay is built around the extended metaphor of a developing Polaroid photograph. As you read, notice how effectively Lamott weaves in references to the Polaroid to clarify points she wishes to make about the process of writing.

Reflecting on What You Know

Do you or does someone in your family enjoy taking photographs or looking back on old family albums and memories? How have digital photography and the convenience of smartphone cameras changed the way we take, view, and display photographs? Have we lost something in the shift to digital photography?

Writing a first draft is very much like watching a Polaroid develop. You can't — and, in fact, you're not supposed to — know exactly what the picture is going to look like until it has finished developing. First you just point at what has your attention and take the picture. In the last chapter, for instance, what had my 1 attention were the contents of my lunch bag. But as the picture developed, I found I had a really clear image of the boy against the fence. Or maybe *your* Polaroid was supposed to be a picture of that boy against the fence, and you didn't notice until the last minute that a family was standing a few feet away from him. Now, maybe it's his family, or the family of one of the kids in his class, but at any rate these people are going to be in the photograph, too. Then the film emerges from the camera with a grayish green murkiness that gradually becomes clearer and clearer, and finally you see the husband and wife holding their baby with two children standing beside them. And at first it all seems very sweet, but then the shadows begin to appear, and then you start to see the animal tragedy, the baboons baring their teeth. And then you see a flash of bright red flowers in the bottom left quadrant that you didn't even know were in the picture when you took it, and these flowers evoke a time or a memory that moves you mysteriously. And finally, as the portrait comes into focus, you begin to notice all the props surrounding these people, and you begin to understand how props define us and comfort us, and show us what we value and what we need, and who we think we are.

You couldn't have had any way of knowing what this piece of work would look like when you first started. You just knew that there was something about these people that compelled you, and you stayed with that something long enough for it to show you what it was about. 2

Watch this Polaroid develop: 3

Six or seven years ago I was asked to write an article on the Special Olympics. I had been going to the local event for years, partly because a couple of friends of mine compete. Also, I love sports, and I love to watch athletes, special or otherwise. So I showed up this time with a great deal of interest but no real sense of what the finished article might look like. 4

Things tend to go very, very slowly at the Special Olympics. It is not like trying to cover the Preakness. Still, it has its own exhilaration, and I cheered and took notes all morning. 5

The last track-and-field event before lunch was a twenty-five-yard race run by some unusually handicapped runners and walkers, many of whom seemed completely confused. They lumped and careened along, one man making a snail-slow break for the stands, one heading out toward the steps where the winners receive their medals; both of them were shepherded back. The race took just about forever. And here it was nearly noon and we were all so hungry. Finally, though, 6 everyone crossed over the line, and those of us in the stands got up to go—when we noticed that way down the track, four or five yards from the starting line, was another runner.

She was a girl of about sixteen with a normal-looking face above 7
a wracked and emaciated body. She was on metal crutches, and she was just plugging along, one tiny step after another, moving one crutch forward two or three inches, then moving a leg, then moving the other crutch two or three inches, then moving the other leg. It was just excruciating. Plus, I was starving to death. Inside I was going, Come on, come on, come on, swabbing at my forehead with anxiety, while she kept taking these two- or three-inch steps forward. What felt like four hours later, she crossed the finish line, and you could see that she was absolutely stoked, in a shy, girlish way.

A tall African American man with no front teeth fell into step 8
with me as I left the bleachers to go look for some lunch. He tugged on the sleeve of my sweater, and I looked up at him, and he handed me a Polaroid someone had taken of him and his friends that day. "Look at us," he said. His speech was difficult to understand, thick and slow as a warped record. His two friends in the picture had Down's syndrome. All three of them looked extremely pleased with themselves. I admired the picture and then handed it back to him. He stopped, so I stopped, too. He pointed to his own image. "That," he said, "is one cool man."

And this was the image from which an article began forming, 9
although I could not have told you exactly what the piece would end up being about. I just knew that something had started to emerge.

After lunch I wandered over to the auditorium, where it turned 10
out a men's basketball game was in progress. The African American man with no front teeth was the star of the game. You could tell that he was because even though no one had made a basket yet, his teammates almost always passed him the ball. Even the people on the *other* team passed him the ball a lot. In lieu of any scoring, the men stampeded in slow motion up and down the court, dribbling the ball thunderously. I had never heard such a loud game. It was all sort of crazily beautiful. I imagined describing the game for my article and then for my students: the loudness, the joy. I kept replaying the scene of the girl on crutches making her way up the track to the finish line—and all of a sudden my article began to appear out of the grayish green murk. And I could see that it was about tragedy transformed over the years into joy. It was about the beauty of sheer effort. I could see it almost

as clearly as I could the photograph of that one cool man and his two friends.

The auditorium bleachers were packed. Then a few minutes later, still with no score on the board, the tall black man dribbled slowly from one end of the court to the other, and heaved the ball up into the air, and it dropped into the basket. The crowd roared, and all the men on both teams looked up wide-eyed at the hoop, as if it had just burst into flames. 11

You would have loved it, I tell my students. You would have felt like you could write all day. 12

Thinking Critically about This Reading

In what way does the African American man's perception of himself in the Polaroid picture help Lamott with her writing assignment?

Questions for Study and Discussion

1. This entire essay is based on an extended metaphor or analogy. (Glossary: **Analogy**) What is the metaphor? How does it serve to clarify Lamott's central idea?
2. Besides the extended metaphor, Lamott uses several figures of speech in this essay. Find at least one metaphor and one simile. How does each contribute to the effect of the piece on the reader?
3. Lamott uses the phrase "grayish green murkiness" in the first paragraph and refers again to "grayish green murk" near the end of the essay, in paragraph 10. Why does she repeat these words? What does this phrase mean to a photographer? To a writer? For which of them does it function as a metaphor?
4. In paragraph 1, Lamott identifies four elements in "*your* Polaroid" that you didn't expect to find. What are they? Why does she include them?
5. Although the diction of this essay is simple and informal (Glossary: **Diction**), the structure is quite complicated. It is almost like an essay within an essay. What purpose is served by the long embedded narrative about the Special Olympics? (Glossary: **Example**) How does Lamott succeed in achieving unity? (Glossary: **Unity**)

Classroom Activity Using Figurative Language

Imagine each of the following abstract nouns as a character. What would each character look like? How would it act or talk? Choose one of these characters, and write a substantial descriptive paragraph, developing your ideas. What does this imaginative leap to personification reveal about the abstraction?

1. Friendship
2. Jealousy
3. Justice
4. Frustration
5. Perfection

Suggested Writing Assignments

1. With sudden insight, Lamott understands what the Special Olympics meant to her: "It was about tragedy transformed over the years into joy. It was about the beauty of sheer effort" (paragraph 10). Everyone has experiences in life that take on special meaning. Look back on a significant event you have witnessed or in which you took part, one that has come to represent to you some important truth about life. Write a narrative essay describing the event. Wait until you are at or approaching the end of your narrative to reveal explicitly your insight into its meaning.
2. When we think about our daily activities, we often clarify our understanding of some aspect of them by seeing one activity in terms of another. Not everyone's perceptions will be the same: A good horseback rider, for example, might come back from a relaxing day on the trail thinking, "Riding a horse is a form of meditation," while the novice bumping around in the saddle thinks, "Riding a horse is a form of torture." A computer expert finds that surfing the web is like traveling on a magic carpet, while someone else might find it more like being lost in a labyrinth. Choose an activity in your daily life that suggests such a simile or metaphor. Write an essay about the activity that begins with a figure of speech and explores its implications.

p a r t ⁝⁝⁝ *f o u r*

Types of Essays

CHAPTER **13**

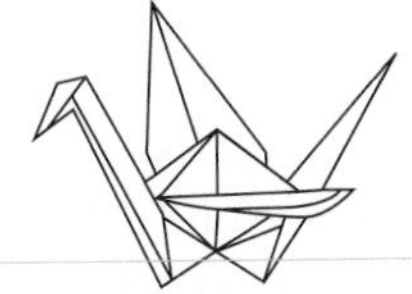

Illustration

Illustration is the use of **examples**—facts, opinions, samples, and anecdotes or stories—to make ideas more concrete and generalizations more specific and detailed. Examples enable writers not just to tell but also to show what they mean. The more specific the example, the more effective it is. For instance, in an essay about alternative sources of energy, a writer might offer an example of how a local architecture firm designed a home heated by solar collectors instead of by a conventional oil, gas, or electric system.

A writer uses examples to clarify or support the thesis in an essay and the main ideas in paragraphs. Sometimes a single striking example suffices; at other times a whole series of related examples is necessary. The following paragraph presents a single extended example—an explanation of weather as a chaotic system:

> The weather provides the most familiar example of a chaotic system. Meteorologists make thousands upon thousands of measurements of wind speed, air temperature, and barometric pressure in their efforts to predict the weather. They do pretty well with 24- and 48-hour forecasts, and sometimes they even get the seven-day predictions right. But no matter how fancy the measurements and the computer simulations, there is no way to predict what the weather will be a year from now. The chaotic nature of atmospheric motion is sometimes dramatized as the "butterfly effect," which says that in a chaotic system an effect as small as a butterfly's flapping its wings in Singapore may eventually make it rain in Texas.
>
> –Robert M. Hazen and James Trefil, *Science Matters: Achieving Scientific Literacy*

This single example is effective because it is familiar to many readers. Hazen and Trefil explain the idea of a chaotic system in a simple manner and using an example familiar to all so readers better understand the point they are trying to make.

In contrast, another writer supports his topic sentence about the growth of the fast-food industry with several examples:

> The extraordinary growth of the fast food industry has been driven by fundamental changes in American society. Adjusted for inflation, the hourly wage of the average U.S. worker peaked in 1973 and then steadily declined for the next twenty-five years. During that period, women entered the workforce in record numbers, often motivated less by a feminist perspective than by a need to pay the bills. In 1975, about one-third of American mothers with young children worked outside the home; today almost two-thirds of such mothers are employed. As the sociologists Cameron Lynne Macdonald and Carmen Sirianni have noted, the entry of so many women into the workforce has greatly increased demand for the types of services that housewives traditionally perform: cooking, cleaning, and child care. A generation ago, three-quarters of the money used to buy food in the United States was spent to prepare meals at home. Today about half of the money used to buy food is spent at restaurants—mainly at fast food restaurants.
>
> –Eric Schlosser, *Fast Food Nation*

Schlosser uses numerous examples to support his topic sentence with adequate supporting evidence. By citing specific examples of key changes in American society that have led to tremendous growth in the fast-food industry, Schlosser makes his point strong and convincing.

To use illustration effectively, use the following strategies:

- Begin by thinking of ideas and generalizations about your topic that you can make clearer and more persuasive by illustrating them with facts, anecdotes, or specific details.
- Focus primarily on your main point—the central generalization that you will develop in your essay.
- Be alert for other statements or references that may benefit from illustration.

Points that are already clear and uncontroversial and that your readers will understand and immediately agree with can stand on their own as you pass along quickly to your next idea; belaboring the obvious wastes your time and energy, as well as your reader's. Often, however, you will find that examples add clarity, color, and weight to what you say.

Consider the following generalization:

> Americans are a pain-conscious people who would rather get rid of pain than seek and cure its root causes.

This assertion is broad and general; it raises the following questions: How so? What does this mean exactly? Why does the writer think so? The statement could be the topic sentence of a paragraph or even the thesis of an essay or of an entire book. You could make the generalization stronger and more meaningful through illustrations. You might support this statement by citing situations or cases in which Americans have gone to the drugstore instead of to a doctor, as well as by supplying sales figures per capita of painkillers in the United States as compared with other countries.

Illustration is so useful and versatile a strategy that it is found in all kinds of writing, and it is essential for writing a successful argument essay. In an essay arguing that non-English-speaking students starting school in the United States should be taught English as a second language, student writer Hilda Alvarado could have made her point in a few words with an unsupported generalization:

> Not only are non-English-speaking students in English-only schools unable to understand the information they are supposed to be learning, but they are also subject to frequent embarrassment and teasing from their classmates.

Instead, Alvarado supports her argument with the following illustration, drawn from her own experience as a Spanish-speaking child in an English-only school:

> Without the use of Spanish, unable to communicate with the teacher or students, for six long weeks we guessed at everything we did. When we lined up to go anywhere, neither my sister nor I knew what to expect. Once, the teacher took the class on a bathroom break, and I mistakenly thought we were on our way to the cafeteria for lunch. Before we left, I grabbed our lunch money, and one of the girls in line began sneering and pointing. Somehow

> she figured out my mistake before I did. When I realized why she was laughing, I became embarrassed and threw the money into my sister's desk as we walked out of the classroom.
>
> –Hilda Alvarado, student

By offering an illustration, Alvarado makes her point more vividly and effectively.

Becoming a Writer

Russell Baker

Richard Howard/Getty Images

Russell Baker has had a long and distinguished career as a newspaper reporter and columnist. He was born in Morrisonville, Virginia, in 1925 and graduated from Johns Hopkins University in 1947. He got his first newspaper job with the *Baltimore Sun* and moved to the *New York Times* in 1954, where he wrote the "Observer" column from 1962 to 1998. His columns have been collected in numerous books over the years. In 1979, he was awarded the Pulitzer Prize, journalism's highest award, as well as the George Polk Award for commentary. Baker's memoir, *Growing Up* (1983), also received a Pulitzer. His autobiographical follow-up, *The Good Times*, appeared in 1989. His other works include *Russell Baker's Book of American Humor* (1993); *Inventing the Truth: The Art and Craft of Memoir* (1998, with William Zinsser and Jill Ker Conway); and *Looking Back* (2002), a collection of his essays for the *New York Review of Books*. From 1992 to 2004, he hosted the PBS television series *Masterpiece Theater*.

The following selection is from *Growing Up*. As you read, notice how Baker uses the extended example of his English class with Mr. Fleagle to show how he discovered his abilities as a writer and how the possibility of becoming a writer took hold.

Reflecting on What You Know

Life is full of moments that change us, for better or worse, in major and minor ways. Identify an event that changed your life or helped you make an important decision. How did it clarify your situation? How might your life be different if the event had never happened?

The notion of becoming a writer had flickered off and on in my head . . . but it wasn't until my third year in high school that the possibility took hold. Until then I'd been bored by everything associated with English courses. I found English grammar dull and baffling. I hated the assignments to turn out "compositions," and went at them 1 like heavy labor, turning out leaden, lackluster paragraphs that were agonies for teachers to read and for me to write. The classics thrust on me to read seemed as deadening as chloroform.[1]

When our class was assigned to Mr. Fleagle for third-year English I anticipated another grim year in that dreariest of subjects. Mr. Fleagle was notorious among City students for dullness and inability to inspire. He was said to be stuffy, dull, and hopelessly out of date. To me he looked to be sixty or seventy and prim to a fault. He wore primly severe eyeglasses, his wavy hair was primly cut and primly combed. He wore prim vested suits with neckties blocked primly against the collar buttons of his primly starched white shirts. He had a primly pointed jaw, a primly straight nose, and a prim manner of speaking that was so correct, so gentlemanly, that he seemed a comic antique. 2

I anticipated a listless, unfruitful year with Mr. Fleagle and for a long time was not disappointed. We read *Macbeth*. Mr. Fleagle loved *Macbeth* and wanted us to love it too, but he lacked the gift of infecting others with his own passion. He tried to convey the murderous ferocity of Lady Macbeth one day by reading aloud the passage that concludes 3

> . . . I have given suck, and know
> How tender 'tis to love the babe that milks me.
> I would, while it was smiling in my face,
> Have plucked my nipple from his boneless gums . . .

The idea of prim Mr. Fleagle plucking his nipple from boneless gums was too much for the class. We burst into gasps of irrepressible[2] snickering. Mr. Fleagle stopped.

"There is nothing funny, boys, about giving suck to a babe. It is the—the very essence of motherhood, don't you see." 4

He constantly sprinkled his sentences with "don't you see." It wasn't a question but an exclamation of mild surprise at our ignorance. "Your pronoun needs an antecedent, don't you see," he would say, very primly. "The purpose of the Porter's scene, boys, is to provide comic relief from the horror, don't you see." 5

Late in the year we tackled the informal essay. "The essay, don't you see, is the . . ." My mind went numb. Of all forms of writing, none seemed so boring as the essay. Naturally we would have to write 6

[1]*chloroform:* a chemical that puts one to sleep.
[2]*irrepressible:* unable to be restrained or controlled.

informal essays. Mr. Fleagle distributed a homework sheet offering us a choice of topics. None was quite so simpleminded as "What I Did on My Summer Vacation," but most seemed to be almost as dull. I took the list home and dawdled until the night before the essay was due. Sprawled on the sofa, I finally faced up to the grim task, took the list out of my notebook, and scanned it. The topic on which my eye stopped was "The Art of Eating Spaghetti."

This title produced an extraordinary sequence of mental images. 7
Surging up from the depths of memory came a vivid recollection of a night in Belleville when all of us were seated around the supper table—Uncle Allen, my mother, Uncle Charlie, Doris, Uncle Hal—and Aunt Pat served spaghetti for supper. Spaghetti was an exotic treat in those days. Neither Doris nor I had ever eaten spaghetti, and none of the adults had enough experience to be good at it. All the good humor of Uncle Allen's house reawoke in my mind as I recalled the laughing arguments we had that night about the socially respectable method for moving spaghetti from plate to mouth.

Suddenly I wanted to write about that, about the warmth and 8
good feeling of it, but I wanted to put it down simply for my own joy, not for Mr. Fleagle. It was a moment I wanted to recapture and hold for myself. I wanted to relive the pleasure of an evening at New Street. To write it as I wanted, however, would violate all the rules of formal composition I'd learned in school, and Mr. Fleagle would surely give it a failing grade. Never mind. I would write something else for Mr. Fleagle after I had written this thing for myself.

When I finished it the night was half gone and there was no time 9
left to compose a proper, respectable essay for Mr. Fleagle. There was no choice next morning but to turn in my private reminiscence of Belleville. Two days passed before Mr. Fleagle returned the graded papers, and he returned everyone's but mine. I was bracing myself for a command to report to Mr. Fleagle immediately after school for discipline when I saw him lift my paper from his desk and rap for the class's attention.

"Now, boys," he said, "I want to read you an essay. This is titled 10
'The Art of Eating Spaghetti.'"

And he started to read. My words! He was reading *my words* out 11
loud to the entire class. What's more, the entire class was listening. Listening attentively. Then somebody laughed, then the entire class was laughing, and not in contempt and ridicule, but with open-hearted enjoyment. Even Mr. Fleagle stopped two or three times to repress a small prim smile.

I did my best to avoid showing pleasure, but what I was feeling was pure ecstasy at this startling demonstration that my words had the power to make people laugh. In the eleventh grade, at the eleventh hour as it were, I had discovered a calling. It was the happiest moment of my entire school career. When Mr. Fleagle finished he put the final seal on my happiness by saying, "Now that, boys, is an essay, don't you see. It's—don't you see—it's of the very essence of the essay, don't you see. Congratulations, Mr. Baker." 12

For the first time, light shone on a possibility. It wasn't a very heartening possibility, to be sure. Writing couldn't lead to a job after high school, and it was hardly honest work, but Mr. Fleagle had opened a door for me. After that I ranked Mr. Fleagle among the finest teachers in the school. 13

Thinking Critically about This Reading

In paragraph 11, Baker states, "And he started to read. My words! He was reading *my words* out loud to the entire class. What's more, the entire class was listening. Listening attentively." Why was this episode so key to Baker's decision to become a writer?

Questions for Study and Discussion

1. What is Baker's thesis and where is it stated? How effectively does his account of being in Mr. Fleagle's English class support this main idea? (Glossary: **Thesis**)
2. What were Baker's expectations about English classes (and Mr. Fleagle's in particular) at the beginning of the school year? Why did Baker think that he needed to give us this information?
3. How does Baker describe his English teacher, Mr. Fleagle, in the second paragraph? (Glossary: **Description**) Why does he repeat the word *prim* throughout the paragraph? Why is the vivid description important to the essay as a whole?
4. What does Baker write about in his informal essay for Mr. Fleagle? Why does he write about this subject? Why doesn't he want to turn the essay in?
5. In the end, why do you suppose Baker "ranked Mr. Fleagle among the finest teachers in the school" (13)?

Classroom Activity Using Illustration

Baker illustrates his thesis by using the single example of his own experience in Mr. Fleagle's third-year English class. Using the model statement and example that follows, find a single example that might be used to best illustrate each of the following potential thesis statements:

MODEL: Seat belts save lives. (*Possible example*: Your aunt was in a car accident but a seat belt saved her life.)

Friends can be very handy.

Having good study skills can improve a student's grades.

Loud music can damage your hearing.

Humor can often make a bad situation more tolerable.

Suggested Writing Assignments

1. Using Baker's inspirational writing about eating spaghetti as a model, write something from your own experience that you would like to record for yourself, not necessarily for the teacher. Don't worry about writing a formal essay. Simply use language with which you are comfortable to convey why the event or experience is important to you.
2. Using one of the following sentences as your thesis statement, write an essay giving examples from your personal experience or from your reading to support your opinion.
   - Most products do (or do not) measure up to the claims of their advertisements.
   - Religion is (or is not) alive and well in the United States.
   - The U.S. government works far better than its critics claim.
   - Being able to write well is more than a basic skill.
   - Today's college students are (or are not) serious about academics.

Be Specific

Natalie Goldberg

Born in 1948 in Brooklyn, New York, Natalie Goldberg has made a specialty of writing about writing. Her first and best-known work, *Writing Down the Bones: Freeing the Writer Within*, was published in 1986. Goldberg's advice to would-be writers is, on the one hand, practical and pithy; on the other, it is almost mystical in its call to know and appreciate the world. Her other books about writing include *Wild Mind: Living the Writer's Life* (1990), *Living Color* (1996), *Thunder and Lightning: Cracking Open the Writer's Craft* (2000), and *Old Friend from Far Away: The Practice of Writing Memoir* (2008). Goldberg has also written fiction. Her first novel, *Banana Rose*, was published in 1994. She is also a painter whose work is exhibited in Taos, New Mexico. *Living Color: A Writer Paints Her World* (1997) is about painting as her second art form, and *Top of My Lungs* (2002) is a collection of poetry and paintings. Her most recent book is *The Great Spring: Writing, Zen, and This Zig-Zag Life* (2016), a memoir of her life.

In "Be Specific," a chapter from *Writing Down the Bones*, Goldberg brings us out of abstract ideas and "close to the ground." As you read, pay attention to how Goldberg uses illustration to demonstrate her point about being specific in one's writing.

Reflecting on What You Know

Suppose someone says to you, "I walked in the woods." What do you envision? Write down what you see in your mind's eye. Now suppose someone says, "I walked in the redwood forest." Again, write down what you see. How are the two descriptions different, and why?

Be specific. Don't say "fruit." Tell what kind of fruit—"It is a pomegranate." Give things the dignity of their names. Just as with human beings, it is rude to say, "Hey, girl, get in line." That "girl" has a name. (As a matter of fact, if she's at least twenty years old, she's a woman, not a "girl" at all.) Things, too, have names. It is much better 1 to say "the geranium in the window" than "the flower in the window." "Geranium"—that one word gives us a much more specific picture. It penetrates more deeply into the beingness of that flower. It immediately gives us the scene by the window—red petals, green circular leaves, all straining toward sunlight.

About ten years ago I decided I had to learn the names of plants and flowers in my environment. I bought a book on them and walked down the tree-lined streets of Boulder,[1] examining leaf, bark, and seed, trying to match them up with their descriptions and names in the book. Maple, elm, oak, locust. I usually tried to cheat by asking people working in their yards the names of the flowers and trees growing there. I was amazed how few people had any idea of the names of the live beings inhabiting their little plot of land. 2

When we know the name of something, it brings us closer to the ground. It takes the blur out of our mind; it connects us to the earth. If I walk down the street and see "dogwood," "forsythia," I feel more friendly toward the environment. I am noticing what is around me and can name it. It makes me more awake. 3

If you read the poems of William Carlos Williams,[2] you will see how specific he is about plants, trees, flowers—chicory, daisy, locust, poplar, quince, primrose, black-eyed Susan, lilacs—each has its own integrity. Williams says, "Write what's in front of your nose." It's good for us to know what is in front of our nose. Not just "daisy," but how the flower is in the season we are looking at it—"The days-eye hugging the earth / in August . . . brownedged, / green and pointed scales / armor his yellow."* Continue to hone your awareness: to the name, to the month, to the day, and finally to the moment. 4

Williams also says: "No idea, but in things." Study what is "in front of your nose." By saying "geranium" instead of "flower," you are penetrating more deeply into the present and being there. The closer we can get to what's in front of our nose, the more it can teach us everything. "To see the World in a Grain of Sand, and a heaven in a Wild Flower . . ."** 5

[1]*Boulder:* a city in Colorado.

[2]*William Carlos Williams* (1883–1963): American poet.

*William Carlos Williams, "Daisy," in *The Collected Earlier Poems* (New York: New Directions, 1938). [Goldberg's note]

**William Blake, "The Auguries of Innocence." [Goldberg's note]

In writing groups and classes too, it is good to quickly learn the names of all the other group members. It helps to ground you in the group and make you more attentive to each other's work. 6

Learn the names of everything: birds, cheese, tractors, cars, buildings. A writer is all at once everything—an architect, French cook, farmer—and at the same time, a writer is none of these things. 7

Thinking Critically about This Reading

What does Goldberg mean when she states, "Give things the dignity of their names" (paragraph 1)? Why, according to Goldberg, should writers refer to things by their specific names?

Questions for Study and Discussion

1. What examples of flowers and fruits does Goldberg use to prove her point about illustration? How do these examples support her thesis? (Glossary: **Thesis**)
2. Goldberg states, "I was amazed how few people had any idea of the names of the live beings inhabiting their little plot of land" (2). How well do you know the names of the plants, flowers, and trees that grow either where you live? Would you be able to write in detail about the flora and fauna surrounding you, even if you didn't know their names? How?
3. How does Goldberg "specifically" follow the advice she gives writers in this essay?
4. Goldberg makes several lists of the names of things. What purpose do these lists serve? (Glossary: **Purpose**)
5. Throughout the essay, Goldberg instructs the reader to be specific and to be aware of the physical world. Of what besides names is the reader advised to be aware? Why?
6. In paragraphs 3, 5, and 6, Goldberg cites a number of advantages to be gained by knowing the names of things. What are these advantages? Do they ring true to you?
7. What specific audience does Goldberg address? (Glossary: **Audience**) How do you know?

Classroom Activity Using Illustration

Consider the following paragraph from the rough draft of a student paper on Americans' obsession with losing weight. The student writer wanted to show the extreme actions people sometimes take to improve their appearance.

> Americans have long been obsessed with thinness—even at the risk of dying. In the 1930s, people took di-nitrophenol, an industrial poison, to lose weight. It boosted metabolism but caused blindness and some deaths. Since that time, dieters have experimented with any number of bizarre schemes that seemed to work wonders in the short term but often end in disappointment or disaster in the long term. Some weight-loss strategies have even led to life-threatening eating disorders.
>
> –Harry Crouse, student

Try your hand at revising this paragraph, supplying specific examples of "bizarre schemes" or "weight-loss strategies" you have tried, observed, or read about. Share your examples with others in your class. Which examples best illustrate and support the central idea in the writer's topic sentence?

Suggested Writing Assignments

1. Goldberg likes William Carlos Williams's statement, "No idea, but in things" (5). What does this statement mean to you? Using this line as both a title and a thesis, write your own argument for the use of the specific over the general in a certain field—news reporting, writing poetry, or making music, for example. (Glossary: **Argumentation**) Use illustration to support your argument, providing specific, appropriate examples.
2. Write a brief essay advising your readers of something they should do. Title your essay, as Goldberg does, with a directive ("Be Specific"). Tell your readers how they can improve their lives by taking your advice, and give strong examples of the behavior you are recommending. Support your argument with specific and appropriate examples.

The Power of Conformity

Jonah Berger

Jonah Berger was born in Washington, D.C., in 1980 and graduated from Stanford University and the Stanford Graduate School of Business. He is a marketing professor at the Wharton School at the University of Pennsylvania, and his research interests include how people's decisions are influenced by their social environment. Aside from publishing in numerous scholarly journals in his field, Berger has written for publications such as the *New York Times*, the *Atlantic*, *Harvard Business Review*, and the *Wall Street Journal*. In 2011 he won Wharton's Iron Professor Competition for faculty research presented to students, and in 2012 he received Early Career Awards from the Association for Consumer Research and the Society for Consumer Psychology. Berger is the author of two popular books: *Contagious: Why Things Catch On* (2013) and *Invisible Influence: Hidden Factors That Shape Behavior* (2016).

In the following excerpt from *Invisible Influence*, Berger observes how people's behavior and use of language are shaped by their social environments. As you read, note how Berger uses illustration to give life to his abstract ideas.

Reflecting on What You Know

How is your vocabulary influenced by the social environment in which you live? Think of words and phrases—everyday expressions or even slang—you use that may not be used by others in different areas of the country. To what extent is what you say influenced by where you live?

Imagine a hot day. Really hot. So sweltering that the birds won't even sing. You're parched, so you drop into a local fast-food restaurant to grab a cold drink. You walk up to the counter and the clerk asks what you'd like. 1

What generic term would you use if you wanted a sweetened car- 2
bonated beverage? What would you say to the clerk? If you had to fill in the blank "I'd like a ______________, please," how would you do it?

People's answers depend a lot on where they grew up. New York- 3
ers, Philadelphians, or people from the northeastern United States would ask for a "soda." But Minnesotans, Midwesterners, people who grew up in the Great Plains region of the country would probably ask for a "pop." And people from Atlanta, New Orleans, and much of the South would ask for a "Coke." Even if they wanted a Sprite.

(For fun, try ordering a Coke next time you're in the South. The 4
clerk will ask you what kind, and then you can tell them a Sprite, Dr Pepper, root beer, or even a regular Coke.)*

Where we grow up, and the norms and practices of people around 5
us, shape everything from the language we use to the behaviors we engage in. Kids adopt their parents' religious beliefs and college students adopt their roommates' study habits. Whether making simple decisions, like which brand to buy, or more consequential ones, like which career path to pursue, we tend to do as others around us do.

The tendency to imitate is so fundamental that even animals do it. 6

Vervets are small, cute monkeys found mostly in South Africa. 7
Similar in size to a small dog, they have light-grey bodies, black faces, and a fringe of white around their stomachs. The monkeys live in groups of ten to seventy individuals, with males striking out on their own and changing groups once they reach sexual maturity.

Scientists often study vervets because of their humanlike charac- 8
teristics. The monkeys display hypertension,[1] anxiety, and even social

---

*Or imagine you're at the office, chatting with some coworkers. You're about to grab lunch, but the rest of your office mates are on deadline and can't go with you. Being the polite person you are, you ask the group whether you can get them something. How would you address the group—that is, what word(s) would you use to address a group of two or more people? How would you fill in the blank: Would ______________ like me to get you anything? The answer seems even easier. But again, it depends on the people around you. People from the West or Northeast tend to say "you guys." People from the South tend to say "y'all." People from Kentucky tend to say "you all." Some people from Philadelphia or Boston might even say "youse," as in "Youse guys want something from the store?" [Berger's note]

[1]*hypertension:* high blood pressure.

and abusive alcohol consumption. Like humans, most prefer drinking in the afternoon, rather than morning, but heavy drinkers will drink even in the morning and some will even drink until they pass out.

In one clever study, researchers conditioned wild vervets to avoid 9
certain food. Scientists gave the monkeys two trays of corn, one containing pink corn and the other blue corn. For one group of monkeys, the scientists soaked the pink corn in a bitter, repulsive liquid. For another group of monkeys, the researchers flipped the colors—blue tasted bad and pink normal.

Gradually, the monkeys learned to avoid whichever color tasted 10
bad. The first group of monkeys avoided the pink corn while the other group avoided the blue. Just like soda in the Northeast and pop in the Midwest, local norms had been created.

But the scientists weren't just trying to condition the monkeys, 11
they were interested in social influence. What would happen to new, untrained monkeys who joined each group?

To see what would happen, the researchers took the colored corn 12
away and waited a few months until new baby monkeys were born. Then, they placed trays of pink and blue corn in front of the monkeys. Except this time they removed the bad taste. Now the pink corn and the blue corn both tasted fine.

Which would the baby monkeys choose? 13

Pink and blue corn were just as tasty, so the baby monkeys should 14
have gone after both. But they didn't. Even though the infants weren't around when one color of corn tasted bitter, they imitated the other members of their group. If their mothers avoided the blue corn, they did the same. Some babies even sat on the avoided color to eat the other, ignoring it as potential food.

Conformity was so strong that monkeys who switched groups 15
also switched colors. Some older male monkeys happened to change groups during the study. Some moved from the Pink Avoiders to the Blue Avoiders, and vice versa. And as a result, these monkeys also changed their food preferences. Switchers adopted the local norms, eating whichever color was customary among their new group.

We might have grown up calling carbonated fizzy beverages 16
"soda," but move to a different region of the country and our language starts to shift. A couple years surrounded by people calling it "Coke" and we might find ourselves doing the same. Monkey see, monkey do.

Thinking Critically about This Reading

Berger states his thesis in paragraph 5: "Where we grow up, and the norms and practices of people around us, shape everything from the language we use to the behaviors we engage in." If so, then what role does free will—the idea that people make conscious choices about their actions—play? What are the benefits of conforming, for humans or animals like vervets?

Questions for Study and Discussion

1. Berger begins by examining how different regions of the country have different terms to identify a "sweetened carbonated beverage" (paragraph 2). How does Berger use this illustration to make his point?
2. What are some possible explanations for why the word *Coke* is used in the South as a generic description of all different varieties of sweetened carbonated beverages?
3. In the footnote to paragraph 4, how did you fill in the blank? What do you think your answer says about you and your region?
4. Berger notes that in making decisions both big and small, we "tend to do as others around us do" (5). What examples does Berger use to illustrate this point? (Glossary: **Example**) What other explanations for these behaviors could there be, and what examples could you use to support them?
5. Berger cites the example of scientists who used vervets, a type of monkey, to study human behavior. List some of the similarities that vervets have to humans. (Glossary: **Comparison and Contrast**) Were you surprised by any? Why?
6. As Berger notes in paragraph 15, male vervets that switched groups also switched their choice of colored corn, even though now both colors of corn tasted the same. What does this say about the role of social conformity as opposed to the influence of habit?
7. In the end, Berger says, "Monkey see, monkey do." Aside from the humor, what does this suggest about larger, important human issues?

Classroom Activity Using Illustration

Read the following application letter for a summer internship. In her second paragraph, in addition to directing the recipient's attention to her résumé, the writer highlights relevant experience. Identify the point she makes about her skills; then discuss how the examples she chooses help support that point.

Dear Ms. Crandell:

I have learned from your website that you are hiring undergraduates for summer internships. An internship with Abel's buyer training program interests me because I have learned that your program is one of the best in the industry.

The professional and analytical qualities that my attached résumé describes match the job description on your website. My experience with the Alumni Relations Program and the University Center Committee has enhanced my communication and persuasive abilities as well as my understanding of negotiation and compromise. For example, in the alumni program, I persuaded both uninvolved and active alumni to become more engaged with the direction of the university. On the University Center Committee, I balanced students' demands with the financial and structural constraints of the administration. With these skills, I can ably assist the buyers in your department with their summer projects and successfully juggle multiple responsibilities.

I would appreciate the opportunity to meet with you to discuss your summer internship program further. If you have questions or would like to speak with me, please contact me at (412) 555-2289 any weekday after 3:00 p.m., or you can e-mail me at msparker@ubi.edu. Thank you for your consideration.

Sincerely,

Marta S. Parker

Marta S. Parker

Suggested Writing Assignments

1. Berger's thesis is that we are shaped by the norms and practices of those around us when we grow up (paragraph 5). Write an essay in which you examine the norms and practices of those who were around you as you grew up. How did they affect you? Argue whether, in your case, Berger's thesis appears to be true or not. Include specific examples.
2. Research an example from history of a person who made notable accomplishments in some area of life, such as politics, science, academics, the military, athletics, the arts, human rights, or philanthropy. Consider how much influence upbringing and environment had on that person's life. Write an essay in which you argue that social environment did (or did not) influence that person to do what he or she was able to accomplish. Use specific examples to illustrate your points.
3. The scientists that Berger cites used vervet monkeys in their study of social influence. Can (or should) animals such as vervet monkeys be used to illustrate human behavior? Why or why not? Write an essay in which you use specific examples to argue your position. You may wish to research and consider uses of animals in scientific and psychological experiments, including their use in the testing of pharmaceuticals, surgeries, and cosmetics.

CHAPTER **14**

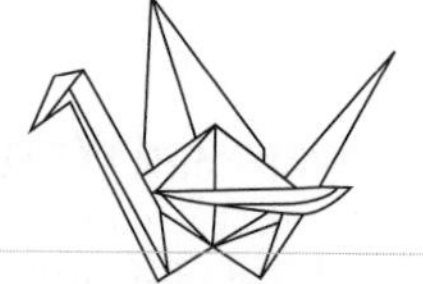

Narration

To *narrate* is to tell a story or to recount a series of events. Whenever you relate an incident or use an **anecdote** (a very brief story) to make a point, you use narration. In its broadest sense, **narration** is any account of any event or series of events. We all love to hear stories; some people believe that sharing stories is a part of what defines us as human beings. Good stories are interesting, sometimes suspenseful, and always instructive because they give us insights into the human condition. Although most often associated with fiction, narration is effective and useful in all kinds of writing. For example, in "The Power of Conformity" (p. 334), Jonah Berger narrates a hypothetical scene to put the reader in the action and set up his illustration.

ELEMENTS OF NARRATION

Good narration has five essential features:

- a clear context
- well-chosen and thoughtfully emphasized detail
- a logical, often chronological organization
- an appropriate and consistent point of view
- a meaningful point or purpose

Consider the following narrative from a student essay titled "I Remember Love":

> I remember standing in my driveway that evening after we got back from dinner; her eyes sparkled in the dim light from my truck's interior as she stood beside it with the door open. I held her hands while we talked about spending Christmas morning with our families, and that we would not see each other until the

evening. I told her that I had a Christmas gift for her so she did not have to wait until the following evening. I recall the excitement in her eyes when I handed her the wrapped present with a card attached to the top of the package. She asked me if she could open it right then, and I told her I didn't mind; however, I recommended that she at least save the card for Christmas morning. She agreed, and she seemed so happy after opening the gift; she hugged me tightly, and we kissed as we held on to each other in the cold night air.

I remember when she was walking away, I wanted to yell out "I love you," but in that moment, I also remember thinking that there was no reason to rush it. I figured there would be plenty of time to tell her that I loved her, and I remember that she meant more to me than anyone or anything I had ever known. The few seconds it took her to leave my sight may have been the same few seconds in which I experienced the deepest thoughts of my life as I realized the woman of my dreams was right in front of me, and I finally found the person who made me feel complete. I thought about how she was all I wanted as I stood spellbound by everything from the kiss to her eyes. Even after she had driven out of view, I still stood there for several minutes in the cold of night, thinking that she would be the last girl I would ever kiss; I recall being completely all right with this idea, and I hoped she felt the same way. As I walked inside the house, I felt better than I ever had before or since.

–Skyler Waid, student

This story contains all the elements of good narration. The writer begins by establishing a clear context for his narrative by telling when, where, and to whom the action happened. He has chosen details well, including enough details so that we know what is happening but not so many that we become overwhelmed, confused, or bored. The writer organizes his narration logically with a beginning that sets the scene, a middle that relates an exchange between him and his girlfriend, and an end that makes his point, all arranged chronologically. He tells the entire story from the first-person point of view. The writer could have chosen to tell his story from the third-person point of view. In this point of view, the narrator is not a participant in the action and uses the pronouns *he* and *she* instead of *I*. Finally, he reveals the purpose of his narration: to recount his experience of the first time he fell in love.

In the following example, Carl T. Rowan tells a story of being scolded by a teacher, one whom he would grow to revere. Again we experience the event directly through the writer's eyes, and also through his ears, as he includes dialogue to make us feel that we had been there with him that day.

> I shall never forget the day she scolded me into reading *Beowulf*.
>
> "But Miss Bessie," I complained, "I ain't much interested in it."
>
> Her large brown eyes became daggerish slits. "Boy," she said, "how dare you say 'ain't' to me! I've taught you better than that."
>
> "Miss Bessie," I pleaded, "I'm trying to make first-string end on the football team, and if I go around saying 'it isn't' and 'they aren't,' the guys are gonna laugh me off the squad."
>
> "Boy," she responded, "you'll play football because you have guts. But do you know what *really* takes guts? Refusing to lower your standards to those of the crowd. It takes guts to say you've got to live and be somebody fifty years after all the football games are over."
>
> I started saying "it isn't" and "they aren't," and I still made first-string end—and class valedictorian—without losing my buddies' respect.
>
> –Carl T. Rowan, "Unforgettable Miss Bessie" (p. 370)

As you begin to write your own narration, take time to ask yourself why you are telling your story. Your purpose in writing will influence which events and details you include and which you leave out. You should include enough details about the action and its context so that your readers can understand what's going on. However, you should not get so carried away with details that your readers become confused or bored by an excess of information. In good storytelling, deciding what to leave out is as important as deciding what to include.

NARRATIVE ORGANIZATION

Be sure to give some thought to the organization of your narrative. Chronological organization is natural in narration because it is a reconstruction of the original order of events, but it is not always the most interesting. To add interest to your storytelling, try using a technique common in the movies and theater called *flashback*.

Begin your narration midway through the story with an important or exciting event, and then use flashback to fill in what happened earlier. Notice how one student uses this very technique. She disrupts the chronological organization of her narrative by beginning in the recent past and then uses a flashback to take us back to when she was a youngster:

Essay opens in recent past

It was a Monday afternoon, and I was finally home from track practice. The coach had just told me that I had a negative attitude and should contemplate why I was on the team. My father greeted me in the living room.

Dialogue creates historical present

"Hi, honey. How was practice?"

"Not good, Dad. Listen, I don't want to do this anymore. I hate the track team."

"What do you mean *hate*?"

"The constant pressure is making me crazy."

"How so?"

"It's just not fun anymore."

"Well, I'll have to talk to the coach—"

"No! You're supposed to be my father, not my coach."

"I am your father, but I'm sure . . ."

"Just let me do what I want. You've had your turn."

Essay returns in time to when troubles began

He just let out a sigh and left the room. Later he told me that I was wasting my "God-given abilities." The funny part was that none of my father's anger hit me at first. All I knew was that I was free.

My troubles began the summer I was five years old. It was late June . . .

–Trena Isley, student, "On the Sidelines" (pp. 55-56)

What's in a Name?

Henry Louis Gates Jr.

Frederick M. Brown/Getty Images

The preeminent African American scholar of our time, Henry Louis Gates Jr. was born in West Virginia in 1950. He is the Alphonse Fletcher University Professor and director of the W. E. B. Du Bois Institute for African and African American Research at Harvard University. Among his impressive list of publications are *The Signifying Monkey: A Theory of Afro-American Literary Criticism* (1988), *Loose Canons: Notes on Culture Wars* (1992), *Thirteen Ways of Looking at a Black Man* (1999), *Mr. Jefferson and Miss Wheatley* (2003), and *Black in Latin America* (2011). He is also the host of an acclaimed PBS documentary series, *The African Americans* (2013), which received the 2015 Alfred I. duPont–Columbia University Award. His *Colored People: A Memoir* (1994) recollects his youth growing up in Piedmont, West Virginia, and his emerging sexual and racial awareness. Gates studied history at Yale University. Then, with the assistance of an Andrew W. Mellon Foundation Fellowship and a Ford Foundation Fellowship, he pursued advanced degrees in English at Clare College at the University of Cambridge. He has been honored with a MacArthur Foundation Fellowship, inclusion on *Time* magazine's "25 Most Influential Americans" list, a National Humanities Medal, and election to the American Academy of Arts and Letters.

In this essay, excerpted from a longer article published in the fall 1989 issue of *Dissent* magazine, Gates tells the story of an early encounter with the language of prejudice. As you read, notice that in learning how one of the "bynames" used by white people to define African Americans robs them of their identity, he feels the sting of racism firsthand. Pay attention to how Gates's use of dialogue gives immediacy and poignancy to his narration.

Reflecting on What You Know

Reflect on the use of racially charged language. For example, has anyone ever used a racial epithet or name to refer to you? When did you first become aware that such names existed? How do you feel about being characterized by your race? If you yourself have ever used such names, what was your intent in using them? What was the response of others?

The question of color takes up much space in these pages, but the question of color, especially in this country, operates to hide the graver questions of the self.

–James Baldwin, 1961

. . . blood, darky, Tar Baby, Kaffir, shine . . . moor, blackamoor, Jim Crow, spook . . . quadroon, meriney, red bone, high yellow . . . Mammy, porch monkey, home, homeboy, George . . . spearchucker, schwarze, Leroy, Smokey . . . mouli, buck, Ethiopian, brother, sistah . . .

–Trey Ellis, 1989

I had forgotten the incident completely, until I read Trey Ellis's essay, "Remember My Name," in a recent issue of the *Village Voice*[1] (June 13, 1989). But there, in the middle of an extended italicized list of the bynames of "the race" ("the race" or "our people" being the terms my parents used in polite or reverential discourse, "jigaboo" or "nigger" more commonly used in anger, jest, or pure disgust), it was: "George." Now the events of that very brief exchange return to mind so vividly that I wonder why I had forgotten it. 1

My father and I were walking home at dusk from his second job. He "moonlighted" as a janitor in the evenings for the telephone company. Every day but Saturday, he would come home at 3:30 from his regular job at the paper mill, wash up, eat supper, then at 4:30 head downtown to his second job. He used to make jokes frequently about a union official who moonlighted. I never got the joke, but he and his friends thought it was hilarious. All I knew was that my family always ate well, that my brother and I had new clothes to wear, and that all of the white people in Piedmont, West Virginia, treated my parents with an odd mixture of resentment and respect that even we understood at the time had something directly to do with a small but certain measure of financial security. 2

He had left a little early that evening because I was with him and I had to be in bed early. I could not have been more than five or six, and we had stopped off at the Cut-Rate Drug Store (where no black person 3

[1] *Village Voice:* a nationally distributed weekly newspaper published in New York City.

in town but my father could sit down to eat, and eat off real plates with real silverware) so that I could buy some caramel ice cream, two scoops in a wafer cone, please, which I was busy licking when Mr. Wilson walked by.

4 Mr. Wilson was a very quiet man, whose stony, brooding, silent manner seemed designed to scare off any overtures of friendship, even from white people. He was Irish, as was one-third of our village (another third being Italian), the more affluent among whom sent their children to "Catholic School" across the bridge in Maryland. He had white straight hair, like my Uncle Joe, whom he uncannily resembled, and he carried a black worn metal lunch pail, the kind that Riley[2] carried on the television show. My father always spoke to him, and for reasons that we never did understand, he always spoke to my father.

5 "Hello, Mr. Wilson," I heard my father say.

6 "Hello, George."

7 I stopped licking my ice cream cone, and asked my Dad in a loud voice why Mr. Wilson had called him "George."

8 "Doesn't he know your name, Daddy? Why don't you tell him your name? Your name isn't George."

9 For a moment I tried to think of who Mr. Wilson was mixing Pop up with. But we didn't have any Georges among the colored people in Piedmont; nor were there colored Georges living in the neighboring towns and working at the mill.

10 "Tell him your name, Daddy."

11 "He knows my name, boy," my father said after a long pause. "He calls all colored people George."

12 A long silence ensued. It was "one of those things," as my Mom would put it. Even then, that early, I knew when I was in the presence of "one of those things," one of those things that provided a glimpse, through a rent[3] curtain, at another world that we could not affect but that affected us. There would be a painful moment of silence, and you would wait for it to give way to a discussion of a black superstar such as Sugar Ray[4] or Jackie Robinson.[5]

---

[2]*Riley:* Chester A. Riley, the lead character on the U.S. television show *The Life of Riley*, a blue-collar, ethnic sitcom popular in the 1950s.

[3]*rent:* torn.

[4]*Sugar Ray:* Walker Smith Jr. (1921–1989), American professional boxer and six-time world champion.

[5]*Jackie Robinson:* Jack Roosevelt Robinson (1919–1972), the first black baseball player in the major leagues in the modern era.

"Nobody hits better in a clutch than Jackie Robinson." 13

"That's right. Nobody." 14

I never again looked Mr. Wilson in the eye. 15

Thinking Critically about This Reading

What is "one of those things," as Gates's mom put it (paragraph 12)? In what ways is "one of those things" really Gates's purpose in telling this story?

Questions for Study and Discussion

1. Gates prefaces his essay with two quotations. What is the meaning of each quotation? Why do you suppose Gates uses both quotations? How does each relate to his purpose? (Glossary: **Purpose**)
2. Gates begins by explaining where he got the idea for his essay. How well does this approach work? Is it an approach you could see yourself using often? Explain.
3. In his first paragraph, Gates sets the context for his narrative. He also reveals that his parents used terms of racial abuse among themselves. Why does Gates make so much of Mr. Wilson's use of the word *George* when his own parents used words that were much more obviously offensive?
4. Gates describes and provides some background information about Mr. Wilson in paragraph 4. (Glossary: **Description**) What is Gates's purpose in providing this information? (Glossary: **Purpose**)

Classroom Activity Using Narration

Beginning at the beginning and ending at the end is not the only way to tell a story. Think of the events in a story that you would like to tell. Don't write the story, but simply list the events that need to be included. Be sure to include at least ten major events in your story. Now play with the arrangement of those events so as to avoid the chronological sequencing of them that would naturally come to mind. Try to develop as many patterns as you can, but be careful that you have a purpose in developing each sequence and that you do not create something that might confuse a listener or reader. Discuss your results with your classmates.

Suggested Writing Assignments

1. Using Gates's essay as a model, identify something that you have recently read that triggers in you a story from the past. Perhaps a newspaper article about how local high school students helped the community reminds you of a community project you and your classmates were involved in. Or perhaps reading about some act of heroism reminds you of a situation in which you performed (or failed to perform) a similar deed. Make sure that you have a purpose in telling the story, that you establish a clear context for it, and that you have enough supporting details to enrich your story. (Glossary: **Purpose; Details**) Also think about how to begin and end your story and which narrative sequence you will use. (Glossary: **Beginnings and Endings**)
2. How do you feel about your name? Do you like it? Does it sound pleasant? Do you think that your name shapes your identity in a positive or a negative way, or do you think that it has no effect on your sense of who you are? Write an essay about your name and the way it helps or fails to help you present yourself to the world. Be sure to develop your essay using narration by including several anecdotes or a longer story involving your name. (Glossary: **Anecdote**)

The Story of an Hour

Kate Chopin

Kate Chopin (1851–1904) was born in St. Louis of Creole Irish descent. Following her marriage, she lived in Louisiana, where she acquired the intimate knowledge of Creole Cajun culture that provided the impetus for much of her work and earned her a reputation as a writer who captured the ambience of the bayou region. When her first novel, *The Awakening* (1899), was published, however, it generated scorn and outrage for its explicit depiction of a southern woman's sexual awakening. Only relatively recently has Chopin been recognized for her literary talent and originality. Besides *The Awakening*, her works include two collections of short fiction, *Bayou Folk* (1894) and *A Night in Acadie* (1897). In 1969, *The Complete Works of Kate Chopin* was published by Louisiana State University Press, and the Library of America published *Kate Chopin: Complete Novels and Stories* in 2002. In 2012, a bronze bust of Chopin was dedicated at Writers' Corner in St. Louis, alongside busts of Tennessee Williams and T. S. Eliot.

As you read the following story, first published as "The Dream of an Hour" in *Vogue* magazine in 1894, try to gauge how your reactions to Mrs. Mallard are influenced by Chopin's use of third-person narration.

Reflecting on What You Know

How do you react to the idea of marriage—committing to someone for life? What are the advantages of such a union? What are the disadvantages?

Knowing that Mrs. Mallard was afflicted with a heart trouble, great care was taken to break to her as gently as possible the news of her husband's death. 1

It was her sister Josephine who told her, in broken sentences; veiled hints that revealed in half concealing. Her husband's friend Richards 2 was there, too, near her. It was he who had been in the newspaper office when intelligence of the railroad disaster was received, with Brently Mallard's name leading the list of "killed." He had only taken the time to assure himself of its truth by a second telegram, and had hastened to forestall any less careful, less tender friend in bearing the sad message.

She did not hear the story as many women have heard the same, with a paralyzed inability to accept its significance. She wept at once, with sudden, wild abandonment, in her sister's arms. When the storm of grief had spent itself she went away to her room alone. She would have no one follow her. 3

There stood, facing the open window, a comfortable, roomy armchair. Into this she sank, pressed down by a physical exhaustion that haunted her body and seemed to reach into her soul. 4

She could see in the open square before her house the tops of trees that were all aquiver with the new spring life. The delicious breath of rain was in the air. In the street below a peddler was crying his wares. The notes of a distant song which someone was singing reached her faintly, and countless sparrows were twittering in the eaves. 5

There were patches of blue sky showing here and there through the clouds that had met and piled one above the other in the west facing her window. 6

She sat with her head thrown back upon the cushion of the chair, quite motionless, except when a sob came up into her throat and shook her, as a child who has cried itself to sleep continues to sob in its dreams. 7

She was young, with a fair, calm face, whose lines bespoke repression and even a certain strength. But now there was a dull stare in her eyes, whose gaze was fixed away off yonder on one of those patches of blue sky. It was not a glance of reflection, but rather indicated a suspension of intelligent thought. 8

There was something coming to her and she was waiting for it, fearfully. What was it? She did not know; it was too subtle and elusive to name. But she felt it, creeping out of the sky, reaching toward her through the sounds, the scents, the color that filled the air. 9

Now her bosom rose and fell tumultuously. She was beginning to recognize this thing that was approaching to possess her, and she was striving to beat it back with her will—as powerless as her two white slender hands would have been. 10

When she abandoned herself a little whispered word escaped her slightly parted lips. She said it over and over under her breath: "free, 11 free, free!" The vacant stare and the look of terror that had followed it went from her eyes. They stayed keen and bright. Her pulses beat fast, and the coursing blood warmed and relaxed every inch of her body.

She did not stop to ask if it were or were not a monstrous joy that held her. A clear and exalted perception enabled her to dismiss the suggestion as trivial. 12

She knew that she would weep again when she saw the kind, tender hands folded in death; the face that had never looked save with love upon her, fixed and gray and dead. But she saw beyond that bitter moment a long procession of years to come that would belong to her absolutely. And she opened and spread her arms out to them in welcome. 13

There would be no one to live for her during those coming years; she would live for herself. There would be no powerful will bending hers in that blind persistence with which men and women believe they have a right to impose a private will upon a fellow-creature. A kind intention or a cruel intention made the act seem no less a crime as she looked upon it in that brief moment of illumination. 14

And yet she had loved him—sometimes. Often she had not. What did it matter! What could love, the unsolved mystery, count for in face of this possession of self-assertion which she suddenly recognized as the strongest impulse of her being! 15

"Free! Body and soul free!" she kept whispering. 16

Josephine was kneeling before the closed door with her lips to the keyhole, imploring for admission. "Louise, open the door! I beg; open the door—you will make yourself ill. What are you doing, Louise? For heaven's sake open the door." 17

"Go away. I am not making myself ill." No; she was drinking in a very elixir of life through that open window. 18

Her fancy was running riot along those days ahead of her. Spring days, and summer days, and all sorts of days that would be her own. She breathed a quick prayer that life might be long. It was only yesterday she had thought with a shudder that life might be long. 19

She arose at length and opened the door to her sister's importunities.[1] There was a feverish triumph in her eyes, and she carried herself unwittingly like a goddess of Victory. She clasped her sister's waist, and together they descended the stairs. Richards stood waiting for them at the bottom. 20

---

[1]*importunities:* urgent requests or demands.

Some one was opening the front door with a latchkey. It was Brently Mallard who entered, a little travel-stained, composedly carrying his grip-sack and umbrella. He had been far from the scene of the accident, and did not even know there had been one. He stood amazed at Josephine's piercing cry; at Richards' quick motion to screen him from the view of his wife. 21

But Richards was too late. 22

When the doctors came they said she had died of heart disease—of joy that kills. 23

Thinking Critically about This Reading

Chopin describes Mrs. Mallard as "beginning to recognize this thing that was approaching to possess her, and she was striving to beat it back with her will—as powerless as her two white slender hands would have been" (paragraph 10). Why does Mrs. Mallard fight her feeling of freedom, however briefly? How does she come to accept it?

Questions for Study and Discussion

1. What assumptions do Mrs. Mallard's sister and acquaintance make about her feelings toward her husband? What are her true feelings?
2. Reread paragraphs 5–9. What is Chopin's purpose in this section? (Glossary: **Purpose**) Do these paragraphs add to the story's effectiveness? Explain.
3. All the events of Chopin's story take place in an hour. Would the story be as poignant if they had taken place over the course of a day or even several days? Explain. Why do you suppose the author selected the time frame as a title for her story? (Glossary: **Title**)
4. Chopin could have written an essay detailing the oppression of women in marriage, but she chose instead to write a fictional narrative. This allows her to show readers the type of situation that can arise in an outwardly happy marriage rather than tell them about it. Why else do you think she chose to write a fictional narrative? What other advantages does it give her over nonfiction?
5. Why do you think Chopin narrates her story in the third person? (Glossary: **Point of View**)

Classroom Activity Using Narration

Using cues in the following sentences, rearrange them in chronological order.

1. The sky was gray and gloomy for as far as she could see, and sleet hissed off the glass.
2. "Oh, hi. I'm glad you called," she said happily, but her smile dimmed when she looked outside.
3. As Betty crossed the room, her phone rang, startling her.
4. "No, the weather's awful, so I don't think I'll get out to visit you today," she said, disappointed.
5. "Hello," she said, and she wandered over to the window.

Write five sentences of your own that cover a progression of events. Try to include dialogue. (Glossary: **Dialogue**) Then scramble them, and see if a classmate can put them back in the correct order.

Suggested Writing Assignments

1. Write a narrative essay in which you describe your reaction to a piece of news you once received—good or bad—that provoked a strong emotional response. What were your emotions? What did you do in the couple of hours after you received the news? How did your perceptions of the world around you change? What made the experience memorable?
2. Write an anecdote about a married couple you know—perhaps your grandparents or a pair of friends. Choose a specific story to narrate to readers, and choose your details well to illustrate the scene as you saw it. Then use the anecdote as the foundation for an essay that explores your current views on marriage. Are you married, or have you been? Do you look forward to marriage hopefully, or do you intend to avoid it? How does the story you narrate make you think about marriage?

Life in Motion

Misty Copeland

Noam Galai/WireImage/Getty Images

Born in Kansas City, Missouri, in 1982, Misty Copeland was raised in Los Angeles, California. Copeland began dancing as a member of the drill team in her middle school. The coach of the team took note of Copeland's skills, and soon she was learning ballet at the San Pedro Dance Center. Misty's career in dance has been nothing short of outstanding and includes first-place prize at the Music Center Spotlight Awards and scholarships to attend ballet school. She joined the American Ballet Theatre (ABT) in 2001 and by 2007 had become a soloist. In 2015, she was named a principal dancer for ABT, the first African American woman to be so named in the seventy-five-year history of the company. In 2014, she was appointed by Barack Obama to the President's Council on Fitness, Sports, and Nutrition.

This selection, which comes from her autobiography *Life in Motion* (2014), details the tumultuous time in Copeland's life when her family—her mother, her mother's new boyfriend Alex, and her five brothers and sisters—were living in a motel. Her dance instructor, Cindy Bradley, invited Copeland to live with her so they could continue their dance studies together. As you read, think about the context Copeland establishes for her story of her dance career and the details she uses to bring to life both her life's problems and her love for dance.

Reflecting on What You Know

Think about interests you have held throughout your life. It might be dance, like Misty Copeland, or something entirely different, such as sports, art, music, science, theater, writing, or cooking. How supportive have other people been of you in your pursuit of that interest? Can you cite particular ways in which that interest has (or has not) been supported?

We stayed with Ray for about a year before moving even farther away from our onetime home in San Pedro to a town called Montebello, where we lived in another cramped apartment with Mommy's next boyfriend, Alex. He was Latino and seemed a little more at ease in his own skin than Ray, but he wasn't much more stable. We were never sure if Alex had a real job. And just like at Ray's, Mommy and Alex slept in the one bedroom while we kids spread blankets and pillows wherever we could find a clear spot on the living room floor. 1

The neighborhoods where Ray and Alex lived weren't dicey like the streets where Auntie Monique and Uncle Charles lived, but their apartments were meant as basic, temporary housing for young men who partied all night and woke up at noon, not for a family with six children. And in those cramped spaces, the scraping back of a kitchen chair or the ringing of the telephone seemed louder, as if the smallness and clutter amplified the sound. . . . 2

Then, a few months after we began living with Alex, he lost his apartment. Again, we moved, this time into a motel. He came with us. 3

It was called the Sunset Inn, two stories of stucco[1] just off a busy highway. We were now in Gardena, a town right next to San Pedro. We were closer to our old neighborhood, but this place, this part of town, didn't feel like home. 4

Our room was toward the back of the top story. We children slept on the couch and the floor in the large front room, but I would often disappear into Mommy's bedroom after school, trying to drift away in a dream or a dance. Our front porch looking out over the Pacific was long gone, replaced by an outdoor hallway that we and the other motel tenants shared. 5

I tried to make the best of it. I would pretend the hallway was a veranda and I'd sit there, soaking up the sun. And I turned the rail into my very own barre, which I would grab hold of to balance as I stretched toward the sky. Or I would place [my brother] Cameron's tiny hands on the cool metal and shift him into various ballet positions, the way Cindy had first done with me. . . . 6

Often we had no money at all. We would run our hands around the couch cushions and through the carpet to find change. Then we'd go to the corner store to see if we could afford something to eat. Eventually, Mommy applied for food stamps. 7

---

[1]*stucco*: a type of plaster used to cover and decorate walls.

I still tried to appear perfect at school, arriving long before the first bell, carrying out my duties as hall monitor and as leader of the drill team. I withdrew even more inside myself as I tried to keep it all a secret, not telling my friends that we'd moved again, that I didn't have my own room . . . let alone a bed. I'd always spent more time at my friends' homes than they'd spent at mine, so it wasn't that hard to pretend my life was as it should be. 8

It was harder to make myself forget. I was grateful to hide from the chaos for a little while at the dance studio, inside ballet, where there were rules and life was dignified. Beautiful. I had continued to go to the studio every day despite the turmoil at home, taking the half hour drive with Cindy from school, and then riding an hour on the bus to get home to the motel. 9

The weeks rushed by. My mastery of ballet deepened, and soon I had my first show. It was at the Palos Verdes Art Center and billed as an "afternoon of art, music, and cultural enrichment," performed for a mostly elderly and white audience of about two hundred. 10

On the program was an older teenage girl who sang some forgettable pop standard, a group of high schoolers who performed a modern-dance routine, and me, the only ballerina in the bunch. Cindy had created a simple routine that blended the positions, spins, and leaps that I had managed to learn up to that point. I wore my black leotard with a pink chiffon skirt, with a blush-colored rose tucked in my hair. 11

Mommy wasn't there. Neither were my brothers or sisters. Only Cindy. 12

But I had performed ballet solo in front of a crowd for the first time, and by then I was in love. It was fun, exciting—and each day I couldn't wait for the bell to ring after sixth period so I could rush out the door, jump into Cindy's car, and head to the studio. 13

Mommy, however, was starting to change her mind about my ballet dreams. 14

When Jeff couldn't give her a lift, Erica would catch the bus, riding an hour each way to pick me up from class so I wouldn't have to take public transportation by myself. The two of us would get home after dark, often exhausted. 15

One night after Erica and I returned home from our long trek from the studio, Mommy sat down beside me. She said ballet class, so far away, wasn't working out. 16

"It's too much," she said, shaking her head, sadness faintly clouding her eyes. "You need to be able to get home earlier to spend time with your brothers and sisters. And both you and Erica are missing out on time with your friends. I know you're liking this class, but you'll only be a kid once." 17

I knew that Mommy meant well, that she was speaking from a place of concern, but I don't think she really understood that for me, ballet had become more than a hobby—it was what helped me stand alone, even shine bright. I desperately needed it. 18

The day after Mommy told me I would have to quit ballet, Cindy was waiting for me in front of the school, rifling through her organizer, looking up from time to time to see if I'd appeared. 19

I opened the car door and got in beside her. 20

"I'm going to have to stop dancing," I blurted out before breaking down in tears. "My mother says that the studio's too far. That it's too much, that I'm missing out on time with my friends and family." 21

Perhaps she would have been better able to understand if, like many concerned parents of ballerinas, my mother had been worried about my struggling schoolwork or fatigue. But this excuse seemed flimsy, even to me. 22

Cindy looked as though she'd forgotten how to breathe. Her eyes were wide and glistening. We sat there for a few minutes, silent. 23

"Well then," she finally said, "at least I can drive you home." 24

I was too tired to protest, too grief-stricken to guard my secret. I gave her my address. 25

We were quiet in the car. I tried to imagine what would fill the space that ballet had occupied, and I kept coming up empty. Finally, Cindy pulled to a stop. Staring at the run-down motel where my family was living, she looked as stunned as she had when I told her that I couldn't dance with her anymore. 26

"Thanks for the ride," I whispered as I hurried out of the car. Upstairs, I fumbled for the room key and entered the living room, blankets rolled up near the spots where they would later be unfurled as makeshift beds. 27

I'm sure Mommy didn't believe she was being neglectful. After all, we hadn't always lived that way, with pallets on the floor. We hadn't always called a motel—with a lobby window to slide our rent check through—home. We didn't always sleep around the corner from a highway lined with liquor stores and sketchy taco joints. 28

But that's how we lived now. That's what Cindy saw. 29

There was a knock on the door. Mommy, who'd been in the bedroom with Alex, came out and opened it. 30

Cindy stood there tentatively. I could feel the tension building in the small space, a nearly tangible thing. I just wanted to disappear. She met my eyes where I sat withdrawn on the floor. I believe that she knew this was it: she either brought me with her that night and into the world she believed I was born to be a part of, or I would never dance again. 31

The two women huddled a while, talking softly, crying, too. Mommy made it very clear that she had five other children. I was not, nor could I be, the center of her universe. I knew that—but I needed to be that to someone. "I can't leave her," Cindy said, tears steaming down her face. "I want Misty to come live with me." Then Mommy sighed and looked around the crowded motel room. 32

And she let me go. 33

Thinking Critically about This Reading

Did Copeland's early living conditions and family life bring her down or motivate her to realize her aspirations? What evidence do you have to support your conclusion?

Questions for Study and Discussion

1. In paragraph 1, Copeland recounts how her family moved from the home of one boyfriend (Ray) to another (Alex). How important—or unimportant—are these boyfriends of her mother in Copeland's life? What details does Copeland use to give you this impression?
2. Often in narration, writers adhere to the mantra "show, don't tell." Identify three examples of where Copeland "shows" rather than "tells," and discuss how effective those passages are.
3. In paragraph 2, Copeland describes the effect of the "scraping back of a kitchen chair or the ringing of the telephone." What mood does this detail set for the reader, and what does it tell you about the family's living conditions? (Glossary: **Dominant Impression**)

4. In paragraph 8, Copeland says, "I still tried to appear perfect at school." What does this statement reveal about her character? How might this quality have helped her succeed in dance?
5. Copeland tells her dance instructor, Cindy, that her mother says she must stop dancing (21). Why is this so devastating to Copeland? What has dance come to mean to her?
6. What is the mother's rationale for letting Copeland go live with her dance instructor? How powerful to you was this ending? Why?

Classroom Activity Using Narration

One of Copeland's themes in *Life in Motion* is that external circumstances outside one's own control can either help or hinder one's personal, educational, or professional development. To practice chronological order, consider a situation in which you encountered a difficulty in your development, particularly from a circumstance that was not entirely within your ability to control. Recount how you overcame, or were not able to overcome, that barrier. Rather than write a draft of an essay at this point, simply list the events that occurred in chronological order. If you like to draw or direct films, compose the sequence in a comic or storyboard. Then consider whether there is a more dramatic order you might use if you were actually to write an essay.

Suggested Writing Assignments

1. Narrate a story from your family's history. It may be based on a meaningful photograph or family home video. It may be a story you have heard told by someone else in your family, such as a parent or grandparent, and one that is told in different ways (depending on who is telling it!). Use plenty of strong relevant details, a consistent viewpoint, and a logical organization. Be sure that a reader who is not a member of your family can follow the storyline and all of the characters.

2. Sadly, the relationship between Misty Copeland, her mother Sylvia, and her dance teacher, Cindy, went sour in the time after this excerpt. There was much acrimony and even lawsuits before a peace was achieved between the parties, all of which played out in the Los Angeles-area media because of Copeland's growing popularity as a ballet prodigy. Research child custody cases like Copeland's and others. Write an essay in which you argue under what circumstances children can and should be removed from their parents' care and authority.

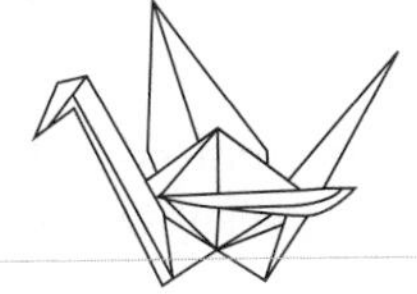

CHAPTER **15**

Description

To describe is to create a verbal picture. A person, a place, a thing—even an idea or a state of mind—can be made vividly concrete through **description.** In the following passage, Mark Twain describes the Mississippi River in the late afternoon:

> I still kept in mind a certain wonderful sunset which I witnessed when steamboating was new to me. A broad expanse of the river was turned to blood; in the middle distance the red hue brightened into gold, through which a solitary log came floating, black and conspicuous; in one place a long, slanting mark lay sparkling upon the water; in another the surface was broken by boiling, tumbling rings that were as many tinted as an opal; where the ruddy flush was faintest was a smooth spot that was covered with graceful circles and radiating lines, ever so delicately traced; the shore on our left was densely wooded, and the somber shadow that fell from this forest was broken in one place by a long, ruffled trail that shone like silver; and high above the forest wall a clean-stemmed dead tree waved a single leafy bough that glowed like a flame in the unobstructed splendor that was flowing from the sun. There were graceful curves, reflected images, woody heights, soft distances, and over the whole scene, far and near, the dissolving lights drifted steadily, enriching it every passing moment with new marvels of coloring.
>
> –Mark Twain, "Two Ways of Seeing a River," p. 451

Writing any description requires that the writer gather many details about a subject, relying not only on what the eyes see but on the other sense impressions—touch, taste, smell, and hearing—as well. From this catalog of details, the writer selects those that will create a **dominant impression**—the single quality, mood, or atmosphere the writer wishes to emphasize. Consider, for example, the details Cherokee Paul McDonald uses to evoke the dominant impression in the following passage, and contrast them with those in the subsequent example by student Dan Bubany:

> I was coming up on the little bridge in the Rio Vista neighborhood of Fort Lauderdale, deepening my stride and my breathing to negotiate the slight incline without altering my pace. And then, as I neared the crest, I saw the kid.
>
> He was a lumpy little guy with baggy shorts, a faded T-shirt and heavy sweat socks falling down over old sneakers.
>
> Partially covering his shaggy blond hair was one of those blue baseball caps with gold braid on the bill and a sailfish patch sewn onto the peak. Covering his eyes and part of his face was a pair of those stupid-looking '50s-style wrap-around sunglasses.
>
> He was fumbling with a beat-up rod and reel, and he had a little bait bucket by his feet. I puffed on by, glancing down into the empty bucket as I passed.
>
> –Cherokee Paul McDonald, "A View from the Bridge," pp. 117–18

> For this particular Thursday game against Stanford, Fleming wears white gloves, a maroon sport coat with brass buttons, and gray slacks. Shiny silver-framed bifocals match the whistle pressed between the lips on his slightly wrinkled face, and he wears freshly polished black shoes so glossy that they reflect the grass he stands on. He is not fat, but his coat neatly conceals a small, round pot belly.
>
> –Dan Bubany, student

The dominant impression that McDonald creates of the young boy is one of a scruffy little urchin. There is nothing about the boy's appearance that suggests any thought was given to what he is wearing. Bubany, on the other hand, creates a dominant impression of a neat, polished man.

Writers must also carefully plan the order in which to present their descriptive details. The pattern of organization must fit the subject of the description logically and naturally and must be easy to follow. For example, visual details can be arranged spatially—from left to right, top to bottom, near to far—or in any other logical order. Other patterns include smallest to largest, softest to loudest, least significant to most significant, and most unusual to least unusual.

How much detail is enough? There is no fixed answer. A good description includes enough vivid details to create a dominant impression and to bring a scene to life but not so many that readers are distracted, confused, or bored. In an essay that is purely descriptive, there is room for much detail. Usually, however, writers use description to create the setting for a story, to illustrate ideas, to help clarify a definition or a comparison, or to make the complexities of a process more understandable. Such descriptions should be kept short and should include just enough detail to make them clear and helpful.

The Corner Store

Eudora Welty

Philip Gould/Getty Images

One of the most honored and respected writers of the twentieth century, Eudora Welty was born in 1909 in Jackson, Mississippi, where she lived most of her life and where she died in 2001. Her first book, *A Curtain of Green* (1941), is a collection of short stories. Although she went on to become a successful writer of novels, essays, and book reviews, among other genres (as well as a published photographer), she is most often remembered as a master of the short story. In 1980, Welty was awarded the prestigious Presidential Medal of Freedom, and in 1996, she won the French Legion of Honor. *The Collected Stories of Eudora Welty* was published in 1982. Her other best-known works include a collection of essays, *The Eye of the Story* (1975); her autobiography, *One Writer's Beginnings* (1984); and a collection of book reviews and essays, *The Writer's Eye* (1994). Welty's novel *The Optimist's Daughter* won the Pulitzer Prize for Fiction in 1973. In 1999, the Library of Congress published two collections of her work: *Welty: Collected Novels* and *Welty: Collected Essays and Memoirs.*

Welty's description of the corner store, taken from an essay in *The Eye of the Story* about growing up in Jackson, recalls for many readers the neighborhood store in the town or city where they grew up. As you read, pay attention to the effect Welty's spatial arrangement of descriptive details has on the dominant impression of the store.

Reflecting on What You Know

Write about a store you frequented as a child. Maybe it was the local supermarket, the hardware store, or the corner convenience store. Using your five senses (sight, smell, taste, touch, and hearing), describe what you remember about the place.

Our Little Store rose right up from the sidewalk; standing in a street of family houses, it alone hadn't any yard in front, any 1 tree or flower bed. It was a plain frame building covered over with brick. Above the door, a little railed porch ran across on an upstairs level and four windows with shades were looking out. But I didn't catch on to those.

Running in out of the sun, you met what seemed total obscurity inside. There were almost tangible smells—licorice recently sucked in a child's cheek, dill pickle brine[1] that had leaked through a paper sack in a fresh trail across the wooden floor, ammonia-loaded ice that had been hoisted from wet croker sacks[2] and slammed into the ice-box with its sweet butter at the door, and perhaps the smell of still untrapped mice. 2

Then through the motes of cracker dust, cornmeal dust, the Gold Dust of the Gold Dust Twins[3] that the floor had been swept out with, the realities emerged. Shelves climbed to high reach all the way around, set out with not too much of any one thing but a lot of things—lard, molasses, vinegar, starch, matches, kerosene, Octagon soap (about a year's worth of octagon-shaped coupons cut out and saved brought a signet ring[4] addressed to you in the mail). It was up to you to remember what you came for, while your eye traveled from cans of sardines to tin whistles to ice-cream salt to harmonicas to flypaper (over your head, batting around on a thread beneath the blades of the ceiling fan, stuck with its testimonial catch). 3

Its confusion may have been in the eye of its beholder. Enchantment is cast upon you by all those things you weren't supposed to have need for, to lure you close to wooden tops you'd outgrown, boys' marbles and agates in little net pouches, small rubber balls that wouldn't bounce straight, frail, frazzly kite string, clay bubble pipes that would snap off in your teeth, the stiffest scissors. You could contemplate those long narrow boxes of sparklers gathering dust while you waited for it to be the Fourth of July or Christmas, and noisemakers in the shape of tin frogs for somebody's birthday party you hadn't been invited to yet, and see that they were all marvelous. 4

You might not have even looked for Mr. Sessions when he came around his store cheese (as big as a doll's house) and in front of the 5

[1]*brine:* salty water used to preserve or pickle food.
[2]*croker sacks:* sacks or bags made of burlap—a coarse, woven fabric.
[3]*Gold Dust Twins:* twins named Goldie and Dusty who advertised the Gold Dust washing powder, developed in the late 1880s.
[4]*signet ring:* a ring bearing an official-looking seal.

counter looking for you. When you'd finally asked him for, and received from him in its paper bag, whatever single thing it was that you had been sent for, the nickel that was left over was yours to spend.

Down at a child's eye level, inside those glass jars with mouths in their sides through which the grocer could run his scoop or a child's hand might be invited to reach for a choice, were wineballs, all-day suckers, gumdrops, peppermints. Making a row under the glass of a counter were the Tootsie Rolls, Hershey bars, Goo Goo Clusters, Baby Ruths. And whatever was the name of those pastilles that came stacked in a cardboard cylinder with a cardboard lid? They were thin and dry, about the size of tiddledy-winks,[5] and in the shape of twisted rosettes. A kind of chocolate dust came out with them when you shook them out in your hand. Were they chocolate? I'd say, rather, they were brown. They didn't taste of anything at all, unless it was wood. Their attraction was the number you got for a nickel. 6

Making up your mind, you circled the store around and around, around the pickle barrel, around the tower of Crackerjack boxes; Mr. Sessions had built it for us himself on top of a packing case like a house of cards. 7

If it seemed too hot for Crackerjacks, I might get a cold drink. Mr. Sessions might have already stationed himself by the cold-drinks barrel, like a mind reader. Deep in ice water that looked black as ink, murky shapes—that would come up as Coca-Colas, Orange Crushes, and various flavors of pop—were all swimming around together. When you gave the word, Mr. Sessions plunged his bare arm in to the elbow and fished out your choice, first try. I favored a locally bottled concoction called Lake's Celery. (What else could it be called? It was made by a Mr. Lake out of celery. It was a popular drink here for years but was not known universally, as I found out when I arrived in New York and ordered one in the Astor bar.) You drank on the premises, with feet set wide apart to miss the drip, and gave him back his bottle and your nickel. 8

But he didn't hurry you off. A standing scale was by the door, with a stack of iron weights and a brass slide on the balance arm, that would weigh you up to three hundred pounds. Mr. Sessions, whose hands were gentle and smelled of carbolic,[6] would lift you up and set 9

---

[5]*tiddledy-winks:* playing pieces from the game Tiddledy-Winks, flat and round in shape, the size of quarters (tiddledies) and dimes (winks).

[6]*carbolic:* a sweet, musky-smelling chemical once used in soap.

your feet on the platform, hold your loaf of bread for you, and taking his time while you stood still for him, he would make certain of what you weighed today. He could even remember what you weighed the last time, so you could subtract and announce how much you'd gained. That was goodbye.

Thinking Critically about This Reading

What does Mr. Sessions himself contribute to the overall experience of Welty's store? What does Welty's store contribute to the community?

Questions for Study and Discussion

1. Which of the three patterns of organization does Welty use in this essay—chronological, spatial, or logical? (Glossary: **Organization**) If she uses more than one, where precisely does she use each type?
2. In paragraph 2, Welty describes the smells that a person encountered when entering the corner store. Why do you think she presents these smells before giving any visual details of the inside of the store?
3. What dominant impression does Welty create in her description of the corner store? (Glossary: **Dominant Impression**) How does she create this dominant impression?
4. What impression of Mr. Sessions does Welty create? What details contribute to this impression? (Glossary: **Details**)
5. Why does Welty place certain pieces of information in parentheses? What, if anything, does this information add to your understanding of the corner store? Might this information be left out? Explain.
6. Comment on Welty's ending. (Glossary: **Beginnings and Endings**) Is it too abrupt? Why or why not?

Classroom Activity Using Description

Make a long list of the objects and people in your classroom as well as the physical features of the room—desks, windows, chalkboard, students, professor, dirty walls, burned-out lightbulb, a clock that is always ten minutes fast, and so on. Determine a dominant impression that you would like to create in describing the classroom. Now choose from your list those items that would best illustrate the dominant impression you have chosen. Your instructor may wish you to compare your response with those of other students.

Suggested Writing Assignments

1. Using Welty's essay as a model, describe your neighborhood store or supermarket. Gather a large quantity of detailed information from memory and from an actual visit to the store if that is still possible. You may find it helpful to reread what you wrote in response to the Reflecting on What You Know prompt for this selection. Then, try to select those details that will help you create a dominant impression of the store. Finally, organize your examples and illustrations according to a clear organizational pattern.
2. Write a short essay about a special event—or choose a normal day to capture. Consider the feeling of the day you're describing: celebratory, anxious, sleepy, bustling, and so on. Using Welty's essay as a model, write a description of the scene from your memory, choosing details that capture the dominant impression you identified.

Unforgettable Miss Bessie

Carl T. Rowan

Bettmann/Getty Images

In addition to being a popular syndicated newspaper columnist, Carl T. Rowan (1925–2000) was an ambassador to Finland and director of the U.S. Information Agency. Born in Ravenscroft, Tennessee, he received degrees from Oberlin College and the University of Minnesota. He worked as a columnist for the *Minneapolis Tribune* and the *Chicago Sun-Times* before moving to Washington, D.C. In 1996, Washington College awarded Rowan an honorary doctor of letters degree in recognition of his achievements as a writer and his contributions to minority youth, most notably through the organization he founded in 1987, Project Excellence. In 1991, Rowan published *Breaking Barriers: A Memoir*. He is also the author of two biographies, one of baseball great Jackie Robinson and the other of former Supreme Court justice Thurgood Marshall. His last book, *The Coming Race War in America*, was published in 1996.

In the following essay, first published in the March 1985 issue of *Reader's Digest*, Rowan describes a high school teacher whose lessons went far beyond the subjects she taught. Through telling details about Miss Bessie's background, behavior, and appearance, Rowan creates a dominant impression of her—the one he wants to leave readers with. As you read, notice how he begins with some factual information about Miss Bessie and concludes by showing why she was "so vital to the minds, hearts, and souls" of her students.

Reflecting on What You Know

Perhaps you have at some time taught a friend or a younger brother or sister how to do something—tie a shoe, hit a ball, read, solve a puzzle, drive a car—but you never thought of yourself as a teacher. Did you enjoy the experience of sharing what you know with someone else? Would you consider becoming a teacher someday?

She was only about five feet tall and probably never weighed more than 110 pounds, but Miss Bessie was a towering presence in the classroom. She was the only woman tough enough to make me read *Beowulf*[1] and think for a few foolish days that I liked it. From 1938 to 1942, when I attended Bernard High School in McMinnville, Tennessee, she taught me English, history, civics—and a lot more than I realized. 1

I shall never forget the day she scolded me into reading *Beowulf*. 2

"But Miss Bessie," I complained, "I ain't much interested in it." 3

Her large brown eyes became daggerish slits. "Boy," she said, "how dare you say 'ain't' to me! I've taught you better than that." 4

"Miss Bessie," I pleaded, "I'm trying to make first-string end on the football team, and if I go around saying 'it isn't' and 'they aren't,' the guys are gonna laugh me off the squad." 5

"Boy," she responded, "you'll play football because you have guts. But do you know what *really* takes guts? Refusing to lower your standards to those of the crowd. It takes guts to say you've got to live and be somebody fifty years after all the football games are over." 6

I started saying "it isn't" and "they aren't," and I still made first-string end—and class valedictorian—without losing my buddies' respect. 7

During her remarkable 44-year career, Mrs. Bessie Taylor Gwynn taught hundreds of economically deprived black youngsters—including my mother, my brother, my sisters, and me. I remember her now with gratitude and affection—especially in this era when Americans are so wrought-up about a "rising tide of mediocrity"[2] in public education and the problems of finding competent, caring teachers. Miss Bessie was an example of an informed, dedicated teacher, a blessing to children, and an asset to the nation. 8

Born in 1895, in poverty, she grew up in Athens, Alabama, where there was no public school for blacks. She attended Trinity School, a private institution for blacks run by the American Missionary Association, and in 1911 graduated from the Normal School (a "super" high school) at Fisk University in Nashville. Mrs. Gwynn, the essence of pride and privacy, never talked about her years in Athens; only in the months before her death did she reveal that she had never attended Fisk University itself because she could not afford the four-year course. 9

---

[1]*Beowulf:* an epic poem written in Old English by an anonymous author in the early eighth century.

[2]*mediocrity:* state of being second-rate; not outstanding.

At Normal School she learned a lot about Shakespeare, but most of all about the profound importance of education—especially for a people trying to move up from slavery. "What you put in your head, boy," she once said, "can never be pulled out by the Ku Klux Klan,[3] the Congress, or anybody." 10

Miss Bessie's bearing of dignity told anyone who met her that she was "educated" in the best sense of the word. There was never a discipline problem in her classes. We didn't dare mess with a woman who knew about the Battle of Hastings, the Magna Carta, and the Bill of Rights—and who could also play the piano. 11

This frail-looking woman could make sense of Shakespeare, Milton, Voltaire, and bring to life Booker T. Washington and W. E. B. Du Bois. Believing that it was important to know who the officials were that spent taxpayers' money and made public policy, she made us memorize the names of everyone on the Supreme Court and in the President's Cabinet. It could be embarrassing to be unprepared when Miss Bessie said, "Get up and tell the class who Frances Perkins[4] is and what you think about her." 12

Miss Bessie knew that my family, like so many others during the Depression,[5] couldn't afford to subscribe to a newspaper. She knew we didn't even own a radio. Still, she prodded me to "look out for your future and find some way to keep up with what's going on in the world." So I became a delivery boy for the Chattanooga *Times*. I rarely made a dollar a week, but I got to read a newspaper every day. 13

Miss Bessie noticed things that had nothing to do with schoolwork, but were vital to a youngster's development. Once a few classmates made fun of my frayed, hand-me-down overcoat, calling me "Strings." As I was leaving school, Miss Bessie patted me on the back of that old overcoat and said, "Carl, never fret about what you *don't* have. Just make the most of what you *do* have—a brain." 14

Among the things that I did not have was electricity in the little frame house that my father had built for $400 with his World War I 15

---

[3]*Ku Klux Klan:* a secret organization in the United States hostile toward African Americans (and eventually other groups as well), founded in 1915 and continuing to the present.

[4]*Frances Perkins* (1882–1965): U.S. secretary of labor during the presidency of Franklin D. Roosevelt and the first woman appointed to a cabinet post.

[5]*Depression:* the longest and most severe modern economic slump in North America, Europe, and other industrialized areas of the world so far; it began in 1929 and ended around 1939. Also called the Great Depression.

bonus. But because of her inspiration, I spent many hours squinting beside a kerosene lamp reading Shakespeare and Thoreau, Samuel Pepys and William Cullen Bryant.

No one in my family had ever graduated from high school, so there was no tradition of commitment to learning for me to lean on. Like millions of youngsters in today's ghettos and barrios, I needed the push and stimulation of a teacher who truly cared. Miss Bessie gave plenty of both, as she immersed me in a wonderful world of similes, metaphors and even onomatopoeia. She led me to believe that I could write sonnets as well as Shakespeare, or iambic-pentameter verse to put Alexander Pope to shame. 16

In those days the McMinnville school system was rigidly "Jim Crow,"[6] and poor black children had to struggle to put anything in their heads. Our high school was only slightly larger than the once-typical little red schoolhouse, and its library was outrageously inadequate—so small, I like to say, that if two students were in it and one wanted to turn a page, the other one had to step outside. 17

Negroes, as we were called then, were not allowed in the town library, except to mop floors or dust tables. But through one of those secret Old South arrangements between whites of conscience and blacks of stature, Miss Bessie kept getting books smuggled out of the white library. That is how she introduced me to the Brontës, Byron, Coleridge, Keats and Tennyson. "If you don't read, you can't write, and if you can't write, you might as well stop dreaming," Miss Bessie once told me. 18

So I read whatever Miss Bessie told me to, and tried to remember the things she insisted that I store away. Forty-five years later, I can still recite her "truths to live by," such as Henry Wadsworth Longfellow's lines from "The Ladder of St. Augustine": 19

> The heights by great men reached and kept
> Were not attained by sudden flight.
> But they, while their companions slept,
> Were toiling upward in the night.

Years later, her inspiration, prodding, anger, cajoling, and almost osmotic[7] infusion of learning finally led to that lovely day when Miss 20

---

[6] *"Jim Crow":* a term referring to the racial segregation laws in the U.S. South between the late 1800s and the mid-1900s.

[7] *osmotic*: related to *osmosis*, the process of absorption.

Bessie dropped me a note saying, "I'm so proud to read your column in the Nashville *Tennessean.*"

Miss Bessie was a spry 80 when I went back to McMinnville and visited her in a senior citizens' apartment building. Pointing out proudly that her building was racially integrated, she reached for two glasses and a pint of bourbon. I was momentarily shocked, because it would have been scandalous in the 1930s and '40s for word to get out that a teacher drank, and nobody had ever raised a rumor that Miss Bessie did. 21

I felt a new sense of equality as she lifted her glass to mine. Then she revealed a softness and compassion that I had never known as a student. 22

"I've never forgotten that examination day," she said, "when Buster Martin held up seven fingers, obviously asking you for help with question number seven, 'Name a common carrier.' I can still picture you looking at your exam paper and humming a few bars of 'Chattanooga Choo Choo.' I was so tickled, I couldn't punish either of you." 23

Miss Bessie was telling me, with bourbon-laced grace, that I never fooled her for a moment. 24

When Miss Bessie died in 1980, at age 85, hundreds of her former students mourned. They knew the measure of a great teacher: love and motivation. Her wisdom and influence had rippled out across generations. 25

Some of her students who might normally have been doomed to poverty went on to become doctors, dentists, and college professors. Many, guided by Miss Bessie's example, became public-school teachers. 26

"The memory of Miss Bessie and how she conducted her classroom did more for me than anything I learned in college," recalls Gladys Wood of Knoxville, Tennessee, a highly respected English teacher who spent 43 years in the state's school system. "So many times, when I faced a difficult classroom problem, I asked myself, *How would Miss Bessie deal with this?* And I'd remember that she would handle it with laughter and love." 27

No child can get all the necessary support at home, and millions of poor children get *no* support at all. This is what makes a wise, educated, warm-hearted teacher like Miss Bessie so vital to the minds, hearts, and souls of this country's children. 28

Thinking Critically about This Reading

Rowan states that Miss Bessie "taught me English, history, civics—and a lot more than I realized" (paragraph 1). Aside from the standard school subjects, what did Miss Bessie teach Rowan? What role did she play in his life?

Questions for Study and Discussion

1. Throughout the essay, Rowan offers details of Miss Bessie's physical appearance. What specific details does he give, and in what context does he give them? (Glossary: **Details**) Do Miss Bessie's physical characteristics match the quality of her character? Explain.
2. At what point in the essay does Rowan give us the details of Miss Bessie's background? Why do you suppose he delays giving us this important information?
3. Do you think Rowan's first few paragraphs make for an effective introduction? Explain.
4. Does Miss Bessie's drinking influence your opinion of her? Why or why not? Why do you think Rowan mentions this aspect of her behavior in his essay?
5. How does dialogue serve Rowan's purpose? (Glossary: **Dialogue; Purpose**)
6. How would you sum up the character of Miss Bessie? Make a list of the key words Rowan uses that you believe best describe her.

Classroom Activity Using Description

Important advice for writing well is to show rather than tell. Your task with this activity is to reveal a person's character. For example, to indicate that someone is concerned about current events without coming out and saying so, you might show her reading the morning newspaper. Or you might show a character's degree of formality by including his typical greeting: *How ya doing?* In other words, the things a person says and does are often important indicators of personality. Choose one of the following traits, and make a list of at least four ways to show that someone possesses that trait. Share your list with the class, and discuss the "show-not-tell" strategies you have used.

plain and uncomplicated	thoughtful	independent
reckless	politically involved	quick-witted
artistic	irresponsible	public-spirited
a sports lover	conversationalist	loyal

Suggested Writing Assignments

1. In paragraph 18, Rowan writes the following: "'If you don't read, you can't write, and if you can't write, you might as well stop dreaming,' Miss Bessie once told me." Write an essay in which you explore this theme (which, in essence, is also the theme of *Models for Writers*).
2. Think of all the teachers you have had, and then write a description of the one who has had the greatest influence on you. (Glossary: **Description**) Remember to give some consideration to the balance you want to achieve between physical attributes and personality traits.

My Lost Mother's Last Receipt

Mara Wilson

Suzi Pratt/Getty Images

Mara Wilson was born in Burbank, California, in 1987. She became a child actress and is known for her roles in *Mrs. Doubtfire* (1993) with Robin Williams and Sally Field and in *Matilda* (1996) with Danny DeVito and Rhea Perlman. After the death of her mother in 1996, Wilson appeared in only two more feature films, *A Simple Wish* (1997) with Martin Short and *Thomas and the Magic Railroad* (2000). She has continued to do work on television and the Internet, but her interests have expanded to include writing scripts. Her book *Where Am I Now? True Stories of Girlhood and Accidental Fame* (2016) is a memoir of her years as a child actress.

In this article, which was originally published in the *New York Times* on September 11, 2016, Wilson uses the story of finding an old purse to recollect what kind of woman her mother was. As you read, notice how Wilson uses the simple everyday items that might be found in anyone's purse to create a revealing portrait of her mother.

Reflecting on What You Know

What simple everyday items do you own and keep with you? What items are in your bag or in your pockets? What would they tell someone about your life?

It was my little sister, Anna, who found the purse. 1

"Was this hers?" she asked. 2

One of our brothers nodded. "Must be the last one she ever used." 3

It had been 20 years since our mother died. Twenty to the day since her funeral. 4

But we hadn't been looking for mementos; we'd just been cleaning out the garage. I'd unearthed a painting of the Roald Dahl title 5 character Matilda dedicated to me by the book's illustrator, Quentin Blake. Anna stumbled on a writing assignment from second grade, where she said she wanted to grow up to "be an art-school girl" but also "study shells and emotions."

Earlier that week, my sister and I had visited our mother's grave, me for the first time. She had been a beloved daughter, wife and mother—"devoted to children," the marker read. I was 8 when she died. My brothers were 17, 15 and 13. Anna had just turned 3. 6

"Tell me things you remember about her," Anna said while we sat by her grave. Not the big things, which she already knew, but the small, day-to-day things. 7

"Her favorite movie was *Sullivan's Travels*. She hated *Love Story*. She had a low speaking voice, but could sing soprano. She was so good at calligraphy she hand-lettered her own wedding invitations. She would help me write notes to the Tooth Fairy and set out grapes and raisins for her. She ate tomatoes like they were apples." 8

Our mother was known as the only Burbank Unified School District board member who could use two expletives in one sentence. Many seemed to find her intimidating, but after her death, several people told us, "Your mother was my best friend." She was talented and theatrical, and yet she never had a career. Instead she had five children. None of us could imagine anyone smarter or stronger than her. 9

I became a child actor at 5, and after some unexpected successes, my mother took on the role of manager. She never would have called herself that—her biggest fear was being labeled a "stage mother"—but it's what she was, and she was good at it. On film sets, she never let me out of her sight. I was there to do a job, and she was there to make sure I did it safely and took it seriously. Out of all of us, she and I probably spent the most time together. I'm grateful I had that, though I regret every day the time I took away from my siblings. 10

Our father remarried when I was a teenager, and Anna was adopted by our stepmother, whom she calls "Mom" or "Inay," the Filipino word for mother. She has since taken on several of our stepmother's mannerisms—saying she is going to "close the lights," eating with a fork and spoon, instead of a fork and knife. She remembers very little of her birth mother. As a child, she once told me, "You made a face like Mama just now," and another time, she cried when I sang her a song our mother used to sing. But that was all she seemed to remember. For a long time, she had only one photo of herself with our mother, and none of them alone together. 11

We took the purse upstairs. The leather was worn, and the hinge didn't quite close. 12

"She never zipped or buttoned her purses shut," my brother said. I smiled. I never seem to do that, either. 13

Gingerly, we started looking through it. The first thing we found was a date and address book. There, in her handwriting, were entries for people like Sally Field and Danny DeVito, my earliest co-stars. A week after what would be her last day, she had written, "Fly to D.C." 14

"Oh, that's right," my brother said. "We were supposed to go to Virginia. But ..." 15

We found unopened makeup, a pill bottle full of medicine to be taken "as needed." We found a photo of a guru and an invoice from a yoga instructor. When traditional medicine failed to halt her cancer, our mother had turned to herbs and acupuncture. I don't know if she believed in that stuff, but it did seem to make her more comfortable. Except the time I found her in the kitchen, dumping a smoothie down the drain. "Ugh!" she sputtered, "Fish oil!" 16

At the bottom of the purse, we pulled out a receipt. 17

"This is from the day she died," our brother said. "I remember talking to her that day before school. That morning, she was lucid. That night, she...wasn't." 18

I remembered, too. Do you think she knew, I wanted to ask? But I couldn't. "What's it for?" 19

He hesitated for a moment. "Baby clothes. Toddler size." 20

We turned to look at Anna. She sat still, looking straight ahead. 21

"Can I take the purse?" she said, at last, quietly. "I want to get it fixed." 22

We nodded. 23

We don't know who our mother would have been if she hadn't worked menial jobs and raised five children. We don't know who she would have been if she had beat cancer, the way she had promised us she would. But with her last act, she showed us who she was: a woman devoted to her children, to the very end. 24

"Is there anything you want to keep?" Anna asked me the next morning, before we said our goodbyes. 25

I thought of all the photos of me and my mother, the years I got to spend with her that Anna never had. 26

"No, that's O.K.," I told Anna. "You keep it all." 27

Thinking Critically about This Reading

The article begins with Wilson and her siblings going through a garage with their mother's things, a full twenty years after their mother's death. How does that length of time create perspectives for Wilson and her younger sister on the death of their mother? How are those perspectives different?

Questions for Study and Discussion

1. In paragraph 7, Wilson writes that when her sister asks about their deceased mother, she means "Not the big things, which she already knew, but the small day-to-day things." What does she mean by the small things, and why are they important? How does Wilson show their importance? What does Wilson's mother's fondness for *Sullivan's Travels* (1941) and dislike of *Love Story* (1970) tell the reader about her personality? (If you're not familiar with the films, do some quick research to respond to this question.)
2. Wilson states that her mother was the only member of the local school board who could use "two expletives in one sentence" (9). What does that detail tell the reader about her? Why is it important that it is followed by the statement that when Wilson's mother died, many people told her that her mother was their best friend?
3. Wilson points out that her younger sister, Anna, hardly knew their birth mother and became more like her stepmother as she matured (11). What tone does Wilson use in reflecting on this? (Glossary: **Tone**). What details and word choice reveal her tone?
4. What is significant about the receipt that the children find in their mother's purse?
5. At the end, why does Wilson tell her younger sister to keep all of the mementos that they found? Do you think this is an effective ending? (Glossary: **Beginnings and Endings**) Why or why not?

Classroom Activity Using Description

One of the best ways to make a description of a person memorable is to use a simile (making a comparison using *like* or *as*, such as "Her feet floated like a feather in a breeze") or a metaphor (making a comparison without the use of *like* or *as*, such as "His fists were iron"). (Glossary: **Figurative Language**) Think of a time when you were one of a group of people assembled to do something most or all of you didn't really want to do. People in such a situation show their discomfort in various ways. One might stare at the ground, for example. A writer describing the scene could use a metaphor to make this detail more vivid: "With his gaze he drilled a hole in the ground between his feet." Other people in an uncomfortable situation might fidget, lace their fingers together, breathe rapidly, squirm, or tap an object, such as a pen or a key. Create a simile or a metaphor to describe each of these behaviors. Compare your metaphors and similes with those of your classmates. Discuss which ones work best for each behavior.

Suggested Writing Assignments

1. Write a descriptive essay about someone that you know or have known. Focus on using good descriptive details that will not only show the person physically but also reveal his or her personality. In addition to strong details, you may consider adding narrative anecdotes and dialogue to write about a memory or to explain how someone acts. (Glossary: **Narration; Anecdote; Dialogue**)
2. Most descriptive writing is primarily visual: it appeals to our sense of sight. Good description, however, often goes beyond the visual by appealing to one or more of the other senses: hearing, smell, taste, and touch. One way to heighten your awareness of these other senses is to purposefully deemphasize the visual impressions you receive. For example, while standing on a busy street corner, sitting in a small Chinese restaurant, or walking into a movie theater after the show has started, carefully note what you hear, smell, taste, and feel. (It may help if you close your eyes to eliminate visual distractions.) Use these sense impressions to write a brief description of the street corner, the Chinese restaurant, the movie theater, or another spot of your choosing.

CHAPTER **16**

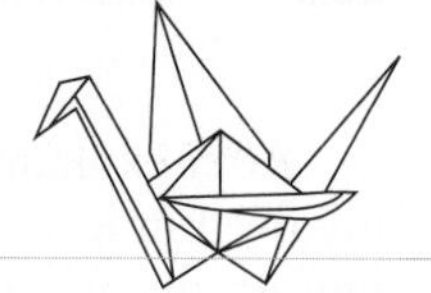

Process Analysis

When you give someone directions to your home, tell how to make ice cream, or explain how a president is elected, you are using **process analysis.** Process analysis usually arranges a series of events in order and relates them to one another, as narration and cause and effect do, but process analysis has a different emphasis. Whereas narration tells mainly *what* happens and cause and effect focuses on *why* it happens, process analysis tries to explain—in detail—*how* it happens.

There are two types of process analysis: directional and informational.

DIRECTIONAL PROCESS ANALYSIS

The *directional* type of process analysis provides instructions on how to do something. These instructions can be as brief as the directions for making instant coffee printed on the label or as complex as the directions in a manual for assembling a new gas grill. The purpose of directional process analysis is to give the reader directions to follow that will lead to the desired results.

Consider these directions for performing the Heimlich maneuver:

> Stand behind the victim, wrap your arms around the victim's waist, and make a fist. Place the thumb side of your fist against the victim's upper abdomen, below the ribcage and above the navel. Grasp your fist with your other hand and press into her upper abdomen with a quick upward thrust. Do not squeeze the ribcage. Repeat until the stuck object is expelled.
>
> –Joshua Piven and David Borgenicht, *The Worst-Case Scenario Survival Handbook: Life*

Piven and Borgenicht present clear, step-by-step directions for performing the Heimlich maneuver on a choking victim, being careful to present enough detail and instruction so that any person would be able to perform the maneuver.

After explaining in two previous paragraphs the first two steps involved in learning how to juggle, a student writer moves to the important third step. Notice here how he explains the third step, offers advice on what to do if things go wrong, and encourages his readers' efforts—all useful in directional process analysis:

> Step three is merely a continuum of "the exchange" with the addition of the third ball. Don't worry if you are confused—I will explain. Hold two balls in your right hand and one in your left. Make a perfect toss with one of your balls in your right hand and then an exchange with the one in your left hand. The ball coming from your left hand should now be exchanged with the, as of now, unused ball in your right hand. This process should be continued until you find yourself reaching under nearby chairs for bouncing tennis balls. It is true that many persons' backs and legs become sore when learning how to juggle because they've been picking up balls that they've inadvertently tossed around the room. Try practicing over a bed; you won't have to reach down so far. Don't get too upset if things aren't going well; you're probably keeping the same pace as everyone else at this stage.
>
> –William Peterson, student

INFORMATIONAL PROCESS ANALYSIS

The *informational* type of process analysis, on the other hand, tells how something works, how something is made, or how something occurs. You would use informational process analysis if you wanted to explain how the human heart functions, how an atomic bomb works, how hailstones are formed, how you selected the college you are attending, or how the polio vaccine was developed. Rather than giving specific directions, informational process analysis explains and informs.

In the following illustration, Jim Collins uses informational process analysis to explain a basic legislative procedure—how a bill becomes a law.

Clarity is crucial for successful process analysis. The most effective way to explain a process is to divide it into steps and to present those steps in a clear (usually chronological) sequence. Transitional words and phrases such as *first, next, after,* and *before* help to connect steps to one another. Naturally, you must be sure that no step is omitted or given out of order. Also, you may sometimes have to explain *why* a certain step is necessary, especially if it is not obvious. With intricate, abstract, or particularly difficult steps, you might use analogy or comparison to clarify the steps for your reader.

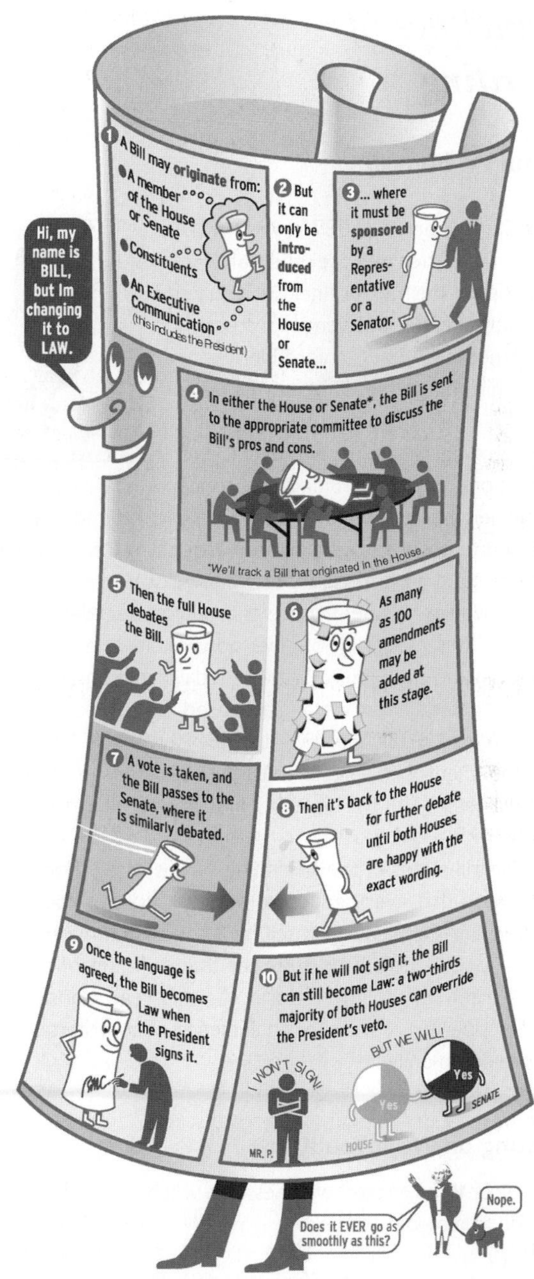

Graphic by Nigel Holmes

The Principles of Poor Writing

Paul W. Merrill

Courtesy of the Carnegie Observatories

Paul Willard Merrill (1887–1961) was a noted astronomer whose specialty was spectroscopy—the measurement of a quantity as a function of either wavelength or frequency. Merrill earned his AB at Stanford University in 1908 and his PhD at the University of California in 1913. After spending three years at the University of Michigan, Merrill went to work at the National Bureau of Standards, concentrating on aerial photography in the visible and infrared spectra. He was the first to propose doing infrared astronomy from airplanes. In 1919, he joined the Mt. Wilson Observatory, located near Pasadena, California, where he spent more than three decades researching peculiar stars, especially long-period variables. He received the Bruce Medal and the Henry Draper Medal, had an asteroid and a lunar crater named after him, and authored four books: *The Nature of Variable Stars* (1938), *Spectra of Long-Period Variable Stars* (1940), *Lines of the Chemical Elements in Astronomical Spectra* (1956), and *Space Chemistry* (1963). This essay first appeared in the January 1947 issue of *Scientific Monthly*.

As Merrill states in the beginning of this essay, "Poor writing is so common that every educated person ought to know something about it." As a scientist himself, he suspects that many scientists who write poorly do so more by ear than by a set of principles, which he freely offers in this essay. As you read, consider how Merrill describes his process for an audience of all writers, including his science community.

Reflecting on What You Know

Describe your three greatest weaknesses in writing. What do you think you can do to remedy each one?

Books and articles on good writing are numerous, but where can you find sound, practical advice on how to write poorly? Poor writing is so common that every educated person ought to know something about it. Many scientists actually do write poorly, but they probably perform by ear without perceiving clearly how their results are achieved. An article on the principles of poor writing might help. The author considers himself well qualified to prepare such an article; he can write poorly without half trying. 1

The average student finds it surprisingly easy to acquire the usual tricks of poor writing. To do a consistently poor job, however, one must grasp a few essential principles: 2

1. Ignore the reader.
2. Be verbose, vague, and pompous.
3. Do not revise.

Ignore the Reader

The world is divided into two great camps: yourself and others. A little obscurity or indirection in writing will keep the others at a safe distance. Write as if for a diary. Keep your mind on a direct course between yourself and the subject; don't think of the reader—he makes a bad triangle. This is fundamental. Constant and alert consideration of the probable reaction of the reader is a serious menace to poor writing; moreover, it requires mental effort. A logical argument is that if you write poorly enough, your readers will be too few to merit any attention whatever. 3

Ignore the reader wherever possible. If the proposed title, for example, means something to you, stop right there; think no further. If the title baffles or misleads the reader, you have won the first round. Similarly, all the way through you must write for yourself, not for the reader. Practice a dead-pan technique, keeping your facts and ideas all on the same level of emphasis with no telltale hints of relative importance or logical sequence. Use long sentences containing many ideas loosely strung together. *And* is the connective most frequently employed in poor writing because it does not indicate cause and effect, nor does it distinguish major ideas from subordinate ones. *Because* seldom appears in poor writing, nor does the semicolon—both are replaced by *and.* 4

Camouflage transitions in thought. Avoid such connectives as *moreover, nevertheless, on the other hand*. If unable to resist the 5 temptation to give some signal for a change in thought, use *however*. A poor sentence may well begin with *however* because to the reader, with no idea what comes next, *however* is too vague to be useful. A good sentence begins with the subject or with a phrase that needs emphasis.

The "hidden antecedent" is a common trick of poor writing. Use a pronoun to refer to a noun a long way back, or to one decidedly subordinate in thought or syntax; or the pronoun may refer to something not directly expressed. If you wish to play a little game with the reader, offer him the wrong antecedent as bait; you may be astonished how easy it is to catch the poor fish. 6

In ignoring the reader, avoid parallel constructions which give the thought away too easily. I need not elaborate, for you probably employ inversion frequently. It must have been a naive soul who said, "When the thought is parallel, let the phrases be parallel." 7

In every technical paper omit a few items that most readers need to know. You had to discover these things the hard way; why make it easy for the reader? Avoid defining symbols: never specify the units in which data are presented. Of course it will be beneath your dignity to give numerical values of constants in formulae. With these omissions, some papers may be too short; lengthen them by explaining things that do not need explaining. In describing tables, give special attention to self-explanatory headings; let the reader hunt for the meaning of *Pr*. 8

Be Verbose, Vague, and Pompous

The cardinal sin of poor writing is to be concise and simple. Avoid being specific: it ties you down. Use plenty of deadwood: include many superfluous words and phrases. Wishful thinking suggests to a writer that verbosity somehow serves as a cloak or even as a mystic halo by which an idea may be glorified. A cloud of words may conceal defects in observation or analysis, either by opacity or by diverting the reader's attention. Introduce abstract nouns at the drop of a hat—even in those cases where the magnitude of the motion in a downward direction is inconsiderable. Make frequent use of the words *case, character, condition, former* and *latter, nature, such, very*. 9

Poor writing, like good football, is strong on razzle-dazzle, weak on information. Adjectives are frequently used to bewilder the reader. It isn't much trouble to make them gaudy or hyperbolic; at the least they can be flowery and inexact. 10

Deadwood

BIBLE:	Render to Caesar the things that are Caesar's.
POOR:	In the case of Caesar it might well be considered appropriate from a moral or ethical point of view to render to that potentate all of those goods and materials of whatever character or quality which can be shown to have had their original source in any portion of the domain of the latter.
SHAKESPEARE:	I am no orator as Brutus is.
POOR:	The speaker is not, what might be termed as adept in the profession of public speaking, as might be properly stated of Mr. Brutus. (Example from P. W. Swain. *Amer. J. Physics,* 13, 318, 1945.)
CONCISE:	The dates of several observations are in doubt.
POOR:	It should be mentioned that in the case of several observations there is room for considerable doubt concerning the correctness of the dates on which they were made.
REASONABLE:	Exceptionally rapid changes occur in the spectrum.
POOR:	There occur in the spectrum changes which are quite exceptional in respect to the rapidity of their advent.
REASONABLE:	Formidable difficulties, both mathematical and observational, stand in the way.
POOR:	There are formidable difficulties of both a mathematical and an observational nature that stand in the way.

Case

REASONABLE:	Two sunspots changed rapidly.
POOR:	There are two cases where sunspots changed with considerable rapidity.

REASONABLE: Three stars are red.

POOR: In three cases the stars are red in color.

Razzle-Dazzle

Immaculate precision of observation and extremely delicate calculations . . .

It would prove at once a world imponderable, etherealized. Our actions would grow grandific.

Well for us that the pulsing energy of the great life-giving dynamo in the sky never ceases. Well, too, that we are at a safe distance from the flame-licked whirlpools into which our earth might drop like a pellet of waste fluff shaken into the live coals of a grate fire.

Do Not Revise

Write hurriedly, preferably when tired. Have no plan; write down items as they occur to you. The article will thus be spontaneous and poor. Hand in your manuscript the moment it is finished. Rereading a few days later might lead to revision—which seldom, if ever, makes the writing worse. If you submit your manuscript to colleagues (a bad practice), pay no attention to their criticisms or comments. Later, resist firmly any editorial suggestion. Be strong and infallible; don't let anyone break down your personality. The critic may be trying to help you or he may have an ulterior motive, but the chance of his causing improvement in your writing is so great that you must be on guard. 11

Thinking Critically about This Reading

Why do you think Merrill might have written "The Principles of Poor Writing"? What special motivation do you think his career as a scientist might have provided him? Explain.

Questions for Study and Discussion

1. *Irony* is the use of words to suggest something different from their meaning. At what point in the essay did you realize that Merrill is being ironic? (Glossary: **Irony**) Did his title, introduction, or actual advice tip you off? Explain.

2. Is the author's process analysis the directional type or the informational type? What leads you to this conclusion?
3. Why has Merrill ordered his three process steps in this particular way? Could he have used a different order? (Glossary: **Organization**) Explain.
4. How useful are the author's examples in helping you understand his principles? Do you agree with all his examples? (Glossary: **Example**) Explain.
5. Why do you suppose Merrill chose to use irony to show his readers that they needed to improve their writing? (Glossary: **Irony**) What do you see as the potential advantages and disadvantages to such a strategy?
6. In what types of writing situations is irony especially useful?

Classroom Activity Using Process Analysis

Most do-it-yourself jobs require that you follow a set process to achieve results. Imagine you are writing an online How To article for one of the following household activities:

cleaning windows

repotting a plant

making burritos

changing a flat tire

unclogging a drain

doing laundry

Would you list the steps by number? Write paragraphs? Include images or illustrations? Work with classmates to create your article, either as a prototype on paper or, if you have the resources, as a Web page.

Suggested Writing Assignments

1. Write a process analysis in which you explain the steps you usually follow when deciding to make a purchase of some importance or expense to you. *Hint:* It's best to analyze your process with a specific product in mind. Do you compare

brands, store prices, and so on? What are your priorities—that the item be stylish or durable, offer good overall value, or give high performance?

2. Try writing a process analysis essay in which you are ironic about the steps that need to be followed. For example, in an essay on how to lose weight by changing your diet or increasing your exercise, you might cast in a positive light all the things that absolutely should not be done. These might include parking as close as you can to your destination to avoid walking, or buying a half gallon of your favorite ice cream instead of a pint because the half gallons are on sale.

Designate a Place for Each Thing

Marie Kondo

Taylor Hill / Getty Images

Marie Kondo was born in Japan in 1985 and studied at Tokyo Woman's Christian University. At age nineteen, while still a student, Kondo started her own consulting business teaching people how to be organized. She created what is known as the KonMari system: gathering one's possessions together by category and then keeping only the items that "spark joy" in one's life. She is now a world-famous organizing consultant and lifestyle expert, and her books have been published in over forty languages. Her first English-language book was *The Life-Changing Magic of Tidying Up: The Japanese Art of Decluttering and Organizing* (2014); her newest is *Spark Joy: An Illustrated Master Class on the Art of Organizing and Tidying Up* (2016). In 2015, she was named one of *Time* magazine's 100 Most Influential People.

In this excerpt from *The Life-Changing Magic of Tidying Up*, Kondo demonstrates the benefits of making sure that every item one owns has its particular place. As you read, notice how the process of simply stepping into her home reveals the benefits of her organized life.

Reflecting on What You Know

Do you consider yourself to be an organized or disorganized person? How important is being organized to you? Does your level of organization affect how you get tasks done for school, work, or home?

This is the routine I follow every day when I return from work. First, I unlock the door and announce to my house, "I'm home!" Picking up the pair of shoes I wore yesterday and left out in the entranceway, I say, "Thank you very much for your hard work," and put them away in the shoe cupboard. Then I take off the shoes 1

I wore today and place them neatly in the entranceway. Heading to the kitchen, I put the kettle on and go to my bedroom. There I lay my handbag gently on the soft sheepskin rug and take off my outdoor clothes. I put my jacket and dress on a hanger, say, "Good job!" and hang them temporarily from the closet doorknob. I put my tights in a laundry basket that fits into the bottom right corner of my closet, open a drawer, select the clothes I feel like wearing inside, and get dressed. I greet the waist-high potted plant by the window and stroke its leaves.

My next task is to empty the contents of my handbag on the rug and put each item away in its place. First I remove all the receipts. Then I put my wallet in its designated box in a drawer under my bed with a word of gratitude. I place my train pass and my business card holder beside it. I put my wristwatch in a pink antique case in the same drawer and place my necklace and earrings on the accessory tray beside it. Before closing the drawer, I say, "Thanks for all you did for me today." 2

Next, I return to the entrance and put away the books and notebooks I carried around all day (I have converted a shelf of my shoe cupboard into a bookshelf). From the shelf below it I take out my "receipt pouch" and put my receipts in it. Then I put my digital camera that I use for work in the space beside it, which is reserved for electrical things. Papers that I've finished with go in the recycle bin beneath the kitchen range. In the kitchen, I make a pot of tea while checking the mail, disposing of the letters I've finished with. 3

I return to my bedroom, put my empty handbag in a bag, and put it on the top shelf of the closet, saying, "You did well. Have a good rest." From the time I get in the door to the moment I close the closet, a total of only five minutes has passed. Now I can go back to the kitchen, pour myself a cup of tea, and relax. 4

I did not give you this account to boast about my beautiful lifestyle, but rather to demonstrate what it's like to have a designated spot for everything. Keeping your space tidy becomes second nature. You can do it effortlessly, even when you come home tired from work, and this gives you more time to really enjoy life. 5

The point in deciding specific places to keep things is to designate a spot for *every* thing. You may think, "It would take me forever to do that," but you don't need to worry. Although it seems like deciding on a place for every item must be complicated, it's far simpler than 6 deciding what to keep and what to discard. Since you have already decided what to keep according to type of item and since those items all belong to the same category, all you need to do is store them near each other.

The reason every item must have a designated place is because the existence of an item without a home multiplies the chances that your space will become cluttered again. Let's say, for example, that you have a shelf with nothing on it. What happens if someone leaves an object that has no designated spot on that shelf? That one item will become your downfall. Within no time that space, which had maintained a sense of order, will be covered with objects, as if someone had yelled, "Gather round, everybody!" 7

You only need to designate a spot for every item once. Try it. You'll be amazed at the results. No longer will you buy more than you need. No longer will the things you own continue to accumulate. In fact, your stock on hand will decrease. The essence of effective storage is this: designate a spot for every last thing you own. If you ignore this basic principle and start experimenting with the vast range of storage ideas being promoted, you will be sorry. Those storage "solutions" are really just prisons within which to bury possessions that spark no joy. 8

One of the main reasons for rebound[1] is the failure to designate a spot for each item. Without a designated spot, where are you going to put things when you finish using them? Once you choose a place for your things, you can keep your house in order. So decide where your things belong and when you finish using them, put them there. This is the main requirement for storage. 9

Thinking Critically about This Reading

Kondo describes the routine that she uses every day when she comes home. Instead of being a mindless activity, the process is deliberate and reveals her theory of organization. Why is it important to include her philosophy rather than just detailing her routine? What does this philosophy reveal about Kondo's values? Or her purpose? (Glossary: **Purpose**)

[1]*rebound*: in Kondo's method, this means falling back into patterns of disorganization or clutter.

Questions for Study and Discussion

1. Why does Kondo talk to the inanimate objects in her home? What tone does that give to her writing? (Glossary: **Tone**)
2. Kondo gives the reader a step-by-step rendering of the process that she goes through when she comes home from work. What type of process is it—directional or informational? What leads you to that conclusion?
3. What transitional words or phrases does Kondo use to keep the process clear?
4. In paragraph 6, the first sentence is typed in a boldface font and the word *every* is italicized. Why does Kondo use this extra emphasis?
5. Kondo states, "The reason every item must have a designated place is because the existence of an item without a home multiplies the chances that your space will become cluttered again" (7). Have you found this to be true? Explain.
6. One benefit to Kondo's organizational technique is that she says you'll never buy more than you need of something. Why is this?
7. Making sure everything has a place seems like simple advice. Why do you think this is so difficult for so many people to follow?

Classroom Activity Using Process Analysis

Review the following illustrations detailing the process of making an origami crane, like the ones depicted on the cover of this book. Try to make one yourself. Then, working with your classmates, try writing instructions to supplement these visual directions. Discuss what the written instructions add to the visual ones. Do they make the process easier?

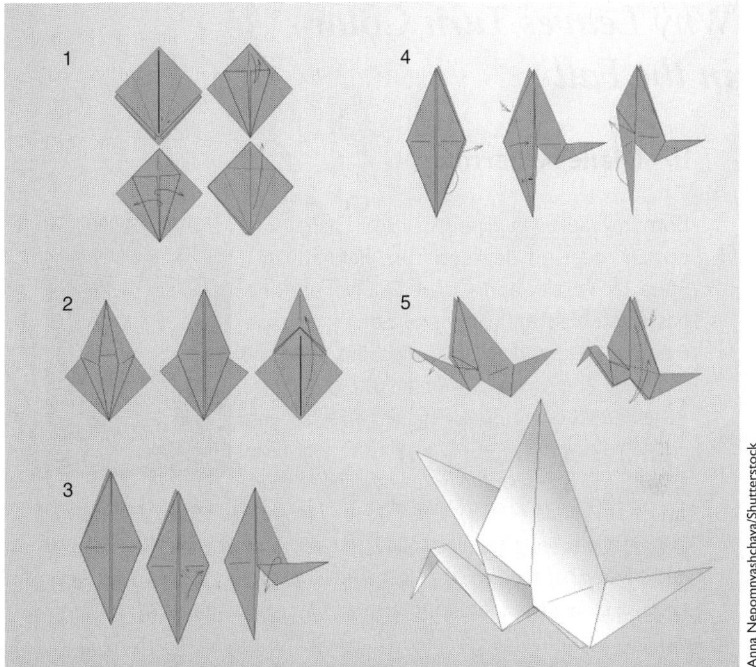

Anna Nepomnyashchaya/Shutterstock

Suggested Writing Assignments

1. Kondo's work is about organizing the things in one's life. Write a process analysis in which you create your own lifestyle advice. Choose something that many people do in life, perhaps on a daily basis, and write about how they can do that activity better if they follow your advice. Make the steps of the process clear to your readers with good transitions and appropriate detail.
2. A central theme behind Kondo's work is that an organized and clutter-free life is a better, more productive, and happier life. Do you agree? Write an argument in defense of your answer. Provide specific details to support your argument, based on your own life, observations, and reading.

Why Leaves Turn Color in the Fall

Diane Ackerman

Ulf Andersen/Getty Images

Born in Waukegan, Illinois, in 1948, Diane Ackerman received degrees from Pennsylvania State University and Cornell University. She has written several books of poetry, a prose memoir, a play, and several collections of essays, including *The Moon by Whale Light, and Other Adventures among Bats, Penguins, Crocodilians, and Whales* (1991); *A Natural History of Love* (1994); *The Rarest of the Rare: Vanishing Animals, Timeless Worlds* (1995); *The Curious Naturalist* (1998); *Deep Play* (1999); *Cultivating Delight* (2002); *An Alchemy of Mind: The Marvel and Mystery of the Brain* (2004); *The Zookeeper's Wife: A War Story* (2007); *Dawn Light: Dancing with Cranes and Other Ways to Start the Day* (2009); *One Hundred Names for Love: A Stroke, a Marriage, and the Language of Healing* (2011); and *The Human Age: A World Shaped by Us* (2014). Ackerman has worked as a writer-in-residence at several major universities, has directed the Writers' Program at Washington University in St. Louis, and has been a staff writer at The *New Yorker.* She currently lives in upstate New York.

Every October, residents of the northeastern United States are dazzled by a spectacular color show that sets them to wondering, "Where do the colors come from?" In the following selection from Ackerman's acclaimed *A Natural History of the Senses* (1990), she lets us in on one of nature's secrets. As you read, notice the way Ackerman shares her enthusiasm for the natural world as she explains the process by which autumn leaves assume their brilliant colors.

Reflecting on What You Know

What is your favorite season? What about this season makes it your favorite—the weather, the activities and memories, the time of year, or a combination of these and other factors?

The stealth of autumn catches one unaware. Was that a goldfinch perching in the early September woods, or just the first turning leaf? A red-winged blackbird or a sugar maple closing up shop for the winter? Keen-eyed as leopards, we stand still and squint hard, looking for signs of movement. Early-morning frost sits heavily on the grass, and turns barbed wire into a string of stars. On a distant hill, a small square of yellow appears to be a lighted stage. At last the truth dawns on us: Fall is staggering in, right on schedule, with its baggage of chilly nights, macabre holidays, and spectacular, heart-stoppingly beautiful leaves. Soon the leaves will start cringing on the trees, and roll up in clenched fists before they actually fall off. Dry seedpods will rattle like tiny gourds. But first there will be weeks of gushing color so bright, so pastel, so confetti-like, that people will travel up and down the East Coast just to stare at it—a whole season of leaves. 1

Where do the colors come from? Sunlight rules most living things with its golden edicts. When the days begin to shorten, soon after the summer solstice on June 21, a tree reconsiders its leaves. All summer it feeds them so they can process sunlight, but in the dog days of summer the tree begins pulling nutrients back into its trunk and roots, pares down, and gradually chokes off its leaves. A corky layer of cells forms at the leaves' slender petioles, then scars over. Undernourished, the leaves stop producing the pigment chlorophyll, and photosynthesis ceases. Animals can migrate, hibernate, or store food to prepare for winter. But where can a tree go? It survives by dropping its leaves, and by the end of autumn only a few fragile threads of fluid-carrying xylem[1] hold leaves to their stems. 2

A turning leaf stays partly green at first, then reveals splotches of yellow and red as the chlorophyll gradually breaks down. Dark green seems to stay longest in the veins, outlining and defining them. During the summer, chlorophyll dissolves in the heat and light, but it is also being steadily replaced. In the fall, on the other hand, no new pigment is produced, and so we notice the other colors that were always there, right in the leaf, although chlorophyll's shocking green hid them from view. With their camouflage gone, we see these colors for the first time all year, and marvel, but they were always there, hidden like a vivid secret beneath the hot glowing greens of summer. 3

The most spectacular range of fall foliage occurs in the northeastern United States and in eastern China, where the leaves are robustly 4

[1]*xylem*: a complex tissue in plants that transports water and food and makes up the woody part of a plant stem.

colored, thanks in part to a rich climate. European maples don't achieve the same flaming reds as their American relatives, which thrive on cold nights and sunny days. In Europe, the warm, humid weather turns the leaves brown or mildly yellow. Anthocyanin, the pigment that gives apples their red and turns leaves red or red-violet, is produced by sugars that remain in the leaf after the supply of nutrients dwindles. Unlike the carotenoids, which color carrots, squash, and corn, and turn leaves orange and yellow, anthocyanin varies from year to year, depending on the temperature and amount of sunlight. The fiercest colors occur in years when the fall sunlight is strongest and the nights are cool and dry (a state of grace scientists find vexing to forecast). This is also why leaves appear dizzyingly bright and clear on a sunny fall day: The anthocyanin flashes like a marquee.[2]

Not all leaves turn the same colors. Elms, weeping willows, and the ancient ginkgo all grow radiant yellow, along with hickories, aspens, bottlebrush buckeyes, cottonweeds, and tall, keening poplars. Basswood turns bronze, birches bright gold. Water-loving maples put on a symphonic display of scarlets. Sumacs turn red, too, as do flowering dogwoods, black gums, and sweet gums. Though some oaks yellow, most turn a pinkish brown. The farmlands also change color, as tepees of cornstalks and bales of shredded-wheat-textured hay stand drying in the fields. In some spots, one slope of a hill may be green and the other already in bright color, because the hillside facing south gets more sun and heat than the northern one. 5

An odd feature of the colors is that they don't seem to have any special purpose. We are predisposed to respond to their beauty, of course. They shimmer with the colors of sunset, spring flowers, the tawny buff of a colt's pretty rump, the shuddering pink of a blush. Animals and flowers color for a reason—adaptation to their environment—but there is no adaptive reason for leaves to color so beautifully in the fall any more than there is for the sky or ocean to be blue. It's just one of the haphazard marvels the planet bestows every year. We find the sizzling colors thrilling, and in a sense they dupe us. Colored like living things, they signal death and disintegration. In time, they will become fragile and, like the body, return to dust. They are as we hope our own fate will be when we die: Not to vanish, just to sublime from one beautiful state into another. Though leaves lose their green life, they bloom 6

[2]*marquee*: a brightly lit or flashing sign, usually placed over the entrance of a theater or entertainment venue to announce featured attractions, performances, or deals.

with urgent colors, as the woods grow mummified day by day, and Nature becomes more carnal[3], mute, and radiant.

We call the season "fall," from the Old English *feallan,* to fall, which leads back through time to the Indo-European *phol,* which also means to fall. So the word and the idea are both extremely ancient, and haven't really changed since the first of our kind needed a name for fall's leafy abundance. As we say the word, we're reminded of that other Fall, in the garden of Eden, when fig leaves never withered and scales fell from our eyes. Fall is the time when leaves fall from the trees, just as spring is when flowers spring up, summer is when we simmer, and winter is when we whine from the cold. 7

Children love to play in piles of leaves, hurling them into the air like confetti, leaping into soft unruly mattresses of them. For children, leaf fall is just one of the odder figments of Nature, like hailstones or snowflakes. Walk down a lane overhung with trees in the never-never land of autumn, and you will forget about time and death, lost in the sheer delicious spill of color. Adam and Eve concealed their nakedness with leaves, remember? Leaves have always hidden our awkward secrets. 8

But how do the colored leaves fall? As a leaf ages, the growth hormone, auxin, fades, and cells at the base of the petiole divide. Two or three rows of small cells, lying at right angles to the axis of the petiole, react with water, then come apart, leaving the petioles hanging on by only a few threads of xylem. A light breeze, and the leaves are airborne. They glide and swoop, rocking in invisible cradles. They are all wing and may flutter from yard to yard on small whirlwinds or updrafts, swiveling as they go. Firmly tethered to earth, we love to see things rise up and fly—soap bubbles, balloons, birds, fall leaves. They remind us that the end of a season is capricious, as is the end of life. We especially like the way leaves rock, careen, and swoop as they fall. Everyone knows the motion. Pilots sometimes do a maneuver called a "falling leaf," in which the plane loses altitude quickly and on purpose, by slipping first to the right, then to the left. The machine weighs a ton or more, but in one pilot's mind it is a weightless thing, a falling leaf. She has seen the motion before, in the Vermont woods where she played as a child. Below her the trees radiate gold, copper, and red. Leaves are falling, although she can't see them fall, as she falls, swooping down for a closer view. 9

At last the leaves leave. But first they turn color and thrill us for weeks on end. Then they crunch and crackle underfoot. They *shush,* 10

[3]*carnal*: relating to crude appetites and base pleasures.

as children drag their small feet through leaves heaped along the curb. Dark, slimy mats of leaves cling to one's heels after a rain. A damp, stuccolike mortar of semidecayed leaves protects the tender shoots with a roof until spring, and makes a rich humus. An occasional bulge or ripple in the leafy mounds signals a shrew or a field mouse tunneling out of sight. Sometimes one finds in fossil stones the imprint of a leaf, long since disintegrated, whose outlines remind us how detailed, vibrant, and alive are the things of this earth that perish.

Thinking Critically about This Reading

In paragraphs 2 and 6, Ackerman attributes some human qualities to nature and to the trees. What effect does her personification have on you as a reader? Why do you think she chose to use these figures of speech in a process analysis essay? (Glossary: **Figure of Speech**)

Questions for Study and Discussion

1. According to Ackerman, exactly what causes leaves to change color? What particular conditions cause the brightest colors in autumn leaves?
2. Briefly summarize the steps of the process by which leaves change color.
3. Not only does Ackerman describe the process by which leaves change color, but she includes other information as well. For example, she uses cause-and-effect analysis to explain why leaves are particularly bright some years, why trees turn color at different rates, and why leaves lose their grip and fall from the trees. (Glossary: **Cause and Effect**) Did you find this information useful? What, if anything, did it add to your appreciation of Ackerman's process analysis?
4. How has Ackerman organized her essay? (Glossary: **Organization**) Explain why this organization seems most appropriate for her subject.
5. Identify several figures of speech—simile, metaphor, and personification—that Ackerman uses, and explain how each functions in the context of her essay. (Glossary: **Figure of Speech**)
6. Reread Ackerman's concluding sentence. What does she mean? Why do you suppose she chose to end her essay this way? In what ways, if any, is it a particularly appropriate ending for her essay? (Glossary: **Beginnings and Endings**)

Classroom Activity Using Process Analysis

To give another person clear directions on how to do something, you need to have a thorough understanding of the process yourself. Analyze one of the following activities by listing any materials you might need and the steps you would follow in completing it:

studying for an exam
setting up a date through a mobile app
determining miles per gallon for an automobile
finding a person's contact information
beginning an exercise program
getting from home to where your writing class meets to where you normally have lunch
installing new software on your computer
writing an essay
adding or dropping a class from your course schedule

Have at least one other person read your list of materials and the steps involved, checking for anything you may have omitted.

Suggested Writing Assignments

1. Our world is filled with hundreds of natural processes—for example, the cycle of the moon, the rising and setting of the sun, the germination of a seed, the movement of the tides, the formation of a tornado, the transformation of a caterpillar into a butterfly or moth, and the flowering of a tree. Using Ackerman's essay as a model, write an informational process analysis explaining one such natural process.
2. Select one of the tasks listed in the Classroom Activity, and write a brief essay in which you give directions for successfully performing the task. As you write, consider how you can enhance your essay by combining the process analysis with other rhetorical modes such as cause and effect, as Ackerman does. (Glossary: **Rhetorical Modes**) (See Chapter 22 for more on combining models.)

CHAPTER 17

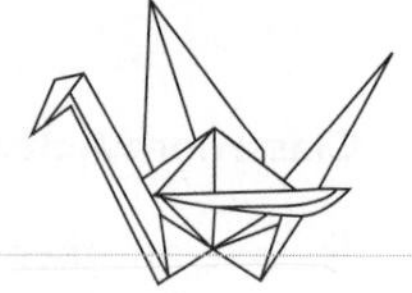

Definition

Definition allows you to communicate precisely what you want to say. At its most basic level, you will frequently need to define key words. Your reader needs to know just what you mean when you use unfamiliar words (such as *accoutrement*), words that are open to various interpretations (such as *liberal*), or familiar words that are used in a particular sense. Important terms that are not defined or that are defined inaccurately confuse readers and hamper communication.

Consider the opening paragraph from a student essay titled "Secular Mantras":

> Remember *The Little Engine That Could*? That's the story about the tiny locomotive that hauled the train over the mountain when the big, rugged locomotives wouldn't. Remember how the Little Engine strained and heaved and chugged, "I think I can — I think I can — I think I can" until she reached the top of the mountain? That's a perfect example of a secular mantra in action. You have probably used a secular mantra (pronounce it "mantruh") already today. It's any word or group of words that helps you use your energy when you consciously repeat it to yourself. You must understand two qualities about secular mantras to be able to recognize one.
>
> –Keith Eldred, student

Eldred engages his readers with the story of the Little Engine and then uses that example to lead into a definition of *secular mantra*. He concludes the paragraph with a sentence that tells readers what is coming next.

You can define a word by giving a synonym, a formal definition, or an extended definition. Each approach is useful in its own way.

SYNONYMS

The first method of definition is to give a *synonym*—that is, to use a word that has nearly the same meaning as the word you wish to define (*face* for *countenance, nervousness* for *anxiety*). No two words have exactly the same meaning, but you can pair an unfamiliar word with a familiar one to clarify your meaning.

FORMAL DEFINITIONS

Another way to define a word quickly, often within a single sentence, is to give a *formal definition*—to place the term in a general class and then distinguish it from other members of that class by describing its particular characteristics, as in the following examples:

Word	*Class*	*Characteristics*
A watch	is a mechanical device	that is used for telling time and is usually carried or worn.
Semantics	is an area of linguistics	that is concerned with the study of the meaning of words.

EXTENDED DEFINITIONS

The third method of defining a word is to give an *extended definition*—that is, to use one or more paragraphs (or even an entire essay) to define a new or difficult term or to rescue a controversial word from misconceptions that may obscure its meaning. In an essay-length extended definition, you provide your readers with information about the meaning of a single word, a concept, or an object. You must consider what your readers already know, or think they know, about your topic. Are there popular misconceptions that need to be corrected? Are some aspects of the topic seldom considered? Have particular experiences helped you understand the topic? You can use synonyms or formal definitions in an extended definition, but you must convince readers to accept your particular understanding of the word, concept, or object.

In the following two-paragraph sequence, the writers provide an extended definition of *restorative justice,* an important concept in the field of criminal justice:

> The criminal justice response focuses on arresting, convicting, and punishing the offender for his actions. During such

> tragedies, the losses suffered by the offender and his family members typically are overlooked. Restorative justice, by recognizing the connections and relationships (whether healthy, strained, or contemptuous) among offenders, victims, their family members, and the community seeks to address crime in a more holistic manner. It seeks to heal and strengthen communities by providing a restorative process for everyone affected by a serious crime.
>
> Howard Zehr, a pioneer in restorative justice theory, practice, and scholarship, outlines the key principles of restorative justice: "1) crime is a violation of people and of interpersonal relationships; 2) violations create obligations; 3) the central obligation is to put right the wrongs." Too often the criminal justice system loses sight of human nature, causing it to ignore many of the emotional consequences of the entire process. Even though the present criminal justice system leads to a verdict and a judgment that purports to right the scales of justice, the collateral damage can be staggering. The offender is often encouraged by his lawyers to deny or minimize responsibility. Though punished, the offender is rarely held personally accountable by publicly acknowledging his guilt, facing his victims, and offering an apology or the truth. In fact, the traditional justice system encourages many offenders to continue to deny responsibility, even in prison, and to blame others for their own actions. Restorative justice encourages offender accountability by stressing dialogue and truth-telling as central to putting things right and repairing personal relationships.
>
> –Elizabeth Beck, Sarah Britto, and Arlene Andrews, *In the Shadow of Death*

Another term that illustrates the usefulness of extended definition is *obscene*. What is obscene? Books that are banned in one school system are considered perfectly acceptable in another. Movies that are shown in one town cannot be shown in a neighboring town. The meaning of *obscene* has been clouded by contrasting personal opinions as well as by conflicting social norms. Therefore, if you use the term *obscene* (and especially if you tackle the issue of obscenity itself), you must define clearly and thoroughly what you mean by that term—that is, you have to give an extended definition. There are a number of methods you might use to develop such a definition. You could define *obscene* by explaining what it does not mean. You could also make your meaning clear by narrating an experience, by comparing and contrasting it to related terms (such as *pornographic* or *erotic*), by citing specific examples, or by classifying the various types of obscenity. Any of these methods could help you develop an effective definition.

The Meanings of a Word

Gloria Naylor

Tom Keller/AP Images

American novelist, essayist, and screenwriter Gloria Naylor (1950–2016) was born in New York City. She worked first as a missionary for the Jehovah's Witnesses from 1967 to 1975 and then as a telephone operator until 1981. That year she graduated from Brooklyn College of the City University of New York. She also held a graduate degree in African American studies from Yale University. Naylor taught writing and literature at George Washington University, New York University, and Cornell University, in addition to publishing several novels: *The Women of Brewster Place* (1982), *Linden Hills* (1985), *Mama Day* (1988), *Bailey's Cafe* (1992), and *The Men of Brewster Place* (1998). Naylor's final book was *1996* (2005), which has been described as a "fictionalized memoir."

The following essay first appeared in the *New York Times* in 1986. In it Naylor examines the ways in which words can take on meaning, depending on who uses them and for what purpose. As you read, notice how Naylor develops her definition of the word *nigger* by giving the word multiple meanings based on how it is used in different situations.

Reflecting on What You Know

Have you ever been called a derogatory name? What was the name, and how did you feel about it?

Language is the subject. It is the written form with which I've managed to keep the wolf away from the door and, in diaries, to keep my sanity. In spite of this, I consider the written word inferior to the spoken, and much of the frustration experienced by novelists is the awareness that whatever we manage to capture in even the most transcendent[1] passages falls far short of the richness of life. 1

[1]*transcendent:* preeminent; above all others.

Dialogue achieves its power in the dynamics of a fleeting moment of sight, sound, smell, and touch.

2 I'm not going to enter the debate here about whether it is language that shapes reality or vice versa. That battle is doomed to be waged whenever we seek intermittent reprieve from the chicken and egg dispute. I will simply take the position that the spoken word, like the written word, amounts to a nonsensical arrangement of sounds or letters without a consensus that assigns "meaning." And building from the meanings of what we hear, we order reality. Words themselves are innocuous;[2] it is the consensus that gives them true power.

3 I remember the first time I heard the word *nigger*.[3] In my third-grade class, our math tests were being passed down the rows, and as I handed the papers to a little boy in back of me, I remarked that once again he had received a much lower mark than I did. He snatched his test from me and spit out that word. Had he called me a nymphomaniac or a necrophiliac, I couldn't have been more puzzled. I didn't know what a nigger was, but I knew that whatever it meant, it was something he shouldn't have called me. This was verified when I raised my hand, and in a loud voice repeated what he had said and watched the teacher scold him for using a "bad" word. I was later to go home and ask the inevitable question that every black parent must face—"Mommy, what does *nigger* mean?"

4 And what exactly did it mean? Thinking back, I realize that this could not have been the first time the word was used in my presence. I was part of a large extended family that had migrated from the rural South after World War II and formed a close-knit network that gravitated around my maternal grandparents. Their ground-floor apartment in one of the buildings they owned in Harlem[4] was a weekend mecca for my immediate family, along with countless aunts, uncles, and cousins who brought along assorted friends. It was a bustling and open house with assorted neighbors and tenants popping in and out to exchange bits of gossip, pick up an old quarrel, or referee the ongoing checkers game in which my grandmother cheated shamelessly. They

[2]*innocuous:* harmless; lacking significance or effect.

[3]"The use of the word 'nigger' is reprehensible in today's society. This essay speaks to a specific time and place when that word was utilized to empower African-Americans; today it is used to degrade them even if spoken from their own mouths."–Gloria Naylor

[4]*Harlem:* a predominantly African American neighborhood located in New York City.

were all there to let down their hair and put up their feet after a week of labor in the factories, laundries, and shipyards of New York.

5 Amid the clamor, which could reach deafening proportions—two or three conversations going on simultaneously, punctuated by the sound of a baby's crying somewhere in the back rooms or out on the street—there was still a rigid set of rules about what was said and how. Older children were sent out of the living room when it was time to get into the juicy details about "you-know-who" up on the third floor who had gone and gotten herself "p-r-e-g-n-a-n-t!" But my parents, knowing that I could spell well beyond my years, always demanded that I follow the others out to play. Beyond sexual misconduct and death, everything else was considered harmless for our young ears. And so among the anecdotes[5] of the triumphs and disappointments in the various workings of their lives, the word *nigger* was used in my presence, but it was set within contexts and inflections[6] that caused it to register in my mind as something else.

6 In the singular, the word was always applied to a man who had distinguished himself in some situation that brought their approval for his strength, intelligence, or drive:

7 "Did Johnny *really* do that?"

8 "I'm telling you, that nigger pulled in $6,000 of overtime last year. Said he got enough for a down payment on a house."

9 When used with a possessive adjective by a woman—"my nigger"—it became a term of endearment for her husband or boyfriend. But it could be more than just a term applied to a man. In their mouths it became the pure essence of manhood—a disembodied force that channeled their past history of struggle and present survival against the odds into a victorious statement of being: "Yeah, that old foreman found out quick enough—you don't mess with a nigger."

10 In the plural, it became a description of some group within the community that had overstepped the bounds of decency as my family defined it. Parents who neglected their children, a drunken couple who fought in public, people who simply refused to look for work, those with excessively dirty mouths or unkempt households were all "trifling niggers." This particular circle could forgive hard times, unemployment, the occasional bout of depression—they had gone through all of that themselves—but the unforgivable sin was a lack of self-respect.

[5]*anecdotes:* short accounts or stories of life experiences.

[6]*inflections:* alterations in pitch or tone of voice.

A woman could never be a "nigger" in the singular, with its connotation of confirming worth. The noun *girl* was its closest equivalent in that sense, but only when used in direct address and regardless of the gender doing the addressing. *Girl* was a token of respect for a woman. The one-syllable word was drawn out to sound like three in recognition of the extra ounce of wit, nerve, or daring that the woman had shown in the situation under discussion. 11

"G-i-r-l, stop. You mean you said that to his face?" 12

But if the word was used in a third-person reference or shortened so that it almost snapped out of the mouth, it always involved some element of communal disapproval. And age became an important factor in these exchanges. It was only between individuals of the same generation, or from any older person to a younger (but never the other way around), that *girl* would be considered a compliment. 13

I don't agree with the argument that use of the word *nigger* at this social stratum of the black community was an internalization of racism. The dynamics were the exact opposite: the people in my grandmother's living room took a word that whites used to signify worthlessness or degradation and rendered it impotent.[7] Gathering there together, they transformed *nigger* to signify the varied and complex human beings they knew themselves to be. If the word was to disappear totally from the mouths of even the most liberal of white society, no one in that room was naive enough to believe it would disappear from white minds. Meeting the word head-on, they proved it had absolutely nothing to do with the way they were determined to live their lives. 14

So there must have been dozens of times that *nigger* was spoken in front of me before I reached the third grade. But I didn't "hear" it until it was said by a small pair of lips that had already learned it could be a way to humiliate me. That was the word I went home and asked my mother about. And since she knew that I had to grow up in America, she took me in her lap and explained. 15

Thinking Critically about This Reading

What does Naylor mean when she states that "words themselves are innocuous; it is the consensus that gives them true power" (paragraph 2)? How does she use the two meanings of the word *nigger* to illustrate her point?

[7]*impotent:* weak; powerless.

Questions for Study and Discussion

1. What are the two meanings of the word *nigger* as Naylor uses it in her essay? Where is the clearest definition of each use of the word presented? (Glossary: **Definition**)
2. Naylor states her thesis in the last sentence of paragraph 2. (Glossary: **Thesis**) How do the first two paragraphs build unity by connecting to her thesis statement? (Glossary: **Unity**)
3. Naylor says she must have heard the word *nigger* many times while she was growing up, yet she "heard" it for the first time when she was in the third grade. How does she explain this seeming contradiction?
4. Naylor gives a detailed narration of her family and its lifestyle in paragraphs 4 and 5. (Glossary: **Narration**) What kinds of details does she include in her brief story? (Glossary: **Details**) How does this narration contribute to your understanding of the word *nigger* as used by her family? Why do you suppose she barely defines the other use of the word *nigger*? Explain.
5. Would you characterize Naylor's tone as angry, objective, cynical, or something else? (Glossary: **Tone**) Cite examples of her diction to support your answer. (Glossary: **Diction**)
6. What is the meaning of Naylor's last sentence? How well does it work as an ending for her essay? (Glossary: **Beginnings and Endings**)

Classroom Activity Using Definition

Define one of the following terms formally by putting it in a class and then by describing its characteristics to differentiate it from other words in the same class. (See p. 403.)

EXAMPLE: Friendship (word) is a type of human relationship (class) that forms by choice and circumstance rather than by genetic relation or forced interaction (characteristics).

lasagna	cosmetic surgery	Monopoly (game)
pride	French (the language)	Hinduism
cello	Pomeranian	

Suggested Writing Assignments

1. Naylor disagrees with the notion that use of the word *nigger* in the African American community can be taken as an "internalization of racism" (14). Reexamine her essay, and discuss in what ways her definition of the word *nigger* affirms or denies her position. Draw on your own experiences, observations, and reading to support your answer.
2. Write a short essay in which you write an extended definition of an abstract word—for example, *hero, feminist, failure,* or *intelligence*—that has more than one meaning depending on one's point of view. (Glossary: **Concrete/Abstract**)

Who Gets to Be "Hapa"?

Akemi Johnson

Twitter/Akemi Johnson

Born in Oakland, California, in 1982, Akemi Johnson received a bachelor's degree in East Asian Studies at Brown University before studying at the famed Iowa Writer's Workshop, where she received her MFA in fiction writing. She has been the recipient of a Fulbright grant to Japan, a Pushcart Prize nomination, and the James D. Phelan Award from the San Francisco Foundation. Johnson has written for a variety of publications, including the *Nation*, the *Asian American Literary Review*, and *Roads and Kingdoms*. She has also contributed to National Public Radio's *All Things Considered* and *Code Switch*, a channel concerned with "the overlapping themes of race, ethnicity and culture." This essay initially appeared on NPR's *Code Switch* on August 8, 2016.

As you read, notice how Johnson defines the Hawaiian word *hapa* and explores its different uses and connotations, including its connection to the Hawaiian people, their history, and their culture.

Reflecting on What You Know

What words have you heard used to describe your own ethnic or racial identity? Were those words largely positive, negative, or mixed? How do you feel when you hear those words?

Sunset in Waikiki: Tourists sipping mai tais[1] crowded the beachside hotel bar. When the server spotted my friend and me, he seemed to relax. "Ah," he said, smiling. "Two hapa girls." 1

He asked if we were from Hawaii. We weren't. We both have lived in Honolulu — my friend lives there now — but hail from California. It didn't matter. In that moment, he recognized our mixed racial backgrounds and used "hapa" like a secret handshake, suggesting we were aligned with him: insiders and not tourists. 2

[1] *mai tai*: popular beach cocktail made with rum and fruit juices.

Like many multiracial Asian-Americans, I identify as hapa, a Hawaiian word for "part" that has spread beyond the islands to describe anyone who's part Asian or Pacific Islander. When I first learned the term in college, wearing it felt thrilling in a tempered[2] way, like trying on a beautiful gown I couldn't afford. Hapa seemed like the identity of lucky mixed-race people far away, people who'd grown up in Hawaii as the norm, without "Chink" taunts, mangled name pronunciations, or questions about what they were. 3

Over time, as more and more people called me hapa, I let myself embrace the word. It's a term that explains who I am and connects me to others in an instant. It's a term that creates a sense of community around similar life experiences and questions of identity. It's what my fiancé and I call ourselves, and how we think of the children we might have: second-generation hapas. 4

But as the term grows in popularity, so does debate over how it should be used. Some people argue that hapa is a slur and should be retired. "[It] is an ugly term born of racist closed-mindedness much like '*half-breed*' or '*mulatto*,'" design consultant Warren Wake wrote to Code Switch after reading my piece on a "hapa Bachelorette." 5

Several scholars told me it's a misconception that hapa has derogatory[3] roots. The word entered the Hawaiian language in the early 1800s, with the arrival of Christian missionaries who instituted a Hawaiian alphabet and developed curriculum for schools. Hapa is a transliteration of the English word "half," but quickly came to mean "part," combining with numbers to make fractions. (For example, hapalua is half. Hapaha is one-fourth.) Hapa haole—part foreigner—came to mean a mix of Hawaiian and other, whether describing a mixed-race person, a fusion song, a bilingual Bible, or pidgin[4] language itself. 6

This original use was *not* negative, said Kealalokahi Losch, a professor of Hawaiian studies and Pacific Island studies at Kapi'olani Community College. "The reason [hapa] feels good is because it's always felt good," he told me. Losch has been one of the few to study the earliest recorded uses of the term, buried in Hawaiian-language newspapers, and found no evidence that it began as derogatory. Because the Hawaiian kingdom was more concerned with genealogy than race, he 7

[2]*tempered*: balanced; not too extreme.
[3]*derogatory*: negative or insulting; showing a low opinion of someone or something.
[4]*pidgin*: a common, simplified language used to communicate between speakers of different languages.

explained, if you could trace your lineage to a Hawaiian ancestor, you were Hawaiian. Mixed Hawaiian did not mean less Hawaiian.

Any use of hapa as a slur[5] originated with outsiders, Losch said. 8
That includes New England missionaries, Asian plantation workers and the U.S. government, which instituted blood quantum laws to limit eligibility for Hawaiian homestead lands. On the continental U.S., some members of Japanese-American communities employed hapa to make those who were mixed "feel like they were not really, truly Japanese or Japanese-American," said Duncan Williams, a professor of religion and East Asian languages and cultures at the University of Southern California. He said this history may have led some to believe the word is offensive.

For Losch, "hapa haole"—meaning part Hawaiian, part other— 9
always has been positive. "This is absolutely who I am," he said. The license plate on his car reads, "HAPA H." His family members have been proud hapa haole for generations. An issue for him is when non-Hawaiians call themselves hapa. "There are times when it feels like identity theft," he said.

This is arguably the trickier and more significant conflict around 10
the term. Hapa, middle school teacher Piikea Kalakau told me, means part Native Hawaiian—not part Asian. "I . . . am personally frustrated with the world misusing this word . . . ," she wrote in an e-mail.

I followed up with Kalakau by phone. The widespread use of hapa, 11
she said, is a form of cultural appropriation, just as offensive as hula dancer dolls shaking their hips on car dashboards. She said correcting the definition of hapa is part of a larger Native Hawaiian "movement to take back our culture." She said her people were fighting to thrive again after surviving colonization and its damage to their language, culture and population. Kalakau encouraged me and other mixed Asian-Americans to find labels from our own heritages. "I wouldn't use a Japanese word or a Filipino word to describe myself because it doesn't fit," she said.

Mixed-race Chinese-American scholar Wei Ming Dariotis works 12
through this dilemma in her 2007 essay, "Hapa: The Word of Power." In it, she details her difficult decision to stop using hapa, though the term had formed the foundation of her identity and community. "To have this symbolic word used by Asians, particularly by Japanese Americans, as though it is their own," she writes, "seems to symbolically mirror the way Native Hawaiian land was first taken by European Americans,

[5]*slur*: an insulting name or remark.

and is now owned by European Americans, Japanese and Japanese Americans and other Asian American ethnic groups that numerically and economically dominate Native Hawaiians in their own land."

The desire of many Native Hawaiians to reclaim this word is often linked to a larger call for change. In Hawaii, a growing sovereignty[6] movement maintains that the late 19th-century overthrow and annexation of the kingdom were illegal and the islands should again exercise some form of self-governance. But even within that movement opinions on hapa vary. I spoke with attorney Poka Laenui, who said he has been involved in the Hawaiian sovereignty movement for more than 40 years. He told me, in the "idea of aloha"—the complex blend that includes love, compassion and generosity—he doesn't mind if the term is shared. "If our word can be used to assist people in identifying and understanding one another, who am I to object?" he said. . . . 13

Hapa has become a meaningful part of who I am. But now I understand this frustrates and offends others. Now, when I think of hapa, I think about the history of Hawaii and identity theft. I think about helping obscure a group of people by swapping my story for theirs. 14

Hapa is a word I don't think I should use anymore. But I also don't know how I will let it go. 15

Thinking Critically about This Reading

Johnson states that when she encountered the word *hapa* in college, she embraced the term: "Hapa seemed like the identity of lucky mixed-raced people far away . . ." (paragraph 3). Why were those people lucky, in Johnson's mind? What does this suggest about growing up as a mixed-race person—particularly a part-Asian person—in America?

Questions for Study and Discussion

1. The server in Waikiki is happy to see Johnson and her friend. What does their interaction suggest about living in Hawaii?
2. In paragraph 5, Johnson introduces the issue of whether the word *hapa* is a slur. What is the evidence that it is a slur? What is the evidence that it's not? Which do you find more convincing?
3. Kealalokahi Losch states, "The reason [hapa] feels good is that it's always felt good" (7). Why is that?

[6]*sovereignty*: freedom from control.

4. Johnson says that identity theft is the "trickier and more significant conflict around the term [hapa]" (10). What is the meaning of "identity theft" in this context? Who is the thief and who is the victim?
5. How does Johnson show that the use of the word *hapa* is connected to the history of the colonization of Hawaii?
6. Why does Johnson ultimately decide to avoid the use of the term *hapa*, as it applies to herself?

Classroom Activity Using Definition

The connotation of a term depends on the context. Choose one of the following terms, and provide two definitions—one positive and one negative—that could apply to the term in different contexts.

player	intellectual
overachiever	salt-of-the-earth

Suggested Writing Assignments

1. In Johnson's essay, the issue of "cultural appropriation" becomes central to whether or not she feels comfortable using the term *hapa* to describe herself. Write an essay in which you define a term like *hapa* and argue that cultural appropriation is or is not a problem. Use specific examples to support your viewpoint.
2. Johnson's essay discusses her relationship to the word *hapa*. Choose a word or term that you use to identify yourself. Perhaps it is a word or identity that you have come to question, as Johnson does. Write an essay explaining your relationship to the term and why you identify with it. Define the term as it is used today, and also investigate its history: how it was created, who created it, and under what circumstances. Provide examples that illustrate how the use of the term may be empowering or problematic. (Glossary: **Illustration**)

What Happiness Is

Eduardo Porter

Miriam Berkley

Eduardo Porter was born in 1963, in Phoenix, Arizona, of a Mexican mother and an American father. When he was six, his family moved to Mexico City, where he lived until he graduated from the Universidad Nacional Autónoma de México in 1987 with a degree in physics. Later he earned an MSc from the Imperial College of Science and Technology in London, England. Porter started his career in journalism at Notimex, a Mexican news agency, where he wrote mostly in Spanish about the stock market and the financial world. In 2000, he moved to the Los Angeles bureau of the *Wall Street Journal*, where he covered issues related to the Hispanic community, then to the *New York Times* in 2004, first as an economics writer in the newsroom and later as a member of the editorial board. Once at the *Times*, he had the opportunity to explore his long-standing interest in the ubiquity of prices. "Slowly," he shared, "the broader idea that prices are involved in every one of our decisions, that economics affect people's behavior gelled for me." His research resulted in *The Price of Everything: Solving the Mystery of Why We Pay What We Do*, published in 2011. He now writes the Economic Scene column for the *Times*.

In the following selection, taken from the "The Price of Happiness" chapter in *The Price of Everything*, Porter sheds some light on the "slippery concept" of happiness. As you read his essay, notice how he explores many different perspectives—from Gandhi, Lincoln, and Kennedy to Freud and even Snoopy—on the meaning of happiness, the pursuit of which is guaranteed in the U.S. Constitution, before settling on a broad definition from the world of economics.

Reflecting on What You Know

What makes you happy—a good relationship? A delicious meal? Satisfying or rewarding work? Money? Is *happiness* a term that's easy for you to define, or do you find it somewhat elusive? Explain.

Happiness is a slippery concept, a bundle of meanings with no precise, stable definition. Lots of thinkers have taken a shot at it. "Happiness is when what you think, what you say, and what you do are in harmony," proposed Gandhi. Abraham Lincoln argued "most people are about as happy as they make up their minds to be." Snoopy, the beagle-philosopher in *Peanuts*, took what was to my mind the most precise stab at the underlying epistemological problem. "My life has no purpose, no direction, no aim, no meaning, and yet I'm happy. I can't figure it out. What am I doing right?" 1

Most psychologists and economists who study happiness agree that what they prefer to call "subjective well-being" comprises three parts: satisfaction, meant to capture how people judge their lives measured up against their aspirations; positive feelings like joy; and the absence of negative feelings like anger. 2

It does exist. It relates directly to objective measures of people's quality of life. Countries whose citizens are happier on average report lower levels of hypertension in the population. Happier people are less likely to come down with a cold. And if they get one, they recover more quickly. People who are wounded heal more quickly if they are satisfied with their lives. People who say they are happier smile more often, sleep better, report themselves to be in better health, and have happier relatives. And some research suggests happiness and suicide rates move in opposite directions. Happy people don't want to die. 3

Still, this conceptual mélange[1] can be difficult to measure. Just ask yourself how happy you are, say, on a scale of one to three, as used by the General Social Survey. Then ask yourself what you mean by that. Answers wander when people are confronted with these questions. We entangle gut reactions with thoughtful analysis, and confound sensations of immediate pleasure with evaluations of how life meshes with our long-term aspirations. We might say we know what will make us happy in the future—fame, fortune, or maybe a partner. But when we get to the future, it rarely does. While we do seem to know how to tell the difference between lifelong satisfaction and immediate well-being, the immediate tends to contaminate the ontological. 4

During an experiment in the 1980s, people who found a dime on top of a Xerox machine before responding to a happiness survey reported a much higher sense of satisfaction with life than those who didn't. Another study found that giving people a chocolate bar 5

[1]*mélange*: a mixture of often incongruous elements.

improved their satisfaction with their lives. One might expect that our satisfaction with the entire span of our existence would be a fairly stable quantity—impervious to day-to-day joys and frustrations. Yet people often give a substantially different answer to the same question about lifetime happiness if it is asked again one month later.

Sigmund Freud argued that people "strive after happiness; they want to become happy and to remain so." Translating happiness into the language of economics as "utility," most economists would agree. This simple proposition gives them a powerful tool to resist Bobby Kennedy's proposal to measure not income but something else. For if happiness is what people strive for, one needn't waste time trying to figure out what makes people happy. One must only look at what people do. The fact of the matter is that people mostly choose to work and make money. Under this optic, economic growth is the outcome of our pursuit of well-being. It is what makes us happy. 6

This approach has limitations. We often make puzzling choices that do not make us consistently happier. We smoke despite knowing about cancer and emphysema. We gorge on chocolate despite knowing it will make us unhappy ten pounds down the road. Almost two thirds of Americans say they are overweight, according to a recent Gallup poll. But only a quarter say they are seriously trying to lose weight. In the 1980s a new discipline called Prospect Theory—also known as behavioral economics—deployed the tools of psychology to analyze economic behavior. It found all sorts of peculiar behaviors that don't fit economics' standard understanding of what makes us happy. For instance, losing something reduces our happiness more than winning the same thing increases it—a quirk known as loss aversion. We are unable to distinguish between choices that have slightly different odds of making us happy. We extrapolate from a few experiences to arrive at broad, mostly wrong conclusions. We herd, imitating successful behaviors around us. 7

Still, it remains generally true that we pursue what we think makes us happy—and though some of our choices may not make us happy, some will. Legend has it that Abraham Lincoln was riding in a carriage one rainy evening, telling a friend that he agreed with economists' theory that people strove to maximize their happiness, when he caught sight of a pig stuck in a muddy riverbank. He ordered the carriage to stop, got out, and pulled the pig out of the muck to safety. When the friend pointed out to a mud-caked Lincoln that he had just disproved 8 his statement by putting himself through great discomfort to save a pig, Lincoln retorted: "What I did was perfectly consistent with my theory. If I hadn't saved that pig I would have felt terrible."

So perhaps the proper response to Bobby Kennedy's angst is to agree that pursuing economic growth often has negative side effects—carbon emissions, environmental degradation—that are likely to make us unhappy down the road. Still, it remains true that American citizens—and the citizens of much of the world—expend enormous amounts of time and energy pursuing more money and a bigger GDP because they think it will improve their well-being. And that will make them happy. 9

Thinking Critically about This Reading

What do you think Porter means when he says, "While we do seem to know how to tell the difference between lifelong satisfaction and immediate well-being, the immediate tends to contaminate the ontological" (paragraph 4). Do you agree with Porter?

Questions for Study and Discussion

1. Porter opens his essay with the statement, "Happiness is a slippery concept, a bundle of meanings with no precise, stable definition." How does he illustrate this generalization? (Glossary: **Example**) How effective did you find this beginning? (Glossary: **Beginnings and Endings**)
2. According to Porter, what are the three parts of what psychologists and economists call "subjective well-being" (2)? Why is it useful to have this information when discussing the meaning of happiness? Explain.
3. In what ways is happiness related to a person's "quality of life" (3)? What character traits, according to Porter, do happy people possess?
4. What point does Porter make with the story about Abraham Lincoln and the pig?
5. How does Porter use economics to explain what he thinks happiness is? What are the limitations, if any, of his economic model?

Classroom Activity Using Definition

Definitions often depend on perspective, as Porter illustrates in his essay with the word *happiness*. Discuss with your classmates other words or terms (*competition*, *wealth*, *success*, *jerk*, *superstar*, *failure*, *poverty*, *luxury*, *beauty*) whose definitions depend on one's perspective. Choose several of these words, and write brief definitions for each of them from your perspective. Share your definitions with your classmates, and discuss how perspective affects the way we define things in our world differently.

Suggested Writing Assignments

1. Using Porter's essay as a model, write a short essay in which you define one of the following abstract terms or another similar term of your choosing. Before beginning to write, you may find it helpful to review what you and your classmates discovered in the Classroom Activity for this selection.

friendship	freedom	trust
commitment	love	hate
peace	liberty	charm
success	failure	beauty

2. How much stock do you put in Porter's claim that "people mostly choose to work and make money. . . . It is what makes us happy" (6)? Or do you side with Bobby Kennedy's "proposal to measure not income but something else"? Write an essay in which you present your position in this debate on what happiness is.

CHAPTER **18**

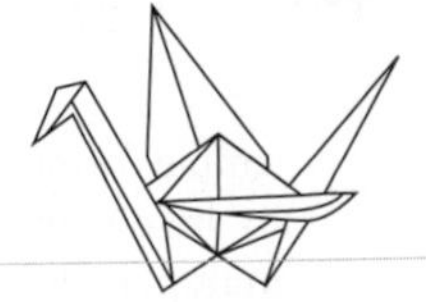

Division and Classification

A writer practices **division** by separating a class of things or ideas into categories following a clear principle or basis. In the following paragraph, journalist Robert MacNeil establishes categories of speech according to their level of formality:

> It fascinates me how differently we all speak in different circumstances. We have levels of formality, as in our clothing. There are very formal occasions, often requiring written English: the job application or the letter to the editor—the dark suit, serious-tie language, with everything pressed and the lint brushed off. There is our less formal out-in-the-world language—a more comfortable suit, but still respectable. There is language for close friends in the evenings, on weekends—bluejeans-and-sweat-shirt language, when it's good to get the tie off. There is family language, even more relaxed, full of grammatical short cuts, family slang, echoes of old jokes that have become intimate shorthand—the language of pajamas and uncombed hair. Finally, there is the language with no clothes on; the talk of couples—murmurs, sighs, grunts—language at its least self-conscious, open, vulnerable, and primitive.
>
> –Robert MacNeil, *Wordstruck: A Memoir*

With **classification**, on the other hand, a writer groups individual objects or ideas into already established categories. Division and classification can operate separately but often accompany each other. Here, for example, is a passage about levers in which the writer first discusses generally how levers work. In the second paragraph, the writer uses division to establish three categories of levers and then uses classification to group individual levers into those categories:

> Every lever has one fixed point called the "fulcrum" and is acted on by two forces—the "effort" (exertion of hand muscles) and the "weight" (object's resistance). Levers work according to a

simple formula: the effort (how hard you push or pull) multiplied by its distance from the fulcrum (effort arm) equals the weight multiplied by its distance from the fulcrum (weight arm). Thus two pounds of effort exerted at a distance of four feet from the fulcrum will raise eight pounds located one foot from the fulcrum.

There are three types of levers, conventionally called "first kind," "second kind," and "third kind." Levers of the first kind have the fulcrum located between the effort and the weight. Examples are a pump handle, an oar, a crowbar, a weighing balance, a pair of scissors, and a pair of pliers. Levers of the second kind have the weight in the middle and magnify the effort. Examples are the handcar crank and doors. Levers of the third kind, such as a power shovel or a baseball batter's forearm, have the effort in the middle and always magnify the distance.

The following paragraph introduces a classification of the kinds of decisions one has to make when purchasing a smartphone:

When you are shopping for a smartphone, you have a great number of options from which to choose. Among these are manufacturer, model, price, carrier, and phone features. In the area of features alone, one has to consider the different kinds of operating systems, battery, screen sizes and resolutions, storage capacities, and types of cameras that are available.

–Freddy Chessa, student

In writing, division and classification are affected directly by the writer's practical purpose—what the writer wants to explain or prove. That purpose determines the class of things or ideas being divided and classified. For instance, a writer might divide television programs according to their audiences (adults, families, or children) and then classify individual programs into each category to show that television networks value certain audiences more than others. A writer who is concerned about violence in television programming would divide programs into those with and without fights and murders and then classify various programs into those categories. Writers with other purposes would divide television programs differently (by the day and time of broadcast, for example, or by the number of women featured in prominent roles) and then classify individual programs accordingly.

Another example may help clarify how division and classification work hand in hand in writing. Suppose a sociologist wants to determine whether income level influences voting behavior in a particular neighborhood. The sociologist chooses as her subject the fifteen families living on Maple Street. Her goal then becomes to group these families in a way that is relevant to her purpose. She knows that she wants to divide the neighborhood in two ways—according to (1) income level (low, middle, and high) and (2) voting behavior (voters and nonvoters)—but her process of division won't be complete until she can classify the fifteen families into her five groupings.

In confidential interviews with each family, the sociologist learns what the family's income is and whether any member of the household voted in a state or federal election in the last four years. Based on this information, she classifies each family according to her established categories and at the same time divides the neighborhood into the subclasses that are crucial to her study. Her work leads her to construct the following diagram of her divisions and classifications.

Purpose: To group 15 families according to income and voting behavior and to study the relationships between the two.

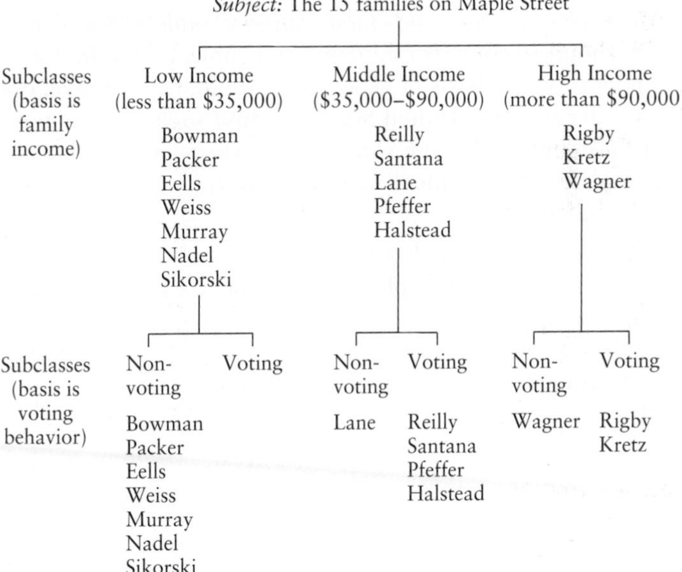

Conclusion: On Maple Street, there seems to be a relationship between income level and voting behavior: the low-income families are nonvoters.

The diagram showing the relationship between voting practices and income allows the sociologist to visualize her division and classification system and its essential components—subject, basis or principle of division, subclasses or categories, and conclusion. Her ultimate conclusion depends on her ability to work back and forth among divisions, subclasses, and the actual families to be classified.

The following guidelines can help you use division and classification in your writing:

1. *Identify a clear purpose, and use a principle of division that is appropriate to that purpose.* If you want to examine the common characteristics of four-year athletic scholarship recipients at your college or university, you might consider the following principles of division: program of study, sport, place of origin, or gender. It would not be useful to divide students on the basis of their favorite type of music because that seems irrelevant to your purpose.
2. *Divide your subject into unique categories.* An item can belong to only one category. For example, don't divide students as men, women, and athletes.
3. *Make your division and classification complete.* Your categories should account for all items in a subject class. In dividing students on the basis of geographic origin, for example, don't consider only the United States because such a division does not account for foreign students. For your classification to be complete, every student must be placed in one of the established categories.
4. *State the conclusion that your division and classification lead you to draw.* For example, after conducting your division and classification of athletic scholarship recipients, you might conclude that the majority of male athletes with athletic scholarships come from the western United States.

The Ways of Meeting Oppression

Martin Luther King Jr.

Martin Luther King Jr. (1929–1968) was the leading spokesman for the rights of African Americans during the 1950s and 1960s. He established the Southern Christian Leadership Conference, organized many civil rights demonstrations, and opposed the Vietnam War and the draft. Beginning in 1960, King was a pastor at the Ebenezer Baptist Church in Atlanta, where both his father and his grandfather had served. In 1964, he was awarded the Nobel Peace Prize for his resistance to racial oppression and discrimination. King was assassinated at the age of thirty-nine in Memphis, Tennessee, where he had traveled to provide leadership and support to striking sanitation workers. In 1983, President Ronald Reagan signed a bill creating a national holiday to honor King's life and legacy.

Bettmann/Getty Images

In the following essay, taken from his book *Strive Toward Freedom* (1958), King classifies the three ways that oppressed people throughout history have reacted to their oppressors. As you read, pay particular attention to how King orders his discussion of the three types of oppression to support his argument, which is expressed in his conclusion.

Reflecting on What You Know

Isaac Asimov once said, "Violence is the last refuge of the incompetent." What are your thoughts on the reasons for violent behavior on either a personal or a national level? Is violence ever justified? If so, under what circumstances?

Oppressed people deal with their oppression in three characteristic ways. One way is acquiescence: the oppressed resign themselves to their doom. They tacitly adjust themselves to oppression, and thereby become conditioned to it. In every movement toward freedom 1 some of the oppressed prefer to remain oppressed. Almost 2800 years ago Moses[1] set out to lead the children of Israel from the slavery of Egypt to the freedom of the promised land. He soon discovered that slaves do not always welcome their deliverers. They become accustomed to being slaves. They would rather bear those ills they have, as Shakespeare pointed out, than flee to others that they know not of. They prefer the "fleshpots of Egypt" to the ordeals of emancipation.

There is such a thing as the freedom of exhaustion. Some people are so worn down by the yoke of oppression that they give up. A few years ago in the slum areas of Atlanta, a Negro guitarist used to sing almost daily: "Been down so long that down don't bother me."[2] This is the type of negative freedom and resignation that often engulfs the life of the oppressed. 2

But this is not the way out. To accept passively an unjust system is to cooperate with that system; thereby the oppressed become as evil as the oppressor. Noncooperation with evil is as much a moral obligation as is cooperation with good. The oppressed must never allow the conscience of the oppressor to slumber. Religion reminds every man that he is his brother's keeper. To accept injustice or segregation passively is to say to the oppressor that his actions are morally right. It is a way of allowing his conscience to fall asleep. At this moment the oppressed fails to be his brother's keeper. So acquiescence—while often the easier way—is not the moral way. It is the way of the coward. The Negro cannot win the respect of his oppressor by acquiescing; he merely increases the oppressor's arrogance and contempt. Acquiescence is interpreted as proof of the Negro's inferiority. The Negro cannot win the respect of the white people of the South or the peoples of the world if he is willing to sell the future of his children for his personal and immediate comfort and safety. 3

A second way that oppressed people sometimes deal with oppression is to resort to physical violence and corroding hatred. Violence often brings about momentary results. Nations have frequently won their independence in battle. But in spite of temporary victories, violence never brings permanent peace. It solves no social problem; it merely creates new and more complicated ones. 4

---

[1]*Moses:* a Hebrew prophet, teacher, and leader in the fourteenth to thirteenth centuries B.C.E.

[2]*"Been down . . . bother me":* lyric possibly adapted from "Stormy Blues" by American jazz singer Billie Holiday (1915–1959).

Violence as a way of achieving racial justice is both impractical 5
and immoral. It is impractical because it is a descending spiral ending in destruction for all. The old law of an eye for an eye leaves everybody blind. It is immoral because it seeks to humiliate the opponent rather than win his understanding; it seeks to annihilate rather than to convert. Violence is immoral because it thrives on hatred rather than love. It destroys community and makes brotherhood impossible. It leaves society in monologue rather than dialogue. Violence ends by defeating itself. It creates bitterness in the survivors and brutality in the destroyers. A voice echoes through time saying to every potential Peter, "Put up your sword."[3] History is cluttered with the wreckage of nations that failed to follow this command.

If the American Negro and other victims of oppression succumb 6
to the temptation of using violence in the struggle for freedom, future generations will be the recipients of a desolate night of bitterness, and our chief legacy to them will be an endless reign of meaningless chaos. Violence is not the way.

The third way open to oppressed people in their quest for freedom 7
is the way of nonviolent resistance. Like the synthesis in Hegelian[4] philosophy, the principle of nonviolent resistance seeks to reconcile the truths of two opposites—acquiescence and violence—while avoiding the extremes and immoralities of both. The nonviolent resister agrees with the person who acquiesces that one should not be physically aggressive toward his opponent; but he balances the equation by agreeing with the person of violence that evil must be resisted. He avoids the nonresistance of the former and the violent resistance of the latter. With nonviolent resistance, no individual or group need submit to any wrong, nor need anyone resort to violence in order to right a wrong.

It seems to me that this is the method that must guide the actions 8
of the Negro in the present crisis in race relations. Through nonviolent resistance the Negro will be able to rise to the noble height of opposing the unjust system while loving the perpetrators of the system. The Negro must work passionately and unrelentingly for full stature as a citizen, but he must not use inferior methods to gain it. He must never come to terms with falsehood, malice, hate, or destruction.

---

[3] *"Put up your sword":* the apostle Peter had drawn his sword to defend Jesus from arrest; the voice was Jesus's, who surrendered himself for trial and crucifixion (John 18:11).

[4] *Georg Wilhelm Friedrich Hegel* (1770–1831): German philosopher.

Nonviolent resistance makes it possible for the Negro to remain in the South and struggle for his rights. The Negro's problem will not be solved by running away. He cannot listen to the glib suggestion of those who would urge him to migrate en masse to other sections of the country. By grasping his great opportunity in the South he can make a lasting contribution to the moral strength of the nation and set a sublime example of courage for generations yet unborn. 9

By nonviolent resistance, the Negro can also enlist all men of good will in his struggle for equality. The problem is not a purely racial one, with Negroes set against whites. In the end, it is not a struggle between people at all, but a tension between justice and injustice. Nonviolent resistance is not aimed against oppressors but against oppression. Under its banner consciences, not racial groups, are enlisted. 10

Thinking Critically about This Reading

King states "There is such a thing as the freedom of exhaustion" (paragraph 2). Why, according to King, is this type of freedom "negative"?

Questions for Study and Discussion

1. What is King's thesis? (Glossary: **Thesis**)
2. How does classifying the three types of resistance to oppression help him develop his thesis?
3. Why do you suppose King discusses acquiescence, violence, and nonviolent resistance in that order? What organizational principle does he use to rank them?
4. How does King's organizational pattern help him build his argument and support his thesis? Would his argument work as well if he had changed the order of his discussion? Why or why not?
5. King states that he favors nonviolent resistance over the other two ways of meeting oppression. What disadvantages does he see in meeting oppression with acquiescence or with violence?

Classroom Activity Using Division and Classification

Discuss in class why you believe that division and classification are important ways of thinking about everyday life. Give examples of how you use the two complementary strategies when you use a computer search engine, shop online, select items in your local supermarket, or look for textbooks in your college bookstore.

Suggested Writing Assignments

1. Using King's essay as a model, write an essay on various solutions to a current social or personal problem. Organize your ideas according to a rational scheme relying on the principles of division and classification. Be sure that you have a clear thesis statement and that the division and classification you employ help convince your reader of your ideas and beliefs.
2. King's use of division and classification in "The Ways of Meeting Oppression" is simple, logical, and natural. He knows that the oppressed can't give in to their oppressors, can't answer violence with violence, and therefore must take a third path of nonviolent resistance to rise above their enemies. Using King's essay as a model, write an essay in which you discuss how to respond to prejudice, hatred, competition, greed, aggression, or some other social force that we all find difficult to overcome.

Cheating Is Good for You

Mia Consalvo

Born in 1969, Mia Consalvo has a PhD from the University of Iowa in Mass Communications. Her area of interest is game studies, with a particular focus on players and the culture of gameplay. Consalvo has held positions at Massachusetts Institute of Technology, Chubu University (Japan), Ohio University, the University of Wisconsin-Milwaukee, and the University of Iowa. She is currently the Canada Research Chair in Game Studies and Design at Concordia University in Montreal, Canada. She has authored or coauthored numerous works, including *Women and Everyday Uses of the Internet: Agency and Identity* (2002) with Susanna Paasonen, *The Handbook of Internet Studies* (2012) with Charles Ess, *Players and Their Pets: Gaming Communities from Beta to Sunset* (2015) with Jason Begy, and *Atari to Zelda: Japan's Videogames in Global Context* (2016).

This excerpt is adapted from *Cheating: Gaining an Advantage in Videogames* (2007) and was originally published by *Forbes* on December 14, 2006. In it, Consalvo argues that there are benefits to (some) cheating. As you read, notice how Consalvo uses division to explain the major reasons for cheating in videogaming and to argue that it has resulting benefits.

Reflecting on What You Know

What is your attitude toward cheating when playing games? Under what circumstances, if any, would you cheat? Do you think of cheating when playing video games differently than cheating in other types of games, such as sports or board games? Why?

Most of the time, we think of cheating as despicable. Cheating is what lazy people do. It's the easy way out. Calling someone a cheater is rarely a compliment, and being cheated is never a good thing. 1

At least, in everyday life it isn't—outside of the occasional "cheat day" on a diet. But what about in the world of video games? After 2 spending the last five years talking with game players, game developers, security experts and others, I've learned a few counterintuitive things about cheating.

First, everybody cheats. Some may justify it, others proudly proclaim it, and others will deny their cheating vigorously, but it's a common activity. Players use walkthroughs, cheat codes, social engineering techniques (basically being crafty and tricking others), hacks and other unauthorized software. Cheats are popular, big business and not going away anytime soon. Individual gamers set boundaries for what they will or won't do, and there are several general reasons why people cheat. But either way, can the activity be good for you? 3

When I first started examining the practice of cheating, I took it as a given that most people viewed it as a negative activity. Cheating implies that you aren't a good enough player to finish a game on your own, or that you want an unfair—and unearned—advantage over other players. Yet in researching why people cheat and how they cheat, I've found that, much of the time, cheating actually implies a player is actively engaged in a game and wants to do well, even when the game fails *them*. 4

There are four major reasons why players cheat in a game: they're stuck, they want to play God, they are bored with the game, or they want to be a jerk. The overwhelming reason most players cheat is because they get stuck. Either the game is poorly designed, too hard, or the players are so inexperienced that they can't advance. A boss monster can't be beaten, or a puzzle solved, or the right direction found. In such situations, players face a choice: They either cheat or stop playing altogether. 5

The next most common reason is that we all like to play God sometimes. We want all the weapons or all the goodies, and we want them now. We don't want to wade through 20 levels to get to the one we like best—we want to beam directly there. We don't want to drive around in a boring car—we want to "unlock" the invincible bicycle instead. In those situations, cheating is about extending the play experience for ourselves. No one is harmed in the process. 6

Third, we can get bored with games. But as with an annoying novel, we still want the option of flipping to the last page to see how things turn out. In a game, we may find the fighting tedious, or the storyline dreary, or the never-ending grind to reach higher levels in World of Warcraft just too much trouble, and so we use some sort of cheat to jump ahead in the game's timeline, maybe all the way to the conclusion. 7

And finally, some people just can't resist cheating others. We want to overwhelm others, not just defeat them. We'll use "aimbots" (programs that automatically aim and shoot for us) or "wall hacks" (programs that allow you to see and even walk through walls) to gain every advantage in an online shooting game. Or we'll intercept the data stream in an online poker game to find out what cards our opponent is actually holding. 8

But even if everyone does it, why is cheating actually good for us? 9

First, players get stuck all the time. It doesn't matter if you are a master at real-time strategy games—if it's your first action-adventure game, you might be really bad at it. Likewise, maybe the game developer rushed the game out the door with less than perfect directions or a less than perfect design. In those situations, cheating lets the player keep playing the game they spent good money on. It can mean the difference between completing a game and abandoning it mid-stream. 10

Imagine reading a book and getting to a difficult passage in chapter three. And then imagine the book won't let you skip to chapter four until you have signified you understand that passage. This is how many video games are designed. 11

Now imagine instead that players can consult walkthroughs (in essence, detailed, step-by-step directions to winning a game) on an "as-needed" basis to help them through the troublesome spots, or receive "hints" that help them figure things out on their own. Players who have completed the game create these walkthroughs for later players. In short, players are teaching one another and learning from each other, and getting only the information they need to keep going. Everyone is taking an active part in playing and learning how to play. This is a good thing for everyone involved. 12

Next, players often use cheat codes, which unlock special items or powers, to get the most value from a game. This suggests that players enjoy the game so much that when they reach the end, they want to play it more. That means more opportunities for interaction with the game. Cheat codes can be hidden in a game for players to find and then share with others. Or, codes can be awarded to excellent players, or given to newer, more tentative players to encourage them to keep playing. Cheat codes can keep the experience enjoyable in different ways for different players. 13

What about when players get bored? Game designers don't usually want them skipping to the end of a game. Yet does the game need 14 to have a linear progression? Could players choose where in the game to go next, or the elements they want to tackle? Are there different ways to succeed–through battle, through puzzle solving, through dialog? Different players have different skill sets, so giving everyone an equal shot at doing well is preferable. As is allowing players to more quickly get to the sections they find rewarding.

But what about the jerks? Everyone wants a perfect opponent like 15
Lisa Simpson, but more often we end up playing with her brother Bart. In EVE Online, for instance, one player, Nightfreeze, allegedly cheated his in-game friends and rivals out of hundreds of millions of in-game "credits" using nothing but fake accounts, a public library's telephone, some help from friends, and his wits.

In such situations, the value is found not in the cheating itself, but 16
in our reaction to it.

There are a couple of things that can be done to either stop this 17
sort of cheating or make it a positive aspect of play. Users themselves often encourage a culture of non-cheating, making cheating not cool. Most commonly, player communities can take an active role in deciding what happens when people are discovered cheating. Psychologists have found that when playing games, if players aren't allowed to punish others they suspect of cheating, the game community falls apart. People will even pay money out of their own pocket to punish cheaters. So figuring out ways to keep the larger community involved in dealing with cheaters can keep the group engaged in ways that "regular" game play might never allow for.

As counter-intuitive as it may seem, cheating can sometimes be 18
good for you. It can keep you active and involved in a game, reward game play and allow expert players to teach others. It can indicate to developers when games are too hard or flawed, and it can even help a community form. We will never get rid of cheating, but at least in games, we can make it a positive thing, even a way to teach and learn.

Thinking Critically about This Reading

Consalvo states that "cheating actually implies a player is actively engaged in a game and wants to do well, even when the game fails *them*" (paragraph 4). Why is cheating a way to "do well" in a game and not a failure based on the player's lack of integrity and ability?

Questions for Study and Discussion

1. In paragraph 2, Consalvo says that cheating in everyday life isn't a good thing. Why then could it be considered acceptable in a gaming environment?
2. What was your reaction to the comment that "everybody cheats" (3)?
3. What is the principle of division that Consalvo presents in paragraph 5? What are the divisions?
4. Can you think of a reason people cheat at video games besides what Consalvo presents?
5. What is the analogy that Consalvo uses in paragraph 7 and again in paragraph 11? (Glossary: **Analogy**) Is the analogy helpful in explaining particular aspects of video game cheating? Why or why not?
6. How does Consalvo use division in describing the benefits of cheating?
7. In paragraph 15, Consalvo states, "But what about the jerks?" Did you find her explanation of the benefits from jerks cheating to be convincing? Why or why not?

Classroom Activity Using Division and Classification

Examine the following list of entertainers, movies, and occupations. Determine at least three principles that could be used to divide the items listed in each group. Finally, classify the items in each group according to one of the principles you have established.

Entertainers

Brad Pitt	Mariah Carey
Kelly Ripa	Kevin Hart
Jay Z	Jennifer Lawrence

Movies

Star Wars	*The Hangover*
A Christmas Story	*Psycho*
Silence of the Lambs	*The Notebook*

Occupations

physician's assistant	elementary school teacher
attorney	plumber
firefighter	accountant

Suggested Writing Assignments

1. Consalvo argues that there are benefits to cheating when playing video games. Consider, however, whether cheating in other areas of life can be beneficial. Write an argument in which you defend your conclusion. Use division and classification to organize the essay, such as by types of cheating, situations in which cheating occurs, which persons are being victimized, or other principles.
2. The strategy of division and classification is most effective when used to reveal something surprising or to help readers recognize nuance. For example, some people might have thought "cheating is cheating," but division helps show that it is a more complex concept. Think of another concept or controversial term that is mistakenly regarded as simple. Write an essay using division and classification to show the complexity of the concept, and use strong examples to illustrate the categories you develop.

Mother Tongue

Amy Tan

Amy Tan was born in 1952 in Oakland, California, to parents who had emigrated from China. Though her mother and teachers encouraged her to pursue a career in math or science, she found an irrepressible interest in literature, and in her first year at college, she changed her major from pre-med to English. She earned bachelor's and master's degrees from San Jose State University, but she did not begin writing fiction until she was thirty-three. Her first book, *The Joy Luck Club* (1987), was published two years later to great acclaim and was later adapted into a successful film. Her other novels include *The Kitchen God's Wife* (1991), *The Hundred Secret Senses* (1995), *The Bonesetter's Daughter* (2000), and, most recently, *The Valley of Amazement* (2013).

This essay, "Mother Tongue," first appeared in *The Threepenny Review* in 1990. It is born out of Tan's realization that she speaks not one but many "Englishes." As you read, pay careful attention to how she divides these forms of the language into categories, and consider how multiple Englishes make her writing richer.

Reflecting on What You Know

How different is the language you speak at home from the one you speak at school? Do you talk differently with your mother than you do with your friends or your boss? How many different languages do you speak on any given day?

I am not a scholar of English or literature. I cannot give you much more than personal opinions on the English language and its variations in this country or others. 1

I am a writer. And by that definition, I am someone who has always loved language. I am fascinated by language in daily life. I spend a great deal of my time thinking about the power of language—the way it can evoke an emotion, a visual image, a complex idea, or a simple truth. Language is the tool of my trade. And I use them all—all the Englishes I grew up with. 2

Recently, I was made keenly aware of the different Englishes I do use. I was giving a talk to a large group of people, the same talk I had already given to half a dozen other groups. The nature of the talk was about my writing, my life, and my book, *The Joy Luck Club*. The talk was going along well enough, until I remembered one major difference that made the whole talk sound wrong. My mother was in the room. And it was perhaps the first time she had heard me give a lengthy speech, using the kind of English I have never used with her. I was saying things like, "The intersection of memory upon imagination" and "There is an aspect of my fiction that relates to thus-and-thus"—a speech filled with carefully wrought grammatical phrases, burdened, it suddenly seemed to me, with nominalized[1] forms, past perfect tenses, conditional phrases, all the forms of standard English that I had learned in school and through books, the forms of English I did not use at home with my mother. 3

Just last week, I was walking down the street with my mother, and I again found myself conscious of the English I was using, the English I do use with her. We were talking about the price of new and used furniture and I heard myself saying this: "Not waste money that way." My husband was with us as well, and he didn't notice any switch in my English. And then I realized why. It's because over the twenty years we've been together I've often used that same kind of English with him, and sometimes he even uses it with me. It has become our language of intimacy, a different sort of English that relates to family talk, the language I grew up with. 4

So you'll have some idea of what this family talk I heard sounds like, I'll quote what my mother said during a recent conversation which I videotaped and then transcribed. During this conversation, my mother was talking about a political gangster in Shanghai who had the same last name as her family's, Du, and how the gangster in his early years wanted to be adopted by her family, which was rich by comparison. Later, the gangster became more powerful, far richer than my mother's family, and one day showed up at my mother's wedding to pay his respects. Here's what she said in part: "Du Yusong having business like fruit stand. Like off the street kind. He is Du like Du Zong—but not Tsung-ming Island people. The local people call putong, the river east side, he belong to that side local people. That 5

[1]*nominalized*: describing when a word is used as a noun. For example, the adjective *Asian* is nominalized to identify a group of people, *Asians*.

man want to ask Du Zong father take him in like become own family. Du Zong father wasn't look down on him, but didn't take seriously, until that man big like become a mafia. Now important person, very hard to inviting him. Chinese way, came only to show respect, don't stay for dinner. Respect for making big celebration, he shows up. Mean gives lots of respect. Chinese custom. Chinese social life that way. If too important won't have to stay too long. He come to my wedding. I didn't see, I heard it. I gone to boy's side, they have YMCA dinner. Chinese age I was nineteen."

You should know that my mother's expressive command of English belies how much she actually understands. She reads the *Forbes* report, listens to *Wall Street Week*, converses daily with her stockbroker, reads all of Shirley MacLaine's books with ease—all kinds of things I can't begin to understand. Yet some of my friends tell me they understand 50 percent of what my mother says. Some say they understand 80 to 90 percent. Some say they understand none of it, as if she were speaking pure Chinese. But to me, my mother's English is perfectly clear, perfectly natural. It's my mother tongue. Her language, as I hear it, is vivid, direct, full of observation and imagery. That was the language that helped shape the way I saw things, expressed things, made sense of the world. 6

Lately, I've been giving more thought to the kind of English my mother speaks. Like others, I have described it to people as "broken" or "fractured" English. But I wince when I say that. It has always bothered me that I can think of no way to describe it other than "broken," as if it were damaged and needed to be fixed, as if it lacked a certain wholeness and soundness. I've heard other terms used, "limited English," for example. But they seem just as bad, as if everything is limited, including people's perceptions of the limited English speaker. 7

I know this for a fact, because when I was growing up, my mother's "limited" English limited my perception of her. I was ashamed of her English. I believed that her English reflected the quality of what she had to say. That is, because she expressed them imperfectly her thoughts were imperfect. And I had plenty of empirical evidence to support me: the fact that people in department stores, at banks, and at restaurants did not take her seriously, did not give her good service, pretended not to understand her, or even acted as if they did not hear her. 8

My mother has long realized the limitations of her English as well. When I was fifteen, she used to have me call people on the phone to pretend I was she. In this guise, I was forced to ask for information or 9 even to complain and yell at people who had been rude to her. One time it was a call to her stockbroker in New York. She had cashed out her small portfolio and it just so happened we were going to go to New York the next week, our very first trip outside California. I had to get on the phone and say in an adolescent voice that was not very convincing, "This is Mrs. Tan."

And my mother was standing in the back whispering loudly, "Why he don't send me check, already two weeks late. So mad he lie to me, losing me money." 10

And then I said in perfect English, "Yes, I'm getting rather concerned. You had agreed to send the check two weeks ago, but it hasn't arrived." 11

Then she began to talk more loudly. "What he want, I come to New York tell him front of his boss, you cheating me?" And I was trying to calm her down, make her be quiet, while telling the stockbroker, "I can't tolerate any more excuses. If I don't receive the check immediately, I am going to have to speak to your manager when I'm in New York next week." And sure enough, the following week there we were in front of this astonished stockbroker, and I was sitting there red-faced and quiet, and my mother, the real Mrs. Tan, was shouting at his boss in her impeccable broken English. 12

We used a similar routine just five days ago, for a situation that was far less humorous. My mother had gone to the hospital for an appointment, to find out about a benign brain tumor a CAT scan had revealed a month ago. She said she had spoken very good English, her best English, no mistakes. Still, she said, the hospital did not apologize when they said they had lost the CAT scan and she had come for nothing. She said they did not seem to have any sympathy when she told them she was anxious to know the exact diagnosis, since her husband and son had both died of brain tumors. She said they would not give her any more information until the next time and she would have to make another appointment for that. So she said she would not leave until the doctor called her daughter. She wouldn't budge. And when the doctor finally called her daughter, me, who spoke in perfect English—lo and behold—we had assurances the CAT scan would be found, promises that a conference call on Monday would be held, and apologies for any suffering my mother had gone through for a most regrettable mistake. 13

I think my mother's English almost had an effect on limiting my possibilities in life as well. Sociologists and linguists probably will tell 14 you that a person's developing language skills are more influenced by peers. But I do think that the language spoken in the family, especially in immigrant families which are more insular, plays a large role in shaping the language of the child. And I believe that it affected my results on achievement tests, I.Q. tests, and the SAT. While my English skills were never judged as poor, compared to math, English could not be considered my strong suit. In grade school I did moderately well, getting perhaps B's, sometimes B-pluses, in English and scoring perhaps in the sixtieth or seventieth percentile on achievement tests. But those scores were not good enough to override the opinion that my true abilities lay in math and science, because in those areas I achieved A's and scored in the ninetieth percentile or higher.

This was understandable. Math is precise; there is only one cor- 15
rect answer. Whereas, for me at least, the answers on English tests were always a judgment call, a matter of opinion and personal experience. Those tests were constructed around items like fill-in-the-blank sentence completion, such as, "Even though Tom was ______, Mary thought he was ______." And the correct answer always seemed to be the most bland combinations of thoughts, for example, "Even though Tom was shy, Mary thought he was charming," with the grammatical structure "even though" limiting the correct answer to some sort of semantic opposites, so you wouldn't get answers like, "Even though Tom was foolish, Mary thought he was ridiculous." Well, according to my mother, there were very few limitations as to what Tom could have been and what Mary might have thought of him. So I never did well on tests like that.

The same was true with word analogies, pairs of words in which 16
you were supposed to find some sort of logical, semantic relationship—for example, "*Sunset* is to *nightfall* as ______ is to ______." And here you would be presented with a list of four possible pairs, one of which showed the same kind of relationship: *red* is to *stoplight*, *bus* is to *arrival*, *chills* is to *fever*, *yawn* is to *boring*: Well, I could never think that way. I knew what the tests were asking, but I could not block out of my mind the images already created by the first pair, "*sunset* is to *nightfall*"—and I would see a burst of colors against a darkening sky, the moon rising, the lowering of a curtain of stars. And all the other pairs of words—*red, bus, stoplight, boring*—just threw up a mass of confusing images, making it impossible for me to sort out something as logical as saying: "A sunset precedes nightfall" is the same as "a chill precedes a fever." The only way I would have gotten that answer right

would have been to imagine an associative situation, for example, my being disobedient and staying out past sunset, catching a chill at night, which turns into feverish pneumonia as punishment, which indeed did happen to me.

I have been thinking about all this lately, about my mother's English, about achievement tests. Because lately I've been asked, as a writer, why there are not more Asian Americans represented in American literature. Why are there few Asian Americans enrolled in creative writing programs? Why do so many Chinese students go into engineering? Well, these are broad sociological questions I can't begin to answer. But I have noticed in surveys—in fact, just last week—that Asian students, as a whole, always do significantly better on math achievement tests than in English. And this makes me think that there are other Asian American students whose English spoken in the home might also be described as "broken" or "limited." And perhaps they also have teachers who are steering them away from writing and into math and science, which is what happened to me. 17

Fortunately, I happen to be rebellious in nature and enjoy the challenge of disproving assumptions made about me. I became an English major my first year in college, after being enrolled as premed. I started writing nonfiction as a freelancer the week after I was told by my former boss that writing was my worst skill and I should hone my talents toward account management. 18

But it wasn't until 1985 that I finally began to write fiction. And at first I wrote using what I thought to be wittily crafted sentences, sentences that would finally prove I had mastery over the English language. Here's an example from the first draft of a story that later made its way into *The Joy Luck Club*, but without this line: "That was my mental quandary in its nascent state." A terrible line, which I can barely pronounce. 19

Fortunately, for reasons I won't get into today, I later decided I should envision a reader for the stories I would write. And the reader I decided upon was my mother, because these were stories about mothers. So with this reader in mind—and in fact she did read my early drafts—I began to write stories using all the Englishes I grew up with: the English I spoke to my mother, which for lack of a better term might be described as "simple"; the English she used with me, which for lack of a better term might be described as "broken"; my translation of her Chinese, which could certainly be described as "watered down"; and what I imagined to be her translation of her Chinese if she could 20 speak in perfect English, her internal language, and for that I sought to preserve the essence, but neither an English nor a Chinese structure. I wanted to capture what language ability tests can never reveal: her intent, her passion, her imagery, the rhythms of her speech and the nature of her thoughts.

Apart from what any critic had to say about my writing, I knew I had succeeded where it counted when my mother finished reading my book and gave me her verdict: "So easy to read." 21

Thinking Critically about This Reading

How does Tan's essay play on the phrase "mother tongue"? What does this term mean in common usage, and how does Tan add to or alter this definition?

Questions for Study and Discussion

1. How does Tan's profession affect her discussion of language in this essay? How does she describe a writer's special relationship to language?
2. Where and how does Tan use the English she learned in school? Besides this "standard English" (paragraph 3), what other categories does her language fit into?
3. Tan describes her mother's English as "vivid, direct, full of observation and imagery" (6). Reread the transcript of Tan's mother's side of the conversation in paragraph 5, and note places where you see these qualities in her speech.
4. As she tries to classify her mother's English, Tan finds that all of the terms she can think of unsatisfying are unsatisfying. What is wrong with "broken" and "limited" as descriptors?
5. There is an apparent contradiction in the scene with the stockbroker when Tan describes her mother's "impeccable broken English" (12). What does she mean by this? How would you explain the contradiction?
6. What is "terrible" about the line Tan quotes from an early draft of a story that became part of *The Joy Luck Club* (19)? How does she find a solution to this problem with her writing?

Classroom Activity Using Division and Classification

The drawing on page 444 is a basic exercise in classification. Use annotations, a list, a chart, or another method to determine the features all the figures have in common, and establish the general class to which they belong. Next, establish subclasses by determining the distinctive features that distinguish one subclass from another. Finally, place each figure in an appropriate subclass within your classification system. You may wish to compare your system with those developed by other members of the class, and discuss any differences that exist.

Suggested Writing Assignments

1. Think back to your response to the Reflecting on What You Know prompt, and create a set of classifications for the kinds of language you speak. Then write versions of the same brief story (you might choose a family legend like the one Tan's mother recounts) in each of these languages. How is the telling of the story different when you write with different audiences in mind? (Glossary: **Audience**)
2. Music can be classified into many different types (jazz, country, pop, rock, soul, rap, classical, big band, western, blues, gospel). Each of these large classifications has a lot of variety within it. Write an essay in which you identify your favorite type of music as well as at least three subclassifications of that music. Explain the characteristics of each category, and use two or three artists and their songs as examples.

a
b
c
d
e
f
g
h
i
j
k
l
m
n
o

CHAPTER 19

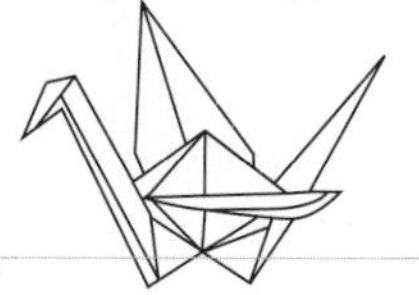

Comparison and Contrast

A **comparison** points out the ways that two or more people, places, or things are alike. A **contrast** points out how they differ. The subjects of a comparison or contrast should be in the same class or general category; if they have nothing in common, there is no good reason for setting them side by side.

The function of any comparison or contrast is to clarify and explain. The writer's purpose may be simply to inform or to make readers aware of similarities or differences that are interesting and significant in themselves. Or the writer may explain something unfamiliar by comparing it with something very familiar, perhaps explaining the game of squash by comparing it with tennis. Finally, the writer can point out the superiority of one thing by contrasting it with another—for example, showing that one product is the best by contrasting it with all its competitors.

ORGANIZING A COMPARISON OR CONTRAST

As a writer, you have two main options for organizing a comparison or contrast: the subject-by-subject pattern or the point-by-point pattern. For a short essay comparing and contrasting Philadelphia, Pennsylvania, and San Diego, California, as vacation destinations, you would probably follow the *subject-by-subject* pattern of organization. With this pattern, you first discuss the points you wish to make about one city and then discuss the corresponding points for the other city. An outline of the body of your essay might look like this:

Subject-by-Subject Pattern

I. Philadelphia
   A. Climate
   B. Public transportation
   C. Tourist attractions (museums, zoos, theme parks)
   D. Accommodations

II. San Diego
  A. Climate
  B. Public transportation
  C. Tourist attractions (museums, zoos, theme parks)
  D. Accommodations

The subject-by-subject pattern presents a unified discussion of each city by emphasizing the cities and not the four points of comparison. Because these points are relatively few, readers should easily remember what you said about Philadelphia's climate when you later discuss San Diego's climate and should be able to make the appropriate connections between them.

For a somewhat longer essay comparing and contrasting solar energy and wind energy, however, you should consider using the *point-by-point* pattern of organization. With this pattern, your essay is organized according to the various points of comparison. Discussion alternates between solar and wind energy for each point of comparison. An outline of the body of your essay might look like this:

Point-by-Point Pattern

I. Installation expenses
  A. Solar
  B. Wind

II. Efficiency
  A. Solar
  B. Wind

III. Operating costs
  A. Solar
  B. Wind

IV. Convenience
  A. Solar
  B. Wind

V. Maintenance
  A. Solar
  B. Wind

VI. Safety
  A. Solar
  B. Wind

With the point-by-point pattern, the writer makes immediate comparisons between solar and wind energy so that readers can consider each similarity and difference separately.

Each organizational pattern has its advantages. In general, the subject-by-subject pattern is useful in short essays, in which few points are being considered; the point-by-point pattern is preferable in long essays, in which numerous points are being considered.

MAKING THE COMPARISON OR CONTRAST SIGNIFICANT

A good essay of comparison and contrast tells readers something significant that they do not already know—that is, it must do more than merely point out the obvious. As a rule, therefore, writers tend to draw contrasts between things that are usually perceived as being similar or comparisons between things usually perceived as being different. In fact, comparison and contrast often go together. For example, an essay about the twin cities of Minneapolis and St. Paul might begin by showing how much they are alike but end with a series of contrasts revealing how much they differ. A consumer magazine might report the contrasting claims made by six car manufacturers and then go on to demonstrate that all the cars actually do much the same thing in the same way.

The following student essay about hunting and photography explores the increasing popularity of photographic safaris. After first pointing out the obvious differences between hunting with a gun and hunting with a camera, the writer focuses on the similarities between the two activities, which make many hunters willing to trade their guns for cameras. Notice how she successfully uses the subject-by-subject organizational plan in the body of her essay to explore three key similarities between hunters and photographers.

Guns and Cameras

The hunter has a deep interest in the apparatus he uses to kill his prey. He carries various types of guns, different kinds of ammunition, and special sights and telescopes to increase his chances of success. He knows the mechanics of his guns and understands how and why they work. This fascination with the hardware of his sport is practical—it helps him achieve his goal—but it frequently becomes an end, almost a hobby in itself.

Not until the very end of the long process of stalking an animal does a game hunter use his gun. First he enters into the animal's world. He studies his prey, its habitat, its daily habits, its watering holes and feeding areas, its migration patterns, its enemies and allies, its diet and food chain. Eventually the hunter himself becomes animal-like, instinctively sensing the habits and moves of his prey. Of course, this instinct gives the hunter a better chance of killing the animal; he knows where and when he will get the best shot. But it gives him more than that. Hunting is not just pulling the trigger and killing the prey. Much of it is a multifaceted and ritualistic identification with nature.

After the kill, the hunter can do a number of things with his trophy. He can sell the meat or eat it himself. He can hang the animal's head on the wall or lay its hide on the floor or even sell these objects. But any of these uses is a luxury, and its cost is high. An animal has been destroyed; a life has been eliminated.

Like the hunter, the photographer has a great interest in the tools he uses. He carries various types of cameras, lenses, and film to help him get the picture he wants. He understands the way cameras work, the uses of telephoto and micro lenses, and often the technical procedures of printing and developing. Of course, the time and interest a photographer invests in these mechanical aspects of his art allow him to capture and produce the image he wants. But as with the hunter, these mechanics can and often do become fascinating in themselves.

The wildlife photographer also needs to stalk his "prey" with knowledge and skill in order to get an accurate "shot." Like the hunter, he has to understand the animal's patterns, characteristics, and habitat; he must become animal-like in order to succeed. And like the hunter's, his pursuit is much more prolonged and complicated than the shot itself. The stalking processes are almost identical and give many of the same satisfactions.

The successful photographer also has something tangible to show for his efforts. A still picture of an animal can be displayed in a home, a gallery, a shop; it can be printed in a publication, as a postcard, or as a poster. In fact, a single photograph can be used in all these ways at once; it can be reproduced countless times. And despite all these ways of using his "trophies," the photographer continues to preserve his prey.

—Barbara Bowman, student

USING ANALOGY

Analogy is a special form of comparison. When a subject is unobservable, complex, or abstract—when it is so unfamiliar that readers may have trouble understanding it—analogy can be effective. By pointing out certain similarities between a difficult subject and a more familiar or concrete subject, writers can help their readers grasp the difficult subject. Unlike a true comparison, though, which analyzes items that belong to the same class (breeds of dogs or types of engines), analogy pairs things from different classes that have nothing in common except through the imagination of the writer. In addition, whereas comparison seeks to illuminate specific features of both subjects, the primary purpose of analogy is to clarify the one subject that is complex or unfamiliar. For example, to explore the similarities (and differences) between short stories and novels (two forms of fiction), you would probably choose comparison. Short stories and novels belong to the same class (fiction), and your purpose is to reveal something about both. If, however, your purpose is to explain the craft of fiction writing, you might note its similarities to the craft of carpentry. In this case you would be drawing an analogy because the two subjects clearly belong to different classes. Carpentry is the more concrete subject and the one more people will have direct experience with. If you use your imagination, you will easily see many ways that the tangible work of the carpenter can be used to help readers understand the abstract work of the novelist.

Depending on its purpose, an analogy can be made in a sentence or in several paragraphs to clarify a particular aspect of the larger topic being discussed, or it can provide the organizational strategy for an entire essay. Consider the following analogy:

> People are like stained-glass windows. They sparkle and shine when the sun is out, but when the darkness sets in, their true beauty is revealed only if there is a light from within.
>
> —Elisabeth Kübler-Ross

An analogy can also help a writer address an abstract issue. In the following, the Harvard Nuclear Study Group raise the questions "What is the balance between American and Soviet nuclear arsenals? Who is ahead?"

> When the question is asked in this manner, it might appear easy to give a definitive and objective answer. Unfortunately, this is not the case. No definitive answer is possible.
>
> This can best be understood by way of analogy. Comparing the nuclear arsenals of the superpowers is like comparing the strengths of two football teams. Each team may be stronger in some departments: one in running, the other in passing; one in special teams, the other in placekicking. Specialists try to predict the winner by comparing, for example, one side's aerial attack with the other side's pass defense. This is a better comparison than contrasting the quarterbacks or receivers. But the accuracy of such complicated predictions cannot be known until the game is over.
>
> —The Harvard Nuclear Study Group, *Living with Nuclear Weapons*

Two Ways of Seeing a River

Mark Twain

Library of Congress, Prints & Photographs Division, Reproduction number LC-USZ62-5513

Samuel L. Clemens (1835–1910), who wrote under the pen name of Mark Twain, was born in Florida, Missouri, and raised in Hannibal, Missouri. He wrote the novels *Tom Sawyer* (1876), *The Prince and the Pauper* (1882), *Huckleberry Finn* (1884), and *A Connecticut Yankee in King Arthur's Court* (1889), as well as many other works of fiction and nonfiction. One of America's most popular writers, Twain is generally regarded as the most important practitioner of the realistic school of writing, a style that emphasizes observable details.

The following passage is taken from *Life on the Mississippi* (1883), Twain's study of the great river and his account of his early experiences learning to be a river steamboat pilot. As you read the passage, notice how Twain makes use of figurative language in describing two very different ways of seeing the Mississippi River.

Reflecting on What You Know

As we age and gain experience, our interpretation of the same memory—or how we view the same scene—can change. For example, the way we view our own appearance changes all the time, and photos from our childhood or teenage years may surprise us in the decades that follow. Perhaps something we found amusing in our younger days may make us feel uncomfortable or embarrassed now, or perhaps the house we grew up in later seems smaller or less appealing than it used to. Write about a memory that has changed for you over the years. How does your interpretation of it now contrast with how you experienced it earlier?

Now when I had mastered the language of this water and had come to know every trifling feature that bordered the great river as familiarly as I knew the letters of the alphabet, I had made a 1 valuable acquisition. But I had lost something, too. I had lost something which could never be restored to me while I lived. All the grace, the beauty, the poetry, had gone out of the majestic river! I still kept in mind a certain wonderful sunset which I witnessed when steamboating was new to me. A broad expanse of the river was turned to blood; in the middle distance the red hue brightened into gold, through which a solitary log came floating, black and conspicuous; in one place a long, slanting mark lay sparkling upon the water; in another the surface was broken by boiling, tumbling rings that were as many tinted as an opal;[1] where the ruddy flush was faintest was a smooth spot that was covered with graceful circles and radiating lines, ever so delicately traced; the shore on our left was densely wooded, and the somber shadow that fell from this forest was broken in one place by a long, ruffled trail that shone like silver; and high above the forest wall a clean-stemmed dead tree waved a single leafy bough that glowed like a flame in the unobstructed splendor that was flowing from the sun. There were graceful curves, reflected images, woody heights, soft distances, and over the whole scene, far and near, the dissolving lights drifted steadily, enriching it every passing moment with new marvels of coloring.

I stood like one bewitched. I drank it in, in a speechless rapture. The 2
world was new to me and I had never seen anything like this at home. But as I have said, a day came when I began to cease from noting the glories and the charms which the moon and the sun and the twilight wrought upon the river's face; another day came when I ceased altogether to note them. Then, if that sunset scene had been repeated, I should have looked upon it without rapture and should have commented upon it inwardly after this fashion: "This sun means that we are going to have wind tomorrow; that floating log means that the river is rising, small thanks to it; that slanting mark on the water refers to a bluff reef which is going to kill somebody's steamboat one of these nights, if it keeps on stretching out like that; those tumbling 'boils' show a dissolving bar and a changing channel there; the lines and circles in the slick water over yonder are a warning that that troublesome place is shoaling up dangerously; that silver streak in the shadow of the forest is the 'break' from a new snag and he has located himself in the very best place he could have found to fish for steamboats; that tall dead tree, with a single living branch, is not going to last long, and then how is a body ever going to get through this blind place at night without the friendly old landmark?"

---

[1]*opal*: a multicolored, iridescent gemstone.

No, the romance and beauty were all gone from the river. All the value any feature of it had for me now was the amount of usefulness it could furnish toward compassing the safe piloting of a steamboat. Since those days, I have pitied doctors from my heart. What does the lovely flush in a beauty's cheek mean to a doctor but a "break" that ripples above some deadly disease? Are not all her visible charms sown thick with what are to him the signs and symbols of hidden decay? Does he ever see her beauty at all, or doesn't he simply view her professionally and comment upon her unwholesome condition all to himself? And doesn't he sometimes wonder whether he has gained most or lost most by learning his trade? 3

Thinking Critically about This Reading

In the opening paragraph, Twain exclaims, "All the grace, the beauty, the poetry, had gone out of the majestic river!" What is "the poetry," and why was it lost for him?

Questions for Study and Discussion

1. What method of organization does Twain use in this selection? (Glossary: **Organization**) What alternative methods might he have used? What would have been gained or lost?
2. Explain the analogy Twain uses in paragraph 3. (Glossary: **Analogy**) What is his purpose in using this analogy?
3. Twain uses a number of similes and metaphors in this selection. (Glossary: **Figure of Speech**) Identify three of each, and explain what Twain is comparing in each case. What do these figures of speech add to Twain's writing?
4. Now that he has learned the trade of steamboating, does Twain believe that he has "gained most or lost most" (paragraph 3)? What has he gained, and what has he lost?
5. Twain points to a change of attitude he underwent as a result of seeing the river from a new perspective, that of a steamboat pilot. What role does knowledge play in Twain's inability to see the river as he once did?

Classroom Activity Using Comparison and Contrast

Using the sample outlines on pages 445–46 as models, prepare both subject-by-subject and point-by-point outlines for one of the following topics:

dogs and cats as pets
Snapchat and Instagram
an SUV and a hybrid car
your local newspaper and the *New York Times* or *USA Today*
a high school–level course and a college-level course
the Golden State Warriors and the Cleveland Cavaliers basketball teams

Before starting your outline, determine the key points you wish to compare and contrast. Be prepared to explain any advantages you see of one organizational plan over the other.

Suggested Writing Assignments

1. Twain's essay contrasts the perception of one person before and after acquiring a particular body of knowledge. Different people also usually perceive the same scene or event differently, even if they are experiencing it simultaneously. To use an example from Twain's writing, a poet and a doctor might perceive a rosy-cheeked young woman in entirely different ways. Write a comparison and contrast essay in which you show how two people with different experiences might perceive the same subject. It can be a case of profound difference (such as a musician and an electrician at the same pyrotechnic rock concert) or one more subtle (such as a novelist and a screenwriter seeing the same lovers' quarrel in a restaurant). Add a short postscript in which you explain your choice of subject-by-subject comparison or point-by-point comparison for your essay.
2. Learning how to drive a car may not be as involved as learning how to pilot a steamboat on the Mississippi River, but it has a tremendous effect on how we function and on how we perceive our surroundings. Write an essay about short trips you took as a passenger and as a driver. Compare and contrast your perceptions and actions. What is most important to you as a passenger? What is most important to you as a driver? How do your perceptions shift between the two roles? What changes in terms of what you notice around you and the way you notice it?

Taking My Son to College, Where Technology Has Replaced Serendipity

Christina Baker Kline

Karin Diana

Christina Baker Kline was born in Cambridge, England, and grew up in Maine. She is a graduate of Yale University, where she majored in English, and received graduate degrees from Cambridge University in England and the University of Virginia. She is the author of many novels, including *Sweet Water* (1993), *Desire Lines* (1999), *The Way Life Should Be* (2007), *Bird in Hand* (2009), and the *New York Times* best-seller *Orphan Train* (2013). She is also the coeditor, with Anne Burt, of *About Face: Women Write about What They See When They Look in the Mirror* (2008). Kline was a writer-in-residence at Fordham University from 2007 to 2011, and she has been the recipient of several fellowships from the Geraldine R. Dodge Foundation. She is currently at work on a new novel, inspired by Andrew Wyeth's famous painting *Christina's World.* She lives in Montclair, New Jersey.

In this essay, which first appeared in the *New Jersey Star-Ledger,* Kline drops her son off at college and looks back on memories of her own first year at college. As you read, note the ways Kline thinks her son's time in college will contrast with what she experienced.

Reflecting on What You Know

How does technology affect the way you experience college? In what ways does it make the experience better? Do you think you lose anything by having more technology available than did previous generations of students?

My son Hayden started college last week. Like many parents of freshmen, my husband and I drove him to school together, the back of the car filled with essentials like extra-long twin sheets, a clip-on light for his bunk bed and a random mix of extension cords. 1

The milk crates, shower caddy and three-ring binders we helped him carry up the stairs flashed me back to my own first days of college—but they weren't the only reason this experience felt so familiar. 2

Three decades ago I was a freshman at the same university. Unlike Hayden, who grew up outside of New York and attended a competitive suburban high school, I was the only student from my small town in Maine to go to Yale, one of the few to even venture out of state. And I had no idea what I was getting into. 3

I was lucky, in a way, to be so naive; I didn't know what I didn't know. I floated through my first year obliviously unaware of the social currencies being exchanged around me, only dimly perceiving markers of wealth and status. 4

When a fellow student bragged about his Alfa Romeo, I thought he meant a Camaro, the fanciest car I'd ever seen. When a classmate casually mentioned that she was meeting her parents in Gstaad[1] for the long weekend, I assumed it was a town in Connecticut. Imagine my surprise when I realized that actual Vanderbilts lived in Vanderbilt Hall. 5

But it wasn't just my relative lack of sophistication that made my experience so vastly different from my son's. Typewriters and carbon paper, telephones with curly cords, TVs with a few channels and no remotes, cassette tapes; compared with the tools Hayden has at his disposal, I went to college in the Stone Age. 6

Without even thinking about it, my son uses technology in almost everything he does, large and small. He installed Yale-specific apps on his phone that provide information about when the washers and dryers in the basement of his dorm are available, the daily menus of each dining hall, ratings of local restaurants, student contact information, the entire list of classes, and an interactive campus map that shows you where you are and where you're going. 7

Within minutes of learning his three suitemates' names this summer, he knew an incredible amount about them: They friended and followed each other on Facebook and Twitter and Instagram and immediately had access to each other's prom pictures, family vacation shots, performance videos, philosophical musings. They established an ongoing group text, exchanging information such as who was bringing an Xbox and who had a coffeemaker. Soon after arriving on campus, Hayden made a spreadsheet of potential classes, vetting them in 8

[1]*Gstaad*: a German-speaking village in Switzerland.

advance by using teacher rating sites and watching videos of potential professors on YouTube.

There's no question that my son is better prepared for college than 9
I was. He manages his time better, is more efficient and more directed, and spends less time in lines and more time doing exactly what he sets out to do.

But I wonder what may be lost. I suspect it's unlikely that he will 10
ever, as I did, trek all the way across campus on a snowy day to a friend's dorm room, only to find that person gone but another roommate available, and making a new friend in the process. He won't have to type and retype his papers—using Wite-Out, no less!—to make revisions, finding in that process new insights into what he's written. I doubt that he'll make his way to a common room at 9 p.m. every Sunday to watch a specific TV show (*L.A. Law*, I'm thinking of you), bonding with a hearty group of loyalists.

I think fondly of the rabbit holes I disappeared down when I 11
researched papers for history and English because I couldn't find quite what I was looking for, or because I had to go through so much material to find examples for my thesis. When you can type a few words into a search engine and land on your topic—or when you can scan a Shakespeare play for specific words or symbols—what opportunities might you miss to expand your thinking in unexpected ways?

I worry that students today are more connected and more frag- 12
mented, learning more about one another from afar but watching programs on their iPads in their rooms. The knowledge they have at their fingertips may make them more productive, but it may also blunt the thrill of unanticipated discovery.

Sometime in my first week on that long-ago campus, I found 13
myself hopelessly lost, scrutinizing an indecipherable map, when a freshman boy came up to me. "Can I help you with that?" he asked, and though he didn't know his way around any better than I did, we figured it out together. Twenty-three years of marriage later, we're still figuring it out.

As Hayden navigates his own journey, I wish for him the satis- 14
faction of productivity and the joy of tapping his potential. But I also hope for him at least some of the wide-eyed wonder I felt as a freshman, the delight of discovering a world that was as remote and unknown to me as a foreign country.

And I hope he'll experience the unexpected pleasures of getting 15
lost, of chance encounters, and the incalculable benefits of time wasted for no good reason at all.

Thinking Critically about This Reading

Kline makes an argument for valuing what some might consider setbacks: "getting lost," "time wasted," and so on. Why? What benefits can come from these apparent problems?

Questions for Study and Discussion

1. Kline's essay focuses on the contrast between her son's initial college experience and her own, but she sets up this series of contrasts by establishing what they have in common. How is his first year like hers?
2. Why does Kline say she was lucky to be naive when she first arrived at college? What sorts of things did she not understand as a first-year student?
3. In paragraphs 6 and 7, Kline contrasts the old technology she used as a student and the new technology available to Hayden. How do these two lists illustrate her point about what has changed? How foreign does her list of tools sound to you?
4. Notice that as she contrasts the two college experiences, Kline primarily uses a point-by-point organization. How does she think technology will change college students' social lives? Their intellectual work?
5. Find a definition for the word *serendipity,* which Kline uses in her title. Then choose examples from her essay that show what she means by this word. (Glossary: **Illustration**)
6. Near the end of the essay, Kline hopes that Hayden will benefit from technology and also put it aside at times. How does she imagine him finding a middle ground?

Classroom Activity Using Comparison and Contrast

We can use comparison and contrast to analyze everything from ideas to sounds to images. Even if the message of two different items is the same, the delivery may be different, which might cause an audience to respond differently. Working in a group, consider the following excerpt from an essay by student writer Jean Brandt, who narrates a time when she stole a button from a store at the mall.

> I walked back to the basket where I had found the button and was about to drop it in when suddenly, instead, I took a quick

glance around, assured myself no one could see, and slipped the button into the pocket of my sweatshirt.

I hesitated for a moment, but once the item was in my back pocket, there was no turning back. I had never before stolen anything; but what was done was done. A few seconds later, my sister appeared and asked, "So, did you decide to buy the button?"

"No, I guess not." I hoped my voice didn't quaver. As we headed for the entrance, my heart began to race. Only a few more yards to go and I'd be safe. As we crossed the threshold, I heaved a sigh of relief. I was home free.

An unexpected tap on my shoulder startled me. I whirled around to find a middle-aged man, dressed in street clothes, flashing a badge.

Brandt then decided to reimagine her story as a comic:

In a group, compare and contrast the two versions of the same story. What details are the same? What is different? Which do you think is more effective, and why?

Suggested Writing Assignments

1. How might Kline's essay look different if it were written from Hayden's perspective instead of his mother's? Write an essay

in which you contrast some aspect of your life (in school or otherwise) with what your parents experienced. You will probably want to start with what you share before discussing how your experiences are different.

2. How did you decide on the college you would attend? Think about the important factors that influenced your decision, and then write a point-by-point comparison of your school with another you considered or another nearby.

On a Plate

Toby Morris

The Wireless

Toby Morris is a cartoonist and illustrator who lives and works in Auckland, New Zealand. His webcomic, *The Pencilsword*, presents a series of comics that, through image and text, address issues such as social inequality, the meaning of success, and what gets omitted in history. Morris has also authored a graphic novel using his experiences as a first-time father, *Don't Puke on Your Dad: A Year in the Life of a New Father* (2013), which was shortlisted for the Random House New Zealand Award for best illustrated book in 2014.

Morris's comic "On a Plate" was published on the *Wireless* in May 2015. In this graphic essay, Morris describes the incremental development of privilege by contrasting two characters, Richard and Paula, who grow up with different socioeconomic statuses and family situations. This graphic essay is intended to be read from left to right, top to bottom, and the images and text interact to create meaning. As you read the first two comic panels (boxes that contain image and text), pay attention to the contrasting details and try to predict which character will wind up in a place of greater privilege.

Reflecting on What You Know

How do you define *privilege?* List several different types of privilege and describe where you see certain privileges at work in our society. How and why do these privileges happen?

THIS IS RICHARD. HIS PARENTS ARE DOING OK.

AND THIS IS PAULA. HER PARENTS? NOT SO MUCH.

RICHARD'S HOUSE IS WARM AND DRY. HIS SHELVES ARE FULL OF BOOKS AND HIS FRIDGE IS FULL OF FOOD.

PAULA'S HOUSE IS FULL OF PEOPLE AND NOT MUCH ELSE. IT'S DAMP AND NOISY AND SHE KEEPS GETTING SICK.

RICHARD'S PARENTS WILL DO ANYTHING FOR THEIR BABY...
Good boy!
Clever!

...AND SO WILL PAULA'S. THAT'S WHY THEY'RE WORKING TWO JOBS.

RICHARD GOES TO A GREAT SCHOOL. WELL RESOURCED, GOOD KIDS. HIS TEACHERS LOVE THEIR JOB.

AT PAULA'S SCHOOL, THE CLASS SIZES ARE LARGE, THE SCHOOL IS UNDERFUNDED, AND LOOKS IT. HER TEACHERS ARE TIRED, STRETCHED THIN FROM THE STRESS.
Oh man, I need a new job...

SO MAYBE WE CAN SEE WHY THE EXPECTATIONS SET FOR RICHARD...
B+? Oh dear, we need to get you a tutor...
REPORT

...MIGHT BE SLIGHTLY DIFFERENT TO THOSE SET FOR PAULA...
B? Hey, not bad!
REPORT

...AND OVER THE YEARS ALL THESE LITTLE DIFFERENCES...
(PARENTS PAYING FOR UNI)
(JUGGLING WORK AND POLYTECH, STILL GETTING IN DEBT)

...THEY START TO ADD UP. TO BUILD INTO SOMETHING BIGGER.
I have friends working there - I'll have a word, and get you an internship.
Thanks Dad.
You should be finishing your studies, not looking after me...
Dad, you're sick.

AND BECAUSE EACH LITTLE DIFFERENCE SNEAKS BY UNNOTICED...
Yep, the loan is approved. Congratulations!
Look, we just can't help you. Maybe try Eazee Finance?

THEN MAYBE RICHARD STARTS TO BELIEVE THAT HE DESERVES TO BE ON TOP. THAT HE DID IT ALL HIMSELF.
Oh you're Roger's boy right? I've heard good things, keeping my eye on you...

AND MAYBE PAULA STARTS TO SETTLE. LEARNS TO 'KNOW HER PLACE'.
OK, you've got the job, but I'm watching you sweetie...

Thinking Critically about This Reading

What did you think about the author's choice to convey his ideas in the form of a comic? Did you find it as effective as other essays you have read so far? What, if anything, confused or impressed you about his work?

Questions for Study and Discussion

1. Which pattern of organization does Morris's graphic essay follow? How do you know?
2. List the points of contrast that Morris presents.
3. What pattern of organization would Morris have been using if he had placed all of the images and text about Paula on one

page, and all of the images and text about Richard on the next page? What would have been gained or lost by this organizational method?

4. A good comparison or contrast should inform readers of something they do not know or haven't fully considered. Did Morris's comic make you think of something you didn't know or hadn't fully considered? If so, what?
5. "On a Plate" is Morris's most widely shared comic on social media. Why do you think this piece has reached such a large audience? (Glossary: **Audience**)
6. Richard's and Paula's paths do not cross until the final two panels, when Richard says, "No one ever handed me anything on a plate." Being handed something on a plate is an idiom for being given something without having to work for it. (Glossary: **Idiom**) In the final panel, the reader sees Paula literally handing Richard oysters on a plate. Why does Morris conclude his comic in this way? Why does he keep the multiple panel format rather than concluding his graphic essay in one large panel?

Classroom Activity Using Comparison and Contrast

In groups of two or three, decide on two people, places, or things worthy of comparison and/or contrast, and be prepared to explain why. Choose an artist from your group who is anywhere between skilled cartoonist and partial master of the stick figure. The artist will draw eight panels (medium-sized squares) on a sheet of paper in the same layout used by Morris. Next, as a group, decide on the points of comparison that each pair of panels will make. Group members should guide the artist in drawing images and text in the panels. Keep in mind that the role of the artist is not merely to illustrate the text, but to add new dimensions to it. If your group finishes before everyone else is done, switch your comic with another group who has finished. Write the other group's reason for comparison or contrast as you understand it at the bottom of their paper. Switch your papers back and discuss what made your reason for comparison or contrast come across or how you might have conveyed your reason more clearly.

Suggested Writing Assignments

1. Look back at Morris's graphic essay. Using your own words, and no pictures, write an essay contrasting Richard's experience with Paula's. Use Morris's captions (words in boxes) to help inspire your topic sentences and the visual details as examples for your paragraphs.
2. Think about the kinds of privileges you enjoy or have never experienced. Plan and write a comparison or contrast essay that explores the relationship between your unique privilege profile and someone else's unique privilege profile. If you are stuck, think back to the Reflecting on What You Know question, which asked you to list different types of privilege. You may choose either pattern of organization, but make sure your reason for comparison and/or contrast is clear to your reader.

Two Ways to Belong in America

Bharati Mukherjee

Marty Lederhandler/AP Images

Bharati Mukherjee (1940–2017) was born into an aristocratic family in Calcutta (now Kolkata), India, in 1940. She earned bachelor's and master's degrees from the University of Calcutta, and in 1961, she pursued her long-held desire to become a writer by earning an MFA at the University of Iowa and eventually a PhD in English and comparative literature. She lived in Canada for fourteen years, until legislation against South Asians prompted her to move with her American husband back to the United States. Mukherjee taught at McGill University; Skidmore College; Queens College, City University of New York; and the University of California–Berkeley. She published several novels, including *The Tiger's Daughter* (1971), *Jasmine* (1989), *The Holder of the World* (1993), and *Miss New India* (2011); two collections of short stories, *Darkness* (1985) and *The Middleman and Other Stories* (1988), for which she won the National Book Critics Circle Award; and works of nonfiction, including *Political Culture and Leadership in India* (1991) and *Regionalism in Indian Perspective* (1992).

The following essay was first published in the *New York Times* in 1996 in response to legislation that gave expedited citizenship for legal immigrants living in the United States. As you read Mukherjee's essay, notice how she has organized her presentation of the different views that she and her sister hold toward citizenship.

Reflecting on What You Know

The word *immigrant* has many connotations. If you have moved to the United States from another country, what associations does the word have for you and your family? If you were born in the United States, what associations does the word have for you? Discuss the word *immigrant* with your classmates. How does one's perspective affect the associations that this word has for them? Explain.

This is a tale of two sisters from Calcutta, Mira and Bharati, who have lived in the United States for some thirty-five years, but who find themselves on different sides in the current debate over the status of immigrants. I am an American citizen and she is not. I am moved that thousands of long-term residents are finally taking the oath of citizenship. She is not. 1

Mira arrived in Detroit in 1960 to study child psychology and preschool education. I followed her a year later to study creative writing at the University of Iowa. When we left India, we were almost identical in appearance and attitude. We dressed alike, in saris; we expressed identical views on politics, social issues, love and marriage in the same Calcutta convent-school accent. We would endure our two years in America, secure our degrees, then return to India to marry the grooms of our father's choosing. 2

Instead, Mira married an Indian student in 1962 who was getting his business administration degree at Wayne State University. They soon acquired the labor certifications necessary for the green card of hassle-free residence and employment. 3

Mira still lives in Detroit, works in the Southfield, Michigan, school system, and has become nationally recognized for her contributions in the fields of preschool education and parent-teacher relationships. After thirty-six years as a legal immigrant in this country, she clings passionately to her Indian citizenship and hopes to go home to India when she retires. 4

In Iowa City in 1963, I married a fellow student, an American of Canadian parentage. Because of the accident of his North Dakota birth, I bypassed labor-certification requirements and the race-related "quota" system that favored the applicant's country of origin over his or her merit. I was prepared for (and even welcomed) the emotional strain that came with marrying outside my ethnic community. In thirty-three years of marriage, we have lived in every part of North America. By choosing a husband who was not my father's selection, I was opting for fluidity, self-invention, blue jeans and T-shirts, and renouncing three thousand years (at least) of caste-observant, "pure culture" marriage in the Mukherjee family. My books have often been read as unapologetic (and in some quarters overenthusiastic) texts for cultural and psychological "mongrelization." It's a word I celebrate. 5

Mira and I have stayed sisterly close by phone. In our regular Sunday morning conversations, we are unguardedly affectionate. I am her only blood relative on this continent. We expect to see each other 6 through the looming crises of aging and ill health without being asked. Long before Vice President Gore's "Citizenship USA" drive, we'd had our polite arguments over the ethics of retaining an overseas citizenship while expecting the permanent protection and economic benefits that come with living and working in America.

Like well-raised sisters, we never said what was really on our minds, but we probably pitied one another. She, for the lack of structure in my life, the erasure of Indianness, the absence of an unvarying daily core. I, for the narrowness of her perspective, her uninvolvement with the mythic depths or the superficial pop culture of this society. But, now, with the scapegoating of "aliens" (documented or illegal) on the increase, and the targeting of long-term legal immigrants like Mira for new scrutiny and new self-consciousness, she and I find ourselves unable to maintain the same polite discretion. We were always unacknowledged adversaries, and we are now, more than ever, sisters. 7

"I feel used," Mira raged on the phone the other night. "I feel manipulated and discarded. This is such an unfair way to treat a person who was invited to stay and work here because of her talent. My employer went to the INS and petitioned for the labor certification. For over thirty years, I've invested my creativity and professional skills into the improvement of *this* country's preschool system. I've obeyed all the rules, I've paid my taxes, I love my work, I love my students, I love the friends I've made. How dare America now change its rules in midstream? If America wants to make new rules curtailing benefits of legal immigrants, they should apply only to immigrants who arrive after those rules are already in place." 8

To my ears, it sounded like the description of a long-enduring, comfortable yet loveless marriage, without risk or recklessness. Have we the right to demand, and to expect, that we be loved? (That, to me, is the subtext of the arguments by immigration advocates.) My sister is an expatriate, professionally generous and creative, socially courteous and gracious, and that's as far as her Americanization can go. She is here to maintain an identity, not to transform it. 9

I asked her if she would follow the example of others who have decided to become citizens because of the anti-immigration bills in Congress. And here, she surprised me. "If America wants to play the manipulative game, I'll play it too," she snapped. "I'll become a U.S. citizen for now, then change back to Indian when I'm ready to go home. I feel some kind of irrational attachment to India that I don't to America. Until all this hysteria against legal immigrants, I was totally 10 happy. Having my green card meant I could visit any place in the world I wanted to and then come back to a job that's satisfying and that I do very well."

In one family, from two sisters alike as peas in a pod, there could not be a wider divergence of immigrant experience. America spoke to me—I married it—I embraced the demotion from expatriate aristocrat to immigrant nobody, surrendering those thousands of years of "pure culture," the saris[1], the delightfully accented English. She retained them all. Which of us is the freak? 11

Mira's voice, I realize, is the voice not just of the immigrant South Asian community but of an immigrant community of the millions who have stayed rooted in one job, one city, one house, one ancestral culture, one cuisine, for the entirety of their productive years. She speaks for greater numbers than I possibly can. Only the fluency of her English and the anger, rather than fear, born of confidence from her education, differentiate her from the seamstresses, the domestics, the technicians, the shop owners, the millions of hardworking but effectively silenced documented immigrants as well as their less fortunate "illegal" brothers and sisters. 12

Nearly twenty years ago, when I was living in my husband's ancestral homeland of Canada, I was always well-employed but never allowed to feel part of the local Quebec or larger Canadian society. Then, through a Green Paper that invited a national referendum on the unwanted side effects of "nontraditional" immigration, the Government officially turned against its immigrant communities, particularly those from South Asia. 13

I felt then the same sense of betrayal that Mira feels now. I will never forget the pain of that sudden turning, and the casual racist outbursts the Green Paper elicited. That sense of betrayal had its desired effect and drove me, and thousands like me, from the country. 14

Mira and I differ, however, in the ways in which we hope to interact with the country that we have chosen to live in. She is happier to live in America as an expatriate Indian than as an immigrant American. I need to feel like a part of the community I have adopted (as I tried to feel in Canada as well). I need to put roots down, to vote and make the difference that I can. The price that the immigrant willingly pays, and that the exile avoids, is the trauma of self-transformation. 15

---

[1]*saris*: garments worn by South Asian women consisting of fabric, usually brightly colored, draped to form a long skirt and shoulder or head covering.

Thinking Critically about This Reading

What do you think Mukherjee's sister means when she says in paragraph 10, "If America wants to play the manipulative game, I'll play it too"? How do you react to her decision and her possible plans if and when she eventually returns to India?

Questions for Study and Discussion

1. What is Mukherjee's thesis? (Glossary: **Thesis**)
2. Mukherjee has used comparison and contrast as her organizing principle. What type of comparison and contrast has she used?
3. Why is the pattern of organization that Mukherjee used appropriate for her subject and her purpose?
4. Why might Mukherjee have ordered her points of discussion in the way that she has? Explain.
5. What arguments does Mukherjee make for becoming a U.S. citizen? What arguments does her sister make for retaining her Indian citizenship?
6. Why does Mukherjee's sister feel "used" by attempts to change U.S. laws regarding benefits for noncitizens?
7. What does Mukherjee mean when she says in paragraph 15, "The price that the immigrant willingly pays, and that the exile avoids, is the trauma of self-transformation"?

Classroom Activity Using Comparison and Contrast

In preparation for writing an essay of comparison and contrast on two world leaders (or popular singers, actors, or sports figures), write out answers to the following questions:

1. Who could I compare and contrast?
2. What is my purpose?
3. Which are more interesting—their similarities or their differences?
4. What specific points should I discuss?
5. What organizational pattern will best suit my purpose: subject-by-subject or point-by-point?

Suggested Writing Assignments

1. Mukherjee writes about the relationship she had with her sister in paragraph 7 by saying that "we never said what was really on our minds, but we probably pitied one another." These types of differences are played out on a larger scale when immigrants who have transformed themselves into Americans are confronted by those who have chosen to retain their ethnic identity, and these tensions often lead to name-calling and aggressive prejudice. Similar situations also exist within the Latino, African American, and Southeast Asian American communities and perhaps among all immigrant groups. Write an essay comparing and contrasting the choices of lifestyle that members of an ethnic or cultural community you are familiar with make as they try to find a comfortable place in American society.
2. Mukherjee presents her sister's reasons for not becoming a citizen and supports them with statements her sister has made. Imagine that you are Mira Mukherjee. Write a counterargument to the one presented by your sister that gives your reasons for remaining an Indian citizen. Consider that you have already broken with tradition by marrying a man not of your father's choosing and also that the "trauma of self-transformation" is much deeper and more complicated than your sister has represented it in the conclusion of her essay. Can you say that you are holding to tradition when you are not? Can you engage in a challenging self-transformation if it is not genuinely motivated?

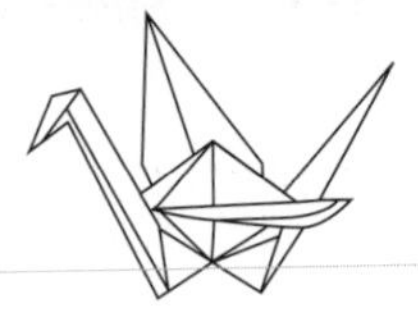

CHAPTER **20**

Cause and Effect

Every time you answer a question that asks *why*, you engage in *causal analysis*—you try to determine a *cause* or series of causes for a particular *effect*. When you answer a question that asks *what if*, you try to determine what *effect* will result from a particular *cause*. You will have many opportunities to use **cause and effect** in your college writing. For example, in history, you might be asked to determine the causes for the 1991 breakup of the former Soviet Union; in political science, you might be asked to determine the critical issues in the 2016 presidential election; in sociology, you might be asked to analyze the effects that the AIDS epidemic has had on sexual-behavior patterns among Americans; and in economics, you might be asked to predict what will happen to our country if we enact large tax cuts.

Fascinated by the effects that private real estate development was having on his neighborhood, a student writer decided to find out what was happening in the older sections of cities across the country. In his first paragraph, Kevin Cunningham describes three possible effects (or fates) of a city's aging. In his second paragraph, he singles out one effect—redevelopment—and discusses in detail the effect it has had on Hoboken, New Jersey.

Effect: *decay*

Effect: urban renewal

Effect: redevelopment

Effects of redevelopment

One of three fates awaits the aging neighborhood. Decay may continue until the neighborhood becomes a slum. It may face urban renewal, with old buildings being razed and ugly new apartment houses taking their place. Or it may undergo redevelopment, in which government encourages the upgrading of existing housing stock by offering low-interest loans or outright grants; thus, the original character of the neighborhood may be retained or restored, allowing the city to keep part of its identity.

An example of redevelopment at its best is Hoboken, New Jersey. In the early 1970s, Hoboken was a dying city, with rundown housing and many abandoned buildings. However, low-interest loans enabled some younger residents to refurbish their homes, and soon the area began to show signs of renewed vigor. Even outsiders moved in and rebuilt some of the abandoned houses. Today, whole blocks have been restored, and neighborhood life is active again. The city does well, too, because property values are higher and so are property taxes.

—Kevin Cunningham, student

In the following example, popular author Bill Bryson explains why the transition from being hunter-gatherers to farmers and city dwellers did not have a beneficial effect on humans:

Even on Orkney, where prehistoric life was probably as good as it could get, an analysis of 340 ancient skeletons showed that hardly any people lived beyond their twenties.

What killed the Orcadians was not dietary deficiency but disease. People living together are vastly more likely to spread illness from household to household, and the close exposure to animals through domestication meant that flu (from pigs or fowl), smallpox and measles (from cows and sheep), and anthrax (from horses and goats, among others) could become part of the human condition, too. As far as we can tell, virtually all of the infectious diseases have become endemic only since people took to living together. Settling down also brought a huge increase in "human commensals"—mice, rats, and other creatures that live with and off us—and these all too often acted as disease vectors.

So sedentism meant poorer diets, more illness, lots of toothache and gum disease, and earlier deaths. What is truly extraordinary is that these are all still factors in our lives today.

—Bill Bryson, *At Home: A Short History of Private Life*

Determining causes and effects is usually a complex process. One reason is that *immediate causes* are readily apparent (because they are closest to the effect) and *ultimate causes* are not as apparent (because they are somewhat removed and even hidden). Furthermore, ultimate causes may bring about effects that themselves become immediate causes, thus creating a *causal chain.* Consider the following causal chain: Sally, a computer salesperson, prepared extensively for a meeting with an important client (ultimate cause), impressed the client (immediate cause), and made a very large sale (effect). The chain did not stop there: the large sale caused her to be promoted by her employer (effect). For a detailed example of a causal chain, read Barry Commoner's analysis of the near disaster at the Three Mile Island nuclear facility in the introduction to Chapter 5 (p. 114).

A second reason causal analysis can be complex is that an effect may have several possible or actual causes, and a cause may have several possible or actual effects. An upset stomach may be caused by eating spoiled food, but it may also be caused by overeating, flu, allergy, nervousness, pregnancy, or any combination of factors. Similarly, the high cost of electricity may have multiple effects—higher profits for utility companies, fewer sales of electrical appliances, higher prices for other products, and the development of alternative sources of energy.

AVOIDING LOGICAL FALLACIES

Sound reasoning and logic are present in all good writing, but they are central to any causal analysis. Writers of believable causal analysis examine their material objectively and develop their essays carefully. They examine all causes and effects methodically and then evaluate them. They are convinced by their own examination of the material but are not afraid to admit that other causes and effects might exist. Above all, they do not let their own prejudices interfere with the logic of their analyses and presentations.

Because people are accustomed to thinking of causes with their effects, they sometimes commit an error in logic known as the "after this, therefore because of this" fallacy (in Latin, *post hoc, ergo propter hoc*). This **logical fallacy** leads people to believe that one event somehow caused a second event, just because the second event followed the first—that is, they sometimes make causal connections that are not proven. For example, if students perform better after a free breakfast program is instituted at their school, one cannot assume that the improvement was caused by the breakfast program. There could be any number of other causes for this effect, and a responsible writer would analyze and consider them all before suggesting a cause.

For more on logical fallacies and how to avoid them, see Chapter 21, pages 502–4.

Our Vanishing Night

Verlyn Klinkenborg

Fred R. Conrad/The New York Times/Redux

Born in 1952 in Meeker, Colorado, Verlyn Klinkenborg grew up on farms in Iowa and Minnesota, where he developed his keen observation skills and love for life in rural America. After graduating from Pomona College and receiving a PhD from Princeton University, he embarked on a career as a writer and farmer. His first book, *Making Hay* (1986), reflects Klinkenborg's fascination with small family farms. *The Last Fine Time* (1991) is a history of immigrant life in Buffalo, New York, where his father-in-law owned a neighborhood bar. From 1997 to 2013, his column The Rural Life appeared regularly on the editorial pages of the *New York Times*, and those essays were later published in the collection *The Rural Life* (2007) and *More Scenes from the Rural Life* (2013). His most recent book is *Several Short Sentences about Writing* (2013). Klinkenborg's essays have also appeared in *Harper's, Smithsonian, Audubon, National Geographic*, and the *New Yorker*. He has taught literature and creative writing at Fordham University, St. Olaf College, Bennington College, Bard College, Sarah Lawrence College, Harvard University, and Yale University.

The following essay first appeared in the November 2008 issue of *National Geographic*. Notice how Klinkenborg builds his essay with striking examples of the negative effects of light pollution.

Reflecting on What You Know

As a child, did you ever go outside on a clear night to look at the stars? Do you remember the names of some of the constellations and planets—like Orion, the Big Dipper, or Venus—that you were able to identify? When you find yourself outside walking now, do you look up at the evening sky? Are the heavens still as you remember them as a child? If not, what's changed?

If humans were truly at home under the light of the moon and stars, we 1
would go in darkness happily, the midnight world as visible to us as it

is to the vast number of nocturnal species on this planet. Instead, we are diurnal creatures, with eyes adapted to living in the sun's light. This is a basic evolutionary fact, even though most of us don't think of ourselves as diurnal beings any more than we think of ourselves as primates or mammals or Earthlings. Yet it's the only way to explain what we've done to the night: We've engineered it to receive us by filling it with light.

This kind of engineering is no different than damming a river. Its benefits come with consequences—called light pollution—whose effects scientists are only now beginning to study. Light pollution is largely the result of bad lighting design, which allows artificial light to shine outward and upward into the sky, where it's not wanted, instead of focusing it downward, where it is. Ill-designed lighting washes out the darkness of night and radically alters the light levels—and light rhythms—to which many forms of life, including ourselves, have adapted. Wherever human light spills into the natural world, some aspect of life—migration, reproduction, feeding—is affected. 2

For most of human history, the phrase "light pollution" would have made no sense. Imagine walking toward London on a moonlit night around 1800, when it was Earth's most populous city. Nearly a million people lived there, making do, as they always had, with candles and rushlights and torches and lanterns. Only a few houses were lit by gas, and there would be no public gaslights in the streets or squares for another seven years. From a few miles away, you would have been as likely to *smell* London as to see its dim collective glow. 3

Now most of humanity lives under intersecting domes of reflected, refracted light, of scattering rays from overlit cities and suburbs, from light-flooded highways and factories. Nearly all of nighttime Europe is a nebula of light, as is most of the United States and all of Japan. In the south Atlantic the glow from a single fishing fleet—squid fishermen luring their prey with metal halide lamps—can be seen from space, burning brighter, in fact, than Buenos Aires or Rio de Janeiro. 4

In most cities the sky looks as though it has been emptied of stars, leaving behind a vacant haze that mirrors our fear of the dark and resembles the urban glow of dystopian science fiction. We've grown so used to this pervasive orange haze that the original glory of an unlit night—dark enough for the planet Venus to throw shadows on Earth—is wholly beyond our experience, beyond memory almost. And yet above the city's pale ceiling lies the rest of the universe, utterly undiminished by the light we waste—a bright shoal of stars and planets and galaxies, shining in seemingly infinite darkness. 5

We've lit up the night as if it were an unoccupied country, when nothing could be further from the truth. Among mammals alone, the number of nocturnal species is astonishing. Light is a powerful biological force, and on many species it acts as a magnet, a process being studied by researchers such as Travis Longcore and Catherine Rich, co-founders of the Los Angeles–based Urban Wildlands Group. The effect is so powerful that scientists speak of songbirds and seabirds being "captured" by searchlights on land or by the light from gas flares on marine oil platforms, circling and circling in the thousands until they drop. Migrating at night, birds are apt to collide with brightly lit tall buildings; immature birds on their first journey suffer disproportionately. 6

Insects, of course, cluster around streetlights, and feeding at those insect clusters is now ingrained in the lives of many bat species. In some Swiss valleys the European lesser horseshoe bat began to vanish after streetlights were installed, perhaps because those valleys were suddenly filled with light-feeding pipistrelle bats. Other nocturnal mammals—including desert rodents, fruit bats, opossums, and badgers—forage more cautiously under the permanent full moon of light pollution because they've become easier targets for predators. 7

Some birds—blackbirds and nightingales, among others—sing at unnatural hours in the presence of artificial light. Scientists have determined that long artificial days—and artificially short nights—induce early breeding in a wide range of birds. And because a longer day allows for longer feeding, it can also affect migration schedules. One population of Bewick's swans wintering in England put on fat more rapidly than usual, priming them to begin their Siberian migration early. The problem, of course, is that migration, like most other aspects of bird behavior, is a precisely timed biological behavior. Leaving early may mean arriving too soon for nesting conditions to be right. 8

Nesting sea turtles, which show a natural predisposition for dark beaches, find fewer and fewer of them to nest on. Their hatchlings, which gravitate toward the brighter, more reflective sea horizon, find themselves confused by artificial lighting behind the beach. In Florida alone, hatchling losses number in the hundreds of thousands every year. Frogs and toads living near brightly lit highways suffer nocturnal light levels that are as much as a million times brighter than normal, throwing nearly every aspect of their behavior out of joint, including their nighttime breeding choruses. 9

Of all the pollutions we face, light pollution is perhaps the most easily remedied. Simple changes in lighting design and installation yield immediate changes in the amount of light spilled into the atmosphere and, often, immediate energy savings. 10

It was once thought that light pollution only affected astronomers, who need to see the night sky in all its glorious clarity. And, in fact, some of the earliest civic efforts to control light pollution—in Flagstaff, Arizona, half a century ago—were made to protect the view from Lowell Observatory, which sits high above that city. Flagstaff has tightened its regulations since then, and in 2001 it was declared the first International Dark Sky City. By now the effort to control light pollution has spread around the globe. More and more cities and even entire countries, such as the Czech Republic, have committed themselves to reducing unwanted glare. 11

Unlike astronomers, most of us may not need an undiminished view of the night sky for our work, but like most other creatures we do need darkness. Darkness is as essential to our biological welfare, to our internal clockwork, as light itself. The regular oscillation of waking and sleep in our lives—one of our circadian rhythms—is nothing less than a biological expression of the regular oscillation of light on Earth. So fundamental are these rhythms to our being that altering them is like altering gravity. 12

For the past century or so, we've been performing an open-ended experiment on ourselves, extending the day, shortening the night, and short-circuiting the human body's sensitive response to light. The consequences of our bright new world are more readily perceptible in less adaptable creatures living in the peripheral glow of our prosperity. But for humans, too, light pollution may take a biological toll. At least one new study has suggested a direct correlation between higher rates of breast cancer in women and the nighttime brightness of their neighborhoods. 13

In the end, humans are no less trapped by light pollution than the frogs in a pond near a brightly lit highway. Living in a glare of our own making, we have cut ourselves off from our evolutionary and cultural patrimony—the light of the stars and the rhythms of day and night. In a very real sense, light pollution causes us to lose sight of our true place in the universe, to forget the scale of our being, which is best measured against the dimensions of a deep night with the Milky Way—the edge of our galaxy—arching overhead. 14

Thinking Critically about This Reading

According to Klinkenborg, are there any benefits to lighting up the night? What are the consequences? For you, do the benefits outweigh the consequences? Explain.

Questions for Study and Discussion

1. What does Klinkenborg mean when he says that "we are diurnal creatures" (paragraph 1)?
2. What is light pollution? According to Klinkenborg, what is the primary cause, or causes, of light pollution?
3. In what ways is light "a powerful biological force" (6)?
4. In addition to people, Klinkenborg lists many other animals that are affected by light pollution. What effects does light pollution have on these creatures? How do the effects differ for each species?
5. What can be done to remedy the problem of light pollution?
6. Klinkenborg claims that "light pollution causes us to lose sight of our true place in the universe" (14). What do you think he means? Do you agree or disagree? Why?

Classroom Activity Using Cause and Effect

Develop a causal chain in which you examine the ramifications of an action you took in the past. Identify each part in the chain. For example, you decided that you wanted to do well in a course (ultimate cause), so you got started on a research project early (immediate cause), which enabled you to write several drafts of your paper (immediate cause), which earned you an A for the project (effect), which led to an excellent grade for the class (effect), which enabled you to take the advanced seminar you wanted (effect). Create a visual representation of your chain, such as a flow chart or Prezi, and present it to your group or the class.

Suggested Writing Assignments

1. What examples of light pollution can you identify on campus or in town? You might consider overilluminated parking lots, walkways, and streets; lights not properly shielded;

and lighting left on in buildings after closing. How might the light pollution be corrected? Write a letter to the building and grounds administrator at your school or to your town manager in which you argue to have the light pollution reduced or eliminated. Be sure that all of your reasons support your thesis.

2. Klinkenborg claims, "Wherever human light spills into the natural world, some aspect of life—migration, reproduction, feeding—is affected" (2). Do some research in your library or on the Internet about how human light affects the migration and feeding patterns of certain migratory birds or the reproduction of certain animals, such as sea turtles. Write a cause-and-effect essay in which you report your findings.

Why We Crave Horror Movies

Stephen King

Kenzo Tribouillard/Getty Images

Stephen King's name is synonymous with horror stories. Born in 1947, King is a 1970 graduate of the University of Maine. He worked as a janitor in a knitting mill, a laundry worker, and a high school English teacher before he struck it big with his writing. Many consider King to be the most successful writer of modern horror fiction today, and in 2015 the National Endowment for the Arts awarded him the National Medal of Arts for his contributions as an author. To date, King has written dozens of novels, collections of short stories, and screenplays, among other works. His books have sold hundreds of millions of copies worldwide, and many of his novels have been made into popular motion pictures, including *Stand by Me, Misery, The Green Mile,* and *Dreamcatcher.* His books, starting with *Carrie* in 1974, include *Salem's Lot* (1975), *The Shining* (1977), *The Dead Zone* (1979), *Christine* (1983), *Pet Sematary* (1983), *The Dark Half* (1989), *The Girl Who Loved Tom Gordon* (1999), *From a Buick 8* (2002), *Under the Dome* (2009), *Joyland* (2013), *Doctor Sleep* (2013), and *End of Watch* (2016). His other works include *Danse Macabre* (1980), a nonfiction look at horror in the media, and *On Writing: A Memoir of the Craft* (2000). The widespread popularity of horror books and films shows that many people share King's fascination with the macabre.

In the following selection, originally published in *Playboy* in 1982—a variation on "The Horror Movie as Junk Food" chapter in *Danse Macabre*—King analyzes the reasons we flock to horror movies.

Reflecting on What You Know

What movies have you seen recently? Do you prefer watching any one particular kind of movie—comedy, drama, science fiction, or horror, for example—over others? How do you explain your preference?

I think that we're all mentally ill; those of us outside the asylums only hide it a little better—and maybe not all that much better, after all. We've all known people who talk to themselves, people who sometimes squinch their faces into horrible grimaces when they believe no one is watching, people who have some hysterical fear—of snakes, the dark, the tight place, the long drop . . . and, of course, those final worms and grubs that are waiting so patiently underground. 1

When we pay our four or five bucks and seat ourselves at tenth-row center in a theater showing a horror movie, we are daring the nightmare. 2

Why? Some of the reasons are simple and obvious. To show that we can, that we are not afraid, that we can ride this roller coaster. Which is not to say that a really good horror movie may not surprise a scream out of us at some point, the way we may scream when a roller coaster twists through a complete 360 or plows through a lake at the bottom of the drop. And horror movies, like roller coasters, have always been the special province of the young; by the time one turns forty or fifty, one's appetite for double twists or 360-degree loops may be considerably depleted. 3

We also go to reestablish our feelings of essential normality; the horror movie is innately conservative, even reactionary. Freda Jackson as the horrible melting woman in *Die, Monster, Die!* confirms for us that no matter how far we may be removed from the beauty of a Robert Redford or a Diana Ross, we are still light-years from true ugliness. 4

And we go to have fun. 5

Ah, but this is where the ground starts to slope away, isn't it? Because this is a very peculiar sort of fun, indeed. The fun comes from seeing others menaced—sometimes killed. One critic has suggested that if pro football has become the voyeur's[1] version of combat, then the horror film has become the modern version of the public lynching. 6

It is true that the mythic, "fairy-tale" horror film intends to take away the shades of gray. . . . It urges us to put away our more civilized and adult penchant for analysis and to become children again, seeing things in pure blacks and whites. It may be that horror movies provide psychic relief on this level because this invitation to lapse into simplicity, irrationality, and even outright madness is extended so rarely. We are told we may allow our emotions a free rein . . . or no rein at all. 7

[1]*voyeur:* one who observes from a distance.

If we are all insane, then sanity becomes a matter of degree. If your insanity leads you to carve up women like Jack the Ripper or the Cleveland Torso Murderer,[2] we clap you away in the funny farm (but neither of those two amateur-night surgeons was ever caught, heh-heh-heh); if, on the other hand, your insanity leads you only to talk to yourself when you're under stress or to pick your nose on your morning bus, then you are left alone to go about your business . . . though it is doubtful that you will ever be invited to the best parties. 8

The potential lyncher is in almost all of us (excluding saints, past and present; but then, most saints have been crazy in their own ways), and every now and then, he has to be let loose to scream and roll around in the grass. Our emotions and our fears form their own body, and we recognize that it demands its own exercise to maintain proper muscle tone. Certain of these emotional muscles are accepted—even exalted—in civilized society; they are, of course, the emotions that tend to maintain the status quo of civilization itself. Love, friendship, loyalty, kindness—these are all the emotions that we applaud, emotions that have been immortalized in the couplets of Hallmark cards and in the verses (I don't dare call it poetry) of Leonard Nimoy.[3] 9

When we exhibit these emotions, society showers us with positive reinforcement; we learn this even before we get out of diapers. When, as children, we hug our rotten little puke of a sister and give her a kiss, all the aunts and uncles smile and twit and cry, "Isn't he the sweetest little thing?" Such coveted treats as chocolate-covered graham crackers often follow. But if we deliberately slam the rotten little puke of a sister's fingers in the door, sanctions follow—angry remonstrance from parents, aunts, and uncles; instead of a chocolate-covered graham cracker, a spanking. 10

But anticivilization emotions don't go away, and they demand periodic exercise. We have such "sick" jokes as, "What's the difference between a truckload of bowling balls and a truckload of dead babies?" (You can't unload a truckload of bowling balls with a pitchfork . . . a joke, by the way, that I heard originally from a ten-year-old.) Such a joke may surprise a laugh or a grin out of us even as we recoil, a 11

---

[2]*Jack the Ripper or the Cleveland Torso Murderer:* serial murderers who were active in the 1880s and the 1930s, respectively.

[3]*Leonard Nimoy* (1931–2015): an actor famous for playing Mr. Spock on the U.S. television series *Star Trek,* which aired from 1966 to 1969, and in its many film versions.

possibility that confirms the thesis: if we share a brotherhood of man, then we also share an insanity of man. None of which is intended as a defense of either the sick joke or insanity but merely as an explanation of why the best horror films, like the best fairy tales, manage to be reactionary, anarchistic,[4] and revolutionary all at the same time.

The mythic horror movie, like the sick joke, has a dirty job to do. It deliberately appeals to all that is worst in us. It is morbidity unchained, our most base instincts let free, our nastiest fantasies realized . . . and it all happens, fittingly enough, in the dark. For those reasons, good liberals often shy away from horror films. For myself, I like to see the most aggressive of them—*Dawn of the Dead,* for instance—as lifting a trap door in the civilized forebrain and throwing a basket of raw meat to the hungry alligators swimming around in that subterranean river beneath. 12

Why bother? Because it keeps them from getting out, man. It keeps them down there and me up here. It was Lennon and McCartney who said that all you need is love, and I would agree with that. 13

As long as you keep the gators fed. 14

Thinking Critically about This Reading

What does King mean when he states that "the horror movie is innately conservative, even reactionary" (paragraph 4)?

Questions for Study and Discussion

1. What, according to King, causes people to crave horror movies? What other reasons can you add to King's list?
2. Identify the analogy King uses in paragraph 3, and explain how it works. (Glossary: **Analogy**)
3. What emotions does society applaud? Why? Which ones does King label "anticivilization emotions" (11)?
4. In what ways is a horror movie like a sick joke? What is the "dirty job," or effect, that the two have in common (12)?
5. King starts his essay with the attention-grabbing sentence "I think that we're all mentally ill." How does he develop this idea of insanity in his essay? What does King mean when he

[4]*anarchistic:* against any authority; favoring anarchy.

says, "The potential lyncher is in almost all of us" (9)? How does King's last line relate to the theme of mental illness?

6. What is King's tone? (Glossary: **Tone**) Point to particular words or sentences that lead you to this conclusion.

Classroom Activity Using Cause and Effect

Use the following test, developed by William V. Haney, to determine your ability to accurately analyze evidence that is presented to you. After completing Haney's test, discuss your answers with other members of your class.

The Uncritical Inference Test

Directions

1. You will read a brief story. Assume that all of the information presented in the story is definitely accurate and true. Read the story carefully. You may refer back to the story whenever you wish.
2. You will then read statements about the story. Answer them in numerical order. *Do not go back* to fill in answers or to change answers. This will only distort your test score.
3. After you read each statement carefully, determine whether the statement is:
   a. "T"—meaning: On the basis of the information presented in the story the statement is *definitely true.*
   b. "F"—meaning: On the basis of the information presented in the story the statement is *definitely false.*
   c. "?"—The statement *may* be true (or false) but on the basis of the information presented in the story you cannot be definitely certain. (If any part of the statement is doubtful, mark the statement "?".)
4. Indicate your answer by circling either "T" or "F" or "?" opposite the statement.

The Story

Babe Smith has been killed. Police have rounded up six suspects, all of whom are known gangsters. All of them are known to have been near the scene of the killing at the approximate time that it occurred. All had substantial motives for wanting Smith killed. However, one of these suspected gangsters, Slinky Sam, has positively been cleared of guilt.

Statements about the Story

1. Slinky Sam is known to have been near the scene of the killing of Babe Smith. T F ?
2. All six of the rounded-up gangsters were known to have been near the scene of the murder. T F ?
3. Only Slinky Sam has been cleared of guilt. T F ?
4. All six of the rounded-up suspects were near the scene of Smith's killing at the approximate time that it took place. T F ?
5. The police do not know who killed Smith. T F ?
6. All six suspects are known to have been near the scene of the foul deed. T F ?
7. Smith's murderer did not confess of his own free will. T F ?
8. Slinky Sam was not cleared of guilt. T F ?
9. It is known that the six suspects were in the vicinity of the cold-blooded assassination. T F ?

Suggested Writing Assignments

1. Write an essay in which you analyze, in light of King's remarks about the causes of our cravings for horror movies, a horror movie you've seen. In what ways did the movie satisfy your "anticivilization emotions" (11)? How did you feel before going to the theater? How did you feel when leaving?
2. One way to understand a person's life is as a series of causes and effects in which decisions large and small lead to present circumstances. Take a look back at a decision you've made in your life and examine the dynamics of the situation. For instance, perhaps you didn't want to go to college but decided to do it anyway. Why weren't you interested, what changed your mind, and what has been the difference? Maybe your dreams were crushed and you made an unwise decision that has had reverberating effects. Once you've settled on your past decision, write a letter to your former self, giving yourself specific advice for living your life, using specific details about the causes and effects of your actions to support your main idea. For instance, you might tell your younger self that it isn't wise to seek immediate gratification and put off college. (For an example of this kind of letter, look up famous tennis player Pete Sampras's "Letter to My Younger Self," published in *The Players' Tribune* on June 29, 2015.)

3. Horror films offer many haunting images—the shower scene in Hitchcock's *Psycho,* the man chasing his son with an axe in *The Shining,* or the girl crawling out of the TV in *The Ring.* Choose a scary movie scene you think is iconographic—an unforgettable symbol of the essence of terror. Write an essay examining the scene, considering the causes of your fright.

Black Men and Public Space

Brent Staples

Brent Staples

Brent Staples was born in Chester, Pennsylvania, in 1951, the oldest of nine children. He earned a BA at Widener University and a PhD at the University of Chicago. He worked for the *New York Times* as an assistant editor for metropolitan news and as editor of the *Book Review* before he joined the paper's editorial board in 1990. His writing, focusing on the areas of education, criminal justice, and economics, appears frequently in the opinion pages. He is also the author of a memoir, *Parallel Time: Growing Up in Black and White* (1994), winner of the Anisfield-Wolf Book Award.

In "Black Men and Public Space," first published in *Ms.* magazine in 1986, Staples describes his nighttime experiences on city streets. He tries to understand the effects he has on other pedestrians, even as he recognizes that the ultimate causes of the tension in these encounters are persistent and damaging stereotypes about African American men.

Reflecting on What You Know

Have you ever felt scared or intimidated when you were out in public? Have you ever sensed that someone felt scared or intimidated by you? What do you think causes these anxieties?

1 My first victim was a woman—white, well dressed, probably in her late twenties. I came upon her late one evening on a deserted street in Hyde Park, a relatively affluent neighborhood in an otherwise mean, impoverished section of Chicago. As I swung onto the avenue behind her, there seemed to be a discreet, uninflammatory distance between us. Not so. She cast back a worried glance. To her, the youngish black man—a broad six feet two inches with a beard and billowing hair, both hands shoved into the pockets of a bulky military

jacket—seemed menacingly close. After a few more quick glimpses, she picked up her pace and was soon running in earnest. Within seconds, she disappeared into a cross street.

That was more than a decade ago. I was twenty-two years old, a graduate student newly arrived at the University of Chicago. It was in the echo of that terrified woman's footfalls that I first began to know the unwieldy inheritance I'd come into—the ability to alter public space in ugly ways. It was clear that she thought herself the quarry of a mugger, a rapist, or worse. Suffering a bout of insomnia, however, I was stalking sleep, not defenseless wayfarers. As a softy who is scarcely able to take a knife to a raw chicken—let alone hold one to a person's throat—I was surprised, embarrassed, and dismayed all at once. Her flight made me feel like an accomplice in tyranny. It also made it clear that I was indistinguishable from the muggers who occasionally seeped into the area from the surrounding ghetto. The first encounter, and those that followed, signified that a vast, unnerving gulf lay between nighttime pedestrians—particularly women—and me. And I soon gathered that being perceived as dangerous is a hazard in itself. I only needed to turn a corner into a dicey situation, or crowd some frightened, armed person in a foyer somewhere, or make an errant move after being pulled over by a policeman. Where fear and weapons meet—and they often do in urban America—there is always the possibility of death. 2

In that first year, my first away from my hometown, I was to become thoroughly familiar with the language of fear. At dark, shadowy intersections, I could cross in front of a car stopped at a traffic light and elicit the *thunk, thunk, thunk, thunk* of the driver—black, white, male, or female—hammering down the door locks. On less traveled streets after dark, I grew accustomed to but never comfortable with people crossing to the other side of the street rather than pass me. Then there were the standard unpleasantries with policemen, doormen, bouncers, cabdrivers, and others whose business it is to screen out troublesome individuals *before* there is any nastiness. 3

I moved to New York nearly two years ago and I have remained an avid night walker. In central Manhattan, the near-constant crowd cover minimizes tense one-on-one street encounters. Elsewhere—in SoHo, for example, where sidewalks are narrow and tightly spaced buildings shut out the sky—things can get very taut indeed. 4

After dark, on the warrenlike[1] streets of Brooklyn where I live, I 5
often see women who fear the worst from me. They seem to have set their faces on neutral, and with their purse straps strung across their chests bandolier[2]-style, they forge ahead as though bracing themselves against being tackled. I understand, of course, that the danger they perceive is not a hallucination. Women are particularly vulnerable to street violence, and young black males are drastically overrepresented among the perpetrators of that violence. Yet these truths are no solace against the kind of alienation that comes of being ever the suspect, a fearsome entity with whom pedestrians avoid making eye contact.

It is not altogether clear to me how I reached the ripe old age of 6
twenty-two without being conscious of the lethality nighttime pedestrians attributed to me. Perhaps it was because in Chester, Pennsylvania, the small, angry industrial town where I came of age in the 1960s, I was scarcely noticeable against a backdrop of gang warfare, street knifings, and murders. I grew up one of the good boys, had perhaps a half-dozen fistfights. In retrospect, my shyness of combat has clear sources.

As a boy, I saw countless tough guys locked away; I have since 7
buried several, too. They were babies, really—a teenage cousin, a brother of twenty-two, a childhood friend in his mid-twenties—all gone down in episodes of bravado played out in the streets. I came to doubt the virtues of intimidation early on. I chose, perhaps unconsciously, to remain a shadow—timid, but a survivor.

The fearsomeness mistakenly attributed to me in public places 8
often has a perilous flavor. The most frightening of these confusions occurred in the late 1970s and early 1980s, when I worked as a journalist in Chicago. One day, rushing into the office of a magazine I was writing for with a deadline story in hand, I was mistaken for a burglar. The office manager called security and, with an ad hoc posse, pursued me through the labyrinthine halls, nearly to my editor's door. I had no way of proving who I was. I could only move briskly toward the company of someone who knew me.

Another time I was on assignment for a local paper and killing 9
time before an interview. I entered a jewelry store on the city's affluent Near North Side. The proprietor excused herself and returned with an enormous red Doberman pinscher straining at the end of a leash.

---

[1]*warrenlike*: maze-like or crowded.

[2]*bandolier*: a belt worn across the body, often with pockets to hold ammunition.

She stood, the dog extended toward me, silent to my questions, her eyes bulging nearly out of her head. I took a cursory look around, nodded, and bade her good night.

Relatively speaking, however, I never fared as badly as another black male journalist. He went to nearby Waukegan, Illinois, a couple of summers ago to work on a story about a murderer who was born there. Mistaking the reporter for the killer, police officers hauled him from his car at gunpoint and but for his press credentials would probably have tried to book him. Such episodes are not uncommon. Black men trade tales like this all the time. 10

Over the years, I learned to smother the rage I felt at so often being taken for a criminal. Not to do so would surely have led to madness. I now take precautions to make myself less threatening. I move about with care, particularly late in the evening. I give a wide berth to nervous people on subway platforms during the wee hours, particularly when I have exchanged business clothes for jeans. If I happen to be entering a building behind some people who appear skittish, I may walk by, letting them clear the lobby before I return, so as not to seem to be following them. I have been calm and extremely congenial on those rare occasions when I've been pulled over by the police. 11

And on late-evening constitutionals I employ what has proved to be an excellent tension-reducing measure: I whistle melodies from Beethoven and Vivaldi and the more popular classical composers. Even steely New Yorkers hunching toward nighttime destinations seem to relax, and occasionally they even join in the tune. Virtually everybody seems to sense that a mugger wouldn't be warbling bright, sunny selections from Vivaldi's *Four Seasons*. It is my equivalent of the cowbell that hikers wear when they know they are in bear country. 12

Thinking Critically about This Reading

Staples finds that he has "the ability to alter public space in ugly ways" (paragraph 2). What does he mean by "ugly" in this sentence? What is ugly about the encounters he describes in the rest of the essay?

Questions for Study and Discussion

1. One of the challenges Staples takes up in this essay is to recognize himself as a cause. What effects does he have on other people? How does he explain those reactions?

2. Discuss Staples's word choice in the first paragraph. How does the language contribute to the feeling of the scene? Which words do you find most telling? (Glossary: **Diction**)
3. How does Staples see himself? How does he believe others see him? Discuss the contrast between these two views. (Glossary: **Comparison and Contrast**)
4. How does Staples describe the complex emotions he felt after the encounter with his "first victim"? Discuss the mix of feelings he mentions in paragraph 2.
5. Learning that others fear him becomes, in turn, a source of fear for Staples. Why? Why is causing fear "a hazard in itself" (2)?
6. What technique does Staples come up with for diminishing the tension in these public encounters? Why does he think it works? What do you think of this solution?
7. Staples ends with a metaphor that likens him to a hiker in "bear country." Discuss the implications of this comparison. (Glossary: **Figure of Speech**)

Classroom Activity Using Cause and Effect

In preparation for writing a cause-and-effect essay, list four effects (two on society and two on personal behavior) for one of the following: television, airplanes, microwave ovens, smartphones, the Internet, social media, entertainment streaming services, or an item of your choice. For example, the automobile could be said to have had the following effects:

Society

A national highway system developed, based on asphalt roads.
petroleum and insurance industries expanded in size and influence.

Personal Behavior

People with cars can live far from public transportation.
Suburban and rural drivers walk less than urban dwellers.

Suggested Writing Assignments

1. In 2012, twenty-five years after Staples published his essay, a young black man, Trayvon Martin, was shot and killed by

George Zimmerman on a street in Sanford, Florida. Martin's death and Zimmerman's subsequent acquittal in 2013 sparked nationwide protests and helped start the Black Lives Matter movement. First, do a little research to familiarize yourself with the Martin case and to be sure you have the facts. (Refer to Evaluating Your Print and Online Sources in Chapter 23, to ensure that you consult credible, unbiased sources.) Then, consider whether you agree with some or all of the ideas Staples presents in his essay and why. Finally, write an essay applying Staples's cause-and-effect analysis to the Martin case. What might his experiences have to tell us about Martin's death? You might also look up, and incorporate into your discussion, the editorial in which Staples addresses the Trayvon Martin case ("Young, Black, Male, and Stalked by Bias," published in the *New York Times* on April 14, 2012).

2. One way to think of ourselves is in terms of the influences that have caused us to be who we are. What contributed to making you who you are—parents, teachers, or coaches? Your neighborhood or cultural heritage? Friends you identify with or heroes you look up to? Write an essay in which you discuss two or three of your most important influences, considering the effects they have had on your life.

CHAPTER **21**

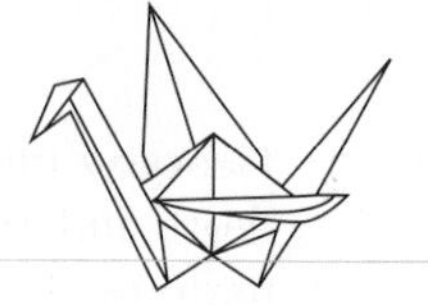

Argument

The word *argument* probably brings to mind a verbal disagreement of the sort that nearly everyone has participated in. Such disputes are satisfying when you convert someone to your point of view. More often, though, verbal arguments are inconclusive and frustrating because you might fail to make your position understood or may believe that your opponent has been stubborn and unreasonable. Because verbal arguments generally arise spontaneously, they cannot be thoughtfully planned or researched. Indeed, it is often not until later that the convincing piece of evidence or the forcefully phrased assertion finally comes to mind.

Written arguments share common goals with spoken ones: they attempt to convince a reader to agree with a particular point of view, to make a particular decision, or to pursue a particular course of action. Written arguments, however, usually involve more deliberate **argumentation**, including the presentation of well-chosen evidence and the artful control of language. Writers of arguments must imagine their probable audience and predict the sorts of objections that may be raised. In written arguments such as academic essays, writers must also choose in advance a specific, sufficiently detailed thesis or proposition. There is a greater need to be organized; to choose the most effective types of evidence from all that is available; and to determine the strategies of rhetoric, language, and style that will best suit the argument's subject, purpose, and thesis and ensure its effect on the intended audience. Such work can be far more satisfying than spontaneous oral argument.

True arguments make assertions about which there is a legitimate and recognized difference of opinion. Readers probably do not need to be convinced that falling in love is a beautiful and intense experience, that crime rates should be reduced, or that computers are changing the world; most people would agree with such assertions. But not everyone would agree that women experience love more intensely than men, that the death penalty reduces the incidence of crime, or that computers are changing the world for the worse; these assertions are arguable and reveal differing perspectives. Regardless of an argument's form or structure, an argument's primary purpose is to set forth a particular point of view and rebut any opposing views, with the hope of creating change, whether that means changing someone's mind or spurring action. Here are a few more examples of arguments that seek to create change:

- A leading heart specialist might argue in a popular magazine that too many doctors are advising patients to have pacemakers implanted when the devices are not necessary.
- A writer for a small-town newspaper might write an editorial urging that a local agency supplying food to needy families be given a larger percentage of the town's budget.
- A foreign-policy specialist might produce a long and complex book attempting to prove that the current administration exhibits no consistent policy in its relationship with other countries and that the Department of State needs to be overhauled.

Argumentation often uses the other rhetorical strategies covered in Chapters 13 to 20. You may find it necessary to define, to compare and contrast, to analyze causes and effects, to classify, to describe, or to narrate. For more on combining strategies, see Chapter 22.

THINKING CRITICALLY ABOUT ARGUMENT

Consider Ethos, Logos, and Pathos

Classical thinkers believed that all rhetorical communication has three parts: the *speaker* (or writer) who comments on a *subject* to an *audience*. We may discuss these parts separately, but in actual rhetorical situations they are inseparable, with each influencing the other two. Moreover, the ancients recognized the importance of three elements of argumentation: *ethos*, which is related to the speaker/writer; *logos*, which is related to the subject; and *pathos*, which is related to the audience.

Ethos (the Greek word for "character") has to do with the authority, credibility, and, to a certain extent, morals of the speaker/writer. The classical rhetoricians believed that the speaker/writer must be credible and argue for a worthwhile cause. Arguing for a questionable cause was not acceptable. But how does one establish credibility? Sometimes it is gained through achievements—that is, the speaker has had experience with an issue, has argued the subject before, and has been judged to be honest and sincere. In your own writing, establishing such credentials is not always possible, so you will need to be especially concerned with presenting your argument reasonably, sincerely, and without excessive emotion. Finally, you should always respect your audience—as well as your opposition—in your writing.

Logos (Greek for "word") is related to the subject and is the effective presentation of the argument itself. Is the thesis or claim worthwhile? Is it logical, consistent, and well supported by evidence? Is the evidence factual, reliable, and convincing? Finally, Is the argument thoughtfully organized and clearly presented so that it will affect the audience? This aspect of argumentation is the most difficult to accomplish and the most rewarding.

Logical appeals are directed at the audience's intellect, understanding, and knowledge. Writers move carefully from assertion to evidence to conclusion and sometimes use an almost mathematical system of proof and counterproof. Logical argument is often found in scientific or philosophical articles, legal decisions, and technical proposals, but also in many disciplines in which writers use rational thought or hard evidence such as statistics.

Arguing logically also means avoiding **logical fallacies**, or errors that result from faulty reasoning. You can learn more about these in the box on pages 502–3.

Pathos (Greek for "emotion") relates to the audience and their emotions—their feelings, values, and even their biases and prejudices. These appeals involve diction, figurative language, analogy, rhythmic patterns of speech, and a tone that will encourage a positive response—or a strategic angry response. Persuasion often tries to get the audience to take action. Visuals such as photographs or even certain fonts can also appeal to emotion; music used in film or presentations can have a similar emotional effect.

☑ **For more practice, visit the LaunchPad for *Models for Writers*: LearningCurve** > Persuasive Appeals

Be careful in your appeals to emotion. Certain buzzwords, slanted diction, or loaded language can be used by the audience to counterattack or may cause resentment. Remember that audiences can range from friendly and sympathetic to hostile and resistant, with myriad possibilities in between. A friendly audience will welcome new information and support your position; a hostile audience will look for flaws in your logic and examples of dishonest manipulation. When addressing an uncommitted audience, use caution, subtlety, and critical thinking.

Use Inductive and Deductive Reasoning

It is the writer's attempt to convince, not explain, that is of primary importance in an argumentative essay. In this respect, it is helpful to keep in mind that there are two basic patterns of thinking and presenting our thoughts that are followed in argumentation: **induction** and **deduction.**

Inductive reasoning, the more common type of reasoning, moves from specific examples to a general statement. The writer makes an *inductive leap* from the evidence to the generalization. For example, after considering enrollment statistics, a writer might conclude that students do not like to take courses offered early in the morning or late in the afternoon.

Deductive reasoning, in contrast, moves from a general statement to a specific conclusion. It works on the model of the **syllogism,** a three-part argument that consists of a major premise, a minor premise, and a conclusion, as in the following example:

a. All women are mortal. *(Major premise)*
b. Jeanne is a woman. *(Minor premise)*
c. Jeanne is mortal. *(Conclusion)*

A syllogism will fail to work if either of the premises is untrue:

a. All living creatures are mammals. *(Major premise)*
b. A butterfly is a living creature. *(Minor premise)*
c. A butterfly is a mammal. *(Conclusion)*

The problem is immediately apparent. The major premise is false: many living creatures are not mammals, and a butterfly happens to be one of the nonmammals. Consequently, the conclusion is invalid.

WRITING ARGUMENTS

Writing an argument is a challenging assignment that can be very rewarding. By nature, an argument must be carefully reasoned and thoughtfully structured to have maximum effect. Therefore, allow yourself enough time to think about your thesis; to gather the evidence you need; and to draft, revise, edit, and proofread your essay. Fuzzy thinking, confused expression, and poor organization will be immediately evident to your reader and will diminish your chances for completing the assignment successfully. The following seven steps will remind you of some key features of arguments and help you sequence your activities as you research and write.

1. Determine the Thesis or Proposition

Begin by deciding on a topic that interests you and that has some significant differences of opinion or some points that you have questions about. Find out what's in the news about your topic, what people are saying about it, and what authors and instructors are emphasizing as important intellectual arguments. As you pursue your research, consider what assertion or assertions you can make about your topic. The more specific you make the thesis or proposition, the more directed your research can become and the more focused your ultimate argument will be. Don't hesitate to modify or even reject an initial thesis as your research warrants.

A thesis can be placed anywhere in an argument, but while learning to write arguments, you should place the statement of your controlling idea near the beginning of your composition. Explain the importance of the thesis, and make clear to your reader that you share a common concern or interest in this issue. State your central assertion directly in your first or second paragraph so that your reader will have no doubt or confusion about your position. You may also wish to lead off with a striking piece of evidence to capture your reader's interest.

2. Take Account of Your Audience

In no other type of writing is the question of audience more important than in argumentation. The tone you establish, the type of

☑ **For more practice, visit the LaunchPad for *Models for Writers*:**
LearningCurve > Arguable Claims
LearningCurve > Topic, Purpose, and Audience

diction you choose, the kinds of evidence you select to buttress your assertions, and the organizational pattern you follow can influence your audience to trust you and believe your assertions. If you judge the nature of your audience accurately; respect its knowledge of the subject; and correctly envision whether it is likely to be hostile, neutral, complacent, or receptive, you will be able to tailor the various aspects of your argument appropriately. (For more on audience, refer to the discussion of ethos, pathos, and logos on pp. 497–99.)

3. Gather the Necessary Supporting Evidence

For each point of your argument, provide appropriate and sufficient evidence: verifiable facts and statistics, illustrative examples and narratives, or quotations from authorities. Don't overwhelm your reader with evidence, but don't skimp, either. Demonstrate your command of the topic and control of the thesis by choosing carefully from all the evidence at your disposal.

4. Settle on an Organizational Pattern

Once you think that you have sufficient evidence to make your assertion convincing, consider how best to organize your argument. To some extent, your organization will depend on your method of reasoning—inductive, deductive, or a combination of the two. For example, is it necessary to establish a major premise before moving on to discuss a minor premise? Should most of your evidence precede your direct statement of an assertion or follow it? Will induction work better with the particular audience you have targeted? As you present your primary points, you may find it effective to move from least important to most important or from most familiar to least familiar. A scratch outline can help, but often a writer's most crucial revisions in an argument involve rearranging its components into a sharper, more coherent order. Often it is difficult to tell what that order should be until the revision stage of the writing process.

5. Consider and Address Opposition to Your Argument

As you proceed with your argument, you may wish to take into account well-known and significant opposing arguments. To ignore opposing views would be to suggest to your reader any one of the following: you don't know about the opposing views, you know about them and are obviously and unfairly weighting the arguments in your favor, or you know about them and have no reasonable answers for them. Grant the validity of opposing arguments or refute them, but respect your reader's intelligence by addressing the objections to your assertion. Your reader will in turn respect you for doing so.

6. Avoid Faulty Reasoning

Have someone read your argument for errors in judgment and for faulty reasoning. Sometimes others can more easily see problems because they aren't intimately tied to your assertion. These errors are typically called **logical fallacies**. Review the Logical Fallacies box below, making sure that you have not made any of these errors in reasoning.

Logical Fallacies

Oversimplification: A simple solution to what is clearly a complex problem or a simple solution to a problem that the writer does not fully understand: *We have a balance-of-trade deficit because foreigners make better products than we do*. This fallacy often occurs when the writer attempts to offer a cause for an event—such as a fire, a natural disaster, or a mechanical failure—and doesn't consider other possibilities.

Hasty generalization: A fallacy often found in inductive reasoning (reasoning from the particular to the general) wherein the writer uses too little evidence or evidence that is not representative to reach a conclusion: *My grandparents, like most older folks, don't understand their Social Security benefits.*

Post hoc, ergo propter hoc: (Latin for "After this, therefore because of this.") Confusing chance with causation. Just because one event comes after another in time does not mean the first event caused the second: *I went swimming yesterday, and the next thing I knew, I had a cold. Every time I wear my orange sweater to a basketball game, we win*. Swimming may or may not be the cause of the cold, and one fan's clothing is not the reason a team wins or loses.

☑ **For more practice, visit the LaunchPad for *Models for Writers*: LearningCurve** > Reasoning and Logical Fallacies

Begging the question: Arriving at a conclusion based on a premise (a statement used as the basis of an argument) that does not have adequate support: *Gambling is wrong because people should stay away from games of chance. Lying is wrong because it's always best to tell the truth.* The first example describes gambling as a game of chance but does not offer proof of what is wrong with it. In the second example, the arguer has failed to provide proof of anything.

False analogy: An analogy compares something unfamiliar to something familiar with the hope that the unfamiliar becomes more clearly understood. False analogies ignore important dissimilarities between the items being compared and therefore do not serve as proof: *If we can put a man on the moon, we should be able to cure the common cold.* Although the two tasks are scientifically complex, there is no reason to believe that accomplishing them involves the same knowledge, skills, or processes.

Either/or thinking: The fallacy of seeing only two alternatives in a situation when, in fact, there may be other possibilities. During the great protest era of the 1960s, many citizens demonstrated against the government. Those who were opposed to the demonstrators simplified the problems our country was facing at the time with posters and bumper stickers reading: *America: Love it or leave it!* This either/or thinking ignores the many possibilities for thought and action that lie between the two extremes of loving the country or leaving it.

Non sequitur: (Latin for "It does not follow.") The writer uses an inference or a conclusion that is not clearly related to the established premises or evidence: *The witness was very sincere and convincing. Her testimony was reliable.* Showing sincerity or being convincing does not necessarily prove the witness's reliability. One can be sincere and convincing but also inaccurate.

If you are having difficulty identifying various kinds of logical fallacies, you are not alone. Whereas they are sometimes easier to identify in the writing of others, they are often difficult to identify in our own writing. Logical fallacies sometimes occur because the argument is based on premises that are not true, the evidence is insufficient for the claims, and erroneous conclusions are drawn. One way to identify logical fallacies in your own writing is to take the position of someone arguing against you. What would you find wrong with your argument and for what reasons? Becoming your own adversary will help you detect and avoid errors in reasoning and strengthen your arguments. Complete the activity in the box below to practice identifying and correcting logical fallacies.

Detecting Logical Fallacies

Each of the following may contain one or more examples of faulty reasoning. Analyze each to determine what, if anything, is wrong with it. If you find an error in logic, determine which of the logical fallacies is occurring and do your best to correct it.

1. Don't lend books to friends. They never return them.
2. I am not in favor of his argument for a new school because he's so liberal and likes to spend money.
3. Don't ever invest in the stock market. You could lose a ton of money.
4. Osama bin Laden has been killed, so we don't need to be afraid of terrorism any longer.
5. Larry the Cable Guy said to take the medicine he was advertising and not "get heartburn in the first place."
6. He'll make a great coach. He was an excellent quarterback when he played.
7. We ought to close the pool at the hotel because too many people have drowned there.
8. The juror was released from the drunk-driving case because he had been a binge drinker in college.
9. Reducing the number of unemployment checks a person can receive will result in more people finding jobs.
10. Exit exams for college seniors will improve the quality of instruction.

7. Conclude Forcefully

In the conclusion of your essay, be sure to restate your position in new language, at least briefly. Besides persuading your reader to accept your point of view, you may also want to encourage some specific course of action. Above all, your conclusion should not introduce new information that may surprise your reader. It should seem to follow naturally, almost seamlessly, from the series of points that you have carefully established in the body of the essay. Don't overstate your case, but at the same time don't qualify your conclusion with the use of too many words or phrases like *I think, in my opinion, maybe, sometimes,* and *probably.* These words can make you sound indecisive and fuzzy-headed rather than rational and sensible.

TAKING A STAND

Even though you have chosen a topic, gathered information about it, and established a thesis statement or proposition, you need to take a stand—to fully commit yourself to your beliefs and ideas about the issue before you. If you try to work with a thesis that you have not clearly thought through or are confused about, or if you take a position you do not fully believe in or care about, it will show in your writing. Your willingness to research, to dig up evidence, to find the most effective organizational pattern for your material, to construct strong paragraphs and sentences, and to find just the right diction to convey your argument is a direct reflection of just how strongly you take a stand—and how much you believe in that stand. With a strong stand, you can argue vigorously and convincingly.

Becoming Disabled

Rosemarie Garland-Thomson

Courtesy Rosemarie Garland-Thomson

Born in 1946, Rosemarie Garland-Thomson earned a PhD in English from Brandeis University. She is currently a professor of English and bioethics at Emory University. A strong proponent of disability rights, Garland-Thomson has spent much of her career pioneering the field of critical disability studies, which seeks to analyze the experiences of individuals with disabilities and to develop better strategies for the inclusion of those with disabilities in society. Garland-Thomson was inspired by the disability rights movement and other civil rights movements to assert her identity as a person with a disability and to encourage others with disabilities to assert their identities as well. Garland-Thomson's essays have appeared in the *New York Times*, the *New Yorker*, and the *Huffington Post*. She is also the author of the books *Staring: How We Look* (2009), *Extraordinary Bodies: Figuring Physical Disability in American Culture and Literature* (2010), *Disabilities Studies: Enabling the Humanities* (2002), and *Freakery: Cultural Spectacles of the Extraordinary Body* (1996). Garland-Thomson has lectured internationally and has been presented with many awards and honors, including the 2010 Society for Disabilities Senior Scholar Award.

In the following essay, published in the *New York Times* on August 19, 2016, Garland-Thomson advocates for those who have disabilities to assert their identities and for those who do not have disabilities to learn how to cooperate with people in the disability community rather than seeing them as fundamentally broken. As you read, think about Garland-Thomson's intended audience and how both her evidence and organizational pattern gradually reveal an expanded target audience.

Reflecting on What You Know

Have others ever made a comment that revealed lack of awareness about an aspect of your identity or personality? If so, how did you react and why? Did you choose to educate them about yourself? Have you ever made such a comment to someone else? How did he or she react?

Not long ago, a good friend of mine said something revealing to me: "I don't think of you as disabled," she confessed. 1

I knew exactly what she meant; I didn't think of myself as disabled until a few decades ago, either, even though my two arms have been pretty significantly asymmetrical[1] and different from most everybody else's my whole life. 2

My friend's comment was meant as a compliment, but followed a familiar logic—one that African-Americans have noted when their well-meaning white friends have tried to erase the complications of racial identity by saying, "I don't think of you as black," or when a man compliments a woman by saying that he thinks of her as "just one of the guys." 3

This impulse to rescue people with disabilities from a discredited identity, while usually well meaning, is decidedly at odds with the various pride movements we've come to know in recent decades. Slogans like "Black Is Beautiful" and "We're Here, We're Queer, Get Used to It!" became transformative taunts for generations of people schooled in the self-loathing of racism, sexism and heterosexism. Pride movements were the psycho-emotional equivalents of the antidiscrimination and desegregation laws that asserted the rights of full citizenship to women, gay people, racial minorities and other groups. More recently, the Black Lives Matter and the L.G.B.T. rights movement have also taken hold. 4

Yet pride movements for people with disabilities—like Crip Power or Mad Pride—have not gained the same sort of traction in the American consciousness. Why? One answer is that we have a much clearer collective notion of what it means to be a woman or an African-American, gay or transgender person than we do of what it means to be disabled. 5

A person without a disability may recognize someone using a wheelchair, a guide dog or a prosthetic[2] limb, or someone with Down syndrome, but most don't conceptualize these people as having a shared social identity and a political status. "They" merely seem to 6

[1]*asymmetrical*: having two sides or parts that are not the same.
[2]*prosthetic*: relating to an artificial part or device.

be people to whom something unfortunate has happened, for whom something has gone terribly wrong. The one thing most people do know about being disabled is that they don't want to be that.

Yet disability is everywhere once you start noticing it. A simple awareness of who we are sharing our public spaces with can be revelatory. Wheelchair users or people with walkers, hearing aids, canes, service animals, prosthetic limbs or breathing devices may seem to appear out of nowhere, when they were in fact there all the time. 7

A mother of a 2-year-old boy with dwarfism who had begun attending Little People of America events summed this up when she said to me with stunned wonder, "There are a lot of them!" Until this beloved child unexpectedly entered her family, she had no idea that achondroplasia is the most common form of short stature or that most people with the condition have average-size parents. More important, she probably did not know how to request the accommodations, access the services, enter the communities or use the laws that he needs to make his way through life. But because he is hers and she loves him, she will learn a lot about disability. 8

The fact is, most of us will move in and out of disability in our lifetimes, whether we do so through illness, an injury or merely the process of aging. 9

The World Health Organization defines disability as an umbrella term that encompasses impairments, activity limitations and participation restrictions that reflect the complex interaction between "features of a person's body and features of the society in which he or she lives." The Americans With Disabilities Act tells us that disability is "a physical or mental impairment that substantially limits one or more major life activities." 10

Obviously, this category is broad and constantly shifting, so exact statistics are hard to come by, but the data from our most reliable sources is surprising. The Centers for Disease Control and Prevention estimates that one in five adults in the United States is living with a disability. The National Organization on Disability says there are 56 million disabled people. Indeed, people with disabilities are the largest minority group in the United States, and as new disability categories such as neurodiversity, psychiatric disabilities, disabilities of aging and learning disabilities emerge and grow, so does that percentage. 11

Disability growth areas—if you will—include diagnostic categories such as depression, anxiety disorders, anorexia, cancers, traumatic brain injuries, attention-deficit disorder, autoimmune disease, spinal 12 cord injuries, autistic spectrum disabilities and dementia. Meanwhile, whole categories of disability and populations of people with certain disabilities have vanished or diminished significantly in the 20th century with improved public health measures, disease prevention and increased public safety.

Because almost all of us will experience disability sometime in our lives, having to navigate one early in life can be a great advantage. Because I was born with six fingers altogether and one quite short arm, I learned to get through the world with the body I had from the beginning. Such a misfit between body and world can be an occasion for resourcefulness. Although I certainly recognized that the world was built for what I call the fully fingered, not for my body, I never experienced a sense of losing capacity, and adapted quite readily, engaging with the world in my preferred way and developing practical work-arounds for the life demands my body did not meet. (I used talk-to-text technology to write this essay, for example.) 13

Still, most Americans don't know how to be disabled. Few of us can imagine living with a disability or using the technologies that disabled people often need. Since most of us are not born into disability but enter into it as we travel through life, we don't get acculturated[3] the way most of us do in our race or gender. Yet disability, like any challenge or limitation, is fundamental to being human—a part of every life. Clearly, the border between "us" and "them" is fragile. We just might be better off preparing for disability than fleeing from it. 14

Yet even talking about disability can be a fraught experience. The vocabulary of this status is highly charged, and for even the most well-meaning person, a conversation can feel like stepping into a maze of courtesy, correctness and possible offense. When I lecture about disability, someone always wants to know—either defensively, earnestly or cluelessly—the "correct" way to refer to this new politicized identity. 15

What we call ourselves can also be controversial. Different constituencies have vibrant debates about the politics of self-naming. "People first" language asserts that if we call ourselves "people with disabilities," we put our humanity first and consider our impairment a modification. Others claim disability pride by getting our identity right up front, making us "disabled people." Others, like many sign language users, reject the term "disability." 16

[3]*acculturated*: accustomed or modified to belong to a group or culture, usually through a long process of exposure and learning.

The old way of talking about disability as a curse, tragedy, misfortune or individual failing is no longer appropriate, but we are unsure about what more progressive, more polite, language to use. "Crippled," "handicapped" and "feebleminded" are outdated and derogatory. Many pre-Holocaust eugenic categories that were indicators for state-sponsored sterilization or extermination policies—"idiot," "moron," "imbecile" and even "mentally retarded"—have been discarded in favor of terms such as "developmentally delayed" or "intellectually disabled." In 2010, President Obama signed Rosa's Law, which replaced references to "mental retardation" with "intellectual disability" in federal statutes. 17

The author and scholar Simi Linton writes about learning to be disabled in a hospital after a spinal cord injury—not by way of her rehabilitation but rather by bonding with other young people new to disability. She calls this entering into community "claiming disability." In "Sight Unseen," an elegant explication of blindness and sight as cultural metaphors, Georgina Kleege wryly suggests the difference between medical low vision and blindness as a cultural identity by observing that, "Writing this book made me blind," a process she calls gaining blindness rather than losing sight. 18

Like them, I had no idea until the 1980s what it meant to be disabled, that there was a history, culture and politics of disability. Without a disability consciousness, I was in the closet. 19

Since that time, other people with disabilities have entered the worlds in which I live and work, and I have found community and developed a sturdy disability identity. I have changed the way I see and treat myself and others. I have taken up the job of teaching disability studies and bioethics[4] as part of my work. I have learned to be disabled. 20

What has been transformed is not my body, but my consciousness. 21

As we manage our bodies in environments not built for them, the social barriers can sometimes be more awkward than the physical ones. Confused responses to racial or gender categories can provoke the question "What are you?" Whereas disability interrogations are "What's wrong with you?" Before I learned about disability rights and disability pride, which I came to by way of the women's movement, I always squirmed out a shame-filled, "I was born this way." Now I'm likely to begin one of these uncomfortable encounters with, "I have a disability," and to complete it with, "And these are the accommodations I need." This is a claim to inclusion and right to access resources. 22

[4]*bioethics*: the study of the ethics of biological research, especially medical research.

This coming out has made possible what a young graduate student with a disability said to me after I gave a lecture at her university. She said that she understood now that she had a right to be in the world. 23

We owe much of this progress to the Americans With Disabilities Act of 1990 and the laws that led up to it. Starting in the 1960s, a broad disability rights movement encouraged legislation and policy that gradually desegregated the institutions and spaces that had kept disabled people out and barred them from exercising the privileges and obligations of full citizenship. Education, transportation, public spaces and work spaces steadily transformed so that people with disabilities came out of hospitals, asylums, private homes and special schools into an increasingly rebuilt and reorganized world. 24

That changed landscape is being reflected politically, too, so much so that when Donald Trump mocked the movement of a disabled reporter, most of the country reacted with shock and outrage at his blatant discrimination, and that by the time the Democratic National Convention rolled round, it seemed natural to find the rights and dignity of people with disabilities placed front and center. Hillary Clinton's efforts early in her career to secure the right to an education for all disabled children was celebrated; Tom Harkin, the former Iowa senator and an author of the Americans With Disabilities Act, marked the law's 26th anniversary and called for improvements to it. People with disabilities were featured speakers, including Anastasia Somoza, who received an ovation for her powerful speech. President Obama, in his address, referred to "black, white, Latino, Asian, Native American; young, old; gay, straight; men, women, folks with disabilities, all pledging allegiance, under the same proud flag." 25

Becoming disabled demands learning how to live effectively as a person with disabilities, not just living as a disabled person trying to become nondisabled. It also demands the awareness and cooperation of others who don't experience these challenges. Becoming disabled means moving from isolation to community, from ignorance to knowledge about who we are, from exclusion to access, and from shame to pride. 26

Thinking Critically about This Reading

According to Garland-Thomson, "[The] impulse to rescue people with disabilities from a discredited identity, while usually well meaning, is decidedly at odds with the various pride movements we've come to know in recent decades" (paragraph 4). What does

Garland-Thomson mean that people with disabilities have a "discredited identity"? What might cause a group with a discredited identity to avoid a public display of pride in that identity?

Questions for Study and Discussion

1. Quote an example of at least one line that reveals Garland-Thomson's appeal to *pathos* (Greek for "emotion") in the first nine paragraphs of her essay. What emotion is she attempting to evoke in her reader? Is it effective in convincing you to agree with her argument?
2. Why does Garland-Thomson include the World Health Organization's definition of disability in the middle of her essay? Does this kind of support help her argument? How?
3. Garland-Thomson writes that "most of us will move in and out of disability in our lifetimes" (9). How does this statement expand her audience? (Glossary: **Audience**)
4. One of the important aspects of argumentation is judging the nature of your audience correctly. As you began to read "Becoming Disabled," were you hostile, neutral, complacent, or receptive? Why? Describe a part of the essay that kept you as the same type of reader or that helped you change your position. (Glossary: **Audience**)
5. Garland-Thomson writes of the definition of disability, "Obviously, this category is broad and constantly shifting, so exact statistics are hard to come by, but the data from our most reliable sources is surprising" (11). Here, Garland-Thomson includes a disclaimer to prove that she is avoiding faulty reasoning. Does this disclaimer strengthen or weaken her argument? Explain.
6. Name at least one strategy that Garland-Thomson uses to create a forceful conclusion.

Classroom Activity Using Argument

Take a stand! Literally. This is a movement activity that will help you generate a successful thesis statement and build a strong sense of audience for your next essay.

1. On a piece of scrap paper or a notecard, write down an arguable claim or thesis statement, which your professor will then collect.
2. Stand in the front of the classroom. If you are unable to stand, ask your professor to provide necessary accommodation for you, such as a chair in front of the class.
3. Your professor will read aloud one of the thesis statements that he or she has collected.
4. Move to your right as far you can go if you agree with the thesis statement that your professor read aloud (think "right" = "correct"). Move to your far left if you disagree with the statement. Move to the middle if the thesis statement sounds unclear to you or you hold a perspective somewhere in the middle. Feel free to stand anywhere on the continuum between disagreement and agreement and to move your position at any time if you hear ideas from the classroom audience that shift your perspective.
5. Your professor will call on a select number of individuals standing at the front of the class to say why they are standing where they are (according to how much they agree with the statement) and to give examples of their perspectives. He or she will then read as many thesis statements as time permits.
6. When the activity is done, write a paragraph to reflect on what you learned from your classmates (your classroom audience), and to think how what you learned affects your thesis statement. For example, do you need to revise your thesis statement for greater clarity? Even if your thesis statement was not read aloud, the kinds of comments made during this activity should help you reflect on your own thesis and essay.

Suggested Writing Assignments

1. Write an essay using (or inspired by) one of the following thesis statements:
    - Elementary school students with intellectual disabilities should be placed in mainstream classrooms.
    - Rather than build separate facilities for those with physical disabilities, architects should design buildings that are

as accessible to those with physical disabilities as to those without physical disabilities (example: Each bathroom stall should be as accessible to people who use wheelchairs as to people who do not).

- Online classes empower people with disabilities.

2. Begin the introduction paragraph of an argument essay on a topic of your choice with an anecdote that will appeal to *pathos* (emotion) in your audience. You might start with a story from your life with which you feel some emotional connection or a story that you have recently seen on the news that would create sympathy in your audience. Then try writing the same introduction beginning with an appeal to *logos* (logic and reason). Select the introduction that works best and write a draft of your essay.

In Praise of the F Word

Mary Sherry

Carrie Bender Coughlin

Mary Sherry was born in Bay City, Michigan. She received a BA from Dominican University and an MBA from the University of St. Thomas. She later founded a research and publishing company specializing in information for economic and development organizations. About her early writing career, Sherry comments: "My interest in writing began in high school. I wrote for the school paper and wound up as editor my senior year. I started out majoring in math in college but found my writing skills were stronger, so I switched, thinking I would be good at writing technical materials. That eventually happened, but my first nationally published work was based on an experience at a church meeting. I have been observing events, writing about them and getting such essays published ever since." Sherry has taught in adult-literacy programs and has written essays on educational problems for various newspapers, including the *Wall Street Journal* and *America* magazine. She also serves on the city council in her current home of Burnsville, Minnesota.

In the following essay, originally published in *Newsweek* in 1991, Sherry takes a provocative stance—that the threat of flunking is a "positive teaching tool." She believes students would be better off if they had a "healthy fear of failure," and she marshals a series of logical appeals to both clarify and support her argument.

Reflecting on What You Know

Comment on what you see as the relationship between learning and grades. Do teachers and students pay too much attention to grades at the expense of learning? Or are grades not seen as that important?

Tens of thousands of eighteen-year-olds will graduate this year and be handed meaningless diplomas. These diplomas won't look any different from those awarded their luckier classmates. Their validity 1 will be questioned only when their employers discover that these graduates are semiliterate.

Eventually a fortunate few will find their way into educational-repair shops—adult-literacy programs, such as the one where I teach basic grammar and writing. There, high-school graduates and high-school dropouts pursuing graduate-equivalency certificates will learn the skills they should have learned in school. They will also discover they have been cheated by our educational system. 2

As I teach, I learn a lot about our schools. Early in each session I ask my students to write about an unpleasant experience they had in school. No writers' block here! "I wish someone would have made me stop doing drugs and made me study." "I liked to party and no one seemed to care." "I was a good kid and didn't cause any trouble, so they just passed me along even though I didn't read well and couldn't write." And so on. 3

I am your basic do-gooder, and prior to teaching this class I blamed the poor academic skills our kids have today on drugs, divorce, and other impediments to concentration necessary for doing well in school. But, as I rediscover each time I walk into the classroom, before a teacher can expect students to concentrate, he has to get their attention, no matter what distractions may be at hand. There are many ways to do this, and they have much to do with teaching style. However, if style alone won't do it, there is another way to show who holds the winning hand in the classroom. That is to reveal the trump card[1] of failure. 4

I will never forget a teacher who played that card to get the attention of one of my children. Our youngest, a world-class charmer, did little to develop his intellectual talents but always got by. Until Mrs. Stifter. 5

Our son was a high-school senior when he had her for English. "He sits in the back of the room talking to his friends," she told me. "Why don't you move him to the front row?" I urged, believing the embarrassment would get him to settle down. Mrs. Stifter looked at me steely-eyed over her glasses. "I don't move seniors," she said. "I flunk them." I was flustered. Our son's academic life flashed before my eyes. No teacher had ever threatened him with that before. I regained my composure and managed to say that I thought she was right. By the time I got home I was feeling pretty good about this. It was a radical 6

[1]*trump card:* a secret weapon; hidden advantage.

approach for these times, but, well, why not? "She's going to flunk you," I told my son. I did not discuss it any further. Suddenly English became a priority in his life. He finished out the semester with an A.

I know one example doesn't make a case, but at night I see a parade of students who are angry and resentful for having been passed along until they could no longer even pretend to keep up. Of average intelligence or better, they eventually quit school, concluding they were too dumb to finish. "I should have been held back" is a comment I hear frequently. Even sadder are those students who are high-school graduates who say to me after a few weeks of class, "I don't know how I ever got a high-school diploma." 7

Passing students who have not mastered the work cheats them and the employers who expect graduates to have basic skills. We excuse this dishonest behavior by saying kids can't learn if they come from terrible environments. No one seems to stop to think that—no matter what environments they come from—most kids don't put school first on their list unless they perceive something is at stake. They'd rather be sailing. 8

Many students I see at night could give expert testimony on unemployment, chemical dependency, abusive relationships. In spite of these difficulties, they have decided to make education a priority. They are motivated by the desire for a better job or the need to hang on to the one they've got. They have a healthy fear of failure. 9

People of all ages can rise above their problems, but they need to have a reason to do so. Young people generally don't have the maturity to value education in the same way my adult students value it. But fear of failure, whether economic or academic, can motivate both. 10

Flunking as a regular policy has just as much merit today as it did two generations ago. We must review the threat of flunking and see it as it really is—a positive teaching tool. It is an expression of confidence by both teachers and parents that the students have the ability to learn the material presented to them. However, making it work again would take a dedicated, caring conspiracy between teachers and parents. It would mean facing the tough reality that passing kids who haven't learned the material—while it might save them grief for the short term—dooms them to long-term illiteracy. It would mean that teachers would have to follow through on their threats, and parents would have to stand behind them, knowing their children's best interests are indeed at stake. This means no more doing Scott's assignments for him because he might fail. No more passing Jodi because she's such a nice kid. 11

This is a policy that worked in the past and can work today. A wise teacher, with the support of his parents, gave our son the opportunity to succeed—or fail. It's time we return this choice to all students. 12

Thinking Critically about This Reading

According to Sherry, "We must review the threat of flunking and see it as it really is—a positive teaching tool. It is an expression of confidence by both teachers and parents that the students have the ability to learn the material presented to them" (paragraph 11). How can flunking students be "an expression of confidence" in them?

Questions for Study and Discussion

1. What is Sherry's thesis? (Glossary: **Thesis**) What evidence does she use to support her argument?
2. Sherry uses dismissive language to characterize objections to flunking—*cheats* and *dooms.* In your opinion, does she do enough to acknowledge the other side of the argument? Explain.
3. What is the "F word" discussed in the essay? Does referring to it in this way increase the effectiveness of the essay? Why?
4. Who makes up Sherry's audience? (Glossary: **Audience**) Are they receptive to the "F word"? Explain your answer.
5. In what way is Sherry qualified to comment on the potential benefits of flunking students? Do you think her induction is accurate?

Classroom Activity Using Argument

A first-year composition student, Marco Schmidt, is preparing to write an essay in which he will argue that music should be a required course for all public high school students. He has compiled the following pieces of evidence:

- Informal interviews with four classmates. Three of the classmates stated that they would have enjoyed and benefited from taking a music course in high school, and the fourth stated that she would not have been interested in taking music.

- An article from a professional journal for teachers comparing the study habits of students who were involved in music and those who were not. The author, a psychologist, found that students who play an instrument or sing regularly have better study habits than students who do not.
- A brief article from a national newsmagazine praising an inner-city high school's experimental curriculum, in which music classes play a prominent part.
- The personal website of a high school music teacher who posts information about the successes and achievements of her former students.

Discuss these pieces of evidence with your classmates. Which are most convincing? Which provide the least support for Marco's argument? Why? What other types of evidence might Marco find to support his argument?

Suggested Writing Assignments

1. Write an essay in which you argue against Sherry's thesis. (Glossary: **Thesis**) In what ways is flunking bad for students? Are there techniques more positive than a "fear of failure" that can be used to motivate students?
2. Think of something that involves short-term pain or sacrifice but that can be beneficial in the long run. For example, exercising requires exertion, but it may help prevent health problems. Studying and writing papers when you'd rather be having fun or even sleeping may seem painful, but earning a college degree leads to personal growth and development. Even if the benefits are obvious, imagine a skeptical audience, and write an argument in favor of the short-term sacrifice over the long-term consequences of avoiding it. (Glossary: **Audience**)

The Declaration of Independence

Thomas Jefferson

President, governor, statesman, lawyer, architect, philosopher, and writer, Thomas Jefferson (1743–1826) is one of the most important figures in U.S. history. He was born in Albemarle County, Virginia, in 1743 and attended the College of William and Mary. After being admitted to law practice in 1767, he began a long and illustrious career of public service to the colonies and, later, the new republic. In 1809, after two terms as president, Jefferson retired to Monticello, a home he had designed and helped build. Ten years later, he founded the University of Virginia. Jefferson died at Monticello on July 4, 1826, the fiftieth anniversary of the signing of the Declaration of Independence.

Jefferson drafted the Declaration in 1776. Although it was revised by Benjamin Franklin and his colleagues at the Continental Congress, the Declaration retains in its sound logic and forceful, direct style the unmistakable qualities of Jefferson's prose.

Reflecting on What You Know

In your mind, what is the meaning of democracy? Where do your ideas about democracy come from?

When in the course of human events, it becomes necessary for one people to dissolve the political bands which have connected them with another, and to assume among the Powers of the earth, the separate and equal station to which the Laws of Nature and of Nature's God entitle them, a decent respect to the opinions of mankind requires that they should declare the causes which impel them to the separation. 1

We hold these truths to be self-evident, that all men are created equal, that they are endowed by their Creator with certain unalienable Rights, that among these are Life, Liberty and the pursuit of Happiness. That to secure these rights, Governments are instituted among 2

Men deriving their just powers from the consent of the governed. That whenever any Form of Government becomes destructive of these ends, it is the Right of the People to alter or to abolish it, and to institute new Government, laying its foundation on such principles and organizing its powers in such form, as to them shall seem most likely to effect their Safety and Happiness. Prudence, indeed, will dictate that Governments long established should not be changed for light and transient[1] causes; and accordingly all experience hath shown, that mankind are more disposed to suffer, while evils are sufferable, than to right themselves by abolishing the forms to which they are accustomed. But when a long train of abuses and usurpations pursuing invariably the same Object evinces a design to reduce them under absolute Despotism, it is their right, it is their duty, to throw off such government, and to provide new Guards for their future security. Such has been the patient sufferance of these Colonies; and such is now the necessity which constrains them to alter their former Systems of Government. The history of the present King of Great Britain[2] is a history of repeated injuries and usurpations, all having in direct object the establishment of an absolute Tyranny over these States. To prove this, let Facts be submitted to a candid world.

He has refused his Assent to Laws, the most wholesome and necessary for the public good. 3

He has forbidden his Governors to pass Laws of immediate and pressing importance, unless suspended in their operation till his Assent should be obtained; and when so suspended, he has utterly neglected to attend to them. 4

He has refused to pass other Laws for the accommodation of large districts of people, unless those people would relinquish the right of Representation in the Legislature, a right inestimable to them and formidable to tyrants only. 5

He has called together legislative bodies at places unusual, uncomfortable, and distant from the depository of their Public Records, for the sole purpose of fatiguing them into compliance with his measures. 6

He has dissolved Representative Houses repeatedly, for opposing with manly firmness his invasions on the rights of the people. 7

He has refused for a long time, after such dissolutions, to cause others to be elected; whereby the Legislative Powers, incapable of 8

[1]*transient:* not lasting; not permanent.

[2]*King of Great Britain:* King George III (1738–1820), who ruled the British Empire from 1760 to 1820.

Annihilation, have returned to the People at large for their exercise; the State remaining in the mean time exposed to all the dangers of invasion from without, and convulsions within.

He has endeavoured to prevent the population of these States; for that purpose obstructing the Laws of Naturalization of Foreigners; refusing to pass others to encourage their migration hither, and raising the conditions of new Appropriations of Lands. 9

He has obstructed the Administration of Justice, by refusing his Assent to Laws for establishing Judiciary Powers. 10

He has made Judges dependent on his Will alone, for the tenure of their offices, and the amount and payment of their salaries. 11

He has erected a multitude of New Offices, and sent hither swarms of Officers to harass our People, and eat out their substance. 12

He has kept among us, in time of peace, Standing Armies without the Consent of our Legislature. 13

He has affected to render the Military independent of and superior to the Civil Power. 14

He has combined with others to subject us to jurisdictions foreign to our constitution, and unacknowledged by our laws; giving his Assent to their acts of pretended Legislation: 15

For quartering large bodies of armed troops among us: 16

For protecting them, by a mock Trial, from Punishment for any Murders which they should commit on the Inhabitants of these States: 17

For cutting off our Trade with all parts of the world: 18

For imposing Taxes on us without our Consent: 19

For depriving us in many cases, of the benefits of Trial by Jury: 20

For transporting us beyond Seas to be tried for pretended offenses: 21

For abolishing the free System of English Laws in a Neighbouring Province, establishing therein an Arbitrary government, and enlarging its boundaries so as to render it at once an example and fit instrument for introducing the same absolute rule into these Colonies: 22

For taking away our Charters, abolishing our most valuable Laws, and altering fundamentally the Forms of our Governments: 23

For suspending our own Legislatures, and declaring themselves invested with Power to legislate for us in all cases whatsoever. 24

He has abdicated Government here, by declaring us out of his Protection and waging War against us. 25

He has plundered our seas, ravaged our Coasts, burnt our towns and destroyed the Lives of our people. 26

He is at this time transporting large Armies of foreign Mercenaries to compleat works of death, desolation and tyranny, already begun 27 with circumstances of Cruelty & perfidy[3] scarcely paralleled in the most barbarous ages, and totally unworthy the Head of a civilized nation.

He has constrained our fellow Citizens taken Captive on the high Seas to bear Arms against their Country, to become the executioners of their friends and Brethren, or to fall themselves by their Hands. 28

He has excited domestic insurrections amongst us, and has endeavoured to bring on the inhabitants of our frontiers, the merciless Indian Savages, whose known rule of warfare is an undistinguished destruction of all ages, sexes and conditions. 29

In every stage of these Oppressions We Have Petitioned for Redress in the most humble terms: Our repeated petitions have been answered only by repeated injury. A Prince, whose character is thus marked by every act which may define a Tyrant, is unfit to be the ruler of a free People. 30

Nor have We been wanting in attention to our British brethren. We have warned them from time to time of attempts by their legislature to extend an unwarrantable jurisdiction over us. We have reminded them of the circumstances of our emigration and settlement here. We have appealed to their native justice and magnanimity[4] and we have conjured them by the ties of our common kindred to disavow these usurpations, which would inevitably interrupt our connections and correspondence. They too have been deaf to the voice of justice and of consanguinity. We must, therefore, acquiesce[5] in the necessity, which denounces our Separation, and hold them, as we hold the rest of mankind, Enemies in War, in Peace Friends. 31

We, therefore, the Representatives of the United States of America, in General Congress, Assembled, appealing to the Supreme Judge of the world for the rectitude of our intentions, do, in the Name, and by Authority of the good People of these Colonies, solemnly publish and declare, That these United Colonies are, and of Right ought to be Free and Independent States; that they are Absolved from all Allegiance to the British Crown, and that all political connection between them and the State of Great Britain, is and ought to be totally dissolved; and that as Free and Independent States, they have full power to levy War, conclude Peace, contract Alliances, establish Commerce, and to do all other Acts and Things which Independent States may of right do. And for the support of this Declaration, with a firm reliance on the 32

---

[3]*perfidy*: disloyalty; treachery.
[4]*magnanimity:* quality of being calm, generous, upstanding.
[5]*acquiesce:* comply; accept.

protection of Divine Providence, we mutually pledge to each other our lives, our Fortunes and our sacred Honor.

Thinking Critically about This Reading

What, according to the Declaration of Independence, is the purpose of government?

Questions for Study and Discussion

1. In paragraph 2, Jefferson presents certain "self-evident" truths. What are these truths, and how are they related to his argument? Do you consider them self-evident?
2. The Declaration of Independence is a deductive argument; therefore, it can be presented in the form of a syllogism. (Glossary: **Syllogism**) Identify the major premise, the minor premise, and the conclusion of Jefferson's argument.
3. The list of charges against the king is given as evidence in support of Jefferson's minor premise. (Glossary: **Evidence**) Does Jefferson offer any evidence in support of his major premise?
4. How does Jefferson refute the possible charge that the colonists should have tried to solve their problems by less drastic means?
5. Where in the Declaration does Jefferson use parallel structure? (Glossary: **Parallelism**) What does he achieve by using it?
6. Although the basic structure of the Declaration reflects sound deductive reasoning, Jefferson's language, particularly when he lists the charges against the king, tends to be emotional. (Glossary: **Diction**) Identify as many examples of this emotional language as you can, and discuss possible reasons for why Jefferson uses this kind of language.

Classroom Activity Using Argument

Choose one of the following controversial subjects, and think about how you would write an argument for or against it. Write three sentences that summarize three important points, two based on logic and one based on persuasion/emotion. Then write one sentence that acknowledges the opposing point of view. For example, if you were to argue for stricter enforcement of a leash law and waste-pickup ordinance for dog owners in your town, you might write the following:

Logic	Dogs allowed to run free can be a menace to joggers and local wildlife.
Logic	Dog waste poses a health risk, particularly in areas where children play.
Emotion	How would you feel if you hit an unleashed dog with your car?
Counterargument	Dogs need fresh air and exercise, too.

Gun control
The effectiveness of standardized testing
Women in combat
Paying college athletes
Assisted suicide for the terminally ill
Government surveillance programs

Suggested Writing Assignments

1. The issue of human rights is often discussed. Review the arguments for and against the U.S. government's active and outspoken promotion of a human rights issue as reported in the press. Then write an argument of your own in favor of or opposed to a continued strong human rights policy on the part of U.S. governmental leaders.
2. Using one of the subjects listed below, develop a thesis, and then write an essay in which you argue in support of that thesis:

   Minimum wage
   Social Security
   Capital punishment
   Erosion of individual rights
   Welfare
   Separation of church and state
   First Amendment rights

The Case for Short Words

Richard Lederer

Courtesy of Richard Lederer

Born in 1938, Richard Lederer holds degrees from Haverford College, Harvard University, and the University of New Hampshire. He has been a prolific and popular writer about language and is the author of more than 40 books about language, history, and humor, including his best-selling *Anguished English* series. He frequently appears on radio as a commentator on language, and his column, "Lederer on Language," appears in newspapers and magazines throughout the United States. Dr. Lederer has been named International Punster of the Year and Toastmasters International's Golden Gavel winner.

In the following essay, taken from *The Miracle of Language* (1999), pay attention to the structure of his argument. He begins with a strong proposition and returns at the end to this proposition, which he expects might contradict what readers have assumed or have been taught about what makes good writing.

Reflecting on What You Know

We all carry with us a vocabulary of short, simple-looking words that possess a special personal meaning. For example, to some the word *rose* represents not just a flower but a whole array of gardens, ceremonies, and romantic occasions. What little words have special meaning for you? What images do they bring to mind?

When you speak and write, there is no law that says you have to use big words. Short words are as good as long ones, and short, old words—like *sun* and *grass* and *home*—are best of all. A lot of small words, more than you might think, can meet your needs with a strength, grace, and charm that large words do not have. 1

Big words can make the way dark for those who read what you write and hear what you say. Small words cast their clear light on big things—night and day, love and hate, war and peace, and life and death. Big words at times seem strange to the eye and the ear and the 2 mind and the heart. Small words are the ones we seem to have known from the time we were born, like the hearth fire that warms the home.

Short words are bright like sparks that glow in the night, prompt like the dawn that greets the day, sharp like the blade of a knife, hot like salt tears that scald the cheek, quick like moths that flit from flame to flame, and terse like the dart and sting of a bee. 3

Here is a sound rule: Use small, old words where you can. If a long word says just what you want to say, do not fear to use it. But know that our tongue is rich in crisp, brisk, swift, short words. Make them the spine and the heart of what you speak and write. Short words are like fast friends. They will not let you down. 4

The title of this [essay] and the four paragraphs that you have just read are wrought entirely of words of one syllable. In setting myself this task, I did not feel especially cabined, cribbed, or confined. In fact, the structure helped me to focus on the power of the message I was trying to put across. 5

One study shows that twenty words account for twenty-five percent of all spoken English words, and all twenty are monosyllabic. In order of frequency they are: *I, you, the, a, to, is, it, that, of, and, in, what, he, this, have, do, she, not, on,* and *they.* Other studies indicate that the fifty most common words in written English are each made of a single syllable. 6

For centuries our finest poets and orators have recognized and employed the power of small words to make a straight point between two minds. A great many of our proverbs punch home their points with pithy monosyllables: "Where there's a will, there's a way," "A stitch in time saves nine," "Spare the rod and spoil the child," "A bird in the hand is worth two in the bush." 7

Nobody used the short word more skillfully than William Shakespeare, whose dying King Lear laments: 8

And my poor fool is hang'd! No, no, no life!
Why should a dog, a horse, a rat have life,
And thou no breath at all? . . .
Do you see this? Look on her, look, her lips.
Look there, look there!

Shakespeare's contemporaries made the King James Bible a centerpiece of short words—"And God said, Let there be light: and there was light. And God saw the light, that it was good." The descendants of such mighty lines live on in the twentieth century. When asked to explain his policy to Parliament, Winston Churchill[1] responded with 9

[1]*Winston Churchill* (1874–1965): British orator, author, and statesman.

these ringing monosyllables: "I will say: it is to wage war, by sea, land, and air, with all our might and with all the strength that God can give us." In his "Death of the Hired Man" Robert Frost[2] observes that "Home is the place where, when you have to go there, / They have to take you in." And William H. Johnson[3] uses ten two-letter words to explain his secret of success: "If it is to be, / It is up to me."

You don't have to be a great author, statesman, or philosopher to 10
tap the energy and eloquence of small words. Each winter I ask my ninth graders at St. Paul's School to write a composition composed entirely of one-syllable words. My students greet my request with obligatory moans and groans, but, when they return to class with their essays, most feel that, with the pressure to produce high-sounding polysyllables relieved, they have created some of their most powerful and luminous prose. Here are submissions from two of my ninth graders:

> What can you say to a boy who has left home? You can say that he has done wrong, but he does not care. He has left home so that he will not have to deal with what you say. He wants to go as far as he can. He will do what he wants to do.
>
> This boy does not want to be forced to go to church, to comb his hair, or to be on time. A good time for this boy does not lie in your reach, for what you have he does not want. He dreams of ripped jeans, shorts with no starch, and old socks.
>
> So now this boy is on a bus to a place he dreams of, a place with no rules. This boy now walks a strange street, his long hair blown back by the wind. He wears no coat or tie, just jeans and an old shirt. He hates your world, and he has left it.
>
> –Charles Shaffer

> For a long time we cruised by the coast and at last came to a wide bay past the curve of a hill, at the end of which lay a small town. Our long boat ride at an end, we all stretched and stood up to watch as the boat nosed its way in.
>
> The town climbed up the hill that rose from the shore, a space in front of it left bare for the port. Each house was a clean white with sky blue or gray trim; in front of each one was a small yard, edged by a white stone wall strewn with green vines.
>
> As the town basked in the heat of noon, not a thing stirred in the streets or by the shore. The sun beat down on the sea, the land, and the back of our necks, so that, in spite of the breeze

[2] *Robert Frost* (1874–1963): American poet.

[3] *William H. Johnson* (1771–1834): associate justice of the U.S. Supreme Court, 1804–1834.

> that made the vines sway, we all wished we could hide from the glare in a cool, white house. But, as there was no one to help dock the boat, we had to stand and wait.
>
> At last the head of the crew leaped from the side and strode to a large house on the right. He shoved the door wide, poked his head through the gloom, and roared with a fierce voice. Five or six men came out, and soon the port was loud with the clank of chains and creak of planks as the men caught ropes thrown by the crew, pulled them taut, and tied them to posts. Then they set up a rough plank so we could cross from the deck to the shore. We all made for the large house while the crew watched, glad to be rid of us.
>
> –Celia Wren

You too can tap into the vitality and vigor of compact expression. Take a suggestion from the highway department. At the boundaries of your speech and prose place a sign that reads "Caution: Small Words at Work." 11

Thinking Critically about This Reading

In his opening paragraph, Lederer states that "short, old words—like *sun* and *grass* and *home*—are best of all." Does this claim surprise you by running counter to what we've always heard about "big words" and a large vocabulary?

Questions for Study and Discussion

1. How does Lederer support his argument? What types of evidence does he provide to support his claim that "short, old words . . . are best of all" (paragraph 1)? (Glossary: **Evidence**)
2. In this essay, written to encourage the use of short words, Lederer himself employs many polysyllabic words in paragraphs 5–11. What is his purpose in doing so? (Glossary: **Purpose**)
3. Lederer quotes a variety of passages to illustrate the effectiveness of short words. For example, he quotes from famous, universally familiar sources, such as Shakespeare and the King James Bible, as well as his own ninth-grade students. How does the variety of his illustrations serve to inform his readers? How does each example gain impact from the inclusion of the others and support his argument?

4. To make clear to the reader why short words are effective, Lederer relies heavily on metaphors and similes, especially in the first four paragraphs. (Glossary: **Figure of Speech**) Choose at least one metaphor and one simile from these paragraphs, and explain the comparison implicit in each.
5. In paragraph 10, Lederer refers to the relief his students feel when released from "the pressure to produce high-sounding polysyllables." Where does this pressure come from? How does it relate to the central purpose of this essay?
6. This essay has many striking sentences and passages consisting entirely of one-syllable words. Choose four of the single-sentence examples or a section of several sentences from one of the longer examples and rewrite them, using primarily words of two or more syllables. Notice how each revision differs from the original.

Classroom Activity Using Argument

Write a short argument essay that begins with an opposite proposition: "When you speak and write, there is no law that says you have to use small words." As you write, incorporate as many polysyllabic words as you can to support your claim. Then compare your brief essay with Lederer's "The Case for Short Words." Afterwards, consider which argument you find more convincing. Do you agree with Lederer that small words are more effective than big words? In your opinion, did this activity support or contradict his argument? To make the argument more effective when you explain your answer, consider which audiences might respond better to small words or polysyllabic words.

Suggested Writing Assignments

1. Follow the assignment Lederer gives his own students, and write a composition composed entirely of one-syllable words. Make your piece approximately the length of his student examples or of his own four-paragraph opening.
2. Write a persuasive essay attempting to convince readers to give up a widely held belief. Using Lederer's essay as a model, state your argument directly in the first paragraph, and use the final paragraph to reiterate the value of your proposition.

CONFLICT: USING LANGUAGE TO SEEK RESOLUTION

We have all seen how people use ethnic slurs, stereotypes, and profanity to talk about a so-called "problem" group or individual and how such language only fans the flames and makes the "problem" worse. The authors of the three essays in this casebook on conflict resolution are concerned with how language can both create conflict and help resolve it. Many conflicts can be positively addressed by examining how we articulate the problem and solution. Inevitably, understanding the conflict and coming to some kind of resolution will require changing the language we use to talk about it. For example, Germany is now called an "ally" and "friend," not an "enemy." Words change as conflicts shift or end.

Once started, however, conflicts seem to have a life of their own, and at the heart of every conflict is usually a disagreement or misunderstanding about how the parties use or interpret words. Hardly a day goes by that social media and news networks do not call out some celebrity, politician, diplomat, organization, or country for starting a fight or escalating one with some sloppy or insensitive use of language. Even on a personal level, we can find ourselves enmeshed in arguments because we express ourselves in a text or on social media before we think something through and end up using language carelessly. By analyzing conflicts that have happened in the past or that are currently unfolding, we can better understand how our words affect others and their words affect us.

Most people will agree that it seems easier to get into a conflict than it is to get out of one, resolve one, or even find some common ground on which to stand. The acts of apology and forgiving and the concept of dignity—and the language we use to convey an apology and a forgiving and to create or nurture dignity—are all important ingredients in any effort to resolve a conflict or restore justice. By including the readings in this cluster, our purpose is to help you think critically about and be sensitive to the language used in ongoing conflicts as well as the language being used to seek resolution so that you can function as a responsible citizen.

In "Independence," Donna Hicks illustrates her belief that independence is one of the essential elements of human dignity. When people or governments seek to dominate other people or countries, they take away their enemy's physical and psychological independence. The oppressed often feel intimidated, shamed, and humiliated—they are no longer in control of their own lives and identity. Hicks believes that when all parties in a conflict are encouraged to act on their own behalf, a pathway to peace is at least possible. In "Tarring Opponents as Extremists Really Can Work," Emily Badger enters the political arena and discusses how people and organizations use labels such as *socialist, right-winger, racist, radical, Christian fundamentalist, Islamic extremist,* and *high-booted feminist* to tarnish or call into question an opponent's positions, especially when American values are at issue. This tactic, she finds, is surprisingly more effective than one might expect. Finally, in "Adventures of the Dork Police," Cincinnati police officer Michael Gardner tells how he and his partner developed strategies to use when called to respond to domestic disputes. Gardner and his partner learned how using language creatively and being spontaneous and untraditional in critical situations often resulted in magical solutions to dangerous disputes.

Independence

Donna Hicks

Donna Hicks

Donna Hicks is an associate at the Weatherhead Center for International Affairs and speaker on topics of conflict resolution and human dignity. She holds a PhD in Educational Psychology from the University of Wisconsin and completed postdoctoral work in International Conflict Analysis. In 2006, Hicks was a cohost with Archbishop Desmond Tutu on *Facing the Truth*, a British Broadcasting Corporation (BBC) series that established dialogue between both sides of the Northern Ireland conflict. In a 2013 TEDx talk entitled "Declare Dignity," she lectured about an unspoken dialogue that occurs when people come together to resolve conflict—a dialogue that reveals the human need for dignity. Hicks's ideas about the role of dignity in conflict resolution have been featured on NPR, Fox News, and the BBC and in publications like *Psychology Today* and *Newsday*.

The following chapter was published in Hicks's best-selling book *Dignity: The Essential Role It Plays in Resolving Conflict* (2011). In this chapter, Hicks begins by writing that it is important to "encourage people to act on their own behalf so that they feel in control of their lives and experience a sense of hope and possibility." As you read, consider how the examples Hicks uses support this argument.

Reflecting on What You Know

Explain a situation when you felt you lost a sense of personal dignity, and then explain a situation when you were able to maintain your dignity. What factors were at play in each situation? How did the circumstances differ?

War is the inevitable consequence of choosing to resolve differences by force. Domination and control are the goals of war. Prisoners may be taken, and we all know that torture is not uncommon when they are questioned, even though international law forbids it. 1

At the end of a conflict-resolution workshop between warring parties held at Harvard, I had an opportunity to speak privately with one of the participants, someone who played a leadership role in his community, about the time he had spent in prison as a political prisoner. I wasn't planning to have an intimate conversation. We were seated next to one another at dinner and made small talk for quite a while. He asked me questions in an effort to get to know me, which doesn't happen often with influential people—they are usually busy telling you all about themselves. At one point, he jokingly mentioned his time in prison. 2

I was surprised to hear that he had been a prisoner and asked him what it was like. For a few seconds he studied my face. I am not sure what he was looking for, but after a short pause, he started to tell me stories about the day-to-day abuse by guards who were younger than his children and about being humiliated during interrogations. 3

One thing he told me will stay with me forever. I asked him how he reacted when he was being humiliated. He said: "From the time I was a little boy, my mother told me that I should never react when someone treats me badly. I should not lose my temper. She said it didn't matter whether someone hurt me with words or with a stick. Never let them know they are hurting you. And that wasn't all. She said I should always maintain a smile on my face because you never want to give the person the satisfaction of thinking he has injured you. *You are the one in control of your dignity, not the person hurting you.*" 4

The last sentence struck home. I added the emphasis mentally. I realized that what he said was true: ultimately we are the ones in control of our own dignity, even if we are being held against our will. My dinner partner's words reminded me of a quotation of Eleanor Roosevelt's: "No one can make you feel inferior without your permission." 5

At the end of our conversation, after listening to him intently for nearly an hour, I told him, "I don't know how you did it. I don't think I would have had the strength to endure what you did with such dignity." 6

He looked at me and began to cry. It was only for a second, but he cried. He quickly composed himself, momentarily put his hand over mine, and then turned to his aide, sitting on the other side of him, who was tapping him on the shoulder. "Mr. X-----------, the waiter wants to know what you would like for dessert: créme brûlée or chocolate gateau?" 7

This story is about the inhumanity of war and how it strips us of our freedom, but the impulse to control and dominate others is not confined to the battleground. The imperative of war—to use power to 8 deprive others of power—is all too often the imperative in our everyday lives as well.

Minority groups often find their freedom restricted by the imposition of the norms of the dominant culture, and that restriction has been enough to incite serious political unrest. Members of the minority group want to express themselves and their unique identity freely. Without coercion[1], it is difficult to repress a group's desire to speak their own language and practice their own religion—to choose how to live their lives in a way that gives them meaning. 9

We can see the impulse to restrict the freedom of others in most of our relationships, not just at the national level. Imagine the domineering husband who wants to control his wife, the overprotective mother who fails to see the importance of letting her daughter experience herself as an independent being with her own dreams to fulfill, or the executive who refuses to hear the concerns of employees out of fear of losing authority. 10

The real problem with domination is that it takes away a person's independence, thereby violating one of the essential elements of dignity. Like any other dignity violation, taking away a person's independence creates resentment. Resentment contaminates relationships, setting the stage for the transformation of the other into an enemy. In contrast, using power to empower others not only guarantees them their freedom and protects our own but is a step toward fulfilling our primal longing to be connected with others. 11

Thinking Critically about This Reading

Hicks writes, "The imperative of war—to use power to deprive others of power—is all too often the imperative in our everyday lives as well" (paragraph 8). Do you think that war and personal conflict are an apt comparison in Hicks's essay? Do you feel that individuals try to take power away from other individuals too often in everyday life? Explain your opinions.

Questions for Study and Discussion

1. After stating her thesis, Hicks provides a definition of war. (Glossary: **Thesis; Definition**) Would you define war the same

[1]*coercion*: the act of compelling or forcing someone to act or choose, often with force or threat.

way? How does Hicks's definition of war relate to her overall argument?

2. Hicks's *ethos* (Greek for "character") is established by her impressive biography, which includes work in top-tier academic institutions and the international exposure of her ideas. In paragraph 2, she also appeals to *ethos* when she introduces one of the participants in a conflict-resolution workshop. How does she appeal to *ethos* in her description of this person? Does this gesture help her argument? If so, how? If not, why not?
3. Consider the quotations from the conflict-resolution participant (4), Eleanor Roosevelt (5), and the participant's aide (7). What is the function of each quotation in Hicks's argument? How does the placement of these quotations contribute to her argument? (Glossary: **Organization**)
4. In paragraph 10, Hicks gives various examples of "the impulse to restrict the freedom of others." Does this paragraph fall into the trap of any logical fallacies? (Glossary: **Logical Fallacy**) If so, explain. If you do not think the paragraph contains any logical fallacies, talk about why it is effective.
5. In the last paragraph of her essay, how does Hicks use deductive reasoning? How does the conclusion of this chapter relate to Hicks's thesis?

Classroom Activity Using Argument

As a class, brainstorm a list of groups of people who may not be afforded the same dignity as others. Start by naming the groups that Hicks writes about. With a partner, select one of the groups listed on the board and brainstorm your experiences or observations regarding any members of this group. Then, using inductive reasoning, draw a conclusion about one effective way to afford this group of people more dignity.

Suggested Writing Assignments

1. In your opinion, what is the most important element in conflict resolution? Write an essay that argues why this element is most important. Hicks writes about dignity, but you might write about an element like cooperation, respect, loyalty, or

another that strikes you as crucial. Develop your argument with a clear thesis, strong supporting evidence, and good organization.

2. Hicks writes that "minority groups often find their freedom restricted by the imposition of the norms of the dominant culture" (9). Consider whether these norms are imposed on minority groups through social media. Write an essay arguing that social media challenges the ability of minority groups (or a particular group) to maintain their cultural dignity, that social media gives minority groups (or a particular group) new opportunities for maintaining cultural dignity, or some position in between.

Tarring Opponents as Extremists Really Can Work

Emily Badger

The Washington Post/Getty Images

Emily Badger is a journalist and essayist who was born in Chicago and currently works in San Francisco as a staff writer for the *Washington Post*. She holds a BS in journalism from Northwestern University and an MA in nonfiction writing from Johns Hopkins University. In her writing, she explores a variety of topics from urban planning and the environment to politics. Some of her article titles include "There Is No Such Thing as a City That Has Run Out of Room," "Debating the Local Food Movement," and "How Poverty Taxes the Brain."

In the following article, published in *Pacific Standard* in 2011, Badger argues that the rhetoric of extremism, which includes words such as *radical, extreme*, and *dogmatic*, can change people's minds about their own beliefs. As you read, pay attention to how Badger summarizes political science research published in the journal *Political Psychology* to support her controlling idea that calling the proponents of an ideology extreme can cause people to reject the entire ideology.

Reflecting on What You Know

Cognitive dissonance is a term in psychology used to describe the experience of having inconsistent beliefs, attitudes, and values. Think about an ideology or belief that you were sure of when you were a child but you are not as sure of now. What makes you less certain now? How do you deal with this uncertainty?

1 Back in 2002, when the male-only, members-only Augusta National golf club was picked to host the Masters Tournament, advocates of equality for women were taken aback. They wanted the tournament moved or the storied golf club opened to women. And their cause

resonated with many Americans in an age when the public supports little outright gender discrimination.

The campaign ran into a hitch, though: for many people, it became synonymous with Martha Burk, a feminist leader whose name frequently appeared in the national press alongside words like "radical," "extreme," and "dogmatic." 2

That story is a classic example of a tactic prevalent in politics. Tar a policy's proponents as "extreme," and maybe the policy will start to look that way, too. Political strategists clearly bank on this idea. And new political science research reveals that it works on many of us. 3

Researchers Thomas Nelson, Gregory Gwiasda, and Joseph Lyons studied the strategy in a paper published in the journal *Political Psychology*. To understand their findings, it's helpful to view political disputes—even the Augusta National story—as a clash of conflicting values, in this case gender equality and the rights of private organizations to determine their own rules. 4

Most values are generally thought to be positive, although people may rank them with different priorities. Most of us are on the same page about freedom, security, equality, and even the environment. No one *dislikes* those things. 5

"We think of [values] as kind of rules that can never be violated, sacred rules that must be protected," Nelson said. "The problem, of course, is you can't have everything. Sooner or later those things are going to come into conflict. This happens in our everyday lives." 6

And it happens constantly in politics. 7

When two of these values come into conflict—in, say, a policy question pitting national security against personal liberties—strategists must figure out how to advocate one at the expense of the other. No one wants to go on record attacking the value of security, or liberty. But you can do the next best thing: attack the people standing near it. 8

Nelson offers this example: "Everybody loves national parks, everybody loves the environment, nobody wants to be perceived as anti-environment. So if you are, say, the snowmobile manufacturer, and you want to push for greater access to public land for snowmobiles, you can't say, 'Well the environment is stupid, nobody cares about the environment. The only thing that's important is riding a snowmobile.'" 9

You could, however, say, "Sporting outdoorsmen may not get to enjoy our national parks this winter because radical environmentalists care more about owls than the local economy." 10

Such rhetoric helps ambivalent voters find their way out of a conflict between competing values. 11

In their study, the researchers had undergraduate students read and respond to an account of the Augusta National dispute with three small changes: one referred to critics of the policy as "people" and "citizens;" another as "radical feminists," "militant feminists" and "extremists"; and the third with extended descriptions of the type of world such radical feminists advocate (one with coed locker rooms!). The policy itself remained constant as these descriptions changed. As a result, the students exposed to the extremist language were less likely to support moving the tournament or welcoming female members to the club—even though a self-assessment of their values would suggest that they might. 12

The researchers performed similar experiments with opinion pieces and blog posts about environmental issues and immigration. 13

Most surprising to them was their discovery that sometimes the label itself is enough. Sometimes, simply calling advocates "feminists" or "environmentalists" is sufficient to tap into extremist associations people already have about those groups (perhaps the same negative associations that underlie the odd phenomenon that many people who care about the environment and gender equality don't want to be called "environmentalists" or "feminists"). Other times, it's apparently necessary to dress up that label, maybe "wild-eyed radical feminists," or even "extreme feminists who would go so far as to advocate unisex toilets." 14

The authors don't know where that line is drawn. They also don't know what distinguishes the people unfazed by this trick from those who are persuaded by it. In their studies, only some of the students were lulled by extremist labels into opposing policies that otherwise align with their values. 15

Perhaps other voters know the tactic when they see it, or they've seen it so many times that extremist labels themselves become off-putting (Nelson calls this the "tactic tactic," calling out an opponent for using just such a tactic). 16

"For a lot of people, that does raise a red flag. This looks like a last desperate measure of somebody who doesn't have anything better to say," he said. "But what distinguishes those people from others who are susceptible to it?" 17

Thinking Critically about This Reading

By using the word *tar,* Badger makes a historical allusion to tarring and feathering, a form of torture and humiliation in which someone was covered first in tar and then in feathers. (Glossary: **Allusion**) What does it mean to "tar a policy's proponents" (paragraph 3)? Does Badger's allusion help her argument? Why or why not?

Questions for Study and Discussion

1. Badger begins her article with an anecdote about the Augusta National golf club. What is the "hitch" that the golf club ran into? Why does Badger choose to explain that "hitch" in her second paragraph rather than making the entire anecdote one paragraph?
2. What is Badger's thesis, located in the third paragraph of this essay? (Glossary: **Thesis**) Why does she wait until the third paragraph to directly state her thesis?
3. Badger writes that the rhetoric of extremism "helps ambivalent voters find their way out of a conflict between competing values" (11). What does she mean by this statement? When you are writing an essay, what tactics have you used or might you use to help convince an ambivalent audience of your ideas? (Glossary: **Audience**)
4. Badger writes that "sometimes, simply calling advocates 'feminists' or 'environmentalists' is sufficient to tap into extremist associations people already have about those groups" (14). Do you have extremist associations with labels such as "feminist" or "environmentalist"? Could you be convinced to reject an ideology if you felt that there were extremists associated with that ideology?
5. The author's main example is a summary of the research of Nelson, Gwiasda, and Lyons, the political science researchers mentioned at the start of the essay. Toward the end of her essay, she writes that these authors "don't know what distinguishes the people unfazed by [the trick of tarring proponents of an ideology to make it look extreme] from those who are persuaded by it" (15). Does this statement undermine the *ethos* (Greek for "character"), or credibility, of Badger's sources? Why or why not?

6. How does Emily Badger conclude her essay? Is her conclusion forceful enough?

Classroom Activity Using Argument

Language can be accurate, or it can be manipulative. It's all in how you label it. Whether you consider your classroom state-of-the-art or not, imagine that you are trying to argue the following point:

> This classroom needs to be updated for the twenty-first century.

Label the items in the classroom using sticky notes: "broken desk," "malfunctioning computer," and so on. Take a look at all of the sticky notes and write the best label in your notebook.

Now, label the classroom to argue this thesis:

> This classroom is the model of a superb twenty-first-century educational space.

Take a look at all of the sticky notes and write the best label in your notebook.

When you are done with the second activity, write down which thesis statement you think is more accurate for your classroom. Consider whether readers might be convinced otherwise if they read an essay that used the labels for the other thesis statement without seeing the classroom for themselves. How would you address their concerns about the "extreme" nature of the classroom?

Suggested Writing Assignments

1. Write an essay in which you argue that there is a particularly effective strategy for resolving cognitive dissonance. What is that strategy? Why should your readers pay attention to it? Use inductive reasoning in your argument.
2. Think about a label for people that you feel should either be changed or removed from common use. Write an essay persuading the reader about why that label should be modified or eliminated. Make sure that you use *logos* or *pathos* in your essay.
3. Write a counterargument to Emily Badger's essay entitled "Tarring Opponents as Extremists Really Doesn't Work." Refute some of Badger's evidence to build your argument.

Adventures of the Dork Police

Michael Gardner

Mark Andreas

Michael Gardner is a retired police officer from the Cincinnati Police Department and an innovator in the use of verbal persuasion tactics rather than physical force in conflict resolution. In 1981, he and his wife Debbie, a retired sheriff, founded the Survive Institute, which helps companies, schools, and communities learn empowering self-defense strategies. Gardner and his wife have written a book called *Raising Kids That Can Protect Themselves* (2004).

The following excerpt was published in *Sweet Fruit from the Bitter Tree: 61 Stories of Creative Compassionate Ways Out of Conflict*, edited by Mark Andreas (2011). In this excerpt, Gardner explores how disputes can be solved through "visual and verbal persuasion." As you read, consider the function of anecdotes in the development of Gardner's argument and whether you find these stories compelling.

Reflecting on What You Know

Reflect on a time when you or someone you know took a nontraditional approach to a situation and still achieved a good result. Why did your approach lead to this desirable outcome? What are the benefits or drawbacks to taking a nontraditional approach?

A lot of the calls we got on night shift were domestic violence runs. Cops hate making domestic runs because they're so dangerous, but for research purposes my partner and I asked other cops, "Do you mind if we start taking over your domestic runs so we can experiment with defusing hostile situations?" Of course we got no objections. 1

Traditionally, police officers are limited to only four choices for controlling situations—visual and verbal persuasion, chemical irritant, impact weapon, and deadly force. In training, most emphasis 2 was on weaponry defense, without nearly enough on visual and verbal defense. My partner and I saw the need to stretch our flexibility to hundreds of choices in this uncharted territory.

The traditional approach in police work for a domestic run was to show up at an apartment and bang on the door using a raid-type knock with the police night stick, BAM BAM BAM BAM! I even hate it when the UPS or mail carrier bangs on my door to give me something I *want,* so I tried to imagine how someone already in emotional distress would be angered even more with a raid-type bang on their door. To be less intrusive and confrontational we started showing up and doing the "shave and haircut" knock, a very light "Rap ta-ta tap tap, tap tap." Even if the people inside didn't catch on to the jingle, it was a less invasive knock, and its association with a harmless advertisement was more to relax *us* than the people inside. It kept us at a condition orange—alert, but not the red of alarmed. We would even joke sometimes going into an apartment, "Hey let's be condition purple." What we were really saying was, "Hey let's not get red, because if we go in there red, we're going to have a fight." 3

The usual question police were trained to ask when entering a home was, "What's the problem here?" Well, if you enter after a loud raid-type knock and ask them, "What's the problem here?" they'll give you a problem, usually several. They may tell you their problems from twenty years ago. 4

Instead we'd ask something like, "What have you decided to do between the time you called us and the time we got here?" That put them in solution mode. Other times we'd ask people to step out into the hallway so they wouldn't feel the need to defend their turf. We also purposely wore our hats when we approached, so when we did enter their house or apartment we could take them off as a sign of respect. 5

My partner and I became known to our fellow officers as the Dork Police, because no one knew what crazy thing we were going to do next. They were equally amazed at our success in non-violent control of tense situations. We experimented daily with ways of startling subjects into confusion in order to interrupt their dangerous mental patterns and provide a space for something more positive. 6

For example, we would sometimes approach potentially dangerous domestic disputes with our jackets purposely buttoned improperly, or with our caps pulled down so our ears stuck out. Other times we'd say "no" while nodding our heads up and down. Unless the combatants were too intoxicated or high to observe this odd behavior, they stopped, 7 at least temporarily. They couldn't help responding to what they saw. Then it was hard for them to pick up their fight where they had left off.

Sometimes we'd walk into a shouting match between a couple, and we'd just run over and switch the channel on the TV set. If one of them said, "Hey, what the hell are you doing?" We'd say cheerfully, "Hey, you're not going to listen to us anyway, so we're going to watch some TV." 8

All we were trying to do was get them to refocus out of their anger and onto something else. We would do anything to create a change. Once that was accomplished, we'd offer suggestions for where couples could go for longer-term help. 9

Using humor was particularly useful when performing routine, uncomfortable tasks like patting down or frisking a suspect. While maintaining physical control, we would like to say, "You don't have any hand grenades, swords, or bazookas hidden on you, do you?" Subjects generally laughed it off. Now and then, one would disclose that he had a knife or razor. 10

When couples were screaming at each other we'd start sniffing and shouting out. "Oh, do you smell gas? Where's your stove? There must be a burner on!" While the fight was temporarily stopped, my partner and I would go to the kitchen and pretend to check the stove for gas leaks. After a few minutes of sniffing the stove and kitchen area, we would advise the people that everything was OK, then ask "What else can we help you with?" The response was amazing. Often they said, "Nothing, officer . . ." If the argument did begin again, all my partner and I had to do was to sniff with a concerned look on our faces. With this pattern interruption, the subjects' personal fighting became secondary to the threat of a gas explosion in their home. They may even start getting an unconscious connection of, *Every time I start getting nasty there's danger, maybe I should try something else.* 11

Other times, we would enter a residence and be greeted by someone standing in a fighting position and shouting, "You two think you can take me? Come on!" We would mirror his stance, but hold our palms up instead of making fists, saying, "No way. We heard how tough you are. We can't beat you, we'd have to call ten more guys in here." If that statement had any effect, we would follow up with, "Why don't we talk first, then you can kick our butts." On several occasions the potentially violent subject changed his mind. And if he didn't respond to our initial statement, that signaled us to try something else. Initially it was hard for us to give this kind of "pull" 12 statement when a violent subject "pushed" us verbally. We instinctively wanted to "push" back with an "attack" statement. Yet the patience of our "pull" statement always minimized the force of our arrest.

One time we had a husband and wife close to killing each other. They were shouting countless obscenities at each other, and their hand gestures were disjointed and out of sync with the tone and tempo of their verbal language. I remembered the metaphor of an orchestra conductor—when people talk in rhythm with their gestures it tends to be good venting; letting their anger come out verbally rather than physically. But when their gestures are short, choppy, stab-like motions, disconnected from their language, it is likely that they're about to explode physically. This couple was actually making verbal threats like, "I'm going to kill you, you son of a bitch!" "You're dead, mother-fucker!" 13

In a flash I said, "In all my years of police work, I've never seen somebody able to express their anger like you can! I appreciate that, because sometimes things really piss me off and I wish I could express my anger like you are!" I was empathizing with them to bring their attention to me and to the importance of what they were feeling, and away from a fight. 14

Another time we came into an argument with the woman yelling and screaming at her husband. I said to her, "I bet you don't talk to the mailman this way, do you?" 15

"What? Of course not!" 16

"And I bet you don't talk to your car mechanic that way, do you?" 17

"No, of course not!" 18

"Well the reason you talk to your husband like that is obviously because you care a whole lot more about what he says than what the mailman or the mechanic says." 19

"Yeah, well I guess so." 20

My questions first took her attention away from her emotions and what she was mad about. Then I offered her a new meaning for her outburst—it was because she *cared* about her husband. After about 15–20 minutes of me telling them how frustrated I was at not being able to express my feelings the way they could, they started counseling me. Soon it was apparent by the way they were sitting next to each other and looking at each other that they were eager to be left alone. I think we reframed their anger toward each other to such an extent that they wanted us gone so they could make up! 21

Once we came into a heated dispute and I said to the man, "Hey, you don't work for the city, do you?" 22

"NO!" 23

"That car out there with the lights on, that's not your car, is it?" 24

"NO!" 25

"You don't want us here, do you?" 26

"NO!" 27

"You'll be happy when we leave here, won't you?" 28

"F--K yeah!" 29

This way I matched him and let him express himself. He was in 30 the mood to disagree, so I started with questions all of which let him say "No." Then I shifted to a "Yes" question, leading him to a more positive place and getting his explicit agreement that when we left he'd be happy. It might sound like a small thing, but it made a huge difference. Now we were on the same page and he was more relaxed—no longer disagreeing with everything we said.

We'd also do a thing I called "word salad." I never did it in a dis- 31 respectful way, but when people get violent they're behaving worse than childish. Sometimes I'd say, "What you're saying here sounds like a phonological ambiguity to me, so rather than jeopardize any other litigation circumstances why don't you just take a walk and let things cool off?"

They got so confused by the first part of my sentence, they would 32 jump on the first thing that made sense, usually responding. "I'll just take a walk and cool off a bit."

I'd say, "Great, I appreciate that." 33

Often we would use many of these different tactics one after the 34 other, until we found what worked. By systematically attempting to stop violence by using our appearance or words, we put ourselves in a position where we would be much more justified—both emotionally and legally—if we ended up having to resort to a higher degree of force. Yet in all these experiments on permanent night shift, and during my thirty-year police career, I never fired my gun. I had to use mace on a person only once, simply because the man was so intoxicated I couldn't communicate with him. We had tried many things, but he just wasn't there because of the alcohol. He had a little paring knife that he wouldn't drop. Technically I could have shot him, but I had been relaxed and aware enough to keep a table between us, so I was able to subdue him with the mace. As amazing as these techniques were for defusing violence in the moment, our biggest success was that we stopped getting return calls from the places we visited. Before we started using these techniques, it was common to get calls from the same location two or three times a night. Sometimes my partner and I would spend 15 or 30 minutes out on a call, and we'd get in trouble from our supervisor because he wanted us in and out. If they didn't straighten up right away he wanted us to simply arrest them. But we knew we could save time in the long run by coming to a peaceful resolution. . . .

35 Unfortunately, it's very difficult to measure what *doesn't* happen, but I can say confidently that I was involved in hundreds of peaceful resolutions that would have ended up in arrests or fights had we used traditional police procedure. Ever since my eyes were opened to what is possible, I've been studying and researching how police officers everywhere can increase their choices by using visual and verbal persuasion to prevent, or at least minimize, their use of force in violent situations. Believe me, police officers all over this country need new tools for accomplishing their duties. They are hungry for positive education that will enhance their control over themselves and others. No group of professionals needs flexibility more than police officers.

Thinking Critically about This Reading

Gardner describes the goal of his persuasion tactics when he states, "All we were trying to do was get them to refocus out of their anger and onto something else" (paragraph 9). What does he mean by this? What are the potential merits or faults of this goal?

Questions for Study and Discussion

1. Gardner sets up his argument by describing the traditional approach that most police officers must take when they encounter conflict. What are the four choices usually available to police officers? Why did Gardner decide to describe these first? (Glossary: **Beginnings and Endings**)
2. Name one reason that the traditional approaches that police officers take may not work, according to Gardner.
3. Why do you think Gardner tells specific stories about some situations and generalizes other situations? Does this strategy make his argument more effective or not? Explain.
4. When speaking about frisking a suspect, Gardner writes "humor was particularly useful" (10). Identify another situation

in which Gardner reports using humor to resolve conflict, and comment on the sentence-level tactics that Gardner uses to make the situation funny—or to make his writing funny.

5. Gardner writes that when threatened he and his partner "instinctively wanted to 'push' back with an 'attack' statement. Yet the patience of our 'pull' statement always minimized the force of our arrest" (12). Come up with a definition of a "push" statement and a "pull" statement. What would be the equivalent of a "push" statement and a "pull" statement in an argument essay?
6. Gardner's essay alludes to but does not directly describe situations in which Gardner's persuasion tactics did not work. Why does Gardner make the decision not to go into depth about such moments?

Classroom Activity Using Argument

In groups of three or four people, choose a conflict that one of you is experiencing or has recently experienced and that you are willing to share with your group members and later with the full class. If you do not have an example, type "common conflicts" into any search engine for inspiration. After explaining the conflict and discussing how or if you resolved it, come up with alternate solutions. Then, devise and agree on an approach to conflict resolution that does the following:

- Uses *logos* (Greek for "word," referring to logic)
- Uses *pathos* (Greek for "emotion")
- Involves a physical or nonverbal response
- Is creative and unexpected (you may add visual or verbal persuasion tactics like humor)

Present the conflict and any one of your approaches to resolution to the class. If there is time, the class will discuss one potential benefit and one potential drawback of your group's approach.

Suggested Writing Assignments

1. Write an essay that argues for an innovative strategy to resolve a particular type of conflict. Describe the type of conflict clearly with an appropriate level of detail, and build your

argument by using at least two personal anecdotes. (Glossary: **Details; Anecdotes**)

2. The heavily reported police shootings of black men and boys such as Philando Castile, Alton Sterling, Tamir Rice, and Trayvon Martin make Gardner's ideas important to consider and relevant to current social and political movements. Look up the events associated with one of these shootings and write an essay arguing for a different way or ways that the conflict could have been handled. Apply at least one idea from "Adventures of the Dork Police" in your essay.

CRIME: FINDING AN EFFECTIVE PUNISHMENT

The authors of the three essays in this mini-casebook on punishment are concerned with the role that shame and guilt should play, if any, in discouraging nonviolent crimes. Their interest in this topic is instigated by several recent trends in our society, namely public-shaming sentences that have been imposed by judges and the emergence of social media, which has allowed the public to anonymously engage in the public humiliation of offenders as a kind of hoped-for retribution. Oddly enough, both these attempts at justice fail to consider the unintended negative consequences of such actions.

Although recent judicial practices and a social environment fashioned by technological innovation have put a new face on shaming, the practice is nothing new. Shaming lies at the heart of one of our most artistically brilliant and psychologically complicated classical novels, *The Scarlet Letter* by Nathaniel Hawthorne. Written in the nineteenth century but set in a seventeenth-century Puritan New England village, the novel examines the life of young Hester Prynne, who has borne a child out of wedlock and is punished by being made to wear an elaborately embroidered red letter A on the bosom of her dress as an ever-present sign of her crime and humiliation, or so it is intended. How all this plays out is another matter. Shame and guilt and the public's need for retribution are ageless impulses and need to be recognized and tended to, if not always resolved.

June Tangney in "Condemn the Crime, Not the Person" emphasizes the need to understand the difference between shame and guilt and what contemporary research reveals about the way each emotion plays out in the public arena of punishment. Dan M. Kahan, a prominent professor of law, advocates in "Shame Is Worth a Try" that we not reject using shame in our judicial practices, as has been urged, but that we use it wisely and appropriately as a low-cost form of punishment. Finally, student writer Libby Marlowe considers Tangney's and Kahan's arguments in the context of a new form of shaming on social media, and she focuses on the negative effects shaming can have on those who perpetrate it. In sum, these essays provide ideas to ponder and material to substantiate our own views about how best to make the punishment fit the crime.

Condemn the Crime, Not the Person

June Tangney

Psychology educator and researcher June Tangney was born in Buffalo, New York, in 1958. After graduating from the State University of New York at Buffalo in 1979, she attended the University of California–Los Angeles, where she earned a master's degree in 1981 and a doctorate in 1985. Tangney taught briefly at Bryn Mawr College and held a research position at the Regional Center for Infants and Young Children in Rockville, Maryland. Since 1988 she has been a professor of psychology at George Mason University, where she was recognized with a Teaching Excellence Award. She is the coauthor of five books—*Self-Conscious Emotions: The Psychology of Shame, Guilt, Embarrassment, and Pride* (1995), with Kurt W. Fisher; *Shame and Guilt* (2002), with Rhonda L. Dearing; *Handbook of Self and Identity* (2005), with Mark R. Leary; *Social Psychological Foundations of Clinical Psychology* (2010), with James E. Maddux; and *Shame in the Therapy Hour* (2011), with Rhonda L. Dearing—and is an associate editor of the journal *Self and Identity*.

In the following essay, first published in the *Boston Globe* on August 5, 2001, Tangney argues against the use of public humiliation as punishment. She bases her position on recent scientific evidence, much of which comes from her own work on shame and guilt.

Reflecting on What You Know

For you, what is the difference between *shame* and *guilt*? Provide an example from your own experience to illustrate your understanding of each concept.

As the costs of incarceration mount and evidence of its failure as a deterrent grows, judges understandably have begun to search for creative alternatives to traditional sentences. One recent trend is the 1 use of "shaming" sentences—sanctions explicitly designed to induce feelings of shame.

Judges across the country are sentencing offenders to parade around in public carrying signs broadcasting their crimes, to post signs on their front lawns warning neighbors of their vices, and to display "drunk driver" bumper stickers on their cars. 2

A number of social commentators have urged America to embrace public shaming and stigmatization as cheaper and effective alternatives for curbing a broad range of nonviolent crimes. Punishments aimed at public humiliation certainly appeal to our sense of moral righteousness. They do indeed appear fiscally attractive when contrasted with the escalating costs of incarceration. 3

But recent scientific evidence suggests that such attempts at social control are misguided. Rather than fostering constructive change, shame often makes a bad situation worse. 4

The crux[1] of the matter lies in the distinction between shame and guilt. Recent research has shown that shame and guilt are distinct emotions with very different implications for subsequent moral and interpersonal behavior. Feelings of shame involve a painful focus on the self—the humiliating sense that "I am a bad person." 5

Such humiliation is typically accompanied by a sense of shrinking, of being small, worthless, and powerless, and by a sense of being exposed. Ironically, research has shown that such painful and debilitating feelings of shame do not motivate constructive changes in behavior. 6

Shamed individuals are no less likely to repeat their transgressions (often more so), and they are no more likely to attempt reparation[2] (often less so). Instead, because shame is so intolerable, people in the midst of the experience often resort to any one of a number of defensive tactics. 7

They may seek to hide or escape the shameful feeling, denying responsibility. They may seek to shift the blame outside, holding others responsible for their dilemma. And not infrequently, they become irrationally angry with others, sometimes resorting to overtly aggressive and destructive actions. In short, shame serves to escalate the very destructive patterns of behavior we aim to curb. 8

Contrast this with feelings of guilt which involve a focus on a specific behavior—the sense that "I did a bad thing" rather than "I am a bad person." 9

[1]*crux:* the essential or deciding point.

[2]*reparation:* a making of amends; repayment.

Feelings of guilt involve a sense of tension, remorse, and regret 10
over the "bad thing done."

Research has shown that this sense of tension and regret typically 11
motivates reparative action (confessing, apologizing, or somehow repairing the damage done) without engendering[3] all the defensive and retaliative responses that are the hallmark of shame.

Most important, feelings of guilt are much more likely to foster 12
constructive changes in future behavior because what is at issue is not a bad, defective self, but a bad, defective behavior. And, as anyone knows, it is easier to change a bad behavior (drunken driving, slumlording, thievery) than to change a bad, defective self.

How can we foster constructive feelings of guilt among America's 13
offenders? Well, one way is to force offenders to focus on the negative consequences of their behavior, particularly on the painful negative consequences for others.

Community service sentences can do much to promote construc- 14
tive guilt when they are tailored to the nature of the crime. What is needed are imposed activities that underscore the tangible destruction caused by the offense and that provide a path to redemption by ameliorating[4] similar human misery.

Drunk drivers, for example, could be sentenced to help clear sites 15
of road accidents and to assist with campaigns to reduce drunken driving. Slumlords could be sentenced to assist with nuts and bolts repairs in low-income housing units. In this way, offenders are forced to see, first-hand, the potential or actual destructiveness of their infractions and they become actively involved in constructive solutions.

Some critics have rejected community service as an alternative to 16
incarceration, suggesting that such community-based sentences somehow cheapen an otherwise honorable volunteer activity while at the same time not adequately underscoring the criminal's disgrace.

Scientific research, however, clearly indicates that public shaming 17
and humiliation is not the path of choice. Such efforts are doomed to provoke all sorts of unintended negative consequences.

In contrast, thoughtfully constructed guilt-oriented community 18
service sentences are more likely to foster changes in offenders' future behaviors, while contributing to the larger societal good. My guess is that any honorable community service volunteer would welcome such constructive changes.

---

[3]*engendering:* causing or producing.

[4]*ameliorating:* improving or making better.

Thinking Critically about This Reading

Tangney states, "A number of social commentators have urged America to embrace public shaming and stigmatization as cheaper and effective alternatives for curbing a broad range of nonviolent crimes" (paragraph 3). What evidence does she present to counter these arguments?

Questions for Study and Discussion

1. What is a "shaming" sentence (1)? According to Tangney, why do judges use such sentences in place of more traditional ones?
2. What is Tangney's position on using sentences intended to shame offenders? Briefly state her thesis in your own words. (Glossary: **Thesis**)
3. What for Tangney is the key difference between shame and guilt? Why does she believe that guilt works better than shame as a form of punishment?
4. Paragraph 13 begins with a rhetorical question: "How can we foster constructive feelings of guilt among America's offenders?" (Glossary: **Rhetorical Question**) How does Tangney answer this question? What suggestions would you add to her solution?
5. How does Tangney counter the critics of community service? Do you find her counterarguments convincing? Why or why not?

Classroom Activity Using Argument

The effectiveness of a writer's argument depends in large part on the writer's awareness of audience. For example, a writer arguing that there is too much violence portrayed on television might present different kinds of evidence, reasoning, and diction for different audiences, such as parents, lawmakers, or television producers and writers.

Review several of the argument essays in this chapter. In your opinion, for what primary audience is each essay intended? List the evidence you found in each essay that helped you determine your answer. (Glossary: **Evidence**)

Suggested Writing Assignments

1. Write an essay in which you tell the story of a childhood punishment that you received or witnessed. (Glossary: **Narration**) How did you feel about the punishment? Was it justified? Appropriate? Effective? Why or why not? In retrospect, did the punishment shame or humiliate you, or did it bring out feelings of guilt? What did you learn from this experience? Before beginning to write, read or review Dick Gregory's "Shame" (pp. 145–49).
2. Tangney writes, "As the costs of incarceration mount and evidence of its failure as a deterrent grows, judges understandably have begun to search for creative alternatives to traditional sentences" (1). Ideally, knowing what the punishment will be should deter people from doing the wrong thing in the first place, but do punishments really act as deterrents? Are certain punishments more effective as deterrents than others? What are the deterrent benefits of both shame and guilt punishments? Conduct library and Internet research to answer these questions, and then report your findings and conclusions in an essay.

Shame Is Worth a Try

Dan M. Kahan

Courtesy of Dan M. Kahan

Dan M. Kahan was born in 1963 and graduated from Middlebury College in 1986 and Harvard Law School in 1989, where he served as president of the *Harvard Law Review*. He clerked for Judge Harry Edwards of the U.S. Court of Appeals for the District of Columbia circuit in 1989–1990 and for Justice Thurgood Marshall of the U.S. Supreme Court in 1990–1991. After practicing law for two years in Washington, D.C., Kahan launched his teaching career, first at the University of Chicago Law School and later at Yale Law School, where since 2003 he has been the Elizabeth K. Dollard Professor of Law. From 2005 to 2006, he served as deputy dean of Yale Law School, and in spring 2016 he served as a distinguished resident scholar at the Annenberg Public Policy Center at the University of Pennsylvania. Kahan is also a senior fellow at the National Center for Science and Civic Engagement and an elected member of the American Academy of Arts and Sciences. His teaching and research interests include science communication, criminal law, risk perception, punishment, and evidence. Kahan, who has written widely in legal journals on current social issues including climate change and gun control, is coauthor, with Tracey Meares, of *Urgent Times: Policing and Rights in Inner-City Communities* (1999).

In the following essay, first published in the *Boston Globe* on August 5, 2001, Kahan argues in favor of the use of shame as "an effective, cheap, and humane alternative to imprisonment."

Reflecting on What You Know

Think about the times you were punished as a child. Who punished you—parents, teachers, or other authority figures? What kinds of bad behavior were you punished for? What type of punishment worked best to deter you from behaving badly later on? Explain.

Is shame an appropriate criminal punishment? Many courts and legislators around the country think so. Steal from your employer in Wisconsin and you might be ordered to wear a sandwich board proclaiming your offense. Drive drunk in Florida or Texas and you might be required to place a conspicuous "DUI" bumper sticker on your car. Refuse to make your child-support payments in Virginia and you will find that your vehicle has been immobilized with an appropriately colored boot (pink if the abandoned child is a girl, blue if a boy). 1

Many experts, however, are skeptical of these new shaming punishments. Some question their effectiveness as a deterrent. Others worry that the new punishments are demeaning and cruel. 2

Who's right? As is usually the case, both sides have their points. But what the shame proponents seem to be getting, and the critics ignoring, is the potential of shame as an effective, cheap, and humane alternative to imprisonment. 3

There's obviously no alternative to imprisonment for murderers, rapists, and other violent criminals. But they make up less than half the American prison population. 4

Liberal and conservative reformers alike have long believed that the remainder can be effectively punished with less severe "alternative sanctions," like fines and community service. These sanctions are much cheaper than jail. They also allow the offender to continue earning an income so he can compensate his victim, meet his child-support obligations, and the like. 5

Nevertheless, courts and legislators have resisted alternative sanctions—not so much because they won't work, but because they fail to express appropriate moral condemnation of crime. Fines seem to say that offenders may buy the privilege of breaking the law; and we can't very well condemn someone for purchasing what we are willing to sell. 6

Nor do we condemn offenders to educate the retarded, install smoke detectors in nursing homes, restore dilapidated low income housing, and the like. Indeed, saying that such community service is punishment for criminals insults both those who perform such services voluntarily and those whom the services are supposed to benefit. 7

There's no confusion about the law's intent to condemn, however, when judges resort to public shaming. As a result, judges, legislators, and the public at large generally do accept shame as a morally appropriate punishment for drunken driving, nonaggravated assaults, 8 embezzlement,[1] small-scale drug distribution, larceny,[2] toxic waste dumping, perjury, and a host of other offenses that ordinarily would result in a short jail term.

The critics' anxieties about shame, moreover, seem overstated. Clearly, shame hurts. People value their reputations for both emotional and financial reasons. In fact, a series of studies by Harold Grasmick, a sociologist at the University of Oklahoma, suggests that the prospect of public disgrace exerts greater pressure to comply with the law than does the threat of imprisonment and other formal punishments. 9

There's every reason to believe, then, that shaming penalties will be an effective deterrent, at least for nonviolent crimes. Indeed, preliminary reports suggest that certain shaming punishments, including those directed at deadbeat dads, are extraordinarily effective. 10

At the same time, shame clearly doesn't hurt as much as imprisonment. Individuals who go to jail end up just as disgraced as those who are shamed, and lose their liberty to boot. Those who've served prison time are also a lot less likely to regain the respect and trust of their law-abiding neighbors—essential ingredients of rehabilitation. Given all this, it's hard to see shame as cruel. 11

Consider the case of a Florida mother sentenced to take out a newspaper ad proclaiming "I purchased marijuana with my kids in the car." 12

The prospect that her neighbors would see the ad surely caused her substantial embarrassment. But the alternative was a jail sentence, which would not only have humiliated her more but could also have caused her to lose custody of her children. Not surprisingly, the woman voluntarily accepted the shaming sanction in lieu of[3] jail time, as nearly all offenders do. 13

Shame, like any other type of criminal punishment, can definitely be abused. Some forms of it, like the public floggings imposed by authoritarian states abroad, are pointlessly degrading. 14

In addition, using shame as a supplement rather than a substitute for imprisonment only makes punishment more expensive for society and destructive for the offender. Accordingly, requiring sex offenders to register with local authorities is harder to defend than are other types of shaming punishments, which are true substitutes for jail. 15

[1]*embezzlement:* stealing money or goods entrusted to one's care.
[2]*larceny:* theft.
[3]*in lieu of:* in place of; instead of.

These legitimate points, however, are a reason to insist that shaming be carried out appropriately, not to oppose it across the board. 16

In short, shame is cheap and effective and frees up scarce prison space for the more serious offenses. Why not at least give it a try? 17

Thinking Critically about This Reading

What does Kahan mean when he states that "requiring sex offenders to register with local authorities is harder to defend than are other types of shaming punishments" (paragraph 15)?

Questions for Study and Discussion

1. What is Kahan's thesis? (Glossary: **Thesis**) Where does he state it most clearly?
2. What examples of shaming punishments does Kahan provide? For you, do these punishments seem to fit the crime? Explain.
3. How does Kahan handle the opposition argument that public shaming is cruel?
4. According to Kahan, why have courts and legislators resisted alternative punishments such as fines and community service?
5. What evidence does Kahan present to show that shaming punishments work? (Glossary: **Evidence**)
6. How convincing is Kahan's argument? What is the strongest part of his argument? The weakest part? Explain.

Classroom Activity Using Argument

Is public shaming justifiable? Hold a class debate, dividing into teams that will argue for and against such punishment. Team members should divide themselves among different aspects of their position (for example, psychological repercussions of the punishment, more traditional sentences it could replace, and examples of judges who have used shaming) and then do library and Internet research to develop ideas and evidence. The teams should be allowed equal time to present their assertions and the evidence they have to support them. Finally, the class as a whole should be prepared to discuss the effectiveness of the presentations on both sides of the question.

Suggested Writing Assignments

1. Write an essay in which you argue your position on the issue of using public shaming as a punishment. Is public shaming appropriate for some or all offenses that would otherwise result in a short jail term? Explain. Support your argument with evidence from Kahan's essay, June Tangney's "Condemn the Crime, Not the Person" (pp. 552–54), and your own experiences and observations. (Glossary: **Evidence**) You may find it helpful to review your Reflecting on What You Know response for this selection.
2. Identify several current problems at your college or university involving violations of campus rules for parking, cheating on exams, plagiarizing papers, recycling waste, using drugs or alcohol, defacing school property, and so on. Select one of these problems, and write a proposal to treat violators with a shaming punishment of your own design. Address your proposal to your school's student government organization or administration office.
3. What is your position on the issue of whether convicted sex offenders should be required to register with local authorities? Should registration be required even though they have already served their sentences in prison? Should people have the right to know the identity of any sex offenders living in their neighborhoods, or is this an invasion of privacy? Conduct library and Internet research on the subject of sex offender registration, and write an essay arguing for or against the measure.

The Ultimate Clickbait

Libby Marlowe

Student writer Libby Marlowe wrote this essay while she was a student. Her instructor in her first-year English course assigned an argument essay with a clear thesis and support from sources, but students were encouraged to use only readings found in their textbook. This allowed students to focus not on an extensive research project but on using sources well.

Libby selected sources on the topic of shame and punishment because of posts she saw on her social media feeds, especially posts following the charged 2016 presidential election. Her essay uses synthesis, an argument strategy by which the writer brings together the ideas of multiple authors, often to support a new claim. (Glossary: **Synthesis**) As you read, consider how Marlowe integrates ideas from authors in *Models for Writers* to support her argument and redirects the academic conversation on shaming.

Reflecting on What You Know

Describe an incidence of shaming that you have seen recently in the news or on social media. Who was doing the shaming? Why?

Click. That is all it takes to shame somebody on social media. One "share" or "retweet" and someone's poor choice is seen by a new group of friends and followers. In a few hours, the shamed person or organization can be the next international trending topic. But what about the shamers? The people who *do* the shaming to embarrass or make examples of others, especially online, are doing as much—if not more—harm to themselves as to their victims. 1

Not all shaming is so quick and easy. Recently, judges have been using shaming as punishment for small crimes, and criminal justice and social commentators have suggested shaming is a good alternative to jail time because it would help solve the problem of America's overpopulated and expensive prison system. Dan M. Kahan, a professor of law at Yale Law School and former clerk for U.S. Supreme Court Justice Thurgood Marshall, sees "the potential of shame as 2 an effective, cheap, and humane alternative to imprisonment" (558) that "frees up scarce prison space for the more serious offenses" (560). More importantly, Kahan argues that shame is effective because there is a better chance criminals will see the error of their ways, shape up, and obey the law in the future. A shame punishment is a better alternative than being remembered by the community as someone who served jail time (559). The challenge of earning back neighbors' trust with a criminal record could lead to a lifetime of fewer job choices and poor living conditions, eventually leading back to crime.

June Tangney, a professor of psychology at George Mason University, agrees that the current state of prisons and their poor results is a "failure," and even though she acknowledges that courts' sentencing practices are "understandbl[e]," she argues that shaming will not improve most criminals: "Rather than fostering constructive change, shame often makes a bad situation worse" (553). Shaming sentences send the message that a person is being punished not because they made a bad choice but because they are a bad person worthy of shame, so they might as well keep breaking the law: "In short, shame serves to escalate the very destructive patterns of behavior we aim to curb" (553). As a solution, Tangney advocates for another alternative form of punishment, community service, to show criminals the damage they caused to their communities (554). 3

Tangney insists that "thoughtfully constructed guilt-oriented community service sentences" should be delivered by judges (554). Kahan, too, points out that "the law's intent [is] to condemn...when judges resort to public shaming" (558). It is important to see that these arguments by Tangney, Kahan, and commenters like them depend on the presence of a judge who has been elected or appointed to the position and bears the responsibility of upholding the law. Kahan notes that punishments such as fines or community service have not been popular "not so much because they don't work, but because they fail to express appropriate moral condemnation of crime" (558). If being effective is not at issue, then what the courts—and the public—want is to be right and feel justified for being right by making sure someone else knows they're wrong. As Tangney says, "Punishments aimed at public humiliation certainly appeal to our sense of moral righteousness" (553). Both Kahan's and Tangney's arguments support the idea that shaming serves the punisher as much as—if not more than—the punished. 4

Some of the examples Kahan and Tangney use to introduce public shaming show creativity: offenders may carry signs, post them in their lawns, or use bumper stickers to announce their crimes, and failing to pay child-support could even lead to a boot on the offender's car, "(pink if the abandoned child is a girl, blue if a boy)" (Tangney 551, Kahan 558). These sentences show off the cleverness of the judge more than they promise to help the criminal avoid crime. Outside of the courtroom, creative shaming—and talk of shaming—has also become more widespread. "Shaming" pets became a meme; pet owners would display a sign near a dog or cat (sometimes around their necks) proclaiming an offense like chewing a shoe or walking through paint, then post it on the Internet. The purpose of the photograph is to create laughter and showcase the humor and good nature of the pet owner; dogs do not care if their image is shared on the internet. Shame has completely ignored the offender and become a conversation between the shame-giver and the audience. 5

Pet shaming may be a silly example with few real consequences, but it reveals how popular the practice of shaming has become – and how quick people are to give out shame, especially online. Court decisions set an example for how law and society should be upheld, and people will start to think they can take justice into their own hands by shaming other people, just like the courts would. Social media channels in particular have become a weapon meant to harm and to give the shamer the moral high ground. When people are separated by physical distance and a computer screen, and appear only as pictures, not living, breathing bodies, it becomes easier to shame them. They are easier to attack because it is easier to ignore the consequences of what shaming will do to them in real life (or "IRL"). In other words, the shamer is not accountable for his or her actions, and the practice of shaming without the authority of being a judge teaches the shamer that they don't need to take responsibility. 6

As a result, shaming becomes less about offense or punishment and more about venting. People who feel wronged may find individuals to shame simply for the sake of shaming or yelling. Online, the practice has been called trolling and "defined as the act of posting inflammatory, derogatory or provocative messages in public forums" (Zhuo 130). Because the Internet allows users to comment and post anonymously, there is even less accountability or need for authority. People who would not normally shame someone publicly may do so once they know they will face no consequences; psychological researchers 7 call this "the online disinhibition effect" (Zhuo 130). Even if someone does not directly participate in shaming, they can spread shame by sharing or liking a post, which could be shared across a broad web of networks. The person shamed—whether they have committed an offense or not—may face more public retaliation than they deserve (if they deserve any). In other cases, a viral post may actually glorify the offense. The impulse to shame and feed anger and moral righteousness is the basis for websites who feature "clickbait" titles such as "You won't believe this celebrity's fashion disaster!" These headlines rely on embarrassment and misfortune, and they encourage an unhealthy desire to click and take part in the public humiliation.

Not all viral stories or public shaming on the Internet is meant 8
to be harmful. Shaming has entered the public consciousness partly because of efforts to call out "slut-shaming" or "fat-shaming" practices that are against women expressing their sexuality or that treat overweight people unfairly. This kind of shaming raises awareness of these issues and promotes equal treatment. However, the most effective examples of this positive shaming are made by people who are already famous or who have a social media or Internet following that most people do not have. More importantly, these instances are intended to shame the society more than shame one person. When people shame others in social media or troll them in comments, they are usually just being spiteful.

When people shame others and claim no responsibility, simply for 9
the sake of throwing stones or gaining the moral high ground, shaming is no longer a form of constructive punishment or activism. If there is more attention on the punishers than on the punished, or if the culture of shame harms the community by victimizing people who do not deserve such public embarrassment, then public shaming becomes more damaging to the community than the original offense. Denying people's right to criticize would violate the right of free speech, but it is worth pursuing ways to keep people accountable for their actions and comments online, to show them the potential harm they're doing, not only to their fellow citizens but to themselves.

Works Cited

Kahan, Dan M. "Shame Is Worth a Try." Rosa and Eschholz, pp. 557–60.

Rosa, Alfred, and Paul Eschholz, editors. *Models for Writers*. 13th ed., Bedford/St. Martin's, 2018.

Tangney, June. "Condemn the Crime, Not the Person." Rosa and Eschholz, pp. 552–54.

Zhuo, Julie. "Where Anonymity Breeds Contempt." Rosa and Eschholz, pp. 129–32.

Thinking Critically about This Reading

Marlowe identifies "clickbait" titles as a source of public shaming and writes, "These headlines rely on embarrassment and misfortune, and they encourage an unhealthy desire to click and take part in the public humiliation" (paragraph 7). Do you see the point of "clickbait" as feeding a human desire to participate in public humiliation? Why or why not?

Questions for Study and Discussion

1. Like the "clickbait" that Marlowe discusses, her essay begins with a word to hook the reader. What is Marlowe's hook? Did you find it effective? (Glossary: **Beginnings and Endings**)
2. Before synthesizing ideas, Marlowe presents her thesis that "The people who *do* the shaming to embarrass or make examples of others, especially online, are doing as much—if not more—harm to themselves as to their victims" (1). (Glossary: **Synthesis; Thesis**) Do you agree with her argument? Why or why not?
3. Why does Marlowe state her controlling idea at the end of the first paragraph?
4. After the first paragraph of her essay, Marlowe does not directly discuss her main point. Instead she spends the bulk of the paper expressing the parts of Kahan's and Tangney's arguments that imply support of her controlling idea. Why does she use this strategy? Do you think it is effective?
5. Identify and quote an example of Marlowe's representation of an author's *ethos*. Why does she include biographical information of the authors whose ideas she is bringing into her essay?
6. Marlowe writes, "Not all viral stories or public shaming on the Internet is meant to be harmful" (8). How do the points in this paragraph support her opening sentence?

7. Do you see any logical fallacies in Marlowe's argument? Does knowing that this article was written by a student make you more likely to think critically about it? Why or why not?

Classroom Activity Using Argument

In your notebook, write down three experiences that caused you to decide to come to college. Your instructor will ask the class for volunteers to read their experiences aloud. As a class, come up with a controlling idea that synthesizes the collection of experiences. Using this controlling idea, write an outline for an argument essay. Be sure to include strong supporting ideas and evidence and to address possible opposition.

Suggested Writing Assignments

1. Look at any of the thematic clusters listed in the beginning of *Models for Writers* (pp. xxxi–xxxvi) and write an essay that synthesizes ideas from this cluster to create a new argument. You might want to list points that the articles have in common. Next, identify a point not covered by the articles that you would like to argue. Use Marlowe's rhetorical strategies for inspiration.
2. Write an essay that argues that a particular aspect of social media is positive and why. Use at least one point in Marlowe's essay to support your ideas. If you'd prefer, summarize her main ideas in one of the early body paragraphs.
3. Write an essay arguing that authors of Internet articles should stop using "clickbait" strategies. In your essay, explain whether you feel that a clickbait title takes away from the author's ethos.

CHAPTER **22**

Combining Models

Each of the preceding chapters in Part Four: Types of Essays in *Models for Writers* emphasizes a particular writing strategy or rhetorical mode: Illustration, Narration, Description, Process Analysis, Definition, Division and Classification, Comparison and Contrast, Cause and Effect, and Argument. The essays and selections within each of these chapters use the given strategy as the dominant method of development. It is important to remember, however, that the *dominant strategy* is rarely the *only* one used to develop a piece of writing. Using other strategies or modes in combination with the dominant strategy enables writers to both explore their topics and strengthen their presentations. This is especially true when argumentation is the dominant strategy; writers can use a number of strategies—such as illustration, definition, comparison and contrast, cause and effect—to support a thesis or persuade an audience.

In this chapter on combining strategies—or what we're calling "combining models" in the chapter title—we offer a collection of essays that make notable use of several different strategies. You encounter such combinations of strategies in other reading selections in earlier chapters of this book, as well as in the reading and writing you do in your other college courses. Beyond the classroom, you might write a community proposal using both description and comparison and contrast to make an argument for a new parking garage in the downtown business area; description and process analysis to apply for a patent for a new product you have engineered; or narration, description, and illustration to write a review of a new art show at a gallery.

In the following essay, student Courtney Smith uses several strategies effectively, even in a brief piece of writing. Inspired by a pest control commercial on television, Smith chose an unusual topic: cockroaches. Before writing, she did some preliminary reading in the library, spoke to a biology professor who had several interesting exhibits to show her, and surveyed the pest control products available at her local hardware store. Smith decided to focus on the ability of cockroaches to survive under almost any circumstances. As she began to search for reasons for the cockroaches' resiliency, three main causes emerged. Although primarily an essay of cause and effect, notice how Smith uses description, process analysis, and illustration to develop each of her three main paragraphs.

Cockroaches

Beginning: A question captures readers' attention.

Have you ever tried to get rid of cockroaches? Those stupid little bugs refuse to go. You can chase them, starve them, spray them, and even try to squash them. But no matter what you do, they always come back. I have read that they are the only creatures that can survive a nuclear explosion. How have cockroaches survived in such extreme conditions? What has enabled them to be such resilient insects? The answer is simple. Cockroaches have survived in some of the Earth's most hostile environments because they possess several unique physical features, an amazing reproductive process, and an immune system that has frustrated even the best efforts of exterminators to get rid of them.

Thesis statement

Cause #1: Writer uses description to detail physical features.

Cockroaches are thin, torpedo-shaped insects. Their body shape allows them to squeeze into small cracks or holes in walls and ceilings or dart into drains, thus avoiding many dangers. Their outer shell is unusually hard, making them almost impossible to crush. Cockroaches have sticky pads on their claws that enable them to climb walls or crawl upside down on ceilings. They also have two little tails, called "cerci," to alert them to danger. These cerci are covered with tiny hairs that, like antennae, are sensitive to things as small as a speck of dust or as seemingly innocent as a puff of air. Finally, if cockroaches cannot find food, they can sustain themselves for up to a month without food, as long as they have water. Combined with their other physical features, this ability to go without food for long periods has made the cockroach almost invincible.

Cause #2: Writer uses process analysis to explain reproduction.

Cockroaches give credence to the old adage that there is safety in numbers. They reproduce at a truly amazing rate. About two months after mating, a new generation of cockroaches is born. One cockroach can produce about two dozen offspring each time it mates. To get some idea of the process behind their reproductive power, imagine that you start with three pairs of cockroaches. Approximately three weeks after mating the females lay their eggs, which hatch some forty-five days later. If we assume two dozen eggs from each female, the first generation would number seventy-two. These cockroaches would continue to multiply geometrically so that by year's end the colony would total more than 10,000 cockroaches. Stopping this process is almost impossible because, even if we were successful in annihilating the adult population, it is more than likely that a new generation would already be on the verge of hatching.

Cause #3: Writer uses illustration to show scientists' frustrations.

Finally, cockroaches have frustrated scientists with their ability to immunize themselves against drugs, poisons, and bomb gases. Cockroaches then pass this new immunity on to the next generation quicker than a new insecticide can be developed. Although scientists have studied the cockroach for decades, they have not yet discovered the biological mechanism that enables them to develop immunity so rapidly. It is not surprising that many scientists are now focusing on a "birth control" solution for cockroaches. By rendering at least some portion of the adult population sterile, scientists hope to gain a measure of control over these pesky insects.

Ending: Writer restates the thesis and predicts the future of cockroaches.

Today there are approximately 3,500 different species of cockroaches. They have survived on this planet since the time of the dinosaurs some 350 million years ago. Whether or not scientists are successful in their latest efforts to rid us of cockroaches is yet to be determined. Odds are that they will not succeed. Given the cockroach's amazing record of survivability, it is not likely to turn up on anyone's list of endangered species.

How do you now begin to write an essay that utilizes a combination of strategies? Do you need to make sure you build a variety of strategies into an essay? Do you need to start with a list? Do you have to use a certain number of strategies? Of course not!

In your own writing you will find yourself using a combination of strategies to get the job done. Indeed, it might be more difficult for you to develop your writing using only one strategy. Sometimes you might use several developmental strategies in a piece of writing without being conscious of the fact. You simply do what you need to do—describe, narrate, compare and contrast, argue, and so on—as your topic and purpose require.

By the time you have finished your draft, you should be able to identify the dominant strategy you have been using. If it's definition, make sure your essay defines. If it's cause and effect, make sure that the causal links are in place and are logical. Then read your draft, looking for opportunities to use a supporting strategy to strengthen your essay, such as adding another example to make a point clearer or a personal narrative to make your argument more persuasive. Finally, examine those passages in which you have employed a supporting strategy to assure yourself that each one supports the dominant strategy and your overall purpose and is crafted in accordance with the writing techniques you have learned in *Models for Writers*.

An Indian Father's Plea

Robert G. Lake-Thom (Medicine Grizzly Bear)

Robert G. Lake-Thom, also known as Medicine Grizzly Bear, is a traditional Native American healer and spiritual teacher, following methods he learned from healers, ceremonial leaders, and religious leaders of several tribes. His ancestry is Karuk, Seneca, Cherokee, and Anglo. He was a professor of Native American studies for over twenty years, teaching at Gonzaga University, Humboldt State University, and Eastern Montana College (now Montana State University Billings). Lake-Thom is the author of multiple books on Native American shamanic life and ceremonies, including *Chilula* (1982) *Native Healer* (1991), *Spirits of the Earth* (1997), and *The Call of the Great Spirit* (2001).

Courtesy of Robert Lake-Thom

Lake-Thom wrote "An Indian Father's Plea" in response to the negative effects Western education practices were having on his children as well as Native American children across the nation. In this piece—which has been used for over two decades in both teacher training workshops and Indian education programs—Lake-Thom responds to a teacher who labeled his child a "slow learner," explaining the education his son has already received. Although he acknowledges that this education may seem foreign to the teacher, he explains that it has developed the boy's sensitivity to the world and honed skills important to his culture. As you read, notice how Lake-Thom's argument is enhanced by a number of supporting strategies such as cause and effect and process analysis, and consider how well these strategies help the teacher better understand the stages of his son's education.

Reflecting on What You Know

Think about a time when your way of learning and understanding seemed out of sync with what you were being taught. What does it tell you about your education? Under what circumstances or with what methods do you learn best?

Wind-Wolf knows the names and migration patterns of more 1
than 40 birds. He knows there are 13 tail feathers on a perfectly balanced eagle. What he needs is a teacher who knows his full measure.

Dear teacher, I would like to introduce you to my son, Wind-Wolf. 2
He is probably what you would consider a typical Indian kid. He was born and raised on a reservation. He has black hair, dark brown eyes, olive complexion. And like so many Indian children his age, he is shy and quiet in the classroom. He is 5 years old, in kindergarten, and I can't understand why you have already labeled him a "slow learner."

At the age of 5, he has already been through quite an education 3
compared with his peers in Western society. At his first introduction into this world, he was bonded to his mother and to the Mother Earth in a traditional native childbirth ceremony. And he has been continuously cared for by his mother, father, sisters, cousins, uncles, grandparents, and extended tribal family since this ceremony.

From his mother's warm and loving arms, Wind-Wolf was placed 4
in a secure and specially designed Indian baby basket. His father and the medicine elders conducted another ceremony with him that served to bond him with the essence of his genetic father, the Great Spirit, the Grandfather Sun, and the Grandmother Moon. This was all done in order to introduce him properly into the new and natural world, not the world of artificiality, and to protect his sensitive and delicate soul. It is our people's way of showing the newborn respect, ensuring that he starts his life on the path of spirituality.

The traditional Indian baby basket became his "turtle's shell" and 5
served as the first seat for his classroom. He was strapped in for safety, protected from injury by the willow roots and hazel wood construction. The basket was made by a tribal elder who had gathered her materials with prayer and in a ceremonial way. It is the same kind of basket that our people have used for thousands of years. It is specially designed to provide the child with the kind of knowledge and experience he will need in order to survive in his culture and environment.

Wind-Wolf was strapped in snuggly with a deliberate restric- 6
tion upon his arms and legs. Although you in Western society may argue that such a method serves to hinder motor-skill development and abstract reasoning, we believe it forces the child to first develop his intuitive faculties, rational intellect, symbolic thinking, and five senses. Wind-Wolf was with his mother constantly, closely bonded physically, as she carried him on her back or held him in front while

breast-feeding. She carried him everywhere she went, and every night he slept with both parents. Because of this, Wind-Wolf's educational setting was not only a "secure" environment, but it was also very colorful, complicated, sensitive, and diverse. He has been with his mother at the ocean at daybreak when she made her prayers and gathered fresh seaweed from the rocks, he has sat with his uncles in a rowboat on the river while they fished with gill nets, and he has watched and listened to elders as they told creation stories and animal legends and sang songs around the campfires.

He has attended the sacred and ancient White Deerskin Dance of his people and is well-acquainted with the cultures and languages of other tribes. He has been with his mother when she gathered herbs for healing and watched his tribal aunts and grandmothers gather and prepare traditional foods such as acorn, smoked salmon, eel, and deer meat. He has played with abalone shells, pine nuts, iris grass string, and leather while watching the women make beaded jewelry and traditional native regalia. He has had many opportunities to watch his father, uncles, and ceremonial leaders using different kinds of songs while preparing for the sacred dances and rituals. 7

As he grew older, Wind-Wolf began to crawl out of the baby basket, develop his motor skills, and explore the world around him. When frightened or sleepy, he could always return to the basket as a turtle withdraws into its shell. Such an inward journey allows one to reflect in privacy on what he has learned and to carry the new knowledge deeply into the unconscious and the soul. Shapes, sizes, colors, texture, sound, smell, feeling, taste, and the learning process are therefore functionally integrated—the physical and spiritual, matter and energy, conscious and unconscious, individual and social. 8

For example, Wind-Wolf was with his mother in South Dakota while she danced for seven days straight in the hot sun, fasting, and piercing herself in the sacred Sun Dance Ceremony of a distant tribe. He has been doctored in a number of different healing ceremonies by medicine men and women from diverse places ranging from Alaska and Arizona to New York and California. He has been in more than 20 different sacred sweat-lodge rituals—used by native tribes to purify the mind, body, and soul—since he was 3 years old, and he has already been exposed to many different religions of his racial brothers: Protestant, Catholic, Asian Buddhist, and Tibetan Lamaist. 9

It takes a long time to absorb and reflect on these kinds of experiences, so maybe that is why you think my Indian child is a slow 10 learner. His aunts and grandmothers taught him to count and know his numbers while they sorted out the complex materials used to make the abstract designs in the native baskets. He listened to his mother count each and every bead and sort out numerically according to color while she painstakingly made complex beaded belts and necklaces. He learned his basic numbers by helping his father count and sort the rocks to be used in the sweat-lodge—seven rocks for a medicine sweat, say, or 13 for the summer solstice ceremony. (The rocks are later heated and doused with water to create purifying steam.) And he was taught to learn mathematics by counting the sticks we use in our traditional native hand game. So I realize he may be slow in grasping the methods and tools that you are now using in your classroom, ones quite familiar to his white peers, but I hope you will be patient with him. It takes time to adjust to a new cultural system and learn new things.

He is not culturally "disadvantaged," but he is culturally "different." 11 If you ask him how many months there are in a year, he will probably tell you 13. He will respond this way not because he doesn't know how to count properly, but because he has been taught by our traditional people that there are 13 full moons in a year according to the native tribal calendar and that there are really 13 planets in our solar system and 13 tail feathers on a perfectly balanced eagle, the most powerful kind of bird to use in ceremonial healing.

But he also knows that some eagles may only have 12 tail feathers, 12 or seven, that they do not all have the same number. He knows that the flicker has exactly 10 tail feathers; that they are red and black, representing the directions of east and west, life and death; and that this bird is considered a "fire" bird, a power used in native doctoring and healing. He can probably count more than 40 different kinds of birds, tell you and his peers what kind of bird each is and where it lives, the seasons in which it appears, and how it is used in a sacred ceremony. He may also have trouble writing his name on a piece of paper, but he knows how to say it and many other things in several different Indian languages. He is not fluent yet because he is only 5 years old and required by law to attend your educational system, learn your language, your values, your ways of thinking, and your methods of teaching and learning.

So you see, all of these influences together make him somewhat 13 shy and quiet—and perhaps "slow" according to your standards. But if Wind-Wolf was not prepared for his first tentative foray into your world, neither were you appreciative of his culture. On the first day of class, you had difficulty with his name. You wanted to call him Wind, insisting that Wolf must somehow be his middle name. The students in the class laughed at him, causing further embarrassment.

While you are trying to teach him your new methods, helping him learn new tools for self-discovery and adapt to his new learning environment, he may be looking out the window as if daydreaming. Why? Because he has been taught to watch and study the changes in nature. It is hard for him to make the appropriate psychic switch from the right to the left hemisphere of the brain when he sees the leaves turning bright colors, the geese heading south, and the squirrels scurrying around for nuts to get ready for a harsh winter. In his heart, in his young mind, and almost by instinct, he knows that this is the time of the year he is supposed to be with people gathering and preparing fish, deer meat, and native plants and herbs, and learning his assigned tasks in this role. He is caught between two worlds, torn by two distinct cultural systems. 14

Yesterday, for the third time in two weeks, he came home crying and said he wanted to have his hair cut. He said he doesn't have any friends at school because they make fun of his long hair. I tried to explain to him that in our culture, long hair is a sign of masculinity and balance and is a source of power. But he remained adamant in his position. 15

To make matters worse, he recently encountered his first harsh case of racism. Wind-Wolf had managed to adopt at least one good school friend. On the way home from school one day, he asked his new pal if he wanted to come home to play with him until supper. That was OK with Wind-Wolf's mother, who was walking with them. When they all got to the little friend's house, the two boys ran inside to ask permission while Wind-Wolf's mother waited. But the other boy's mother lashed out: "It is OK if you have to play with him at school, but we don't allow those kind of people in our house!" When my wife asked why not, the other boy's mother answered, "Because you are Indians, and we are white, and I don't want my kids growing up with your kind of people." 16

So now my young Indian child does not want to go to school anymore (even though we cut his hair). He feels that he does not belong. He is the only Indian child in your class, and he is well-aware of this fact. Instead of being proud of his race, heritage, and culture, he feels ashamed. When he watches television, he asks why the white people 17 hate us so much and always kill our people in the movies and why they take everything away from us. He asks why the other kids in school are not taught about the power, beauty, and essence of nature or provided with an opportunity to experience the world around them firsthand. He says he hates living in the city and that he misses his Indian cousins and friends. He asks why one young white girl at school who is his friend always tells him, "I like you, Wind-Wolf, because you are a good Indian."

Now he refuses to sing his native songs, play with his Indian artifacts, learn his language, or participate in his sacred ceremonies. When I ask him to go to an urban powwow or help me with a sacred sweat-lodge ritual, he says no because "that's weird" and he doesn't want his friends at school to think he doesn't believe in God. 18

So, dear teacher, I want to introduce you to my son, Wind-Wolf, who is not really a "typical" little Indian kid after all. He stems from a long line of hereditary chiefs, medicine men and women, and ceremonial leaders whose accomplishments and unique forms of knowledge are still being studied and recorded in contemporary books. He has seven different tribal systems flowing through his blood; he is even part white. I want my child to succeed in school and in life. I don't want him to be a dropout or juvenile delinquent or to end up on drugs and alcohol because he is made to feel inferior or because of discrimination. I want him to be proud of his rich heritage and culture, and I would like him to develop the necessary capabilities to adapt to, and succeed in, both cultures. But I need your help. 19

What you say and what you do in the classroom, what you teach and how you teach it, and what you don't say and don't teach will have a significant effect on the potential success or failure of my child. Please remember that this is the primary year of his education and development. All I ask is that you work with me, not against me, to help educate my child in the best way. If you don't have the knowledge, preparation, experience, or training to effectively deal with culturally different children, I am willing to help you with the few resources I have available or direct you to such resources. 20

Millions of dollars have been appropriated by Congress and are being spent each year for "Indian Education." All you have to do is take advantage of it and encourage your school to make an effort to use it in the name of "equal education." My Indian child has a constitutional right to learn, retain, and maintain his heritage and culture. By the same token, I strongly believe that non-Indian children also have 21 a constitutional right to learn about our Native American heritage and culture, because Indians play a significant part in the history of Western society. Until this reality is equally understood and applied in education as a whole, there will be a lot more schoolchildren in grades K-2 identified as "slow learners."

My son, Wind-Wolf, is not an empty glass coming into your class 22 to be filled. He is a full basket coming into a different environment and society with something special to share. Please let him share his knowledge, heritage, and culture with you and his peers.

Thinking Critically about This Reading

The ritual introducing the child to his baby basket is a "way of showing the newborn respect" (paragraph 4). In what ways is Lake-Thom's essay more generally a call for showing respect? How would you expect the teacher to whom he is writing to respond?

Questions for Study and Discussion

1. Lake-Thom begins this essay by describing his son and listing a few examples of what his son knows. Why do you think he starts in this way? Is this an appropriate writing strategy? Explain.
2. Identify the supporting strategies that Lake-Thom uses in his letter to his son's teacher. (Glossary: **Rhetorical Modes**) Explain how each supporting strategy enhances Lake-Thom's argument.
3. Lake-Thom describes the specially designed baby basket as a "turtle's shell" (5). Why does he use this metaphor? What similarities is he pointing out? (Glossary: **Figure of Speech**)
4. Discuss why Wind-Wolf would say there are thirteen months in a year. How does his father explain this "mistake" to the teacher?
5. What does Lake-Thom suggest are the advantages to the way his son has learned about the world? In what areas does he have greater knowledge than his classmates, who are not from Native American families?
6. What are the benefits of having Wind-Wolf attend school? What will this new form of education add to what he already knows?

7. Discuss Wind-Wolf's emotional reaction to his new school. What experiences have most affected him?
8. How does Lake-Thom think the teacher can make the school environment better for his child? Make note of where the essay transitions from describing Wind-Wolf's early education to making its "plea" to the teacher.

Classroom Activity Using Combining Models

Brainstorm some points in a response to Lake-Thom from the perspective of his son's teacher. How might the teacher make sure the child's needs are addressed? What steps should the teacher take after reading this letter? What concerns might she have? Which rhetorical modes would you consider using in your response to make your point more effectively? (Glossary: **Rhetorical Modes**) Then, work with a partner or small group and have a discussion, playing the roles of the teacher and Lake-Thom (and, perhaps, Lake-Thom's son, if you have enough people). After your discussion, reflect on which rhetorical modes were most convincing.

Suggested Writing Assignments

1. Write a history of your education, both inside and outside the classroom. When did you begin to learn? What have your greatest achievements and hardest challenges been? You might find it helpful to think of the history of your education as a simple narrative. (Glossary: **Narration**) Look for opportunities where you can use supporting strategies such as comparison and contrast or process analysis to strengthen your essay.
2. Though Lake-Thom is writing for a specific audience — the teacher — he published his letter so that the public could also learn from his experience with Wind-Wolf's first weeks of school. Think of a subject on which you have strong feelings, and write an open letter to persuade readers of your view. Using "An Indian Father's Plea" as a model, try to combine passionate expression with careful planning and structure. (Glossary: **Persuasion**)

The Myth of the Catty Woman

Sheryl Sandberg and Adam Grant

Gaetan Bally/Keystone/Redux

Sheryl Sandberg was born in Washington, D.C., in 1969. A 1991 graduate of Harvard University with a BA in economics, she went on to receive an MBA from Harvard Business School in 1995. Sandberg is the chief operating officer of Facebook and was named one of the 100 most influential people in the world by *Time* magazine in 2012. As an author and speaker, Sandberg often focuses on issues of women and work. In 2010, she delivered a TED talk entitled "Why We Have Too Few Women Leaders" that brought her great acclaim. In 2013, she and coauthor Nell Scovell published the best-selling book *Lean In: Women, Work, and the Will to Lead*. In 2014, she sponsored a campaign to ban the word *bossy* from media because of its potential harm to young girls.

Adam Grant was born in 1981 and spent his childhood in suburban Detroit. He has a BA from Harvard University and a PhD in organizational psychology from the University of Michigan. Currently, he is a tenured professor and top-rated teacher at the Wharton School at the University of Pennsylvania. He is the author of *Give and Take: Why Helping Others Drives Our Success* (2013) and *Originals: How Non-Conformists Move the World* (2016). Grant has been recognized as one of the world's most influential management thinkers, *Fortune's* "40 under 40," and his 2016 TED talk, "The Surprising Habits of Original Thinkers," earned a standing ovation.

The following article was published in the *New York Times* on June 26, 2016. In the article, Sandberg and Grant use a variety of rhetorical modes to confront the stereotype that women are "catty." As you read, consider how the authors strengthen their argument by using a number of supporting rhetorical strategies. How many of the supporting strategies can you identify?

Reflecting on What You Know

What are some stereotypes you have about women, and where do they come from? Be as specific as possible. For example, rather than saying "the media portrays women as sex objects," talk about a particular ad you saw online recently that characterizes women in this way. Is there a social purpose to spreading stereotypes about gender? Explain.

At the 2014 Winter Olympic Games, the Norwegian cross-country skier Therese Johaug was vying for her first individual gold medal. Fresh off a world championship in the 10-kilometer race, she was now competing in the 30-kilometer. More than a grueling hour later, Ms. Johaug landed the silver, finishing less than three seconds behind the gold medalist—her training partner, Marit Bjorgen. 1

The two Norwegians are the top two female cross-country skiers in the world and fierce competitors. Instead of being bitter rivals, they are best friends. 2

Ms. Bjorgen, 36, has been the reigning queen for more than a decade. When Ms. Johaug burst onto the scene, a wunderkind eight years younger threatening to unseat her, Ms. Bjorgen took her under her wing. 3

"She has given me an incredible amount of confidence," Ms. Johaug said, "and because she has done that I have become the cross-country skier I am." When Ms. Bjorgen announced last year that she was pregnant, Ms. Johaug joked that she was prepared to be the baby's "spare aunt." 4

This is an extreme example of something that happens every day: women helping one another, professionally and personally. Yet the popular idea is that women are not supportive of other women. At school, we call them "mean girls" and later, we call them "catty" or "queen bees." (What's the derogatory male equivalent? It doesn't exist.) 5

The biggest enemy of women, we're warned, is a powerful woman. Queen bees refuse to help other women. If you approach one for advice, instead of opening a door, she'll shut the door before you can even get your foot in. We've often heard women lower their voices and confess, "It hurts me to say this, but the worst boss I ever had was a woman." 6

But statistically that isn't true. 7

According to the queen bee theory, a female senior manager should have a more negative impact on the other women trying to climb into 8 professional ranks. When strategy professors studied the top management of the Standard & Poor's 1,500 companies over 20 years, they found something that seemed to support the notion. In their study, when one woman reached senior management, it was 51 percent less likely that a second woman would make it.

But the person blocking the second woman's path wasn't usually 9
a queen bee; it was a male chief executive. When a woman was made chief executive, the opposite was true. In those companies, a woman had a better chance of joining senior management than when the chief executive was a man.

In business and in government, research supports the notion that 10
women create opportunities for women. On corporate boards, despite having stronger qualifications than men, women are less likely to be mentored—unless there's already a woman on the board. And when women join the board, there's a better chance that other women will rise to top executive positions. We see a similar pattern in politics: In Latin America between 1999 and 2013, female presidents appointed 24 percent more female ministers to their cabinets than the average for their region.

Queen bees exist, but they're far less common than we think. 11
Women aren't any meaner to women than men are to one another. Women are just expected to be nicer. We stereotype men as aggressive and women as kind. When women violate those stereotypes, we judge them harshly. "A man has to be Joe McCarthy to be called ruthless," Marlo Thomas once lamented. "All a woman has to do is put you on hold."

In one experiment, researchers asked people to read about a work- 12
place conflict between two women, two men, or a man and a woman. The conflict was identical, but when the case study was between two women, the participants saw it as more damaging to the relationship and expected them to be more likely to quit. When men argue, it's a healthy debate. When women argue...meow! It's a catfight.

Queen bees aren't a reason for inequality but rather a result of 13
inequality. In the past, structural disadvantages forced women to protect their fragile turf. Some of those disadvantages persist. Research shows that in male-dominated settings, token women are more likely to worry about their standing, so they're reluctant to advocate for other women. A talented woman presents a threat if there's only one seat for a woman at the table. A marginally qualified woman poses a different type of threat: "Hiring you will make me look bad."

This behavior isn't inherently female. It's a natural way we react to discrimination when we belong to a nondominant group. Fearing that their group isn't valued, some members distance themselves from their own kind. They internalize cultural biases and avoid affiliating with groups that are seen as having low status. 14

As more women advance in the workplace, queen bees will go the way of the fax machine. One survey of high-potential leaders involved in mentoring showed that women were mentored by 73 percent of the women but only 30 percent of the men. And 65 percent of high-potential women who received support paid it forward by mentoring others, compared with only 56 percent of men. There is even evidence that there are concrete benefits to supporting others: Research reveals that when women negotiate on behalf of other women on their team, they are able to boost their own salaries, too. 15

Yet women can still pay a price when they advocate for other women. In a recent study of more than 300 executives, when men promoted diversity, they received slightly higher performance ratings. They were good guys who cared about breaking down the old boys' network. When female executives promoted diversity, they were punished with significantly *lower* performance ratings. They were perceived as nepotistic—trying to advantage their own group. 16

The same findings held true for race. White leaders got credit for championing diversity, while nonwhite leaders were penalized for it. And in a controlled experiment on hiring decisions, male leaders were not penalized for choosing a woman or nonwhite candidate over an equally qualified white man. But when female and nonwhite leaders chose the same diversity candidate, they were rated as 10 percent less effective. 17

It's time to stop punishing women and minorities for promoting diversity. In the meantime, there are many ways that women can help one another without hurting themselves. There's no penalty for women mentoring women—and when they do, they're more likely to be seen by their protégés as role models. They share advice about how to break glass ceilings and escape sticky floors, which helps the group and costs them nothing but time. When a woman's accomplishments are overlooked, other women can celebrate them, showing that they care and giving public credit where it's due. 18

And it's time for all of us to stop judging the same behavior more harshly when it comes from a woman rather than a man. Women can disagree—even compete—and still have one another's backs. 19

20 Therese Johaug and Marit Bjorgen are competitors in each individual race; only one can win. But in the long run, training together has made them both stronger. As teammates in Sochi, they won three golds, a silver and a bronze for Norway. When a woman helps another woman, they both benefit. And when women celebrate one another's accomplishments, we're all lifted up.

Thinking Critically about This Reading

Before explaining their ideas, Sandberg and Grant write, "The biggest enemy of women, we're warned, is a powerful woman" (paragraph 6). To what extent have the stereotypes of the catty woman and queen bee been a part of your life or the lives of those you know?

Questions for Study and Discussion

1. Sandberg and Grant begin their essay with narration. (Glossary: **Beginnings and Endings; Narration**) What story do they narrate and why?
2. After their narration, Sandberg and Grant move on to definition. (Glossary: **Definition**) What terms do they define? Why do they choose not to start their essay with definitions?
3. To illustrate their points, Sandberg and Grant use many statistics. (Glossary: **Illustration**) Comment on the placement and function of one of the statistics that Sandberg and Grant mention.
4. How does Sandberg and Grant contrast of men and women contribute to their idea of the catty woman myth? (Glossary: **Comparison and Contrast**) Explain one point of contrast between men and women that they develop.
5. Why do you think this article was written collaboratively? Is there a relationship between the multiple writing strategies and the joint authorship?

Classroom Activity Using Combining Models

Write a short paragraph about an interesting moment in your life in the past week. Focus on narration rather than interpretation. In other words, describe events and give details without saying what you think they mean. You will have five to seven minutes for this activity. When time is called, exchange your paragraph with a partner. Use inductive reasoning to come up with an argument based on your partner's narration, and write that argument in a paragraph beneath your partner's narration. Be sure to create an argument that is sympathetic to your partner's story and that is respectful of your partner's efforts. Your job is not to critique or judge the story; it is simply to write an argument based on the story you read. For example, your partner might have written a paragraph about trouble finding a parking space. You could then write a paragraph arguing for the school to build below-ground parking. You will have five to seven minutes for this part of the activity as well.

When the activity is complete and (time permitting) several pieces have been shared, discuss as a class how it felt to write collaboratively. What were some of the challenges of creating an argument based on someone else's story? How did it feel to shift from narration to argument? What types of narration lent themselves to the best arguments?

Suggested Writing Assignments

1. Write a story from your life in one paragraph and then switch to another essay-writing mode after this paragraph. Then write a paragraph reflecting on how effective your rhetorical switch was.
2. Write an essay about a societal myth that you feel needs to be dispelled. Make sure to use at least three writing modes in your essay. Highlight each mode in a different color. Next, write a separate reflection essay of two paragraphs. The first paragraph should be about which mode seems to take up the most space in your essay and why. The second paragraph should be about what you learned from writing an essay with multiple modes. You (or your instructor) may choose to do this essay in pairs, with a partner highlighting the different modes you use.

Fahrenheit 59: What a Child's Fever Might Tell Us about Climate Change

Audrey Schulman

Miriam Berkley

Novelist Audrey Schulman was born in Montreal, Quebec, Canada, in 1963. She attended Sarah Lawrence College from 1981 to 1983 and graduated from Barnard College in 1985. Schulman has worked as a scriptwriter, a computer consultant, and an Internet Web site designer while developing her skills as a writer. In her first novel, *The Cage* (1995), Schulman tells the story of a young female photographer who is sent to the wilds of northern Canada to study polar bears. She followed this with *Swimming with Jonah* (1999), *A House Named Brazil* (2000), *The Third Way* (2009), and *Three Weeks in December* (2010). She is also the cofounder of Home Energy Efficiency Team (HEET), a nonprofit organization dedicated to increasing energy efficiency education to reduce the effects of climate change. Her articles on global climate change and severe climatic events have appeared in *E Magazine, Conservation Matters, Ms.*, and *Grist.*

In "Fahrenheit 59," first published in the January–February 2007 issue of *Orion* magazine, Schulman explores the inner workings of climate change. As you read, pay attention to how she makes an argument, organizes a vivid analogy (her son's body and its ability to deal with temperature changes and illness), and uses other writing strategies to explain how the earth deals with the complexities of climate change.

Reflecting on What You Know

How concerned are you about climate changes or global warming? What, if anything, do you think needs to be done? Have you personally made any lifestyle changes as a result of your concerns? If so, describe what you have done.

Yesterday afternoon, my six-year-old son practiced swimming with me. Delighted with the water and my attention, Corey stayed in for forty minutes. Despite the water's chill, I knew if I took his temperature it would be close to 98.6° Fahrenheit. For an hour afterward he ran through the humid July heat, playing tag with his cousins, his hair damp with sweat. Still, a reading would have shown his body to be within a degree or two of 98.6°. 1

This stability is a product of homeostasis. A holy word for biologists, *homeostasis* refers to an organism's ability to maintain its ideal temperature and chemistry. 2

Each species has its own preferred level of warmth, but among most mammals the possible range is surprisingly narrow, generally between 97° and 103°F. Each body's temperature works to optimize the function of its enzymes, which are critical to its every chemical interaction. Too cold, and these catalysts slow down. Too hot, and they break down entirely. 3

Such homeostatic regulation depends on a mechanism known as negative feedback: a response that maintains a system's balance. Yesterday, for example, when Corey ran in the hot sun, his cheeks got rosy as more blood moved to the surface, maximizing heat loss off his skin. No, his body said to his increasing temperature. 4

It turns out that our bodies' homeostasis can provide an analogy with which to understand the complexities of climate change—and the human response to it. Over geological time, the biosphere uses negative feedbacks in a way that maintains a stable global average temperature. When the earth's oceans heat up past a certain point, for example, hurricanes (which thrive only on warm water) increase their intensity, leaving a trail of stirred-up nutrients. The food creates a massive bloom of phytoplankton,[1] which suck in enough of the greenhouse gas carbon dioxide to start cooling the global climate. 5

Conversely, when temperatures fall too low, vast quantities of methane are released into the atmosphere, possibly in part because ice sheets build up, lowering sea levels and exposing coastal methane hydrates. As a greenhouse gas twenty times more powerful than carbon dioxide, the methane warms the biosphere quickly. 6

Through a large array of negative feedbacks like these, the biosphere has managed to maintain a relatively stable temperature, despite massive volcanic eruptions of greenhouse gasses and orbital 7

[1]*phytoplankton*: ocean-dwelling microscopic plants.

and solar irregularities. To earth-based organisms, the fluctuations may have seemed severe, allowing ice sheets to roll in or crocodiles to paddle across the Arctic. But through its self-corrections, the biosphere has remained habitable.

According to New York University biology professor Tyler Volk, the 8
sun's temperature has increased 30 percent over the course of earth's history, which would have increased temperatures about one hundred degrees were it not for the cooling effect of phytoplankton and other life. And scientists calculate that the earth would be a frigid fifty to sixty degrees colder without any greenhouse gases. Over the last million years, the biosphere has remained within about eighteen degrees of 59°F.

Humanity's intemperate carbon emissions, however, have severely 9
tested these negative feedbacks. Since 1900 alone, the earth has warmed more than a full degree—one-fifth the entire temperature range over the past ten thousand years. The earth is now within two degrees of its warmest levels in one million years.

The increased heat dries up the soil faster and pumps water vapor 10
into the clouds, exaggerating the severity of drought, then rain. Gentle summer days turn into baking onslaughts, temperate-zone drizzles become tropical monsoons, tropical diseases and pests have whole new latitudes to conquer, and temperate-zone animals and plants are fleeing toward the poles. The increased heat has also warmed the oceans, causing hurricanes to grow in intensity.

And when a situation becomes extreme enough, biological systems 11
can abandon their attempts at moderation. Corey crawled into bed with me in the middle of last night, saying his head hurt. His hands and face felt hot. Touching his ribs I could feel his heart racing. Ill with the flu, his body no longer fought to maintain its normal temperature. Instead it was using positive feedbacks, reactions that amplify a change, to create a fever. Holding him close in bed, I could feel his muscles violently shivering, creating heat and more heat. Within an hour of the first symptoms, his temperature was 102°.

Positive feedbacks can also shift the earth's climate quickly, with 12
the kind of results seen in the latest global warming news. As ice sheets melt near the poles, for example, the water slips through the crevasses to the rock below. At some point the water pools up enough to raise the glacier just a fraction, greasing its slide into the ocean. James Hansen of the Goddard Institute, whose science has been uncannily accurate since he alerted Congress in 1988 to signs of human-induced climate change, points out that this phenomenon can cause millennia-old ice sheets to disappear

with an explosive splash. At that point, white ice no longer reflects sunlight into space. Instead, dark water draws the sunlight in as heat, accelerating the rise in the earth's temperature. Yes, the water says, yes.

The thaw of the Siberian permafrost may provide another example of a positive feedback. Roughly 400,000 megatons of dead plant matter that has never finished decaying because it has been frozen, the permafrost is now thawing more rapidly than expected, according to recent reports. Because all this plant flesh is wet—under snow that's now melting—the decay is engineered by anaerobic bacteria, which metabolize the plants straight into methane, that muscular greenhouse gas. Once truly underway, this release of methane would dwarf any effect humans have on climate change. There'd be no more discussion of Energy Star appliances or raising the emission standards of cars. The rising temperatures would effectively no longer be powered by us, or subject to our influences. The system would take over. 13

As medical researchers have discovered in the past decade, our bodies give us fevers for a specific reason: certain antibodies and other infection-fighting agents function optimally at 100°F or higher. When Corey's body detected the presence of overly aggressive microbes, it turned its thermostat up high. His hypothalamus made his muscles shiver, minimized the blood flow to his skin, conserved heat in his gut. For a little while, his body could withstand a high temperature while the immune system brought out its heavy artillery. Overall this strategy tends to work well: Corey slept straight through the day, and, late in the afternoon, he sat up, skinnier and ferociously thirsty, but healthy again. Research shows, however, that while the feverish response may preserve the human organism as a whole, some of the immune system's agents have side effects: their activity can kill many "innocent" nonaggressive cells. 14

We should take note. It may seem a poetic stretch to say the earth itself ever sickens or has a fever. Seen from a distance, the earth itself does not become more or less "healthy"—just more or less populated with life. But as seen from the ground, the view is rather different. If our planet's feedback systems switch over from negative to positive and the biosphere heats up fast, the earth will certainly seem feverishly ill to a number of species, many of which will not survive. 15

In terms of our planetary climate, it's easy to guess which species is playing the role of overly aggressive microbe. But we do have a choice. Some human cultures, through their agriculture and hunting, have respected and adapted to ecological limits. We have the ability to shape our destiny—to be microbial attackers, or humble cells inside a living body. 16

Thinking Critically about This Reading

In her final paragraph, Schulman says that "it's easy to guess which species is playing the role of overly aggressive microbe." In terms of her analogy, in what ways can human beings be considered "overly aggressive microbes"? Does this analogy help you explain what is happening to our planetary climate? Explain.

Questions for Study and Discussion

1. How does Schulman's organizational pattern help her develop the analogy between her son's illness and the earth's climate changes? Would her essay work as well if she changed the order of her discussion? Why or why not?
2. Schulman begins her essay with narration, describing what happens to her son Corey before discussing what is happening to the earth's climate and the relationship between the two subjects. Why does she begin this way? Is her combination of writing strategies effective here? Explain.
3. What is homeostasis? How does it work in humans? Why is it an important concept to understand? Why does Schulman need to explain it early in her essay?
4. What is negative feedback? How does the author use her son to explain this concept?
5. According to Schulman, how has the biosphere used negative feedback to maintain a relatively constant temperature over time?
6. How does Schulman use her son's fever to explain what is happening to the earth's climate today? What writing strategies does she combine in these passages? Does her analogy help you better understand climate change? Explain.

Classroom Activity Using Combining Models

Which writing strategies might you use in an essay on one of the following topics? Working in a small group, identify one strategy as your primary mode and list at least two other supporting rhetorical modes; then explain how each one could be used in an essay on the topic. (Glossary: **Rhetorical Modes**)

1. What to do when a tornado threatens
2. What we can do about the homeless
3. What we mean by freedom of speech
4. A description of a painting
5. How a musical instrument works
6. Why we need a flat income tax
7. What happened at your friend's birthday party
8. Why we can't let languages become extinct
9. The case for the legalization of certain drugs

Suggested Writing Assignments

1. Schulman concludes: "Some human cultures, through their agriculture and hunting, have respected and adapted to ecological limits. We have the ability to shape our destiny—to be microbial attackers, or humble cells inside a living body" (16). Which choice do you think Schulman recommends? Write an essay in which you propose measures that could be taken on your college campus to make it more climate-friendly. What energy-saving measures are already being taken? What can be done to control carbon dioxide emissions? What measures do you think would have the greatest effect? You may find it helpful to review your response to the Reflecting on What You Know prompt for this selection before you start writing.
2. Using Schulman's essay as a model, write an essay in which you create an analogy to explain a complex idea or concept such as freedom, capitalism, populism, life insurance, air pollution, or metabolism. (Glossary: **Analogy**)

part five

Guides to Research and Editing

CHAPTER **23**

A Brief Guide to Writing a Research Paper

The research paper is an important part of a college education—and for good reason. In writing a research paper, you gain a number of indispensable skills that you can adapt to other college assignments and to situations after graduation.

The real value of writing a research paper, however, goes beyond acquiring basic skills; it is a unique hands-on learning experience. The purpose of a research paper is not to present a collection of quotations that show you can report what others have said about your topic. Rather, your goal is to **analyze, evaluate**, and **synthesize** the materials you research on a topic, gathering skills you can apply to research on other topics and in other disciplines. You learn how to view the results of research from your own perspective and to arrive at an informed opinion of a topic.

Writing a research paper is not very different from the other writing you will be doing in your college writing course. First you determine what you want to write about. Then you decide on a purpose, consider your audience, develop a thesis, collect your evidence, write a first draft, revise and edit, and prepare a final copy. What differentiates the research paper from other kinds of papers is your use of outside sources and how you acknowledge them. Your research will involve working with print and electronic sources and selecting the most appropriate sources from the many that are available on your topic. (See also Chapter 10, Writing with Sources.)

In this chapter, you will learn some valuable research techniques:

- How to establish a realistic schedule for your research project
- How to conduct research on the Internet using keyword searches
- How to evaluate sources
- How to analyze sources
- How to develop a working bibliography

- How to take useful notes
- How to acknowledge your sources using either Modern Language Association (MLA) style in-text citations and a list of works cited or American Psychological Association (APA) style in-text citations and a list of references
- How to present/format your research paper

ESTABLISHING A REALISTIC SCHEDULE

A research project easily spans several weeks. To avoid losing track of time and finding yourself facing an impossible deadline at the last moment, establish a realistic schedule for completing key tasks. By thinking of the research paper as a multistage process, you avoid becoming overwhelmed by the size of the whole undertaking.

Your schedule should allow at least a few days to accommodate unforeseen needs and delays. Use the following template, which lists the essential steps in writing a research paper, to plan your research schedule.

Research Paper Schedule

	Task	Completion Date
1.	Choose a research topic, and pose a worthwhile question.	___/___/___
2.	Locate print and electronic sources.	___/___/___
3.	Develop a working bibliography.	___/___/___
4.	Evaluate and analyze your sources.	___/___/___
5.	Read your sources, taking complete and accurate notes.	___/___/___
6.	Develop a preliminary thesis, and make a working outline.	___/___/___
7.	Write a draft of your paper, including sources that you have summarized, paraphrased, and quoted.	___/___/___
8.	Visit your college writing center for help with your revision.	___/___/___
9.	Decide on a final thesis, and modify your outline.	___/___/___
10.	Revise your paper, and properly cite all borrowed materials.	___/___/___
11.	Prepare a list of works cited.	___/___/___
12.	Prepare the final manuscript, and proofread.	___/___/___
13.	Submit your research paper.	___/___/___

FINDING AND USING SOURCES

You should use materials found through a search of your school library's holdings in print or online—including books, newspapers, journals, magazines, encyclopedias, pamphlets, brochures, and government documents—as your primary tools for research. These sources, unlike many sources found through a generic Internet search, are often reviewed by experts in the field before they are published, are generally overseen by a reputable publishing company or organization, and are examined by editors and fact checkers for accuracy and reliability.

The best place to start any search for print and online sources is your college library's home page. There you will find links to the computerized catalog of book holdings, online reference works, periodical databases, and electronic journals, as well as a list of full-text databases. You'll also find links for subject study guides and for help conducting your research.

To get started, decide on some likely keyword search terms and try them out. You might have to try a number of different terms related to your topic to generate the best results. (For tips on refining your keyword searches, see the box on p. 598.) Your goal is to create a preliminary listing of books, magazine and newspaper articles, public documents and reports, and other sources that may be helpful in exploring your topic. At this early stage, it is better to err on the side of listing too many sources so that, later on, you will not have to relocate sources you discarded too hastily.

Internet sources can be informative and valuable additions to your research, and they are especially useful in providing recent data, stories, and reports. For example, you might find a just-published article from a university laboratory or a news story in your local newspaper's online archives. The Internet offers a vast number of useful and carefully maintained resources, but it also contains much unreliable information. It is your responsibility to determine whether a given Internet source should be trusted. (For advice on evaluating sources, see pp. 599–601.)

CONDUCTING KEYWORD SEARCHES

When searching for sources about your topic in an electronic database, in the library's computerized catalog, or on the Internet, you should start with a keyword search. As obvious or simple as it may sound, the key to a successful keyword search is the quality of the keywords you generate about your topic. You might find it helpful to start a list of potential keywords as you begin your search and add to it as your work proceeds. Often you will discover meaningful combinations of keywords that will lead you directly to the sources you need.

Databases and library catalogs index sources by author, title, year of publication, and subject headings (which are assigned by a cataloger who has previewed the source). The object here is to find a keyword that matches one of the subject headings. Once you begin to locate sources on your topic, be sure to note the subject headings that are listed for each source. You can use these subject headings as keywords to lead you to additional book sources, as well as articles that are gathered in full-text databases (such as InfoTrac, LexisNexis, Expanded Academic ASAP, and JSTOR) to which your library subscribes.

The keyword search process is somewhat different when you are searching on the Internet. It is always a good idea to look for search tips on the help screens or advanced search instructions for the search engine you are using before initiating a keyword search. When you type a keyword in the "Search" box, the search engine electronically scans Internet sites to match your keyword to titles and texts. A search on the Internet might yield a million hits, but the search engine's algorithm puts the sources with the most relevant hits up front. After you scan the first couple of pages of results, you can decide whether these sites seem on topic. If they seem off topic, you will need to refine your search terms to narrow or broaden your search (for tips, see the Refining Keyword Searches on the Web box).

Refining Keyword Searches on the Web

Command terms and characters vary somewhat among electronic databases and popular Internet search engines, but the following functions are almost universally accepted. You can click on the site's "Help" or "Advanced Search" links to ask questions about refining your keyword search.

- Use quotation marks when you are searching for words in exact sequence—for example, "whooping cough"; "Supreme Court."
- Use AND or a plus sign (+) between words to narrow your search by specifying that all words need to appear in a document—for example, tobacco AND cancer; Shakespeare + sonnet.
- Use NOT or a minus sign (–) between words to narrow your search by eliminating unwanted words—for example, monopoly NOT game; cowboys – Dallas.
- Use an asterisk (*) to indicate that you will accept variations of a term—for example, "food label*" for food labels, food labeling, and so forth.

EVALUATING PRINT AND ONLINE SOURCES

You will not have to spend much time in the library to realize that you cannot read every print and online source that appears relevant. Given the abundance of print and Internet sources, the key to successful research is identifying those books, articles, websites, and other online sources that will help you the most. You must evaluate your potential sources to determine which materials you will read, which you will skim, and which you will simply eliminate. (See the Strategies for Evaluating Print and Online Sources box that follows for some evaluation strategies and questions to assist you in identifying your most promising sources.)

Strategies for Evaluating Print and Online Sources

Evaluating a Book

- Read the dust jacket or cover copy for insights into the book's coverage, its relevance, and the author's expertise. In the library catalog, read the summary, if there is one.
- Scan the copyright page or look at the online catalog record to check the publication year.
- Scan the table of contents, and identify any promising chapters.
- Read the author's preface, looking for his or her thesis and purpose. Do the thesis and purpose clearly relate to your topic?
- Check the index for key words or key phrases related to your research topic.
- In the online catalog record, check the subject terms associated with the book.
- Read the opening and concluding paragraphs of any promising chapters. If you are unsure about a chapter's usefulness, skim the whole chapter.
- Ask yourself: Does the source appear to be too general or too technical for my needs or audience?

Evaluating an Article

- Ask yourself what you know about the journal or magazine publishing the article:
  - Is the publication scholarly or popular? Scholarly journals (*American Economic Review, Journal of Marriage and the Family, Wilson Quarterly*) publish articles representing original research written by authorities in the field. Such articles always cite their sources in notes, reference lists, or works cited, which means that you can check their accuracy and delve deeper into the topic by locating these sources. Popular news and

general-interest magazines (*National Geographic, Smithsonian, Time, Ebony*), on the other hand, publish informative, entertaining, and easy-to-read articles written by editorial staff or freelance writers. Popular essays sometimes cite sources but often do not, making them somewhat less authoritative and less helpful in terms of extending your research.
  - What is the reputation of the journal or magazine? Determine the publisher or sponsor. Is it an academic institution, a commercial enterprise, or an individual? Does the publisher or publication have a reputation for accuracy and objectivity?
  - Who are the readers of this journal or magazine?
- Try to determine the author's credentials. Is he or she an expert?
- Consider the title or headline of the article, the opening paragraph or two, and the conclusion. Does the source appear to be too general or too technical for your needs and audience?
- For articles in journals, read the abstract (a summary of the main points), if there is one at the beginning of the essay or in the online record.
- Examine any photographs, charts, graphs, or other illustrations that accompany the article. Determine how useful they might be for your research purposes.

Evaluating a Website

- Consider the type of website. Is this site a personal blog or professional publication? Often the URL, especially the top-level domain name, can give you a clue about the kinds of information provided and the type of organization behind the site. Common suffixes include:

  .com — business, commercial, or personal
  .edu — educational institution
  .gov — government-sponsored
  .net — various types of networks
  .org — nonprofit organization, but also some commercial or personal
- Examine the home page of the site:
  - Does the content appear to be related to your research topic?
  - Is the home page well maintained and professional in appearance?
  - Is there an *About* link on the home page that takes you to background information on the site's sponsor? Is there a mission statement, history, or statement of philosophy? Can you verify whether the site is official—that is, is it actually sanctioned by the organization or company?

- Identify the author of the site or article. What are the author's qualifications for writing on this subject?
- Determine when the site was last updated. Is the content current enough for your purposes?

On the basis of your evaluation, select the most promising books, articles, and websites to pursue in depth for your research project.

ANALYZING SOURCES FOR POSITION AND BIAS

Before beginning to take notes, analyze each source carefully. Look for the writer's main ideas, key examples, strongest arguments, and conclusions. How would you summarize the writer's position? Does the writer have a discernible bias? In what ways, if any, has the writer's bias colored his or her claims and evidence? It is important to ask yourself where each writer stands relative to the other writers as well as to your own position on the subject. Be sure to read critically; it is easy to become absorbed in sources that support your beliefs. Ask yourself whether these like-minded sources consider the possible merits of alternative points of view. If only to test your own position, you should always seek out several independent sources with opposing viewpoints. By knowing exactly where each of your sources is positioned, you can more effectively use them in the context of your research paper.

Look for information about the authors themselves—information like that provided in the writer headnote that accompanies each selection in *Models for Writers*. Such information will help you determine the writer's authority and perspective or bias on the issue. You should also consider the reputation and special interests of book publishers and magazines, because you are likely to get different views—conservative, liberal, international, feminist—on the same topic depending on which publication you read. Use the Checklist for Analyzing a Writer's Position and Bias that follows to assist you in analyzing each of your print and online sources for the writer's position and bias.

Checklist for Analyzing a Writer's Position and Bias

- What is the writer's thesis or claim?
- How does the writer support this thesis? Does the **evidence** seem reasonable and representative, or is it mainly vague, anecdotal, or sensational?
- What is the writer's attitude toward the subject (tone)?
- Is the author's **purpose** to inform? Or is it to argue for a particular position? If it's to argue, is the writer's appeal logical and reasoned, or is it largely emotional?
- Does the writer consider opposing viewpoints?
- What are the writer's basic assumptions? Which of these are stated, and which are implied? Are they acceptable?
- Does the writer have any discernible cultural, political, religious, or gender biases? Is the writer associated with a special-interest group, such as the American Medical Association, the National Organization for Women, the American Immigration Council, the Sierra Club, the National Education Association, the National Rifle Association, or Amnesty International?
- Is the writer an expert on the subject? Do other writers on the subject mention this author in their work?
- Does the publisher or publication have a reputation for accuracy and objectivity? Or does it have an inclination for a particular viewpoint?
- Is important information documented in notes or links so that it can be verified or corroborated in other sources?
- Does the source reflect current thinking and research in the field?

DEVELOPING A WORKING BIBLIOGRAPHY

As you discover books, journal and magazine articles, newspaper stories, and websites that you think might be helpful for writing your paper, you need to start maintaining a record of important information about each source. This record, called a *working bibliography,* will enable you to know where sources are located when it comes time to consult and acknowledge them in your paper and list of works cited (for MLA) or list of references (for APA). See pages 608–16 (MLA) and 625–30 (APA) for an explanation of how to prepare these lists. In all likelihood, your working bibliography will contain more sources than you actually consult and include in your final list.

You may find it easy to make a separate bibliography document or index note for each work that you think might be helpful to your research. Alphabetize them by the authors' last names. By using a separate document or card for each book, article, or website, you can continually edit your working bibliography, dropping sources that do not prove helpful and adding new ones.

When conducting your research through your library's online offerings, you can copy bibliographic information from the online catalog and periodical indexes or from the Internet and paste it directly into your document. Unlike hard copy notes or an index card, electronic documents allow you to search these sources throughout the research process. You can also track your project online with a citation manager. One advantage of the copy/paste option over the index card method is accuracy, especially in punctuation, spelling, and capitalization—details that are essential when accessing Internet sites. One danger, however, is accidental plagiarism if you copy and paste information without acknowledging that it came from a source.

Checklist for a Working Bibliography

For Books

- Library call number
- Names of all authors, editors, and translators
- Title and subtitle
- Publication data:
  - Publisher's name
  - Date of publication
- Edition number (if not the first) and volume number (if applicable)
- Online location information, if an online book

For Periodical Articles

- Names of all authors
- Title and subtitle of article
- Title of journal, magazine, or newspaper (the "container" in which the article appears)
- Publication data:
  - Volume number and issue number and/or date of issue
  - Page numbers
  - DOI (digital object identifier), a permanent code, or URL (permalink preferred)

For Internet Sources

Names of all authors, editors, compilers, or sponsoring agents
Title and subtitle of the source
Title of the longer work (or "container") in which the source appears (an online periodical or book, blog, website, or similar work)
Editor, compiler, publisher, or sponsor of the larger work in which the document is contained
Date of release, online posting, or latest revision
Name of database or other type of even larger work (or "container") that houses the longer work
Format of online source (web page, e-mail, scholarly journal article, blog or Twitter post, and so on)
DOI (digital object identifier) or direct, stable URL
Date of access (if no date of release, online posting, or latest revision is provided)

For Other Sources

Name of author, government agency, organization, company, recording artist, personality
Title of the work
Format (pamphlet, unpublished diary, interview, television broadcast, government document, legal document, address or lecture)
Publication or production data:
    Name of publisher or producer
    Date of publication, production, or release
    Identifying codes or numbers (if applicable), including URL if accessed online and version number for apps, software, and so on

TAKING NOTES

As you read, take notes. You're looking for ideas, facts, opinions, statistics, examples, and other evidence that you think will be useful as you write your paper. Look for recurring themes, and notice where writers are in agreement and where they differ. The effectiveness of your paper is largely determined by the quality—not necessarily the quantity—of your notes. Your purpose is not to present a collection of quotes showing that you've read all the material and know what others have said about your topic. Rather, your goal is to **analyze**, **evaluate**, and **synthesize** the information you collect—to enter into the discussion of the issues and take ownership of your topic. You want to view the results of your research from your own perspective and arrive at an informed opinion of your topic. (For more on writing with sources, see Chapter 10.)

Now for some practical advice on taking notes. First, be systematic in your note taking. If you keep notes electronically, consider creating a separate file for each topic or source, or using an electronic research manager like Zotero. Title all documents using the same naming conventions. If you keep your notes by hand or on note cards, write one note per page or card and include the author's full name, the complete title of the source, and a page number indicating the origin of the note. If you keep your notes organized, when you get to the planning and writing stage you will be able to sequence them according to the plan you have envisioned for your paper. Furthermore, should you decide to alter your organizational plan, you can easily reorder your notes to reflect those revisions.

Be very careful, though, when taking notes electronically—especially if you are taking your notes from an online source. It is easy and tempting to simply copy and paste phrases or whole paragraphs into your notes. This can get you into trouble, however, when you go to write your paper if you do not keep careful track of which words belong to the author and which are your own. For tips on avoiding plagiarism, see Chapter 10, pages 238–42.

Second, try not to take too many notes. Ask yourself, "How exactly does this material help prove or disprove my thesis?" Try to envision where in your paper you could use the information. If it does not seem relevant to your thesis, don't bother to take a note.

Once you decide to take a note, you must decide whether to summarize, paraphrase, or quote directly. The approach you take should be determined by the content of the passage and the way you plan to use it in your paper. For detailed advice on summaries, paraphrases, and quotations, see Chapter 10, pages 228–32.

DOCUMENTING SOURCES

Whenever you summarize, paraphrase, or quote a person's thoughts and ideas and whenever you use facts or statistics that are not commonly known or believed, you must properly acknowledge the source of your information. If you do not properly acknowledge ideas and information created by someone else, you are guilty of **plagiarism**—of using someone else's material but making it look as if it were your own (see pp. 238–42). You must document the source of your information whenever you do the following:

- Quote a source word for word
- Refer to information and ideas from another source that you present in your own words as either a paraphrase or a summary
- Cite statistics, tables, charts, or graphs

You do not need to document these types of information:

- Your own observations, experiences, and ideas
- Factual information available in a number of reference works (known as "common knowledge")
- Proverbs, sayings, and familiar quotations

A reference to the source of your borrowed information is called a **citation**. There are many systems for making citations, and your citations must consistently follow one of these systems. The documentation style recommended by the Modern Language Association is commonly used in English and the humanities and is the style used throughout this book. Another common system is the American Psychological Association (APA) style, which is generally used in the social sciences. Your instructor will probably tell you which style to use. For more information on documentation styles, consult the appropriate manual or handbook.

MLA-STYLE DOCUMENTATION

There are two components of MLA-style documentation. *In-text citations* are placed in the body of your paper, and the *list of works*

For more practice, visit the LaunchPad for *Models for Writers*:
Tutorial > Do I Need to Cite That?
LearningCurve > Working with Sources (MLA)

cited provides complete publication data for your in-text citations and is placed at the end of your paper. Both of these components are necessary for complete documentation.

In-Text Citations

In-text citations, also known as *parenthetical citations*, give the reader citation information immediately, at the point at which it is most meaningful. Rather than having to find a footnote or an endnote, the reader sees the citation as part of the writer's text.

Most in-text citations consist of only the author's last name and a page reference. Usually the author's name is given in an introductory, or *signal*, phrase at the beginning of the borrowed material, and the page reference is given in parentheses at the end. If the author's name is not given in a signal phrase, put it in parentheses along with the page reference. (For more information on signal phrases, see pp. 233–35.) When you borrow material from two or more works by the same author, you must include the title of the work in the signal phrase or a shortened version of it parenthetically at the end. (To shorten a title, use the first noun and any adjectives, minus any words like *The*, *A*, or *An*: "The Greatest Woman on the Planet" becomes "Greatest Woman.") The parenthetical reference signals the end of the borrowed material and directs your readers to the list of works cited should they want to pursue a particular source. Treat electronic sources as you do print sources, keeping in mind that some electronic sources use paragraph numbers instead of page numbers. Consider the following examples of in-text citations, taken from the opening paragraph of student Charley Horton's paper "How Humans Affect Our Global Environment."

In-Text Citations (MLA Style)

Controversy has always shadowed public discussions of our environment and environmental policy. In her essay "Fable for Tomorrow," Rachel Carson first warned Americans about the dire consequences of the irresponsible use of herbicides and insecticides. As early as 1962, she clearly saw that "a grim specter has crept upon us almost unnoticed" (50). First decried as an alarmist, Carson is now revered as an early leader in the ecology movement. Today the debate is not limited to pesticides, where controversy still swirls around the use of certain lawn care products and their commercial agricultural counterparts. It has expanded to include often uncivil discussions about the causes of climate change. Audrey Schulman has written extensively on severe climatic events, and she concludes that human behavior has had a direct impact on global climate change. She knows that while "some human cultures, through their agriculture and hunting, have respected and adapted to ecological limits" (589), others have not. Like her predecessor Rachel Carson, Schulman believes that Americans must act to avoid an ecological tragedy: "We have the ability to shape our destiny" (589).

List of Works Cited (MLA Style)

Carson, Rachel. "Fable for Tomorrow." *Models for Writers*, edited by Alfred Rosa and Paul Eschholz, 13th ed., Bedford/St. Martin's, 2018, pp. 47–50.

Schulman, Audrey. "Fahrenheit 59: What a Child's Fever Might Tell Us about Climate Change." *Models for Writers*, edited by Alfred Rosa and Paul Eschholz, 13th ed., Bedford/St. Martin's, 2018, pp. 586–89.

In the preceding example, the student followed MLA style guidelines for his list of works cited. When constructing the list of works cited page for your paper, consult the following MLA guidelines, based on the *MLA Handbook*, 8th ed. (2016), where you will find model entries for a range of common sources.

List of Works Cited

In this section, you will find general MLA guidelines for creating a works-cited list, followed by sample entries that cover the citation situations you will encounter most often. Make sure that you follow the formats as they appear on these pages. Although most college libraries and databases provide programs that will format citations, you will need to check the citations carefully, since these programs are often inaccurate.

Guidelines for Constructing Your Works Cited Page

1. Begin the list on a fresh page following the last page of text.
2. Center the title *Works Cited* at the top of the page.
3. Double-space both within and between entries on your list.
4. Alphabetize your sources by the authors' last names. If you have two or more authors with the same last name, alphabetize first by last names and then by first names.
5. If you have two or more works by the same author, alphabetize by the first word of the titles, not counting *A*, *An*, or *The*. Use the author's name in the first entry and three unspaced hyphens followed by a period in subsequent entries: (---.).
6. For two authors, reverse only the name of the first author. For three or more authors, provide only the first author's name followed by a comma and *et al.* (and others).
7. If no author is known, alphabetize by title.
8. Begin each entry at the left margin. If the entry is longer than one line, indent the second and subsequent lines half an inch.
9. Italicize the titles of books, journals, magazines, and newspapers. Use quotation marks with titles of periodical articles, chapters, and essays within books, short stories, and poems.
10. Provide the names of other contributors, such as editors, translators, or illustrators, with explanations such as *translated by*.
11. Include edition or version numbers.
12. If the source is part of a sequence, include volume and/or issue numbers.
13. If the source has a publisher whose name differs significantly from the work it embodies or is contained by, include this publisher's name; otherwise, omit it.
14. If your source was accessed through a database, application, streaming service, or other larger "container," include information about that larger container after information about the original source. For a database, for example, include its name and the DOI or URL, separated by a comma.
15. Provide the location where the source was accessed. For print sources, this means page numbers, preceded by the prefix *p.* or *pp*. For online sources, this means a DOI or URL. For lectures or live performances, this means the physical location where they took place.

PERIODICAL PRINT PUBLICATIONS: JOURNALS, MAGAZINES, AND NEWSPAPERS

ARTICLE IN A SCHOLARLY JOURNAL

For all scholarly journals—whether they paginate continuously throughout a given year or not—provide the volume number, the issue number, the publication date, and the page numbers. Separate the volume number and the issue number with a comma.

Masuzawa, Tomoko. "The Bible as Literature?—Note on a Litigious Ferment of the Concept 'Comparative Literature.'" *Comparative Literature*, vol. 65, no. 3, Summer 2013, pp. 306-24.

ARTICLE IN A MAGAZINE

When citing a weekly or biweekly magazine, give the complete date (day, month, year). Abbreviate all months except May, June, and July.

Von Drehle, David. "Broken Trust: Fifty Years after JFK's Assassination." *Time,* 25 Nov. 2013, pp. 40-49.

When citing a magazine published every month or every two months, provide the month or months and year. If the article is not printed on consecutive pages—for example, an article might begin on page 45 and then skip to page 48—include only the first page followed by a plus sign.

Mascarelli, Amanda Leigh. "Fall Guys." *Audubon,* Nov.-Dec. 2009, pp. 44+.

ARTICLE IN A NEWSPAPER

Bilton, Nick. "Internet's Sad Legacy: No More Secrets." *The New York Times,* 16 Dec. 2013, national ed., p. B8.

NONPERIODICAL PRINT PUBLICATIONS: BOOKS, BROCHURES, AND PAMPHLETS

BOOK WITH ONE AUTHOR

Shlaes, Amity. *Coolidge*. Harper Collins, 2013.

Spell out the publisher's name, but omit generic business words or abbreviations, such as *Corporation* or *Inc*. For university presses,

For more practice, visit the LaunchPad for *Models for Writers*:
Video Tutorial: How to Cite an Article in MLA Style
Video Tutorial: How to Cite a Book in MLA Style

replace *university* and *press* with *UP*: Write *Cambridge UP* for Cambridge University Press.

ANTHOLOGY

Eggers, Dave, editor. *The Best American Nonrequired Reading, 2002*. Houghton Mifflin, 2002.

BOOK WITH TWO OR MORE AUTHORS

For a book with two authors, list the authors in the order in which they appear on the title page.

Courtney, Elizabeth, and Eric Zencey. *Greening Vermont: The Search for a Sustainable State*. Vermont Natural Resources Council, 2012.

For a book with three or more authors, list the first author last name first, followed by a comma and the abbreviation *et al.* ("and others").

Beardsley, John, et al. *Gee's Bend: The Women and Their Quilts.* Tinwood Books, 2002.

WORK IN AN ANTHOLOGY

Smith, Seaton. "'Jiving' with Your Teen." *The Best American Nonrequired Reading, 2002*. Edited by Dave Eggers, Houghton Mifflin, 2002, pp. 217-20.

AN ILLUSTRATED BOOK OR GRAPHIC NOVEL

Clemens, Samuel L. *The Adventures of Huckleberry Finn*. Illustrated by Norman Rockwell, Heritage Books, 1940.

Neufeld, Josh, writer and artist. *A.D.: New Orleans after the Deluge*. Pantheon Books, 2009.

BOOK PUBLISHED IN A SECOND OR SUBSEQUENT EDITION

Phillipson, David W. *African Archaeology*. 3rd ed., Cambridge UP, 2005.

GOVERNMENT PUBLICATION

United States, Department of Health and Human Services. *Eat Healthy, Be Active, Community Workshops*. Government Printing Office, 2012.

Give the government and the agency, and any departments with commas between them, followed by a period. Follow the source title with a period. In many cases, the publisher is the Government

Printing Office, for U.S. government documents published before 2014, and Government Publishing Office in 2014 or after.

ONLINE PUBLICATIONS

The following guidelines and models for citing online sources or sources accessed online have been adapted from the most recent advice of the MLA, as detailed in the *MLA Handbook,* 8th ed. (2016), and from the MLA's website, mla.org.

For sources located or accessed online or through an online database, MLA style requires you to include either DOIs or direct URLs as locations for sources in works-cited entries. The following example illustrates an entry with the URL included.

Reychler, Luc. "Peace Building Architecture." *Peace and Conflict Studies*, vol. 9, no. 1, 2002, www.gmu.edu/programs/icar/pcs/LR83PCS.htm.

To format the URL, omit the *http://* prefix, but include the rest of the URL in full, including *www.* when applicable. Precede a DOI with *doi:* (no space). End both with a period. MLA style requires that you break URLs extending over more than one line only after a punctuation mark, ideally a slash, but not a hyphen or period. Do *not* add spaces, hyphens, or any other punctuation to indicate the break.

PERIODICAL ARTICLES PUBLISHED OR ACCESSED ONLINE

To cite an article, a review, an editorial, or a letter to the editor in a periodical (journal, magazine, or newspaper) accessed online, provide the author, the title of the article, the title of the publication, the volume and issue (for scholarly journals), and the date of issue, followed by the page numbers (if available), the publisher (if distinct from the publication), and the article's DOI or direct URL. Because the nature of online news can be fluid and content can change over time, include the time the story was posted, if available.

ARTICLE IN AN ONLINE SCHOLARLY JOURNAL

Rist, Thomas. "Religion, Politics, Revenge: The Dead in Renaissance Drama." *Early Modern Literary Studies*, vol. 9, no. 1, 2003, extra.shu .ac.uk/emls/09-1/ristdead.html.

For more practice, visit the LaunchPad for *Models for Writers*:
Video Tutorial: How to Cite a Web Site in MLA Style

ARTICLE IN AN ONLINE MAGAZINE

Walsh, Joan. "Poverty Nation: How America Created a Low-Wage Work Swamp." *Salon,* 15 Dec. 2013, www.salon.com/2013/12/15/poverty_nation_how_america_created_a_low_wage_work_swamp/.

ARTICLE IN AN ONLINE NEWSPAPER

Garland, Lance. "After Orlando Shooting, Why Visibility Matters for the Gay Community." *The Seattle Times*, 14 June 2016, www.seattletimes.com/opinion/why-visibility-matters-for-the-gay-community/.

STORY FROM AN ONLINE NEWS SERVICE

"Iran Police Clash with Protesters." *CNN,* 7 Dec. 2009, www.cnn.com/2009/WORLD/meast/12/07/iran.protest.warnings/index.html?iref=topnews.

PERIODICAL PUBLICATIONS ACCESSED IN ONLINE DATABASES

Here are some model entries for periodical publications collected in online databases/subscription services.

JOURNAL ARTICLE WITH A DOI

Diaz, Robert. "Transnational Queer Theory and Unfolding Terrorisms." *Criticism,* vol. 50, no. 3, 2009, pp. 533-41. *Project Muse,* doi:10.1353/crt.0.0072.

JOURNAL ARTICLE WITHOUT A DOI (USE URL)

Bachi, Salim, and Alison Rice. "The Place of Islam in Literature, Geography, Memory, and Exile." *Religion and Literature,* vol. 43, no. 1, 2011, pp. 162-66. *JSTOR,* www.jstor.org.proxy.wexler.hunter.cuny.edu/stable/23049365.

MAGAZINE ARTICLE

Keizer, Garret. "Sound and Fury: The Politics of Noise in a Loud Society." *Harper's Magazine,* Mar. 2001, pp. 39-48. *Academic Search Complete,* ebscohost.com.

For more practice, visit the LaunchPad for *Models for Writers*:
Video Tutorial: How to Cite a Database in MLA Style

NEWSPAPER ARTICLE

Porter, Eduardo. "Racial Identity Returns to American Politics." *The New York Times,* 6 Jan. 2016, p. B1. *LexisNexis Academic,* www.nytimes.com/2016/01/06/business/economy/racial-identity-and-its-hostilities-return-to-american-politics.html.

NONPERIODICAL WEB PUBLICATIONS

Nonperiodical web publications include all online content that does not fit into one of the previous two categories—articles published or accessed online, or articles accessed from an online database/subscription service.

BOOK OR PART OF A BOOK ACCESSED ONLINE

For a book available online, provide the author, the title, the editor (if any), original publication date (and other information only if relevant), and the name of the database or website where it was accessed.

Hawthorne, Nathaniel. *The Blithedale Romance.* 1894. *Project Gutenberg,* 2000, www.gutenberg.org/ebooks/2081.

If you are citing only part of an online book, include the title or name of the part directly after the author's name.

Woolf, Virginia. "Kew Gardens." *Monday or Tuesday,* 1921. *Bartleby.com: Great Books Online,* www.bartleby.com/85/7.html.

SPEECH, ESSAY, POEM, OR SHORT STORY FROM AN ONLINE SITE

If there is no date provided for the online publication of a source, include your date of access at the end of the entry after the word *Accessed.*

Faulkner, William. "On Accepting the Nobel Prize." 10 Dec. 1950. *The History Place: Great Speeches Collection,* www.historyplace.com/speeches/faulkner.htm. Accessed 12 Mar. 2014.

ONLINE GOVERNMENT PUBLICATION

United States, Department of the Treasury, Internal Revenue Service. *Your Rights as a Taxpayer.* 23 July 2013, www.tax.ny.gov/tra/rights.htm.

WIKI ENTRY

"C. S. Lewis." *Wikipedia*. 13 June 2016, en.wikipedia.org/w/index.php?title=C._S._Lewis&oldid=725147501.

No author is listed for a Wiki entry because the content is written collaboratively. Be sure to list the date of the exact version you are citing, and to provide a stable URL to this version. Find this URL by selecting the "View history" link at the top right corner of the page.

ADDITIONAL COMMON SOURCES

TELEVISION OR RADIO BROADCAST

"Everyone's Waiting." *Six Feet Under*. Directed by Alan Ball, performances by Peter Krause and Michael C. Hall, season 5, episode 12, HBO, 21 Aug. 2005.

FILM OR VIDEO RECORDING

Spielberg, Steven, director. *Schindler's List*. Performances by Liam Neeson, Ralph Fiennes, and Ben Kingsley. 20th Anniversary ed., Universal Studios, 2013.

TELEVISION SHOW (VIA STREAMING SERVICE)

Pesce, P.J., director. "Murphy's Law." *The 100*, season 1, episode 4, CW, 9 Apr. 2014. *Netflix*, www.netflix.com/watch/70303980.

PODCAST (VIA APP)

"Happy Ending." *Start Up*, season 3, episode 7, Gimlet, 9 June 2016. *Overcast: Podcast Player*, version 2.5.

INTERVIEW

Handke, Peter. "Facing His Critics." Interview by Deborah Solomon, *The New York Times Magazine*, 2 July 2006, p. 13.

Begin with the name of the person being interviewed. For interviews that you conduct, provide the name of the person interviewed, the words *Personal interview*, and the date.

Mosher, Howard Frank. Personal interview. 30 Jan. 2014.

CARTOON OR COMIC STRIP

Luckovich, Mike. *The Atlanta Journal-Constitution*, 24 Nov. 2009, p. 2B. Cartoon.

ADVERTISEMENT

American Cruise Lines. *Smithsonian,* Jan. 2013, p. 7. Advertisement.

AN ANNOTATED STUDENT MLA-STYLE RESEARCH PAPER

Lesley Timmerman's assignment was to write an argument, and she was free to choose her own topic. After considering a number of possible topics and doing some preliminary research on several of them, she turned to a subject that she and her classmates had been discussing: the need for corporations to be socially responsible for their actions.

Timmerman began by brainstorming about her topic. She made lists of ideas, facts, issues, arguments, and opposing arguments. Once she was confident that she had amassed enough information to begin writing, she made a rough outline of an organizational plan she thought she could follow and ran it by her professor. With this plan in mind, she wrote a first draft of her essay. After taking a break from the draft for a day or two, Timmerman went back and examined it carefully, assessing how it could be improved.

After rereading her first draft, Timmerman saw that her organizational plan could be modified to emphasize the examples of PepsiCo and Walmart. She could then develop them as examples of the many socially responsible corporations that measure their success by the "triple bottom line" of "profit, planet, and people." And these two examples would lead naturally into her discussion of what socially responsible corporations mean to employees and consumers alike. Timmerman scoured her sources to make sure that she was using the materials that best either supported or illustrated the points she wanted to make about corporate responsibility as well as the opposition's argument.

The final draft of Timmerman's research paper illustrates that she has learned how the parts of a well-researched and well-written paper fit together and how to make revisions that emulate some of the qualities of the model essays she had read and studied in class. The following is the final draft of her paper, which demonstrates MLA-style documentation and format for research papers.

Timmerman 1

Lesley Timmerman
Professor Jennifer Wilson
English 102
17 April 2017

Title is focused and announces the thesis

An Argument for Corporate Responsibility

Double space between the title and the first paragraph—and throughout the essay

Opponents of corporate social responsibility (CSR) argue that a company's sole duty is to generate profits. According to them, by acting for the public good, corporations are neglecting their primary obligation to make money. However, as people are becoming more and more conscious of corporate impacts on society and the environment, separating profits from company practices and ethics does not make sense. Employees want to work for institutions that share their values, and consumers want to buy products from companies that are making an impact and improving people's lives. Furthermore, businesses exist in an interdependent world where the health of the environment and the well-being of society really do matter. For these reasons, corporations have to take responsibility for their actions, beyond making money for shareholders. For their own benefit as well as the public's, companies must strive to be socially responsible.

Brief statement of one side of the issue

Summary of the opposing view clearly introduced with signal phrase

In his article "The Case against Corporate Responsibility," *Wall Street Journal* writer Aneel Karnani argues that CSR will never be able to solve the world's problems. Thinking it can, Karnani says, is a dangerous illusion. He recommends that instead of expecting corporate managers to act in the public interest, we should rely on philanthropy and government regulation. Karnani maintains that "Managers who sacrifice profit for the common good . . . are in effect imposing a tax on their shareholders and arbitrarily deciding how that money should be spent." In other words, according to Karnani, corporations should not be determining what constitutes socially responsible behavior; individual donors and the

Lead-in to quotation

1" margin on each side and at bottom

government should. Certainly, individuals should continue to make charitable gifts, and governments should maintain laws and regulations to protect the public interest. However, Karnani's reasoning for why corporations should be exempt from social responsibility is flawed. With very few exceptions, corporations' socially responsible actions are not arbitrary and do not sacrifice long-term profits.

Essayist's response to the quotation

In fact, corporations have already proven that they can contribute profitably and meaningfully to solving significant global problems by integrating CSR into their standard practices and long-term visions. Rather than focusing on shareholders' short-term profits, many companies have begun measuring their success by "profit, planet, and people" — what is known as the "triple bottom line." Businesses operating under this principle consider their environmental and social impacts, as well as their financial impacts, and make responsible and compassionate decisions. For example, such businesses use resources efficiently, create healthy products, choose suppliers who share their ethics, and improve economic opportunities for people in the communities they serve. By doing so, companies often save money. They also contribute to the sustainability of life on earth and ensure the sustainability of their own businesses. In their book *The Triple Bottom Line: How Today's Best-Run Companies Are Achieving Economic, Social, and Environmental Success*, coauthors Savitz and Weber demonstrate that corporations need to become sustainable, in all ways. They argue that "the only way to succeed in today's interdependent world is to embrace sustainability" (xi). The authors go on to show that for the vast majority of companies, a broad commitment to sustainability enhances profitability (Savitz and Weber 39).

Author concisely states her position

Transitions ("For example," "also") alert readers to where the writer is taking them

Signal phrase introduces both the direct quotation and the paraphrase directly following

For example, PepsiCo has been able to meet the financial expectations of its shareholders while demonstrating its

Timmerman 3

Parenthetical citations clearly document what the author has borrowed

commitment to the triple bottom line. In addition to donating over $16 million to help victims of natural disasters, Pepsi has woven concerns for people and for the planet into its company practices and culture (Bejou 4). For instance, because of a recent water shortage in an area of India where Pepsi runs a plant, the company began a project to build community wells (Savitz and Weber 160). Though Pepsi did not cause the water shortage nor was its manufacturing threatened by it, "Pepsi realizes that the well-being of the community is part of the company's responsibility" (Savitz and Weber 161). Ultimately, Pepsi chose to look beyond the goal of maximizing short-term profits. By doing so, the company improved its relationship with this Indian community, improved people's daily lives and opportunities, and improved its own reputation. In other words, Pepsi embraced CSR and ensured a more sustainable future for everyone involved.

Another example of a wide-reaching company that is working toward greater sustainability on all fronts is Walmart. The corporation has issued a CSR policy that includes three ambitious goals: "to be fully supplied by renewable energy, to create zero waste and to sell products that sustain people and the environment" ("From Fringe"). As Dr. Doug Guthrie, dean of George Washington University's School of Business, noted in a recent lecture, if a company as powerful as Walmart were to succeed in these goals, the impact would be huge. To illustrate Walmart's potential influence, Dr. Guthrie pointed out that the corporation's exports from China to the United States are equal to Mexico's total exports to the United States. In committing to CSR, the company's leaders are acknowledging how much their power depends on the earth's natural resources, as well as the communities who produce, distribute, sell, and purchase Walmart's products. The company is also well aware that achieving its goals will "ultimately save the company a great deal of money" ("From Fringe"). For good reason, Walmart, like other companies around the world, is choosing to act in *everyone's* best interest.

Author now introduces statistical evidence that might have turned the reader off if introduced earlier

Recent research on employees' and consumers' social consciousness offers companies further reason to take corporate responsibility seriously. For example, studies show that workers care about making a difference (Meister). In many cases, workers would even take a pay cut to work for a more responsible, sustainable company. In fact, 45 percent of workers said they would take a 15 percent reduction in pay "for a job that makes a social or environmental impact" (Meister). Even more said they would take a 15 percent cut in pay to work for a company with values that match their own (Meister). The numbers are most significant among Millennials (those born between, approximately, 1980 and the early 2000s). Eighty percent of Millennials said they "wanted to work for a company that cares about how it impacts and contributes to society," and over half said they would not work for an "irresponsible company" (Meister). Given this more socially conscious generation, companies are going to find it harder and harder to ignore CSR. To recruit and retain employees, employers will need to earn the admiration, respect, and loyalty of their workers by becoming "good corporate citizen[s]" (qtd. in "From Fringe").

Similarly, studies clearly show that CSR matters to today's consumers. According to an independent report, 80 percent of Americans say they would switch brands to support a social cause. Eighty-eight percent say they approve of companies' using social or environmental issues in their marketing. And 83 percent say they "wish more of the products, services and retailers would support causes" (Cone Communications 5–6). Other independent surveys corroborate these results, confirming that today's customers, especially Millennials, care about more than just price ("From Fringe"). Furthermore, plenty of

Timmerman 5

companies have seen what happens when they assume that consumers do not care about CSR. For example, in 1997, when Nike customers discovered that their shoes were manufactured by child laborers in Indonesia, the company took a huge financial hit (Guthrie). Today, information-age customers are even more likely to educate themselves about companies' labor practices and environmental records. Smart corporations will listen to consumer preferences, provide transparency, and commit to integrating CSR into their long-term business plans.

Author argues that it is in the companies' interest to be socially responsible

In this increasingly interdependent world, the case against CSR is becoming more and more difficult to defend. Exempting corporations and relying on government to be the world's conscience does not make good social, environmental, or economic sense. Contributors to a recent article in the online journal *Knowledge@Wharton,* published by the Wharton School of Business, agree. Professor Eric Orts maintains that "it is an outmoded view to say that one must rely only on the government and regulation to police business responsibilities. What we need is re-conception of what the purpose of business is" (qtd. in "From Fringe"). The question is, what should the purpose of a business be in today's world? Professor of Business Administration David Bejou of Elizabeth City State University has a thoughtful and sensible answer to that question. He writes:

Author's lead-in to the quotation guides the readers' response to the quotation (long quotation is indented ½")

> [I]t is clear that the sole purpose of a business is not merely that of generating profits for its owners. Instead, because compassion provides the necessary equilibrium between a company's purpose and the needs of its communities, it should be the new philosophy of business. (Bejou 1)

As Bejou implies, the days of allowing corporations to act in their own financial self-interest with little or no regard for their effects on others are over. None of us can afford such a

Timmerman 6

narrow view of business. The world is far too interconnected. A seemingly small corporate decision — to buy coffee beans directly from local growers or to install solar panels — can affect the lives and livelihoods of many people and determine the environmental health of whole regions. A business, just like a government or an individual, therefore has an ethical responsibility to act with compassion for the public good.

Author ends on an upbeat note

Fortunately, corporations have many incentives to act responsibly. Customer loyalty, employee satisfaction, overall cost-savings, and long-term viability are just some of the advantages businesses can expect to gain by embracing comprehensive CSR policies. Meanwhile, companies have very little to lose by embracing a socially conscious view. These days, compassion is profitable. Corporations would be wise to recognize the enormous power, opportunity, and responsibility they have to effect positive change.

Works Cited

Alphabetical by author's last name

Bejou, David. "Compassion as the New Philosophy of Business." *Journal of Relationship Marketing*, vol. 10, no. 1, 2011, pp. 1–6. *Business Source Complete*, doi:10.1080/15332667.2011.550098.

Hanging indent ½"

Cone Communications. *2010 Cone Cause Evolution Study*, ppqty.com/2010_Cone_Study.pdf. Accessed 15 Mar. 2014.

An article on a blog without a known author

"From Fringe to Mainstream: Companies Integrate CSR Initiatives into Everyday Business." *Knowledge@Wharton*, 14 Mar. 2014, knowledge.wharton.upenn.edu/article/from-fringe-to-mainstream-companies-integrate-csr-initiatives-into-everyday-business/.

A clip from YouTube

Guthrie, Doug. "Promoting a Comprehensive Approach to Corporate Social Responsibility (CSR)." George P. Schultz National Training College, Arlington, VA, 26 Apr. 2012. Address. YouTube, www.youtube.com/watch?v=99cJMe6wERc.

Timmerman 7

Karnani, Aneel. "The Case against Corporate Social Responsibility." *The Wall Street Journal,* Dow Jones, 23 Aug. 2010, www.wsj.com/articles/SB10001424052748703338004575230112664504890.

Meister, Jeanne. "Corporate Social Responsibility: A Lever for Employee Attraction & Engagement." *Forbes*, 7 June 2012, www.forbes.com/sites/jeannemeister/2012/06/07/corporate-social-responsibility-a-lever-for-employee-attraction-engagement/#.

Savitz, Andrew W., with Karl Weber. *The Triple Bottom Line: How Today's Best-Run Companies Are Achieving Economic, Social, and Environmental Success*. Jossey-Bass, 2006.

APA-STYLE DOCUMENTATION

The American Psychological Association (APA) recommends a simple, two-part system for documenting sources. The system consists of a brief *in-text citation* at the point where words or ideas have been borrowed from a source, and a *list of references* at the end of the paper, which includes complete bibliographical information for all sources cited in the text. The following recommendations are based on the *Publication Manual of the American Psychological Association*, 6th ed. (2010), as well as APA's website.

In-Text Citations

APA style recommends the author-date citation system for sources cited in the text. At the appropriate point in the text, give the author's last name and year of publication. For all direct quotations, you must also include the page number preceded by *p.* (page numbers are not required with paraphrases and summaries). You can present this information in several different ways—at the beginning of the borrowed material: *According to DeAngelus (2017)*; at the end of the borrowed material: *(DeAngelus, 2017)*; or divided between the beginning and the end of the borrowed material: *According to DeAngelus, cognitive development can vary greatly from one child to another even within the same family (2017)*. When presenting the information parenthetically, use commas to separate the author's last name, year, and page number: *(DeAngelus, 2017, p. 27)*. For a discussion of using signal phrases to integrate quotations, paraphrases, and summaries smoothly into your research paper, see pages 233–35. If you are citing more than one source, list them in alphabetical order, in the same order as they appear in the references list, separated by semicolons: (*Andros, 2016; Carter, 2017; Zulin, 2007, p. 3*).

Each in-text citation directs your readers to the list of references should they want to pursue a particular source. Treat electronic sources as you would print sources, keeping in mind that some electronic sources use paragraph numbers instead of page numbers. Consider the following examples of APA in-text citations found in the opening paragraph of student Nancy Magnusson's paper "The English-Only Controversy."

In-Text Citations (APA Style)

Many people are surprised to discover that English is not the official language of the United States. Today, even as English literacy becomes a necessity for people in many parts of the world, some people in the United States believe its primacy is being threatened right at home. Much of the current controversy focuses on Hispanic communities with large Spanish-speaking populations who may feel little or no pressure to learn English. Columnist and cultural critic Charles Krauthammer (2006) believes English should be America's official language. He notes that this country has been "blessed . . . with a linguistic unity that brings a critically needed cohesion to a nation as diverse, multiracial and multiethnic as America" and that communities such as these threaten the bond created by a common language (p. 112). There are others, however, who think that the threat has been sensationalized, that "language does not threaten American unity. Benign neglect is a good policy for any country when it comes to language, and it's a good policy for America" (King, 1997, p. 64). Let's revisit the arguments on both sides of the English-only debate to determine what options are available to best serve America's growing number of non-English-speaking residents.

References

King, R. D. (1997, April). Should English be the law? *Atlantic Monthly, 279,* 55–64.

Krauthammer, C. (2006, June 12). In plain English: Let's make it official. *Time, 174,* 112.

In the preceding example, the student followed APA style guidelines for her reference list. When constructing the reference page for your paper, consult the following APA guidelines, where you will find model entries for common print and online sources.

List of References

In this section, you will find general APA guidelines for creating a list of references, followed by model entries that cover the citation situations you will encounter most often.

Guidelines for Constructing Your Reference Page

1. Place your list of sources on a separate page at the end of your paper.
2. Center the title *References* at the top of the page. (See the model above.)
3. Double-space both within and between entries on your list.
4. Arrange your sources alphabetically by the authors' or editors' last names. If you have two or more authors with the same last name, alphabetize by the initials of the first name.
5. If you have two or more works by the same author, arrange them chronologically by year of publication, starting with the one published earliest. Arrange works published in the same year alphabetically by title, and use lowercase letters

☑ **For more practice, visit the LaunchPad for *Models for Writers*: LearningCurve** > Working with Sources (APA) to differentiate them: (2013a), (2013b), (2013c). Include the author's name, including any initials, with all entries.

6. Reverse *all* authors' names within each entry, and use initials, not first and middle names (Burns, E. A.). Name up to seven authors, separating names and parts of names with commas. Use an ampersand (&) instead of *and* before the last author's name. If there are more than seven authors, use an ellipsis after the sixth author, followed by the last author's name.
7. If no author or editor is known, alphabetize by the first word of the title, not counting *A*, *An*, or *The*.
8. Begin each entry at the left margin, and indent subsequent lines five spaces.
9. Give the date of publication in parentheses after the last author's name. For some journal, magazine, and newspaper articles, you will need to include the month and sometimes the day as well as the year (2017, December 2).
10. For book and article titles, capitalize the first word of the title, the first word of the subtitle if there is one, and any proper names. Begin all other words with lowercase letters. With titles of journals, capitalize all significant words (*Social Work with Groups: A Journal of Community and Clinical Practice*).
11. Italicize the titles of books, journals, magazines, and newspapers. Do not italicize or put quotation marks around article titles.
12. For book publications, provide the city of publication followed by a comma and the two-letter postal abbreviation of the state (Davenport, IA). Follow the city and state with a colon.
13. For book publications, provide the publisher's name after the place of publication. For many commercial publishers, use shortened names, such as *Houghton* for Houghton Mifflin. Provide the full name of university presses, corporations, and professional associations. Omit such terms as *Publishers, Co.,* and *Inc.* Retain the term *Books* and, for academic publishers, *Press.*
14. Use the abbreviations *p.* and *pp.* for page numbers of all newspaper articles and for chapters or articles in edited books. Do *not* use these abbreviations for articles in journals or magazines. When citing inclusive page numbers, give complete figures: 217–223.
15. For an online source, APA format stresses that you include the same elements, in the same order, as you would for a reference

to a print source, and add as much electronic retrieval information as needed for others to locate each source. APA also recommends using a DOI (digital object identifier), when available, in place of a URL in references to electronic texts. The DOI is more permanent and consistent than a URL. No retrieval date is necessary if the content is not likely to be updated or changed.

16. When dividing a URL at the end of a line, never insert a hyphen to mark the break. Break line immediately *before* most marks of punctuation (an exception would be http://, which should never break). Do not italicize, underline, or use angle brackets with URLs, and do not add a period at the end of a URL.

PERIODICALS

JOURNAL ARTICLE WITH A DOI

Niedt, C. (2013). The politics of eminent domain: From false choices to community benefits. *Urban Geography, 34,* 1047–1069. doi:10.1080/02723638.2013.819683.

If the journal is paginated by volume, the issue number is not needed. When a journal is paginated by issue, APA requires that the issue number be given parenthetically after the volume number.

Nock, M. K. (2008). Actions speak louder than words: An elaborated theoretical model of the social functions of self-injury and other harmful behaviors. *Applied and Preventive Psychology, 12*(4), 159–168. doi:10.1016/j.appsy.22008.5.002.

JOURNAL ARTICLE WITH A DOI AND MULTIPLE AUTHORS

When an article has up to seven authors, present all the authors' names in your reference entry.

Brown, L. F., Rand, K. L., Bigatti, S. M., Stewart, J. C., Theobald, D. E., Wu, J., & Kroenke, K. (2013). Longitudinal relationships between fatigue and depression in cancer patients with depression and/or pain. *Health Psychology, 32,* 1199–1208. doi:10.1037/a0029773.

For more practice, visit the LaunchPad for *Models for Writers*:
Video Tutorial: How to Cite a Database in APA Style

JOURNAL ARTICLE WITHOUT A DOI

Stephens, R. (2012). What if? Preparing schools and communities for the unthinkable. *Law Enforcement Executive Forum, 12*(4), 1–7.

If there is no DOI assigned and the article is retrieved online, provide the URL of the home page of the journal.

Nordhall, O., & Agerstrom, J. (2013). Future-oriented people show stronger moral concerns. *Current Research in Social Psychology, 18*, 52–63. Retrieved from http://www.uiowa.edu/-grpproc/crisp/crisp.html

MAGAZINE ARTICLE (MONTHLY OR WEEKLY)

Tucker, A. (2012, October). The great New England vampire panic. *Smithsonian, 43*, 58–65.

Abend, L. (2013, December 16). Boys won't be boys. *Time, 182*, 40–44.

ONLINE MAGAZINE ARTICLE

DeAngelis, T. (2013, December). When the conflict comes home. *Monitor on Psychology, 44*(11). Retrieved from http://www.apa.org/monitor/

NEWSPAPER ARTICLE (DAILY OR WEEKLY)

Casey, N. (2017, March 12). Meet Diego, the centenarian whose sex drive saved his species. *The New York Times*, p. A1.

When the article appears on discontinuous pages, provide all page numbers.

Goode, E. (2013, December 16). Sheriffs refuse to enforce laws on gun control. *The New York Times*, pp. A1, A15.

ONLINE NEWSPAPER ARTICLE

Weeks, L. (2006, February 8). Burdens of the modern beast. *The Washington Post*. Retrieved from http://www.washingtonpost.com

For more practice, visit the LaunchPad for *Models for Writers*:
Video Tutorial: How to Cite a Web Site in APA Style

BOOKS, REFERENCE BOOKS, AND BOOK CHAPTERS

BOOK WITH ONE AUTHOR

Gladwell, M. (2013). *David and Goliath: Underdogs, misfits, and the art of battling giants*. New York, NY: Little, Brown.

BOOK WITH TWO TO SEVEN AUTHORS

Beck, E., Britto, S., & Andrews, A. (2007). *In the shadow of death: Restorative justice and death row families*. New York, NY: Oxford University Press.

ELECTRONIC VERSION OF A PRINT BOOK

Dewey, J. (1916). *Democracy and education: An introduction to the philosophy of education*. Retrieved from http://www.gutenberg.org/etext/852

BOOK WITH A GROUP OR AN INSTITUTIONAL AUTHOR

National Association for the Advancement of Colored People. (1994). *Beyond the Rodney King story: An investigation of police conduct in minority communities*. Boston, MA: Northeastern University Press.

EDITED BOOK

Clark, V., Eschholz, P., Rosa, A., & Simon, B. L. (Eds.). (2008). *Language: Introductory readings* (7th ed.). Boston, MA: Bedford/St. Martin's.

EDITION OTHER THAN THE FIRST

Leopold, Aldo. (1989). *A Sand County almanac and other sketches here and there* (commemorative ed.). New York, NY: Oxford University Press.

ARTICLE OR CHAPTER IN AN EDITED BOOK OR ANTHOLOGY

Lawson, W. (2003). Remembering school. In M. Prior (Ed.), *Learning and behavior problems in Asperger syndrome* (pp. 177–193). New York, NY: Guilford.

ARTICLE IN A REFERENCE BOOK

Anagnost, G. T. (2005). Sandra Day O'Connor. In *The Oxford Companion to the Supreme Court* (2nd ed., pp. 701–704). New York, NY: Oxford University Press.

ENTRY IN AN ONLINE REFERENCE BOOK

Jaworska, A. (2009). Advance directives and substitute decision-making. In E. N. Zalta (Ed.), *The Stanford encyclopedia of philosophy* (Summer 2009 ed.). Retrieved from http://plato.stanford.edu/entries/advance-directives/

GOVERNMENT PUBLICATION, PRINT AND ONLINE

U.S. Department of Housing and Urban Development. (2000). *Welfare to work: Reaching a new workforce*. Washington, DC: Government Printing Office.

U. S. Department of Health and Human Services. (2009). *Keep the beat recipes: Deliciously healthy dinners*. Retrieved from http://healthyeating.nhlbi.nih.gov/pdfs/Dinners_Cookbook_508-compliant.pdf

ADVERTISEMENT, PRINT AND ONLINE

Sprint. (2013, November 25). [Advertisement]. *Time, 182*, 5.

Ford Motor Company. (2017). 2017 Fusion [Advertisement]. Retrieved from http://www.ford.com/cars/fusion/

AN ANNOTATED STUDENT APA-STYLE RESEARCH PAPER

Laura DeVeau was free to choose her own topic when it came time to write a research paper for her English 102 class. After considering a number of possible topics and doing some research on several of them, she turned to a subject that interested her: the effects of religion and spirituality on the mental health of society.

DeVeau was particularly interested to learn that historically, psychology professionals saw little value in religion and spirituality and, in fact, viewed them as having a negative impact on the mental health of individuals and society in general. This jarred with her own experience, and DeVeau set out in her first draft to document the psychological benefits and value of spiritual and religious beliefs. Once finished with the draft, she put it aside for a day before reading it carefully in an effort to see how she could strengthen it. DeVeau reworked her opening two paragraphs. In the first paragraph, she clearly described her research dilemma: the wide variety of opinions about the impact of religion on a person's life. In the second paragraph, she focused the scope of her project on her disagreement with professionals in the field of psychology who claim that religious feelings are not compatible with sound mental health. DeVeau then looked at all of her examples to make sure that they were well organized and persuasive. Finally, she scoured her sources to make sure that she was using the materials that best supported or illustrated the points she wanted to make about the value of spirituality and religion.

The final draft of DeVeau's research paper shows that she has learned how the parts of a well-researched and well-written paper fit together and how to make revisions that emulate some of the qualities of the model essays she has read and studied in class. On the following pages you will see the cover page (required for all APA-style research papers), first page, and list of references from DeVeau's paper.

Running head

Running head: RELIGION IN MENTAL HEALTH 1

The APA-style cover page gives title, author, and course information

The Role of Spirituality and Religion
in Mental Health

Laura DeVeau

English 102

Professor Gardner

April 12, 2010

Short form of title and page number as running head

The Role of Spirituality and Religion
in Mental Health

It has been called "a vestige of the childhood of mankind," "the feeling of something true, total and absolute," "an otherworldly answer as regards the meaning of life" (Jones, 1991, p. 1; Amaro, 1998; Kristeva, 1987, p. 27). It has been compared to medicine, described as a psychological cure for mental illness, and also referred to as the cause of a dangerous fanaticism. With so many differing opinions on the impact of religion in people's lives, where would one begin a search for the truth? Who has the answer: Christians, humanists, objectivists, atheists, psychoanalysts, Buddhists, philosophers, cults? This was my dilemma at the advent of my research into how religion and spirituality affect the mental health of society as a whole.

Citation of multiple works from references

In this paper, I explore the claims, widely accepted by professionals in the field of psychology, that religious and spiritual practices have a negative impact on mental health. In addition, though, I cannot help but reflect on how this exploration has changed my beliefs as well. Religion is such a personal experience that one cannot be dispassionate in reporting it. One can, however, subject the evidence provided by those who have studied the issue to critical scrutiny. Having done so, I find myself in disagreement with those who claim religious feelings are incompatible with sound mental health. There is a nearly limitless number of beliefs regarding spirituality. Some are organized and involve rituals like mass or worship. Many are centered around the existence of a higher being, while others focus on the self. I have attempted to uncover the perfect set of values that lead to a better lifestyle, but my research has pointed me in an entirely different direction, where no single belief seems to be adequate but where spiritual belief in general should be valued more highly than it is currently in mental health circles.

Acknowledgment of opposing viewpoints

Thesis explicitly introduced

RELIGION IN MENTAL HEALTH 7

References begin on a new page

References

An online source

Amaro, J. (1998). *Psychology, psychoanalysis and religious faith. Nielsen's psychology of religion page*. Retrieved from http://www.psywww.com/psyrelig/amaro.html

A book

Beyerman A. K. (1989). *The holistic health movement*. Tuscaloosa, AL: Alabama University Press.

Dein, S. (2010, January). Religion, spirituality, and mental health. *Psychiatric Times, 20*(1): 1–3. Retrieved from http://www.psychiatrictimes.com/articles/religion-spirituality-and-mental-health

An article or a chapter in a book

Ellis, A. (1993). Dogmatic devotion doesn't help, it hurts. In B. Slife (Ed.), *Taking sides: Clashing views on controversial psychological issues* (pp. 297–301). New York, NY: Scribner.

Jones, J. W. (1991). *Contemporary psychoanalysis and religion: Transference and transcendence*. New Haven, CT: Yale University Press.

Kristeva, J. (1987). *In the beginning was love: Psychoanalysis and faith*. New York, NY: Columbia University Press.

Larson, D. (1998). Does religious commitment improve mental health? In B. Slife (Ed.), *Taking sides: Clashing views on controversial psychological issues* (pp. 292–296). New York, NY: Scribner.

An article in a journal

Pargament, K. I., Smith, B. W., Koening, H. G., & Perez, L. (1998). Patterns of positive and negative religious coping with major life stressors. *Journal for the Scientific Study of Religion, 37*, 710–724.

Anonymous source alphabetized by title

"Psychological benefits." (1999). *Walking the labyrinth*. Retrieved April 3, 2000, from http://www.labyrinthway.com/html/benefits.html

Verghese, A. (2008). Spirituality and mental health. *Indian Journal of Psychiatry, 50*(4): 233–237. doi:10.4103/0019-5545.44742

CHAPTER **24**

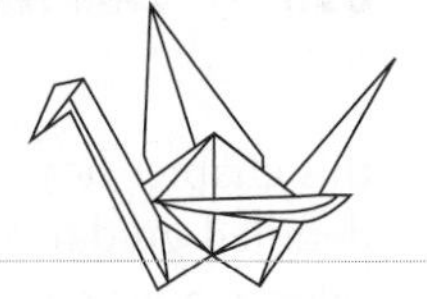

Editing for Grammar, Punctuation, and Sentence Style

Once you have revised your essay and you are confident that you have said what you wanted to say, you are ready to begin editing your essay. Remember that when you are *revising*, you are (re)considering the most important elements of your essay: thesis, purpose, content, organization, and paragraph structure. If these pieces are not in place and clear to your reader, you will be adding and changing sentences to communicate your ideas, which might lead you to eliminate editing errors or introduce new ones. Therefore, you typically move on to *editing* after revision (though it is important to note that you can—and should—return to revision often because the writing process does not always move easily from one step to another).

It is at the editing stage of the writing process that you identify and correct errors in grammar, punctuation, and sentence style. You don't want a series of small errors to detract from your paper. Such errors can also cause readers to have second thoughts about your credibility as an author, leading them to distrust *what* you are saying because of *how* you say or write it.

However, you may have difficulty identifying editing errors because they are not easy to spot and they take time to learn. To help you, this chapter addresses ten common writing problems that instructors from around the country told us trouble their students most. As you edit your essay, you can use this chapter as a guide, checking for these specific errors (see, especially, the Questions for Editing Sentences checklist on p. 646). Or, if you know you struggle with one or more of these errors—or if your instructor or peer has pointed out an error to you in their feedback—you can learn from the examples in

☑ For more help with grammar, punctuation, and sentence style, visit the LaunchPad for *Models for Writers* and navigate to LearningCurve, game-like quizzing activities that help you practice and improve your writing skills.

this chapter how to identify the error and how to correct it. For more detailed guidance with these and other editing concerns, be sure to refer to a writer's handbook or ask your instructor for help.

RUN-ONS: FUSED SENTENCES AND COMMA SPLICES

Writers can become so absorbed in getting their ideas down on paper that they often combine two independent clauses (complete sentences that can stand alone when punctuated with a period) incorrectly, creating a *run-on sentence*. A run-on sentence fails to show where one thought ends and where another begins and can confuse readers. There are two types of run-on sentences: the fused sentence and the comma splice.

A *fused sentence* occurs when a writer combines two independent clauses with no punctuation at all. To correct a fused sentence, divide the independent clauses into separate sentences, or join them by adding words, punctuation, or both.

INCORRECT Jen loves Harry Potter she was the first in line to buy the latest book.

EDITED Jen loves Harry Potter ~~she~~ [. She] was the first in line to buy the latest book.

EDITED Jen loves Harry Potter [; in fact,] she was the first in line to buy the latest book.

A *comma splice* occurs when writers use only a comma to combine two independent clauses. To correct a comma splice, divide the independent clauses into separate sentences or join them by adding words, punctuation, or both.

INCORRECT The e-mail looked like spam, Marty deleted it.

EDITED The e-mail looked like spam[.] Marty deleted it.

EDITED The e-mail looked like spam, [so] Marty deleted it.

☑ **LearningCurve** > Run-ons and Comma Splices; Commas
☑ **LearningCurve** > Fragments

SENTENCE FRAGMENTS

A *sentence fragment* is a word group that cannot stand alone as a complete sentence. Even if a word group begins with a capital letter and ends with punctuation, it is not a sentence unless it has a subject (the person, place, or thing the sentence is about) and a verb (a word that tells what the subject does) and expresses a complete thought. Word groups that do not express complete thoughts often begin with a subordinating conjunction such as *although, because, since,* or *unless*. To correct a fragment, add a subject or a verb, or integrate the fragment into a nearby sentence to complete the thought.

INCORRECT	Divided my time between work and school last semester.
EDITED	~~Divided~~ *I divided* my time between work and school last semester.
INCORRECT	Terry's essay was really interesting. Because it brought up good points about energy conservation.
EDITED	Terry's essay was really interesting/ ~~Because~~ *because* it brought up good points about energy conservation.

Creative use of intentional sentence fragments is occasionally acceptable—in narration essays, for example—when writers are trying to establish a particular mood or tone.

> I asked him about his recent trip. He asked me about work. Short questions. One-word answers. Then an awkward pause.
>
> –David P. Bardeen, "LIVES; Not Close Enough for Comfort"

SUBJECT-VERB AGREEMENT

Subjects and verbs must agree in number—that is, a singular subject (one person, place, or thing) must take a singular verb, and a plural subject (more than one person, place, or thing) must take a plural verb. Most native speakers of English use proper subject-verb

☑ **LearningCurve** > Subject-Verb Agreement

agreement in their writing without conscious awareness. Even so, some sentence constructions can be troublesome.

When a prepositional phrase (a phrase that includes a preposition such as *on*, *of*, *in*, *at*, or *between*) falls between a subject and a verb, it can obscure their relationship. To make sure the subject agrees with its verb in a sentence with an intervening prepositional phrase, mentally cross out the phrase (*of basic training* in the following example) to isolate the subject and verb and determine if they agree.

INCORRECT The first three weeks of basic training is the worst.

EDITED The first three weeks of basic training ~~is~~ *are* the worst.

Writers often have difficulty with subject-verb agreement in sentences with compound subjects (two or more subjects joined together with the word *and*). As a general rule, compound subjects take plural verbs.

INCORRECT My mother, sister, and cousin is visiting me next month.

EDITED My mother, sister, and cousin ~~is~~ *are* visiting me next month.

However, in sentences with subjects joined by *either . . . or*, *neither . . . nor*, or *not only . . . but also*, the verb must agree with the subject closest to it.

INCORRECT Neither the mechanics nor the salesperson know what's wrong with my car.

EDITED Neither the mechanics nor the salesperson ~~know~~ *knows* what's wrong with my car.

While editing your essay, be sure to identify the subjects and verbs in your sentences and to check their agreement.

☑ **LearningCurve** > Pronouns

PRONOUN-ANTECEDENT AGREEMENT

A *pronoun* is a word that takes the place of a noun in a sentence. To avoid repeating nouns in our speech and writing, we use pronouns as noun substitutes. The noun to which a pronoun refers is called its *antecedent*. A pronoun and its antecedent are said to *agree* when the relationship between them is clear. Pronouns must agree with their antecedents in both *person* and *number.*

There are three types of pronouns: first person (*I* and *we*), second person (*you*), and third person (*he, she, they,* and *it*). First-person pronouns refer to first-person antecedents, second-person pronouns refer to second-person antecedents, and third-person pronouns refer to third-person antecedents.

INCORRECT	House hunters should review their finances carefully before you make an offer.
EDITED	House hunters should review their finances carefully before ~~you~~ *they* make an offer.

A pronoun must agree in number with its antecedent; that is, a singular pronoun must refer to a singular antecedent, and a plural pronoun must refer to a plural antecedent. When two or more antecedents are joined by the word *and*, the pronoun must be plural.

INCORRECT	Gina, Kim, and Katie took her vacations in August.
EDITED	Gina, Kim, and Katie took ~~her~~ *their* vacations in August.

When the subject of a sentence is an indefinite pronoun such as *everyone, each, everybody, anyone, anybody, everything, either, one, neither, someone,* or *something,* use a singular pronoun to refer to it or recast the sentence to eliminate the agreement problem.

INCORRECT	Each of the women submitted their résumé.
EDITED	Each of the women submitted ~~their~~ *her* résumé.
EDITED	~~Each~~ *Both* of the women submitted their ~~resume.~~ *résumés*

☑ **LearningCurve** > Verb Tenses and Shifts

VERB TENSE SHIFTS

A verb's tense indicates when an action takes place—sometime in the past, right now, or in the future. Using verb tense consistently helps your readers understand time changes in your writing. Inconsistent verb tenses, or *shifts,* within a sentence confuse readers and are especially noticeable in narration and process analysis writing, which are sequence and time oriented. Generally, you should write in the past or present tense and maintain that tense throughout your sentence.

INCORRECT The painter studied the scene and pulls a fan brush decisively from her cup.

EDITED The painter studied the scene and *pulled* ~~pulls~~ a fan brush decisively from her cup.

MISPLACED AND DANGLING MODIFIERS

A *modifier* is a word or words that describe or give additional information about other words in a sentence. Always place modifiers as close as possible to the words they modify. An error in modifier placement could be unintentionally confusing (or amusing) to your readers. Two common problems arise with modifiers: the misplaced modifier and the dangling modifier.

A *misplaced modifier* unintentionally modifies the wrong word in a sentence because it is placed incorrectly.

INCORRECT The waiter brought a steak to the man covered with onions.

EDITED The waiter brought a steak *covered with onions* to the man. ~~covered with onions.~~

A *dangling modifier* appears at the beginning or end of a sentence and modifies a word that does not appear in the sentence—often an unstated subject.

INCORRECT Staring into the distance, large rain clouds form.

EDITED Staring into the distance, *Jon saw* large rain clouds form.

☑ LearningCurve > Modifier Placement

While editing your essay, make sure you have positioned your modifiers as close as possible to the words they modify, and make sure each sentence has a clear subject that is modified correctly.

FAULTY PARALLELISM

Parallelism means using similar grammatical forms to show that ideas in a sentence are of equal importance. Faulty parallelism can interrupt the flow of your writing and confuse your readers. Writers have trouble with parallelism in three kinds of sentence constructions.

In sentences that include items in a pair or series, make sure the elements of the pair or series are parallel in form. Delete any unnecessary or repeated words.

INCORRECT Nina likes snowboarding, roller skating, and to hike.

EDITED Nina likes snowboarding, roller skating, and ~~to hike.~~ hiking.

In sentences that include connecting words such as *both . . . and, either . . . or, neither . . . nor, rather . . . than,* and *not only . . . but also,* make sure the elements being connected are parallel in form. Delete any unnecessary or repeated words.

INCORRECT The lecture was both enjoyable and it was a form of education.

EDITED The lecture was both enjoyable and ~~it was a form of education.~~ educational.

In sentences that include the comparison word *as* or *than,* make sure the elements of the comparison are parallel in form. Delete any unnecessary or repeated words.

INCORRECT It would be better to study now than waiting until the night before the exam.

EDITED It would be better to study now than ~~waiting~~ to wait until the night before the exam.

WEAK NOUNS AND VERBS

Inexperienced writers often believe that adjectives and adverbs are the stuff of effective writing. They're right in one sense but not wholly so. Although strong adjectives and adverbs are crucial, good writing depends on strong, well-chosen nouns and verbs. The noun *vehicle* is not nearly as descriptive as *Jeep, snowmobile, pickup truck,* or *SUV,* for example. Why use the weak verb *look* when your meaning would be conveyed more precisely with *glance, stare, spy, gaze, peek, examine,* or *witness*? Instead of the weak verb *run,* use *fly, gallop, hustle, jog, race, rush, scamper, scoot, scramble,* or *trot.*

While editing your essay, look for instances of weak nouns and verbs. If you can't form a clear picture in your mind of what a noun looks like or what a verb's action is, your nouns and verbs are likely weak. The more specific and strong you make your nouns and verbs, the more lively and descriptive your writing will be.

WEAK The flowers moved toward the bright light of the sun.

EDITED The ~~flowers moved~~ *tulips stretched* toward the bright light of the sun.

When you have difficulty thinking of strong, specific nouns and verbs, reach for a thesaurus—but only if you are sure you can identify the best word for your purpose. Thesauruses are available free online and in inexpensive paperback editions; most word processing programs include a thesaurus as well. A thesaurus will help you avoid redundancy in your writing and find specific words with just the right meaning.

ACADEMIC DICTION AND TONE

The language that you use in your college courses, known as *American Standard English,* is formal in diction and objective in tone. American Standard English is the language used by educators, civic leaders, the media, and professionals in all fields. Although the standard is fairly narrow in scope, it allows for individual

☑ **LearningCurve** > Appropriate Language

differences in expression and voice so that your writing can retain its personality and appeal.

Tone is the distance that you establish between yourself and your audience and is created by your *diction* (the particular words you choose) and the complexity of your sentences. Formal writing creates a distance between yourself and your audience through the use of third-person pronouns (*he*, *she*, *it*, *they*) and provides the impression of objectivity. Formal writing values logic, evidence, and reason over opinion and bias. Informal writing, on the other hand, uses first-person pronouns (*I*, *we*); is usually found in narratives; and respects feelings, individual tastes, and personal preferences. Similarly, the second-person pronoun (*you*) is used to bring your reader close to you, as is done in this text, but it is too familiar for most academic writing and is best avoided if there is any question about its appropriateness.

INFORMAL	The experiment looked like it was going to be a bust.
FORMAL	After detecting a number of design flaws in the experiment, we concluded that it was going to be a failure.
SUBJECTIVE	The governor said that the shortfall in tax revenues was quite a bit bigger than anyone expected.
OBJECTIVE	The governor reported that tax revenues fell by 9 percent over last year.

When writing in a particular discipline, use discipline-specific language and conventions that reflect your understanding of the discipline. Key resources are your readings and the language you use with your instructors and classmates in each discipline. As you read, note how the writer uses technical language (for example, *point of view* and *denouement* in literature; *mean distribution* in statistics; *derivatives* in financial analysis; *pan, tilt,* and *track* in film study; *exogamy* and *endogamy* in anthropology; and *polyphony* and *atonality* in music) to communicate difficult concepts, recognized phenomena in the discipline, and characteristic nuances of the discipline.

Discipline-Specific Prose (Psychology)

> How does information get "into" long-term memory? One very important function that takes place in short-term memory is *encoding*, or transforming the new information into a form that can be retrieved later. As a student, you may have tried to memorize dates, facts, or definitions by simply repeating them to yourself over and over. This strategy reflects an attempt to use maintenance rehearsal to encode material into long-term memory. However, maintenance rehearsal is *not* a very effective strategy for encoding information into long-term memory.
>
> A much more effective encoding strategy is *elaborative rehearsal*, which involves focusing on the *meaning* of information to help encode and transfer it to long-term memory. With elaborative rehearsal, you relate the information to other information you already know. That is, rather than simply repeating the information, you *elaborate* on the new information in some meaningful way.
>
> —Don H. Hockenbury and Sandra E. Hockenbury, "Encoding Long-Term Memories," from *Psychology*, Sixth Edition

If you listen carefully and read closely, you will be able to discern the discipline-specific language cues that make a writer sound more like, say, a historian or an anthropologist than a psychologist. In turn, you will be able to use the language of your own discipline with greater ease and accuracy and achieve the subtleties of language that will allow you to carry out your research, draw sound conclusions, and write effectively and with authority.

ESL CONCERNS (ARTICLES AND NOUNS)

Two areas of English grammar that can be especially problematic for nonnative speakers of English are articles and nouns. In English, correct use of articles and nouns is necessary for sentences to make sense.

There are two kinds of articles in English: *indefinite* (*a* and *an*) and *definite* (*the*). Use *a* before words beginning with a consonant sound and *an* before words beginning with a vowel sound. Note, too, that *a* is used before an *h* with a consonant sound (*happy*) and *an* is used before a silent *h* (*hour*).

There are two kinds of nouns in English: count and noncount. *Count nouns* name individual things or units that can be counted or separated out from a whole, such as *students* and *pencils*. *Noncount nouns* name things that cannot be counted because they are considered wholes in themselves and cannot be divided, such as *work* and *furniture*.

Use the indefinite article (*a* or *an*) before a singular count noun when you do not specify which one.

> I would like to borrow *a* colored pencil.

Plural count nouns take *the*.

> I would like to borrow *the* colored pencils.

If a plural count noun is used in a general sense, it does not take an article at all.

> I brought colored pencils to class today.

Noncount nouns are always singular and never take an indefinite article.

> We need new living room furniture.

The is sometimes used with noncount nouns to refer to a specific idea or thing.

> *The* furniture will be delivered tomorrow.

When editing your essay, be sure you have used articles and nouns correctly.

INCORRECT	I love an aroma of freshly baked cookies.
EDITED	I love ~~an~~ the aroma of freshly baked cookies.
INCORRECT	I have never had the chicken pox.
EDITED	I have never had ~~the~~ chicken pox.

☑ **LearningCurve for Multilingual Writers** > Articles and Types of Nouns
☑ **LearningCurve for Multilingual Writers** > Prepositions
☑ **LearningCurve for Multilingual Writers** > Sentence Structure
☑ **LearningCurve for Multilingual Writers** > Verbs

Questions for Editing Sentences

1. Do I include any fused sentences or comma splices?
2. Do I include any unintentional sentence fragments?
3. Do my verbs agree with their subjects?
4. Do my pronouns agree with their antecedents?
5. Do I make any unnecessary shifts in verb tense?
6. Do I have any misplaced or dangling modifiers?
7. Are my sentences parallel?
8. Do I use strong nouns and verbs?
9. Do I pair articles and nouns correctly?

Glossary of Useful Terms

Abstract See *Concrete / Abstract.*

Allusion A passing reference to a familiar person, place, or thing, often drawn from history, the Bible, mythology, or literature. An allusion is an economical way for a writer to capture the essence of an idea, atmosphere, emotion, or historical era, as in "The scandal was his Watergate" or "He saw himself as a modern Job." An allusion should be familiar to the reader; if it is not, it will add nothing to the meaning.

Analogy A special form of comparison in which the writer explains something unfamiliar by comparing it to something familiar: "A transmission line is simply a pipeline for electricity. In the case of a water pipeline, more water will flow through the pipe as water pressure increases. The same is true of electricity in a transmission line."

Analysis An examination of a reading or a source to understand the writer's main point and to assess the piece of writing for its relevance, bias, overall argument, and reliability.

Anecdote A short narrative about an amusing or interesting event. Writers often use anecdotes to begin essays as well as to illustrate certain points.

Argumentation The art of arguing, or attempting to persuade the reader to agree with a point of view, to make a given decision, or to pursue a particular course of action. There are two basic types of argumentation: logical and persuasive. See the introduction to Chapter 21 (pp. 496–505) for a detailed discussion of argumentation.

Attitude A reflection of the writer's opinion of a subject. The writer can think very positively or very negatively about a subject or have an attitude that falls somewhere in between. See also *Tone.*

Audience The intended readership for a piece of writing. For example, the readers of a national weekly news magazine come from all walks of life and have diverse interests, opinions, and educational backgrounds. In contrast, the readership of an organic chemistry journal is made up of people whose interests and education are quite similar. The essays in *Models for Writers* are intended for general readers, intelligent people who may lack specific information about the subject being discussed.

Beginnings and Endings A beginning is the sentence, group of sentences, or section that introduces an essay. Good beginnings usually identify the thesis or controlling idea, attempt to interest readers, and establish a tone.

An ending is the sentence or group of sentences that brings an essay to a close. Good endings are purposeful and well planned. Endings satisfy readers when they are the natural outgrowths of the essays themselves and give readers a sense of finality or completion. Good essays do not simply stop; they conclude. See the introduction to Chapter 6 (pp. 136–44) for a detailed discussion of beginnings and endings.

Cause and Effect A type of analysis or writing strategy that explains the reasons for an occurrence or the consequences of an action. See the introduction to Chapter 20 (pp. 473–76) for a detailed discussion of cause and effect.

Citation A reference to a published or unpublished work that indicates that the material being referenced is not original to the present author. A citation allows a reader to find and examine the referenced material to verify its authenticity, accuracy, and appropriateness.

Classification See *Division and Classification.*

Cliché An expression that has become ineffective through overuse. Expressions such as *quick as a flash, jump for joy,* and *slow as molasses* are clichés. Good writers normally avoid such trite expressions and seek instead to express themselves in fresh and forceful language. See also *Diction.*

Coherence A quality of good writing that results when all sentences, paragraphs, and longer divisions of an essay are naturally connected. Coherent writing is achieved through (1) a logical sequence of ideas (arranged in chronological order, spatial order, order of importance, or some other appropriate order), (2) the purposeful repetition of key words and ideas, (3) a pace suitable for your topic and your reader, and (4) the use of transitional words and expressions. Coherence should not be confused with *Unity*. See also *Transition.*

Colloquial Expression An expression that is characteristic of or appropriate to spoken language or to writing that seeks the effect of spoken language. Colloquial expressions are informal, such as *chem,* *gym, come up with, be at wit's end, won't,* and *photo*. These types of expressions are acceptable in formal writing only if they are used purposefully. See also *Diction*.

Combining Models By combining rhetorical strategies, writers are able to develop their ideas in interesting ways. For example, in writing a cause-and-effect essay about a major oil spill, the writer might want to describe the damage the spill caused as well as explain the cleanup process step by step. See the introduction to Chapter 22 (pp. 568–71) for a detailed discussion of combining strategies.

Comparison and Contrast A type of analysis or writing strategy used to point out the similarities and differences between two or more subjects in the same class or category. The function of any comparison and contrast is to clarify — to reach some conclusion about the items being compared and contrasted. See the introduction to Chapter 19 (pp. 445–72) for a detailed discussion of comparison and contrast.

Conclusions See *Beginnings and Endings*.

Concrete/Abstract A concrete word names a specific object, person, place, or action that can be directly perceived by the senses, such as *car, bread, building, book, John F. Kennedy, Chicago,* or *hiking*. An abstract word, in contrast, refers to general qualities, conditions, ideas, actions, or relationships that cannot be directly perceived by the senses, such as *bravery, dedication, excellence, anxiety, stress, thinking,* or *hatred*. See the introduction to Chapter 11 (p. 272) for more on abstract and concrete words.

Connotation/Denotation Both connotation and denotation refer to the meanings of words. Denotation is the dictionary meaning of a word, the literal meaning. Connotation, on the other hand, is the implied or suggested meaning of a word. For example, the denotation of *lamb* is "a young sheep." The connotations of *lamb* are numerous: *gentle, docile, weak, peaceful, blessed, sacrificial, blood, spring, frisky, pure, innocent,* and so on. See the introduction to Chapter 11 (p. 271) for more on connotation and denotation.

Controlling Idea See *Thesis*.

Coordination The joining of grammatical constructions of the same rank (words, phrases, and clauses) to indicate that they are of equal importance. For example, "*They ate hot dogs, and we ate hamburgers.*" See the introduction to Chapter 9 (p. 204) for more on coordination. See also *Subordination.*

Deduction The process of reasoning from stated premises to a conclusion that necessarily follows. This form of reasoning moves from the general to the specific. See the introduction to Chapter 21 (pp. 496–505) for a discussion of deductive reasoning and its role in argumentation. See also *Syllogism.*

Definition The stated meaning of a word or concept. A definition may be either brief or extended, part of an essay, or an entire essay. See the introduction to Chapter 17 (pp. 402–5) for a detailed discussion of definition.

Denotation See *Connotation/Denotation.*

Description A rhetorical pattern that tells how a person, place, or thing is perceived by the five senses. See the introduction to Chapter 15 (pp. 361–63) for a detailed discussion of description.

Details The small elements that collectively contribute to the overall impression of a person, place, thing, or idea. For example, in the sentence "The *organic, whole-grain* dog biscuits were *reddish brown, beef-flavored,* and in the *shape of a bone,*" the italicized words are details.

Dialogue The conversation between two or more people as represented in writing. Dialogue is what people say directly to one another.

Diction A writer's choice and use of words. Good diction is precise and appropriate: the words mean exactly what the writer intends, and the words are well suited to the writer's subject, intended audience, and purpose in writing. The word-conscious writer knows that there are differences among *aged, old,* and *elderly; blue, navy,* and *azure;* and *disturbed, angry,* and *irritated.* Furthermore, that writer knows in which situation to use each word. See the introduction to Chapter 11 (pp. 271–77) for a detailed discussion of diction. See also *Cliché, Colloquial Expression, Connotation/Denotation, Jargon,* and *Slang.*

Direct Quotation Material that has been borrowed word for word and must be placed within quotation marks and properly cited.

Division and Classification Rhetorical patterns used by the writer to first establish categories and then to arrange or sort people, places, or things into these categories according to their different characteristics, thus making them more manageable for the writer and more understandable and meaningful for the reader. See the introduction to Chapter 18 (pp. 421–24) for a detailed discussion of division and classification.

Documentation The act or the instance of providing documents or references as to where documents or other material may be found.

Dominant Impression The single mood, atmosphere, or quality a writer wishes to emphasize [per text] in a piece of descriptive writing. The dominant impression is created through the careful selection of details; it is influenced by the essay's subject, audience, and purpose. See the introduction to Chapter 15 (pp. 361–63) for more on dominant impression.

Emphasis Placing important ideas and words in specific places within sentences and longer units of writing so that they have the greatest impact. In general, what comes at the end has the most impact, while that placed at the beginning has nearly as much; what comes in the middle gets the least emphasis.

Endings See *Beginnings and Endings.*

Ethos One of the key components of argumentation, according to Aristotle. Ethos concerns the authority, credibility, and, to a certain extent, morals of the speaker/writer. See also *Logos* and *Pathos*.

Evaluation An assessment of the effectiveness or merit of a piece of writing. In evaluating a piece of writing, one should ask questions such as the following: What is the writer's purpose? Is it a worthwhile purpose? Does the writer achieve the purpose? Is the writer's information sufficient and accurate? What are the strengths of the essay? What are its weaknesses? Depending on the type of writing and the purpose, more specific questions can also be asked. For example, with an argument essay one could ask: Does the writer follow the principles of logical thinking? Is the writer's evidence sufficient and convincing?

Evidence The information on which a judgment or argument is based or by which proof or probability is established. Evidence usually takes the form of statistics, facts, names, examples or illustrations, and opinions of authorities.

Example Something that illustrates a larger idea or represents something of which it is a part. An example is one of the basic means of developing or clarifying an idea. Furthermore, examples enable writers to show rather than simply tell readers what they mean. See the introduction to Chapter 13 (pp. 321–24) for more on example.

Facts Pieces of information presented as having objective reality — that is, having actual existence. For example, water boils at 212°F, Katharine Hepburn died in 2003, and the USSR no longer exists — these are all facts.

Fallacy See *Logical Fallacy.*

Figure of Speech A brief, imaginative comparison that highlights the similarities between things that are basically dissimilar. Figures of speech make writing vivid, interesting, and memorable. The most common figures of speech are:

Simile: An explicit comparison introduced by *like* or *as*. "The fighter's hands were like stone."

Metaphor: An implied comparison that makes one thing the equivalent of another. "All the world's a stage."

Personification: A special kind of figure of speech in which human traits are assigned to ideas or objects. "The engine coughed and then stopped."

See the introduction to Chapter 12 (pp. 304–10) for a detailed discussion of figurative language.

Focus The limitation a writer gives to his or her subject. The writer's task is to select a manageable topic given the constraints of time, space, and purpose. For example, within the general subject of sports, a writer could focus on government support of amateur athletes or narrow the focus even further to government support of Olympic athletes.

General See *Specific/General.*

Idiom A word or phrase having a special meaning that is used habitually. The meaning of an idiom is not always readily apparent to nonnative speakers of a language. For example, *catch a cold, hold a job, make up your mind,* and *give them a hand* are all idioms in English.

Illustration The use of examples to explain, elucidate, or corroborate. Writers rely heavily on illustration to make their ideas both clear and concrete. See the introduction to Chapter 13 (pp. 321–24) for a detailed discussion of illustration.

Induction The process of reasoning to a conclusion about all members of a class through an examination of only a few members of the class. This form of reasoning moves from the particular to the general. See the introduction to Chapter 21 (p. 496) for a discussion of inductive reasoning and its role in argumentation.

Introduction See *Beginnings and Endings.*

Irony The use of words to suggest something different from their literal meaning. For example, when Jonathan Swift suggested in "A Modest Proposal" that Ireland's problems could be solved if the people of Ireland fattened their babies and sold them to the English landlords for food, he meant that almost any other solution would be preferable. A writer can use irony to establish a special relationship with the reader and to add an extra dimension or twist to the meaning. See the introduction to Chapter 11 (pp. 271–77) for more on irony.

Jargon The special vocabulary, or technical language, of a trade, profession, or group. Doctors, construction workers, lawyers, and teachers, for example, all have a specialized vocabulary that they use on the job. See also *Diction.*

Logical Fallacy An error in reasoning that renders an argument invalid. See the introduction to Chapter 21 (pp. 496–505) for a discussion of common logical fallacies.

Logos One of the key components of argumentation, according to Aristotle. Logos concerns the presentation of an argument through the use of logic and reason. It requires that the thesis or claim is worthwhile, logical, consistent, and supported by evidence. See also *Ethos* and *Pathos.*

Metaphor See *Figure of Speech.*

Narration The writing strategy of telling a story to relate what happened. Although narration is most often used in fiction, it is also important in expository writing, either by itself or in conjunction with other types of prose. See the introduction to Chapter 14 (pp. 340–43) for a detailed discussion of narration.

Opinion A belief or conclusion that may or may not be substantiated by positive knowledge or proof. (If not substantiated, an opinion is a prejudice.) Even when based on evidence and sound reasoning, an opinion is personal and can be changed; it is therefore less persuasive than facts and arguments.

Organization The pattern or order the writer imposes on his or her material. Some often-used patterns of organization include time order, space order, and order of importance. See the introduction to Chapter 5 (pp. 112–16) for a detailed discussion of organization.

Paradox A seemingly contradictory statement that is nonetheless true. For example, "We little know what we have until we lose it" is a paradoxical statement.

Paragraph A unit of a series of closely related sentences. These sentences adequately develop the central or controlling idea of the paragraph. This central idea, usually stated in a topic sentence, is necessarily related to the purpose of the whole composition. A well-written paragraph has several distinguishing characteristics: a clearly stated or implied topic sentence, adequate development, unity, coherence, and an appropriate organizational strategy. See the introduction to Chapter 7 (pp. 162–64) for a detailed discussion of paragraphs.

Parallelism The repetition of word order or grammatical form either within a single sentence or in several sentences that develop the same central idea. As a rhetorical device, parallelism can aid coherence and add emphasis. Franklin Roosevelt's statement "I see one-third of a nation ill-housed, ill-clad, and ill-nourished" illustrates effective parallelism. See the introduction to Chapter 9 (pp. 203–13) for more on parallelism.

Paraphrase A restatement of the information a writer is borrowing. A paraphrase closely parallels the presentation of ideas in the original, but it does not use the same words or sentence structure. See also *Direct Quotation, Plagiarism,* and *Summary.*

Pathos One of the key elements of argumentation, according to Aristotle. Pathos is concerned with using artful, strategic, and well-crafted language and support that appeal to the emotions of the speaker/writer's audience. See also *Ethos* and *Logos*.

Personification See *Figure of Speech*.

Persuasion An attempt to convince readers to agree with a point of view, to make a particular decision, or to pursue a particular course of action.

Plagiarism The use of someone else's ideas in their original form or in a slightly altered form without proper documentation. Writers avoid plagiarism by (1) putting direct quotations within quotation marks and properly citing them, and (2) documenting any idea, explanation, or argument that is borrowed and presented in a quotation, summary, or paraphrase, making it clear where the borrowed material begins and ends. See the introduction to Chapter 10 (pp. 225–42) for a more thorough discussion of plagiarism and Chapter 23 (pp. 595–634) for help documenting sources.

Point of View The grammatical "person" in an essay. For example, the first-person point of view uses the pronoun *I* and is commonly found in autobiography and the personal essay; the third-person point of view uses the pronouns *he, she,* or *it* and is commonly found in objective writing. See the introduction to Chapter 14 (pp. 340–43) for a discussion of point of view in narration.

Process Analysis A rhetorical strategy used to explain how something works or to give step-by-step directions for doing something. See the introduction to Chapter 16 (pp. 381–83) for a detailed discussion of process analysis.

Purpose What the writer wants to accomplish in a particular piece of writing. Purposeful writing seeks to *tell* (narration), to *describe* (description), to *explain* (process analysis, definition, division and classification, comparison and contrast, and cause and effect), or to *convince* (argument).

Rhetorical Modes Spoken or written strategies for presenting ideas or information, the most common of which are argument, cause and effect, comparison and contrast, definition, description, division and classification, illustration, narration, and process analysis.

Rhetorical Question A question asked for dramatic effect or to make a point but that does not require an answer from the reader. "When will nuclear proliferation end?" is such a question. Writers use rhetorical questions to introduce topics they plan to discuss or to emphasize important points. See the introduction to Chapter 6 (pp. 136–44) for another example.

Sentence A grammatical unit that expresses a complete thought. It consists of at least a subject (a noun) and a predicate (a verb). See the introduction to Chapter 9 (pp. 203–08) for a detailed discussion of effective sentences.

Signal Phrase A phrase alerting the reader that borrowed information follows. A signal phrase usually consists of an author's name and a verb (for example, "Coughlan argues" or "Yadav disagrees") and helps integrate direct quotations, paraphrases, and summaries into the flow of a paper. A signal phrase tells the reader who is speaking and indicates exactly where your ideas end and your source's begin.

Simile See *Figure of Speech*.

Slang The unconventional, informal language of particular subgroups in our culture. Slang terms, such as *bummed, hot,* and *cool,* are acceptable in formal writing only if used selectively for specific purposes.

Specific/General General words name groups or classes of objects, qualities, or actions. Specific words, on the other hand, name individual objects, qualities, or actions within a class or group. To some extent the terms *general* and *specific* are relative. For example, *clothing* is a class of things. *Shirt,* however, is more specific than *clothing* but more general than *T-shirt*. See also *Diction*.

Strategy A means by which a writer achieves his or her purpose. Strategy includes the many rhetorical decisions the writer makes about organization, paragraph structure, sentence structure, and diction. In terms of the whole essay, strategy refers to the principal rhetorical mode a writer uses. If, for example, a writer wishes to explain how to make chocolate chip cookies, the most effective strategy would be process analysis. If it is the writer's purpose to analyze why sales of American cars have declined in recent years, the most effective strategy would be cause-and-effect analysis.

Style The individual manner in which a writer expresses his or her ideas. Style is created by the author's particular choice of words, construction of sentences, and arrangement of ideas.

Subordination The use of grammatical constructions to make one part of a sentence dependent on, rather than equal to, another. For example, the italicized clause in the following sentence is subordinate: "They all cheered *when I finished the race.*" See the introduction to Chapter 9 (pp. 204–05) for more on subordination. See also *Coordination.*

Summary A condensed form of the essential idea of a passage, article, or entire chapter. A summary is always shorter than the original. See also *Paraphrase, Plagiarism,* and *Direct Quotation.*

Supporting Evidence See *Evidence.*

Syllogism An argument that uses deductive reasoning and consists of a major premise, a minor premise, and a conclusion:

> All trees that lose leaves are deciduous. (*Major premise*)
>
> Maple trees lose their leaves. (*Minor premise*)
>
> Therefore, maple trees are deciduous. (*Conclusion*)

See the introduction to Chapter 21 (pp. 496–505) for more on syllogisms. See also *Deduction.*

Symbol A person, place, or thing that represents something beyond itself. For example, the bald eagle is a symbol of the United States, and the maple leaf is a symbol of Canada.

Syntax The way in which words are arranged to form phrases, clauses, and sentences, as well as the grammatical relationship among the words themselves.

Synthesis A written discussion that weaves together the ideas of one or more sources with your own. There are two types of synthesis: *informational/explanatory synthesis* and *persuasive/argument synthesis.* See the introduction to Chapter 10 (pp. 225–42) for more on synthesis.

Technical Language See *Jargon.*

Thesis The main idea of an essay, also known as the controlling idea. The thesis may sometimes be implied rather than stated directly. See the introduction to Chapter 3 (pp. 71–74) for more on the thesis statement.

Title A word or phrase given to a text to identify the essay's subject, to state the essay's main idea, or to attract the reader's attention. A title may be explicit or suggestive. A subtitle, when used, explains or restricts the meaning of the main title.

Tone The manner or "voice" in which a writer relates to an audience. Tone may be friendly, serious, distant, angry, humorous, cheerful, bitter, cynical, enthusiastic, morbid, resentful, warm, playful, and so forth. A particular tone results from a writer's diction, sentence structure, purpose, and attitude toward the subject. See the introduction to Chapter 11 (pp. 271–77) for several examples of different tones.

Topic Sentence States the central idea of a paragraph and thus limits the content of the paragraph. Although the topic sentence normally appears at the beginning of the paragraph, it may appear at any other point, particularly if the writer is trying to create a special effect. Not all paragraphs contain topic sentences. See also *Paragraph.*

Transition A word or phrase that links sentences, paragraphs, and larger units of a composition to achieve coherence. Transitions include parallelism, pronoun references, conjunctions, and the repetition of key ideas, as well as many conventional transitional expressions: *moreover, on the other hand, in addition, in contrast, therefore,* and so on. See the introduction to Chapter 8 (pp. 182–85) for a detailed discussion of transitions. See also *Coherence.*

Unity The quality of oneness in an essay that results when all the words, sentences, and paragraphs contribute to the thesis. The elements of a unified essay harmoniously support a single idea or purpose—they do not distract the reader. See the introduction to Chapter 4 (pp. 91–94) for a detailed discussion of unity.

Verb Verbs can be classified as either strong verbs (*scream, pierce, gush, ravage,* and *amble*) or weak verbs (*be, has, get,* and *do*). Good writers prefer to use strong verbs to make their writing more specific, more descriptive, and more action-filled.

Voice Verbs can be classified as being in either the active or the passive voice. In the *active voice,* the doer of the action is the grammatical subject. In the *passive voice,* the receiver of the action is the subject:

Active: Glenda questioned all of the children.
Passive: All the children were questioned by Glenda.

Writing Process The sequence of activities that most writers usually follow when composing a written work. The process typically consists of four stages:

Prewriting: The stage in the writing process in which you select your subject and topic, gather ideas and information, and determine the thesis and organizational pattern or patterns of a written work.

Drafting: The process of creating the first version of your writing in which you lay out your ideas and information and, through subsequent revision, prepare more focused and polished versions, referred to as second and third drafts, and more if necessary.

Revising: The stage in the writing process in which you reconsider and possibly change the large elements of your writing, such as thesis, purpose, content, organization, and paragraph structure.

Editing: The stage in the writing process in which you reconsider and possibly change the small elements of your writing, such as grammar, punctuation, mechanics, and spelling.

Acknowledgments

Diane Ackerman, "Why Leaves Turn Color in the Fall" from *A Natural History of the Senses*, copyright © 1990 by Diane Ackerman. Used by permission of Random House, an imprint and division of Penguin Random House LLC. All rights reserved.

Chimamanda Ngozi Adichie, "Excerpts from *We Should All Be Feminists* by Chimamanda Ngozi Adichie, copyright © 2014 by Chimamanda Ngozi Adichie. Used by permission of Alfred A. Knopf, an imprint of the Knopf Doubleday Publishing Group, a division of Penguin Random House LLC. All rights reserved.

Omar Akram, "Can Music Bridge Cultures and Promote Peace?" from the *Huffington Post*, June 12, 2013. Copyright © 2013 by Omar Akram. Reprinted by permission of the author.

Maya Angelou, "Chapter 24 (Momma, the Dentist and Me)" from *I Know Why the Caged Bird Sings* by Maya Angelou, copyright © 1969 and renewed 1997 by Maya Angelou. Used by permission of Random House, an imprint and division of Penguin Random House LLC. All rights reserved.

Emily Badger, "Tarring Opponents as Extremists Really Can Work." Republished with permission of Miller-McCune, from *Pacific Standard*, December 4, 2011; permission conveyed through Copyright Clearance Center, Inc.

Russell Baker, "Becoming a Writer." Excerpt from Chapter 2 of *Growing Up*. Reprinted by permission of Don Congdon Associates, Inc. Copyright © 1982 by Russell Baker.

Jonah Berger, "The Power of Conformity" from Jonah Berger, *Invisible Influence: The Hidden Forces That Shape Behavior*. Copyright © 2016 by Social Dynamics Group, LLC. Reprinted by permission of Simon & Schuster. All rights reserved.

Rachel Carson, "Fable for Tomorrow" from *Silent Spring*. Copyright © 1962 by Rachel L. Carson. Copyright © renewed 1990 by Roger Christie. Used by permission of Houghton Mifflin Harcourt Publishing Company and by Frances Collin, trustee. All rights reserved. All copying, including electronic, or re-distribution of this text, is expressly forbidden.

Jimmy Carter, "The Home Place" from *An Hour Before Daylight: Memoirs of a Rural Boyhood*. Copyright © 2001 by Jimmy Carter. Reprinted by permission of Simon & Schuster, Inc. All rights reserved.

Bruce Catton, "Grant and Lee: A Study in Contrasts." Originally published in *The American Story*, Earl Schneck Miers, ed. 1956. Copyright © 1956 U.S. Capitol Historical Society. Used by permission.

Judith Ortiz Cofer, "My Rosetta" from *Woman in Front of the Sun: On Becoming a Writer*. Copyright © 2000 by Judith Ortiz Cofer. Used by permission of University of Georgia Press.

James Lincoln Collier, "Anxiety: Challenge by Another Name" from *Reader's Digest*, December 1986. Reprinted with the permission of the author.

Mia Consalvo, "Cheating Is Good for You" from Forbes.com, December 14, 2006. Copyright © 2006 by Forbes Inc. All rights reserved. Used by permission and protected by the Copyright Laws of the United States. The printing, copying, redistribution, or retransmission of this Content without express written permission is prohibited.

Misty Copeland. From *Life in Motion: An Unlikely Ballerina* by Misty Copeland. Copyright © 2014 by Misty Copeland. Reprinted with the permission of Touchstone, a division of Simon & Schuster, Inc. All rights reserved.

Jonathan Safran Foer. From *Eating Animals* **by Jonathan Safran Foer. Copyright © 2009 by Jonathan Safran Foer. Originally appeared as "Against Meat" in the** *New York Times Magazine*, October 7, 2009. By permission of Little, Brown and Company.

Thomas L. Friedman, "Foreign Affairs; My Favorite Teacher" from the *New York Times*, January 9, 2001. Copyright © 2001 by The New York Times. All rights reserved. Used by permission and protected by the Copyright Laws of the United States. The printing, copying, redistribution, or retransmission of this Content without express written permission is prohibited.

Michael Gardner, "The Dork Police" from *Sweet Fruit from the Bitter Tree: 61 Stories of Creative and Compassionate Ways Out of Conflict*, by Mark Andreas. Copyright © 2011 Real People Press. Reprinted by permission of Real People Press.

Rosemarie Garland-Thomson, "Becoming Disabled" from the *New York Times*, August 19, 2016. Copyright © 2016 by The New York Times. All rights reserved. Used by permission and protected by the Copyright Laws of the United States. The printing, copying, redistribution, or retransmission of this Content without express written permission is prohibited.

Henry Louis Gates, Jr., "What's in a Name?" from *Dissent*, Fall 1989. Reprinted by permission of the University of Pennsylvania Press.

Natalie Goldberg, "Be Specific" from *Writing down the Bones: Freeing the Writer Within*, copyright © 1986 by Natalie Goldberg. Reprinted by arrangement with The Permissions Company, Inc., on behalf of Shambhala Publications, Inc. Boulder, Colorado, www.shambhala.com.

Dick Gregory, "Shame." From *Nigger: An Autobiography* by Dick Gregory. Copyright © 1964 by Dick Gregory Enterprises, Inc. Used by permission of Dutton, a division of Penguin Group (USA) LLC. and International Creative Management.

Tara Haelle. © 2016 National Public Radio, Inc. Tara Haelle for NPR news report titled "How to Teach Children That Failure Is the Secret to Success" by Tara Haelle as originally published on npr.org on May 6, 2016, and is used with the permission of NPR. Any unauthorized duplication is strictly prohibited.

Donna Hicks, "Independence" from *Dignity: Its Essential Role in Resolving Conflict*. Copyright © 2011 by Donna Hicks. Reprinted by permission of Yale University Press.

Langston Hughes, "Salvation" from *The Big Sea: An Autobiography*. Copyright © 1940 by Langston Hughes. Copyright renewed 1968 by Arna Bontemps and George Houston Bass. Reprinted with the permission of Hill and Wang, a division of Farrar, Straus & Giroux, LLC.

Jake Jamieson, "The English-Only Movement: Can America Proscribe Language with a Clear Conscience?" Reprinted with the permission of the author.

Akemi Johnson. © 2016 National Public Radio, Inc. Akemi Johnson for NPR news report titled "Who Gets to Be 'Hapa'?" by Akemi Johnson as originally published on npr.org on August 8, 2016, and is used with the permission of NPR. Any unauthorized duplication is strictly prohibited.

Dan M. Kahan, "Shame Is Worth a Try" from the *Boston Globe* (August 5, 2001). Copyright © 2001 by Dan M. Kahan. Reprinted with the permission of the author.

Martin Luther King Jr., "The Ways of Meeting Oppression" from *Stride toward Freedom: The Montgomery Story*. Copyright © 1958 by Dr. Martin Luther King Jr. Copyright © 1986 by Coretta Scott King. Reprinted with the permission of the Estate of Martin Luther King Jr., c/o Writer's House as agent for the proprietor.

Stephen King, "Why We Crave Horror Movies." Copyright © 1982 by Stephen King. Originally appeared in *Playboy*, 1982. Reprinted with permission. All rights reserved.

Christina Baker Kline, "Taking My Son to College, Where Technology Has Replaced Serendipity." Copyright © 2013 Christina Baker Kline. Blog.NJ.com. Reprinted by permission of Writers House LLC acting as agent for the author.

Verlyn Klinkenborg, "Our Vanishing Night" from *National Geographic Magazine*, November 2008. Copyright © 2008 National Geographic Society. Used by permission of the National Geographic Society.

Marie Kondo, "Designate a Place for Each Thing" from *The Life-Changing Magic of Tidying Up: The Japanese Art of Decluttering and Organizing*, translated by Cathy Hirano, copyright © 2014 by Marie Kondo. Used by permission of Ten Speed Press, an imprint of the Crown Publishing Group, a division of Penguin Random House LLC. All rights reserved.

Robert Krulwich. © 2012 National Public Radio, Inc. NPR news report titled "How Do Plants Know Which Way Is Up and Which Way Is Down?" by Robert Krulwich as originally published on June 22, 2012, and is used with the permission of NPR. Any unauthorized duplication is strictly prohibited.

Robert Lake-Thom, aka Medicine Grizzly Bear, "An Indian Father's Plea." Originally published in *Teacher's Magazine*, September 1990. Reprinted with permission of the author.

Anne Lamott, "Polaroids" from *Bird by Bird: Some Instructions on Writing and Life*, copyright © 1994 by Anne Lamott. Used by permission of Pantheon Books, an imprint of the Knopf Doubleday Publishing Group, a division of Random House, Inc. All rights reserved.

Richard Lederer, "The Case for Short Words" from *The Miracle of Language*. Copyright © 1991 by Richard Lederer. Reprinted with the permission of Atria Books, a division of Simon & Schuster, Inc. All rights reserved.

Laura Lee, "Lucy and Her Friends" from *Blame It on the Rain* by Laura Lee. Copyright © 2006 by Laura Lee. Reprinted by permission of HarperCollins Publishers.

Jamie Mackay, "Why We Need to Bring Back the Art of Communal Bathing." AEON, August 26, 2016. Copyright © Aeon Media Group Ltd., 2016.

Cherokee Paul McDonald, "A View from the Bridge" from the *Sun-Sentinel*, February 12, 1989. Reprinted with permission of ICM Partners, LLC.

Sean McElwee, "The Case for Censoring Hate Speech." Sean McElwee is a writer based in New York City. Used by permission of the author.

Paul W. Merrill, "The Principles of Poor Writing" from the *Scientific Monthly*, Vol. 64, No. 1 (Jan. 1947). pp 72–74. Reprinted with permission from SCIENCE/AAAS.

Roland Merullo, "The Phantom Toll Collector" from the *Boston Globe*, July 27, 2016. Reprinted by permission of the Emma Sweeney Agency, LLC. Copyright © 2016 by Roland Merullo.

N. Scott Momaday, "The Flight of the Eagles," excerpt from pp. 16–17 from *House Made of Dawn* by N. Scott Momaday. Copyright © 1966, 1967, 1968 by N. Scott Momaday. Reprinted by permission of HarperCollins Publishers.

Toby Morris, "On a Plate" from the *Pencilsword* #Ten. February 22, 2015 http://thewireless.co.nz/articles/the-pencilsword-on-a-plate. Reprinted by permission of the author.

Bharati Mukherjee, "Two Ways to Belong in America." Copyright © 1996 by Bharati Mukherjee. Originally published in the *New Yorker*. Reprinted by permission of the author.

Erin Murphy, "White Lies" from *Brevity33* (first appeared in May 2010 issue). Reprinted with the permission of the author.

Gloria Naylor, "The Meanings of a Word" from the *New York Times* (February 20, 1986). Reprinted by permission of SLL/Sterling Lord Literistic, Inc. Copyright by Gloria Naylor, 1986.

David Pogue, "Remember All Those Passwords? No Need" from the *New York Times*, June 5, 2013. Copyright © 2013 by The New York Times. All rights reserved. Used by permission and protected by the Copyright Laws of the United States. The printing, copying, redistribution, or retransmission of this Content without express written permission is prohibited.

Eduardo Porter, "What Happiness Is" from *The Price of Everything: Solving the Mystery of Why We Pay What We Do*, copyright © 2011 by Eduardo Porter. Used by permission of Portfolio, an imprint of Penguin Group, a division of Penguin Random House LLC. All rights reserved.

Robert Ramirez, "The Barrio" (original title "The Woolen Serape") from *Pain and Promise: The Chicano Today*, edited by Edward Simmens (New York: New American Library, 1972). Reprinted with the permission of the author.

Carl T. Rowan, "Unforgettable Miss Bessie" originally published in *Reader's Digest*. Copyright © 1985 by Trusted Media Brands, Inc. Used by permission. All rights reserved.

Sheryl Sandberg and Adam Grant, "Sheryl Sandberg on the Myth of the Catty Woman" from the *New York Times Sunday Review*, June 23, 2016.

Audrey Schulman, "Fahrenheit 59: What a Child's Fever Might Tell Us about Climate Change." Reprinted by permission of the author.

David Sedaris, "Me Talk Pretty One Day" from *Me Talk Pretty One Day*. Copyright © 2000 by David Sedaris. Reprinted by permission of Little, Brown & Company and Don Congdon Associates, Inc.

Dan Shaughnessy, "Teammates Forever Have a Special Connection" from the *Boston Globe*, June 24, 2016. Reprinted by permission of the author.

Mary Sherry, "In Praise of the F Word" from *Newsweek*, May 6, 1991. Copyright © 1991 by Mary Sherry. Reprinted with the permission of the author.

The Sierra Club. From "Vietnam Defoliation: A Fable for Our Times." http://content.sierraclub.org/military/vietnam-defoliation-fable-for-our-times Reprinted by permission of Sierra Club.

Brent Staples, "Black Men and Public Space" from *Harper's*. Copyright © 1987 Reprinted by permission of the author.

Amy Tan, "Mother Tongue." Copyright © 1989 by Amy Tan. First appeared in the *Threepenny Review*. Reprinted by permission of the author and the Sandra Dijkstra Literary Agency.

June Tangney, "Condemn the Crime, Not the Person" from the *Boston Globe*, August 5, 2001. Copyright © 2001 by June Tangney. Reprinted with the permission of the author.

Maya Wei-Haas, "How Chuck Taylor Taught America How to Play Basketball." *Smithsonian.com*, August 8, 2016. Copyright © 2016 Smithsonian Institution. Reprinted with permission from Smithsonian Enterprises. All rights reserved. Reproduction in any medium is strictly prohibited without permission from Smithsonian Institution.

Eudora Welty, "The Corner Store" from *The Eye of the Story*. Copyright © 1978 by Eudora Welty. Used by permission of Random House, an imprint and division of Penguin Random House LLC. All rights reserved.

Terry Tempest Williams, "The Clan of the One-Breasted Women" from *Refuge: An Unnatural History of Family and Place* by Terry Tempest Williams. Copyright ©1991 by Terry Tempest Williams. Used by permission of Pantheon Books, an imprint of the Knopf Doubleday Publishing Group, a division of Penguin Random House LLC. All rights reserved.

Mara Wilson, "My Lost Mother's Last Receipt" from the *New York Times*, September 8, 2016. Copyright © 2016 by The New York Times. All rights reserved. Used by permission and protected by the Copyright Laws of the United States. The printing, copying, redistribution, or retransmission of this Content without express written permission is prohibited.

Julie Zhuo, "Where Anonymity Breeds Contempt" from the *New York Times*, November 29, 2010. Copyright © 2010 by The New York Times. All rights reserved. Used by permission and protected by the Copyright Laws of the United States. The printing, copying, redistribution, or retransmission of this Content without express written permission is prohibited.

Index